CANADIAN EDITION

THE
MACRO
ECONOMY
TODAY

D1308144

Bradley R. Schiller
American University

Laurie Craig Phipps
Camosun College

David R. Sabiston
Mount Royal College

McGraw-Hill
Ryerson

Toronto Montréal Boston Burr Ridge, IL Dubuque, IA Madison, WI New York San Francisco St. Louis Bangkok Bogotá Caracas Kuala Lumpur Lisbon London Madrid Mexico City Milan New Delhi Santiago Seoul Singapore Sydney Taipei

The McGraw·Hill Companies

McGraw-Hill Ryerson

The Macro Economy Today
Canadian Edition

ISBN-13: 978-0-07-097312-1
ISBN-10: 0-07-097312-1

1 2 3 4 5 6 7 8 9 10 TCP 0 9 8

Printed and bound in Canada

Care has been taken to trace ownership of copyright material contained in this text; however, the publisher will welcome any information that enables them to rectify any reference or credit for subsequent editions.

Editorial Director: Joanna Cotton
Executive Sponsoring Editor: Leanna MacLean
Sponsoring Editor: Bruce McIntosh
Marketing Manager: Matthew Busbridge
iLearning Sales Specialist: Milene Fort, Laura Lazaruk
Senior Developmental Editor: Maria Chu
Permissions Editor: Alison Derry
Editorial Associate: Stephanie Hess
Supervising Editor: Joanne Limebeer
Copy Editor: Cat Haggert
Senior Production Coordinator: Madeleine Harrington
Cover Design: Sharon Lucas Creative Services
Cover Image: © Photographer's Choice/Sylvain Grandadam
Interior Design: Sharon Lucas Creative Services
Page Layout: Aptara, Inc.
Printer: Transcontinental Printing Group

Library and Archives Canada Cataloguing in Publication Data

Schiller, Bradley R., 1943-
    The macro economy today / Bradley R. Schiller, Laurie Craig Phipps, David R. Sabiston. — 1st Canadian ed.

Includes bibliographical references and index.
ISBN 978-0-07-097312-1

    1. Macroeconomics—Textbooks. I. Phipps, Laurie Craig, 1952- II. Sabiston, David R., 1957- III. Title.

HB172.5.S34 2008   339   C2007-905151-0

To my brother, Jay, whose memory encourages me always; to my wife, Kate, who has convinced me that all things are possible—even co-authoring a text; and to the multitude of students at Camosun College who struggled with me to find a better way to help them learn economics and understand the passion I feel for the study.

L.C.P.

To my parents, Gordon and Alison, who, through example, taught us the value of an honest effort, the value of a kind gesture at the appropriate time, and the importance of accepting people at face value.

D.R.S.

Bradley R. Schiller has over three decades of experience teaching introductory economics at American University, the University of California (Berkeley and Santa Cruz), and the University of Maryland. He has given guest lectures at more than 300 colleges ranging from Fresno, California, to Istanbul, Turkey. Dr. Schiller's unique contribution to teaching is his ability to relate basic principles to current socioeconomic problems, institutions, and public policy decisions. This perspective is evident throughout *The Macro Economy Today.*

Dr. Schiller derives this policy focus from his extensive experience as a Washington consultant. He has been a consultant to most major federal agencies, many congressional committees, and political candidates. In addition, he has evaluated scores of government programs and helped design others. His studies of discrimination, training programs, tax reform, pensions, welfare, Social Security, and lifetime wage patterns have appeared in both professional journals and popular media. Dr. Schiller is also a frequent commentator on economic policy for television, radio, and newspapers.

Dr. Schiller received his PhD from Harvard in 1969. He earned a BA degree, with great distinction, from the University of California (Berkeley) in 1965. He is now a professor of economics in the School of Public Affairs at American University in Washington, D.C.

Laurie C. Phipps completed an MA in Economics from Queen's University, Kingston, and has been a faculty member at Camosun College in Victoria, British Columbia since January, 1995. Over the past thirteen years, he has taught predominantly principles courses in microeconomics and macroeconomics along with some money and banking and quantitative methods courses.

His current focus is on the teaching and learning process and the role and potential of information and communication technologies within that process. To that end, he completed an MA in Distributed Learning from Royal Roads University in 2003 and is taking time this fall to begin PhD studies in Educational Technology and Learning Design at Simon Fraser University. He has worked with learners in both face-to-face and fully online courses, developing an introduction to economics course at the undergraduate level and co-developing a course in online facilitation at the master's level.

Away from the classroom, either as an instructor or student, Laurie takes advantage of beautiful British Columbia to hike in its parks and mountains, kayak its coastline, bike in and around Victoria, and become more acquainted with wines from each of British Columbia's wine-growing areas.

David R. Sabiston received his PhD from the University of Ottawa in 1996 and has taught the principles courses on an annual basis since the early 1990s. He is currently a tenured faculty member with the Department of Policy Studies at Mount Royal College. Prior to joining MRC, he worked part-time at the Department of Finance during his graduate years and later taught at Laurentian University. His research interests lie in the field of international economics and in the pedagogical approaches to teaching economics. He teaches face-to-face, blended, and online sections of principle courses and acts as a consultant for the online assessment company associated with this text (Lyryx Learning Inc.).

Away from the office and the classroom, David enjoys an eclectic assortment of activities. When he is not repotting neglected orchids, replacing broken window cranks, or complaining about the colour of the walls in his bedroom, he may be on the links instructing his children on the finer aspects of the game of golf. He insists that his latest toy—a Ducati ST3—is not a mid-life crisis but rather a motorcycle invented by the Italians to help resolve the world's problems.

CONTENTS IN BRIEF

CONTENTS

THE 24/7 ECONOMY

24/7. That's the way the economy works. While you're sleeping, workers in Malaysia are assembling the electronic circuits that will instruct your alarm clock to go off, relay the news via satellite TV or radio, enable video presentations in class or at remote locations, and help retrieve music files on the iPod you carry around. If you live in eastern Canada, Norwegian and Algerian oil workers are pumping oil that will fuel your drive to class. Ethiopian farmers are harvesting the coffee beans that will help keep you alert. Traders in London, Hong Kong, and Tokyo are pushing the value of the dollar up or down, changing the cost of travel and trade. In an increasingly globalized economy, the economy truly never sleeps. It's in motion 24 hours a day, 7 days a week.

All of this perpetual motion makes teaching economics increasingly difficult. The parameters of the economy are constantly changing. Interest rates are up one day, down the next. The same with oil prices. Inflation looks worrisome one month and benign the next. Job growth looks great one month, then dismal the next. Even economists at Canada's central bank—the Bank of Canada—have trouble keeping track of all these (changing) data, much less the direction of the economy.

At the micro level, incessant changes in the economy create similar problems. Market structures are continuously evolving. Products are always changing. With those changes, even market boundaries are on the move. Is your local cable franchise really a monopoly when satellite and Internet companies offer virtually identical products? Will Apple Computer, Inc., with a 70 percent market share in the portable MP3-player market, behave more like a monopolist or like a perfect competitor? With the Internet creating *global* shopping malls, how should industry concentration ratios be calculated? Canadian regulatory agencies are continuously challenged by ever-changing market boundaries and structures.

There is no less change at the macro level. Federal, provincial, and territorial governments alter their fiscal approaches, the Bank of Canada adjusts the overnight interest rate to control inflation, the Canadian dollar rises to $1.10 ($US) and then falls to $0.98 ($US), new trade agreements are signed and trade disputes happen. At the same time, the Canadian macroeconomy reacts to similar changes in other countries; to changes of policy, changes in government direction, and changes to the domestic economic activity of our trade partners. What occurs outside of Canada can alter the economic activity inside Canada.

Coping with Change

So how do we cope with all this flux in the classroom? Or, for that matter, in a textbook that will be in print for three years? We could ignore the complexities of the real world and focus exclusively on abstract principles, perhaps "enlivening" the presentation with fables about the Acme Widget Company or the Jack and Jill Water Company. That approach not only bores students, but it also solidifies the misperception that economics is irrelevant to their daily life. Alternatively, we could spend countless hours reporting and discussing the economic news of the day. But that approach transforms the principles course into a current-events symposium.

The Macro Economy Today pursues a different strategy. We are convinced that economics is an exciting and extremely relevant field of study and have felt this way since our first undergraduate principles course. For at least two of us, we somehow discerned that economics could be an interesting topic despite an overbearing textbook and a super-sized class (over 250 students). All it needed was a commitment to merging theoretical insights with the daily realities of shopping malls, stock markets, global integration, and policy development. Whew!

What Makes Economies Tick

How does this lofty ambition translate into the nuts and bolts of teaching? It starts by infusing the textbook and the course with a purposeful theme. Spotlighting scarcity and the necessity for choice is not enough; there's a much bigger picture. It's really about why some nations prosper while others languish. As we look around the world, how can we explain why millionaires abound in Canada, the United States, Hong Kong, the United Kingdom, and Australia, while 2.8 *billion* people live on less than $2 a day? How is it that affluent consumers in developed nations carry around videophones while one-fourth of the world's population has never made a phone call? Surely, the way an economy is structured has something to do with this. At the micro level, Adam Smith taught us long ago that the degree of competition in product markets affects the quantity, quality, and price of consumer products.

Markets vs. Government

At the aggregate level, we've also seen that macro structure matters. Specifically, we recognize that the degree of government intervention in an economy is a critical determinant of its performance. The Chinese Communist Party once thought that central control of an economy would not only reduce inequalities but also accelerate growth. Since decentralizing parts of its economy, freeing up some markets, and even legalizing private property (see the World View box, p. 18), China has become the world's fastest-growing economy. India has heeded China's experience and is also pursuing a massive privatization and deregulation strategy (World View, p. 11).

This doesn't imply that *laissez faire* is the answer to all of our economic problems. What it does emphasize, however, is how important the choice between market reliance and government dependence can be.

We know that the three core questions in economics are WHAT, HOW, and FOR WHOM to produce. Instead of discussing them in a political and institutional void, we should energize these issues with more real-world context. We should also ask who should resolve these core questions, the governments or the marketplace? Where, when, and why do we expect market failure—suboptimal answers to the WHAT, HOW, and FOR WHOM questions? Where, when, and why can we expect government intervention to give us better answers—or to fail? This theme of market reliance versus government dependence runs through every chapter of *The Macro Economy Today*.

Real-World Concerns

Within the two-dimensional framework of three core questions and markets-versus-governments decision making, *The Macro Economy Today* pursues basic principles in an unwavering real-world context. The commitment to relevance is evident from the get-go. At the outset, DaimlerChrysler's tradeoff between producing gas-guzzling SUVs or gas-sipping subcompact cars (p. 4) illustrates the concept of opportunity cost in a meaningful context. The discussion also highlights the "economic way of thinking" by documenting the relevant information required to make an informed decision. The recent controversy surrounding the federal government's decision to offer rebates to fuel-efficient automobiles (see the Applications box, p.16) integrates the market reliance vs. government dependence theme. In an effort to provide consumers with an incentive to reduce pollution, has the policy inadvertently favoured one automobile manufacturer over another? These kinds of concrete, page-one examples motivate students to learn *and retain* core economic principles.

Macro Realities

In macro, we begin by emphasizing the macroeconomic system in Chapter 3 rather than waiting until the end of the text to put everything together. The macroeconomy that is discussed on television, in newspapers, by policy makers and activists isn't a single entity at all, but a number of smaller components—markets or economies—that collectively constitute the whole macro economy. The four components addressed in this text are the real economy, the labour market, the monetary economy, and the foreign economy. While each will be examined individually, we must also consider how each is impacted by and impacts each other component.

After Chapter 4 presents the basic vocabulary and process of measuring the real economy, we immediately dive into three of the most "present" and pressing concerns of macroeconomics: unemployment, inflation, and economic growth. But students aren't motivated to learn the origins or potential solutions for these concerns just by citing the latest economic statistics (yawn). Most students don't have enough personal experience to understand why 12 percent unemployment, 5 percent inflation, or 0 percent real economic growth are *serious* concerns. To fill that void, *The Macro Economy*

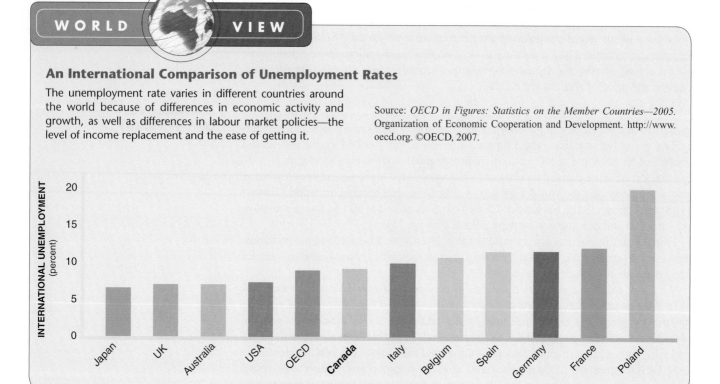

WORLD VIEW

An International Comparison of Unemployment Rates

The unemployment rate varies in different countries around the world because of differences in economic activity and growth, as well as differences in labour market policies—the level of income replacement and the ease of getting it.

Source: *OECD in Figures: Statistics on the Member Countries—2005.* Organization of Economic Cooperation and Development. http://www.oecd.org. ©OECD, 2007.

Analysis: Unemployment rates are typically significantly higher in Europe and Canada than in the United States. Analysts blame both sluggish economic growth and high unemployment benefits.

Today takes students on a tour—telling stories—of unemployment, inflation, and economic growth.

In Chapter 5, they see unemployment statistics translate into personal tragedies and social tensions. They see that unemployment isn't experienced equally by age group, by level of education or by the province where they live (Figure 5.4, p. 94) and how devastating the human costs can be (pp. 96–97). Students will also place Canada's unemployment problem in a broader context through the World View on page 96.

In Chapter 6, the devastation wrought by an inflation rate greater than 200 percent per year in Zimbabwe (Applications box, p. 105) and the redistributive effects of even low levels of inflation (p. 107) drives home the realization that price level changes matter. Chapter 7 takes a longer-term view of economic growth and productivity. Students may feel somewhat hostile to the concept of economic growth because of worries like climate change, pollution, and sustainability. However, without ignoring these important concerns, economic growth and productivity can be demonstrated to be both important and desirable. Growth and productivity can raise standards of living and reduce poverty—helping to create opportunity for the more than 1 billion people in the world surviving on $1 a day (World Bank, 2001). These three chapters lay a global, historical, and personal foundation that gives purpose to the study of macro theory. Few other texts lay this foundation.

Part 3 constructs the workhorse model used in modern macroeconomics: Aggregate Supply and Aggregate Demand. What is unusual in this text is that our model includes both the short-run aggregate supply and long-run aggregate supply curves in each graph. Even when the discussion is focused on short-run deviations, it is important to remind students that the long-run still matters. Chapter 8 builds the complete model and includes a clear and step-by-step algebraic presentation of the model. Students see the model built once and used in one consistent format. Chapter 9 focuses on "change and adjustment" in the model and where the economy, though working as we would expect it, can result in undesirable outcomes. Applications and World View presentations help students connect the theory discussions to current news headlines and remind them of the real-world relevancy of these core macro concepts. Chapter 10 takes a closer look at the role of government and the operation of fiscal policy—taxes and government spending—and the implications of those policy choices. Chapter 11 illustrates the annual consequences of taxing and spending policies through the government budget balance—deficit or surplus—and through the economic "burden" of the public debt.

Part 4 turns the spotlight on the monetary economy. Chapter 12 starts by explaining the role and function of money in our economy—whether the money was printed by the Canadian mint, or by the Salt Spring Island Monetary Foundation (SS IMF, see Webnote, p. 242) the role and function are the same. The chapter also provides an overview of Canada's commercial banks and financial institutions. Chapter 13 describes the development of the Bank of Canada from its creation in 1934 to today and the policy goal and instruments of monetary policy—controlling the supply of money available to the Canadian economy. The "monetary transmission mechanism" provides students with a connection between the monetary and real economies and between fiscal and monetary policy and the implications for the macroeconomy.

Part 5 contains only one chapter, but it is another important "connector" chapter. Chapter 14 takes an in-depth look at the supply side of the economy and the role of expectations—what household and firm decision-makers *think* will happen. This chapter will also take a look at how getting more folks into classrooms can be good for the macroeconomy.

International Realities

Finally, Part 6 completes the components making up the macroeconomic system by discussing the foreign economy. The international trade chapter (15) not only introduces students to a basic model of trade and explains the core concepts of comparative advantage and absolute advantage, but does so by incorporating concerns about globalization, climate change, poverty, and increasing development and opportunity for those around the world who don't share the standard of living many of us take for granted. By identifying the vested interests, political compromises, and the myths that support resistance to trade, *The Macro Economy Today* bridges the gap between abstract free-trade models and real-world trade disputes. Students see not only why trade can be a solution rather than a problem, but also how and why we pay for trade barriers. Chapter 16 describes international finance: Canada's international balance of payments, exchange rates (the external value of the Canadian dollar) and fixed versus flexible exchange rate regimes. We also briefly examine how trade and exchange rates act in a small open economy like Canada and if globalization might be creating a "deadly brew for national currencies" (Applications box, p. 362) and if a "common currency" (like the Euro) might be better.

The bottom line here is simple and straightforward: *by infusing the presentation of core concepts with a unifying theme and pervasive real-world application,* The Macro Economy Today *offers an exciting and motivated introduction to macroeconomics.* This is the kind of reality-based instruction today's students need to think about newspaper headlines through the critical context *thinking like an economist* can bring.

EFFECTIVE PEDAGOGY

Clean, Clear Theory

Despite the abundance of real-world applications, this is at heart a *principles* text, not a compendium of issues. Good theory and interesting applications are not mutually exclusive. This is a text that wants to *teach macroeconomics,* not just increase awareness of policy issues. To that end, *The Macro Economy Today* provides a logically organized and uncluttered theoretical structure for macro and international theory. What distinguishes this text from others on the market is that it conveys theory in a lively, student-friendly manner.

FIGURE 2.3
Shifts vs. Movements

A demand curve shows how a consumer responds to price changes. If the determinants of demand stay constant, the response is a *movement* along the curve to a new quantity demanded. In this case, the quantity demanded increases from 5 (point d_1), to 12 (point g_1), when price falls from $35 to $20 per hour.

If the determinants of demand change, the entire demand curve *shifts*. In this case, an increase in income increases demand. With more income, Tom is willing to buy 12 hours at the initial price of $35 (point d_2), not just the 5 hours he demanded before the lottery win.

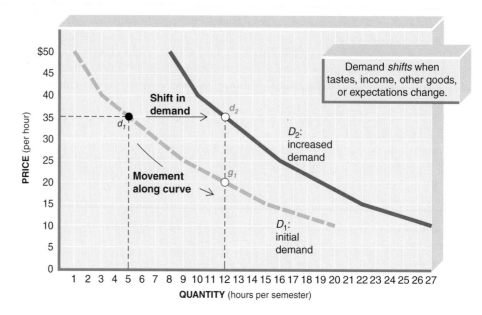

	Price (per hour)	Quantity Demanded (hours per semester)	
		Initial Demand	After Increase in Income
A	$50	1	8
B	45	2	9
C	40	3	10
D	35	5	12
E	30	7	14
F	25	9	16
G	20	12	19
H	15	15	22
I	10	20	27

Concept Reinforcement

Student comprehension of core theory is facilitated with careful, consistent, and effective pedagogy. This distinctive pedagogy includes the following features:

Self-Explanatory Graphs and Tables

Graphs are *completely* labelled, colourful, and positioned on background grids. Because students often enter the principles course as graph-phobics, graphs are frequently accompanied by synchronized tabular data. Every table is also annotated. This shouldn't be a product-differentiating feature but, sadly, it is. Putting a table in a textbook without an annotation is akin to writing a cluster of numbers on the board, then leaving the classroom without any explanation.

Reinforced Key Concepts

Key terms are defined in the margin when they first appear and included in a glossary for easy reference. Web site references are directly tied to the book's content, not hung on like ornaments. End-of-chapter discussion questions use tables, graphs, and boxed news stories from the text, reinforcing key concepts.

Boxed and Annotated Applications

In addition to the real-world applications that run through the body of the text, *The Macro Economy Today* intersperses boxed domestic (Applications) and global (World View) case studies. Although nearly every text on the market now offers boxed applications, *The Macro Economy Today's* presentation is distinctive. First, the sheer number of Applications (46) and World View (37) boxes is unique. Second, and more important, *every* boxed application is referenced in the body of the text. Third, *every* Applications and World View comes with a brief, self-contained explanation. Fourth, the Applications and World View boxes are the subject of the end-of-chapter Discussion Questions and Student Problem Set exercises. In combination, these distinctive features assure that students will actually read the boxed applications and discern their economic content. The *Test Bank* also provides subsets of questions tied to the Applications and World View boxes so that instructors can confirm student use of this feature.

A mini Web site directory is provided in each chapter's marginal Web Notes. These URLs aren't random picks; they were selected because they let students extend and update adjacent in-text discussions.

Web Notes

The text presentation is also enlivened with occasional photos and cartoons that reflect basic concepts. The "Boxing Day Madness" photograph (Applications, p. 44) is a vivid testimony to how goods are often allocated when demand exceeds supply. The "Happy Map" (p. 84) more strikingly illustrates the standard-of-living differences around the world than a table of "World Bank" data. The cartoon on page xvii reminds students that not all economists are of the same mind. Every photo and cartoon is annotated and referenced in the body of the text. These visual features are an integral part of the presentation, not diversions.

Photos and Cartoons

Photo from CBC News, http://www.cbc.ca/money/story/2006/12/26/shopping-boxing.html

In reviews for the early draft of this first Canadian edition of *The Macro Economy Today,* the text was described as "concise and to the point," "engaging," and a text that "students would be inclined to read." The writing style is lively and issue-focused. Unlike other textbooks on the market, every boxed feature, every graph, every table, and every cartoon is explained and analyzed. Every feature is also referenced in the text, so students actually learn the material rather than skipping over it. Because readability is ultimately in the eye of the beholder, you might ask a couple of students to read and compare an analogous chapter in *The Macro Economy Today* with that of another text. This is a test that we feel confident *The Macro Economy Today* will win.

Readability

We firmly believe that students must *work* with key concepts in order to really learn them. Homework assignments are *de rigueur* in our own classes. To facilitate homework assignments, we have prepared the *Student Problem Set,* which includes built-in numerical and graphing problems that build on the tables, graphs, and boxed material in each chapter. Grids for drawing graphs are also provided. The Student Problem Set is located at the end of this book. (Answers are available in the *Instructor's Resource Manual,* in downloadable form on the book's Web site).

Student Problem Set

All of these pedagogical features add up to an unusually supportive learning context for students. With this support, students will learn and retain more economic concepts—and maybe even enjoy the educational process.

APPLICATIONS

Canada Ranks 10th on "Happy Map"

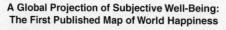

A Global Projection of Subjective Well-Being:
The First Published Map of World Happiness

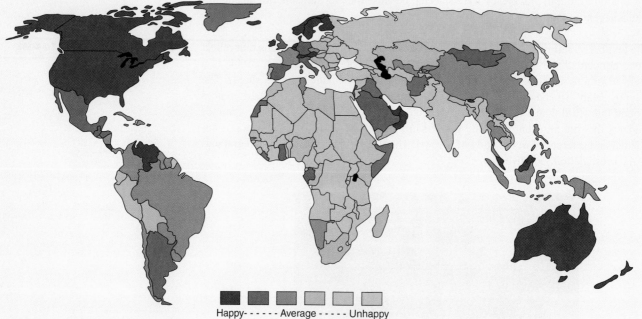

Happy- - - - - Average - - - - - Unhappy

Map created by Adrian White, Analytic Social Psychologist, University of Leicester (2006)
Map and further analysis incorporates data published by UNESCO, the WHO, the New Economics Foundation, the Veenhoven Database, the Latinbarometer, the Afrobarometer, the CIA, and the UN Human Development Report.

Source: Adrian White, University of Leicester, 2006.

TORONTO—Canada has made the top 10 on a "world map of happiness," which rates 178 countries ranging from Albania to Zimbabwe on their populations' overall sense of well-being.

Ranked 10th in the world, Canada scored high on the map's three major measures of happiness—health, wealth and access to education, said one of its creators, Adrian White of the University of Leicester in England.

Mr. White, an analytic social psychologist who is working towards his PhD, believes the map is the first to illustrate levels of happiness and well-being on such a global scale.

"I don't know if it's been the same in Canada, but recently there's been a lot of political interest in looking at happiness as a measure of a country's performance, rather than just GDP [gross domestic product]," Mr. White said Thursday from Leicester.

Sheryl Ubelacker

Source: Sheryl Ubelacker, Canadian Press. July 28, 2006. Used with permission of the Canadian Press.

Analysis: Using an index constructed from "health, wealth, and access to education" measures, Adrian White places Canada in 10th place in the world for "happiness." Perhaps what is more interesting is the consistency across the various measures that Canada is a pretty good place to live.

DISTINCTIVE MACRO

The Macro Economy Today takes a balanced approach in the presentation of different theoretical perspectives, its consistent use of the combined short-run and long-run AS/AD framework, its global perspective, and its explicit juxtaposition of theory and reality.

This tries not to be a highly opinionated text. It doesn't assert that only long-run issues matter or that monetary policy is the only effective lever of short-run stabilization. Rather *The Macro Economy Today* strives to offer students a *balanced* introduction where both short and long-run concerns matter and an array of competing viewpoints need to be considered. Each competing theory is presented in their best possible light, and then subjected to comparative scrutiny. This approach reflects our belief that students need to be exposed to a variety of perspectives—and see the development of those perspectives in some historical context—if they're to understand the range and intensity of ongoing public policy debates. Maybe we can't always answer the question posed in the accompanying cartoon with certainty. But our students should at least know that the question is legitimate.

Too many textbooks still treat the aggregate supply/aggregate demand (AS/AD) framework as a separate theory. The AS/AD model is *not* a separate theory; it is just a convenient framework for illustrating macro theories in a world of changing prices. As David Colander suggests (p. 52), the AS/AD model helps principles teachers tell effective stories. *The Macro Economy Today* also consistently presents the AS/AD model with both the short-run and long-run aggregate supply curve marked. As with the larger macroeconomic system, the full implications of AS/AD cannot be understood without recognizing that policy choices have impacts over both "runs".

The AD multiplier effects are illustrated in Figure 9.10 (p. 191) as sequential AD shifts and measured along a horizontal plane at the prevailing price level (P_0). But each graph also spotlights the fact that AD shifts have both price and output effects (e.g., Figure 10.3, p. 206). Students should *start* their macro tour with this real-world perspective.

In view of the upfront AS/AD depiction of the multiplier, the macro presentation is now exclusively rendered in the context of AS/AD model. This greatly simplifies the presentation for students, who often got lost shuttling between two distinct models, sometimes in the same chapter. Since students have never encountered the Keynesian Cross model, they won't miss it in *The Macro Economy Today*. For instructors who still want to use it, the Keynesian Cross is now contained in the appendix to Chapter 8. As that Appendix explains, the two models are simply different paths for reaching the same conclusions. The advantage of the AS/AD framework is that it generates more useful policy guidelines in a world of changing price levels and policy goals for both the short-run and long-run.

The *Macro Economy Today* consistently places discussions in the context of global linkages. As a small open economy, Canada's economy is impacted by and reacts to international events and economic changes and policies in other countries. The Bank of Canada always looks over its collective shoulder at global markets when making decisions on domestic monetary policy. The impact of changing interest rates on the external value of the dollar and global money flows is always a concern. Likewise, the effectiveness of fiscal-policy initiatives is sensitive to potential "export leakage" and other trade effects. We want students to be constantly aware of how world events impact Canada's economy and constrain Canada's policy choices.

DISTINCTIVE INTERNATIONAL

Canada is a relatively small economy and open to the world. This openness is highlighted by including the global economy in every chapter of *The Macro Economy Today*.

The most visible evidence of this globalism is in the 37 World View boxes that are distributed throughout the text. As noted earlier, these boxed illustrations offer specific

Balance Macro Theory

Analysis: There are different theories about when and how the government should "fix" the economy. Policymakers must decide which advice to follow in specific situations.

World Views

global illustrations of basic principles. To facilitate their use, every World View has a brief caption that highlights the theoretical relevance of the example. The *Test Bank* and Student Problem Set also offer questions based on the World Views.

Vested Interests

Consistent with the reality-based content of the entire text, the discussion of international trade goes beyond basic principles to policy trade-offs and constraints. It's impossible to make sense of trade debates and trade policy without recognizing the vested interests that battle trade principles. Chapter 15 emphasizes that there are both winners and losers associated with every change in trade flows. While DaimlerChrysler works on an agreement to import sub-compact cars from China to benefit Canadian consumers, (see the Applications box on page 325), the Canadian Auto Workers raise concerns about potential job losses in Ontario. Because vested interests are typically highly concentrated and well organized (a single industry group or trade union), they can often bend trade rules and promote policies to their advantage. Trade disputes over appliances "dumped" into Canada, softwood lumber exports to the United States and import restrictions on a key ingredient used to produce cheese help illustrate the realities of trade policy. The on-going protests against the World Trade Organization (WTO) and the North American Free Trade Agreement (NAFTA) are also assessed in terms of competing interests.

Free trade is also not just about Canada and other countries. British Columbia and Alberta recently enacted a Trade, Investment, and Labour Mobility Agreement (TILMA) that "aims to slash trade barriers [between the provinces] and red tape and increase labour mobility in a bid to create the country's second largest economic trade zone behind Ontario."[1] However, this free trade initiative within Canada is also controversial and so far no other provinces have joined.

TECHNOLOGY SOLUTIONS

Lyryx

Lyryx Assessment for Economics is a leading-edge online assessment program designed to support both students and instructors. The assessment takes the form of a homework assignment called a Lab. The assessments are algorithmically generated and automatically graded so that students get instant grades and detailed feedback. New Labs are randomly generated each time, providing the student with unlimited opportunities to try a question. After they submit a Lab for marking, students receive extensive feedback on their work, thus enhancing their learning experience.

For the Student: Lyryx Assessment for Economics offers algorithmically generated and automatically graded assignments. Students get instant grades and instant feedback—no need to wait until the next class to find out how well they did! Grades are instantly recorded in a grade book that the student can view.

Students are motivated to do their labs for two reasons: first because it can be tied to assessment, and second, because they can try the lab as many times as they wish prior to the due date with only their best grade being recorded.

Instructors know from experience that if students are doing their economics homework, they will be successful in the course. Recent research regarding the use of Lyryx has shown that when labs are tied to assessment, even if worth only a small percentage of the total grade of the course, students WILL do their homework—and MORE THAN ONCE!

For the Instructor: The goal of Lyryx Assessment for Economics is for instructors to use the labs for course marks instead of creating and marking their own assignments, saving instructors and teaching assistants valuable time which they can use to help students directly. After registering their courses with Lyryx, instructors can create labs of their choice by selecting problems from our bank of questions, and set a deadline for each one of these labs. The content, marking, and feedback of the problems has been developed and implemented with the help of experienced instructors in economics.

[1]See the Application on page 333 "B.C. Premier shines spotlight on free trade".

Instructors have access to all their students' marks and can view their labs. At any time, the instructors can download the class grades for their own programs.

Please contact your *i*Learning Sales Specialist for additional information on the Lyryx Assessment Economics system.

Visit **http://lyryx.com**

Available 24/7. *i*Study provides instant feedback so you can study when you want, how you want and where you want.

This exciting and innovative online study guide provides students with a completely new way to learn. The motivating interactive exercises are not only enjoyable, but ensure the students' active involvement in the learning process, boosting their ability to retain and apply key concepts. Each chapter of *i*Study includes a chapter quick review, learning objectives, a puzzle using key terms, true and false questions, multiple choice questions, problems and applications with instant feedback, and a glossary available as downloadable MP3 audio files.

To see a sample chapter, go to the Online Learning Centre at **www.mcgrawhill.ca/ olc/schiller.** Full access to *i*Study can be purchased at the Web site or by purchasing a pin code card through your campus bookstore.

Instructors: Contact your *i*Learning Sales Specialist for additional information regarding packaging access to *i*Study with the student text.

The Online Learning Centre (OLC) offers learning aids such as access to Σ-Stat and the CANSIM II database, self-grading multiple-choice and true-or-false questions. *The Macro Economy Today* OLC is located at **www.mcgrawhill.ca/olc/schiller.**

Student Online Learning Centre (OLC)

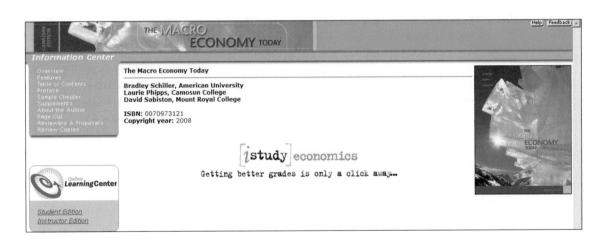

Σ-STAT is Statistics Canada's education resource that allows you to view socio-economic and demographic data in charts, graphs, and maps. Access to Σ-STAT and the CANSIM II database is made available from this Web site by special agreement between McGraw-Hill Ryerson and Statistics Canada to purchasers of the Schiller textbook. Please visit the Online Learning Centre for additional information.

SUPPORT FOR THE INSTRUCTOR

Instructor's Online Learning Centre (OLC)

The OLC includes a password-protected Web site for Instructors; visit us at **www.mcgrawhill.ca/olc/schiller.** The site offers downloadable supplements and PageOut, the McGraw-Hill Ryerson course Web site development centre.

News Flashes. The U.S. author, Brad Schiller, writes two-page News Flashes that discuss major economic events as they occur. Many of these deal with international events and provide excellent lecture material that can be copied for student use. They will be posted to the Instructors portion of the OLC as they become available so check back often.

New Chapter on Global Poverty

Available on the Online Learning Centre
U.S. author, Brad Schiller, is a leading authority in Global Poverty and introduces it to the principles course with this new chapter. An array of global data, theory, and policy combine to make an engaging and eye-opening study of this world-wide issue.

Instructor's CD-ROM

Instructor's Resource Manual. The Canadian authors have prepared the *Instructor's Resource Manual.*

The *Instructor's Resource Manual* is also available online, and it includes chapter summaries, "lecture launchers" to stimulate class discussion, and media exercises to extend the analysis. Other features include a section that details common misconceptions regarding the material in a particular chapter; learning outcomes of the chapter; and answers to the Questions for Discussion and the Student Problem Sets. Also, there are debate projects found in the *Instructor's Resource Manual.* In addition, there is a photocopy-ready Print Media Exercise for each chapter.

Instructor Aids

Computerized Test Bank. Author David Sabiston, Mount Royal College, adapted the *Test Bank* for the Canadian edition. He assures a high level of quality and consistency of the test questions and the greatest possible correlation with the content of the text as well as the *i*Study. All questions are coded according to level of difficulty and have a text-page reference where the student will find a discussion of the concept on which the question is based. The computerized *Test Bank* is available in EZ Test, a flexible and easy-to-use electronic testing program. EZ Test can produce high-quality graphs from the test banks and feature the ability to generate multiple tests, with versions "scrambled" to be distinctive. This software will meet the various needs of the widest spectrum of computer users. The computerized test bank is offered in micro and macro versions, each of which contains nearly 4,000 questions including over 200 essay questions.

PowerPoint Presentations. Angela Chow, Centennial College, prepared presentation slides using Microsoft PowerPoint software. These slides are a step-by-step review of the key points in each chapter, and use animation to show students how graphs build and shift.

Image Bank. All figures and tables are available in digital format in the Instructor's CD and the Online Learning Centre.

COURSE MANAGEMENT

PageOut. McGraw-Hill Ryerson's course management system, PageOut, is the easiest way to create a Web site for your economics course. There is no need for HTML coding, graphic design, or a thick how-to book. Just fill in a series of boxes in plain English and click on one of our professional designs. In no time, your course is online!

For the integrated instructor, we offer *Macroeconomics* content for complete online courses. Whatever your needs, you can customize the *Macroeconomics* Online Learning Centre content and author your own online course materials. It is entirely up to you. You can offer online discussion and message boards that will complement your office hours and reduce the lines outside your door. Content cartridges are also available for course management systems, such as **WebCT** and **Blackboard.** Ask your *i*Learning Sales Specialist for details.

SUPERIOR SERVICE

Service takes on a whole new meaning with McGraw-Hill Ryerson and economics. More that just bringing you the textbook, we have consistently raised the bar in terms of innovation and educational research—both in economics and in educational in general. These investments in learning and the education community have helped us to understand the needs of students and educators across the country and allowed us to foster the growth of truly innovative, integrated learning.

Integrated Learning. Your Integrated Learning Sales Specialist is a McGraw-Hill Ryerson representative who has the experience, product knowledge, training, and support to help you assess and integrate any of your products, technology, and services into your course for optimum teaching and learning performance. Whether it's helping your students improve their grades or putting your entire course online, your *i*Learning Sales Specialist is there to help you do it. Contact your *i*Learning Sales Specialist today to learn how to maximize all of McGraw-Hill Ryerson's resources!

_i_Learning Services. McGraw-Hill Ryerson offers a unique *i*Service package designed for Canadian faculty. Our mission is to equip providers of higher education with superior tools and resources required for excellence in teaching. For additional information, visit **www.mcgrawhill.ca/highereducation/iservices** or contact your local *i*Learning Sales Specialist.

Teaching, Learning & Technology Conference Series. The educational environment has changed tremendously in recent years, and McGraw-Hill Ryerson continues to be committed to helping you acquire the skills you need to succeed in this new milieu. Our innovative Teaching, Learning & Technology Conference Series brings faculty together from across Canada with 3M Teaching Excellence award winners to share teaching and learning best practices in a collaborative and stimulating environment. Preconference workshops on general topics, such as teaching large classes and technology integration, will also be offered. We will also work with you at your own institution to customize workshops that best suit the needs of your faculty.

ACKNOWLEDGMENTS

The birth of this first Canadian edition of *The Macro Economy Today* has been made far easier through the patience, expertise, support, and professionalism of the McGraw-Hill Ryerson team: Bruce McIntosh, Sponsoring Editor; Maria Chu, Senior Developmental Editor; Joanne Limebeer, Supervising Editor; and Cat Haggert, freelance Copy Editor. Many thanks to Bruce for sharing his passion for motorcycles and introducing David to Peter Egan's book, *Leanings*. On countless occasions both Maria and Joanne answered our queries and concerns, no matter how trivial, in their typical efficient and calming manner. And just as we started to tire of the whole process, Cat's probing questions and delightful sense of humour provided the required impetus to finish the task at hand.

The quality of the presentation and readability has been improved by a number of reviewers who were generous enough to tell us what we had done right and helped us to see many areas where we could do better, often providing suggestions that led us to do just that. They include:

Worku Aberra,
Dawson College

Aphy Artopoulo,
Seneca College

Michael Bozzo,
Mohawk College

James Butko,
Niagara College

David Desjardins,
John Abbott College

Livio Di Matteo,
Lakehead University

Bruno Fullone,
George Brown College

Pierre-Pascal Gendron,
Humber College Institute of
Technology & Advanced
Learning

Abdelkrim Hammi,
Vanier College

Susan Kamp,
University of Alberta

George Kennedy,
College of New Caledonia

Borys Kruk,
University College of the
North

Tomi Ovaska,
University of Regina

Kevin Richter,
Douglas College

Jean Louis Rosmy,
Malaspina University-College

Herbert Schuetze,
University of Victoria

Lance Shandler,
Kwantlen University College

Peter Sinclair,
Wilfrid Laurier University

Panagiotis (Peter) Tsigaris,
Thompson Rivers University

Brian Van Blarcom,
Acadia University

Carl Weston,
Mohawk College

A special thank you goes to James Butko, Niagara College, who provided the technical review of the text.

Bradley R. Schiller
Laurie C. Phipps
David R. Sabiston

PART 1

Basic Concepts

he image on the cover depicts beautiful new ice crystals growing on the ancient Canadian Rockies. In some respects, this geographical snapshot captures the fundamental economic concepts outlined in Chapters 1 and 2. Economists' viewpoints on how we decide to allocate our current scarce resources (the growing ice crystals) are frequently based on the foundations created by the perceptive insights of our ancestors (the Canadian Rockies).

As a consumer deciding on how much New Brunswick lobster to purchase, or as an individual trying to find the right amount of labour to supply in a hot Alberta market, or as a producer in the Saguenay deciding whether to shut down an aluminum pot line, the decision-making process has been articulated by great economists from the eighteenth and nineteenth centuries, such as Adam Smith, David Ricardo, and Alfred Marshall. Their research into the decision-making process guides us to the basic concept of opportunity costs (Chapter 1) and the classical demand and supply model (Chapter 2).

Economics: The Core Issues

In February 2004, Intel Corporation announced a research breakthrough that stunned the high-tech industry. The company's engineers had created a new processor with 125 million transistors—the tiny parts that regulate the flow of electricity on a silicon chip. The new transistors were so small (90 nanometers, or less than one thousandth the width of a human hair) that 1 billion of them could be packed onto a single chip. That was a gargantuan leap from the 42-million-transistor Pentium 4 chip that dominated the market: and light-years away from the 2,300-transistor chip that powered IBM computers in 1972. What does all this have to do with you? For starters, it means that every time Intel innovates in this way all electronic goods and services will be able to operate faster and with more options. In other words, the extraordinary array of goods we now confront in the marketplace will continue to expand and improve.

Maybe more isn't always better, but the history of humankind reveals a relentless quest for more and better output. To a large extent, the quest for more output has been driven by necessity. The world's population keeps growing, but the amount of land doesn't. That's why the English economist Thomas Malthus predicted in 1778 that the world would run out of food long before the nineteenth century ended. He didn't know that a few years later someone would invent the iron plow (1808), the reaper (1826), or the milking machine (1878). And Malthus had no conception of what biotechnology's "green revolution" might become and no clues at all about electronic circuits. So his prediction of global starvation turned out to be unduly pessimistic.

Although we've managed to increase global food output faster than the population has grown, we can't be complacent. The United Nations predicts that the world's population, now at 6.4 billion, will increase by another billion every 10 years. Even if we find ways for food output to keep pace, we can't be satisfied. Our future goals are much more ambitious. We want an ever higher standard of living, not just enough food on the table. No matter how fast our incomes grow, we always want more. The living standards earlier generations dreamed of we now take for granted. Today's luxuries—plasma TVs, camera phones, satellite radio—will most likely be viewed as necessities in a few years, but only if we keep squeezing more and more output out of available resources.

LEARNING OBJECTIVES

By the end of this chapter, you should be able to:

1.1 Identify the three core economic questions that all nations must answer

1.2 Explain the importance of scarcity

1.3 Understand how opportunity costs influence decision-making

1.4 Explain the relationship between opportunity costs and production possibilities curves

1.5 Understand the roles of markets and governments in the allocation of resources

1.6 Identify the difference between micro and macro economics

1.7 Recognize the difference between economic theory and reality

WORLD VIEW

Cloudy Days in Tomorrowland

We'd like to think all *our* predictions will prove right. But the highways of history are littered with wrong calls, false insights and bad guesses. Here's a sampler of twentieth-century futurology that flopped.

I confess that in 1901, I said to my brother Orville that man would not fly for 50 years . . . Ever since, I have distrusted myself and avoided all predictions.

—Wilbur Wright, *U.S. aviation pioneer, 1908*

I must confess that my imagination . . . refuses to see any sort of submarine doing anything but suffocating its crew and floundering at sea.

—H. G. Wells, *British novelist, 1901*

Airplanes are interesting toys but of no military value.

—Marshal Ferdinand Foch, *French military strategist and future World War I commander, 1911*

The horse is here to stay, but the automobile is only a novelty—a fad.

—*A president of the Michigan Savings Bank advising* Horace Rackham *(Henry Ford's lawyer) not to invest in the Ford Motor Co., 1903. Rackham ignored the advice, bought $5,000 worth of stock and sold it several years later for $12.5 million.*

Radio has no future.

—Lord Kelvin, *Scottish mathematician and physicist, former president of the Royal Society, 1897*

Everything that can be invented has been invented.

—Charles H. Duell, *U.S. commissioner of patents, 1899*

Who the hell wants to hear actors talk?

—Harry M. Warner, *Warner Brothers, 1927*

There is no reason for any individual to have a computer in their home.

—Kenneth Olsen, *president and founder of Digital Equipment Corp., 1977*

[Man will never reach the moon] regardless of all future scientific advances.

—Dr. Lee De Forest, *inventor of the Audion tube and a father of radio, February 25, 1967*

We don't like their sound. Groups of guitars are on the way out.

—Decca Records, *rejecting the Beatles, 1962*

What use could this company make of an electrical toy?

—*Western Union president* William Orton, *rejecting Alexander Graham Bell's offer to sell his struggling telephone company to Western Union for $100,000*

Computers in the future may . . . perhaps only weigh 1.5 tons.

—Popular Mechanics, *forecasting the development of computer technology, 1949*

Stocks have reached what looks like a permanently high plateau.

—Irving Fisher, *professor of economics, Yale University, October 17, 1929*

The Olympics can no more lose money than a man can have a baby.

—Jean Drapeau, *mayor of Montreal, 1973*

Analysis: No one predicts the future well. But the economic choices we make today about the use of scarce resources will determine the kind of future we have.

Ironically, some people fear we will do exactly that—and end up destroying the environment in the process. They foresee a doomsday in which greenhouse gases generated by ever-rising production levels will overheat the earth, melt the polar icecaps, flood coastal areas, and destroy crops.

As the quotes in the following World View illustrate, no one really knows how the future will unfold. Even some of history's greatest minds have made predictions that turned out to be ludicrous. In gazing into the future, however, we can be certain of some fundamental principles. The first principle is that resources will always be scarce, relative to our desires. Second, how we use those scarce resources will shape our future. If we use resources today to miniaturize electronic circuits, we'll be able to produce more and better products in the future. Likewise, if we build more factories and cyber networks today, we'll be able to produce more output tomorrow. If we install more pollution controls in cars, power plants, and factories today, we'll even have cleaner air tomorrow.

WEB NOTE

Intel Corporation showcases its latest technology at www.intel.com/technology/ silicon/index.htm.

Analysis: Each car manufacturer must decide how to allocate their scarce resources across product lines. More resources allocated to one brand imply fewer resources available for other brands.

economics: The study of how best to allocate scarce resources among competing uses.

The science of economics helps us frame these choices. In a nutshell, **economics** is the study of how people use scarce resources. All decision-makers (individuals, private firms, and public organizations) make choices subject to their particular constraints. How do you decide how much time to spend studying for your economics midterm exam? Would your decision change if your political science midterm was scheduled for the same day? How does DaimlerChrysler decide whether to use its factories to produce sport utility vehicles (e.g., Dodge Durango) or subcompact automobiles (e.g., the Smart Car)? How much do you think their decision is influenced by Canadian demographics, the expected price of oil, or the interest rate policy of the Bank of Canada? How does the provincial government of Ontario decide to allocate their annual budget between health care, education, and social services? Would their decision change if the federal government reduced transfer payments to the provinces?

In each case, alternative ways of using scarce labour, land, and building resources are available, and we have to choose one use over another. The decision-making process, therefore, involves tradeoffs. Choosing one option necessarily implies giving up another. An hour watching the last period of a hockey game, for example, means that hour cannot be used to study for your economics midterm.

In this first chapter we explore the nature of scarcity and the kinds of choices it forces us to make. As we'll see, **three core issues must be resolved:**

- **WHAT to produce with our limited resources.**
- **HOW to produce the goods and services we select.**
- **FOR WHOM goods and services are produced;** that is, who should get them.

We also have to decide who should answer these questions. Should the marketplace decide what gets produced and how and for whom? Or should the government dictate output choices, regulate production processes, and redistribute incomes? Should Microsoft decide what features get included in a computer's operating system, or should the government make that decision? Should private companies provide airport security or should the government assume that responsibility? Should interest rates be set by private banks alone, or should the government try to control interest rates? The battle over *who* should answer the core questions is often as contentious as the questions themselves.

1.1 THE ECONOMY IS US

To learn how the economy works, let's start with a simple truth: *The economy is us.* "The economy" is simply an abstraction referring to the grand sum of all our production and consumption activities. What we collectively produce is what the economy

*"Meaningless statistics were up one-point-five per cent
this month over last month."*

Analysis: Many people think of economics as dull statistics. But economics is really about human behaviour—how people decide to use scarce resources and how those decisions affect market outcomes.

produces; what we collectively consume is what the economy consumes. In this sense, the concept of "the economy" is no more difficult than the concept of "the family." If someone tells you that the Jones family has an annual income of $42,000, you know that the reference is to the collective earnings of all the Joneses. Likewise, when someone reports that the nation's income is $1.5 trillion per year—as it now is—we should recognize that the reference is to the grand total of everyone's income. If we work fewer hours or get paid less, both family income *and* national income decline. The "meaningless statistics" (see accompanying cartoon) often cited in the news are just a summary of our collective market behaviour.

The same relationship between individual behaviour and aggregate behaviour applies to specific output. If we as individuals insist on driving cars rather than taking public transportation, the economy will produce millions of cars each year and consume vast quantities of oil. In a slightly different way, the federal government spends billions of dollars on the protection of persons and property to satisfy our desire for law and order. In each case, the output of the economy reflects the collective behaviour of the individuals who participate in the economy.

We may not always be happy with the output of the economy. But we can't ignore the link between individual action and collective outcomes. If the highways are clogged and the air is polluted, we can't blame someone else for the transportation choices we made. If we're disturbed by the size of our military spending, we must still accept responsibility for our choices. In either case, we continue to have the option of reallocating our resources. We can create a different outcome the next day, month, or year.

1.2 SCARCITY: THE CORE PROBLEM

Although we can change economic outcomes, we can't have everything we want. If you go to the mall with $20 in your pocket, you can only buy so much. The money in your pocket sets a *limit* to your spending.

The output of the entire economy is also limited. The limits in this case are set not by money but by the resources available for producing goods and services. Everyone wants more housing, new schools, better transit systems, and a new car. But even a country as rich as Canada can't produce everything people want. So, like every other nation, we have to grapple with the core problem of **scarcity**—the fact that there aren't enough resources available to satisfy all our desires.

scarcity: Lack of enough resources to satisfy all desired uses of those resources.

Factors of Production

factors of production: Resource inputs used to produce goods and services, such as land, labour, capital, and entrepreneurship.

The resources used to produce goods and services are called **factors of production.** *The four basic factors of production are*

- *Land*
- *Labour*
- *Capital*
- *Entrepreneurship*

These are the *inputs* needed to produce desired *outputs.* To produce this textbook, for example, we needed paper, printing presses, a building, and lots of labour. We also needed people with good ideas who could put it together. To produce the education you're getting in this class, we need not only a textbook but a classroom, a teacher, and a blackboard as well. Without factors of production, we simply can't produce anything.

Land. The first factor of production, land, refers not just to the ground but to all natural resources. Crude oil, water, air, and minerals are all included in our concept of "land."

Labour. Labour too has several dimensions. It's not simply a question of how many bodies there are. When we speak of labour as a factor of production, we refer to the skills and abilities to produce goods and services. Hence, both the quantity and the quality of human resources are included in the "labour" factor.

capital: Final goods produced for use in the production of other goods, e.g., equipment, structures.

Capital. The third factor of production is capital. In economics the term **capital** refers to final goods produced for use in further production. The residents of fishing villages in southern Thailand, for example, braid huge fishing nets. The sole purpose of these nets is to catch more fish. The nets themselves become a factor of production in obtaining the final goods (fish) that people desire. Thus, they're regarded as *capital.* Blast furnaces used to make steel and desks used to equip offices are also capital inputs.

Entrepreneurship. The more land, labour, and capital available, the greater the amount of potential output. A farmer with 10,000 acres, 12 employees, and six tractors can grow more crops than a farmer with half those resources. But there's no guarantee that he will. The farmer with fewer resources may have better ideas about what to plant, when to irrigate, or how to harvest the crops. *It's not just a matter of what resources you have but also of how well you use them.* This is where the fourth factor of production—**entrepreneurship**—comes in. The entrepreneur is the person who sees the opportunity for new or better products and brings together the resources needed for producing them. If it weren't for entrepreneurs, Thai fishermen would still be using sticks to catch fish. Without entrepreneurship, farmers would still be milking their cows by hand. If someone hadn't thought of a way to miniaturize electronic circuits, you wouldn't have a cell phone.

entrepreneurship: The assembling of resources to produce new or improved products and technologies.

The role of entrepreneurs in economic progress is a key issue in the market-versus-government debate. The Austrian economist Joseph Schumpeter argued that free markets unleash the "animal spirits" of entrepreneurs, propelling innovation, technology, and growth. Critics of government regulation argue that government interference in the marketplace, however well intentioned, tends to stifle those very same animal spirits.

Limits to Output

No matter how an economy is organized, there's a limit to how fast it can grow. The most evident limit is the amount of resources available for producing goods and services. These resource limits imply that we can't produce everything we want. One of Prime Minister Stephen Harper's key priorities for his Conservative minority government in 2006 was making "our streets and communities safer by cracking down on crime." While many individuals and organizations applauded the decision to tackle crime issues, a number of Canadians wondered how they would pay for the various, newly-proposed programs (e.g., National Victims' Ombudsman Office, Missing Persons Registry, etc.). In *dollar* terms, the money would have to come from other programs. In *economic* terms, the resources devoted to the creation of these programs would be unavailable for producing other government goods and services such as education, health care, and highways.

"There's no such thing as a free lunch."

Analysis: All goods and services have an opportunity cost. Even the resources used to produce a "free lunch" could have been used to produce something else.

WEB NOTE

To see how wait times for health services vary across provinces, go to the Canadian Institute for Healtha Information's (CIHI) website at www.cihi.ca/ and look under the "Research and Reports" tab.

Opportunity Costs

Every time we use scarce resources in one way, we give up the opportunity to use them in other ways. If more resources are devoted to fighting crime, fewer resources are available to reduce the wait times for health care services. Lengthier wait times represent an **opportunity cost** of fighting crime. *Opportunity cost is what is given up to get something else.* Even a so-called free lunch has an opportunity cost (see cartoon). The resources used to produce the lunch could have been used to produce something else.

Your economics class also has an opportunity cost. The building space used for your economics class can't be used to show movies at the same time. Your professor can't lecture (produce education) and repair motorcycles simultaneously. The decision to use these scarce resources (capital, labour) for an economics class implies producing less of other goods.

Even reading this book is costly. That cost is not measured in dollars and cents. The true (economic) cost is, instead, measured in terms of some alternative activity. What would you like to be doing right now? The more time you spend reading this book, the less time you have available for that alternative use of your time. The opportunity cost of reading this text is the best alternative use of your scarce time. If you are missing your favourite TV show, we'd say that show is the opportunity cost of reading this book. It is what you gave up to do this assignment. Hopefully, the benefits you get from studying will outweigh that cost. Otherwise this wouldn't be the best way to use your scarce time.

opportunity cost: The most desired goods or services that are forgone to obtain something else.

1.3 PRODUCTION POSSIBILITIES

The opportunity costs implied by our every choice can be illustrated easily. Suppose a nation can only produce two goods, wheat and softwood lumber. In addition, assume that both goods use all four basic factors of production (land, labour, capital, and entrepreneurship). Our initial problem is to determine the limits of output. How many metric tonnes of wheat or millions of board-feet[1] of softwood lumber can be produced in one year with all available resources?

Before going any further, notice how opportunity costs affect the answer. If we devote all our available resources to softwood lumber, no resources are available for the production of wheat. In this case, total wheat forgone is the opportunity cost of a decision to employ all our resources in softwood lumber production. In a similar fashion, each and every time we decide to produce more of one good, the opportunity cost can be measured by the amount of the other good forgone.

---

[1]A board-foot (1 foot × 1 foot × 1 inch) is the unit of measurement for lumber in North America.

Production of Wheat (Metric tonnes/year)	Production of Softwood Lumber (Millions of board-feet/year)
A 0	10.0
B 1	9.0
C 2	7.5
D 3	5.5
E 4	3.0
F 5	0.0

TABLE 1.1
Production Possibilities Schedule

As long as resources are limited their use entails an opportunity cost. In this case, resources used to produce softwood lumber cannot simultaneously be used to produce wheat. Hence, the forgone tonnes of wheat are the opportunity cost of producing softwood lumber. If, for example, all our resources were used to produce softwood lumber (row *A*), the opportunity cost of this decision is 5 metric tonnes of wheat—that is, the maximum amount of wheat forgone if all the resources were used to produce wheat instead (row *F*). Similarly, the opportunity cost of producing wheat can be measured in the forgone amount of softwood lumber.

The Production Possibilities Curve

production possibilities: The alternative combinations of final goods and services that could be produced in a given time period with all available resources and technology.

To calculate these opportunity costs we need more details about the production processes involved—specifically, how many resources are required to produce wheat or softwood lumber. Table 1.1 summarizes the hypothetical choices, or **production possibilities,** that are obtainable for this nation given all available resources as well as the current state of technology. Row A of the table shows the consequence of a decision to produce only softwood lumber. With all our resources allocated to the softwood lumber, we can produce a maximum of 10 billion board-feet per year. If we want to produce any wheat, we must cut back on softwood lumber production and move those resources into the wheat production; this is the essential choice (or tradeoff) that we must make.

The remainder of Table 1.1 identifies the full range of production choices. For the production of the first metric tonne of wheat, for example, we see that the required resources amount to the equivalent of one million board-feet of softwood lumber (Row *B*) since production has fallen from 10 to 9. Therefore, the opportunity cost for production of the first metric tonne of wheat is one million board-feet of softwood lumber.

As we proceed down the rows of Table 1.1, the nature of opportunity costs becomes apparent. Each additional tonne of wheat implies the loss (opportunity cost) of softwood lumber production. Similarly, if we start from the bottom of the table and work our way up, additional softwood lumber production necessarily implies the loss of some wheat output.

These tradeoffs between wheat and softwood lumber production are illustrated in the production possibilities curve (PPC) of Figure 1.1. *Each point on the production possibilities curve depicts an alternative mix of output* that could be produced in a year, given total available resources and current technology.

Notice in particular how points *A* through *F* in Figure 1.1 represent the choices described in each row of Table 1.1. A production possibilities curve, then, is simply a graphic summary of production possibilities, as described in Table 1.1. It illustrates the alternative goods and services we could produce and the implied opportunity costs of each choice. In other words, *the production possibilities curve illustrates two essential principles:*

- *Scarce resources.* There's a limit to the amount we can produce in a given time period with available resources and technology.
- *Opportunity costs.* We can obtain additional quantities of any desired good only by reducing the potential production of another good.

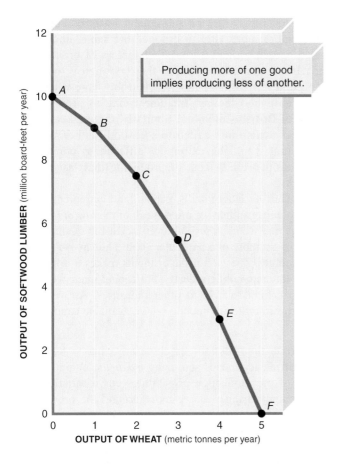

Producing more of one good implies producing less of another.

OUTPUT OF SOFTWOOD LUMBER (million board-feet per year)

OUTPUT OF WHEAT (metric tonnes per year)

FIGURE 1.1
A Production Possibilities Curve (PPC)

A production possibilities curve describes the various output combinations that can be produced in a given time period with available resources and technology. It represents a menu of output choices an economy confronts. Point *B*, for example, indicates that we could produce a combination of one metric tonne of wheat and nine million board-feet of softwood lumber in one year. A move to point *C*, and an increase total output of wheat from one to two metric tonnes, requires reducing production of softwood lumber by one and one-half million board-feet (from nine to seven and one-half million board-feet). This curve is a graphical illustration of the production possibilities schedule in Table 1.1.

Increasing Opportunity Costs

The shape of the production possibilities curve reflects another limitation on our choices. Notice how opportunity costs increase as we move along the production possibilities curve. Recall that our opportunity cost for the first metric tonne of wheat is one million board-feet of softwood lumber (moving from point *A* to point *B*). What is the opportunity cost for the second metric tonne of wheat? As we move from point *B* to point *C*, total production of softwood lumber has fallen from nine million board-feet to seven and one-half million board-feet. Therefore, the opportunity cost of producing the second metric tonne of wheat is one and one-half million board feet of softwood lumber. Notice that as we continue in a similar manner along the PPC, each production of an additional metric tonne of wheat implies a *greater opportunity cost* as measured in millions of board-feet of softwood lumber. These increases in opportunity cost are reflected in the outward bend of the production possibilities curve.

Why do opportunity costs increase? Mostly because it's difficult to move resources from one industry to another. ***Resources tend to be specialized***—that is, they are better suited to the production of one good rather than another good. Consider our example where we start at point *A* with all resources devoted to the production of softwood lumber. If we wanted to produce our first metric tonne of wheat and move to point *B*, what can we say about the resources that we would shift out of the softwood lumber industry and into wheat production? Well, there must be some type of land, for example, currently used in the production of softwood lumber that is better suited for the production of wheat. Imagine trying to grow softwood lumber on the hot, dry, windswept prairies of Saskatchewan! Similarly, there are workers whose skills are better suited to farming as well as capital that could easily be converted to the production of wheat. So, that initial one metric tonne of wheat comes at a relatively low opportunity cost. But what happens if we want to produce another metric tonne of wheat? Since we have already chosen the land best suited for wheat, the subsequent tracts of land will not be as productive and we require more land to produce the same amount of wheat. This statement can also be generalized to the other factors of production. Consider what would happen if we wanted to produce that last metric tonne of wheat (move from point *E* to point *F*). We have now reached the stage where we are using land most suited for softwood lumber. Imagine trying to grow wheat in the temperate, rainy, climate of British Columbia! Similarly, the workers moving into wheat production possess skills more suited to softwood lumber and the remaining softwood lumber capital would be extremely difficult to convert to wheat production. Therefore, the opportunity cost of producing that last metric tonne of wheat is extremely high.

The difficulties entailed in transferring labour skills, capital, and entrepreneurship from one industry to another are so universal that we often speak of the *law of increasing opportunity cost*. This law says that we must give up ever-increasing quantities of other goods and services in order to get more of a particular good. The law isn't based solely on the specialization of resources. The *mix* of factor inputs makes a difference as well. Some industries, such as the automobile industry, are capital-intensive—that is, they use much more physical capital relative to other industries. As we move resources away from other industries into the automobile sector, available capital may restrict our output capabilities.[2]

Efficiency

Not all of the choices on the production possibilities curve are equally desirable. They are, however, all *efficient*. Efficiency means squeezing *maximum* output out of available resources. Every point of the production possibilities curve satisfies this condition. Although the *mix* of output changes as we move around the production possibilities curve, at every point we are getting as much *total* output as physically possible. Since **efficiency** in production means simply "getting the most from what you've got," every point on the production possibilities curve is efficient. At any point on the curve we are using all available resources in the best way we know how.

efficiency: Maximum output of a good from the resources used in production.

Inefficiency

There's no guarantee, of course, that we'll always use resources so efficiently. *A production possibilities curve shows* **potential** *output, not necessarily* **actual** *output.* If we're inefficient, actual output will be less than that potential. This happens. In the real world, workers sometimes loaf on the job. Or they call in sick and go to a baseball game instead of working. Managers don't always give the clearest directions or stay in touch with advancing technology. Even students sometimes fail to put forth their best effort on homework assignments. This kind of slippage can prevent us from achieving maximum production. When that happens, we end up *inside* the production possibilities curve rather than *on* it.

Point *Y* in Figure 1.2 illustrates the consequence of inefficient production. At point *Y*, we are producing only five and one-half million board-feet of softwood lumber and two metric tonnes of wheat. This is less than our potential. We could produce seven and one-half million board-feet of softwood lumber without cutting back wheat production (point *B*). Or we could get an extra metric tonne of wheat without sacrificing any softwood lumber production (point *C*). Instead, we're producing *inside* the production possibilities curve at point *Y*. Such inefficiencies plagued centrally planned economies. Government-run factories guaranteed everyone a job regardless of how much output he or she produced. They became bloated bureaucracies; as many as 40 percent of the workers were superfluous. When communism collapsed, many of these factories were "privatized," that is, sold to private investors. The privatized companies were able to fire thousands of workers and *increase* output. Governments in Europe and Latin America have also

---

[2]Note that the more specialized our resources are, and the greater the difference in the mix of factors of production between products, the greater the "bend" in the PPC. At the other extreme, if resources are perfectly substitutable between goods and the mix of factor inputs is identical, the PPC becomes a linear relationship and we experience *"constant"* opportunity costs.

India's Economy Gets a New Jolt From Mr. Shourie

NEW DELHI—In March 2001, strikers opposed to the Indian government's sale of an aluminum company threatened to fast until they died, an act of civil disobedience made famous by the nation's founding father, Mahatma Gandhi. India's privatization czar, Arun Shourie, was unmoved. "I said you can do what you want," recalls Mr. Shourie, photos of Mr. Gandhi hanging on the office wall in front of him. "But we're still not going to talk to you." The strike folded weeks later.

The sale of Bharat Aluminum Co. was a big test of Mr. Shourie's three-year campaign to sell off the almost 250 companies owned by India's central government. . . .

Since becoming minister of disinvestment in 2000, Mr. Shourie has taken state-owned companies once thought sacrosanct, such as India's long-distance telephone company and its biggest auto maker, and placed them in private hands. . . .

In India, state-owned companies provide a vast patronage system to ministers, party officials, and even petty bureaucrats.

For that system's beneficiaries, privatization represents a "loss of control, prestige, and money," says a banker who has advised the government on privatizations. . . .

What Mr. Shourie learned about the condition of many state-owned companies shocked him. On one fact-finding trip, he toured a state-owned airport hotel in New Delhi that had only a 3% occupancy rate and inoperable toilets. A state-owned tourist hotel in the south of the country had a crematorium and two burial grounds on its land. And a fertilizer company in West Bengal hadn't produced an ounce of product in 14 years. "The employees just sat around all day playing carrom," says Mr. Shourie, referring to an Indian board game.

—Jay Solomon and Joanna Slater

Analysis: When resources are used inefficiently, a nation's output lies *inside* its production possibilities. By privatizing inefficient state enterprises, India hopes to increase total output and reach its production possibilities.

sold off many of their state-owned enterprises in the hopes of increasing efficiency and reaching the production possibilities curve. India's "Minister of Disinvestment" has been pursuing the same strategy, as the World View attests.

Countries may also end up inside their production possibilities curve if all available resources aren't used. In 1993, for example, as many as 1.64 million Canadians (or 11.4% of the labour force) were officially looking for work each week, but no one hired them. As a result, we were stuck inside the production possibilities curve, producing less output than we could have. A basic challenge for policymakers is to eliminate unemployment and keep the economy on its production possibilities curve. By May 2006, Canada was much closer to this goal with unemployment at 1.07 million people (or 6.4% of the labour force—the lowest value in over 30 years).

Unemployment

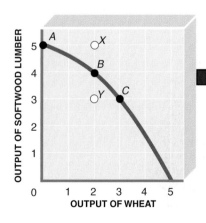

FIGURE 1.2
Points Inside and Outside the Curve

Points outside the production possibilities curve (point *X*) are unattainable with available resources and technology. Points inside the curve (point *Y*) represent the incomplete use of available resources. Only points on the production possibilities curve (*A, B, C*) represent maximum use of our production capabilities.

FIGURE 1.3
Growth: Increasing Production Possibilities

A production possibilities curve is based on *available* resources and technology. If more resources or better technology becomes available, production possibilities will increase. This economic growth is illustrated by the *shift* from PP_1 to PP_2.

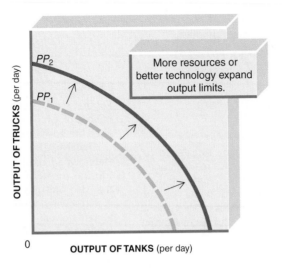

Economic Growth

economic growth: An increase in output (real GDP); an expansion of production possibilities.

Figure 1.2 also illustrates an output mix that everyone would welcome. Point X lies *outside* the production possibilities curve. It suggests that we could get *more* goods than we're capable of producing! Unfortunately, point X is only a mirage: All output combinations that lie outside the production possibilities curve are unattainable with available resources and technology.

Things change, however. Every year, population growth and immigration increase our supply of labour. As we continue building factories and machinery, the stock of available capital also increases. The *quality* of labour and capital also increases when we train workers and pursue new technologies. Entrepreneurs may discover new products or better ways of producing old ones (e.g., Intel's latest chips). All these changes increase potential output. This is illustrated in Figure 1.3 by the outward *shift* of the production possibilities curve. Before the appearance of new resources or better technology, our production possibilities were limited by the curve PP_1. **With more resources or better technology, our production possibilities increase.** This greater capacity to produce is represented by curve PP_2. This outward shift of the production possibilities curve is the essence of **economic growth.** With economic growth, countries can have more of *all* goods and services. Without economic growth, living standards decline as the population grows. This is the problem that plagues some of the world's poorest nations, where population increases every year but output often doesn't.

1.4 BASIC DECISIONS

Production possibilities define the output choices that a nation confronts. From these choices every nation must make some basic decisions. As we noted at the beginning of this chapter, the three core economic questions are

- *WHAT to produce*
- *HOW to produce*
- *FOR WHOM to produce*

WHAT

There are millions of points along a production possibilities curve, and each one represents a different mix of output. We can choose only *one* of these points at any time. The point we choose determines what mix of output gets produced.

The production possibilities curve doesn't tell us which mix of output is best; it just lays out a menu of available choices. It's up to us to pick out the one and only mix of output that will be produced at a given time. This WHAT decision is a basic decision every nation must make.

Decisions must also be made about HOW to produce. Should we generate electricity by burning coal, smashing atoms, or transforming solar power? Should we harvest ancient forests even if that destroys endangered owls or other animal species? Should we dump municipal and industrial waste into nearby rivers, or should we dispose of it in some other way? There are lots of different ways of producing goods and services, and someone has to make a decision about which production methods to use. The HOW decision is a question not just of efficiency but of social values as well.

HOW

After we've decided what to produce and how, we must address a third basic question: FOR WHOM? Who is going to get the output produced? Should everyone get an equal share? Should everyone wear the same clothes and drive identical cars? Should some people get to enjoy seven-course banquets while others forage in garbage cans for food scraps? How should the goods and services an economy produces be distributed? Are we satisfied with the way output is now distributed?

FOR WHOM

1.5 THE MECHANISMS OF CHOICE

Answers to the questions of WHAT, HOW, and FOR WHOM largely define an economy. But who formulates the answers? Who actually decides which goods are produced, what technologies are used, or how incomes are distributed?

Adam Smith had an answer back in 1776. In his classic work *The Wealth of Nations,* Smith said the "invisible hand" determines what gets produced, how, and for whom. The invisible hand he referred to wasn't a creature from a science fiction movie but, instead, a characterization of the way markets work.

The Invisible Hand of a Market Economy

Consider the decision about how many cars to produce in Canada. There's no "auto czar" who dictates production. Not even General Motors can make such a decision. Instead, the *market* decides how many cars to produce. Millions of consumers signal their desire to have a car by browsing the Internet, visiting showrooms, and buying cars. Their purchases flash a green light to producers, who see the potential to earn more profits. To do so, they'll increase auto output. If consumers stop buying cars, profits will disappear. Producers will respond by reducing output, laying off workers, and even closing factories. These interactions between consumers and producers determine how many cars are produced.

Notice how the invisible hand moves us along the production possibilities curve. If consumers demand more cars, the mix of output will include more cars and less of other goods. If auto production is scaled back, the displaced autoworkers will end up producing other goods and services, which will change the mix of output in the opposite direction.

Adam Smith's invisible hand is now called the **market mechanism.** Notice that it doesn't require any direct contact between consumers and producers. Communication is indirect, transmitted by market prices and sales. Indeed, *the essential feature of the market mechanism is the price signal.* If you want something and have sufficient income, you can buy it. If enough people do the same thing, the total sales of that product will rise, and perhaps its price will as well. Producers, seeing sales and prices rise, will want to exploit this profit potential. To do so, they'll attempt to acquire a larger share of available resources and use it to produce the goods we desire. That's how the "invisible hand" works.

market mechanism: The use of market prices and sales to signal desired outputs (or resource allocations).

The market mechanism can also answer the HOW question. To maximize their profits, producers will seek to use the lowest-cost method of producing a good. By observing prices in the marketplace, they can determine if their current production method is the most profitable. If not, they can search for a lower-cost method and adopt it.

The market mechanism can also resolve the FOR WHOM question. A market distributes goods to the highest bidder. In a pure market economy, individuals who are willing and able to pay the most for a good tend to get it.

laissez faire: The doctrine of "leave it alone," of nonintervention by government in the market mechanism.

Adam Smith was so impressed with the ability of the market mechanism to answer the basic WHAT, HOW, and FOR WHOM questions that he urged government to "leave it alone" (**laissez faire**). In his view, the price signals and responses of the marketplace were likely to do a better job of allocating resources than any government could.

Government Intervention and Command Economies

The laissez-faire policy Adam Smith favoured has always had its share of critics. Karl Marx emphasized how free markets tend to concentrate wealth and power in the hands of the few, at the expense of the many. As he saw it, unfettered markets permit the capitalists (those who own the machinery and factories) to enrich themselves while the proletariat (the workers) toil long hours for subsistence wages. Marx argued that the government not only had to intervene but had to *own* all the means of production—the factories, the machinery, the land—to avoid savage inequalities. In *Das Kapital* (1867) and the *Communist Manifesto* (1848), he laid the foundation for a communist state in which the government would be the master of economic outcomes.

The British economist John Maynard Keynes seemed to offer a less drastic solution. The market, he conceded, was pretty efficient in organizing production and building better mousetraps. However, individual producers and workers had no control over the broader economy. The cumulative actions of so many economic agents could easily tip the economy in the wrong direction. A completely unregulated market might veer off in one direction and then another as producers all rushed to increase output at the same time or throttled back production in a herdlike manner. The government, Keynes reasoned, could act like a pressure gauge, letting off excess steam or building it up as the economy needed. With the government maintaining overall balance in the economy, the market could live up to its performance expectations. While assuring a stable, full-employment environment, the government might also be able to redress excessive inequalities. In Keynes's view, government should play an active but not all-inclusive role in managing the economy.

WEB NOTE

For more information on Smith, Malthus, Keynes, and Marx, visit McMaster University's Department of Economics link to the "History of Economic Thought" at http://socserv.mcmaster.ca/econ/ugcm/3ll3/.

Continuing Debates

These historical views shed perspective on today's political debates. The core of most debates is some variation of the WHAT, HOW, or FOR WHOM questions. Much of the debate is how these questions should be answered. Generally speaking, politicians whose ideologies are considered right-of-centre on the political spectrum favour Adam Smith's laissez-faire approach, whereas left-of-centre politicians tend to think government intervention is likely to improve the answers. Similarly, right-leaning politicians often resist workplace regulation, affirmative action, and tax increases on the grounds that such interventions impair market efficiency. Their left-leaning opponents, on the other hand, frequently argue that such interventions help temper excesses of the market and promote both equity and efficiency.

The debate over how best to manage the economy is not unique to Canada. Countries around the world confront the same choice, between reliance on the market and reliance on the government. Few countries have ever relied exclusively on either one or the other to manage their economy. Even the former Soviet Union, where the government owned all the means of production and central planners dictated how they were to be used, made limited use of free markets. In Cuba, the government still manages the economy's resources but encourages farmers' markets and some private trade and investment. As a previous World View indicated, India is now letting the market play a larger role in deciding what is produced, how it is produced, and who gets the resulting output.

The World View below categorizes nations by the extent of their market reliance. Hong Kong scores high on this "Index of Economic Freedom" because its tax rates are relatively low, the public sector is comparatively small, and there are few restrictions on private investment or trade. By contrast, North Korea scores extremely low because the government owns all property, directly allocates resources, sets wages, and limits trade.

The rankings shown in the World View are neither definitive nor stable. In 1989, Russia began a massive transformation from a state-controlled economy to a more

WORLD VIEW

Index of Economic Freedom

Hong Kong ranks number one among the world's nations in economic freedom. It achieves that status with low tax rates, free-trade policies, minimal government regulation, and secure property rights. These and other economic indicators place Hong Kong at the top of the Heritage Foundation's 2006 country rankings by the degree of "economic freedom." The "most free" and the "least free" (repressed) economies on the list of 157 countries are

Greatest Economic Freedom	Least Economic Freedom
Hong Kong	Nigeria
Singapore	Haiti
Ireland	Turkmenistan
Luxembourg	Laos
United Kingdom	Cuba
Iceland	Belarus
Estonia	Venezuela
Denmark	Libya
United States	Zimbabwe
Australia	Burma
New Zealand	Iran
Canada	Korea, North

Source: Heritage Foundation, *2006 Index of Economic Freedom,* Washington, DC, 2006. www.heritage.org

Analysis: All nations must decide whether to rely on market signals or government directives to determine economic outcomes. Nations that rely the least on government intervention score highest on this Index of Economic Freedom.

market-oriented economy. Some of the former republics (e.g., Estonia) became relatively free, while others (e.g., Turkmenistan) still rely on extensive government control of the economy. China has greatly expanded the role of private markets and Cuba is moving in the same direction in fits and starts. Even Libya—one of the second "least-free" nations on the Heritage list—is just now experimenting with some market reforms.

In Canada, the changes have been less dramatic. Over the past few decades, the overall tendency of federal governments—both Conservative and Liberal—has been towards promoting the allocation of resources through the market economy. This does not necessarily reduce the importance of the role of the government.

The recent concern about environmental issues is a good example. Many Canadians believe that without some sort of government intervention, producers (and consumers) will continue to pollute the environment. They argue that there are few market incentives to reduce pollution and that we cannot simply rely on moral convictions to tackle the problem. In an effort to address the pollution associated with automobiles, the 2007 federal budget presented by the Harper government included a Vehicle Efficiency Incentive which provided a rebate of up to $2,000 to people who bought more fuel efficient vehicles and penalized those who purchased gas-guzzlers with new taxes of up to $4,000. Rather than impose specific gas consumption limits, the government is relying on the market mechanism to reduce emissions. The Applications below illustrate some of the problems created with this new legislation.

WEB NOTE

To learn how the Heritage Foundation defines economic freedom, visit its Web site at www.heritage.org.

APPLICATIONS

Controversy over Ottawa's Rebate for Fuel-Efficient Cars

Unhappy auto companies that sell subcompact cars are revising marketing plans and sales forecasts now that Ottawa has provided a competitive advantage to Toyota Canada Inc. with environmental provisions in the new federal budget.

Buyers of cars that use less than 6.5 litres of gas to go 100 kilometres will receive a rebate of at least $1,000. The

Toyota Yaris, rated by Natural Resources Canada at 6.4 litres per 100 kilometres, qualifies for the $1,000. The Honda Fit, which has a rating of 6.6 litres for every 100 kilometres doesn't make the grade. A rebate of $1,000 is a major advantage in segment of the market where the vehicles sell in the $12,000 to $14,000 range.

	Fuel economy	Rebate
Toyota Yaris: $14,605 (four door)	6.4	$1,000
Honda Fit: $14,980 (five-speed manual)	6.6	$0
Hyundai Accent: $12,995 (five-speed manual)	6.9	$0
Nissan Versa: $14,498	7.2	$0
Chevrolet Aveo: $12,995	7.55	$0

"What we're concerned about is letting one [model] in a very price-sensitive segment of the market receive the rebate when all the vehicles in that segment of the market are fuel efficient," Hyundai Auto Canada president Steve Kelleher said yesterday.

Source: Greg Keenan, *The Globe and Mail,* March 22, 2007, page B1.

Analysis: Governments' attempts to influence resource allocation through the market mechanism are often controversial since they can create "winners" and "losers."

A Mixed Economy

mixed economy: An economy that uses both market signals and government directives to allocate goods and resources.

No one wants to rely exclusively on Adam Smith's invisible hand. Nor is anyone willing to have the economy steered exclusively by the highly visible hand of the government. *Canada, like most nations, uses a combination of market signals and government directives to select economic outcomes.* The resulting compromises are called **mixed economies.**

The reluctance of countries around the world to rely exclusively on either market signals or government directives is due to the recognition that both mechanisms can and do fail on occasion. As we've seen, market signals are capable of answering the three core questions of WHAT, HOW, and FOR WHOM. But the answers may not be the best possible ones.

Market Failure

market failure: An imperfection in the market mechanism that prevents optimal outcomes.

When market signals don't give the best possible answers to the WHAT, HOW, and FOR WHOM questions, we say that the market mechanism has *failed.* Specifically, **market failure** means that the invisible hand has failed to achieve the best possible outcomes. If the market fails, we end up with the wrong (*sub*optimal) mix of output, too much unemployment, polluted air, or an inequitable distribution of income.

In a market-driven economy, for example, producers will select production methods based on cost. Cost-driven production decisions, however, may lead a factory to spew pollution into the environment rather than to use cleaner but more expensive methods of production. The resulting pollution may be so bad that society ends up worse off as a result of the extra production. In such a case we may need government intervention to force better answers to the WHAT and HOW questions.

We could also let the market decide who gets to consume cigarettes. Anyone who had enough money to buy a pack of cigarettes would then be entitled to smoke. What if, however, children aren't experienced enough to balance the risks of smoking against the pleasures? What if nonsmokers are harmed by secondhand smoke? In this case as well, the market's answer to the FOR WHOM question might not be optimal.

Government intervention may move us closer to our economic goals. If so, the resulting mix of market signals and government directives would be an improvement over a purely market-driven economy. But government intervention may fail as well. **Government failure** occurs when government intervention fails to improve market outcomes or actually makes them worse.

The collapse of communism revealed how badly government directives can fail. But government failure also occurs in less spectacular ways. For example, the government may intervene to force an industry to clean up its pollution. The government's directives may impose such high costs that the industry closes factories and lays off workers. Some cutbacks in output might be appropriate, but they could also prove excessive. The government might also mandate pollution control technologies that are too expensive or even obsolete. None of this has to happen, but it might. If it does, government failure will have worsened economic outcomes.

The government might also fail if it interferes with the market's answer to the FOR WHOM question. For 50 years, communist China distributed goods by government directive, not market performance. Incomes were more equal, but uniformly low. To increase output and living standards, China has turned to market incentives (see the World View on the next page). As entrepreneurs respond to these incentives, everyone may become better off—even while inequality increases.

The current practice of raising taxes to fund transfer payments may also worsen economic outcomes. If the government raises taxes on the rich to pay welfare benefits for the poor, neither the rich nor the poor may see much purpose in working. In that case, the attempt to give everybody a "fair" share of the pie might end up shrinking the size of the pie. If that happened, society could end up worse off.

None of these failures has to occur, but each might. The challenge for society is to minimize failures by selecting the appropriate balance of market signals and government directives. This isn't an easy task. It requires that we know how markets work and why they sometimes fail. We also need to know what policy options the government has and how and when they might work.

1.6 WHAT ECONOMICS IS ALL ABOUT

Understanding how economies function is the basic purpose of studying economics. We seek to know how an economy is organized, how it behaves, and how successfully it achieves its basic objectives. Then, if we're lucky, we can discover better ways of attaining those same objectives.

Economists don't formulate an economy's objectives. Instead, they focus on the *means* available for achieving given *goals*. Under the preamble of the Bank of Canada Act, for example, the Bank's mandate is "generally to promote the economic and financial welfare of Canada." The economist's job is to help design policies that will best achieve these goals. One of the Bank's responsibilities is for monetary policy; how much money circulates in the economy, and what that money is worth. To that extent, the current cornerstone of the Bank's monetary policy framework is its inflation-control system, the goal of which is to keep the persistent rise over time in the average price of goods and services near 2 percent—the midpoint of a 1 to 3 percent target range. The means by which the Bank attains this end is by influencing short-term interest rates.

Government Failure

> government failure: Government intervention that fails to improve economic outcomes.

Seeking Balance

End vs. Means

China's Leaders Back Private Property

SHANGHAI, Dec. 22—China's Communist Party leaders on Monday proposed amendments to the nation's constitution that would enshrine a legal right to private property while broadening the focus of the party to represent private businesses.

Virtually assured of adoption in the party-controlled National People's Congress, the amendments constitute a significant advance in China's ongoing transition from communism to capitalism. They amount to recognition that the economic future of the world's most populous country rests with private enterprise—a radical departure from the political roots of this land still known as the People's Republic of China.

Not since the Communist Party swept to power in 1949 in a revolution built on antipathy toward landowners and industrialists have Chinese been legally permitted to own property. Under the leadership of Chairman Mao, millions of people suffered persecution for being tainted with "bad" class backgrounds that linked them to landowning pasts.

But in present-day China the profit motive has come to pervade nearly every area of life. The site in Shanghai where the Communist Party was founded is now a shopping and entertainment complex anchored by a Starbucks coffee shop. From the poor villages in which most Chinese still live to the cities now dominated by high-rises, the market determines the price of most goods and decisions about what to produce. Business is widely viewed as a favored, even noble, undertaking.

The state-owned firms that once dominated China's economy have traditionally been sustained by credit from state banks, regardless of their balance sheets. Today, many are bankrupt, and banks are burdened by about $500 billion in bad loans, according to private economists. The government has cast privatization as the prescription for turning them around, creating management incentives to make them profitable.

—Peter S. Goodman

Source: *Washington Post*, December 23, 2003. © 2003 The Washington Post. Reprinted with permission. www.washingtonpost.com

Analysis: Government-directed production, prices, and incomes may increase equalities but blunt incentives. Private property and market-based incomes motivate higher productivity and growth.

Macro vs. Micro

macroeconomics: The study of aggregate economic behaviour, of the economy as a whole.

microeconomics: The study of individual behaviour in the economy, of the components of the larger economy.

The study of economics is typically divided into two parts: macroeconomics and microeconomics. Macroeconomics focuses on the behaviour of an entire economy— the "big picture." In macroeconomics we worry about such national goals as full employment, control of inflation, and economic growth, without worrying about the well-being or behaviour of specific individuals or groups. The essential concern of **macroeconomics** is to understand and improve the performance of the economy as a whole.

Microeconomics is concerned with the details of this big picture. In microeconomics we focus on the individuals, firms, and government agencies that actually compose the larger economy. Our interest here is in the behaviour of individual economic actors. What are their goals? How can they best achieve these goals with their limited resources? How will they respond to various incentives and opportunities?

A primary concern of macroeconomics, for example, is to determine how much money, *in total,* consumers will spend on goods and services. In microeconomics, the focus is much narrower. In micro, attention is paid to purchases of *specific* goods and services rather than just aggregated totals. Macro likewise concerns itself with the level of *total* business investment, while micro examines how *individual* businesses make their investment decisions.

Although they operate at different levels of abstraction, macro and micro are intrinsically related. Macro (aggregate) outcomes depend on micro behaviour, and micro (individual) behaviour is affected by macro outcomes. One can't fully understand how an economy works until one understands how all the participants behave and why they behave as they do. But just as you can drive a car without knowing how its engine is constructed, you can observe how an economy runs without completely disassembling it. In macroeconomics we observe that the car goes faster when the accelerator is depressed and that it slows when the brake is applied. That's all we need to know in most situations. At times, however, the car breaks down. When it does, we have to know something more about how the pedals work. This leads us into micro studies. How does each part work? Which ones can or should be fixed?

Our interest in microeconomics is motivated by more than our need to understand how the larger economy works. The "parts" of the economic engine are people. To the extent that we care about the welfare of individuals in society, we have a fundamental interest in microeconomic behaviour and outcomes. In this regard, we examine how individual consumers and business firms seek to achieve specific goals in the marketplace. The goals aren't always related to output. Gary Becker won the 1992 Nobel Prize in economics for demonstrating how economic principles also affect decisions to marry, to have children, or to engage in criminal activities.

The distinction between macroeconomics and microeconomics is one of many simplifications we make in studying economic behaviour. The economy is much too vast and complex to describe and explain in one course (or one lifetime). Accordingly, we focus on basic relationships, ignoring annoying detail. In so doing, we isolate basic principles of economic behaviour and then use those principles to predict economic events and develop economic policies. This means that we formulate theories, or *models,* of economic behaviour and then use those theories to evaluate and design economic policy.

These models of economic behaviour and subsequent policies rely primarily on data and empirical observation to justify their accuracy. Economists use the term *positive statements* to identify the questions or the relationships of interest. By definition, positive statements can be verified with empirical data. "An increase in the minimum wage will lead to an increase in the unemployment rate for teenagers" or "giving each Albertan a $400 prosperity cheque will lead to higher inflation in the province" are examples of positive statements; the accuracy of each statement can be empirically verified. But statements such as "we should increase minimum wages" or "the province of Alberta should invest more money in health care and not give out prosperity cheques" are examples of *normative statements.* Such statements are based on an individual's principles or value judgments and cannot be deemed true or false through any formal empirical analysis.

Economics—both theory and policy—focuses on positive statements. But these statements frequently need to be set in the proper context. Our model of consumer behaviour assumes, for example, that people buy less of a good when its price rises. In reality, however, people *may* buy *more* of a good at increased prices, especially if those high prices create a certain snob appeal or if prices are expected to increase still further. In predicting consumer responses to price increases, we typically ignore such possibilities by *assuming* that the price of the good in question is the *only* thing that changes. This assumption of "other things remaining equal" (unchanged) (in Latin, **ceteris paribus**) allows us to make straightforward predictions. If instead we described consumer responses to increased prices in any and all circumstances (allowing everything to change at once), every prediction would be accompanied by a book full of exceptions and qualifications. We'd look more like lawyers than economists.

Although the assumption of *ceteris paribus* makes it easier to formulate economic theory and policy, it also increases the risk of error. If other things do change in significant ways, our predictions (and policies) may fail. But, like weather forecasters, we continue to make predictions, knowing that occasional failure is inevitable. In so doing, we're motivated by the conviction that it's better to be approximately right than to be dead wrong.

Theory vs. Reality

ceteris paribus: The assumption of nothing else changing.

Politics. Politicians can't afford to be quite so complacent about economic predictions. Policy decisions must be made every day. And a politician's continued survival in office frequently depends on his or her government's choices. During his tenure (1984–1993), Prime Minister Brian Mulroney introduced free trade agreements with the United States and Mexico, replaced the Manufacturers' Sales Tax with the Goods and Services Tax (GST) and attempted to end Quebec's constitutional grievances with the Meech Lake Accord. Were these the right choices? Did they influence the 1993 elections results? Probably, but economic theory alone can't completely answer these questions. Political decisions are not only derived by examining economic trade-offs (opportunity costs), but also social values. By all accounts, Paul Martin was a well-respected and competent politician. As the Minister of Finance (1993–2003) under the Chrétien government, he successfully turned a $42 billion federal deficit into annual surpluses. Yet, his tenure as Prime Minister (2003–2006) was overshadowed by a major government sponsorship scandal left over from the Chrétien years. While the subsequent investigation by the Gomery Commission cleared Martin of any personal wrongdoing, the damage was done and his party fell to defeat in January 2006.

"Politics"—the balancing of competing interests—is an inevitable ingredient of economic policy. On occasion, political expediency of a policy takes precedence over economic implications. Prime Minister Stephen Harper's decision to reduce the GST from 7 percent to 6 percent in July 2006 received plenty of political support, but many economists argued that *income* tax reform rather than *consumption* tax changes would be a more efficiency manner to reduce the tax burden.

Imperfect Knowledge. One last word of warning before you read further. Economics claims to be a science, in pursuit of basic truths. We want to understand and explain how the economy works without getting tangled up in subjective value judgments. This may be an impossible task. First, it's not clear where the truth lies. For more than 200 years economists have been arguing about what makes the economy tick. None of the competing theories has performed spectacularly well. Indeed, few economists have successfully predicted major economic events with any consistency. Even annual forecasts of inflation, unemployment, and output are regularly in error. Worse still, never-ending arguments about what caused a major economic event continue long after it occurs. In fact, economists are still arguing over the primary causes of the Great Depression of the 1930s!

In part, this enduring controversy reflects diverse sociopolitical views on the appropriate role of government. Some people think a big public sector is undesirable, even if it improves economic performance. But the controversy has even deeper roots. Major gaps in our understanding of the economy persist. We know how much of the economy works, but not all of it. We're adept at identifying all the forces at work, but not always successful in gauging their relative importance. In point of fact, we may *never* find an absolute truth, because the inner workings of the economy change over time. When economic behaviour changes, our theories must be adapted.

In view of all these debates and uncertainties, don't expect to learn everything there is to know about the economy today in this text or course. Our goals are more modest. We want to develop a reasonable perspective on economic behaviour, an understanding of basic principles. With this foundation, you should acquire a better view of how the economy works. Daily news reports on economic events should make more sense. Debates on tax and budget policies should take on more meaning. You may even develop some insights that you can apply toward running a business or planning a career, or—if the Nobel prize-winning economist Gary Becker is right—developing a lasting marriage.

WEB NOTE

Comparative data on the percentage of goods and services the various national governments provide is available from the Penn World Tables at www.pwt.econ.upenn.edu.

SUMMARY

- Scarcity is a basic fact of economic life. Factors of production (land, labour, capital, entrepreneurship) are scarce in relation to our desires for goods and services.

- All economic activity entails opportunity costs. Factors of production (resources) used to produce one output cannot simultaneously be used to produce something else. When we choose to produce one thing, we forsake the opportunity to produce some other good or service.

- A production possibilities curve illustrates the limits to production and the opportunity costs associated with different output combinations. It shows the alternative combinations of final goods and services that could be produced in a given period if all available resources and technology are used efficiently.

- The bent shape of the production possibilities curve reflects the law of increasing opportunity costs. This law states that increasing quantities of any good can be obtained only by sacrificing ever-increasing quantities of other goods.

- Inefficient or incomplete use of resources will fail to attain production possibilities. Additional resources or better technologies will expand them. This is the essence of economic growth.

- Every country must decide WHAT to produce, HOW to produce, and FOR WHOM to produce with its limited resources.

- The choices of WHAT, HOW, and FOR WHOM can be made by the market mechanism or by government directives. Most nations are mixed economies, using a combination of these two choice mechanisms.

- Market failure exists when market signals generate suboptimal outcomes. Government failure occurs when government intervention worsens economic outcomes. The challenge for economic theory and policy is to find the mix of market signals and government directives that best fulfills our social and economic goals.

- The study of economics focuses on the broad question of resource allocation. Macroeconomics is concerned with allocating the resources of an entire economy to achieve aggregate economic goals (e.g., full employment). Microeconomics focuses on the behaviour and goals of individual market participants.

Key Terms

economics 4
scarcity 5
factors of production 6
capital 6
entrepreneurship 6
opportunity cost 7

production possibilities 8
efficiency 10
economic growth 12
market mechanism 13
laissez faire 14
mixed economy 16

market failure 16
government failure 17
macroeconomics 18
microeconomics 18
ceteris paribus 19

Questions for Discussion

1. What opportunity costs did you incur in reading this chapter? If you read four more chapters of this book today, would your opportunity cost (per chapter) increase? Explain.
2. How much time could you spend on homework in a day? How much do you spend? How do you decide?
3. What's the real cost of the food in the free lunch cartoon?
4. What economic benefits might India get from privatizing state enterprises (World View, p. 11)?
5. How might a nation's production possibilities be affected by the following?
   a. A decrease in taxes.
   b. An increase in government regulation.
   c. An increase in military spending.
   d. An increase in college tuition.
   e. Faster, more powerful electronic chips.
6. Markets reward individuals according to their output; communism rewards people according to their needs. How might these different systems affect work effort?
7. How does government intervention affect college admissions? Who would go to college in a completely private (market) college system?
8. How will the Chinese economy benefit from private property? (See World View, page 18.) Is there any downside to greater entrepreneurial freedom?
9. How many resources should we allocate to reducing automobile pollution? How will we make this decision?

EXERCISES

PROBLEMS The Student Problem Set to accompany this chapter can be found at the end of the book.

WEB ACTIVITIES Web Activities to accompany this chapter can be found on the Online Learning Centre at **http://www.mcgrawhill.ca/olc/schiller**.

A P P E N D I X

USING GRAPHS

Economists like to draw graphs. In fact, we didn't even make it through the first chapter without a few graphs. This appendix looks more closely at the way graphs are drawn and used. The basic purpose of a graph is to illustrate a relationship between two *variables*. Consider, for example, the relationship between grades and studying. In general, we expect that additional hours of study time will lead to higher grades. Hence, we should be able to see a distinct relationship between hours of study time and grade-point average.

Suppose that we actually surveyed all the students taking this course with regard to their study time and grade-point averages. The resulting information can be compiled in a table such as Table 1A.1.

According to the table, students who don't study at all can expect an F in this course. To get a C, the average student apparently spends 8 hours a week studying. All those who study 16 hours a week end up with an A in the course.

These relationships between grades and studying can also be illustrated on a graph. Indeed, the whole purpose of a graph is to summarize numerical relationships.

We begin to construct a graph by drawing horizontal and vertical boundaries, as in Figure 1A.1. These boundaries are called the *axes* of the graph. On the vertical axis (often called the *y*-axis) we measure one of the variables; the other variable is measured on the horizontal axis (the *x*-axis).

In this case, we shall measure the grade-point average on the vertical axis. We start at the *origin* (the intersection of the two axes) and count upward, letting the distance between horizontal lines represent half (0.5) a grade point. Each horizontal line is numbered, up to the maximum grade-point average of 4.0.

TABLE 1A.1
Hypothetical Relationship of Grades to Study Time

Study Time (hours per week)	Grade-Point Average
16	4.0 (A)
14	3.5 (B+)
12	3.0 (B)
10	2.5 (C+)
8	2.0 (C)
6	1.5 (D+)
4	1.0 (D)
2	0.5 (F+)
0	0.0 (F)

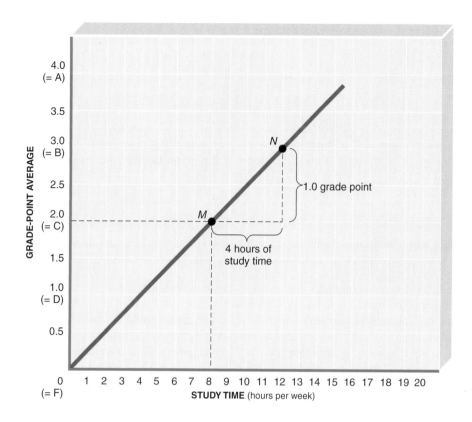

FIGURE 1A.1
The Relationship of Grades to Study Time

The upward (positive) slope of the curve indicates that additional studying is associated with higher grades. The average student (2.0, or C grade) studies 8 hours per week. This is indicated by point *M* on the graph.

The number of hours each week spent doing homework is measured on the horizontal axis. We begin at the origin again, and count to the right. The *scale* (numbering) proceeds in increments of 1 hour, up to 20 hours per week.

When both axes have been labelled and measured, we can begin illustrating the relationship between study time and grades. Consider the typical student who does eight hours of homework per week and has a 2.0 (C) grade-point average. We illustrate this relationship by first locating eight hours on the horizontal axis. We then move up from that point a distance of 2.0 grade points, to point *M*. Point *M* tells us that eight hours of study time per week is typically associated with a 2.0 grade-point average.

The rest of the information in Table 1A.1 is drawn (or *plotted*) on the graph the same way. To illustrate the average grade for people who study 12 hours per week, we move upward from the number 12 on the horizontal axis until we reach the height of 3.0 on the vertical axis. At that intersection, we draw another point (point *N*).

Once we've plotted the various points describing the relationship of study time to grades, we may connect them with a line or curve. This line (curve) is our summary. In this case, the line slopes upward to the right—that is, it has a *positive* slope. This slope indicates that more hours of study time are associated with *higher* grades. Were higher grades associated with *less* study time, the curve in Figure 1A.1 would have a *negative* slope (downward from left to right).

Slopes

The upward slope of Figure 1A.1 tells us that higher grades are associated with increased amounts of study time. That same curve also tells us *by how much* grades tend to rise with study time. According to point *M* in Figure 1A.1, the average student studies 8 hours per week and earns a C (2.0 grade-point average). To earn a B (3.0 average), students apparently need to study an average of 12 hours per week (point *N*). Hence an increase of four hours of study time per week is associated with a one-point increase in grade-point average. This relationship between *changes* in study time and *changes* in grade-point average is expressed by the steepness, or *slope,* of the graph.

The slope of any graph is calculated as

$$\text{Slope} = \frac{\text{vertical distance between two points}}{\text{horizontal distance between two points}}$$

In our example, the vertical distance between M and N represents a change in grade-point average. The horizontal distance between these two points represents the change in study time. Hence the slope of the graph between points M and N is equal to

$$\text{Slope} = \frac{3.0 \text{ grade} - 2.0 \text{ grade}}{12 \text{ hours} - 8 \text{ hours}} = \frac{1 \text{ grade point}}{4 \text{ hours}}$$

In other words, a four-hour increase in study time (from 8 to 12 hours) is associated with a one-point increase in grade-point average (see Figure 1A.1).

Shifts

The relationship between grades and studying illustrated in Figure 1A.1 isn't inevitable. It's simply a graphical illustration of student experiences, as revealed in our hypothetical survey. The relationship between study time and grades could be quite different.

Suppose that the university decided to raise grading standards, making it more difficult to achieve every grade other than an F. To achieve a C, a student now would need to study 12 hours per week, not just 8 (as in Figure 1A.1). Whereas students could previously expect to get a B by studying 12 hours per week, now they'd have to study 16 hours to get that grade.

Figure 1A.2 illustrates the new grading standards. Notice that the new curve lies to the right of the earlier curve. We say that the curve has *shifted* to reflect a change in the relationship between study time and grades. Point R indicates that 12 hours of study time now "produces" a C, not a B (point N on the old curve). Students who now study only four hours per week (point S) will fail. Under the old grading policy,

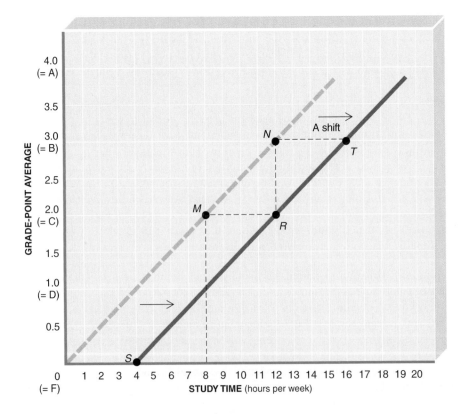

FIGURE 1A.2
A Shift

When a relationship between two variables changes, the entire curve *shifts*. In this case a tougher grading policy alters the relationship between study time and grades. To get a C, one must now study 12 hours per week (point *R*), not just 8 hours (point *M*).

they could have at least gotten a D. ***When a curve shifts, the underlying relationship between the two variables has changed.***

A shift may also change the slope of the curve. In Figure 1A.2, the new grading curve is parallel to the old one; it therefore has the same slope. Under either the new grading policy or the old one, a four-hour increase in study time leads to a one-point increase in grades. Therefore, the slope of both curves in Figure 1A.2 is

$$\text{Slope} = \frac{\text{vertical change}}{\text{horizontal change}} = \frac{1}{4}$$

This too may change, however. Figure 1A.3 illustrates such a possibility. In this case, zero study time still results in an F. But now the payoff for additional studying is reduced. Now it takes six hours of study time to get a D (1.0 grade point), not four hours as before. Likewise, another 4 hours of study time (to a total of 10) raises the grade by only two-thirds of a point. It takes six hours to raise the grade a full point. The slope of the new line is therefore

$$\text{Slope} = \frac{\text{vertical change}}{\text{horizontal change}} = \frac{1}{6}$$

The new curve in Figure 1A.3 has a smaller slope than the original curve and so lies below it. What all this means is that it now takes a greater effort to *improve* your grade.

In Figures 1A.1–1A.3 the relationship between grades and studying is represented by a straight line—that is, a *linear curve*. A distinguishing feature of linear curves is that they have the same (constant) slope throughout. In Figure 1A.1, it appears that *every* four-hour increase in study time is associated with a one-point increase in average grades. In Figure 1A.3, it appears that every six-hour increase in study time leads to a one-point increase in grades. But the relationship between studying and grades may not be linear. Higher grades may be more difficult to attain. You may be able to raise a C to a B by studying four hours more per week. But it may

Linear vs. Nonlinear Curves

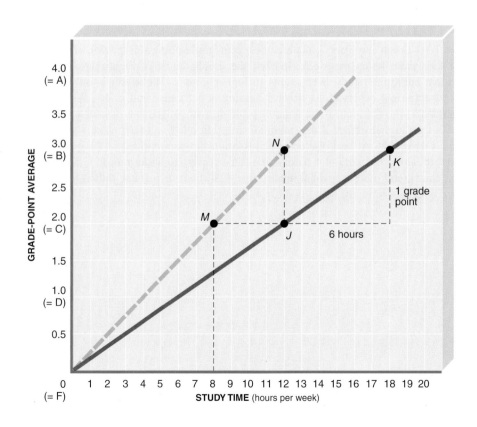

FIGURE 1A.3
A Change in Slope

When a curve shifts, it may change its slope as well. In this case, a new grading policy makes each higher grade more difficult to reach. To raise a C to a B, for example, one must study six additional hours (compare points *J* and *K*). Earlier it took only four hours to move the grade scale up a full point. The slope of the line has declined from 0.25(= 1 ÷ 4) to 0.17(= 1 ÷ 6).

FIGURE 1A.4
A Nonlinear Relationship

Straight lines have a constant slope, implying a constant relationship between the two variables. But the relationship (and slope) may vary. In this case, it takes six extra hours of study to raise a C (point *W*) to a B (point *X*) but eight extra hours to raise a B to an A (point *Y*). The slope decreases as we move up the curve.

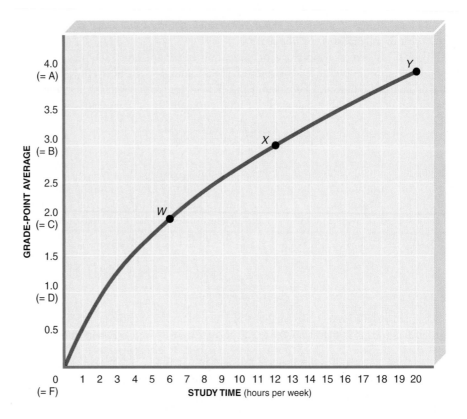

be harder to raise a B to an A. According to Figure 1A.4, it takes an additional eight hours of studying to raise a B to an A. Thus the relationship between study time and grades is *nonlinear* in Figure 1A.4; the slope of the curve changes as study time increases. In this case, the slope decreases as study time increases. Grades continue to improve, but not so fast, as more and more time is devoted to homework. You may know the feeling.

Causation

Figure 1A.4 doesn't by itself guarantee that your grade-point average will rise if you study four more hours per week. In fact, the graph drawn in Figure 1A.4 doesn't prove that additional study ever results in higher grades. The graph is only a summary of empirical observations. It says nothing about cause and effect. It could be that students who study a lot are smarter to begin with. If so, then less-able students might not get higher grades if they studied harder. In other words, the *cause* of higher grades is debatable. At best, the empirical relationship summarized in the graph may be used to support a particular theory (e.g., that it pays to study more). Graphs, like tables, charts, and other statistical media, rarely tell their own story; rather, they must be *interpreted* in terms of some underlying theory or expectation.

WEB NOTE

For online practice with graphs, visit "Math Skills for Introductory Economics" at syllabus.syr.edu/cid/graph/book.html.

Introduction to Supply and Demand

The lights went out in California in January 2001. With only minutes of warning, sections of high-tech Silicon Valley, San Francisco, the state capital of Sacramento, and a host of smaller cities went dark. Schools closed early, traffic signals malfunctioned, ATM machines shut down, and elevators abruptly stopped. "It's like we're living in Bosnia," said Michael Mischer, an Oakland, California baker. "How could this happen?"[1]

The California electricity crisis of 2000–2001—where average prices for wholesale electricity skyrocketed from $30 ($US) per megawatt-hour (MWh) in January 2000 to $300 ($US) per MWh in January 2001—occurred shortly after California moved away from regulated market prices toward unregulated market prices. California's Governor, Grey Davis, argued that out-of-state power company "pirates" were gouging Californian residents with exorbitant prices and suggested price controls, state purchase of transmission lines, and customer refunds from "profiteering" power companies. Critics of the governor's explanation suggested that government intervention, not the market, was the cause of the electricity crisis. The decision to let markets dictate wholesale prices, but still retain caps on retail prices ($100 ($US) per MWh) did not provide consumers with the proper incentives to conserve energy when demand increased. In addition, the previous regulated market did not provide adequate incentives for power producers to expand capacity and now, with California enjoying a boom, the sudden increase in demand for electricity could only result in short-term higher prices. They urged the state to rely more on the market than on state legislators to avoid future blackouts.

As the crises continued, it was clear that both sides had valid arguments. The independent agency regulating transmission of wholesale energy prices, the Federal Energy Regulatory Commission (FERC), testified that the ". . . major factors contributing to the electricity crisis in California were insufficient infrastructure, dysfunctional market rules, and inadequate market oversight and enforcement. These and other factors caused wholesale prices for spot power during the crisis to be unjust and unreasonable . . . the Commission Staff found evidence of significant market manipulation in Western energy markets during 2000 and 2001."[2]

[1] Rene Sanchez and William Booth, "California Forced to Turn the Lights Off," *Washington Post*, January 18, 2001, p. 1.
[2] Summary of Testimony of Pat Wood III, Chairman, Federal Energy Regulatory Commission to US House of Representatives, April 8, 2003. (http://www.ferc.gov/press-room/cong-test/2003/04-08-03-wood.pdf)

California's 2000 to 2001 energy crisis is a classic illustration of why the choice between market reliance and government intervention is so critical and often so controversial. Moreover, the U.S. experience can also help guide Canadian provincial policy-makers as both Alberta and Ontario have started the process of deregulation in electricity markets. The goal of this chapter is to examine that choice in a more coherent framework by focusing on how *unregulated* markets work. How does the market mechanism decide WHAT to produce, HOW to produce, and FOR WHOM to produce? Specifically,

- **What determines the price of a good or service?**
- **How does the price of a product affect its production and consumption?**
- **Why do prices and production levels often change?**

2.1 MARKET PARTICIPANTS

Maximizing Behaviour

A good way to start figuring out how markets work is to see who participates in them. The answer is simple: just about every person and institution on the planet. All these market participants come into the marketplace to satisfy specific goals. Consumers, for example, come with a limited amount of income to spend. Their objective is to buy the most desirable goods and services that their limited budgets will permit. We can't afford *everything* we want, so we must make *choices* about how to spend our scarce dollars. Our goal is to *maximize* the utility (satisfaction) we get from our available incomes.

Businesses also try to maximize in the marketplace. In their case, the quest is for maximum *profits.* Business profits are the difference between sales receipts and total costs. To maximize profits, business firms try to use resources efficiently in producing products that consumers desire.

The public sector also has maximizing goals. The economic purpose of government is to use available resources to serve public needs. The resources available for this purpose are limited too. Hence, local, provincial, and federal governments must use scarce resources carefully, striving to maximize the general welfare of society. International consumers and producers pursue these same goals when participating in our markets.

Market participants sometimes lose sight of their respective goals. Consumers sometimes buy impulsively and later wish they'd used their income more wisely. Likewise, a producer may take a two-hour lunch, even at the sacrifice of maximum profits. And elected officials sometimes put their personal interests ahead of the public's interest. In all sectors of the economy, however, ***the basic goals of utility maximization, profit maximization, and welfare maximization explain most market activity.***

Specialization and Exchange

The notion that buying and selling goods and services in the market might maximize our well-being originates in two simple observations. First, most of us are incapable of producing everything we desire to consume. Second, even if we *could* produce all our own goods and services, it would still make sense to specialize, producing only one product and trading it for other desired goods and services.

Suppose you were capable of growing your own food, stitching your own clothes, building your own shelter, and even writing your own economics text. Even in this little utopia, it would still make sense to decide how *best* to expend your limited time and energy and to rely on others to fill in the gaps. If you were *most* proficient at growing food, you would be best off spending your time farming. You could then exchange some of your food output for the clothes, shelter, and books you wanted. In the end, you'd be able to consume *more* goods than if you'd tried to make everything yourself.

Our economic interactions with others are thus necessitated by two constraints:

1. Our absolute inability as individuals to produce all the things we need or desire.
2. The limited amount of time, energy, and resources we have for producing those things we could make for ourselves.

Together, these constraints lead us to specialize and interact. Most of the interactions that result take place in the market.

2.2 THE CIRCULAR FLOW

Figure 2.1 summarizes the kinds of interactions that occur among market participants. Note first that the figure identifies four separate groups of participants. Domestically, the rectangle labelled "Consumers" includes all 30 million consumers in Canada. In the "Business firms" box are grouped all the domestic business enterprises that buy and sell goods and services. The third participant, "Governments," includes the many separate agencies of the federal government, as well as provincial and local governments. Figure 2.1 also illustrates the role of global actors.

The easiest way to keep track of all this market activity is to distinguish two basic markets. Figure 2.1 makes this distinction by portraying separate circles for product markets and factor markets. In **factor markets,** factors of production are exchanged. Market participants buy or sell land, labour, or capital that can be used in the production process. When you go looking for work, for example, you're making a factor of production—your labour—available to producers. The producers will hire you—purchase

The Two Markets

> **factor market:** Any place where factors of production (e.g., land, labour, capital) are bought and sold.

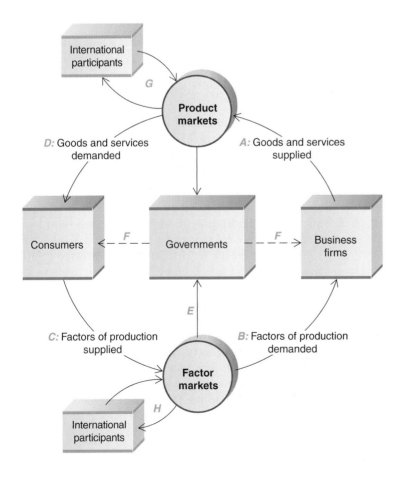

FIGURE 2.1
The Circular Flow

Business firms supply goods and services to product markets (point *A*) and purchase factors of production in factor markets (*B*). Individual consumers supply factors of production such as their own labour (*C*) and purchase final goods and services (*D*). Federal, provincial, and local governments acquire resources in factor markets (*E*) and provide services to both consumers and business (*F*). International participants also take part by supplying imports, purchasing exports (*G*), and buying and selling factors of production (*H*).

your services in the factor market—if you're offering the skills they need at a price they're willing to pay. The same kind of interaction occurs in factor markets when the government enlists workers into the armed services or when the Japanese buy pulp and paper mills in British Columbia.

Interactions within factor markets are only half the story. At the end of a hard day's work, consumers go to the grocery store (or to a virtual store online) to buy desired goods and services—that is, to buy *products.* In this context, consumers again interact with business firms, this time purchasing goods and services those firms have produced. These interactions occur in **product markets.** Foreigners also participate in the product market by supplying goods and services (imports) to Canada and buying some of our output (exports).

> **product market:** Any place where finished goods and services (products) are bought and sold.

The government sector also supplies services. (e.g., education, national defence, health service, highways.) In California, Governor Davis even wanted the state to supply electricity to households and businesses. Most government services aren't explicitly sold in product markets, however. Typically, they're delivered "free," without an explicit price (e.g., public elementary schools, highways). This doesn't mean government services are truly free, though. There's still an opportunity cost associated with every service the government provides. Consumers and businesses pay that cost indirectly through taxes rather than directly through market prices.

In Figure 2.1, the arrow connecting product markets to consumers (point *D*) emphasizes the fact that consumers, by definition, don't supply products. When individuals produce goods and services, they do so within the government or business sector. For instance, a doctor, a dentist, or an economic consultant functions in two sectors. When selling services in the market, this person is regarded as a "business"; when away from the office, he or she is regarded as a "consumer." This distinction is helpful in emphasizing that *the consumer is the final recipient of all goods and services produced.*

Locating Markets. Although we refer repeatedly to two kinds of markets in this book, it would be a little foolish to go off in search of the product and factor markets. Neither market is a single, identifiable structure. The term *market* simply refers to a place or situation where an economic exchange occurs—where a buyer and seller interact. The exchange may take place on the street, in a taxicab, over the phone, by mail, or in cyberspace. In some cases, the market used may in fact be quite distinguishable, as in the case of a retail store, the Toronto Stock Exchange, or a federal employment office. But whatever it looks like, *a market exists wherever and whenever an exchange takes place.*

Dollars and Exchange

Figure 2.1 provides a useful summary of market activities, but it neglects one critical element of market interactions: dollars. Each arrow in the figure actually has two dimensions. Consider again the arrow linking consumers to product markets: It's drawn in only one direction because consumers, by definition, don't provide goods and services directly to product markets. But they do provide something: dollars. If you want to obtain something from a product market, you must offer to pay for it (typically, with cash, cheque, or credit card). Consumers exchange dollars for goods and services in product markets.

The same kinds of exchange occur in factor markets. When you go to work, you exchange a factor of production (your labour) for income, typically a paycheque. Here again, the path connecting consumers to factor markets really goes in two directions: one of real resources, the other of dollars. Consumers receive wages, rent, and interest for the labour, land, and capital they bring to the factor markets. Indeed, nearly *every market transaction involves an exchange of dollars for goods (in product markets) or resources (in factor markets).* Money is thus critical in facilitating market exchanges and the specialization the exchanges permit.

In every market transaction there must be a buyer and a seller. The seller is on the **supply** side of the market; the buyer is on the **demand** side. As noted earlier, we *supply* resources to the market when we look for a job—that is, when we offer our labour in exchange for income. We *demand* goods when we shop in a supermarket—that is, when we're prepared to offer dollars in exchange for something to eat. Business firms may *supply* goods and services in product markets at the same time they're *demanding* factors of production in factor markets. Whether one is on the supply side or the demand side of any particular market transaction depends on the nature of the exchange, not on the people or institutions involved.

2.3 DEMAND

To get a sense of how the demand side of market transactions work, we'll focus first on a single consumer. Then we'll aggregate to illustrate *market* demand.

We can begin to understand how market forces work by looking more closely at the behaviour of a single market participant. Let us start with Tom, who is in his fourth year at Maritime University. Tom has majored in everything from art history to government in his three years at Maritime University. He didn't connect to any of those fields and is on the brink of academic dismissal. To make matters worse, his parents have threatened to cut him off financially unless he gets serious about his course work. By that, they mean he should enroll in courses that will lead to a job after graduation. Tom thinks he has found the perfect solution: Web design. Everything associated with the Internet pays big bucks. Plus, the girls seem to think Webbies are "cool." Or at least so Tom thinks. And his parents would definitely approve. So Tom has enrolled in Web-design courses.

Unfortunately for Tom, he never developed computer skills. Until he got to Maritime University, he thought mastering Sony's latest alien-attack video game was the pinnacle of electronic wizardry. His parents gave him a Wi-Fi laptop, but he used it only for surfing hot video sites. The concept of using his computer for course work, much less developing some Web content, was completely foreign to him. To compound his problems, Tom didn't have a clue about "streaming," "interfacing," "animation," or the other concepts the Web-design instructor outlined in the first lecture.

Given his circumstances, Tom was desperate to find someone who could tutor him in Web design. But desperation is not enough to secure the services of a Web architect. In a market-based economy, you must also be willing to *pay* for the things you want. Specifically, **a demand exists only if someone is willing and able to pay for the good**—that is, exchange dollars for a good or service in the marketplace. Is Tom willing and able to *pay* for the Web-design tutoring he so obviously needs?

Let us assume that Tom has some income and is willing to spend some of it to get a tutor. Under these assumptions, we can claim that Tom is a participant in the *market* for Web-design services.

But how much is Tom willing to pay? Surely, Tom is not prepared to exchange *all* his income for help in mastering Web design. After all, Tom could use his income to buy more desirable goods and services. If he spent all his income on a Web tutor, that help would have an extremely high *opportunity cost.* He would be giving up the opportunity to spend that income on other goods and services. He'd pass his Web-design class but have little else. It doesn't sound like a good idea to Tom. Even though Tom says he would be willing to pay *anything* to pass the Web-design course, he probably has lower prices in mind. Indeed, it would be more reasonable to assume that there are *limits* to the amount Tom is willing to pay for any given quantity of Web-design tutoring. These limits will be determined by how much income Tom has to spend and how many other goods and services he must forsake to pay for a tutor.

Tom also knows that his grade in Web design will depend in part on how much tutoring service he buys. He can pass the course with only a few hours of design help. If he wants a better grade, however, the cost is going to escalate quickly.

Supply and Demand

supply: The ability and willingness to sell (produce) specific quantities of a good at alternative prices in a given time period, *ceteris paribus.*

demand: The ability and willingness to buy specific quantities of a good at alternative prices in a given time period, *ceteris paribus.*

Individual Demand

Naturally, Tom wants it all: an A in Web design and a ticket to higher-paying jobs. But here again the distinction between *desire* and *demand* is relevant. He may *desire* to master Web design, but his actual proficiency will depend on how many hours of tutoring he is willing to *pay* for.

We assume, then, that when Tom starts looking for a Web-design tutor he has in mind some sort of **demand schedule,** like that described in Figure 2.2. According to row *A* of this schedule, Tom is willing and able to buy only one hour of tutoring service per semester if he must pay $50 an hour. At such an outrageous price he will learn minimal skills and pass the course. Just the bare minimum is all Tom is willing to buy at that price.

At lower prices, Tom would behave differently. According to Figure 2.2, Tom would purchase more tutoring services if the price per hour were less. At lower prices, he

> **demand schedule:** A table showing the quantities of a good a consumer is willing and able to buy at alternative prices in a given time period, *ceteris paribus.*

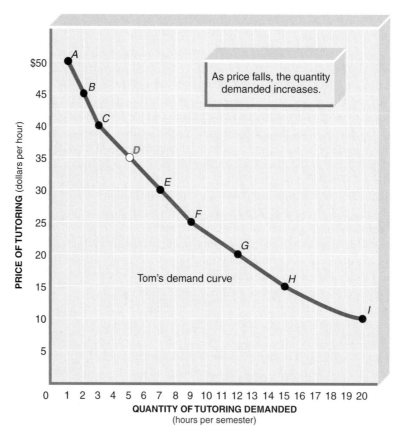

FIGURE 2.2
A Demand Schedule and Curve

A demand schedule indicates the quantities of a good a consumer is able and willing to buy at alternative prices (*ceteris paribus*). The demand schedule below indicates that Tom would buy five hours of Web tutoring per semester if the price were $35 per hour (row *D*). If Web tutoring were less expensive (rows *E–I*), Tom would purchase a larger quantity.

A demand curve is a graphical illustration of a demand schedule. Each point on the curve refers to a specific quantity that will be demanded at a given price. If, for example, the price of Web tutoring were $35 per hour, this curve tells us the consumer would purchase five hours per semester (point *D*). If Web tutoring cost $30 per hour, seven hours per semester would be demanded (point *E*). Each point on the curve corresponds to a row in the schedule.

	Tom's Demand Schedule	
	Price of Tutoring (per hour)	Quantity of Tutoring Demanded (hours per semester)
A	$50	1
B	45	2
C	40	3
D	35	5
E	30	7
F	25	9
G	20	12
H	15	15
I	10	20

would not have to give up so many other goods and services for each hour of technical help. The reduced opportunity costs implied by lower service prices increase the attractiveness of professional help. Indeed, we see from row *I* of the demand schedule that Tom is willing to purchase 20 hours per semester—the whole bag of design tricks—if the price of tutoring is as low as $10 per hour.

Notice that the demand schedule doesn't tell us anything about *why* this consumer is willing to pay specific prices for various amounts of tutoring. Tom's expressed willingness to pay for Web-design tutoring may reflect a desperate need to finish a Web-design course, a lot of income to spend, or a relatively small desire for other goods and services. All the demand schedule tells us is what the consumer is *willing and able* to buy, for whatever reasons.

Also observe that the demand schedule doesn't tell us how many hours of design help the consumer will *actually* buy. Figure 2.2 simply states that Tom is *willing and able* to pay for one hour of tutoring per semester at $50 per hour, for two hours at $45 each, and so on. How much tutoring he purchases will depend on the actual price of such services in the market. Until we know that price, we cannot tell how much service will be purchased. Hence ***"demand" is an expression of consumer buying intentions, of a willingness to buy, not a statement of actual purchases.***

A convenient summary of buying intentions is the **demand curve,** a graphical illustration of the demand schedule. The demand curve in Figure 2.2 tells us again that this consumer is willing to pay for only one hour of tutoring per semester if the price is $50 per hour (point *A*), for two if the price is $45 (point *B*), for three at $40 an hour (point *C*), and so on. Once we know what the market price of tutoring actually is, a glance at the demand curve tells us how much service this consumer will buy.

What the notion of *demand* emphasizes is that the amount we buy of a good depends on its price. We seldom if ever decide to buy only a certain quantity of a good at whatever price is charged. Instead, we enter markets with a set of desires and a limited amount of money to spend. How much we actually buy of any good will depend on its price.

A common feature of demand curves is their downward slope. As the price of a good falls, people purchase more of it. In Figure 2.2 the quantity of Web-tutorial services demanded increases (moves rightward along the horizontal axis) as the price per hour decreases (moves down the vertical axis). This inverse relationship between price and quantity is so common we refer to it as the **law of demand.** Compaq used this law to increase computer sales in 2000 (see Applications).

The demand curve in Figure 2.2 has only two dimensions—quantity demanded (on the horizontal axis) and price (on the vertical axis). This seems to imply that the amount of tutoring demanded depends only on the price of that service. This is surely not the case. A consumer's willingness and ability to buy a product at various prices depend on a variety of forces. ***The determinants of market demand include***

- *Tastes* (desire for this and other goods).
- *Income* (of the consumer).
- *Other goods* (their availability and price).
- *Expectations* (for income, prices, tastes).
- *Number of buyers.*

Tom's "taste" for tutoring has nothing to do with taste buds. *Taste* is just another word for desire. In this case Tom's taste for Web-design services is clearly acquired. If he didn't have to pass a Web-design course, he would have no desire for related services, and thus no demand. If he had no income, he couldn't *demand* any Web-design tutoring either, no matter how much he might *desire* it.

Other goods also affect the demand for tutoring services. Their effect depends on whether they're *substitute* goods or *complementary* goods. A **substitute good** is one that might be purchased instead of tutoring services. In Tom's simple world, pizza is a substitute for tutoring. If the price of pizza fell, Tom would use his limited income

demand curve: A curve describing the quantities of a good a consumer is willing and able to buy at alternative prices in a given time period, *ceteris paribus*.

law of demand: The quantity of a good demanded in a given time period increases as its price falls, *ceteris paribus*.

Determinants of Demand

substitute goods: Goods that substitute for each other; when the price of good *x* rises, the demand for good *y* increases, *ceteris paribus*.

Millions of Albertans Receive Prosperity Cheques

© James Grasdal, http://zone.artizans.com/product.htm?pid=301945

In 2006, the provincial government of Alberta decided to share the wealth associated with high energy prices by giving a tax-free cheque of $400 to each man, woman, and child residing in the province.

These prosperity cheques, fondly known as "Ralph bucks" in honour of the premier, Ralph Klein, amounted to roughly $1.4 billion dollars of additional spending income into the hands of Albertans. Not surprisingly, there were some innovative attempts on the behalf of suppliers of goods and services to get consumers to part with their newly acquired cheques. Resorts in the Rocky Mountains, for example, offered weekend accommodation for exactly $400, and a popular Scandinavian furniture store also offered packages equal to $400.

While there was considerable public debate on the merits of the prosperity cheques, most Albertans took advantage of the one-time offer and spent the money on goods and services.

Analysis: One of the determinants of demand is income—for most goods and services, an increase in income leads to an increase in demand.

---

complementary goods: Goods frequently consumed in combination; when the price of good *x* rises, the demand for good *y* falls, *ceteris paribus*.

to buy more pizzas and cut back on his purchases of Web tutoring. When the price of a substitute good falls, the demand for tutoring services declines.

A **complementary good** is one that's typically consumed with, rather than instead of, tutoring. If textbook prices or tuition increases, Tom might take fewer classes and demand *less* Web-design assistance. In this case, a price increase for a complementary good causes the demand for tutoring to decline.

Expectations also play a role in consumer decisions. If Tom expected to flunk his Web-design course anyway, he probably wouldn't waste any money getting tutorial help; his demand for such services would disappear. On the other hand, if he expects a Web tutor to determine his college fate, he might be more willing to buy such services.

Ceteris Paribus

If demand is in fact such a multidimensional decision, how can we reduce it to only the two dimensions of price and quantity? In Chapter 1 we first encountered this ceteris paribus trick. To simplify their models of the world, economists focus on only one or two forces at a time and *assume* nothing else changes. We know a consumer's tastes, income, other goods, and expectations all affect the decision to hire a tutor. But we want to focus on the relationship between quantity demanded and price. That is, we want to know what *independent* influence price has on consumption decisions. To find out, we must isolate that one influence, price, and assume that the determinants of demand remain unchanged.

The *ceteris paribus* assumption is not as farfetched as it may seem. People's tastes, income, and expectations do not change quickly. Also, the prices and availability of other goods don't change all that fast. Hence, a change in the *price* of a product may be the only factor that prompts a change in quantity demanded.

The ability to predict consumer responses to a price change is important. What would happen, for example, to enrollment at your school if tuition doubled? Must we guess? Or can we use demand curves to predict how the quantity of applications will change as the price of college goes up? *Demand curves show us how changes in market prices alter consumer behaviour.* We used the demand curve in Figure 2.2 to predict how Tom's Web-design ability would change at different tutorial prices.

Although demand curves are useful in predicting consumer responses to market signals, they aren't infallible. The problem is that *the determinants of demand can and do change.* When they do, a specific demand curve may become obsolete. A *demand curve (schedule) is valid only so long as the underlying determinants of demand remain constant.* If the *ceteris paribus* assumption is violated—if tastes, income, other goods, or expectations change—the ability or willingness to buy will change. When this happens, the demand curve will **shift** to a new position.

Suppose, for example, that Tom won $1,000 in a lottery. This increase in his income would greatly increase his ability to pay for tutoring services. Figure 2.3 shows the effect of this windfall on Tom's demand. The old demand curve, D_1, is no longer relevant. Tom's lottery winnings enable him to buy more tutoring at any price, as illustrated by the new demand curve, D_2. According to this new curve, lucky Tom is now willing and able to buy 12 hours per semester at the price of $35 per hour (point d_2). This is a large increase in demand; previously (before winning the lottery) he demanded only five hours at that price (point d_1).

Shifts in Demand

> **shift in demand:** A change in the quantity demanded at any (every) given price.

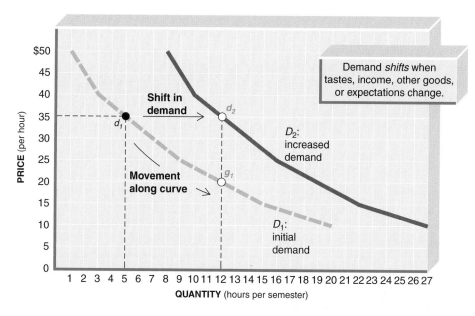

Demand *shifts* when tastes, income, other goods, or expectations change.

	Price (per hour)	Quantity Demanded (hours per semester)	
		Initial Demand	**After Increase in Income**
A	$50	1	8
B	45	2	9
C	40	3	10
D	35	5	12
E	30	7	14
F	25	9	16
G	20	12	19
H	15	15	22
I	10	20	27

FIGURE 2.3
Shifts vs. Movements

A demand curve shows how a consumer responds to price changes. If the determinants of demand stay constant, the response is a *movement* along the curve to a new quantity demanded. In this case, the quantity demanded increases from 5 (point d_1), to 12 (point g_1), when price falls from $35 to $20 per hour.

If the determinants of demand change, the entire demand curve *shifts*. In this case, an increase in income increases demand. With more income, Tom is willing to buy 12 hours at the initial price of $35 (point d_2), not just the 5 hours he demanded before the lottery win.

With his higher income, Tom can buy more tutoring services at every price. Thus, *the entire demand curve shifts to the right when income goes up.* Figure 2.3 illustrates both the old (prelottery) and the new (postlottery) demand curves.

Income is only one of the basic determinants of demand. Changes in any of the other determinants of demand would also cause the demand curve to shift. Tom's taste for Web tutoring might increase dramatically, for example, if his parents promised to buy him a new car for passing Web design. In that case, he might be willing to forgo other goods and spend more of his income on tutors. *An increase in taste (desire) also shifts the demand curve to the right.*

Movements vs. Shifts

It's important to distinguish shifts of the demand curve from movements along the demand curve. *Movements along a demand curve are a response to price changes for that good.* Such movements assume that determinants of demand are unchanged. By contrast, *shifts of the demand curve occur when the determinants of demand change.* When tastes, income, other goods, or expectations are altered, the basic relationship between price and quantity demanded is changed (shifts).

For convenience, movements along a demand curve and shifts of the demand curve have their own labels. Specifically, take care to distinguish

WEB NOTE

Priceline.com is an online service for purchasing airline tickets, vacation packages, and car rentals. The site allows you to specify the *highest* price you're willing to pay for air travel between two cities. In effect, you reveal your demand curve to Priceline. If you use the price naming option and they find a ticket that costs no more than the price you're willing and able to pay, you must buy it. Priceline makes a profit by matching demand and supply. Try it at www.priceline.com.

* *Changes in quantity demanded:* movements along a given demand curve, in response to price changes of that good.
* *Changes in demand:* shifts of the demand curve due to changes in tastes, income, other goods, or expectations.

Tom's behaviour in the Web-tutoring market will change if either the price of tutoring changes (a movement) or the underlying determinants of his demand are altered (a shift). Notice in Figure 2.3 that he ends up buying 12 hours of Web tutoring if either the price of tutoring falls or his income increases. Demand curves help us predict those market responses.

Market Demand

Whatever we say about demand for Web-design tutoring on the part of one wannabe Web master, we can also say about every student at Maritime University (or, for that matter, about all consumers). Some students have no interest in Web design and aren't willing to pay for related services: They don't participate in the Web-tutoring market. Other students want such services but don't have enough income to pay for them: They too are excluded from the Web-tutoring market. A large number of students, however, not only have a need (or desire) for Web tutoring but also are willing and able to purchase such services.

What we start with in product markets, then, is many individual demand curves. Fortunately, it's possible to combine all the individual demand curves into a single **market demand.** The aggregation process is no more difficult than simple arithmetic. Suppose you would be willing to buy one hour of tutoring per semester at a price of $80 per hour. George, who is also desperate to learn Web design, would buy two at that price; and I would buy none, since my publisher (McGraw-Hill) creates a Web page for me (try www.mcgrawhill.ca/olc/schiller). What would our combined (market) demand for hours of tutoring be at that price? Clearly, our individual inclinations indicate that we would be willing to buy a total of three hours of tutoring per semester if the price were $80 per hour. Our combined willingness to buy—our collective market demand— is nothing more than the sum of our individual demands. The same kind of aggregation can be performed for all consumers, leading to a summary of the total market demand for a specific good or service. This *market demand is determined by the number of potential buyers and their respective tastes, incomes, other goods, and expectations.*

market demand: The total quantity of a good or service people are willing and able to buy at alternative prices in a given time period; the sum of individual demand.

The Market Demand Curve

Figure 2.4 provides the basic market demand schedule for a situation in which only three consumers participate in the market. It illustrates the same market situation with demand curves. The three individuals who participate in the market demand for

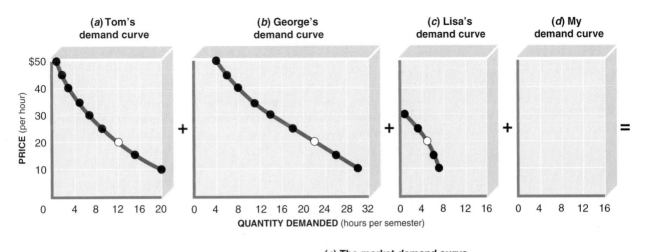

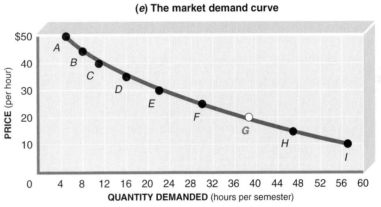

FIGURE 2.4
Construction of the Market Demand Curve

Market demand represents the combined demands of all market participants. To determine the total quantity of Web tutoring demanded at any given price, we add the separate demands of the individual consumers. Row *G* of this schedule indicates that a *total* quantity of 39 hours per semester will be demanded at a price of $20 per hour. This same conclusion is reached by adding the individual demand curves, leading to point *G* on the market demand curve (see above).

	Price (per hour)	Quantity of Tutoring Demanded (hours per semester)									Market Demand
		Tom	+	George	+	Lisa	+	Me	=		
A	$50	1		4		0		0			5
B	45	2		6		0		0			8
C	40	3		8		0		0			11
D	35	5		11		0		0			16
E	30	7		14		1		0			22
F	25	9		18		3		0			30
G	20	12		22		5		0			39
H	15	15		26		6		0			47
I	10	20		30		7		0			57

Web tutoring at Maritime University obviously differ greatly, as suggested by their respective demand schedules. Tom *has* to pass his Web-design classes or confront college and parental rejection. He also has a nice allowance (income), so can afford to buy a lot of tutorial help. His demand schedule is portrayed in the first column of the table (and is identical to the one we examined in Figure 2.2). George is also desperate to acquire some job skills and is willing to pay relatively high prices for Web-design tutoring. His demand is summarized in the second column under Quantity Demanded in the table.

The third consumer in this market is Lisa. Lisa already knows the nuts and bolts of Web design, so she isn't so desperate for tutorial services. She would like to upgrade her skills, however, especially in animation and e-commerce applications. But her limited budget precludes paying a lot for help. She will buy some technical support only if the price falls to $30 per hour. Should tutors cost less, she'd even buy quite a few hours of design services. Finally, there is my demand schedule (column 4 under Quantity Demanded), which confirms that I really don't participate in the Web-tutoring market.

The differing personalities and consumption habits of Tom, George, Lisa, and me are expressed in our individual demand schedules and associated curves in Figure 2.4. To determine the *market* demand for tutoring from this information, we simply add these four separate demands. The end result of this aggregation is, first, a *market* demand schedule and, second, the resultant *market* demand curve. These market summaries describe the various quantities of tutoring that Maritime University students are *willing and able* to purchase each semester at various prices.

How much Web tutoring will be purchased each semester? Knowing how much help Tom, George, Lisa, and I are willing to buy at various prices doesn't tell you how much we're actually going to purchase. To determine the actual consumption of Web tutoring, we have to know something about prices and supplies. Which of the many different prices illustrated in Figures 2.3 and 2.4 will actually prevail? How will that price be determined?

2.4 SUPPLY

market supply: The total quantity of a good that sellers are willing and able to sell at alternative prices in a given time period, *ceteris paribus.*

To understand how the price of Web tutoring is established, we must also look at the other side of the market: the supply side. We need to know how many hours of tutoring services people are willing and able to *sell* at various prices, that is, the **market supply.** As on the demand side, the *market supply* depends on the behaviour of all the individuals willing and able to supply Web tutoring at some price.

Determinants of Supply

Let's return to the Maritime University campus for a moment. What we need to know now is how much tutorial Web service people are willing and able to provide. Generally speaking, Web-page design can be fun, but it can also be drudge work, especially when you're doing it for someone else. Software programs like PhotoShop, Flash, and Fireworks have made Web-page design easier and more creative. And Wi-Fi laptops have made Web tutoring more convenient. But teaching someone else to design Web pages is still work. So few people offer to supply tutoring services just for the fun of it. Web designers do it for money. Specifically, they do it to earn income that they, in turn, can spend on goods and services they desire.

How much income must be offered to induce Web designers to do a job depends on a variety of things. The ***determinants of market supply include***

- *Technology*
- *Factor costs*
- *Prices of other goods*

- *Taxes and subsidies*
- *Expectations*
- *Number of sellers*

The technology of Web design, for example, is always getting easier and more creative. With a program like PageOut, for example, it's very easy to create a bread-and-butter Web page. A continuous stream of new software programs (e.g., Fireworks,

DreamWeaver) keeps stretching the possibilities for graphics, animation, interactivity, and content. These technological advances mean that Web-design services can be supplied more quickly and cheaply. They also make *teaching* Web design easier. As a result, they induce people to supply more tutoring services at every price.

How much Web-design service is offered at any given price also depends on the cost of factors of production. If the software programs needed to create Web pages are cheap (or, better yet, free), Web designers can afford to charge lower prices. If the required software inputs are expensive, however, they will have to charge more money per hour for their services.

Prices of other goods can also affect the willingness to supply Web-design services. If you can make more income waiting tables than you can tutoring lazy students, why would you even boot up the computer? As the prices paid for other goods and services change, they will influence people's decision about whether to offer Web services.

In the real world, the decision to supply goods and services is also influenced by government tax and subsidy policies. Federal, provincial, and local governments impose taxes on income earned in the marketplace. When tax rates are high, people get to keep less of the income they earn. Once taxes start biting into paycheque, some people may conclude that tutoring is no longer worth the hassle and withdraw from the market. Conversely, if governments subsidize certain productive activities, this lowers the costs of production and existing firms have an incentive to produce more at any given price. In addition, subsidies tend to attract new suppliers, since the opportunity costs of allocating resources into the industry are now lower.

Expectations are also important on the supply side of the market. If Web designers expect higher prices, lower costs, or reduced taxes, they may be more willing to learn new software programs. On the other hand, if they have poor expectations about the future, they may just sell their computers and find something else to do.

Finally, we note that the number of available tutors will affect the quantity of service offered for sale at various prices. If there are lots of willing tutors on campus, a large quantity of tutorial service will be available.

All these considerations—factor costs, technology, expectations—affect the decision to offer Web services and at what price. In general, we assume that Web architects will be willing to provide more tutoring if the per-hour price is high and less if the price is low. In other words, there is a **law of supply** that parallels the law of demand. On the supply side the law says that *larger quantities will be offered for sale at higher prices.* Here again, the laws rest on the *ceteris paribus* assumption: The quantity supplied increases at higher prices *if* the determinants of supply are constant. *Supply curves are upward-sloping to the right,* as in Figure 2.5. Note how the *quantity supplied* jumps from 39 hours (point *d*) to 130 hours (point *h*) when the price of Web service doubles (from $20 to $40 per hour).

Figure 2.5 also illustrates how market supply is constructed from the supply decisions of individual sellers. In this case, only three Web masters are available. Ann is willing to provide a lot of tutoring at low prices, whereas Bob requires at least $20 an hour. Cory won't talk to students for less than $40 an hour.

By adding the quantity each Webhead is willing to offer at every price, we can construct the market supply curve. Notice in Figure 2.5, for example, how the quantity supplied to the market at $45 (point *i*) comes from the individual efforts of Ann (93 hours), Bob (33 hours), and Cory (14 hours). *The market supply curve is just a summary of the supply intentions of all producers.*

None of the points on the market supply curve (Figure 2.5) tells us how much Web tutoring is actually being sold on the Maritime University campus. *Market supply is an expression of sellers' intentions—an offer to sell—not a statement of actual sales.* My next door neighbour may be willing to sell his 1994 Honda Civic for $8,000, but most likely he'll never find a buyer at that price. Nevertheless, his *willingness* to sell his car at that price is part of the *market supply* of used cars.

WEB NOTE

Sellers of books and cars post asking prices for their products on the Internet. With the help of search engines such as autoweb.com and www.bookfinder.com, consumers can locate the seller who's offering the lowest price. By examining a lot of offers, you could also construct a supply curve showing how the quantity supplied increases at higher prices.

law of supply: The quantity of a good supplied in a given time period increases as its price increases, *ceteris paribus.*

Market Supply

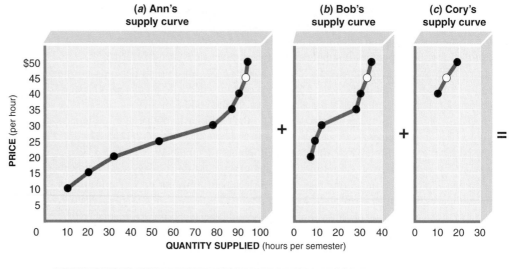

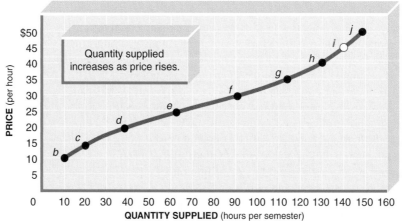

FIGURE 2.5
Market Supply

The market supply curve indicates the *combined* sales intentions of all market participants. If the price of tutoring were $45 per hour (point *i*), the *total* quantity of services supplied would be 140 hours per semester. This quantity is determined by adding the supply decisions of all individual producers. In this case, Ann supplies 93 hours, Bob supplies 33, and Cory supplies the rest.

	Price (per hour)	Quantity of Tutoring Supplied by						
		Ann	+	Bob	+	Cory	=	Market
j	$50	94		35		19		148
i	45	93		33		14		140
h	40	90		30		10		130
g	35	86		28		0		114
f	30	78		12		0		90
e	25	53		9		0		62
d	20	32		7		0		39
c	15	20		0		0		20
b	10	10		0		0		10

Shifts of Supply

As with demand, there's nothing sacred about any given set of supply intentions. Supply curves *shift* when the underlying determinants of supply change. Thus, we again distinguish

- ***Changes in quantity supplied:*** movements along a given supply curve.
- ***Changes in supply:*** shifts of the supply curve.

Our Latin friend *ceteris paribus* is once again the decisive factor. If the price of a product is the only variable changing, then we can ***track changes in quantity supplied***

APPLICATIONS

Wheat Prices Increase as Disaster Hits Prairies

In their annual crop season report, Alberta's Department of Agriculture, Food and Rural Development wrote "The 2002 crop season will be remembered as one of the worst in Alberta's farming history. The season was full of challenges for producers from beginning to end. Major challenges included a cool and dry spring, persistent dryness in much of Alberta, flooding in the Southern Region in June, heat in July, cool and wet conditions in August, early frosts, damp, cool weather conditions during the harvest season and severe insect problems."

The unique weather patterns and insect challenges of 2002, combined with a prolonged drought in the prairies, reduced the overall production of wheat in Alberta to 3.5 million (metric) tonnes, down from 5.8 million tonnes in 2001 and 8.2 million tonnes in 1999. Over this time period, September prices increased from \$137/(metric) tonne in 1999 to \$170/tonne in 2001 and \$204 in 2002. As the graph indicates, for a relatively constant market demand, this considerable reduction in the supply of wheat (leftward shift) substantially increased prices.

Source: Ministry of Agriculture, Food and Rural Development, Government of Alberta, "Alberta 2002 Crop Season in Review with Feed and Harvest Summary Report" (http://www.agric.gov.ab.ca/economic/stats/crpsum02. html) and Statistics Canada: Farm Product Prices, Crops, and Livestock—Table 002–0043.

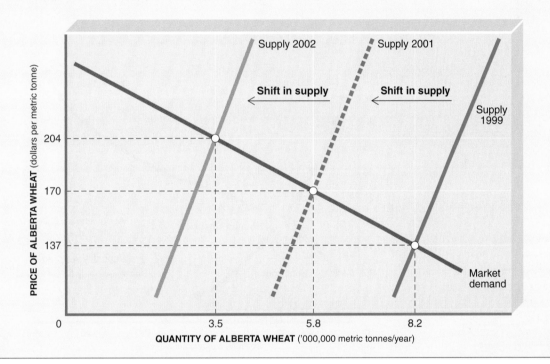

Analysis: When factor costs or availability worsen, the supply curve shifts to the left. Such leftward supply-curve shifts push prices up the market demand curve.

along the supply curve. But if *ceteris paribus* is violated—if technology, factor costs, the profitability of producing other goods, tax rates, expectations, or the number of sellers change—then **changes in supply are illustrated by shifts of the supply curve.**

The Applications box on the next page illustrates how a supply shift sent wheat prices soaring in 2002. When poor weather and insect problems reduced harvests, the wheat supply curve shifted leftward and prices increased substantially.

2.5 EQUILIBRIUM

The abrupt spike in wheat prices offers some clues as to how the forces of supply and demand set, and change, market prices. To get a more detailed sense of how those forces work, we'll return to the mythical Maritime University Web tutoring market for a moment. How did supply and demand resolve the WHAT, HOW, and FOR WHOM questions in that market?

Figure 2.6 helps answer that question by bringing together the market supply and demand curves we've already examined (Figures 2.4 and 2.5). When we put the two curves together, we see that *only one price and quantity are compatible with the existing intentions of both buyers and sellers.* This equilibrium occurs at the intersection of the two curves in Figure 2.6. Once it's established, Web tutoring will cost $20 per hour. At that **equilibrium price,** campus Webheads will sell a total of 39 hours of tutoring per semester—the same amount that students wish to buy at that price. Those 39 hours of tutoring service will be part of WHAT is produced.

An equilibrium doesn't imply that everyone is happy with the prevailing price or quantity. Notice in Figure 2.6, for example, that some students who want to buy Web-design assistance services don't get any. These would-be buyers are arrayed along the demand curve *below* the equilibrium. Because the price they're *willing* to pay is less than the

> **equilibrium price:** The price at which the quantity of a good demanded in a given time period equals the quantity supplied.

Market Clearing

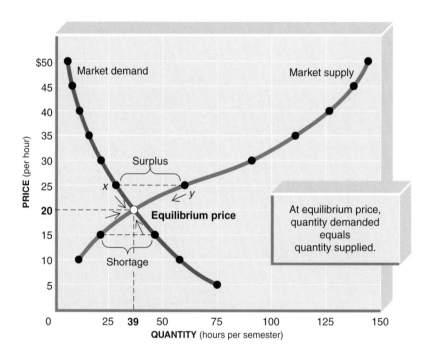

FIGURE 2.6
Equilibrium Price

Only at equilibrium is the quantity demanded equal to the quantity supplied. In this case, the equilibrium price is $20 per hour, and 39 hours is the equilibrium quantity. At higher prices, a market surplus exists—the quantity supplied exceeds the quantity demanded. At prices below equilibrium, a market shortage exists.

The intersection of the demand and supply curves in the graph represents equilibrium price and output in this market.

Price (per hour)	Quantity Supplied (hours per semester)		Quantity Demanded (hours per semester)
$50	148		5
45	140		8
40	130	market	11
35	114	surplus	16
30	90		22
25	62		30
20	39	equilibrium	39
15	20	market	47
10	10	shortage	57

equilibrium price, they don't get any Web-design help. The market's FOR WHOM answer includes only those students willing and able to pay the equilibrium price.

Likewise, some would-be sellers in the market don't sell as much service as they might like. These people are arrayed along the supply curve *above* the equilibrium. Because they insist on being paid a price higher than the equilibrium price, they don't actually sell anything.

Although not everyone gets full satisfaction from the market equilibrium, that unique outcome is efficient. The equilibrium price and quantity reflect a compromise between buyers and sellers. No other compromise yields a quantity demanded that's exactly equal to the quantity supplied.

The Invisible Hand. The equilibrium price isn't determined by any single individual. Rather, it's determined by the collective behaviour of many buyers and sellers, each acting out his or her own demand or supply schedule. It's this kind of impersonal price determination that gave rise to Adam Smith's characterization of the market mechanism as "the invisible hand." In attempting to explain how the *market mechanism* works, the famed eighteenth-century economist noted a certain feature of market prices. The market behaves as if some unseen force (the invisible hand) were examining each individual's supply or demand schedule and then selecting a price that assured an equilibrium. In practice, the process of price determination isn't so mysterious: It's a simple process of trial and error.

An Initial Surplus. To appreciate the power of the market mechanism, consider what occurs if the price of Web-design assistance services differs from the equilibrium price. Suppose, for example, that campus Webheads band together and agree to charge a price of $25 per hour. Figure 2.6 illustrates the consequences of this *dis*equilibrium pricing. At $25 per hour, campus Webheads would be offering more tutoring services (point *y*) than Tom, George, and Lisa were willing to buy (point *x*) at that price. A **market surplus** of Web services would exist in the sense that more tutoring was being offered for sale (supplied) than students cared to purchase at the available price.

As Figure 2.6 indicates, at a price of $25 per hour, a market surplus of 32 hours per semester exists. Under these circumstances, campus Webheads would be spending many idle hours at their keyboards waiting for customers to appear. Their waiting will be in vain because the quantity of Web tutoring demanded will not increase until the price of tutoring falls. That is the clear message of the demand curve. As would-be tutors get this message, they'll reduce their prices. This is the response the market mechanism signals.

As sellers' asking prices decline, the quantity demanded will increase. This concept is illustrated in Figure 2.6 by the movement along the demand curve from point *x* to lower prices and greater quantity demanded. As we move down the market demand curve, the *desire* for Web-design help doesn't change, but the quantity people are *able and willing to buy* increases. When the price falls to $20 per hour, the quantity demanded will finally equal the quantity supplied. This is the *equilibrium* illustrated in Figure 2.6.

An Initial Shortage. A very different sequence of events would occur if a market shortage existed. Suppose someone were to spread the word that Web-tutoring services were available at only $15 per hour. Tom, George, and Lisa would be standing in line to get tutorial help, but campus Web designers wouldn't be willing to supply the quantity desired at that price. As Figure 2.6 confirms, at $15 per hour, the quantity demanded (47 hours per semester) would greatly exceed the quantity supplied (20 hours per semester). In this situation, we may speak of a **market shortage,** that is, an excess of quantity demanded over quantity supplied. At a price of $15 an hour, the shortage amounts to 27 hours of tutoring services.

Surplus and Shortage

market surplus: The amount by which the quantity supplied exceeds the quantity demanded at a given price; excess supply.

market shortage: The amount by which the quantity demanded exceeds the quantity supplied at a given price; excess demand.

APPLICATIONS

Boxing Day Madness

Toronto (CP)—Millions of bargain-hunters across Canada were out in full force Monday on one of the biggest shopping days of the year looking for Boxing Day deals.

Photo from CBC News, http://www.cbc.ca/money/story/2006/12/26/shopping-boxing.html

A Future Shop on Montreal's busy Ste. Catherine Street hired extra security and erected metal barricades to maintain control of about 1,500 people who lined up well around a city block. Extra police cars were also parked along the street. "It's a bit nuts," said Barry McGarr, 23, one of the store's employees who was trying to ensure people stayed in line. "They start pushing each other. I've seen someone fall and people just walking over them just to save a few bucks. I find it's madness."

In Alberta, thousands of shoppers jammed West Edmonton Mall. Many of the stores had security guards posted at the doors to prevent too many people from entering at one time. Cathy Williams said she and her daughter circled the mall in their car for more than half an hour searching for a parking space. In desperation, they convinced a man on his way out to allow them to follow him as he walked to his vehicle so they could take his spot. "It's warfare; you have to do that," Williams explained.

In Vancouver, massive lineups formed outside most of the upscale clothing stores on the city's downtown trendy Robson Street. Some of the queues, like the ones outside designer shops Salvatore Ferragamo and Armani, had three or four dozen people waiting for them to open. "Some of these clothes are 70 per cent off," said Lina Sun, 20, an English student.

Source: Tara Brautigam, Canadian Press, December 26, 2005. http://www.cbc.ca/cp/business/051226/b122618.html, accessed April 19, 2007.

Analysis: When prices fall below equilibrium, the quantity demanded exceeds the quantity supplied. For this shortage, initial allocation of these goods goes to those people willing and able to stand in line.

When a market shortage exists, not all consumer demands can be satisfied. Some people who are *willing* to buy Web help at the going price ($15) won't be able to do so. To assure themselves of sufficient help, Tom, George, Lisa, or some other consumer may offer to pay a *higher* price, thus initiating a move up the demand curve in Figure 2.6. The higher prices offered will in turn induce other enterprising Webheads to tutor more, thus ensuring an upward movement along the market supply curve. Thus, a higher price tends to evoke a greater quantity supplied, as reflected in the upward-sloping supply curve. Notice, again, that the *desire* to tutor Web design hasn't changed; only the quantity supplied has responded to a change in price.

Self-Adjusting Prices. What we observe, then, is that ***whenever the market price is set above or below the equilibrium price, either a market surplus or a market shortage will emerge.*** To overcome a surplus or shortage, buyers and sellers will change their behaviour. Webheads will have to compete for customers by reducing prices when a market surplus exists. If a shortage exists, buyers will compete for service by offering to pay higher prices. Only at the *equilibrium* price will no further adjustments be required.

Sometimes the market price is slow to adjust, and a disequilibrium persists. This is often the case with tickets to rock concerts, football games, and other one-time events. People initially adjust their behaviour by standing in ticket lines for hours, hoping to buy a ticket at the below-equilibrium price. The tickets are typically resold ("scalped"), however, at prices closer to equilibrium.

Business firms can discover equilibrium prices by trial and error. If they find that consumer purchases aren't keeping up with production, they may conclude that their price is above the equilibrium price. They'll have to get rid of their accumulated inventory. To do so they'll have to lower their price (by a Grand End-of-Year Sale, perhaps). In the happy situation where consumer purchases are outpacing production, a firm might conclude that its price was a trifle too low and give it a nudge upward. In any case, the equilibrium price can be established after a few trials in the marketplace.

No equilibrium price is permanent. The equilibrium price established in the Maritime University tutoring market, for example, was the unique outcome of specific demand and supply schedules. Those schedules themselves were based on our assumption of *ceteris paribus*. We assumed that the "taste" (desire) for Web-design assistance was given, as were consumers' incomes, the price and availability of other goods, and expectations. Any of these determinants of demand could change. When one does, the demand curve has to be redrawn. Such a shift of the demand curve will lead to a new equilibrium price and quantity. Indeed, ***the equilibrium price will change whenever the supply or demand curve shifts.***

Changes in Equilibrium

A Demand Shift. We can illustrate how equilibrium prices change by taking another look at the Maritime University tutoring market. Our original supply and demand curves, together with the resulting equilibrium (point E_1), are depicted in Figure 2.7. Now suppose that all the professors at Maritime University begin requiring class-specific Web pages from each student. The increased need (desire) for Web-design ability will affect market demand. Tom, George, and Lisa are suddenly willing to buy more Web tutoring at every price than they were before. That is, the *demand* for Web services has increased. We can represent this increased demand by a rightward *shift* of the market demand curve, as illustrated in Figure 2.7*a*.

Note that the new demand curve intersects the (unchanged) market supply curve at a new price (point E_2), the equilibrium price is now $30 per hour. This new equilibrium price will persist until either the demand curve or the supply curve shifts again.

A Supply Shift. Figure 2.7*b* illustrates a *supply* shift. The decrease (leftward shift) in supply might occur if some on-campus Webheads got sick. Or approaching exams might convince would-be tutors that they have no time to spare. ***Whenever supply decreases (shifts left), price tends to rise,*** as in Figure 2.7*b*.

Market outcomes shifted even more dramatically after eastern Canada's "ice storm of the century" in January 1998. The prolonged freezing rain downed telephone cables and power lines through the area and hundreds of thousands of people were without electricity for up to three weeks. Environmental catastrophes of this magnitude can have serious economic consequences. The demand for generators, for example, increased significantly. As the graphical analysis in the Applications box below indicates, the initial increase in demand gave rise to shortages and eventually the equilibrium price for generators increased.

The World View on the next page shows how rapid price adjustments can alleviate market shortages and surpluses. In this unusual case, a restaurant continuously adjusts its prices to ensure that everything on the menu is ordered.

Simultaneous Shifts. Up to now, we have discussed how *single* shifts in either the demand or the supply curve can influence equilibrium prices and quantities. But what happens if we observe *simultaneous* shifts? That is, what would happen if both the demand curve and the supply curve changed over the time period under consideration? We can use our knowledge about how single shifts affect equilibrium to derive an answer, but as we shall see, there are *three possible outcomes* for each combination of simultaneous shifts. In the final analysis, the important factor is the relative magnitudes of the shifts.

FIGURE 2.7
Changes in Equilibrium

If demand or supply change (shift), market equilibrium will change as well.

Demand shift. In (a), the rightward shift of the demand curve illustrates an increase in demand. When demand increases, the equilibrium price rises (from E_1 to E_2).

Supply shift. In (b), the leftward shift of the supply curve illustrates a decrease in supply. This raises the equilibrium price to E_3.

Demand and supply curves shift only when their underlying determinants change, that is, when *ceteris paribus* is violated.

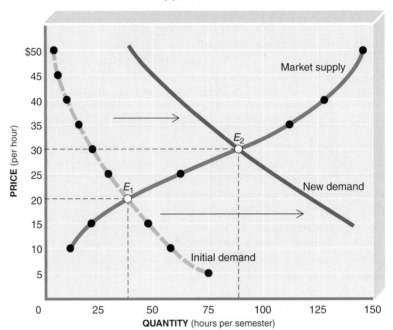

(*a*) A demand shift

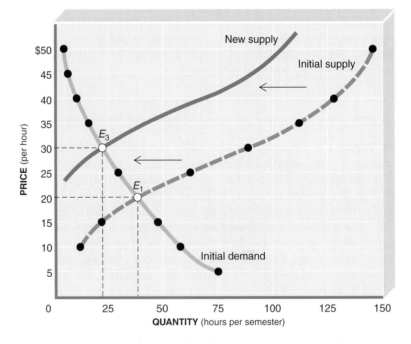

(*b*) A supply shift

In Figure 2.7, we illustrated how equilibrium prices and quantities in Web-tutoring services were affected individually by (a) an increase in demand and (b) a decrease in supply. Now, suppose that over the semester we observed both of these shifts simultaneously. Figure 2.8 illustrates the three potential new equilibrium outcomes. In panel (*a*), we see that the increase in demand is quite large while the decrease in supply is relatively small. Combined, both the new equilibrium price and quantity of Web-tutoring hours has increased. In panel (*b*), however, the increase in demand is relatively small while the decrease in supply is quite large. This combination leads to a higher equilibrium price, but a lower equilibrium in the quantity of Web-tutoring hours. Finally, in panel (*c*), we see that, once again, the equilibrium price has increased.

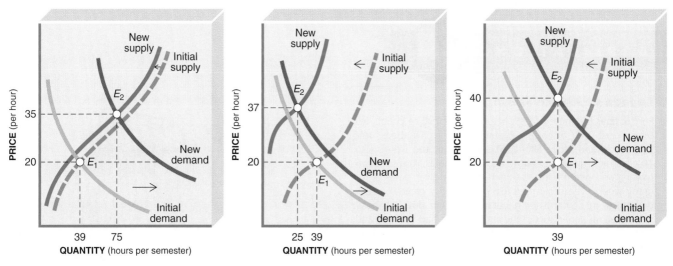

FIGURE 2.8
Simultaneous Shifts and Changes in Equilibrium

Whenever demand and supply curves shift simultaneously, there are three possible outcomes. The actual outcome depends on the relative magnitudes of the shifts. One equilibrium variable (either price or quantity) will move in one direction while the other is indeterminate—that is, it may increase, decrease, or remain constant. In this example, where demand for Web-tutoring services increases and the supply decreases, we see that the equilibrium price always increases, but the equilibrium quantity is indeterminate.

But in this case, the equilibrium quantity of Web-tutoring hours has not changed from its original position.

In each of the three cases, we see that the equilibrium price has increased. What is different, however, is the equilibrium quantity; it can increase, decrease, or remain constant. The magnitude of the demand shift relative to the supply shift determines which of these three cases prevails.

This case captures the basics of simultaneous shifts.[3] Whenever we encounter simultaneous shifts in demand and supply curves, one of the equilibrium variables (either price or quantity) will definitely move in one direction whereas the other variable is indeterminate—it may increase, decrease or remain constant.

2.6 MARKET OUTCOMES

Notice how the market mechanism resolves the basic economic questions of WHAT, HOW, and FOR WHOM.

WHAT

The WHAT question refers to the amount of Web tutorial services to include in society's mix of output. The answer at Maritime University was 39 hours of tutoring per semester. This decision wasn't reached in a referendum, but instead in the market equilibrium (Figure 2.6). In the same way but on a larger scale, millions of consumers and a handful of auto producers decide to include 2.6 million or so cars and trucks in each year's mix of output. Auto prices and quantities adjust until consumers buy the same quantity that auto manufacturers produce.

HOW

The market mechanism also determines HOW goods are produced. Profit-seeking producers will strive to produce Web designs and automobiles in the most efficient way. They'll use market prices to decide not only WHAT to produce but also what resources to use in the production process. If new software simplifies Web design—and is priced

---

[3]Note that there are four possible simultaneous shift examples: (1) both demand and supply increase, (2) both demand and supply decrease, (3) demand increases and supply decreases, and (4) demand decreases and supply increases. Each of these examples has three possible outcomes—can you illustrate these twelve graphs?

APPLICATIONS

Canada's 1998 Ice Storm

For six days in January 1998, freezing rain and ice pellets fell over a vast area of eastern Ontario, western Quebec, New Brunswick, and Nova Scotia. The weight of the ice—up to 10 cm thick in places—downed utility poles, transmission towers, and hydro wires creating massive power outages for many weeks. The prolonged loss of electricity created a sudden surge in demand for generators. Within days, all businesses selling generators in the affected area had sold out and individuals were driving hundreds of kilometres to search of the nearest available source. For those fortunate to find a generator, life became somewhat manageable during this crisis. For those unable to secure a generator, life was challenging during those hectic weeks. For example, Canada's largest aluminum producer, Alcan Aluminum Ltd., had to shut down their Beaurnhois smelting operations for six weeks, since the aluminum metal froze in the pots. It required costly and time-consuming jack hammering to return to normal operations.

Farmers were hit especially hard. Dairy and hog farmers were left without power, frantically sharing generators to run milking machines and to care for new-born piglets. The damage in eastern Ontario and southern Quebec was so severe that major rebuilding, not repairing, of the electrical grid had to be undertaken. What it took human beings a half century to construct took nature a matter of hours to knock down.

Source: Meteorological Services, Environment Canada, "The Worst Storm in Canadian History?" (http://www.msc-smc.ec.gc.ca/media/icestorm98/icestorm98_the_worst_e.cfm).

Analysis: When a determinant of demand (e.g., tastes, expectations) changes, the demand curve shifts. When this happens, the equilibrium price will change.

low enough—Webheads will use it. Likewise, auto manufacturers will use robots rather than humans on the assembly line if robots reduce costs and increase profits.

FOR WHOM

Finally, the invisible hand of the market will determine who gets the goods produced. At Maritime University, who got Web tutoring? Only those students who were willing and able to pay $20 per hour for that service. FOR WHOM are all those automobiles produced each year? The answer is the same: those consumers who are willing and able to pay the market price for a new car.

Optimal, Not Perfect

Not everyone is happy with these answers, of course. Tom would like to pay only $10 an hour for a tutor. And some of the Maritime University students don't have enough income to buy any tutoring. They think it's unfair that they have to design their own Web pages while richer students can have someone else do their design work for them. Students who can't afford cars are even less happy with the market's answer to the FOR WHOM question.

Although the outcomes of the marketplace aren't perfect, they're often optimal. Optimal outcomes are the best possible *given* our incomes and scarce resources. In other words, we expect the choices made in the marketplace to be the best possible choices for each participant. Why do we draw such a conclusion? Because Tom and George and everybody in our little Maritime University drama had (and continue to

Dining on the Downtick

Canadians aren't the only consumers who fall for packaging. Since late January, Parisians (not to mention TV crews from around the world) have been drawn to 6 rue Feydeau to try La Connivence, a restaurant with a new gimmick. The name means "collusion," and yes, of course, La Connivence is a block away from the Bourse, the French stock exchange.

What's the gimmick? Just that the restaurant's prices fluctuate according to supply and demand. The more a dish is ordered, the higher its price. A dish that's ignored gets cheaper.

Customers tune in to the day's menu (couched in trading terms) on computer screens. Among a typical day's options: *forte baisse du haddock* ("precipitous drop in haddock"), *vif recul de la côte de boeuf* ("rapid decline in beef ribs"), *la brochette de lotte au plus bas* ("fish kabob hits bottom"). Then comes the major decision—whether to opt for the price that's listed when you order or to gamble that the price will have gone down by the time you finish your meal.

So far, only main dishes are open to speculation, but co-owners Pierre Guette, an ex-professor at a top French business school, and Jean-Paul Trastour, an ex-journalist at *Le Nouvel Observateur*, are adding wine to the risk list.

La Connivence is open for dinner, but the midday "session" (as the owners call it) is the one to catch. That's when the traders of Paris leave the floor to push their luck *à table*. But here, at least, the return on their $15 investment (the average price of a meal) is immediate—and usually good.

—Christina de Liagre

Source: *New York*, April 7, 1986. © 1986 K-III Magazine Corporation. All rights reserved. Reprinted with the permission of *New York* magazine. www.newyorkmag.com

Analysis: A market surplus signals that price is too high; a market shortage suggests that price is too low. This restaurant adjusts price until the quantity supplied equals the quantity demanded.

---

have) absolute freedom to make their own purchase and consumption decisions. And also because we assume that sooner or later they'll make the choices they find most satisfying. The results are *optimal* in the sense that everyone has done as well as she or he could, given their income and talents.

SUMMARY

- Individual consumers, business firms, government agencies, and foreigners participate in the marketplace by offering to buy or sell goods and services, or factors of production. Participation is motivated by the desire to maximize utility (consumers), profits (business firms), or the general welfare (government agencies) from the limited resources each participant has.

- All market transactions involve the exchange of either factors of production or finished products. Although the actual exchanges can occur anywhere, they take place in product markets or factor markets, depending on what is being exchanged.

- People willing and able to buy a particular good at some price are part of the market demand for that product. All those willing and able to sell that good at some price are part of the market supply. Total market demand or supply is the sum of individual demands or supplies.

- Supply and demand curves illustrate how the quantity demanded or supplied changes in response to a change in the price of that good, if nothing else changes (*ceteris paribus*). Demand curves slope downward; supply curves slope upward.

- Determinants of market demand include the number of potential buyers and their respective tastes (desires), incomes, other goods, and expectations. If any of these determinants change, the demand curve shifts. Movements along a demand curve are induced only by a change in the price of that good.

- Determinants of market supply include factor costs, technology, profitability of other goods, expectations, tax rates, and number of sellers. Supply shifts when these underlying determinants change.

- The quantity of goods or resources actually exchanged in each market depends on the behaviour of all buyers and sellers, as summarized in market supply and demand curves. At the point where the two curves intersect, an equilibrium price—the price at which the quantity demanded equals the quantity supplied—is established.

- A distinctive feature of the equilibrium price and quantity is that it's the only price-quantity combination acceptable to buyers and sellers alike. At higher prices, sellers supply more than buyers are willing to purchase (a market surplus); at lower prices, the amount demanded exceeds the quantity supplied (a market shortage). Only the equilibrium price clears the market.

- Shifts in the demand curve or the supply curve or both curves (i.e., simultaneous shifts) lead to either market surpluses or market shortages at current prices. Adjustments occur in the market and a new equilibrium price and quantity emerges.

Key Terms

factor market   29
product market   30
supply   31
demand   31
demand schedule   32
demand curve   33

law of demand   33
substitute goods   33
complementary goods   34
shift in demand   35
market demand   36
market supply   38

law of supply   39
equilibrium price   42
market surplus   43
market shortage   43

Questions for Discussion

1. In our story of Tom, the student confronted with a Web-design assignment, we emphasized the great urgency of his desire for Web tutoring. Many people would say that Tom had an "absolute need" for Web help and therefore was ready to "pay anything" to get it. If this were true, what shape would his demand curve have? Why isn't this realistic?

2. With respect to the demand for college enrollment, which of the following would cause (1) a movement along the demand curve or (2) a shift of the demand curve?
   a. An increase in incomes.
   b. Lower tuition.
   c. More student loans.
   d. An increase in textbook prices.

3. One of the determinants of demand is income. For most goods, an increase in income leads to increases in demand—these are called *normal goods*. Some goods and services, however, are *inferior*—an increase in income leads to a decrease in demand. List three goods/services that you consider inferior. Illustrate the new equilibrium prices and quantities for one of these goods when there is an increase in income.

4. Which determinants of demand for generators changed when Eastern Canada was ravaged by the ice storm (page 48)?

5. Can you explain the practice of scalping tickets for major sporting events in terms of market shortages? How else might tickets be distributed?

6. How else besides higher prices could the 2001 market shortage in California's electricity market have been alleviated? Consider both demand- and supply-side options.

7. Graphically illustrate what happens to the equilibrium price and quantity of Web-design tutoring if both demand and supply *simultaneously increase*. (Hint: There are three possible outcomes—each depends on the relative magnitude of the shifts.)

8. The World View on page 49 describes the use of prices to achieve an equilibrium in the kitchen. What happens to the food at more traditional restaurants?

9. Is there a shortage of on-campus parking at your school? How might the shortage be resolved?

10. Do Internet price information services tend to raise or lower the price consumers pay for a product?

EXERCISES

PROBLEMS   The Student Problem Set to accompany this chapter can be found at the end of the book.

WEB ACTIVITIES   Web Activities to accompany this chapter can be found on the Online Learning Centre at **http://www.mcgrawhill.ca/olc/schiller**.

PART 2

Macroeconomics, Policy Issues, and Growth

Macroeconomics focuses on the performance of the entire economy rather than on the behaviour of individual participants (a micro concern). The central concerns of macroeconomics are (1) the short-term business cycle and (2) long-term economic growth.

In the short run, the emphasis is on fully using available capacity, thereby maximizing output and minimizing unemployment. This emphasis was described in Chapter 1 through the production possibility curve, PPC, and keeping the economy as close to the curve, or as close to being productively efficient as possible.

In the long run, the focus is on expanding the economy's capacity to produce goods and services, thereby raising future living standards. In the long run, we want the production possibility curve to expand, or be pushed outward to the right.

This part begins with Chapter 3, an introduction to the study of macroeconomics. The introduction provides an overview of where the rest of the book will take you without much of the detail. That comes later on. Keep the overview in mind, though; it will help you better understand how everything fits together.

Chapters 4 through 6 focus on the measurement tools used to gauge the nation's current macroeconomic performance, measuring the size of the real economy—the goods and services produced in a given year—and determining the levels of unemployment and inflation. We also examine the social and economic damage associated with unemployment and inflation.

Chapter 7 concludes this part by taking the focus back to the long run—an examination of economic growth.

An Introduction to the Macroeconomic System

At the introductory economics level, where the models are highly simplified, the storytelling grows in relative importance. A good principles of economics teacher is a good storyteller.[1]

If you open a newspaper, tune into the television news, or wander into a macroeconomics class, you may get the impression that "macroeconomics" is some large, nearly incomprehensible singular entity. However, this is really only true in the way that we might talk about the Tragically Hip or any other band as a singular entity. The band is, in fact, made up of individual players, each operating within their own area of expertise, while at the same time interacting with every other band member. When each member of the band plays the same song in the same key and with the same timing, the song is recognizable and musical. Imagine the crisis if each band member played a different song, or the same song but at a different tempo or in a different key!

Like a band, a nation's macro economy is made up of identifiable and individual components, or markets or economies, that then interact to create the grand macro economy of newspaper, television, or class fame. In other words, for the macro economy as a whole to be in harmony, each of its parts must be in tune and on the same beat.

The approach of this text is to begin by articulating the individual markets or economies that support this larger macroeconomic system: a **real economy**, a **labour market**, a **monetary economy**, and a **foreign economy**. After introducing each, we'll also briefly describe their "expertise"—the variables that are measured, the equilibriums of interest, and the way in which each of these parts interconnect to form the macroeconomic whole.

The subsequent parts and chapters of the text will take a closer, more detailed look at each economy, and, more importantly, examine how each impacts and is impacted by the others. In the end, the purpose is to better understand the whole macro economy by better understanding each of its parts.

LEARNING OBJECTIVES

By the end of this chapter, you should be able to:

3.1 Describe the four "economies" that make up the macroeconomic system

3.2 Discuss the evolution of macroeconomic thought in a Classical and Keynesian context

3.3 Describe the short run business cycle in relation to an economy's long run growth trend

3.4 Differentiate the "determinants" and "outcomes" in a macroeconomic system

real economy: Where the employment of "real" resources (labour, capital, and natural resources) create all the goods and services that are purchased by households, government, firms, and foreigners. Represented as the total value of national output—gross domestic product, GDP.

[1]David C. Colander, "The stories we tell: a reconsideration of AS/AD analysis," *Journal of Economic Perspectives* 9(3):169–88.

Peter E. Kennedy, a professor of economics at Simon Fraser University, has suggested that students should gain "an overall picture of the structure of the macro economy" and by understanding the "essence of important concepts" be able to "demonstrate how what is learned can explain real-world phenomena."[2] This is both the intent and the hope of this text.

3.1 THE ECONOMIES THAT MAKE UP THE MACROECONOMIC SYSTEM

Macroeconomics can be described as the study of aggregate economic behaviour; of the economy as a whole. What is left unsaid in this description is that the macro economy itself isn't a single entity, but rather a system; an integrated network of four individual "economies" that interact and integrate to produce what we observe and discuss as this larger national "economy." The macroeconomic "system" is described by four markets or sub-economies:

- The "*real*" economy—the production and consumption of "real" goods and services.
- The "*labour*" market—the demand and supply of labour services in the production of goods and services.
- The "*monetary*" economy—the demand and supply of money in the macro economy.
- The "*foreign*" economy—the supply and demand of goods and services between the domestic and foreign economies.

So, how does our definition of a macro economy fit within this system? Well, in fact it introduces the variables and topics from each of these sub-economies that we will spend the rest of the course exploring. Figure 3.1 puts this system idea into a visual form, showing each of the economies individually, but also indicating their interaction and integration.

The real economy will take up quite of bit of space in this textbook. That makes sense, of course, because it is in the real economy where we earn our income and purchase our goods and services. Here in Part 2 of the text, our focus will be on how macroeconomic

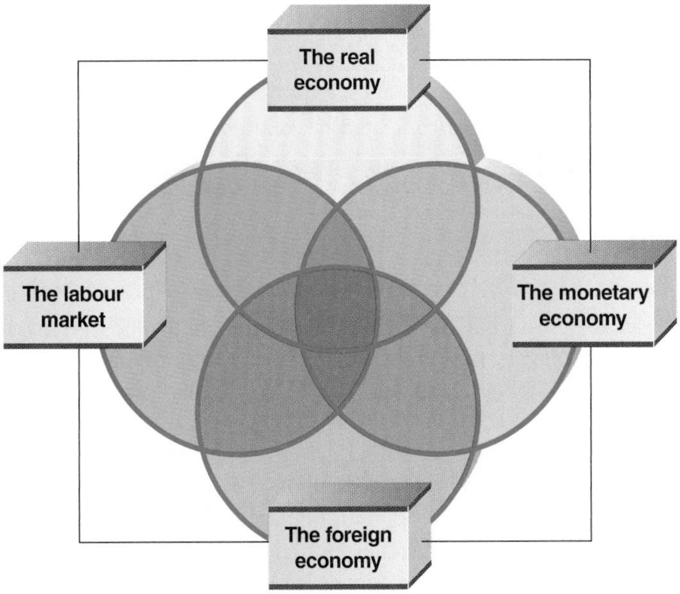

labour market: A part of the larger factor or resource market. Labour is hired by firms and paid wages to produce goods and services. The nature of the market impacts the level of unemployment and the level of wages in the national economy.

monetary economy: The supply and demand for money determines the level of interest rates, and influences inflation and the exchange rate of the currency. The focus of monetary policy determined by the Bank of Canada.

foreign economy: The world economy outside of the borders of the macroeconomy under consideration. Interactions between a domestic economy (like Canada) and all other countries in the world include the exchange of goods and services (international trade) and the exchange of financial assets and currency transactions (foreign direct investment and exchange rates).

The "Real" Economy

FIGURE 3.1
The Macro Economic System

The primary outcomes of the macroeconomic economy are the output of goods and services (the real economy), jobs (the labour market), prices (real and monetary economies), and foreign balances (the foreign economy). These outcomes result from the interplay of internal market forces and the interrelationships among the parts of the system—the centre overlapping area of the four circles—such as changes in population, innovations, and spending or saving decisions; external shocks such as international disputes, weather, trade disruptions, and exchange rates; and changes to fiscal and monetary policy such as tax, expenditure, regulatory, and interest rate decisions. The larger "box" surrounding the four circles provides a sense of what we mean with the term "macro economy."

[2]Peter E. Kennedy, "The Macroeconomics Principles Course: What They Should Be Doing" (lecture, 2006 BC Economics Articulation meeting, Kwantlen University College, May 2, 2005).

WORLD **VIEW**

Comparative GDP

The Canadian economy is often referred to as a "small open economy." That is, the Canadian economy is "small" relative to the entire world economy. As illustrated in the accompanying figure, the Canadian economy is about the same size as Mexico's but approximately 1/3 smaller than the economies of Russia, France, and the United Kingdom. It is only 1/2 the size of the German economy and 1/3 the size of the Japanese economy. However, Canada's economy is barely 1/10 the size of the United States—our largest trading partner—and only 1/8 the size of China, one of the world's fastest growing economies and an increasingly important trade partner to Canada. (The figure is based on purchasing power parity calculations and converted to Canadian dollars.)

Source: IMF, "World Economic and Financial Survey," *World Economic Outlook Database*, September 2006.

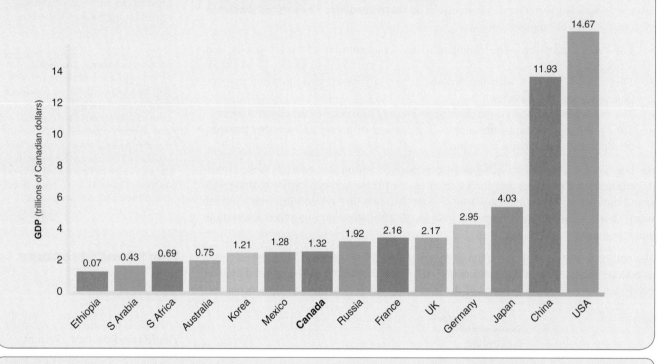

Analysis: Although the Canadian economy ranks in the top ten, it is relatively small compared to countries like the United States and China and represents a small share the entire world's economic output.

outcomes are measured. We get started on the real economy in the next chapter (Chapter 4) as we discuss the players that make up the real economy and measure each of their contributions towards the total value of economic output—gross domestic product, GDP.

The World View box provides a comparative look at economies around the world. The U.S. economy is the world's largest at $14.67 trillion, about 20 percent larger than China's economy, which is about $11.93 trillion, and more than 10 times larger than Canada's $1.32 trillion. All the values in the World View box are in Canadian dollars, and are measured in purchasing power parity terms (measuring what a dollar can buy rather than using official exchange rates).

Chapter 6 looks at the impact of price level changes in the economy with specific focus on the impact of price level changes on consumers. It is important to recognize right from the beginning that talking about price in macroeconomics is different than talking about price in microeconomics. Since macroeconomics is made up of all goods and services produced in an economy—perhaps numbering in the tens of thousands— the term price cannot relate to any particular good but rather in some way to all goods. Hence, the term price level—or to put it another way, a measure of the change in average prices in an economy. The consumer price index, CPI, is the common measure associated with price level change, and in Chapter 6 we will discuss what it is, how it is constructed, what it actually tells us, and what concerns we should be aware of.

Economic growth takes centre stage in Chapter 7. We are interested in what economic growth implies, what its fundamental components are, and how we might get more of it. The chapter takes a brief look at the evolution in thinking associated with economic growth over the past few decades. Understanding the process and policies that encourage long run economic growth help us put many complex current policy debates into some context.

Part 3 discusses cyclical instability and presents a model of the real economy that enables us to consider both the near as well as the not-so-near future. Chapter 8 presents an aggregate demand (AD) and aggregate supply (AS) model that allows us to predict outcomes as a result of changes in policy, unanticipated economic "shocks" arising from either domestic or foreign sources, and changes the behaviour of real economy "players." This model, it turns out, is really the workhorse of understanding the real economy in this course. Chapter 9 follows this up by considering the economy's penchant for change and its ability to self-adjust.

To conclude the discussion of the real economy, Part 3 will take a look at the role and impact of government—fiscal policy levers—in the real economy. It is government that creates programs and determines what to spend and how to spend it. This exercise of fiscal policy—raising revenue through taxes and transferring or spending those funds on economic and social policy goals—is the focus of Chapter 10. Chapter 11 follows up with a look at the annual budgetary implications of government policy—annual deficits or surpluses—and the effect these annual outcomes have on the accumulation of government debt.

The "Labour" Market

A relatively brief discussion of the labour market occurs in Chapter 5. Much of the detail of the labour market is included in the microeconomic view of the economy. The development of a fuller appreciation of macroeconomics and macroeconomic policy requires us to look at labour market outcomes in an aggregate way. Therefore, this chapter explores the measurement of an economy's total labour force and, at the same time, a measurement of the rate of unemployment within that labour force.

We use the same "how we determine it, what it tells us, and what should we be aware of" lens to look at unemployment statistics as we earlier looked at the consumer price index (CPI). Since much of government economic policy relates to increasing employment opportunities within the economy and decreasing unemployment, we will discuss what rate of unemployment is the "right" rate, and how the underlying reasons for unemployment can be moderated through government fiscal policy.

The "Monetary" Economy

The *monetary* economy has two chapters devoted to it in Part 4. The first, Chapter 12, introduces the nature and function of money within a modern economy. It goes on to measure purchasing power in the economy, recognizing that purchasing power arises both from physical holdings of money—change in your pocket and bills in your wallet—as well as from the deposits that are available to you through cheques or debit cards.

While the level of physical money can be controlled through monetary policy, commercial banks can *create* additional purchasing power in the economy depending on their choice of reserves. In other words, the actions of commercial banks can lead to a *multiplication* of purchasing power in the economy. This chapter will explain how this occurs and some of the constraints that affect the final size of that multiplier.

Chapter 12 concludes with an introduction to Canada's monetary authority—the Bank of Canada—and the policy instruments that they have to work with to increase or decrease the level of purchasing power available to the economy. Of course, the idea of "increase and decrease" is itself a simplification, since in reality the level of purchasing power is growing. Technically, what we are describing is either increasing or decreasing the rate at which the purchasing power is growing. But the final impact is the same in either case.

Chapter 13 takes a look at the operation and impact of monetary policy generally and the mechanism that transmits the monetary policy impact back into the real economy. We will also see how monetary policy can affect interest rates in the economy, inflation rates in the economy, and the external exchange rate of the Canadian dollar. However, we will also make the case that the Bank of Canada is only able to sustain a policy goal for one of these at any given time and that the choice of one goal diminishes the ability to pursue a goal in either of the other areas. Finally, this chapter will present alternative perspectives on monetary policy effectiveness and some concerns with policy generally.

The "Foreign" Economy

The final focus on the macroeconomic system takes us out of our own domestic economy and into the wide world beyond. Canada has always been a trading nation—an "open" economy. Figure 3.2 illustrates the importance of trade to the Canadian economy since 1981. In 1981 the combined value of exports and imports to Canadian GDP was about 40 percent. By 2005, that proportion had doubled to slightly more than 80 percent of total GDP. Canada's largest trading partner, the United States, accounts for more than 80 percent of Canada's total exports and about 70 percent of Canada's total imports.

Chapter 15 focuses on the trade in goods and services—exports and imports. While we have already looked at these as part of the real economy (just another relationship within the broader system) this chapter takes a more fundamental view. Understanding trade requires understanding the difference between **absolute** and **comparative advantage**; a difference that economist Paul Krugman writes about as "Ricardo's difficult idea."[3]

Although offering a deeper appreciation of the benefits and gains from trade is important, at least equally important is confronting the counter-arguments and criticisms. Economist Jagdish Bhagwati writes of this in his book *In Defense of Globalization*:

> When all is said the fact is that we lack a clear, coherent, and comprehensive sense of how globalization—and I refer to economic globalization (which embraces diverse forms of international integration, including foreign trade, multinational direct foreign investment, movements of short-term portfolio funds, technological diffusion, and cross-border migration)—works and how it can do better.[4]

absolute advantage: The ability of a country to produce a specific good with fewer resources (per unit of output) than other countries.

comparative advantage: The ability of a country to produce a specific good at a lower opportunity cost than its trading partners.

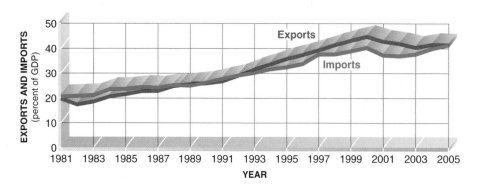

FIGURE 3.2

Canada's Exports and Imports as a Proportion of GDP

Although Canada has been a trading nation from its start, the extent of trade as a proportion of Canadian GDP has doubled since 1981 to 80 percent of total GDP.

Source: Statistics Canada CANSIM Table 380-0017. Statistics Canada information is used with the permission of Statistics Canada.

[3]Paul Krugman, "Ricardo's difficult idea," http://www.pkarchive.org/ accessed November 15, 2006. Click on "International Trade."
[4]Jagdish Bhagwati, (2004). *In Defense of Globalization* (New York: Oxford University Press, 2004), p. ix.

WORLD VIEW

Income Share of the Rich and Poor

Inequality tends to diminish as a country develops. In poor developing nations, the richest tenth of the population typically gets 40 to 50 percent of all income. In developed countries, the richest tenth gets 20 to 30 percent of total income.

Source: World Development Report, *Beyond Scarcity: Power, Poverty and the Global Water Crisis.* (Washington, D.C.: The World Bank, 2007), Table 15, pp. 335–338, http://hdr.undp.org/hdr2006/pdfs/report/HDR_2006_Tables.pdf, accessed May 14, 2007.

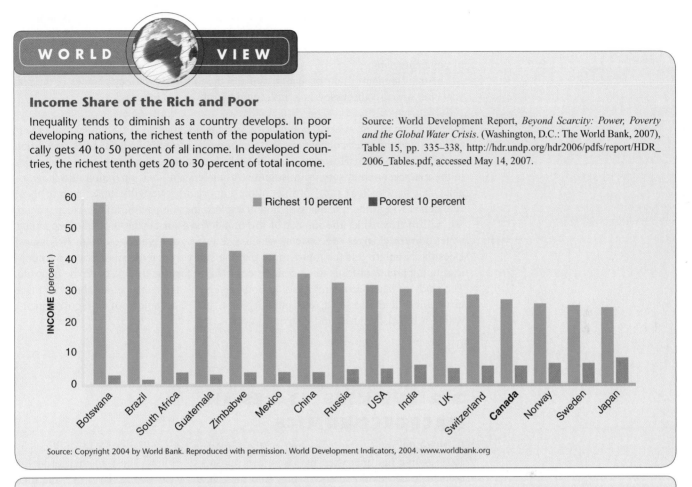

Source: Copyright 2004 by World Bank. Reproduced with permission. World Development Indicators, 2004. www.worldbank.org

Analysis: Although perfect equality doesn't exist, development does lead to a reduction in the disparity between the richest tenth and poorest tenth of a population.

Perhaps even more importantly for a world that appears to be concerned about the economic development and growth in "less developed countries," is the role that liberalized trade can play in achieving that goal. Amartya Sen writes the following in *Development as Freedom*:

> The freedom to exchange words, or goods, or gifts does not need defensive justification in terms of their favourable but distant effects; they are part of the way human beings in society live and interact with each other (unless stopped by regulation or fiat). The contribution of the market mechanism to economic growth is, of course, important, but this comes only after the direct significance of the freedom to interchange—words, goods, gifts—has been acknowledged.[5]

The World View box provides another perspective on economic development—the impact of development on the inequality of wealth within the economy. The evidence presented illustrates that relative inequality tends to diminish as a country develops, although inequalities remain.

Chapter 15 also explores the rise of protectionist pressures, as well as intended (and unintended) barriers to trade. All of this leads to an introduction to international institutions relating to trade, such as the World Trade Organization (WTO) and regional trade arrangements such as the North American Free Trade Agreement (NAFTA).

[5]Amartya Sen, *Development as Freedom* (New York: Anchor Books, 1999).

Chapter 16 completes the look at our international relationships but this time in the context of financial flows—portfolio and direct investments—and the international exchange of currencies. Much of this interaction is summarized in Canada's balance of payments data.

The management of our exchange rate and the impact of various choices in the real economy are also discussed in a little more depth in Chapter 16.

Of course, as we go, we will connect the systems together to get a sense of the inter-relationships and inter-connections that are important to fully understand the operation of a macro economy. However, we will begin by looking at each of these economies in the macroeconomic system in isolation, to understand their operation and the variables that they "solve" for. But then, more importantly, we will situate each of these economies within the broader system and explore their impact in that broader system. We will then consider the impact of the broader system on the individual economy, which in turn changes the system, which again . . . well, you see one of the issues! Does the circularity of the topic imply that the study of macroeconomics is meaningless, unimportant, or leads to no conclusions? No, in fact the truth is quite the opposite. The study of macroeconomics should both engage us and enhance our ability to place our choices and decisions, our public policy, and the choices of our governments within a broader, richer, and deeper context.

Enjoy!

3.2 BUSINESS CYCLES IN MACROECONOMICS

In 1926, the total value of output of the Canadian economy was $5.146 billion; by 1929, output had increased by 19 percent to $6.139 billion. The Canadian economy seemed to be healthy and growing. And then things went wrong. By 1933, the total value of output in Canada had fallen to $3.492 billion. The economy had shrunk by 43 percent!

When firms reduced their production of goods and services, they also reduced their use of economic resources like labour. The number of unemployed persons looking for work in Canada was 65,000 in 1927, rising to 826,000 in 1933.[6] The Great Depression had firmly taken hold of the Canadian economy.

Although the depression of the 1930s represents the most dramatic example of economic downswings, we have experienced a number of smaller ones since, most recently in the 1980s and early 1990s.

The Great Depression shook not only the foundations of the world economy but also the self-confidence of the economics profession. No one had predicted the depression, and few could explain it. The ensuing search for explanations focused on three central questions:

- **How stable is a market-driven economy?**
- **What forces cause instability?**
- **What, if anything, can the government do to promote steady economic growth?**

The basic purpose of *macroeconomics* is to answer these questions—to *explain* how and why economies grow and what causes the recurrent ups and downs of the economy that characterize the **business cycle.** In this chapter we introduce the theoretical model economists use to describe and explain the short-run business cycle.

business cycle: Alternating periods of economic growth and contraction.

[6]F. H. Leacy, ed., *Historical Statistics of Canada*. Catalogue 11-516-XIE. http://www.statcan.ca/english/freepub/11-516-XIE/sectiona/toc.htm, accessed November 8, 2006.

We'll also preview some of the policy options the government might use to dampen those cycles.

Classical Theory. Prior to the 1930s, macro economists thought there could never be a Great Depression. The economic thinkers of the time asserted that a market-driven economy was inherently stable. There was no need for government intervention.

This *laissez-faire* view of macroeconomics seemed reasonable at the time. During the nineteenth century and the first 30 years of the twentieth, the Canadian economy experienced some bad years in which the nation's output declined and unemployment increased. But most of these episodes were relatively short-lived. The dominant feature of the Industrial Era was growth: an expanding economy, with more output, more jobs, and higher incomes nearly every year.

In this environment, classical economists, as they later became known, propounded an optimistic view of the macro economy. *According to the classical view, the economy "self-adjusts" to deviations from its long-term growth trend.* Producers might occasionally reduce their output and throw people out of work, but these dislocations would cause little damage. If output declined and people lost their jobs, the internal forces of the marketplace would quickly restore prosperity. Economic downturns were viewed as temporary setbacks, not permanent problems.

The cornerstones of classical optimism were flexible prices and flexible wages. If producers couldn't sell all their output at current prices, they had two choices. They could reduce the rate of output and throw some people out of work, or they could reduce the price of their output, thereby stimulating an increase in the quantity demanded. According to the *law of demand,* price reductions cause an increase in unit sales. If prices fall far enough, all the output produced can be sold. Thus, flexible prices—prices that would drop when consumer demand slowed—virtually guaranteed that all output could be sold. No one would have to lose a job because of weak consumer demand.

Flexible prices had their counterpart in factor markets. If some workers were temporarily out of work, they'd compete for jobs by offering their services at lower wages. As wage rates declined, producers would find it profitable to hire more workers. Ultimately, flexible wages would ensure that everyone who wanted a job would have a job.

These optimistic views of the macro economy were summarized in Say's Law. **Say's Law**—named after the nineteenth-century economist Jean-Baptiste Say—decreed that "supply creates its own demand." Whatever was produced would be sold. All workers who sought employment would be hired. *Unsold goods and unemployed labour could emerge in this classical system, but both would disappear as soon as people had time to adjust prices and wages.* There could be no Great Depression—no protracted macro failure—in this classical view of the world.

The Great Depression was a stunning blow to classical economists. At the onset of the depression, classical economists assured everyone that the setbacks in production and employment were temporary and would soon vanish. Andrew Mellon, Secretary of the U.S. Treasury, expressed this optimistic view in January 1930, just a few months after the stock market crash. Assessing the prospects for the year ahead, he said: "I see nothing . . . in the present situation that is either menacing or warrants pessimism. . . . I have every confidence that there will be a revival of activity in the spring and that during the coming year the country will make steady progress."[7] Merrill Lynch, one of the nation's largest brokerage houses, was urging that people should buy stocks. But the depression deepened. Indeed, unemployment grew and persisted *despite* falling prices and wages (see Figure 3.3). The classical self-adjustment mechanism simply didn't work.

Stable or Unstable?

Say's Law: Supply creates its own demand.

[7]David A. Shannon, *The Great Depression* (Englewood Cliffs, NJ: Prentice Hall, 1960), p. 4.

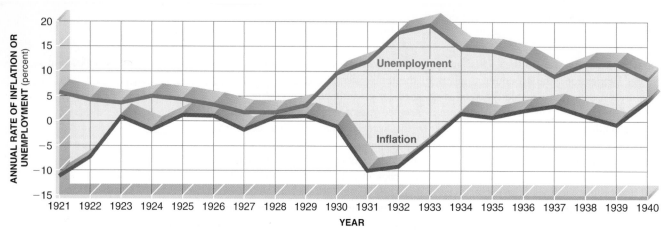

FIGURE 3.3

Inflation and Unemployment, 1921–1940

Unemployment (U) rose to almost 20 percent of the labour force by 1933 and remained above 10 percent through to the beginning of World War II. Even as unemployment was rising between 1930 and 1933, wages and prices were falling (deflation). Falling wages and prices did not restore full employment. This macroeconomic failure prompted calls for new theories and policies to control the business cycle.

Source: Adapted from Statistics Canada publication *Historical Statistics Canada*, Catalogue 11-516, Series D127 and D132, http://www.statcan.ca/bsolc/english/bsolc?catno=11-516-X. Statistics Canada information is used with the permission of Statistics Canada.

The Keynesian Revolution. The Great Depression effectively destroyed the credibility of classical economic theory. As the British economist John Maynard Keynes pointed out in 1935, classical economists

were apparently unmoved by the lack of correspondence between the results of their theory and the facts of observation:—a discrepancy which the ordinary man has not failed to observe... .

The celebrated optimism of [classical] economic theory...is...to be traced, I think, to their having neglected to take account of the drag on prosperity which can be exercised by an insufficiency of effective demand. For there would obviously be a natural tendency towards the optimum employment of resources in a Society which was functioning after the manner of the classical postulates. It may well be that the classical theory represents the way in which we should like our Economy to behave. But to assume that it actually does so is to assume our difficulties away.[8]

Keynes went on to develop an alternative view of the macro economy. Whereas the classical economists viewed the economy as inherently stable, **_Keynes asserted that a market-driven economy is inherently unstable._** Small disturbances in output, prices, or unemployment were likely to be magnified, not muted, by the invisible hand of the marketplace. The Great Depression was not a unique event, Keynes argued, but a calamity that would recur if we relied on the market mechanism to self-adjust.

In Keynes's view, the inherent instability of the market-place required government intervention. When the economy falters, we can't afford to wait for some assumed self-adjustment mechanism but must instead intervene to protect jobs and income. The government can do this by "priming the pump": buying more output, employing more people, providing more income transfers, and making more money available. When the economy overheats, the government must cool it down with higher taxes, spending reductions, and less money.

Keynes's denunciation of classical theory didn't end the macroeconomic debate. On the contrary, economists continue to wage fierce debates about the stability of the economy. Those debates fill the pages of later chapters. But before examining them, let's first take a quick look at the economy's actual performance.

[8]John Maynard Keynes, *The General Theory of Employment, Interest and Money* (London: Macmillan, 1936), pp. 33–34.

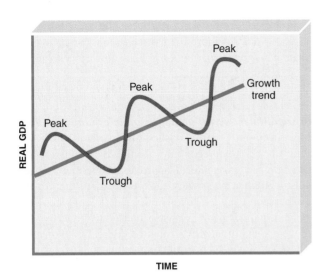

FIGURE 3.4
The Business Cycle

The model business cycle resembles a roller coaster. Output first climbs to a peak, then decreases. After hitting a trough, the economy recovers, with real GDP again increasing.

A central concern of macroeconomic theory is to determine whether a recurring business cycle exists, and if so, what forces cause it.

The upswings and downturns of the business cycle are gauged in terms of changes in total output. An economic upswing, or expansion, refers to an increase in the volume of goods and services produced. An economic downturn, or contraction, occurs when the total volume of production declines. Changes in employment typically mirror these changes in production.

Figure 3.4 depicts the stylized features of a business cycle. Over the long run, the output of the economy grows at roughly 3 percent per year. There's a lot of year-to-year variation around this growth trend, however. The short-run cycle looks like a roller coaster, climbing steeply, then dropping from its peak. Once the trough is reached, the upswing starts again.

In reality, business cycles aren't as regular or as predictable as Figure 3.4 suggests. The Canadian economy has experienced recurrent upswings and downswings, but of widely varying length, intensity, and frequency.

Figure 3.5 illustrates the actual performance of the Canadian economy since 1927. Changes in total output are measured by changes in **real GDP,** the inflation-adjusted

Historical Cycles

real GDP: The value of final output produced in a given period, adjusted for changing prices.

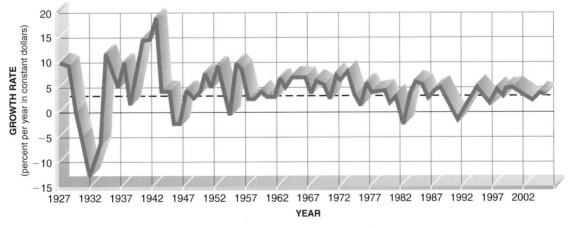

FIGURE 3.5
The Business Cycle in Canadian History

From 1927 to 2005, real national income increased at an average rate of about 3 percent per year. But the year-to-year changes have departed widely from that average. Years of high-growth seem to alternate with years of low-growth (slow growth) and at times, actual decreases in total income (recession).

Source: Adapted from Statistics Canada publication *Historical Statistics Canada,* Catalogue 11-516, Series F33-55, and from Statistics Canada CANSIM Table 380-0017, http://cansim2.statcan.ca and author's calculations. Statistics Canada information is used with the permission of Statistics Canada.

value of all goods and services produced. From a long-run view, the growth of real GDP has been impressive: Real GDP today is more than fifteen times larger than it was in 1929. Canadians now consume a greater variety of goods and services, and in greater quantities, than earlier generations ever dreamed possible.

Our long-term success in raising living standards is clouded, however, by a spate of short-term macro setbacks. On closer inspection, ***the growth path of the Canadian economy isn't a smooth, rising trend but a series of steps, stumbles, and setbacks.*** This short-run instability is evident in Figure 3.5. The dashed line marks the long-run *average* annual real growth rate of the Canadian economy. From 1927 through 2005, the Canadian economy expanded at an average rate of approximately 3 percent per year. However, as Figure 3.5 illustrates, there were very few years where the growth rate was actually equal to that 3 percent average. There were many years when real GDP grew by greater than 3 percent and many years when real GDP grew by less than 3 percent. Worse still, there were years of *negative* growth, with real GDP *declining* from one year to the next. These successive short-run contractions and expansions are the essence of the business cycle.

The Great Depression. The most prolonged departure from our long-run growth path occurred during the Great Depression. Between 1929 and 1933, total Canadian output steadily declined. Notice in Figure 3.5 how the growth rate is negative in each of these years. During these four years of negative growth, real GDP contracted a total of nearly 30 percent. Investment in new plant and equipment virtually ceased. Economies around the world came to a grinding halt (see the World View box).

Although the Canadian economy rebounded after 1933 and experienced positive economic growth each year, it wasn't until 1939 that total output finally surpassed what it had been in 1929.

World War II. World War II greatly increased the demand for goods and services and real GDP grew at unprecedented rates—from 14 percent in 1940 to almost 19 percent in 1942. Virtually everyone was now employed—unemployment had fallen from a high of 19 percent in 1933, to less than 9 percent in 1940, to less than 3 percent by 1942. Throughout the war, Canada's productive capacity was strained to the limit.

WORLD VIEW

Global Depression

The Great Depression wasn't confined to the Canadian economy. Most other countries suffered substantial losses of output and employment over a period of many years. Between 1929 and 1932, industrial production around the world fell 37 percent. The United States and Germany suffered the largest losses, while Spain and the Scandinavian countries lost only modest amounts of output.

Some countries escaped the ravages of the Great Depression altogether. The Soviet Union, largely insulated from Western economic structures, was in the midst of Stalin's forced industrialization drive during the 1930s. China and Japan were also relatively isolated from world trade and finance and so suffered less damage from the depression.

Country	Decline in Industrial Output
Chile	−22%
France	−31
Germany	−47
Great Britain	−17
Japan	−2
Norway	−7
Spain	−12
United States	−46
Canada	**−43**

Analysis: International trade and financial flows tie nations together. When the world economy tumbled in the 1930s, other nations lost export sales. Such interactions made the Great Depression a worldwide calamity.

The Post-World War II Years. Since the extremes of the Great Depression and World War II, the economic performance has been more moderate—but still experiencing periods of above- and below-average positive growth, and periods of negative growth. The reduction in defense spending after World War II pushed the economy into recession until pent-up consumer demand in the 1950s revived Canadian economic fortunes.

From the mid-1950s through to the late 1970s, Canada experienced an extended period of positive economic growth. The 1980s and 1990s, on the other hand, both began with years of slow growth and actual declines in GDP. Growth was only 1.4 percent in 1980 and declined by almost 3 percent in 1982 with an "average" 3 percent year in between. 1990 and 1992 both had growth of less than 1 percent and 1991 had negative growth—an actual decline in GDP—of almost 2 percent.

Canada Since the 1990s. Since 1993, the Canadian economy has had sustained economic expansion, although not at any consistent rate. Real Canadian economic growth has been as low as 1.5 percent (1996) to 4.5 percent or slightly more (1999 and 2000). In fact, eight of the years between 1993 and 2005 had growth above the 3 percent long run average while only four were below.

The years where growth is below the long run average of 3 percent are called **growth recessions**—the economy grows, but at a slower rate that the average: Thus *a growth recession occurs when the economy expands too slowly. A recession occurs when real GDP actually contracts.* A **depression** is an extremely deep and long **recession**—or when you don't even get socks for Christmas.

The Bank of Canada's *Monetary Policy Report* looks forward, estimating that "*the bank's base-case outlook calls for economic growth, on an average annual basis, to be 2.8 percent in 2006, 2.5 percent in 2007, and 2.8 percent in 2008.*"[9] The near-term outlook then is for continued economic growth, but at a rate slightly below the long run average annual rate.

Figure 3.4 on page 61 illustrates the relationship between business cycles and the growth trend. Another way of characterizing these two economic events is to talk about the deviations from the trend in the short run, and the growth of the economy's potential in the long run.

growth recession: A period during which real GDP grows, but at a rate below the long-term trend.

depression: A severe and extended recession.

recession: A decline in total output (real GDP) for two or more consecutive quarters.

The Short Run and the Long Run

ROB ROGERS, reprinted by permission of United Features Syndicate, Inc.

Analysis: Recessions occur when total output in the economy declines. In recessions, household income and spending fall.

[9]Bank of Canada (2006, October 19), *Monetary Policy Report,* (October 19, 2006), p. 28, http://www.bankofcanada.ca/en/mpr/mpr_previous.html, accessed November 18, 2006.

The bumpy record of the Canadian economy—any short-run deviations from the long-run trend—is associated with changes in output and unemployment. Beginning in the next chapter, we'll look at ways of measuring the state of the economy through time, and of comparing the current measure to previous measurements as well as to where the economy should be at its potential level. The result of such comparisons may be to propose a government policy to "fix" whatever is seen to be wrong.

Modern economists are cautious about how big a role government is able to play in setting the economy right. Nearly all economists recognize that policy intervention affects macroeconomic outcomes. But there are disagreements about just how effective any fiscal and monetary policy is. Some economists echo the Classical notion that policy intervention may be either ineffective or, worse still, inherently destabilizing. Others see a positive role for government both in stabilizing the economy and in setting a foundation for future economic growth.

Adding to the cautious approach of many economists is a concern about the impact on the economy's long-run economic growth of policy intended to "fix" short-run problems. If changes in taxes, regulations, and government spending and budget balances—deficits or surpluses—change investment and innovation decisions, the long-run growth trend of the economy may be reduced. A reduction from 3 percent to 2 percent would result in the economy taking 50 percent longer to double in size. So, the price of any short-run gain from government intervention may be offset by slower long-run economic growth.

The rest of this text, in one form or another, attempts to shed light on these disagreements and controversies. Understanding current policy debate is difficult, if not impossible, without understanding the impact and opportunity cost associated with any policy. And developing policy requires balancing today's short-run deviation and tomorrow's long-run trend.

SUMMARY

- A macro economy is best thought of from a "systems" perspective. That is, the macro economy is really made up of four economies—a real economy, a labour market, a monetary economy, and a foreign economy—that are integrated to produce the "whole."
- The "outcomes" of the macroeconomic system—output, jobs, prices, growth, and foreign balances—are the result of "determinants"—internal market forces, external shocks, and fiscal and monetary policy.
- Modern macroeconomics is more often framed as a complex debate between short-run and long-run outcomes rather than the earlier, simpler Classical and Keynesian confrontation.

- The long-term growth rate of the Canadian economy is approximately 3 percent a year. But output doesn't increase 3 percent every year. In some years, real GDP grows much faster than that; in other years growth is slower. Sometimes total output actually declines.
- These short-run variations in GDP growth are a central focus of macroeconomics. Macro theory tries to explain the alternating periods of growth and contraction that characterize the business cycle; macro policy attempts to control the cycle.

Key Terms

Questions for Discussion

1. If business cycles were really inevitable, what purpose would macro policy serve?
2. What events might prompt consumers to demand fewer goods at current prices?
3. If equilibrium is compatible with both buyers' and sellers' intentions, how can it be undesirable?
4. The Bank of Canada publishes a *Monetary Policy Report* in April and October, and *Monetary Policy Report Updates* in January and July each year. The opening paragraph of the October 2006 *Report* overview states that:

   "The Canadian economy continues to operate just above its full production capacity, and the near-term outlook for core inflation has moved slightly higher. However, with the U.S. economy slowing more quickly than expected, the base-case projection for Canadian economic growth has been revised down slightly from that in the July *Monetary Policy Report Update*. Lower energy prices have led to a downward revision of the projection for total consumer price inflation. They have also contributed to moving the Canadian dollar into a somewhat lower trading range." (p. 5)

   Where are each of the macroeconomic system's economies in this paragraph and what are the particular economic variables of interest?
5. What exactly did Say mean when he said "supply creates its own demand"?
6. What's wrong with the Classical theory of self-adjustment? Why didn't sales and employment increase in 1929–1933 in response to declining prices and wages (see Figure 3.3)?

EXERCISES

PROBLEMS   The Student Problem Set to accompany this chapter can be found at the end of the book.

WEB ACTIVITIES   Web Activities to accompany this chapter can be found on the Online Learning Centre at **http://www.mcgrawhill.ca/olc/schiller**.

Describing the Real Economy

A favorite cliché of policymakers is that government likes to tackle only those problems it can measure. Politicians need visible results. They want to be able to brag to their constituents about the kilometres of new highways built, the number of students who graduated, the number of families that left welfare, and the number of unemployed workers who found jobs. To do this, they must be able to measure economic outcomes.

The Great Depression of the 1930s was an abject lesson in the need for better measures of economic performance. There were plenty of anecdotes about factories closing, farms failing, and people selling apples on the streets. But nobody knew the dimensions of the nation's economic meltdown until thousands of workers had lost their jobs. The need for more timely information about the health of the national economy was evident. The Dominion Bureau of Statistics, the predecessor to Statistics Canada, was formed in 1918 through the merger of assorted statistical divisions of the government. The new bureau became responsible for Canadian statistics relating to the national census, foreign trade, industrial production, births and deaths, and other institutional statistics, some of which had been collected as far back as 1665.

In a memorandum to the Committee on National Income Statistics in 1939, Sedley Cudmore, who later was appointed Dominion Statistician, a position now called the Chief Statistician of Canada, noted that "for Canada, where the statistics available are roughly comparable with those of the United States, it has seemed desirable, after making an exhaustive study of the methods used in various countries . . . to follow, as far as possible, United States methods, as exemplified in the publications of the National Bureau of Economic Research and the Department of Commerce."[1] Much of this methodology was developed by the U.S. economist, Simon Kuznets, who in 1971 received the Nobel Prize in economics.

The Dominion Bureau began publishing annual national income measurements for Canada in the mid-1940s. By 1952 they had also constructed a set of data representing the years 1926–1950 and subsequently, a quarterly data series for the years 1947–1952. Other economists, notably M.C. Urquart at Queen's University, Kingston, extended the series of national income statistics back to 1870.

[1]David A. Worton, *The Dominion Bureau of Statistics: A History of Canada's Central Statistical Office and its Antecedents, 1841–1972*. (Montreal and Kingston: McGill—Queen's University Press, 1998), p. 193.

LEARNING OBJECTIVES

By the end of this chapter, you should be able to:

4.1 Identify the real economy participants in the circular flow and explain their interconnectedness

4.2 Describe how gross domestic product (GDP) can be measured from both the expenditure and income sides and the problems of measurement

4.3 Explain the flow relationship between expenditure and income, and foreign and domestic economies

4.4 Explain the difference between "real" and "nominal" values

4.5 Describe alternative measures of "well-being"

The Dominion Bureau of Statistics was transformed into Statistics Canada by an Act of Parliament in February 1971. Today, Statistics Canada is recognized as one of the world's best statistical agencies. The **national-income accounting** system now churns out reams of data that are essential to tracking the economy's performance. They answer such questions as

- **How much output is being produced? What is it being used for?**
- **How much income is being generated in the marketplace?**
- **What's happening to prices and wages?**

It's tempting, of course, to ignore all these measurement questions, especially since they tend to be rather dull. But if we avoid measurement problems, we severely limit our ability to understand how the economy works or how well (or poorly) it's performing. We also limit our ability to design policies for improving economic performance.

National-income accounting also provides a useful perspective on the way the economy works. It shows how factor markets relate to product markets, how output relates to income, and how consumer spending and business investment relate to production. It also shows how the flow of taxes and government spending may alter economic outcomes.

In other words, the focus of national-income accounting is on the four participant groups—or sectors—identified in the circular flow diagram presented in chapter 2 (page 29): consumers (households), business firms, governments, and international participants (foreign). Figure 4.1 presents the circular flow diagram again as a handy reminder to refer to as you work through this chapter.

national-income accounting: The measurement of aggregate economic activity, particularly national income and its components.

WEB NOTE

Statistics Canada publishes *A User Guide to the Canadian System of National Accounts,* which offers a detailed explanation of the conventions, major concepts, definitions, purposes, and the integrated nature of the system of accounts. http://www. statcan.ca/english/neacen/pub/ guide/13589.pdf.

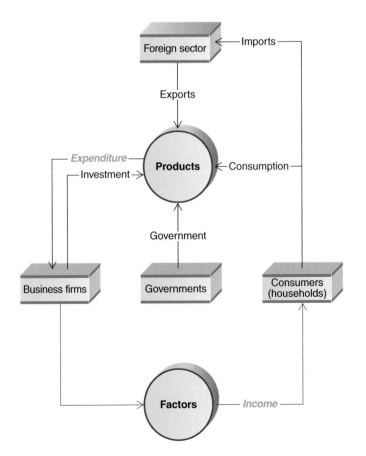

FIGURE 4.1
The Real Economy Circular Flow

Figure 4.1 illustrates the four participants, or sectors, that make up the real economy. The "top half" of the diagram shows the expenditures that arise from each of the sectors (traced through the blue lines), while the "bottom half" follows the income generated from production (traced through the black lines). Expenditures come from household consumption, from governments, from foreigners (net exports), and from business firms (investment) for goods and services. Income arises from the payments to factors required for the production of all those goods and services and owned by households.

4.1 MEASURES OF OUTPUT

The array of goods and services we produce is truly massive, including everything from professional hockey to commercial jets. All these things are part of our total output; the problem is to find a summary measure.

Itemizing the amount of each good or service produced each year won't solve our measurement problems. The resulting list would be so long that it would be both unwieldy and meaningless. We couldn't even add it up, since it would contain diverse goods measured in a variety of units (e.g., kilometres, items, kilograms, litres). Nor could we compare one year's output to another's. Suppose that last year we produced 2 billion apples, 2 million bicycles, and 700 rock concerts, whereas this year we produced 3 billion apples, 4 million bicycles, and 600 rock concerts. Which year's output was larger? With more of some goods, but less of others, the answer isn't obvious.

Gross Domestic Product

To facilitate our accounting chores, we need some mechanism for organizing annual output data into a more manageable summary. The mechanism we use is price. ***Each good and service produced and brought to market has a price. That price serves as a measure of value for calculating total output.*** Consider again the problem of determining how much output was produced this year and last. There's no obvious way to answer this question in physical terms alone. But once we know the price of each good, we can calculate the *value* of output produced. The total dollar value of final output produced each year is called the **gross domestic product (GDP).** GDP is simply the sum of all final goods and services produced for the market in a given time period, with each good or service valued at its market price.

> **gross domestic product (GDP):** The total market value of all final goods and services produced within a nation's borders in a given time period.

Table 4.1 illustrates the use of prices to value total output in two hypothetical years. If apples were 20 cents each last year and 2 billion apples were produced, then the *value* of apple production last year was $400 million ($0.20 × 2 billion). In the same manner, we can determine that the value of bicycle production was $100 million and the value of rock concerts was $700 million. By adding these figures, we can say that the value of last year's production—last year's GDP—was $1,200 million (Table 4.1a).

Output	Amount
a. Last Year's Output	
In physical terms:	
Apples	2 billion
Bicycles	2 million
Rock concerts	700
Total	?
In monetary terms:	
2 billion apples @ $0.20 each	$ 400 million
2 million bicycles @ $50 each	100 million
700 rock concerts @ $1 million each	700 million
Total	$1,200 million
b. This Year's Output	
In physical terms:	
Apples	3 billion
Bicycles	4 million
Rock concerts	600
Total	?
In monetary terms:	
3 billion apples @ $0.20 each	$ 600 million
4 million bicycles @ $50 each	200 million
600 rock concerts @ $1 million each	600 million
Total	$1,400 million

TABLE 4.1

The Measurement of Output

It's impossible to add up all output when output is counted in *physical* terms. Accordingly, total output is measured in *monetary* terms, with each good or service valued at its market price. GDP refers to the total market value of all goods and services produced in a given time period. According to the numbers in this table, the total *value* of the apples, bicycles, and rock concerts produced "last" year was $1.2 million and $1.4 million "this" year.

Now we're in a position to compare one year's output to another's. Table 4.1*b* shows that the use of prices enables us to say that the *value* of this year's output is $1,400 million. Hence, *total output* has increased from one year to the next. ***The use of prices to value market output allows us to summarize output activity and to compare the output of one period with that of another.***

GDP vs. GNP. The concept of GDP is of relatively recent use in national-income accounts. Prior to 1986, statistics focused on gross *national* product or G*N*P. Gross *national* product refers to the output produced by Canadian-owned factors of production regardless of where they're located. In other words, GNP focuses on the income generated by production and which nation receives those payments. GNP therefore, is not geographically focused. ***GNP is the value of the income generated by a nation's factors regardless of where, geographically, the production occurs.*** Gross *domestic* product refers to output produced within Canada's borders. Thus, GNP would include some output from an Apple computer factory in Singapore but exclude some of the income produced by a Honda factory in Ontario. In an increasingly global economy, where factors of production and ownership move easily across international borders, the calculations of GNP became ever more complex. It also became a less dependable measure of the nation's economic health. ***GDP is geographically focused, including all output produced within a nation's borders regardless of whose factors of production are used to produce it.*** Apple's output in Singapore ends up in Singapore's GDP; the cars produced at Honda's Ontario plant are counted in Canada's GDP. GDP is considered a more dependable measure of a nation's macroeconomic health because it measures the extent to which domestic factors of production are being utilized. That is, it measures where in relation to the production possibility curve the economy might be—what proportion of factors, particularly labour, are not employed.

Not every reported market transaction gets included at full value in GDP statistics. If it did, the same output would get counted over and over. The problem here is that the production of goods and services typically involves a series of distinct stages. Consider the production of a bagel, for example. For a bagel to reach Einstein's or some other bagel store, the farmer must grow some wheat, the miller must convert it to flour, and the baker must make bagels with it. Figure 4.2 illustrates this chain of production.

Notice that each of the four stages of production depicted in Figure 4.2 involves a separate market transaction. The farmer sells to the miller (stage 1), the miller to the baker (stage 2), the baker to the bagel store (stage 3), and finally, the store to the consumer. If we added up the separate value of each market transaction, we'd come to the conclusion that $1.75 of output had been produced. In fact, though, only one bagel has been produced, and it's worth only 75 cents. Hence, we should increase GDP—the value of output—only by 75 cents.

Value Added

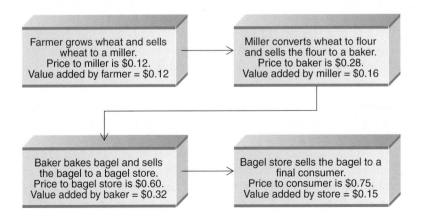

FIGURE 4.2
Value Added in Various Stages of Production

The diagram illustrates the process of turning wheat into bagels and the value added along the way. The value added at each stage of production represents a contribution of total output. Value added equals the price received at each stage less the price paid to acquire the intermediate product. An important connection here is that the sum of the value added at each stage ($0.12 + $0.16 + $0.32 + $0.15) is exactly equal to the final selling price of the bagel ($0.75).

intermediate goods: Goods or services purchased for use as input in the production of final goods or in services.

To get an accurate measure of GDP we must distinguish between *intermediate* goods and *final* goods. **Intermediate goods** are goods purchased for use as input in further stages of production. Final goods are the goods produced at the end of the production sequence, for use by consumers (or other market participants).

We can compute the value of *final* output in one of two ways. The easiest way would be to count only market transactions entailing final sales (stage 4 in Figure 4.2). To do this, however, we'd have to know who purchased each good or service to know when we had reached the end of the process. Such a calculation would also exclude any output produced in stages 1, 2, and 3 in Figure 4.2 but not yet reflected in stage 4.

value added: The increase in the market value of a product that takes place at each stage of the production process.

Another way to calculate GDP is to count only the **value added** at each stage of production. Consider the miller, for example. He doesn't really contribute $0.28 worth of production to total output, but only $0.16. The other $0.12 reflected in the price of his flour represents the contribution of the farmer who grew the wheat. By the same token, the baker *adds* only $0.32 to the value of output, as part of his output was purchased from the miller. By considering only the value *added* at each stage of production, we eliminate double counting. We don't count twice the *intermediate* goods and services that producers buy from other producers, which are then used as inputs. As Figure 4.2 confirms, we can determine that value of final output by summing up the value added at each stage of production. (Note that $0.75 is also the price of a bagel.)

Measurement Problems

Nonmarket Activities. Although the methods for calculating GDP are straightforward, they do create a few problems. For one thing, GDP measures exclude most goods and services that are *produced* but not *sold* in the market. This may appear to be a trivial point, but it isn't. Vast quantities of output never reach the market. For example, the homemaker who cleans, washes, gardens, shops, and cooks definitely contributes to the output of goods and services. Because a market wage is not paid for these services, however, the efforts are excluded from the calculation of GDP. At the same time, we do count the efforts of those workers who sell identical homemaking services in the marketplace. This seeming contradiction is explained by the fact that a homemaker's services aren't sold in the market and therefore carry no explicit, market-determined value.

The exclusion of homemakers' services from the GDP accounts is particularly troublesome when we want to compare living standards over time or between countries. In Canada, most women now work outside the home. As a result households make greater use of *paid* domestic help (e.g., child care, house cleaning). Accordingly, a lot of housework and child care that were previously excluded from GDP statistics (because they were unpaid family help) are now included (because they're done by paid help). In this respect, our historical GDP figures may exaggerate improvements in our standard of living.

Homemaking services aren't the only output excluded. If a friend helps you with your homework, the services never get into the GDP accounts. But if you hire a tutor or engage the services of a term paper-writing agency, the transaction becomes part of GDP. Here again, the problem is simply that we have no way to determine how much output was produced until it enters the market and is purchased.

Unreported Income. The GDP statistics also fail to capture market activities that aren't reported to tax or census authorities. Many people work "off the books," getting paid in unreported cash. This so-called underground economy is motivated by tax avoidance and the need to conceal illegal activities. Although illegal activities capture most of the headlines, tax evasion on income earned in otherwise legal pursuits accounts for most of the underground economy. David Giles and Lindsay Tedds have estimated this "tax gap," suggesting that the loss of tax dollars increased in current dollars

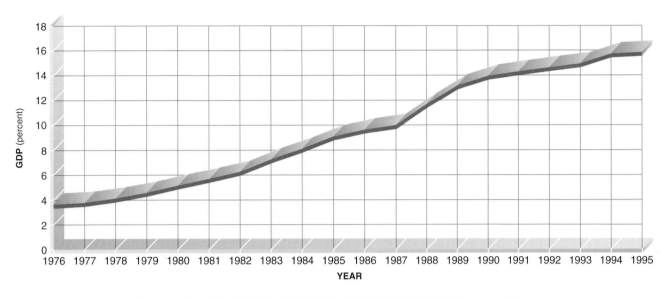

A Classification of Underground Economic Activities		
	Market Activities	**Nonmarket Activities**
Underground activities based on legal activities	Failure to report income from wages, self-employment, benefits, profits, capital gains and dividends; evasion of border taxes via "e-commerce;" unreported sales; excessive employee benefits and discounts.	Barter of legal goods and services.
Illegal activities	Sale of stolen goods, drugs, smuggled gems, tobacco, alcohol, and exotic animals and plants; "fees" for human smuggling; the manufacture of drugs; prostitution; gambling; fraud related to business activities, benefits, and insurance; "zapping;" "curbsiding" software and audio-visual piracy; theft of cash.	Barter of stolen goods, drugs or smuggled tobacco or alcohol; theft of goods for own use; extortion; software and audio-visual piracy for own use or barter.

FIGURE 4.3
The Underground Economy

Source: Adapted from David E. A. Giles and Lindsay M. Tedds, *Taxes and the Canadian Underground Economy* (2002). Canadian Tax Foundation, Canadian Tax Paper No. 106. Toronto, Ontario. Pg. 5 original table 1-1.

from "approximately $2 billion in 1976 to almost $44 billion in 1995."[2] Figure 4.3 shows the increase over the period 1976–1995.

Beneath Figure 4.3 is a classification of activities that are defined as making up the underground economy. The list of underground activities based on legal activities runs the range of products paid in cash yet not reported for tax purposes—from child care to car repairs and the barter of legal goods and services.

[2]David E. A. Giles and Lindsay M. Tedds, *Taxes and the Canadian Underground Economy,* Canadian Tax Paper No. 106, (Toronto: Canadian Tax Foundation, 2002), p. 236.

4.2 THE USES OF OUTPUT—GDP FROM THE EXPENDITURE APPROACH

The role of investment in maintaining or expanding our production possibilities helps focus attention on the uses to which GDP is put. It's not just the total value of annual output that matters, its also the use that we make of that output. ***The GDP accounts also tell us what mix of output we've selected, that is, society's answer to the core issue of WHAT to produce.***

Consumption

The major uses of total output conform to the four sets of market participants we encountered in the circular flow, namely, consumers, business firms, government, and foreigners. Those goods and services used by households are called *consumption goods* and range all the way from doughnuts to online computer services. Included in this category are all goods and services households purchase in product markets. As you can see from Table 4.2, household expenditures account for more than half of our annual output.

Investment

Investment goods represent another use of GDP. Investment goods are the plant, machinery, and equipment we produce. Net changes in business inventories and expenditures for residential construction are also counted as investment. To produce any of these investment goods, we must use scarce resources that could be used to produce something else. Investment spending claims about one-fifth of our total output.

Government Spending

The third major use of GDP is the *public sector*. Federal, provincial, and local governments purchase resources to police the streets, teach classes, write laws, and build highways. The resources purchased by the government sector are unavailable for either consumption or investment purposes. At present, government spending on goods and services (*not* income transfers) claims roughly one-fifth of total output.

Net Exports

exports: Goods and services sold to international buyers.

Finally, remember that some of the goods and services we produce each year are used abroad rather than at home. That is, we **export** some of our output to other countries, for whatever use they care to make of it. Thus, GDP—the value of output produced—will be larger than the sum of our own consumption, investment, and government purchases to the extent that we succeed in exporting goods and services.

imports: Goods and services purchased from foreign sellers.

We **import** goods and services as well. A flight to London on British Air is an imported service; a Jaguar is an imported good. These goods and services aren't part of Canada's GDP since they weren't produced within our borders. In principle, these

TABLE 4.2
GDP at Market Prices for Each Circular Flow Sector

The table indicates the value of GDP arising from each of the four market participants identified in the circular flow diagram, as determined by Statistics Canada for 2005. (See Table 4.3 for an explanation of the statistical discrepancy.)

	2005
Gross domestic product at market prices (in millions of dollars)	**1,371,425**
Household expenditure, C	760,380
Government expenditure, G	298,506
Business Investment, I	260,969
Exports, X	519,680
Deduct: Imports, M	−467,673
Statistical discrepancy	−437

Source: "Value of GDP," adapted from Statistics Canada publication *National Income and Expenditure Accounts, Quarterly Estimates,* Catalogue 13-001 and Statistics Canada CANSIM table 380-0017 and Statistics Canada website http://www40.statcan.ca/l01/cst01/econ04.htm. Last modified: 2006-05-31. Statistics Canada information is used with the permission of Statistics Canada.

imports never enter the GDP accounts. In practice, however, it's difficult to distinguish imports from domestic-made products, especially when goods include value added from both foreign and domestic producers. Even "Canadian-made" cars typically incorporate parts manufactured in Japan, Mexico, Thailand, Britain, Spain, or Germany, with final assembly here in Canada. Should that car be counted as a "Canadian" product or as an import? Rather than try to sort out all these products and parts, Statistics Canada simply subtracts the value of all imports from the value of total spending. Thus, exports are *added* to GDP and *imports* are subtracted. The difference between the two expenditure flows is called **net exports.**

net exports: The value of exports minus the value of imports.

Once we recognize the components of output, we discover a simple method for computing GDP. ***The value of GDP can be computed by adding up the expenditures of market participants.*** Specifically, we note that

GDP Components

$$GDP = C + I + G + (X - M)$$

where C = consumption expenditure
I = investment expenditure
G = government expenditure
X = exports
M = imports

This approach to GDP accounting emphasizes the fact that all the output produced in the economy must be claimed by someone. If we know who's buying our output, we know how much was produced and what uses were made of it. Table 4.2 details the expenditures from each of these sectors for 2005.

4.3 MEASURES OF INCOME—GDP FROM THE INCOME APPROACH

There's another way of looking at GDP. Instead of looking at who's *buying* our output, we can look at who's *being paid* to produce it. Like markets themselves. ***GDP accounts have two sides: One side focuses on expenditure (the demand side), the other side focuses on income (the supply side).***

We've already observed (see Figure 4.1) that every market transaction involves an *exchange* of dollars for a good or resource. Moreover, the *value* of each good or resource is measured by the amount of money exchanged for it (its market price). Hence, ***the total value of market incomes must equal the total value of final output, or GDP.*** In other words, one person's expenditure always represents another person's income.

Figure 4.4 illustrates the link between spending on output and incomes. This is a modified version of the circular flow we saw earlier. The spending that flows into the product market gets funnelled into the factor market when resources are employed to produce the goods people want. The expenditure then flows into the hands of business owners, workers, landlords, and other resource owners. With the exception of sales taxes and depreciation, all spending on output becomes income to factors of production.

The equivalence of output and income isn't dependent on any magical qualities possessed by money. Were we to produce only one product—say, wheat—and pay everyone in bushels and pecks, total income would still equal total output. People couldn't receive in income more wheat than we produced. On the other hand, all the wheat produced would go to *someone*. Hence, one could say that the production possibilities of the economy define the limits to real income. The amount of income actually generated in any year depends on the production and expenditure decisions of consumers, firms, governments, and foreigners.

FIGURE 4.4
Output = Income

All the spending that establishes the value of output also determines the value of incomes. With minor exceptions, the market value of incomes must equal the market value of output.

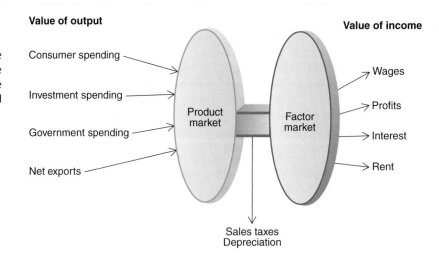

Table 4.3 shows the actual flow of output and income in the Canadian economy during 2005. Total output is made up of the familiar components of GDP: consumption, investment, government goods and services, and net exports. The figures on the left side of Table 4.3 indicate that consumers spent $760.4 billion, businesses spent $261.0 billion on plant and equipment, governments spent $298.5 billion, and net exports were $52.0 billion. Our total output value (GDP) was thus nearly $1.4 trillion in 2005.

The right-hand side of Table 4.3 indicates who received the income generated from these markets transactions. Every dollar spent on goods and services provides income to someone. It may go to a worker (as wage or salary) or to a business firm (as profit and depreciation allowance). It may go to a landlord (as rent), to a lender (as interest), or to government (as sales or property tax). None of the dollars spent on goods and services disappears into thin air.

National Income

Although it may be exciting to know that we collectively received nearly $1.4 trillion of income in 2005, it might be of more interest to know who actually got all

TABLE 4.3
The Equivalence of Expenditure and Income (in millions of dollars)

The value of total expenditure must equal the value of total income. Why? Because every dollar spent on output becomes a dollar of income for someone. (After the calculation of GDP from both the income and expenditure approaches is complete, any difference is divided in two to find the "statistical difference." This difference is then added to the lesser value and subtracted from the higher value so that the value of GDP is equal from both approaches.)

	2005		
Expenditure Approach		**Income Approach**	
Household expenditure	$760,380	Wages and salaries	$688,150
Government expenditure	$298,506	Corporate profits	$189,455
Business investment	$260,969	Government profits	$14,481
Exports	$519,680	Interest and misc. income	$60,403
Imports	−$467,673	Farm operations	$1,706
		Unincorp business	$84,500
		Inventory adjustment	−$326
		Taxes less subsidies/factors	$61,402
		Net domestic product	**$1,099,771**
		Taxes less subsidies/product	$93,895
		Capital cost allowance	$177,322
Statistical discrepancy	−$437	Statistical discrepancy	$437
Total value of expenditure	**$1,371,425**	**Total Value of Income**	**$1,371,425**

Source: Statistics Canada CANSIM table 380-0017 Catalogue 13-001-XIP and CANSIM table 380-0001 Catalogue 13-001-XIB. Statistics Canada information is used with the permission of Statistics Canada.

that income. After all, in addition to the 32.5 million pairs of outstretched palms among us, millions of businesses and government departments were also competing for those dollars and the goods and services they represent. By charting the flow of income through the economy, we can see FOR WHOM our output was produced.

Capital Cost Allowance (CCA). The annual income flow originates in product-market sales. Purchases of final goods and services create a flow of income to producers and, through them, to factors of production. But a major diversion of sales revenues occurs immediately, as a result of depreciation charges made by businesses. As we noted earlier, some of our capital resources are used up in the process of production. For the most part, these resources are owned by business firms that expect to be compensated for such investments. Accordingly, they regard some of the sales revenue generated in product markets as reimbursement for wear and tear on capital plant and equipment. They therefore subtract *depreciation charges* from gross revenues in calculating their incomes. Depreciation charges reduce GDP to the level of **net domestic product (NDP)** before any income is available to current factors of production.

$$NDP = GDP - CCA - \text{taxes less subsidies on products}$$

> **net domestic product (NDP):** The total income earned by factors of production within Canada: GDP less Capital Consumption Allowance, CCA and taxes less subsidies on products and any statistical discrepancy.

Taxes Less Subsidies on Factors of Production. This represents the difference between the taxes levied on factors of production—such as labour—and any subsidies paid to firms for wages or labour. The point here is that these are dollars flowing to government rather than to us consumers.

Net Domestic Income (NDI). This represents the income earned by factors of production within Canada for any given year.

$$NDI = NDP - \text{taxes less subsidies on factors plus any inventory adjustment}$$

As Table 4.3 indicates, in 2005, the net domestic income earned by Canadian factors of production was $1,038,695 billion.

We're not quite through counting the gaps between the total sales revenue that gets registered in product markets and the amount of income actually received by households.

Corporate Taxes and Retained Earnings. Theoretically, all the income corporations receive represents income for their owners—the households who hold stock in the corporations. But the flow of income through corporations to stockholders is far from complete. First, corporations may pay taxes on their profits. Accordingly, some of the income received on behalf of a corporation's stockholders goes into the public treasury rather than into private bank accounts. Second, corporate managers typically find some urgent need for cash. As a result, part of the profit is retained by the corporation rather than passed on to the stockholders in the form of dividends. Accordingly, both *corporate taxes* and *retained earnings* must be subtracted from national income before we can determine how much income flows into the hands of consumers.

Still another deduction must be made for our contributions to social insurance programs such as Employment Insurance, the Canada or Quebec Pension Plans, and Worker's Compensation. Workers never see this income because it is withheld by employers and sent directly to the federal government. Thus, the flow of national income is reduced considerably before it becomes **personal income (PI),** the amount of income received by households before payment of personal taxes.

Not all of our adjustments to national income are negative. Households receive income in the form of transfer payments from government. These transfers include Canada or Quebec pension payments, welfare, and any other payments arising

Personal Income

> **personal income (PI):** Income received by households before payment of personal taxes.

from governments for particular programs (such as for child care). These income transfers represent income for the people who receive them. Accordingly, our calculation of personal income is as follows:

- **National domestic income** (= income earned by factors of production)
  less   corporate taxes
           retained earnings
           Social Insurance plans
  plus   transfer payments
- **Equals personal income** (= income received by households)

The total flow of income generated in production is significantly reduced before it gets into the hands of individual households. But we haven't yet reached the end of the reduction process. We have to set something aside for personal income taxes. Personal income taxes are withheld by the employer, who thus acts as a tax collector. Accordingly, to calculate **disposable income (DI),** which is the amount of income consumers may themselves spend (dispose of), we reduce personal income by the amount of personal taxes:

$$\text{Disposable income} = \text{personal income} - \text{personal taxes}$$

Disposable income is the end of the accounting line. Once consumers get this disposable income in their hands, they face two choices. They may choose to *spend* their disposable income on consumer goods and services. Or they may choose to *save* it. These are the only two choices in GDP accounting. **Saving,** in this context, simply refers to disposable income that isn't spent on consumption. In the analysis of income and saving flows, we don't care whether savings are hidden under a mattress, deposited in the bank, or otherwise secured. All we want to know is whether disposable income is spent. Thus, *all disposable income is, by definition, either consumed or saved; that is,*

$$\text{Disposable income} = \text{consumption} + \text{saving}$$

4.4 THE FLOW OF INCOME

Figure 4.5 summarizes the relationship between expenditure and income. The essential point again is that every dollar spent on goods and services flows into somebody's hands. Thus, *the dollar value of output will always equal the dollar value of income.* Specifically, total income (GDP) ends up distributed in the following way:

- To *households,* in the form of disposable income. Remember our discussion of GNP? We said that the difference between GDP and GNP was the difference between the value of domestic production and the value of the income that remained in Canada. So, not all of this disposable income flows to Canadian households, some will flow to foreign households because they have claims on Canadian produced income through the ownership of Canadian factors of production.
- To *business,* in the form of retained earnings and depreciation allowances.
- To *government,* in the form of taxes.

Income and Expenditure

The annual flow of income to households, businesses, and government is part of a continuing process. Households rarely stash their disposable income under the mattress; they spend most of it on consumption. This spending adds to GDP in the next round of activity, thereby helping to keep the flow of income moving.

Business firms also have a lot of purchasing power tied up in retained earnings and depreciation charges. This income, too, may be recycled—returned to the circular flow—in the form of business investment.

Even the income that flows into public treasuries finds its way back into the marketplace, as governments hire police officers, soldiers, and clerks, or they buy goods

---

disposable income (DI): After-tax income of households; personal income less personal taxes.

saving: That part of disposable income not spent on current consumption; disposable income less consumption.

WEB NOTE

For the latest data on GDP and its components, visit the Statistics Canada Web page at http://www.statcan.ca/start.html.

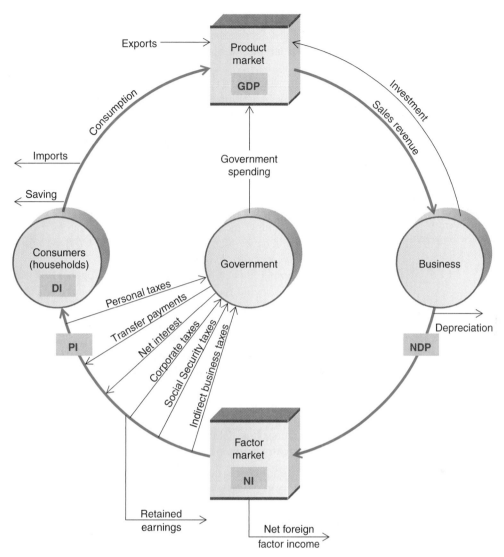

FIGURE 4.5
The Circular Flow of Spending and Income

GDP represents the dollar value of final output sold in the product market. The revenue stream flowing from GDP works its way through NDP, NI, and PI before reaching households in the form of smaller DI. DI is in turn either spent or saved by consumers. This consumption, plus investment, government spending, and net exports, continues the circular flow.

and services. Thus, *the flow of income that starts with GDP ultimately returns to the market in the form of new consumption (C), investment (I), and government purchases (G).* A new GDP arises, and the flow starts all over. In later chapters we examine in detail these *expenditure* flows, with particular emphasis on their ability to keep the economy producing at its full potential.

4.5 REAL VS. NOMINAL GDP

Although prices are a convenient measure of market value, they can also distort perceptions of real output. Imagine what would happen to our calculations of GDP if all prices were to double from one year to the next. Suppose, for example, that the price of oranges, as shown in Table 4.1, rose from $0.20 to $0.40, the price of bicycles to $100, and the price of rock concerts to $2 million each. How would such price changes alter measured GDP? Obviously, the price increases would double the *value* of final output. Measured GDP would rise from $1,400 million to $2,800 million.

Such a rise in GDP doesn't reflect an increase in the *quantity* of goods and services available to us. We're still producing the same quantities shown in Table 4.1; only the prices of those goods have changed. Hence, **changes in GDP brought about by changes in the price level can give us a distorted view of economic activity.** Surely we wouldn't want to assert that our standard of living had improved just because price increases raised measured GDP from $1,400 million to $2,800 million.

To distinguish increases in the quantity of goods and services from increases in their prices, we must construct a measure of GDP that takes into account price-level changes. We do so by distinguishing between *real* GDP and *nominal* GDP. **Nominal GDP** is the value of final output measured in *current* prices, whereas *real GDP* is the value of output measured in *constant* prices. ***To calculate real GDP, we adjust the market value of goods and services for changing prices.***

> **nominal GDP:** The value of final output produced in a given period, measured in the prices of that period (current prices).

Note, for example, that in Table 4.1 prices were unchanged from one year to the next. When prices in the marketplace are constant, interyear comparisons of output are simple. But if all prices double, the comparison becomes more complicated. If all prices doubled from last year to this year, this year's nominal GDP would rise to $2,800 million. But these price increases wouldn't alter the quantity of goods produced. In other words, *real* GDP, valued at constant prices, would remain at $1,400 million. Thus, **the distinction between nominal and real GDP is important whenever the price level changes.**

Because the price level does change every year, both real and nominal GDP are regularly reported. Nominal GDP is computed simply by adding up the current dollar value of production. Real GDP is computed by making an adjustment for changes in prices from year to year as illustrated in Table 4.4.

Chain-Weighted Price Adjustments

Although the distinction between real and nominal GDP is critical in measuring the nation's economic health, the procedure for making inflation adjustments isn't perfect. If we use the prices of some specific year—the method prior to 2001—as the base for computing real GDP, we're implicitly freezing *relative* prices as well as *average* prices. Over time, however, relative prices change markedly. Computer prices for example, have fallen sharply in recent years in both absolute and relative terms. During the same period, unit sales of computers have increased by 20–25 percent each year. If we used the higher computer prices of, say, five years ago to compute that sales growth, we would greatly exaggerate the *value* of today's computer output. If we used today's prices in conjunction with previous years' output we would underestimate the value of computer output produced in the past. To resolve this problem,

TABLE 4.4
Real and Nominal GDP

This table shows both the nominal GDP given earlier as well as the real GDP determined by Statistics Canada for 2005. The difference between these two measures is $213,720 million. That implies that of the $1,371,425 million of nominal GDP in 2005, more than $200 billion was accounted for by price changes since the base year (2002)—no additional production, just higher prices for the same goods and services.

	2005 Real GDP (chained 2002 dollars)	2005 Nominal GDP
Total GDP (millions of dollars)	**1,157,705**	**1,371,425**
Household expenditure, C	663,583	760,380
Government expenditure, G	250,032	298,506
Business investment, I	244,756	260,969
Exports, X	472,037	519,680
Deduct: Imports, M	−474,040	−467,673
Statistical discrepancy	−366	−437

Source: "The Determination of Real GDP" adapted from Statistics Canada CANSIM tables 380-0002 and 380-0017, http://cansim2.statcan.ca, and Statistics Canada publication Catalogue 13-001; Statistics Canada information is used with the permission of Statistics Canada.

Statistics Canada uses a *chain-weighted Fisher* price index to compute real GDP. Instead of using the prices of a single **base year** to compute real GDP, ***chain-weighted indexes use a moving-average of price levels in consecutive years as an inflation adjustment.***[3] When chain-weighted price adjustments are made, real GDP still refers to the inflation-adjusted value of GDP but isn't expressed in terms of the prices prevailing in any specific base year. Since 2001, all official estimates of real national GDP have been based on a chain-weighted Fisher price index. This methodology was also adopted for Provincial economic accounts in October 2002.

We can also use these two calculations to determine an economy-wide measure of **inflation**—this is called the GDP deflator. Although a funny sounding term, it is actually pretty descriptive of exactly what it measures, that is, the percentage that our current nominal GDP must be deflated to arrive at our real GDP.

$$\text{GDP Deflator} = \frac{\text{Nominal GDP}}{\text{Real GDP}} \times 100$$

To demonstrate this for the year 2005 values in Table 4.4:

$$\text{GDP Deflator} = \frac{\$1,371,425}{\$1,157,705} \times 100 = 118.46$$

Since this price index is based on 100, the GDP deflator tells us that our current GDP must be "deflated" by 18.46 percentage points to be equal to our real GDP. To say the same thing in a slightly different fashion, the GDP deflator tells us that since the base period (1997), the price level in Canada has risen by 18.46 percent, or approximately 2 percent each year on average.

GDP per Capita. International comparisons of total output are even more vivid in *per capita terms*. **GDP per capita** relates the total value of annual output to the number of people who share that output; it refers to the average GDP per person. In 2005, Canada's total GDP of $1,371 billion was shared by 32.5 million citizens. Hence, our average, or *per capita,* GDP was nearly $42,197. By contrast, the average GDP for the entire world's inhabitants was only $8,000. In these terms, Canada's position as a rich country in the world clearly stands out.

Statistical comparisons of GDP across nations are abstract and lifeless. They do, however, convey very real differences in the way people live. The accompanying World View boxes examine some everyday realities of living in a poor nation, compared with a rich nation. Disparities in per capita GDP mean that people in low-income countries have little access to telephones, televisions, paved roads, or schools. They also die a lot younger than do people in rich countries.

But even the World Views fail to fully convey how tough life is for people at the *bottom* of the income distribution in both poor and rich nations. Per capita GDP isn't a measure of what every citizen is getting. In Canada, many individuals have access to far more goods and services than our average per capita GDP, while thousands of others must get by with much less. Although per capita GDP in Kuwait is three times larger than that of Brazil's, we can't conclude that the typical citizen of Kuwait is three times as well off as the typical Brazilian. The only thing these figures tell us is that the average Kuwaiti *could have* almost three times as many goods and services each year as the average Brazilian *if* GDP were distributed in the same way in both countries. ***Measures of per capita GDP tell us nothing about the way GDP is actually distributed or used: they're only a statistical average.*** When countries are quite similar in structure, institutions, and income distribution, however—or when historical comparisons are made within a country—per capita GDP can be viewed as a rough-and-ready measure of relative standards of living.

base period: The time period used for comparative analysis; the basis for indexing, for example, of price changes.

inflation: An increase in the average level of prices of goods and services.

GDP per capita: Total GDP divided by total population; average GDP per person.

WEB NOTE

Global data on per capita incomes and other social indicators are available from the United Nations at http://unstats.un.org/unsd/snaama/dnllist.asp.

---

[3]For additional information on the chain-weighted Fisher index, see Statistics Canada Catalogue 13-605-XIE at http://www.statcan.ca/english/freepub/13-605-XIE/2003001/conceptual/fisher/methodology/.

WORLD VIEW

Global Inequalities

The 2.5 billion residents of the world's low-income nations have comparatively few goods and services. Their average income (per capita GDP) is only $2,100 a year, a *fourteenth* of the average income in high-income nations such as the United States, Japan, and Germany. It's not just a colossal *income* disparity; it's also a disparity in the quality and even the duration of life. Some examples:

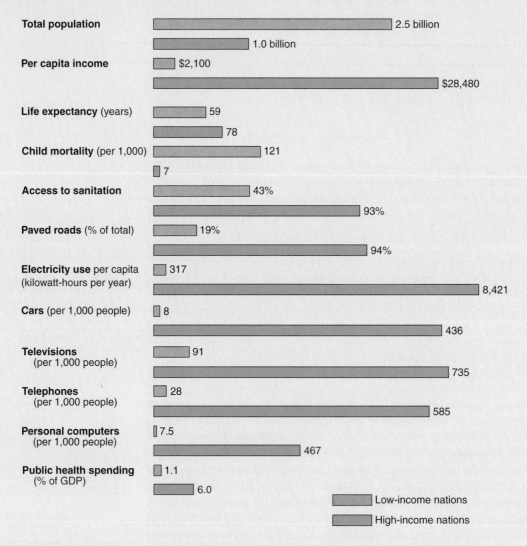

	Low-income nations	High-income nations
Total population		2.5 billion / 1.0 billion
Per capita income	$2,100	$28,480
Life expectancy (years)	59	78
Child mortality (per 1,000)	121	7
Access to sanitation	43%	93%
Paved roads (% of total)	19%	94%
Electricity use per capita (kilowatt-hours per year)	317	8,421
Cars (per 1,000 people)	8	436
Televisions (per 1,000 people)	91	735
Telephones (per 1,000 people)	28	585
Personal computers (per 1,000 people)	7.5	467
Public health spending (% of GDP)	1.1	6.0

Low-income nations

High-income nations

Analysis: Hidden behind dry statistical comparisons of per capita GDP lie very tangible and dramatic differences in the way people live. Low GDP per capita reflects a lot of deprivation.

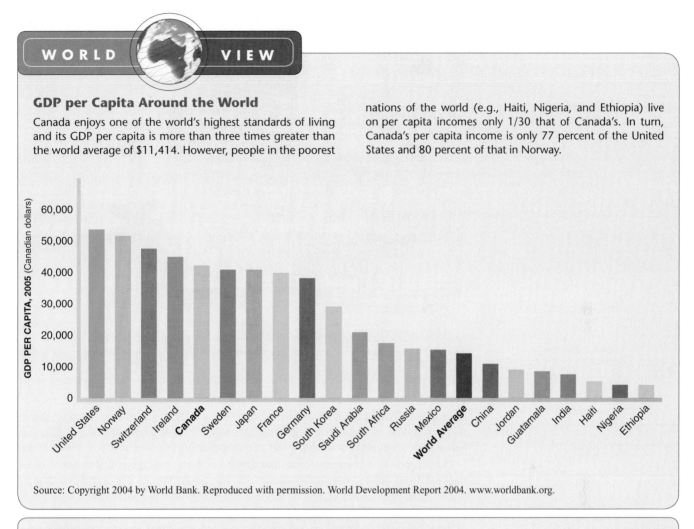

WORLD VIEW

GDP per Capita Around the World

Canada enjoys one of the world's highest standards of living and its GDP per capita is more than three times greater than the world average of $11,414. However, people in the poorest nations of the world (e.g., Haiti, Nigeria, and Ethiopia) live on per capita incomes only 1/30 that of Canada's. In turn, Canada's per capita income is only 77 percent of the United States and 80 percent of that in Norway.

Source: Copyright 2004 by World Bank. Reproduced with permission. World Development Report 2004. www.worldbank.org.

Analysis: Per capita GDP is a measure of output that reflects average living standards. Canada's high GDP per capita implies access to far more goods and services than people in many other nations have.

4.6 ALTERNATE MEASURES OF WELL-BEING

The Quality of Life

Money, money, money—it seems that's all we talk about. Why don't we talk about important things like beauty, virtue, or the quality of life? Will the economy of tomorrow be filled with a glut of products but devoid of real meaning? Do the GDP accounts—either the expenditure side or the income side—tell us anything we really want to know about the quality of life? If not, why should we bother to examine them?

Intangibles. All the economic measures discussed in this chapter are important indexes of individual and collective welfare; they tell us something about how well people are living. They don't, however, capture the completeness of the way in which we view the world or the totality of what makes our lives satisfying. A clear day, a sense of accomplishment, even a smile can do more for a person's sense of well-being than can favourable movements in the GDP accounts. Or, as John Kenneth

Analysis: GDP includes *everything* produced and sold in the product market, no matter how much each good or service contributes to our social well-being.

Galbraith put it, "In a rational lifestyle, some people could find contentment working moderately and then sitting by the street—and talking, thinking, drawing, painting, scribbling, or making love in a suitably discreet way. None of these requires an expanding economy."[4]

The emphasis on economic outcomes arises not from ignorance of life's other meanings but from the visibility of the economic outcomes. We all realize that well-being arises from both material and intangible pleasures, but the intangibles tend to be elusive. It's not easy to gauge individual happiness, much less to ascertain the status of our collective satisfaction. We have to rely on measures we can see, touch, and count. As long as the material components of our environment bear some positive relation to our well-being, they at least serve a useful purpose.

In some situations, however, more physical output may actually worsen our collective welfare. If increased automobile production raises congestion and pollution levels, the rise in GDP occasioned by those additional cars is a misleading index of society's welfare. In such a case, the rise in GDP might actually mask a *decrease* in the well-being of the population. We might also wonder whether more casinos, more prisons, more telemarketing, more divorce litigation, and more Prozac—all of which contribute to GDP growth—are really valid measures of our well-being (see cartoon). Exclusive emphasis on measurable output would clearly be a mistake in many cases.

What is true of automobile production might also be true of other outputs. Increased development of urban areas may cause a loss of social welfare if that development occurs at the expense of space, trees, and tranquillity. Increased mechanization on the farm may raise agricultural output but isolate and uproot farmers. So, too, increased productivity in factories and offices might contribute to a sense of alienation. These ill effects of increased output needn't occur; but if they do, indexes of output tell us less about social or individual well-being.

[4]Cited in Leonard Silk, *Nixonomics,* 2nd ed. (New York: Praeger, 1973), p. 163.

TABLE 4.5
Human Development Index
Rankings, 2002–2006,
Top 10 Countries

| Top 10 Countries | | | | |
2002	2003	2004	2005	2006
1 Norway	Norway	Norway	Norway	Norway
2 Sweden	Iceland	Sweden	Iceland	Iceland
3 **Canada**	Sweden	Australia	Australia	Australia
4 Belgium	Australia	**Canada**	Luxemburg	Ireland
5 Australia	Netherlands	Netherlands	**Canada**	Sweden
6 United States	Belgium	Belgium	Sweden	**Canada**
7 Iceland	United States	Iceland	Switzerland	Japan
8 Netherlands	**Canada**	United States	Ireland	United States
9 Japan	Japan	Japan	Belgium	Switzerland
10 Finland	Switzerland	Ireland	United States	Netherlands

Source: Based on Human Development Index Rankings, 2002–2005, Top 10 Countries. United Nations' Development Programme.

Analysis: The Human Development Index, published by the United Nations Development Program (UNDP), indicates a country's ranking for human development using both economic and social indicators. Canada has consistently ranked at or near the top of the index, ranging from 3rd to 8th in the five years from 2002 to 2006.

Index of Economic Well-Being. The *Index of Economic Well-Being* began as research for the MacDonald Commission done by Professor Lars Osberg of Dalhousie University in the mid-1980s. Osberg suggests that the motivation was the belief "that commonly used indicators of economic welfare, such as GDP per capita, were not truly capturing trends in economic well-being."[5] The Index of Economic Well-Being weights economic measures such as per-capita GDP with measures of social well-being, wealth stocks, income distribution, and economic security.

The *Canadian Index of Well-Being (CIW)* is currently under construction as a national successor to the Genuine Progress Index Atlantic (http://www.gpiatlantic.org/). Like the Index of Economic Well-Being, the Canadian index of well-being goes beyond the common economic statistics to include measures from seven domains: living standards, time allocation, healthy populations, ecosystem health, educated populace, community vitality, and civic engagement.

The *Human Development Report* is published by the United Nations Development Program (UNDP) annually.[6] The *Human Development Index,* which is part of the *Human Development Report,* uses economic and social measures to rank individual countries. The result is a listing of countries as either high human development, medium human development, or low human development. For example, as seen in Table 4.5, in 2005 Canada is ranked 5th of all countries whereas Norway is ranked 1st and the United States 10th. Medium-ranked countries range from Brazil at 63rd to Zimbabwe at 145th. Low ranked countries range from Madagascar at 146th to Niger at 177th.

While all these various measures can be useful, and can add information to what we might think we know, there is a caution. All indexes are a reflection of the choices made by the creators of the particular index—the particular variables chosen and the weights accorded to each variable. Change the variable or the weights or both, and the index can be turned on its head.

WEB NOTE

The United Nations has constructed a Human Development Index that offers a broader view of social well-being than GDP alone. For details and country rankings, visit www.undp.org. Also check the Genuine Progress Indicator at www.rprogress.org.

[5]Lars Osberg and Andrew Sharpe, "The index of economic well-being," *Indicators: The Journal of Social Health,* vol. 1, no. 2, (Spring 2002).
[6]United Nations Development Program, UNDP, "International cooperation at a crossroads: Aid, trade and security in an unequal world," *The Human Development Report.* (2005).

APPLICATIONS

Canada Ranks 10th on "Happy Map"

A Global Projection of Subjective Well-Being: The First Published Map of World Happiness

Happy - - - - - Average - - - - - Unhappy

Map created by Adrian White, Analytic Social Psychologist, University of Leiceter (2006)
Map and further analysis incorporates data published by UNESCO, the WHO, the New Economics Foundation, the Veenhoven Database, the Latinbarometer, the Afrobarometer, the CIA, and the UN Human Development Report.

Source: Adrian White, University of Leicester, 2006.

TORONTO—Canada has made the top 10 on a "world map of happiness," which rates 178 countries ranging from Albania to Zimbabwe on their populations' overall sense of well-being.

Ranked 10th in the world, Canada scored high on the map's three major measures of happiness—health, wealth and access to education, said one of its creators, Adrian White of the University of Leicester in England.

Mr. White, an analytic social psychologist who is working towards his PhD, believes the map is the first to illustrate levels of happiness and well-being on such a global scale.

"I don't know if it's been the same in Canada, but recently there's been a lot of political interest in looking at happiness as a measure of a country's performance, rather than just GDP [gross domestic product]," Mr. White said Thursday from Leicester.

Sheryl Ubelacker

Source: Sheryl Ubelacker, Canadian Press. July 28, 2006. Used with permission of the Canadian Press.

Analysis: Using an index constructed from "health, wealth, and access to education" measures, Adrian White places Canada in 10th place is the world for "happiness." Perhaps what is more interesting is the consistency across the various measures that Canada is a pretty good place to live.

SUMMARY

- The circular flow diagram summarizes the kinds of relationships that occur among market participants—consumers, businesses, governments, and foreigners—through both product and factor markets.
- National-income accounting measures annual output and income flows. The national-income accounts provide a basis for assessing our economic performance, designing public policy, and understanding how all the parts of the economy interact.
- The most comprehensive measure of output is gross domestic product (GDP), the total market value of all final goods and services produced within a nation's borders during a given time period.
- The difference between GDP and GNP is the difference between the value of domestic production and the value of incomes earned by domestic citizens.
- In calculating GDP, we include only the value added at each stage of production. This procedure eliminates the possibility of the double counting that would result because business firms buy intermediate goods from other firms and include the associated costs in their selling price. For the most part, only marketed goods and services are included in GDP.
- Statistics Canada calculates GDP through both an expenditure approach and an income approach. The totals of each of these measures must be equivalent because every dollar spent on output becomes a dollar of income for someone.
- GDP from the expenditure approach measures the total value of goods and services produced in Canada in any given year by adding up the market value of the goods and services consumed by the market participants: consumers, businesses, governments, and foreigners

$$National\ income = C + I + G + [X - M]$$

- To distinguish physical changes in output from monetary changes in its value, we compute both nominal and real GDP. Nominal GDP is the value of output expressed in *current* prices. Real GDP is the value of output expressed in *constant* prices (the prices of some *base* year).
- Each year some of our capital equipment is worn out in the process of production. Hence, GDP is larger than the amount of goods and services we could consume without reducing our production possibilities. The amount of capital used up each year is referred to as *depreciation*.
- The incomes received by households, business firms, and governments provide the purchasing power required to buy the nation's output. As that purchasing power is spent, further GDP is created and the circular flow continues.
- The GDP deflator provides an economy-wide measure of a change in the price level, or *inflation*, in the real economy.
- GDP per capita provides a quick way of comparing average "well-offness" across different countries or different years. However, since per-capita measures assume everyone receives an equal share, it may not accurately capture the actual situation.
- While GDP, and to a lesser extent GNP, are the most commonly talked about measures of "well-being," there are several alternate measures presented.

Key Terms

national-income accounting 67
gross domestic product (GDP) 68
intermediate goods 70
value added 70
exports 72

imports 72
net exports 73
net domestic product (NDP) 75
personal income (PI) 75
disposable income (DI) 76

saving 76
nominal GDP 78
base period 79
inflation 79
GDP per capita 79

Questions for Discussion

1. The manuscript for this book was typed by a friend. Had I hired a secretary to do the same job, GDP would have been higher, even though the amount of output would have been identical. Why is this? Does this make sense?

2. GDP in 1981 was $2.96 trillion. It grew to $3.07 trillion in 1982, yet the quantity of output actually decreased. How is this possible?

3. If gross investment is not large enough to replace the capital that depreciates in a particular year, is net investment greater or less than zero? What happens to our production possibilities?

4. Can we increase consumption in a given year without cutting back on either investment or government services? Under what conditions?

5. Why is it important to know how much output is being produced? Who uses such information?

6. What jobs are likely part of the underground economy?

7. How might the quality of life be adversely affected by an increase in GDP?

8. Would you consider the Index of Economic Well-Being or the Canadian Index of Well-Being (CIW) a better indicator of how well-off Canadians are than GDP? What are the relative advantages and disadvantages of each?

EXERCISES

PROBLEMS   The Student Problem Set to accompany this chapter can be found at the end of the book.

WEB ACTIVITIES   Web Activities to accompany this chapter can be found on the Online Learning Centre at **http://www.mcgrawhill.ca/olc/schiller**.

Unemployment and the Labour Market

In 1989, Statistics Canada reported that 1,060,800 people were unemployed in Canada, a rate of 7.5 percent and less than in the previous two years. The growth in the real economy had resulted in more jobs, more hires, and therefore fewer unemployed persons. All that was about to change; in 1989 the economy's growth slowed and in fact began to decline. This meant that fewer goods and services were being purchased than the previous year and inventories were building up on stores' and manufacturers' shelves. The response was for stores to reduce their orders and manufacturers their production. That meant that both required fewer resources—more to the point—both required fewer hours of labour, and unemployment began to rise. By 1993, an additional 582,000 Canadians, or 11.4 percent of the labour force, were without employment.

Firms found it necessary over these years to "downsize," "restructure," "right-size," and "re-engineer" their labour force, or to simply close their doors and disappear. All of this meant that more Canadians were unable to earn a living, pay their bills, send their kids to college or university, or put gasoline in their cars.

By 2000, the number of persons unemployed in Canada had almost returned to the 1989 level. Statistics Canada reported that the number of unemployed was 1,082,800 persons. But the economic growth slowed and again unemployment began to rise. By 2003, an additional 203,000 Canadians were looking for work.

These two examples are not an isolated or uncommon experience for any macro economy. Rather, these are the human experiences of the business cycle that we talked about back in Chapter 3. Real economies suffer downturns or recessions and the outcome of any recession is an increase in the number of persons unemployed. As these two examples also illustrate, not all recessions are the same—some are longer and some shorter, some are quite disruptive and others far less so.

The pain of joblessness is not confined to those who lose their jobs. In recessions, students discover that jobs are hard to find in the summer. In the recession of 2001, college graduates found out that jobs weren't waiting for them. No matter how good their grades were or how nice their résumés looked, some graduates just didn't get any job offers. Those who did get job offers were dismayed when start dates were postponed—or the offer was rescinded. Even people with jobs felt some economic pain: Their paycheques shrank when hours or wages were scaled back.

In this chapter we take a closer look at the problem of unemployment, focusing on the following questions:

- **When is a person "unemployed"?**
- **What are the costs of unemployment?**
- **What's an appropriate policy goal for "full employment"?**

As we answer these questions, we'll develop a sense of why full employment is a major goal of macro policy and begin to see some of the obstacles we face in achieving it.

5.1 THE LABOUR FORCE

To assess the dimensions of our unemployment problem, we first need to decide who wants a job. Millions of people are jobless, yet they're not part of our unemployment problem. Full-time students, young children playing with their toys, and older people living in retirement are all jobless. We don't expect them to be working, so we don't regard them as part of the unemployment problem. We're not concerned that *everybody* be put to work, only with ensuring jobs for all those persons who are ready and willing to work.

To distinguish between those people who want a job from those who don't, we separate the entire population into two distinct groups. One group consists of *labour-force participants;* the other group encompasses all *nonparticipants.*

That means that not everyone in the population is *eligible* to be part of the labour force, and not all those eligible actually participate in the labour force. The **labour force** includes the civilian, non-institutional population, 15-years of age and over, who are either working or were without a job but were available for work. Individuals are also counted as "working" if they "were not at work due to factors such as own illness or disability, personal or family responsibilities, vacation, labour dispute or other reasons."[1] Also, unpaid family members working in a family enterprise (farming, for example) are counted as employed. *People who are neither employed nor actively seeking work aren't counted as part of the labour force;* they're referred to as **not in the labour force.** As Figure 5.1 shows, approximately two-thirds of those eligible are part of the Canadian labour force.

labour force: The civilian, non-institutional population (non-institutional includes individuals in prison or long-term hospital care), 15 years of age and over, who, during the reference week, were either employed or unemployed as defined by Statistics Canada.

not in the labour force: Anyone 15 years of age or older who is unwilling or unable to participate in the labour market, and who is neither employed nor unemployed.

FIGURE 5.1
The Canadian Labour Force

Of the 32,501.1 million Canadian population as of April 2006, approximately 26,100.2 million were of working age—15-years and older—and therefore eligible to be part of the labour force. 17,334.5 million actually were. That is, these 17,334.50 million were officially either employed or unemployed. An additional 8,765.70 were not in the labour force.

Source: Adapted from Statistics Canada CANSIM database table 282-0001, http://cansim2.statcan.ca. Labour Force survey estimates (LFS) by sex and detailed age group. Unadjusted for seasonality, monthly (persons unless otherwise noted), April 2006. Statistics Canada information is used with the permission of Statistics Canada.

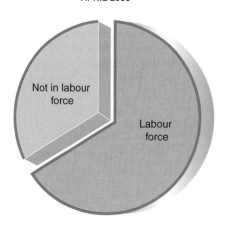

LABOUR FORCE PARTICIPATION
APRIL 2006

Labour Force	17,334.50
Not in Labour Force	8,765.70
Total Eligible Labour Force	26,100.20

[1] *Guide to the Labour Force Survey,* (Statistics Canada, 2006) p. 8.

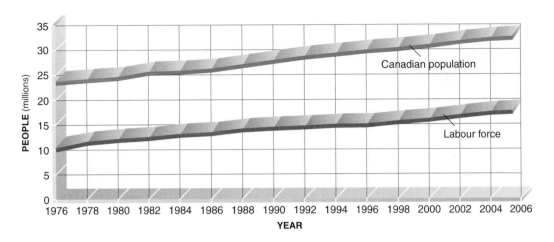

Participation Rates (15 years and older)		
Years	Male	Female
1980	78.3	50.6
1985	76.7	54.9
1990	76.1	58.5
1995	72.5	57.5
2000	72.4	59.4
2006	72.5	62.1

FIGURE 5.2
A Growing Labour Force

The labour force expands as the birth rate and immigration increase. A big increase in the participation rate of women has also added to labour-force growth.

Source: Adapted from Statistics Canada, CANSIM database tables 282-0002 and 051-00011, http://cansim2.statcan.ca. Statistics Canada information is used with the permission of Statistics Canada.

Note that our definition of labour-force participation excludes most household and volunteer activities. A person who chooses to devote their energies to household responsibilities or to unpaid charity work isn't counted as part of the labour force, no matter how hard he or she works. Because they are neither in paid employment nor seeking such employment in the marketplace, they are regarded as outside the labour market (a nonparticipant). But if he or she decides to seek a paid job outside the home, we'd say that they are "entering the labour force." Students too are typically out of the labour force until they leave school. They *enter* the labour force when they go looking for a job, either during the summer or after graduation. People *exit* the labour force when they go back to school, return to household activities, go to prison, or retire. These entrants and exits keep changing the size and composition of the labour force.

Since 1976 the Canadian labour force has increased by slightly more than 65 percent, while the population in Canada increased by slightly less than 38 percent. The implication is that the rise in the labour force is made up of more than just the rise in the population itself. This "extra" increase in the labour force comes from changes in the **labour force participation rate.** Notice in Figure 5.2 that whereas in 1980, just more than half of eligible women were part of the labour force, by 2006, 62 percent of women were. Over this same period, the participation rate of men has actually fallen, though it remains higher for men than for women.

Does this past predict our future? Well, perhaps not. Statistics Canada has projected that by 2036, the Canadian population will be approximately 40.020 million persons, an annual growth rate of 0.07 percent. Does this mean the labour force will also have similar growth? Well, again, perhaps not. Some of this population growth is the result of more of us living longer. In fact, the estimate is that by 2015, the population over 65 will outnumber those under 15. What is the impact of this changing demographic on the "working population"? Currently, the working-age population makes up about 70 percent of the population, by the 2030s, that proportion will fall to about 62 percent and continue to fall to about 60 percent of the population. The result would be fewer working taxpayers supporting those who are no longer part of the labour force.

labour-force participation rate: The percentage of the working-age population working or seeking employment.

Tyson Looks Overseas to Fill Labour Shortage

Tyson Foods, the world's largest meat processor by sales, is recruiting workers from China and the Philippines in an effort to solve a labour shortage at its Canadian operation.

Tyson Foods is also targeting the Ukraine and El Salvador to fill gaps in its plants in the province of Alberta, where the boom in oil sands exploration has driven economic growth to 6.6 percent—twice the national average—and cut unemployment to 3.7 percent.

Source: Excerpt from Doug Cameron, "Tyson looks overseas to fill labour shortage: First firm to recruit under Alberta's 10-year hiring plan," *National Post* (August 1, 2006) p. FP16.

Red Tape Traps Russian Workers Vital to Atlantic's Lobster Season

Two weeks into the peak Atlantic lobster season, a short-staffed seafood processing plant on the eastern tip of Prince Edward Island is hoping to find out as early as today whether the Russian workers it was counting on to keep its operation running full throttle will be allowed into Canada again this year.

Ocean Choice brought over 30 workers from Russia last year under a program that allowed them to stay for a maximum of 10 months.

Source: Excerpt from Allison Hanes, "Red tape traps Russian workers vital to Atlantic's lobster season: Lack of local labourers slows production at plant," *National Post* (May 15, 2007) p. A5.

Analysis: If the economy grows more quickly than the labour force, producers will look to fill job vacancies from outside of their geographic area—even outside of their country.

Statistics Canada offers another way of looking at these same projections, noting that in 2005, each 100 working-age people, were supporting (both directly and through taxes) 44 children and seniors.[2] By the early 2030s, this "dependency ratio" will rise to approximately 61. The actual number of working-age Canadians—the labour force—could be less by the 2030s than today.

Along with the changing demographics, the geography of the labour force in Canada has also shifted. The Canadian labour force is becoming more urban—more likely to be working in a large city rather than a smaller town. According to Statistics Canada, the growth in the labour force between 2001 and 2005 in **census metropolitan areas,** or CMAs (large urban areas together with adjacent suburbs and rural fringes), was 7.2 percent, whereas the growth in non-CMAs was 6.6 percent.

census metropolitan area (CMA): Large urban centres including adjacent urban and rural areas.

As the Applications box illustrates, the problem in some areas of Canada today is a labour shortage. One solution has been to recruit workers from Mexico to work on B.C. vineyards or workers from China or the Philippines to work in Alberta's meat processing industry.

Growth of Production Possibilities

The growth in the labour force over the past thirty years has been an important source of the nation's economic growth. As we first saw in Chapter 1, the quantity of goods and services that can be produced in a real economy is limited by two factors:

- *Availability of factors of production.*
- *Our technological know-how.*

As the available labour force has grown, the nation's *production possibilities* curve has shifted outward, as in Figure 5.3. With those shifts has come an increased capacity for producing goods and services, the essence of long-run *economic growth.* However, if the labour force begins to fall, this will reduce the availability of one factor of production—labour—and, if nothing else changes, lead to an inward or leftward shift of the nation's production possibility curve. What could change so that this inward shift doesn't happen? Either other factors of production, such as capital,

[2]"Population projections: 2005–2031," *The Daily* (Statistics Canada, 2005, December 15), http://statcan.ca/Daily/English/051215/d051215b.htm, accessed August 2, 2005.

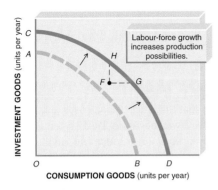

FIGURE 5.3
Labour-Force Growth

The amount of labour available for work—the *labour force*—is a prime determinant of a nation's production possibilities. As the labour force grows, so does the capacity to produce. To produce at capacity, however, the labour force must be fully employed. At point *F*, resources are unemployed.

Source: "The Canadian Labour Force," adapted from Statistics Canada CANSIM database table 282-0048 http://cansim2statcan.ca. Labour Force survey estimates (LFS) by sex and detailed age group. Unadjusted for seasonality, monthly (persons unless otherwise noted), April 2006. Statistics Canada information is used with the permission of Statistics Canada.

would increase and/or our "technological know-how" would have to improve. The official term for this "know-how" is productivity and we'll learn more about it in Chapter 7 when we look in more detail at long-run economic growth.

Institutional Constraints. We could grow the economy even faster if we used more labour and natural resources. But we've chosen to impose institutional constraints on resource exploitation. Child labour laws, for example, prohibit small children from working, no matter how much they or their parents yearn to contribute to total output. Yet we could produce more output this year if we put all those little bodies to work. In fact, we could produce a little more output this year if you were to put down this book and get a job. To the extent that small children, students, and others are precluded from working, both the size of our labour force (our *available* labour) and our potential output shrink. Before you put this book down and rush out to get a job, however, remember that there is another consideration. There is a trade-off between current production and future production. While abandoning your education now might result in a little extra production today, it may at the same time reduce the potential production in the future by some greater amount. Your education increases your "know-how" or technology, and this increase in technology increases the economy's productivity.

Constraints are also imposed on the use of material resources and technology. We won't cut down all the forests this year and build everybody a wooden palace. We've collectively decided to preserve some natural habitat for owls and other endangered species. The federal and provincial governments also set aside land as national or provincial parks to preserve old-growth forest and natural habitat. The need for environmental protection constrains the use of resources or technology and limits annual output. These are *institutional* constraints on our productive capacity. Without such constraints, we could produce more output. Our production possibilities in any year therefore depend not only on what resources and technology are available but also on how we choose to restrict their use.

An expanding labour force not only increases our capacity to produce but also implies the need to keep creating new jobs. Even in the short run (with given resources and technology), we have to confront the issue of job availability.

We can't reach points beyond the production possibilities curve, but we can easily end up somewhere inside that curve, as at point *F* in Figure 5.3. When that happens, we're not producing at (short-run) capacity, and some available resources remain underused. ***To make full use of available production capacity, the labour force must be fully employed.*** If we fail to provide jobs for all labour-force participants, we end up with less than capacity output and the related problem of **unemployment**. With the labour force growing each year, the challenge of keeping all labour-force participants employed never disappears.

Okun's Law. Arthur Okun quantified the relationship between the production possibilities curve and unemployment. According to the original formulation of **Okun's Law,** each additional 1 percent of unemployment translated into a loss of 3 percent

Unemployment

unemployment: The inability of labour-force participants to find jobs.

Okun's Law: One percent more unemployment is estimated to equal 2 percent less output.

in real output. More recent estimates of Okun's Law put the ratio at about 1 to 2, largely due to the changing composition of both the labour force (more women and teenagers) and output (more services).

5.2 MEASURING UNEMPLOYMENT

The **Labour Force Survey (LFS)** is the instrument that Statistics Canada uses to sketch a picture of the Canadian labour market.[3] The survey was begun in 1945 to "satisfy a need for reliable and timely data on the labour market"[4] and is used to divide the eligible population into those employed, unemployed, and not in the labour force.

The labour market estimates are based on a survey of approximately 53,000 households randomly chosen from each province and "allocated to provinces and strata within provinces in the way that best meets the need for reliable estimates at various geographic levels in proportion to the province's size to the total Canadian population."[5] Table 5.1 shows the geographic breakdown that enables Statistics Canada to not only produce estimates for Canada, but also for each province and for the census metropolitan areas within each province, such as Vancouver, Regina, and Halifax.

Each month, Statistics Canada interviewers contact survey participants and ask a series of questions relating to their labour market status for a specific **reference week.** The responses to the survey provide the basis for estimating both the participation rate and the unemployment rate.

Individuals are considered to be employed if, in the reference week, they:

* did any work at all at a job or business, that is, paid work in the context of an employer–employee relationship, or self-employment. It also includes unpaid family work; or
* had a job but were not at work due to certain factors.

Individuals are considered to be unemployed if, in the reference week, they:

* were on temporary layoff and were expecting to be recalled, and were available for work; or
* were without work, had actively looked for work in the past four weeks, and were available for work; or
* had a new job that was to start within four weeks, and were available for work.

> **Labour Force Survey (LFS):** A monthly survey of 53,000 Canadian households across the 10 provinces used to determine the size of the Canadian labour force and the rate of unemployment in Canada.

> **reference week:** One calendar week (Sunday to Saturday) covered by the Labour Force Survey each month.

Province	Sample Size (January 2006)
Newfoundland and Labrador	1,944
Prince Edward Island	1,378
Nova Scotia	2,873
New Brunswick	2,754
Quebec	9,773
Ontario	15,416
Manitoba	3,661
Saskatchewan	3,780
Alberta	5,416
British Columbia	6,377
Canada	**53,372**

Source: "Duration of unemployment," adapted from Statistics Canada CANSIM database table 282-0048, http://cansim2.statcan.ca. Statistics Canada information is used with the permission of Statistics Canada.

TABLE 5.1
Labour Force Survey Sample by Province

[3] *Guide to the Labour Force Survey,* (Statistics Canada, February 2006) Catalogue no. 71-543-GIE.
[4] *Guide to the Labour Force Survey,* (Statistics Canada, February 2006).
[5] *Guide to the Labour Force Survey,* (Statistics Canada, February 2006) Catalogue no. 71-543-GIE, http://www.statcan.ca/english/freepub/71-543-GIE/2007001/part4.htm, accessed May 18, 2007.

Individuals are considered to be not in the labour force if they are neither employed nor unemployed under the definitions of each.

In June 2006, 1.067 million persons were estimated to be unemployed from a labour force of 17.577 million persons, an **unemployment rate** (U) equal to 6.1 percent, the same rate as the month earlier.

When we look at the numbers though, we notice that there were approximately 6 thousand fewer unemployed persons in June as compared to May, 2006. So how can the unemployment rate be the same? Since the estimates of the labour market statistics are determined from the survey each month, each of the categories can, and do, change. Just reading the headline in the newspaper often doesn't give us the complete picture. For instance, in June 2006, it was estimated that there were also 4,600 fewer persons employed and almost 11,000 fewer persons in the labour force.

$$\text{Unemployment rate} = \frac{\text{number of unemployed people}}{\text{labour force}}$$

$$\text{Unemployment rate (U)} = \frac{1,067.1}{17,577.3} = 0.0607 \text{ or } 6.1 \text{ percent}$$

The monthly unemployment figures indicate not only the total amount of unemployment in the economy but also which groups are suffering the greatest unemployment. Typically, teenagers just entering the labour market have the greatest difficulty finding (or keeping) jobs. They have no job experience and relatively few marketable skills. Employers are reluctant to hire them, especially if they must pay at least minimum wage. As a consequence, teenage unemployment rates are typically three times higher than adult unemployment rates (see Figure 5.4b).

Education also affects the chances of being unemployed. If you graduate from college, your chances of being unemployed drop sharply (Figure 5.4c). Advancing technology and a shift to services from manufacturing have put a premium on better-educated workers. Very few people with master's or doctoral degrees stand in unemployment lines.

Although high school dropouts are more likely to be unemployed than college graduates, they don't *stay* unemployed. In fact, most people who become unemployed remain jobless for a relatively brief period of time. As Table 5.2 indicates, almost two-fifths of those unemployed are jobless for less than five weeks, while less than one-fifth are jobless for more than six months (greater than 25 weeks). The average duration of unemployment in 2005 was 17.8 weeks for males and 16.3 weeks for females. People who lose their jobs do find new ones. **When the economy is growing, both unemployment rates and the average duration of unemployment decline.** Recessions have the opposite effect—raising the costs of unemployment significantly.

The reason a person is unemployed or becomes unemployed also affects the length of time the person remains without a job. A person just entering the labour market from high school, college, or university might require more time to identify job opportunities and develop job contacts. By contrast, an autoworker laid off for a temporary plant closing can expect to return to work quickly. People are unemployed for a variety of reasons; they may quit their current job or get laid off or fired. Others who have been out of the labour market raising children or looking after aging parents are re-entering or entering for the first time. Yet others have become eligible for the labour force or finished their desired education. Like the duration of unemployment, the reasons for joblessness are very sensitive to economic conditions. In really bad years, most of the unemployed are job losers, and they remain out of work a long time.

Unemployment statistics don't tell the complete story about the human costs of a sluggish economy. When unemployment persists, job seekers become increasingly frustrated. After repeated rejections, job seekers often get so discouraged that they give up the search and turn to their families, friends, or public welfare for income

The Unemployment Rate

> **unemployment rate:** The proportion of the labour force that is unemployed.

WEB NOTE

Statistics Canada releases the data for each month on *The Daily* and the latest release of the Labour Force Survey is available at http://www.statcan.ca/start.html.

The Duration of Unemployment

Reasons for Unemployment

Discouraged Workers

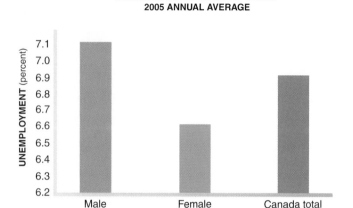

(a) Unemployment by sex

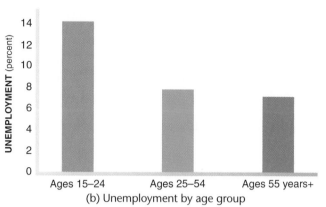

(b) Unemployment by age group

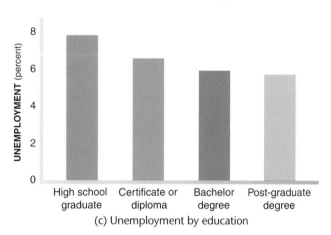

(c) Unemployment by education

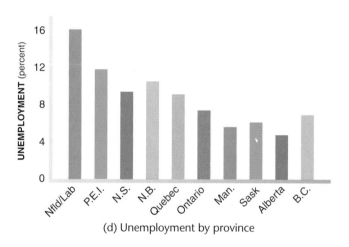

(d) Unemployment by province

FIGURE 5.4

Unemployment Perspectives in 2005: Unemployment Isn't Experienced Equally

Different sexes, different age-groups, different educational backgrounds, and different geographic locations all experience different levels of unemployment. The four graphs above illustrate some of these differences. Figure 5.4a shows the differences between males and females; Figure 5.4b the differences in each age group;

Figure 5.4c the differences among different educational levels; and Figure 5.4d the differences among the Canadian provinces.

Source: Adapted from Statistics Canada CANSIM database tables 282-0086 and 282-0004, http://cansim2.statcan.ca. Statistics Canada information is used with the permission of Statistics Canada.

TABLE 5.2

Duration of Unemployment

The personal cost of unemployment depends on how long the spell of joblessness lasts. During 2005, approximately 38 percent of unemployed male workers and 41 percent of unemployed female workers were unemployed less than five weeks, but many others remain unemployed for six months or longer.

Duration	2005 Percent of People Unemployed	
	Male	Female
Less than 5 weeks	37.65	41.22
5 to 13 weeks	29.46	28.10
14 to 25 weeks	15.07	14.33
Greater than 25 weeks	17.83	16.35

Source: Adapted from Statistics Canada CANSIM database table 282-0048, http://cansim2.statcan.ca. Statistics Canada information is used with the permission of Statistics Canada.

"I've stopped looking for work, which, I believe, helps the economic numbers."

Analysis: People who stop searching for a job aren't officially counted as "unemployed." They are called "discouraged workers."

support. When Statistics Canada asks whether they're actively seeking employment, such **discouraged workers** are apt to reply no. Yet they'd like to be working, and they'd probably be out looking for work if job prospects were better.

Discouraged workers aren't counted as part of our unemployment problem because they're technically out of the labour force (see cartoon). Statistics Canada estimated that throughout 2005, the number of discouraged workers added approximately 0.2 percent to the official unemployment rate. This would add some 35,000 to the number officially unemployed. In years of higher unemployment, this number jumps sharply.

Some people can't afford to be discouraged. Many people who become jobless have family responsibilities and bills to pay: They simply can't afford to drop out of the labour force. Instead, they're compelled to take some job—any job—just to keep body and soul together. The resultant job may be part-time or full-time and may pay very little. Nevertheless, any paid employment is sufficient to exclude the person from the count of the unemployed, though not from a condition of **underemployment.**

Underemployed workers represent labour resources that aren't being fully utilized. They're part of our unemployment problem, even if they're not officially counted as *unemployed.* Although an incomplete measure, Statistics Canada does collect data on those who are "involuntary part-timers," that is, those working part-time who would prefer to be working full-time. The 2005 estimate of these individuals is about 2 percent of the labour force, or some 350,000 Canadian workers.

Although discouraged and underemployed workers aren't counted in official unemployment statistics, some of the people who *are* counted probably shouldn't be. Many people report that they're actively seeking a job even when they have little interest in finding employment. To some extent, public policy actually encourages such behaviour. For example, welfare recipients are often required to look for a job, even though some would prefer to spend all their time raising their children. Their resultant job search is likely to be perfunctory at best. Similarly, some recipients may prefer a brief period of joblessness. Here again, reported unemployment may conceal labour-force nonparticipation. More generous benefits are thought to create similar problems (see the following World View).

discouraged worker: An individual who isn't actively seeking employment but would look for or accept a job if one were available.

Underemployment

underemployment: People seeking full-time paid employment who work only part-time or are employed at jobs below their capability.

The Phantom Unemployed

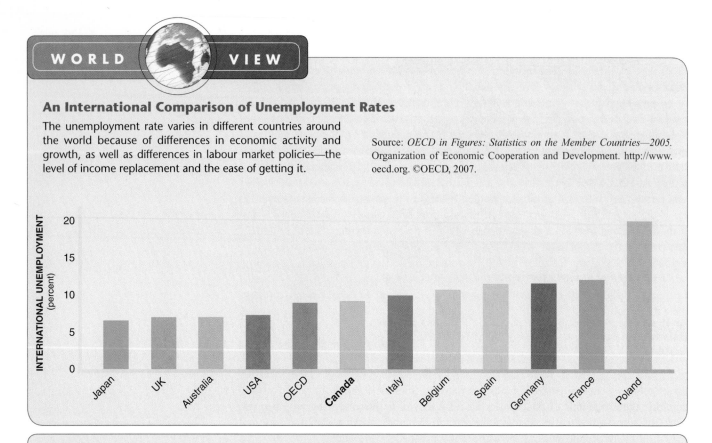

WORLD VIEW

An International Comparison of Unemployment Rates

The unemployment rate varies in different countries around the world because of differences in economic activity and growth, as well as differences in labour market policies—the level of income replacement and the ease of getting it.

Source: *OECD in Figures: Statistics on the Member Countries—2005.* Organization of Economic Cooperation and Development. http://www.oecd.org. ©OECD, 2007.

Analysis: Unemployment rates are typically significantly higher in Europe and Canada than in the United States. Analysts blame both sluggish economic growth and high unemployment benefits.

WEB NOTE

Compare unemployment rates of different countries at http://www.oecd.org/site/ 0,2865,en_21571361_ 34374092_1_1_1_1,00.html.

5.3 THE HUMAN COSTS

Although our measures of unemployment aren't perfect, they're a reliable index to a serious macro problem. Unemployment statistics tell us that more than a million people are jobless. That may be all right for a day or even a week, but if you need income to keep body and soul together, prolonged unemployment can hurt.

The most visible impact of unemployment on individuals is the loss of income. For workers who've been unemployed for long periods of time, such losses can spell financial disaster. Typically, an unemployed person must rely on a combination of savings, income from other family members, and government employment insurance benefits for financial support. After these sources of support are exhausted public welfare is often the only legal support left.

Not all unemployed people experience such a financial disaster, of course. College students who fail to find summer employment are unlikely to end up on welfare the following semester. Similarly, teenagers and others looking for part-time employment won't suffer great economic losses from unemployment. Nevertheless, the experience of unemployment—of not being able to find a job when you want one—can still be painful. This sensation isn't easily forgotten, even after one has finally found employment.

It is difficult to measure all the intangible effects of unemployment on individual workers. Studies have shown, however, that joblessness causes more crime, more health problems, more divorces, and other problems. Such findings underscore the notion that prolonged unemployment poses a real danger; many unemployed workers simply can't cope with the resulting stress. The Canadian Mental Health Association (see the Applications box) describes this stress as "experiencing some of the same

APPLICATIONS

Coping with Unemployment

The Canadian Mental Health Association (CMHA) writes in their *Coping with Unemployment* online pamphlet that:

When you lose your job, not only is your usual source of income gone, but also your personal work relationships, daily structures, and an important sense of self-purpose. Unemployment can be, and often is, a shock to your whole system. You can experience some of the same feelings and stresses that you

would if you were seriously injured, going through a divorce, or mourning the loss of a loved one. You can go through some or all of the stages of grieving just as you would with any other major loss.

Source: Excerpt from *Coping with Unemployment*, (Canadian Mental Health Association, 2007), http://www.cmha.ca/bins/content_page.asp?cid=2-28-62&lang=1, accessed May 18, 2007.

Analysis: The cost of unemployment is not measured in lost wages alone. Unemployment creates stresses that can impair an individual's health, social relationships and responsibilities, and productivity.

feelings and stresses that you would if you were seriously injured, going through a divorce, or mourning the loss of a loved one."

German psychiatrists have also observed that unemployment can be hazardous to your health. They estimate that the anxieties and other nervous disorders that accompany one year of unemployment can reduce life expectancy by as much as five years. In Japan, the suicide rate jumped by more than 50 percent in 1999 when the economy plunged into recession. In New Zealand, suicide rates are twice as high for unemployed workers than for employed ones.

There's an upside to these relationships as well. When the U.S. unemployment rate fell steadily in the late 1990s, so did crime rates, premarital births, divorce rates, and child abuse. Declining unemployment rates weren't the only cause of these trends, but they certainly helped.

5.4 DEFINING FULL EMPLOYMENT

In view of the economic and social losses associated with unemployment, it's not surprising that *full employment* is one of our basic macroeconomic goals. You may be surprised to learn, however, that *full* employment isn't the same thing as *zero* unemployment. There are in fact several reasons for regarding some degree of unemployment as inevitable and even desirable.

Some joblessness is virtually inevitable as long as we continue to grow crops, fish, build houses, go skiing, or catch lobster at certain seasons of the year. At the end of each season some workers must go searching for new jobs, experiencing some **seasonal unemployment** in the process.

Seasonal fluctuations also arise on the supply side of the labour market. Youth unemployment rates, for instance, rise in the spring and summer as high school, college, and university students look for temporary jobs. For example, between April and May of 2005, the number of unemployed youth (aged 15–24) increased by more than 80,000. While the number of unemployed youth fell in June (as college and university students found jobs) the number increased in July, again by 80,000 as more high school students joined the hunt.[6]

Seasonal Unemployment

seasonal unemployment: Unemployment due to seasonal changes in employment or labour supply.

---

[6]Seasonal variation in employment and labour supply not only create some unemployment in the annual averages, but also distort monthly comparisons. Unemployment rates are generally higher just after Christmas and again in the summer months as more youth look for work. Statistics Canada adjusts for these anticipated regular yearly fluctuations—caused by climate and institutional variation—to make the monthly estimates more comparable. Seasonal adjustments don't alter annual averages, however.

Frictional Unemployment

There are other reasons for expecting a certain amount of unemployment. Many workers have sound financial or personal reasons for leaving one job to look for another. In the process of moving from one job to another, a person may well miss a few days or even weeks of work without any serious personal or social consequences. On the contrary, people who spend more time looking for work may find *better* jobs.

The same is true of students first entering the labour market. It's not likely that you'll find a job the moment you leave school. Nor should you necessarily take the first job offered. If you spend some time looking for work, you're more likely to find a job you like. The job-search period gives you an opportunity to find out what kinds of jobs are available, what skills they require, and what they pay. Accordingly, a brief period of job search may benefit labour market entrants and the larger economy. The unemployment associated with these kinds of job searches is referred to as **frictional unemployment.**

frictional unemployment: Brief periods of unemployment experienced by people moving between jobs or into the labour market.

Three factors distinguish frictional unemployment from other kinds of unemployment. First, enough jobs exist for those who are frictionally unemployed—that is, there's adequate *demand* for labour. Second, those individuals who are frictionally unemployed have the skills required for available jobs. Third, the period of job search will be relatively short. Under these conditions, frictional unemployment resembles an unconventional game of musical chairs. There are enough chairs of the right size for everyone, and people dance around them for only a brief period of time.

Structural Unemployment

For many job seekers, the period between jobs may drag on for months or even years because they don't have the skills that employers require. This mismatch of worker's skills and the demands of employers occurs because of the changing structure of the Canadian economy. Much of the transition is talked of as moving toward a "new" economy, one based on worker's knowledge rather than on the extraction of raw resources. The impact of closing coal mines on Cape Breton Island, pulp mills in northern Ontario, or saw mills in British Columbia is the unemployment of workers skilled in coal mining and lumber and pulp mill operation. If other coal mines and pulp and lumber mills are hiring, these workers would experience frictional unemployment as they looked for and accepted jobs with these other firms. However, if the jobs available are in biotechnology, computer science, or teaching economics, skills not held by these workers, the available jobs are unfilled and the workers remain unemployed. These workers would make up the category of **structural unemployment.**

structural unemployment: Unemployment caused by a mismatch between the skills (or location) of job seekers and the requirements (or location) of available jobs.

Structural unemployment violates the second condition for frictional unemployment: that the job seekers can perform the available jobs. Structural unemployment is analogous to a musical chairs game in which there are enough chairs for everyone, but some of them are too small to sit on. It's a more serious concern than frictional unemployment and incompatible with any notion of full employment.

Changes in Structural Unemployment. During the 1970s and early 1980s, the view of our full-employment potential was considered overly optimistic. Unemployment rates that had been around 4 percent in the 1950s and early 1960s (see Figure 5.5) jumped into the 6.5 to 9.0 percent range through the 1970s and reached a high of 14.1 percent in March, 1983. The new normal level of unemployment seemed to be much higher than in previous decades. Critics suggested that structural barriers to full employment had intensified, necessitating a redefinition of the full-employment goal. Some of these structural barriers include:

- *More Youth and Women.* The "baby boom" generation began entering the labour force in the early 1960s and thus the labour force grew. During the same period, the proportion of adult women in the labour force increased significantly. In 1976, the participation rate of women in the labour force was about 45 percent of women in the population. By 2006, this proportion had increased to just greater than 62 percent.

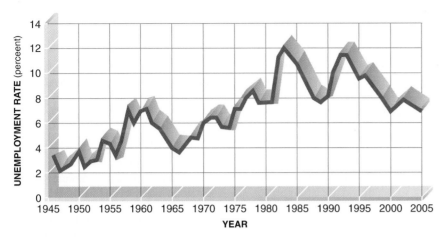

FIGURE 5.5

Canada's Annual Average Rate of Unemployment: 1945–2005

The Canadian rate of unemployment averaged around 4 percent from the end of World War II in 1945 through to the middle of the 1960s (except for the recessionary period in the late 1950s). There was a general upward trend from then until the early 1980s, when the annual average rate rose to 8 percent. The two recessions in the 1980s saw unemployment reach peaks of 12 and 11 percent, returning to about 8 percent in 1998. Since then, the rate has continued to fall, reaching 6.1 percent in 2005.

Source: Adapted from Statistics Canada CANSIM database table 282-00002, http://cansim2.statcan.ca and Statistics Canada publication *Historical Statistics of Canada,* Catalogue 11-516-XIE. Statistics Canada information is used with the permission of Statistics Canada.

- *Increased Benefits.* Higher benefits and easier rules for employment insurance (EI) and welfare made unemployment less painful. As a result, critics suggested, more people were willing to stay unemployed rather than accept just any position.
- *Structural Changes in Demand.* Changes in consumer demand, technology, and trade shrank the markets in steel, textiles, pulp and paper, and other industries. The workers dislocated from these industries couldn't be absorbed fast enough in new high-tech and other service industries and professions.

Declining Structural Pressures. These structural barriers began to recede by the late 1980s and 1990s. The generation following the "baby boomers" (generation "X") was smaller and the labour force grew more slowly. The upsurge in the participation of women in the labour force also levelled off. By 2006, the participation rate of women was 62.1 percent, an increase of less than 4 percentage points from 1990, compared to the 13 percentage point increase between 1976 and 1990 (see Figure 5.2). High school completion rates increased, and attendance at colleges and universities was higher as well. All of these structural changes made it easier to reduce unemployment rates.

The fourth type of unemployment is **cyclical unemployment**—joblessness that occurs when there simply aren't enough jobs to go around. Cyclical unemployment exists when the number of workers demanded falls short of the number of persons supplied (in the labour force). This isn't a case of mobility between jobs (frictional unemployment) or even of job seekers' skills (structural unemployment). Rather, it's simply an inadequate level of demand for goods and services and thus for labour. Cyclical unemployment resembles the most familiar form of musical chairs, in which the number of chairs is always less than the number of players.

Two recent examples of the effect of cyclical unemployment come from the recessions in the early 1980s and again in the early 1990s. In both cases, as indicated in Figure 5.5, the rate of unemployment spiked upwards, reaching slightly more than

Cyclical Unemployment

cyclical unemployment: Unemployment attributable to a lack of job vacancies, that is, to an inadequate level of aggregate demand.

12 percent in 1984 and 11.4 percent in 1993. In each of these examples, the demand for goods and services in the economy declined. To put this in the context of our production possibility curve, the recessions moved the economy inside the curve where our resources, notably labour, were no longer being used to their normal maximum and the economy produced fewer goods and services than it was capable of.

Slow Growth. Cyclical unemployment can emerge even when the economy is expanding. Keep in mind that the labour force is always growing, due to population growth and continuing immigration. If these additional labour-force participants are to find jobs, the economy must grow. Specifically, *the economy must grow at least as fast as the labour force to avoid cyclical unemployment.* When economic growth slows below this threshold, unemployment rates start to rise.

The Full-Employment Goal

No one knows for sure just how much of our unemployment problem is frictional. However, the current Canadian economy is estimated to be operating close to potential—on our production possibility curve—meaning there is little or no cyclical unemployment. A paper in written by Lars Osberg and Zengxi Lin in 2000 suggested that structural unemployment was approximately 0.75 percent.[7] Given an unemployment rate of just over 6 percent, these two things taken together would leave us to estimate that the frictional and seasonal unemployment in Canada would be responsible for an unemployment rate of perhaps 5.25 percent. Accordingly, our definition of *"full employment"* should allow for at least this much unemployment.

In later chapters we examine the causes of cyclical unemployment and explore some potential policy responses. At this point, however, we're just establishing some perspective on the goal of full employment. The preamble to the Bank of Canada Act commits the bank "to mitigate by its influence fluctuations in the general level of . . . employment" and the elected federal and provincial governments are often judged at the ballot box by their ability to keep the economy near the full employment level. Presumably, this means avoiding as much cyclical and structural unemployment as possible while keeping frictional unemployment within reasonable bounds. As guidelines for public policy, these perspectives are admittedly vague.

A "Natural" Rate of Unemployment

natural rate of unemployment: Long-term rate of unemployment determined by structural forces in labour and product markets.

As we've described, even an economy operating at full-employment will experience some level of frictional and structural unemployment. So the rate of unemployment will be greater than zero. Early economists described this full-employment level of unemployment as a **"natural rate."** That is, while the unemployment rate may rise or fall in the short run the economy will tend to gravitate toward this natural rate in the long run.

More commonly today, the level of unemployment is considered more in the context of the pressure it may exert on inflation in the economy. What has been described here as a "natural rate" is therefore more commonly referred to as the *non-accelerating inflation rate of unemployment,* or *NAIRU.*

Although the natural rate concept avoids specifying a short-term inflation trigger, it too is subject to debate. As we've seen, the *structural* determinants of unemployment (e.g., age and composition of the labour force) change over time. When structural forces change, the level of natural unemployment presumably changes as well.

As well as structural forces, other changes to the labour market can cause a natural rate to rise or fall, A more flexible labour market that makes hiring and firing easier can encourage firms to add more employees, and reduce unemployment. Higher benefits ease the financial pain of unemployment and can encourage more frictional unemployment and lead to it having a longer duration.

[7]Lars Osberg and Zengxi Lin, "How much of Canada's unemployment is structural," *Canadian Public Policy* vol. 25, supplement 1, http://myweb.dal.ca/osberg/classification/articles/academic%20journals/HowMuchUEStructural/HowMuchUEStructural.pdf.

"I don't like six-per-cent unemployment, either. But I can live with it."

Analysis: So-called full employment entails a compromise between employment and inflation goals. That compromise doesn't affect everyone equally.

The Employment Insurance Act has undergone significant reforms over the years that attempt to address some issues that may negatively impact the Canadian natural rate of unemployment. Two recent reforms occurred in 1989 and in 1996, with provisions coming into force in two phases, the first phase in July 1996 and the second phase in January 1997.

Generally, the reforms were intended to tighten the rules for qualifying for benefits, reduce the level of benefits, and shorten the time the benefits could be claimed. Each of these reforms would increase the incentive to find and accept employment, or to not leave a job in the first place. The result would be a reduction in the rate of unemployment in Canada.

At least in part, the impetus for these reforms was the fact that the Canadian natural rate estimates were higher than those experienced in other countries. For instance, while the unemployment rate for 2004 in Canada was 7.2 percent, the Bush administration in the United States set their full employment threshold for 2004 at 5.1 percent, two full percentage points lower.

Currently, economists suggest that an unemployment rate of 6 to 8 percent is consistent with either natural or full employment.

5.5 THE HISTORICAL RECORD

Although there's some ambiguity about the specific definition of full employment, the historical record is littered with evident failures. We have already noted two such "failures" in the recessions of the early 1980s and then again after 1989. But Figure 5.5 provides us with a longer sweep of unemployment history in Canada and enables us to see several factors that we have talked about at work.

Throughout the 1940s and into the 1950s, unemployment was less than 4 percent. The economy was returning to civilian goods and services after World War II and consumers were buying and outfitting houses and beginning the "baby boom." A recession in the late 1950s saw unemployment rise to over 6 percent and not return to the 4 percent level until 1965. The demographic changes in Canada, the leading edge of the "baby boom" generation entering the labour market starting in 1961, and the increasing participation of women in the labour force, along with economic dislocations in the 1970s (such as the oil price spikes in 1973 and again in 1976) and, some critics suggest, the introduction of employment insurance benefits, resulted in the rate of unemployment rising to slightly more than 8 percent.

Since 1989, the slowing down of labour force growth and strong real economic growth (with one relatively small "hiccup" after September 11, 2001) has brought the unemployment rate for Canada down to 6 percent by June, 2006, although if we look at the individual provinces, the rate ranges from a high of 14.8 percent in Newfoundland and Labrador to a low of 3.5 percent in Alberta.

Estimates by the Bank of Canada that the Canadian economy is operating at its potential—at the economy's production possibility curve—suggest that this 6 percent rate of unemployment may also represent Canada's current natural rate of unemployment.

SUMMARY

- To understand unemployment, we must distinguish the labour force from the larger population. Only people who are working (employed), are available for work, or who spend some time looking for a job (unemployed) are participants in the labour force. People neither working nor looking for work are outside the labour force.

- The size of the labour force affects production possibilities. As the labour force grows, so does the capacity to produce goods and services.

- Unemployment implies that we're producing inside the production possibilities curve rather than on it.

- The macroeconomic loss imposed by unemployment is reduced output of goods and services. Okun's Law suggests that 1 percentage point in unemployment is equivalent to a 2 percentage point decline in output.

- The human cost of unemployment includes not only financial losses but social, physical, and psychological costs as well.

- The Labour Force Survey (LFS) is conducted each month by Statistics Canada to "satisfy a need for reliable and timely data on the labour market."

- Unemployment is distributed unevenly; teenagers and the less educated have much higher rates of unemployment. Also hurt are discouraged workers—those who've stopped looking for work—and those underemployed

and working at part-time or menial jobs because they can't find full-time jobs equal to their training or potential.

- There are four types of unemployment: seasonal, frictional, structural, and cyclical. Because some seasonal, structural, and frictional unemployment is inevitable and even desirable, full employment is not defined as zero unemployment.

- The economy (output) must grow at least as fast as the labour force to keep the unemployment rate from rising.

- The natural rate of unemployment is based on frictional and structural forces.

- The natural rate of unemployment in Canada is estimated to be approximately 6 to 7 percent. But this is not a stable number and rises or falls depending upon other factors such as economic and social factors and government policy choices.

- Cyclical unemployment follows the "swing" of the business cycle: in the recessions of the early 1980s and early 1990s, the rate of unemployment exceeded 12 and 11 percent respectively.

- The historical record of unemployment in Canada beginning in 1945 shows unemployment rising from 2 percent at the end of World War II to more than 12 percent in 1984 and then falling to approximately 6 percent by 2006.

Key Terms

labour force 88
not in the labour force 88
labour-force participation rate 89
census metropolitan area (CMA) 90
unemployment 91
Okun's Law 91

Labour Force Survey, LFS 92
reference week 92
unemployment rate 93
discouraged worker 95
underemployment 95
seasonal unemployment 97

frictional unemployment 98
structural unemployment 98
cyclical unemployment 99
natural rate of unemployment 100

Questions for Discussion

1. Is it possible for unemployment rates to increase at the same time that the number of employed persons is increasing? How?
2. If more teenagers stay in school longer, what happens to (*a*) production possibilities? (*b*) unemployment rates?
3. What factors might explain (*a*) the rising labour-force participation rate of women and (*b*) the declining participation of men? (See Figure 5.2 for trends.)
4. Why might job (re)entrants have a harder time finding a job than job losers?
5. If the government guaranteed some income to all unemployed persons, how might the unemployment rate be affected? Who should get unemployment benefits?
6. Can you identify three institutional constraints on the use of resources (factors of production)? What has motivated these constraints?
7. Why is frictional unemployment deemed desirable?
8. Why do people expect inflation to "heat up" (increase) when the unemployment rate in Canada falls below the "natural" rate?
9. If Canadian producers are unable to find willing and able workers locally or elsewhere (see the Applications box on page 90), what might be the impact on wages in the labour market and the willingness to produce?
10. Madawaska-Restigouche (New Brunswick) MP Jean-Claude D'Amours has said that there is a need to limit the imports of Chinese textiles into the Canadian market to help the local industry and save local jobs. How can the importing textiles from China actually lead to an increase in jobs in Canadian retail stores and the restaurants?

EXERCISES

PROBLEMS The Student Problem Set to accompany this chapter can be found at the end of the book.

WEB ACTIVITIES Web Activities to accompany this chapter can be found on the Online Learning Centre at **http://www.mcgrawhill.ca/olc/schiller**.

Inflation

Germany set a record in 1923 that no other nation wants to beat. In that year, prices in Germany rose a *trillion* times over. Prices rose so fast that workers took "shopping breaks" to spend their twice-a-day paycheques before they became worthless. Menu prices in restaurants rose while people were still eating! Accumulated savings became worthless, as did outstanding loans. People needed sacks of currency to buy bread, butter, and other staples. With prices more than doubling every *day*, no one could afford to save, invest, lend money, or make long-term plans. In the frenzy of escalating prices, production of goods and services came to a halt, unemployment rose tenfold, and the German economy all but collapsed.

Hungary had a similar episode of runaway inflation in 1946, as did Japan. More recently, Russia, Bulgaria, Brazil, Zaire, Yugoslavia, Argentina, and Uruguay have all witnessed at least a tenfold jump in prices in a single year.

In 2006, Zimbabwe had the distinction of the world's highest rate of inflation at about 1,200 percent. (See the Application box on page 105).

Canada has never experienced inflation on this kind of scale. Near the end of World War I, in 1917, the average annual rate of inflation in Canada hit a year-over-year rate of 19 percent. More recently, Canada experienced rising average annual rates of inflation in the 1970s, beginning at 3 percent in 1971 and peaking at almost 11 percent in 1975. The general anxiety caused by inflation was such that the Prime Minister at the time, Pierre Trudeau, instituted wage and price controls with an Anti-Inflation Act that took effect on December 16, 1975, and was phased out in 1978. The Act created an Anti-Inflation Board and an Anti-Inflation Appeal Tribunal whose purpose was to ensure that important economic sectors in the economy adhered to the government's wage and price guidelines.

In 1991, a target for inflation became a cornerstone of Canadian monetary policy administered by the Bank of Canada. The inflation target initially was to bring inflation from the then nearly 6 percent down to 3 percent. The target was then incrementally reduced, first to 2½ percent and finally to 2 percent. Since 1991, price stability has been a major goal of government. The result of the Bank's focus on inflation has been an average annual rate of inflation within a range of 1 to 3 percent over the past decade.

But if Canada's rate of inflation is so low in world terms, why would there be such "anxiety" about it? Two reasons really: first, any inflation reduces the real purchasing

LEARNING OBJECTIVES

By the end of this chapter, you should be able to:

6.1 Describe both inflation and deflation

6.2 Explain the macroeconomic consequences of inflation

6.3 Describe the consumer price index, the CPI measurement of inflation process, and the potential measurement problems in the CPI

6.4 Discuss the benefits of price stability

6.5 Describe the causes of inflation

APPLICATIONS

$100,000 Doesn't Buy Much in Zimbabwe

HARARE—The 100,000 Zimbabwean dollar note that went into circulation this week was officially worth just over $1 [US]. Yesterday on Zimbabwe's black markets it was valued at about 33¢.

In a country stricken by 1,000% inflation, the world's worst, the new note will not even buy a loaf of bread.

Hours after the national mint started printing the notes, the price of bread shot up by more than 40% to Z$130,000, the third increase this year

Source: Based on Peta Thornycroft, "$100,000 doesn't buy much in Zimbabwe," June 7, 2006, *National Post*, pg. A11.

Analysis: High rates of inflation—rising prices—quickly diminish the purchasing power of money and the value of wages and savings.

APPLICATIONS

Is Inflation Dead?

February's spike in inflation notwithstanding, one of the more remarkable macroeconomic developments of the past decade, both in Canada and in other countries, has been the general disappearance of inflation from the headline news.

How was this achieved? First, after two decades of inflationary pain that eroded purchasing power and magnified social tension, Canadians have accepted that monetary policy has one core role—to maintain purchasing power. Milton Friedman's conclusion that inflation is, everywhere and always, a monetary phenomenon, is now accepted wisdom. In plain words, this means that inflation can only be sustained if central banks

provide the fuel that keeps pumping liquidity into the economic system. No fuel, no inflation.

Second, central banks have developed more sophisticated tools in their analysis of inflationary forces. Potential economic output is now assessed to identify the risks that inflation will accelerate. Moreover, the Bank of Canada, with the support of the federal minister of finance, adopted explicit inflation targets as the foundation for monetary policy.

Source: Glen Hodgson, "Is inflation dead?" *National Post* (March 21, 2007) p. FP19. Material reprinted with the express permission of the National Post Company, a CanWest Partnership.

Analysis: An entire generation (your's) has grown up with inflation rates of less than 5 percent per year. These rates are low enough, that inflation is generally unnoticed on a month-to-month or even year-to-year basis. This is not accidental, however, but rather the result of the Bank of Canada's monetary policy focus of "price stability," or at least low inflation rates.

power of money. Even a 5 percent rate of annual inflation would reduce the real purchasing power of money by half in 15 years. Secondly, inflation creates uncertainty about the future, and uncertainty can reduce investment and slow down future economic growth.

In later chapters we'll examine the role and function of the Bank of Canada and how monetary policy is used to slow the economy down or speed it up. Before looking at the levers of macro policy, however, we need to examine our policy goals. Why is inflation so feared? How much inflation is unacceptable? To get a handle on this basic issue, we'll ask and answer the following questions:

WEB NOTE

For more detailed perspective on Canada's anti-inflation program see http://canadianeconomy. gc.ca/english/economy/ 1975economic.html; and for some background on Canada's inflation targets, http://www.bankofcanada.ca/ en/backgrounders/bg-i3.html.

* **What kind of price increases are referred to as *inflation?***
* **Who is hurt (or helped) by inflation?**
* **What is an appropriate goal for *price stability?***

As we'll discover, inflation is a serious problem, but not for the reasons most people cite. We'll also see why deflation—falling prices—isn't so welcome either.

6.1 WHAT IS INFLATION?

Most people associate *inflation* with price increases on specific goods and services. The economy isn't necessarily experiencing an inflation, however, every time the price of a cup of coffee goes up. We must be careful to distinguish the phenomenon of inflation from price increases for specific goods. ***Inflation is an increase in the average level of prices, not a change in any specific price.***

The Average Price

Suppose you wanted to know the average price of fruit in the supermarket. Surely you wouldn't have much success in seeking out an average fruit—nobody would be quite sure what you had in mind. You might have some success, however, if you sought out the prices of apples, oranges, cherries, and peaches. Knowing the price of each kind of fruit, you could then compute the average price of fruit. The resultant figure wouldn't refer to any particular product but would convey a sense of how much a typical basket of fruit might cost. By repeating these calculations every day, you could then determine whether fruit prices, *on average,* were changing. On occasion, you might even notice that apple prices rose while orange prices fell, leaving the *average* price of fruit unchanged.

The same kinds of calculations are made to measure inflation in the entire economy. We first determine the average price of all output—the average price level—then look for changes in that average. A rise in the average price level is referred to as inflation.

The average price level may fall as well as rise. A decline in average prices—a **deflation**—occurs when price decreases on some goods and services outweigh price increases on all others. This happened in Japan in 1995, and again in 2003 (see World View "Worldwide Inflation," p. 119). Such deflations are rare, however; since 1915, Canada has had only two periods of deflation, the recession of 1921–1924 and the depression years of 1930–1933. In the following seven decades, in only one year, 1951, did Canadians experience any deflation.

> **deflation:** A decrease in the average level of prices of goods and services.

Relative Prices vs. the Price Level

Because inflation and deflation are measured in terms of average price levels, it's possible for individual prices to rise or fall continuously without changing the average price level. We already noted, for example, that the price of apples can rise without increasing the average price of fruit, so long as the price of some other fruit, such as oranges, falls. In such circumstances, **relative prices** are changing, but not average prices. An increase in the *relative* price of apples simply means that apples have become more expensive in comparison with other fruits (or any other good or service).

Changes in relative price may occur in a period of stable average price, or in periods of inflation or deflation. In fact, in an economy as vast as ours—in which literally millions of goods and services are exchanged in the factor and product markets—relative prices are always changing. Indeed, relative price changes are an essential ingredient of the market mechanism. Recall from Chapter 2 what happens when the market price of Web-design services rises relative to other goods and services. This (relative) price rise alerts Web architects (producers) to increase their output, cutting back on other production or leisure activities.

A general inflation—an increase in the average price level—doesn't perform this same market function. If all prices rise at the same rate, price increases for specific goods are of little value as market signals. In less extreme cases, when most but not all prices are rising, changes in relative prices do occur but aren't so immediately apparent. During periods of general inflation, the prices of some goods actually fall. For example, Statistics Canada reported in the April 2007 release of the consumer price index that computer prices fell by 12 percent even though the general inflation rate was rising by 2.4 percent. The prices of digital cameras, cell phones, and MP3 players have also been falling.

> **relative price:** The price of one good in comparison with the price of other goods.

6.2 REDISTRIBUTIVE EFFECTS OF INFLATION

The distinction between relative and average prices helps us determine who's hurt by inflation—and who's helped. Popular opinion notwithstanding, it's simply not true that everyone is worse off when prices rise. ***Although inflation makes some people worse off, it makes other people better off.*** Some people even get rich when prices rise! The micro consequences of inflation are reflected in redistributions of income and wealth, not general declines in either measure of our economic welfare. These redistributions occur because people buy different combinations of goods and services, own different assets, and sell distinct goods or services (including labour). The impact of inflation on individuals therefore depends on how prices change for the goods and services each person actually buys or sells.

Price changes are the most visible consequence of inflation. If you've been paying tuition, you know how painful a price hike can be. Statistics Canada reports in the April 2006 edition of *Education Matters* that between 1995 and 2002, average undergraduate tuition increased approximately 34 percent after accounting for inflation.[1] Some professional programs, such as medicine, experienced tuition increases of as much as 132 percent over this same time period. You don't need a whole course in economics to figure out the implications of these tuition hikes. To stay in school, you (or your parents) must forgo increasing amounts of other goods and services. You end up being worse off since you can't buy as many goods and services as you could before tuition went up.

The effect of tuition increases on your economic welfare can be reflected in the reduction of your purchasing power—the quantity of goods and services your dollars will buy. If the number of dollars you receive every year remains the same, your purchasing power will rise or fall as prices change.

Suppose that you have $6,000 per term while you're in school. Out of that $6,000 you must pay for your tuition, room and board, books, and everything else. The budget for the first term is given in Table 6.1 below.

Now suppose that in the second term, tuition rises by 34 percent, to $3,350, while books and room and board costs remain the same. What happens to your ability to buy "everything else"?

You now have to use more of your income for the term to pay tuition. This means you have less income to spend on other things. Since the cost of room and board and books is unchanged, there's only one place that you can cut: the category of "everything else." After paying for the tuition increase, you only have $150.00 left to spend during the term on movies, clothes, pizzas, and music downloads. Even though your income for the term remains the same, your ability to purchase other goods and services—your purchasing power—has been reduced.

Price Effects

WEB NOTE

For a more detailed analysis of the impact of tuition increases in Canada and their impact on attending post-secondary institutions, see http://www.statcan.ca/english/freepub/81-004-XIE/2006001/tcosts.htm.

	First Term	Second Term
Income for Term	$6,000.00	$6,000.00
Tuition	$2,500.00	$3,350.00
Books	$ 500.00	$ 500.00
Room and Board	$2,000.00	$2,000.00
Everything Else	$1,000.00	$ 150.00

Source: *Education matters: insights on education, learning and training in Canada.* (Statistics Canada, April 2006), Catalogue 81-004-XIE, http://www.statcan.ca/english/freepub/81-004-XIE/81-004-XIE2006001.htm; Statistics Canada information is used with the permission of Statistics Canada.

TABLE 6.1
Real Income Effects from Tuition Increases

[1]*Education matters: insights on education, learning and training in Canada.* (Statistics Canada, April 2006), Catalogue 81-004-XIE, http://www.statcan.ca/english/freepub/81-004-XIE/81-004-XIE2006001.htm; Statistics Canada information is used with the permission of Statistics Canada.

TABLE 6.2
Price Changes in April, 2007

The average rate of inflation conceals substantial differences in the price changes of specific goods and services. The impact of inflation on individuals depends in part on which goods and services are consumed. People who buy goods whose prices are rising fastest lose more real income.

Prices That Rose (%)		Prices That Fell (%)	
Fresh vegetables	+12.9%	Computer equipment	−18.7%
Car insurance	+4.3%	Video equipment	−8.4%
Restaurant meals	+2.3%	Vehicles	−1.1%
Average rate of inflation April 2006 to April 2007: +2.2%			

Source: Adapted from Statistics Canada, "Average Rate of Inflation," *The Daily,* April 2007 release of the Consumer Price Index. Statistics Canada information is used with the permission of Statistical Canada.

Two basic lessons about inflation are to be learned from this sad story:

- *Not all prices rise at the same rate during an inflation.* In our example, tuition increased substantially while other prices remained steady. Hence, the "average" price increase wasn't representative of any particular good or service. Typically, some prices rise rapidly, others only modestly, and some actually fall.
- *Not everyone suffers equally from inflation.* This follows from our first observation. Those people who consume the goods and services that are rising faster in price bear a greater burden of inflation; their real incomes fall further. Other consumers bear a lesser burden, or even none at all, depending on how fast the prices rise for the goods they enjoy.

Table 6.2 illustrates some of the price changes that occurred in April 2007. The average rate of inflation was only 2.2 percent. This was little solace to college students, however, who confronted tuition increases and price hikes on textbooks (sorry!). On the other hand, price reductions on video equipment and computers spared consumers of these products from the pain of the *average* inflation rate.

Although tuition hikes reduce the purchasing power of students, non-students aren't hurt by such price increases. In fact, if tuition doubled, non-students really wouldn't care. They could continue to buy the same bundle of goods and services they'd been buying all along. Tuition increases only reduce the purchasing power of people at college or university.

Income Effects

Even if all prices rose at the *same* rate, inflation would still redistribute income. The redistributive effects of inflation originate not only in *expenditure* patterns but also *income* patterns. Some people have fixed incomes that *don't* go up with inflation. Fixed-income groups include those retired people who depend primarily on private pensions and workers with multiyear contracts that fix wage rates at preinflation levels. Lenders (like banks) that have lent funds at fixed interest rates also suffer real income losses when price levels rise. They continue to receive interest payments fixed in *nominal* dollars that have increasingly less *real* value. All these market participants experience a declining share of real income (and output) in inflationary periods.

Not all market participants suffer a real income decline when prices rise. Some people's **nominal income** rises *faster* than average prices, thereby boosting their **real incomes.** Keep in mind that there are two sides to every market transaction. *What looks like a price to a buyer looks like an income to a seller.* If students all pay higher tuition, the college or university will take in more income. When the nominal incomes colleges and universities receive increase faster than average prices, they actually *benefit* from inflation. They end up being able to buy *more* goods and services (including faculty, buildings, and library books) after a period of inflation than they could before. Their real income rises. When the price of this textbook goes up, our *nominal* income goes up. If the text price rises faster than other prices, our *real* income increases as well. In either case, you lose (sorry!).

nominal income: The amount of money income received in a given time period, measured in current dollars.

real income: Income in constant dollars; nominal income adjusted for inflation.

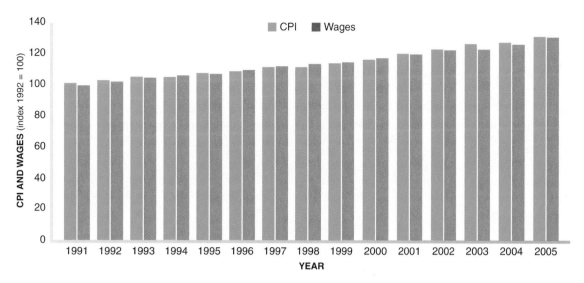

FIGURE 6.1

An Index of the CPI and Average Weekly Wages: 1991–2005

Figure 6.1 illustrates that the pattern of inflation and the index of average weekly wages is very similar. The implication from this is that average weekly wages have increased at approxi-

mately the same rate as CPI inflation, leaving "real" wage relatively unchanged.

Source: Adapted from Statistics Canada CANSIM database tables 326-0002 and 281-0087, http://cansim2.statcan.ca. Statistics Canada information is used with the permission of Statistics Canada.

Once we recognize that nominal incomes and prices don't all increase at the same rate, it makes no sense to say that "inflation hurts everybody." *If prices are rising, incomes must be rising too.* In fact, on *average,* incomes rise just as fast as prices (see Figure 6.1). That fact is of little comfort, however, to those who end up losing real income in the inflation game.

Still more winners and losers of the inflation game are selected on the basis of the assets they hold. Suppose you deposit $100 in a savings account on January 1, where it earns 5 percent interest. At the end of the year you'll have more nominal wealth ($105) than you started with ($100). But what if all prices have doubled in the meantime? In that case, your $105 will buy you no more at the end of the year than $52.50 would have bought you at the beginning. Inflation in this case reduces the *real* value of your savings, and you end up worse off than those individuals who spent all their income earlier in the year!

Wealth Effects

By altering relative prices, incomes, and the real value of wealth, inflation turns out to be a mechanism for redistributing income and wealth. *The redistributive mechanics of inflation include:*

Redistributions

- *Price effects.* People who prefer goods and services that are increasing in price the fastest end up with fewer goods and services.
- *Income effects.* People whose nominal incomes rise more slowly than the rate of inflation end up with fewer goods and services.
- *Wealth effects.* People who own assets that are declining in real value end up with less real wealth.

On the other hand, people whose nominal incomes increase faster than inflation end up with larger shares of total output. The same thing is true of those who enjoy goods that are rising slowest in price or who hold assets whose real value is increasing. In this sense, *inflation acts just like a tax, taking income or wealth from one group and giving it to another.* But we have no assurance that this particular tax will behave like Robin Hood, taking from the rich and giving to the poor. In reality, inflation often redistributes income in the opposite direction.

Demand for Corn Pushes Mexico to Keep Cap on Tortilla Prices

Mexico's government will renew a deal to cap prices of the food staple tortilla to control inflation and placate angry consumers, Agriculture Minister Alberto Cardenas said. Prices for corn, the main ingredient in tortillas, surged in December and January to their highest in a decade because of increased demand for corn from U.S. ethanol fuel producers. A deal with producers and retailers in January to limit corn flour and tortilla prices helped stymie an inflation spike but was set to expire on April 30. Mexico imports millions of tonnes of U.S. corn every year. Corn flour producers agreed in January tonnes limit the price of their product to 5 pesos per kilo.

Source: "Demand for corn pushes Mexico to keep cap on tortilla prices," *National Post* (April 26, 2007), p. FP4.

Analysis: The redistributive effects of inflation can cause a political backlash. No one wants to pay higher prices or fear the uncertainty of potentially higher prices.

Social Tensions

Because of its redistributive effects, inflation also increases social and economic tensions. Tensions—between labour and management, between government and the people, and among consumers—may overwhelm a society and its institutions. As Gardner Ackley of the University of Michigan observed, "A significant real cost of inflation is what it does to morale, to social coherence, and to people's attitudes toward each other." "This society," added Arthur Okun, "is built on implicit and explicit contracts. . . . They are linked to the idea that the dollar means something. If you cannot depend on the value of the dollar, this system is undermined. People will constantly feel they've been fooled and cheated."[2] This is how the middle class felt in Germany in 1923 and in China in 1948, when the value of their savings was wiped out by sudden and unanticipated inflation. A surge in prices also stirred social and political tensions in Russia as it moved from a price-controlled economy to a market-driven economy in the 1990s. A similar political backlash occurred in Mexico in 1999 when tortilla prices jumped (see World View). On a more personal level, psychotherapists report that "inflation stress" leads to more frequent marital spats, pessimism, diminished self-confidence, and even sexual insecurity. Some people turn to crime as a way of solving the problem.

Money Illusion

money illusion: The use of nominal dollars rather than real dollars to gauge changes in one's income or wealth.

Even those people whose nominal incomes keep up with inflation often feel oppressed by rising prices. People feel that they *deserve* any increases in wages they receive. When they later discover that their higher (nominal) wages don't buy any additional goods, they feel cheated. They feel worse off, even though they haven't suffered any actual loss of real income. This phenomenon is called **money illusion.** People suffering from money illusion are forever reminding us that they used to pay only $5 to see a movie or $20 for a textbook. What they forget is that nominal incomes were also a lot lower in the "good old days" than they are today.

6.3 MACRO CONSEQUENCES

Although redistributions of income and wealth are the primary consequences of inflation, inflation has *macroeconomic* effects as well. Inflation can alter the rate and mix of output by changing consumption, work, saving, investment, and trade behaviour.

[2]Quoted in *BusinessWeek,* May 22, 1978, p. 118.

One of the most immediate consequences of inflation is uncertainty. When the average price level is changing significantly in either direction, economic decisions become more difficult. As the accompanying cartoon suggests, even something as simple as ordering a restaurant meal is more difficult if menu prices are changing (as they did during Germany's 1923 runaway inflation). Longer-term decisions are even more difficult. Should you commit yourself to college or university, for example, if you aren't certain that you or your parents will be able to afford the full costs? In a period of stable prices you can be fairly certain of what an education will cost. But if prices are rising, you can no longer be sure how large the bill will be. Under such circumstances, some individuals may decide not to enter school rather than risk the possibility of being driven out later by rising costs.

Price uncertainties affect production decisions as well. Imagine a firm that wants to build a new factory. Typically, the construction of a factory takes two years or more, including planning, site selection, and actual construction. If construction costs change rapidly, the firm may find that it's unable to complete the factory or to operate it profitably. Confronted with this added uncertainty, the firm may decide not to build a new plant. This deprives the economy of new investment and expanded production possibilities.

Inflation threatens not only to reduce the level of economic activity but to change its very nature. If you really expect prices to rise, it makes sense to buy goods and resources now for resale later. If prices rise fast enough, you can make a handsome profit. These are the kinds of thoughts that motivate people to buy houses, precious metals, commodities, and other assets. But such speculation, if carried too far, can detract from the production process. If speculative profits become too easy, few people will engage in production; instead, everyone will be buying and selling existing goods. People may even be encouraged to withhold resources from the production process, hoping to sell them later at higher prices. Such speculation may fuel **hyperinflation,** as spending accelerates and production declines. This happened in Germany in the 1920s, China in 1948–1949, and in Russia in the early 1990s. Russian prices rose by 200 percent in 1991 and by another 1,000 percent in 1992. These price increases rendered the Russian ruble nearly worthless. No one wanted to hold rubles or trade for them. Farmers preferred to hold potatoes rather than sell them. Producers of shoes and clothes likewise decided to hold rather than sell their products. The resulting contraction in supply caused a severe decline in Russian output.

Uncertainty

WEB NOTE

To see the what a basket of goods and services costing $100 the year you were born would cost today, go to http://www.bankofcanada.ca/en/rates/inflation_calc.html. To see the impact of inflation on savings, go to http://www.bankofcanada.ca/en/rates/investment.html.

Speculation

hyperinflation: Formally defined as an inflation rate of 50 percent per month or more—nearly 1300 percent per year—but more commonly used to describe rates of 200 percent per year or greater.

" DO I HAVE YOUR ASSURANCE THAT PRICES WILL NOT BE INCREASED BEFORE WE ARE SERVED ? "

From *The Wall Street Journal*. Permission, Cartoon Features Syndicate.

Analysis: The uncertainty caused by rising prices causes stress and may alter consumption and investment decisions.

Bracket Creep

bracket creep: The movement of taxpayers into higher tax brackets (rates) as nominal incomes grow.

Another reason that savings, investment, and work effort decline when prices rise is that taxes go up, too. Federal income tax rates are *progressive;* that is, tax rates are higher for larger incomes. The intent of these progressive rates is to redistribute income from rich to poor. However, inflation tends to increase *everyone's* income. In the process, people are pushed into higher tax brackets and confront higher tax rates. The process is referred to as **bracket creep.** In recent years, bracket creep has been limited by the inflation indexing of personal income tax rates and a reduction in the number of tax brackets.

When rates of inflation become perceived as "too high" government may try and lessen the impact of "bracket creep" by indexing the brackets themselves. That is, based on the annual rate of inflation, the brackets are adjusted. Similar indexing may also be used to protect fixed income sources, such as government pensions, from diminished purchasing power by increasing nominal income at the rate of average inflation.

In the 1970s and 1980s, many union contracts included another kind of protection from inflation. These were referred to as COLA clauses, or *cost-of-living adjustment clauses*. The clauses generally operated by increasing wages by some amount based on the difference between the CPI rate of inflation and a pre-negotiated threshold of between 1 and 3 percent. So if the CPI rate of inflation was 9 percent and the threshold 2 percent, the contract would adjust wages by 7 percent to increase the real purchasing power of the workers. Since the early 1990s, with the rate of inflation being less than 3 percent, such clauses have become less common.

Although the public sector still reaps some gain from inflation, inflation stress tends to create a political backlash. Voters are quick to blame the government for inflation. If the government doesn't put a stop to inflation, the voters will turn to someone who promises to do so.

Deflation Dangers

Ironically, a *falling* price level—a deflation—might not make people happy either. In fact, a falling price level can do the same kind of harm as a rising price level. When prices are falling, people on fixed incomes and long-term contracts gain more *real* income. Lenders win and creditors lose. People who hold cash or bonds win: Home-owners and stamp collectors lose. A deflation simply reverses the kinds of redistributions caused by inflation.

A falling price level also has similar macro consequences. Time horizons get shorter. Businesses are more reluctant to borrow money or to invest. People lose confidence in themselves and public institutions when declining price levels deflate their incomes and assets.

6.4 MEASURING INFLATION

In view of the macro and micro consequences of price-level changes, the measurement of inflation serves two purposes: to gauge the average rate of inflation and to identify its principal victims.

Consumer Price Index

consumer price index (CPI): A measure (index) of changes in the average price of consumer goods and services.

inflation rate: The annual percentage rate of increase in the average price level.

The most common measure of inflation is the **consumer price index (CPI).** As its name suggests, the CPI is a mechanism for measuring changes in the average price of consumer goods and services. It's analogous to the fruit price index we discussed earlier. The CPI doesn't refer to the price of any particular good but to the average price of all consumer goods.

By itself, the "average price" of consumer goods isn't a very useful number. But once we know the average price of consumer goods, we can observe whether that average rises—that is, whether inflation is occurring. By observing the extent to which prices increase, we can calculate the **inflation rate.**

We can get a better sense of how inflation is measured by observing how the CPI is constructed. The process begins by identifying a market basket of goods and services the typical consumer buys. The set of consumer goods and services that make

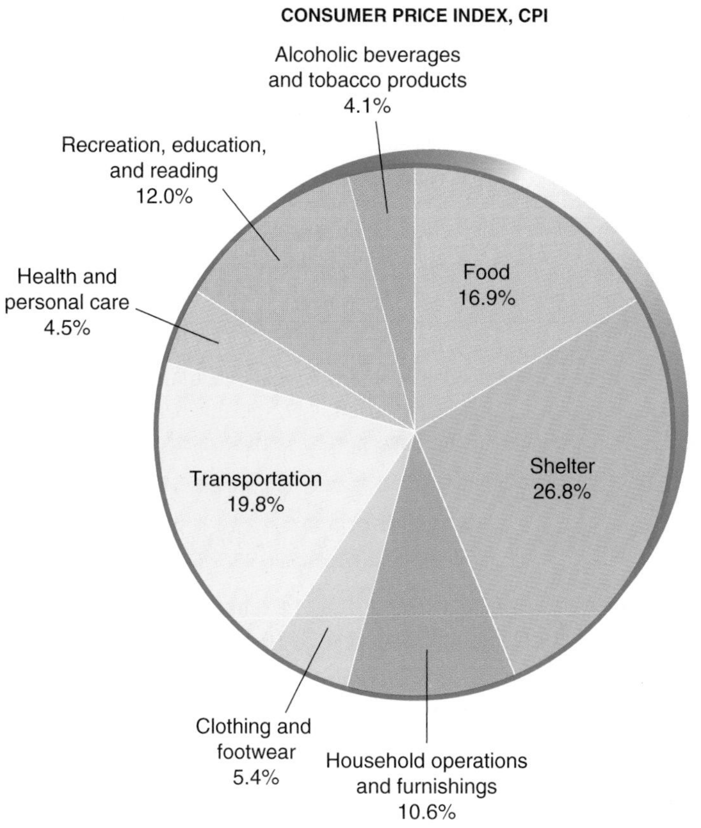

CONSUMER PRICE INDEX, CPI

FIGURE 6.2
Major Component Weights for the CPI

Figure 6.2 provides the weights of each major component that makes up the consumer price index (CPI) and is representative of the average Canadian consumer.

Source: Adapted from Statistics Canada publication *The Consumer Price Index*, Catalogue 62-001, (June 2006), http://www.statcan.ca/english/freepub/62-001-XIB2006006.pdf. Statistics Canada information is used with the permission of Statistics Canada.

up this basket is determined by Statistics Canada and updated based on the expenditures of Canadians during a specific period. Currently, the commodities in the basket reflect expenditures for 2001. As well as reviewing the commodities themselves, Statistics Canada also reviews the weights that each major component is given in the overall index. Figure 6.2 illustrates the weights given to the 2001 basket as of July, 2004. Note that out of each consumer dollar spent, on average, 16.9 cents is spent on food while 19.8 cents is spent on transportation. Only 12 cents is spent on recreation, education, and reading.

Each of these major components are themselves made up of many commodities. Recreation, education, and reading includes individual commodities that relate to, well, recreation, education, and reading, such as traveller accommodation as part of recreation, tuition as part of education, and newspapers as part of reading.

Once we know what the typical consumer buys, it's relatively easy to calculate the average price of a market basket. Statistics Canada employees go shopping in cities and towns across the country. During the first three weeks of each month interviewers collect some 60,000 prices from sellers as diverse as supermarkets, dental offices, and gas stations. As we noted with the Labour Force Survey in the previous chapter, data is collected in each province and census metropolitan area so that a consumer price index can be calculated for these as well as for Canada as a whole. For example, while the CPI determined the April, 2007 annual rate of inflation for Canada as +2.2 percent, Statistics Canada also reported that Alberta consumers experienced inflation of +5.5 percent while those living in New Brunswick only experienced inflation of +1.4 percent.

As a result of these massive, ongoing surveys, Statistics Canada can tell us what's happening to consumer prices. Suppose, for example, that the market basket cost $100 last year and that the same basket of goods and services cost $110 this year. On the basis of those two shopping trips, we could conclude that consumer prices had risen by 10 percent in one year.

WEB NOTE

On the Statistics Canada homepage, http://www.statcan.ca/start.html, you can find the CPI for the most recent month.

TABLE 6.3
Impact of Major Components on the CPI

Item	Item Weight	×	Percent Price Increase for the Item	=	Impact on the CPI
Education	0.120		0.10%		0.0120%
Shelter	0.189		3.70%		0.6993%

Source: Statistics Canada publications *The Consumer Price Index*, Catalogue 62-001-XIB, http://www.statcan.ca/english/freepub/63-224-XIB/0000563-224-XIB.pdf and *The Market Research Handbook—2005*. Statistics Canada information is used with the permission of Statistics Canada.

In practice, the CPI is usually expressed in terms of what the market basket cost in a specific *base period.* Statistics Canada has used 1992 as the base period since January, 1998. The price of the basket in the base period is then used to construct an index number series based on 100:

$$\text{Index number} = \frac{\text{Current basket price}}{\text{Base year basket price}} \times 100$$

In June 2006 the CPI was determined to be 130.6. In other words, a basket of commodities that cost $100 in 1992 would have cost $130.60 in June 2006. Since 1992, prices have inflated by an average 30.6 percent, or slightly less than 2 percent per year.

All price changes don't have the same impact on the inflation rate. Rather, ***the effect of a specific price change on the inflation rate depends on the product's relative importance in consumer budgets.***

The relative importance of a product in consumer budgets is reflected in its **item weight,** which refers to the percentage of a typical consumer budget spent on the item.

Table 6.3 shows the impact on the total CPI of two components of the basket, education and shelter. The table shows both the major component weights and the price increase for that component as determined by Statistics Canada for June 2006. Education has little impact on the overall CPI, just greater than one-tenth of one percent. This is because the recreation, education, and reading category is a smaller proportion of the average consumer's expenditure, and also because of the relatively small annual inflation for the category, 0.10 percent between June 2005 and June 2006. Shelter adds 0.7, or seven-tenths of one percent to the total CPI. Shelter, which includes all forms of housing, is both a greater proportion of the average expenditure and experienced a greater rate of inflation for the period.

Again, we can make the point that if a greater-than-average proportion of your expenditure was spent in recreation, education, and reading, you would have experienced a lower-than-average inflation rate. On the other hand, if more of your expenditure was spent to provide shelter, you would have experienced a higher-than-average inflation rate.

item weight: The percentage of total expenditure spent on a specific product; used to compute inflation indexes.

WEB NOTE

The importance of housing prices is emphasized in Steven Cecchetti's 'Inflation Updates' at http://people.brandeis.edu/~cecchett.

Measurement Problems

Like the Labour Force Survey, while the CPI is a useful and perhaps necessary measure to help us understand how our economy is changing, it is not a perfect measure. There are four particular issues that are of interest to us in relation to the CPI: (1) the fact that none of us is "average," (2) although the CPI basket is fixed, our expenditures each month are not, (3) goods are constantly adding new features and improving functionality, and (4) firms are constantly producing new goods that didn't exist before.

The fact that *none of us is average* has been a theme throughout this chapter, although you might not have noticed it. When we talked about the redistributive aspects of inflation, we suggested that each of us experiences inflation differently depending on the goods and services that we actually buy. If we aren't purchasing goods that have rising prices, then we won't experience that inflation.

APPLICATIONS

How the Inflation Rate Gets Inflated

The Bank of Canada doesn't think StatsCan is doing anything wrong in measuring the price of consumer goods and services. It's just that all inflation measures probably overstate inflation; in Canada, the error is about half a percentage point, maybe more.

This seems to be an odd turn of events for one of the most widely quoted and widely used economic indicators. If the official rates are wrong, the effect shows up in the cheques received by pensioners whose benefits are raised to offset price increases and workers whose collective agreements call for inflation-linked wage increases.

The result of these measurement issues is that the CPI is biased upward, meaning that the rate of inflation actually experienced on average by Canadians may be lower than the official rate calculated by Statistics Canada. That may sound minor, but over a decade, it means the inflation rate is about five percentage points higher than the official numbers suggest. So those getting pensions or wages linked to the official CPI might be getting more than they should be.

The error might also show up in calculations of real incomes per person, which climbed sharply in the 1980s and have fallen in the 1990s. The CPI inflation rate is often used to deflate income figures—so they can be reported in constant dollars. If it's overstated, then the rise and fall of Canadians' incomes was less pronounced than reported.

Source: Bruce Little, "How the inflation rate gets inflated," *The Globe and Mail* (June 8, 1998) p. A7. Reprinted with permission from *The Globe and Mail*.

Analysis: The CPI is often thought to overstate inflation in the economy due to the introduction of new goods and changes in product quality. The CPI may overstate the inflation experience of individuals due to averages and substitution biases.

Although the CPI is calculated with a fixed basket of goods and services, our expenditures are generally decided on when we face the choice of goods. While we may have bought apples last month, this month's low orange prices may sway our decision. In other words, as consumers, *we are free to substitute* one good for another each month, and often do, opting for the relatively cheapest good.

Even when a good appears the same from month-to-month, it may not actually be the same. Older products become better as a result of *quality improvements*. A plasma TV set costs more today than a TV did in 1955, but today's television also delivers a bigger, clearer picture, in digital sound, and with a host of on-screen programming options. Hence, increases in the price of TV sets tend to exaggerate the true rate of inflation; at least some of the higher price represents more product.

Statistics Canada does recognize that the quality of goods change and does attempt to adjust the prices collected to account for any difference in the price due to the new feature or quality. However, as Statistics Canada explains, "the problems encountered in adjusting prices for quality changes are complex and sometimes impossible to solve in a fully satisfactory manner. This is especially true in evaluation the quality change in services."[3]

Finally, firms are constantly producing *new products* entirely. Digital cameras, camera-equipped cellular phones, Blackberrys©, and MP3 players didn't exist a decade ago. And who knows what is coming along in the future to make these cutting-edge products look old-fashioned and become unfashionable!

Statistics Canada periodically reviews the make-up of the basket to keep the CPI relevant. The current basket is based on expenditures from 2001.

The result of these measurement issues is that the CPI estimate may be biased upward—meaning that the rate of inflation experienced on average by Canadians may be lower than that calculated by Statistics Canada. How much lower the "real" inflation

[3] *Your Guide to the Consumer Price Index,* (Statistics Canada, 1996), Catalogue no. 62-557-XPB, p. 7.

rate is, is an important question—but one without a clear answer. However, some estimates have suggested that the "real" rate of inflation may be from ½ to 1 percent lower than the CPI reports.

So far, we have tried to explain what the CPI is. Before we leave this section, however, we also need to explain what it is not. The CPI is a measure of *pure price movements*. That is, the CPI measures the change of price in a "fixed basket of . . . commodities of unchanging or equivalent quantity and quality."[4] The CPI *is not* a *cost-of-living index*. A cost-of-living index would be one that measures the price of maintaining a constant *standard of living* that may include consumers substituting one good for another without reducing their standard of living.

Other Price Indexes

In addition to the familiar consumer price index, there are a number of other price change measures. Some of these other measures focus on producer inputs, such as the raw materials price indexes, or on producer output, such as the industrial product price indexes. Some focus on agriculture, such as the farm input price indexes and farm product price indexes, or on construction, for example the new housing price indexes and the non-residential building construction price indexes. The purpose of approaching prices from different perspectives, as explained by Statistics Canada, is that "depending on the circumstances, it might be more useful to examine the price of gasoline at the gas pump (CPI), the price of gasoline as it leaves the refinery (industrial product price index), or world crude oil prices (raw materials price index)."[5]

Over long periods of time, all these indexes generally reflect the same rate of inflation. In the short run, however, the producer and raw material indexes usually increase before the CPI, because it takes time for raw material and producers' price changes to be reflected in the prices that consumers pay. For this reason, these indexes are watched closely as a *leading indicator* of consumer prices.

The GDP Deflator

> **GDP deflator:** A price index that refers to all goods and services included in GDP.

The broadest price index is the GDP deflator. The GDP deflator covers all output, including consumer goods, investment goods, and government services. Unlike the CPI and other indexes, the **GDP deflator** isn't based on a fixed "basket" of goods or services. Rather, it allows the contents of the basket to change with people's consumption and investment patterns. The GDP deflator therefore isn't a pure measure of price change. Its value reflects both price changes and market responses to those price changes, as reflected in new expenditure patterns. Hence, the GDP deflator typically registers a lower inflation rate than the CPI.

Real vs. Nominal GDP. The GDP deflator is used to adjust nominal output values for changing price levels. Recall that *nominal GDP* refers to the *current*-dollar value of output, whereas *real GDP* denotes the *inflation-adjusted* value of output. These two measures of output are connected by the GDP deflator:

$$\text{Real GDP} = \frac{\text{nominal GDP}}{\text{GDP deflator}} \times 100$$

The nominal values of GDP were $1,371.4 billion in 2005 and $882.7 billion in 1997. At first blush, this would suggest that output (real goods and services) had increased by 55 percent. However, over this same period the price level rose by 18.5 percent. Hence, real GDP in 2005, in the base period prices of 1997 was:

$$\frac{\text{2005 real GDP}}{\text{(in 1997 prices)}} = \frac{\text{Nominal GDP}}{\text{Price deflator}} = \frac{\$1,371.4 \text{ billion}}{1.1846} = \$1,157.7 \text{ billion}$$

---

[4]*Your Guide to the Consumer Price Index,* (Statistics Canada, 1996), Catalogue no. 62-557-XPB, p. 1.
[5]*Your Guide to the Consumer Price Index,* (Statistics Canada, 1996), Catalogue no. 62-557-XPB, p. 2.

In reality, then, output (real goods and services) increased by only 31 percent from 1997 to 2005. Changes in real GDP are a good measure of how output and living standards are changing. Nominal GDP statistics, by contrast, mix up output (real goods and services) increases with price changes (inflation).

6.5 THE GOAL: PRICE STABILITY

While there is a great deal of discussion about the real cost of inflation, and whether the appropriate inflation target might be 2 percent or 0 percent, **price stability** has become the major goal of monetary policy in Canada and many other countries. As we observed at the beginning of this chapter, rising rates of inflation through the 1970s resulted in Prime Minister Pierre Trudeau bringing in the Anti-Inflation Act in 1975 that instituted wage and price controls. Although the Act was phased out in 1978, inflation had become, along with full employment, an important policy consideration for the federal government.

price stability: The absence of significant changes in the average price level; officially defined as a rate of inflation of approximately 2 percent.

A Numerical Goal

In 1991, the federal government and the Bank of Canada (which controls monetary policy) increased the focus on inflation and adopted specific numerical goals for the Canadian rate of inflation. They began by aiming to reduce inflation from the then-actual rate of 6 percent per year to a target of 3 percent per year. They then went further, to 2 percent, as the mid-point of a 1 to 3 percent range. David Dodge, the Governor of the Bank of Canada explained this focus:

> By the early 1990s, the Bank decided to achieve price stability by directly targeting inflation. That inflation-targeting system worked so well that it has been renewed four times, more recently near the end of last year [2006]. This means that we will continue with our goal of holding inflation to 2 percent . . . over the coming five years.[6]

Unemployment Concerns

Why did the federal government and the Bank of Canada agree on 2 percent within a 1–3 percent range for inflation rather than zero inflation as the benchmark for price stability? One reason was concern about unemployment. To keep prices from rising, the government might have to restrain spending in the economy. Such restraint could lead to cutbacks in production and an increase in joblessness. In other words, there might be a trade-off between declining inflation and rising unemployment. From this perspective, a little bit of inflation might be the "price" the economy has to pay to keep unemployment rates from rising.

Recall how the same kind of logic was used to define the goal of full employment. The fear there was that price pressures would increase as the economy approached its production possibilities. This suggested that some unemployment might be the "price" the economy has to pay for price stability. Accordingly, the goal of "full employment" was defined as the lowest rate of unemployment *consistent with stable prices*. The same kind of thinking is apparent here. The amount of inflation regarded as tolerable depends in part on the effect of anti-inflation strategies on unemployment rates.

Full Employment

In Chapter 5 we explained that full employment didn't mean that there was no unemployment; an economy could be considered fully employed even if, as in Canada's case, it experienced approximately 5 percent unemployment. Knowing what we now know about inflation, we can add a little more here to that discussion.

Once an economy is operating at its "natural rate," or on the economy's production possibilities curve, it becomes increasingly difficult to hire more workers at current

[6]David Dodge, (2007, March 8) as cited in the *Monetary Policy Report,* April 2007, p. 2.

wage rates since everyone who wants to work already has a job. Firms, therefore, attract more workers by "bidding up" the price of labour, that is, offering higher wages. Higher wages means higher costs for firms and they recover these higher costs by raising the prices of their goods or services. That's inflation.

So, the level of unemployment can not only be determined as "natural" in the context of the rate of unemployment, it can also be thought of in the context of adding inflationary pressure to the economy. The rate of unemployment that is consistent with price stability is referred to as the **non-accelerating inflation rate of unemployment (NAIRU).** That is, there is a sufficient pool of willing-yet-unemployed workers such that firms can easily increase their workforce at current wage rates. This would be the rate of unemployment that enabled firms to hire workers as needed without having to offer higher wages.

non-accelerating inflation rate of unemployment (NAIRU):
A rate of unemployment that is consistent with price stability (an inflation rate of zero).

WEB NOTE

For a more detailed explanation of the natural rate of unemployment and the non-accelerating inflation rate of unemployment, and their technical differences, check out Wikipedia at http://en.wikipedia.org/wiki/Differences_between_the_Natural_Rate_of_Unemployment_and_the_NAIRU.

6.6 THE HISTORICAL RECORD

Over the past century, Canada's record on inflation is pretty good. Certainly when we compare the experiences of Germany and Hungary in the 1920s and 1940s, or the experience of Zimbabwe today, Canada's annual rate of inflation has been low. That is not to say that we haven't had periods of relatively high inflation (for Canada), or even periods of deflation.

Figure 6.3 provides a snapshot of the Canadian experience since 1915 as measured by the consumer price index. In 1917, the rate of inflation in Canada was 19 percent, but in 1921, the economy suffered a deflation of almost 12 percent. In fact, by 1939, the price level was the same has it had been in 1917.

More recently, we can see the build-up of inflation through the 1970s and the impact of the Anti-Inflation Act and then the period of recurring economic recessions from the early 1980s until the early 1990s. Since 1991, and the policy focus on price stability, the rate of inflation has been almost always within the Bank of Canada's 1–3 percent range.

As the accompanying World View documents, the low rate of inflation Canada has experienced is far below the pace in other nations. In 2005, for example, the inflation rate in Canada was lower than in Europe and incomprehensibly low for Zimbabweans, who saw their prices rise 237.8 percent.

FIGURE 6.3
Annual CPI Inflation Rates: 1915–2005

Source: Adapted from Statistics Canada CANSIM database table 326-0002, http://cansim2.statcan.ca. Statistics Canada information is used with the permission of Statistics Canada.

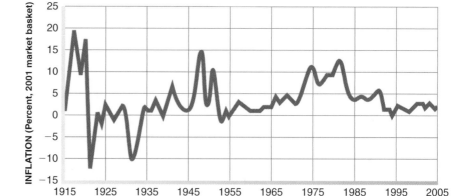

Inflation in Canada (Based on 2001 Market Basket)

Worldwide Inflation

Country	Inflation Rate	Country	Inflation Rate
Zimbabwe	237.8	Germany	1.9
Angola	23.0	Japan	−0.3
Venezuela	15.9	Russia	12.6
Canada	2.2	United Kingdom	2.1
United States	3.4		

Source: International Monetary Fund, *World Economic Outlook,* 2006. www.imf.org

Analysis: Although inflation is regarded as a major macro problem in Canada, inflation rates are comparatively low. Many developing countries have extraordinarily fast price increases.

6.7 CAUSES OF INFLATION

The evident variation in year-to-year inflation rates requires explanation. So do the horrifying bouts of hyperinflation that have erupted in other nations at various times. What causes price levels to rise or fall?

In the most general terms, this is an easy question to answer. Recall that all market transactions entail two converging forces, namely, *demand* and *supply.* Accordingly, any explanation of changing price levels must be rooted in one of these two market forces.

In fact, while supply and demand provide the negotiation that results in higher or lower prices, the amount of money in the economy matters as well. Consider yourself playing a game of Monopoly© and wanting to buy one of the railroads from another player. While you want to get it for the lowest possible price (you're a consumer after all), the highest price you can pay depends on the money (or other money-based assets) that you have. Pass go, collect $200 dollars, and your bid can be $200 higher.

So, inflation is determined in the supply and demand transaction, but is also a function of the amount of money available to the economy. Many economists describe inflation as a monetary phenomenon. This is the monetary economy that we will be dealing with in Part IV. Here, in this chapter, we'll only look at the pressure on inflation arising from first the demand side and then from the supply side.

Excessive pressure on the demand side of the economy is often the cause of inflation. Suppose the economy was already producing at capacity but that consumers were willing and able to buy even more goods. With accumulated savings or easy access to credit, consumers could end up trying to buy more output than the economy was producing. This would be a classic case of "too much money chasing too few goods." As consumers sought to acquire more goods, store shelves (inventory) would begin to empty. Seeing this, producers would begin raising prices. The end result would be a demand-driven rise in average prices, or demand-pull inflation.

Demand-Pull Inflation

Cost-Push Inflation

The pressure on prices could also originate on the supply side. For instance, the price of oil was approximately $20 ($US) a barrel in early 2002. By May, 2007, oil prices were $65 ($US) a barrel. When the price of oil rises, production costs increase in a broad array of industries. To cover these higher costs, producers raise output prices. When hurricane Katrina and others ripped through the Gulf of Mexico in 2005, oil production in the Gulf was reduced and oil refineries located on the coast were unable to operate. As market participants scurried for the remaining output, prices rose across the board. Political events can also have an impact. Strikes in Venezuela or political uncertainty in Nigeria—both significant oil producers—can cause prices to rise.

On the other hand, technological progress can reduce inflationary pressure or even result in reduced prices (deflation). Many economists have suggested that the technological revolution in the 1990s resulted in decreased unit costs (pushing the supply curve to the right) and translated into lower prices. As we saw in Table 6.2, falling prices of computers and video equipment reduced the overall inflation experienced by consumers. In the same way price reductions would also reduce production costs.

Inflationary pressure can also originate from higher wages. Labour shortages cause companies to compete for workers, resulting in wage increases. When the level of unemployment is below the non-accelerating inflation rate of unemployment, NAIRU, producers have a harder time finding and attracting workers at the current wage rate and may bid up prices to acquire labour services.

Inflationary expectations can also matter. If inflation is expected to be 5 percent, for example, then workers will require a 5 percent increase in wages just to keep their purchasing power the same. In this case, the negotiation of wage rates would include both the expected level of inflation as well as a "real" wage increase. Employers would then want to recover the expected inflation in higher prices, which simply makes the expected inflation real.

WEB NOTE

For current news stories on inflation, check out the Excite server money.excite.com/ht/nw/tbeconomy.html. Search for "inflation."

APPLICATIONS

Crude Rallies on Nigeria Unrest, Supply Concerns

Oil surged more than a dollar to more than $70 ($US) a barrel yesterday as unrest in Nigeria kept markets on edge for further supply disruptions ahead of the . . . summer gasoline season.

Unknown assailants broke into an unused Nigerian oil well operated by France's Total SA yesterday, causing a minor spill, a company spokesman said. There were no injuries nor any impact on oil output. Rising violence in Nigeria since February, 2006, has cut a third of the OPEC nation's oil output and forced thousands of expatriates to evacuate.

"The uncertainty over Nigeria oil production and the continuing worries over U.S. gasoline supply seem to be behind this latest rally on crude," said Phil Flynn, analyst at Alaron Trading in Chicago.

The inauguration of a new president in Nigeria could lead to more violence, which would drive up prices. The June crude contract on the New York Mercantile Exchange (NYMex) also expires this week, which could add to price action, and the U.S. federal government will release its updated hurricane outlook.

Source: Based on Matthew Robinson, "Crude rallies on Nigeria unrest, supply concerns," *The Globe and Mail* (May 22, 2007), p. B8.

Analysis: There are many factors at play in determining prices. As this news report indicates, there is seasonal pressure (summer driving season) as well as political unrest (as in Nigeria) and natural events (hurricanes). Each of these can result in inflationary pressure.

APPLICATIONS

The End of Inflation?

The earth spins, the sun shines, prices rise: two generations have grown up believing that inflation is an unalterable fact of life. No wonder. A dollar today is worth only 13 cents in 1945 money; a pound is worth only 6p. Much of the damage was done in the 1970s and early 1980s, and much has improved since then. In the OECD countries inflation is now hovering around its 1960s level of 3–4 percent. That gives governments the best chance they have had for decades to kill it off and achieve price stability. Sadly, they may fluff it.

Historical Stability

Price stability is not as extraordinary as it sounds. It does not mean that all prices stay the same: some will fall, others rise, but the average price level remains constant. Anyway, inflation, in the sense of continuously rising prices, is historically the exception, not the rule. On the eve of the first world war, prices in Britain were on average no higher than at the time of the fire of London in 1666. . . . During those 250 years, the longest unbroken run of rising prices was six years. Since 1946, by contrast, prices in Britain have risen every year, and the same is true of virtually every other OECD country.

It is easy to say that double-digit inflation is bad, but harder to agree on the ideal rate. Should governments aim for 5 percent, 3 percent, or 0 percent? Some claim that the extra benefits of zero inflation are tiny and would be outweighed by the short-term cost—lost output, lost jobs—of pushing inflation lower. A little bit of inflation, they say, acts like a lubricant, helping relative prices and wages to adjust more efficiently, since all wages and most prices are hard to cut in absolute terms. But a little inflation sounds like "a little drink" for an alcoholic. It can too easily accelerate. That is the lesson of the past 40 years—that and the fact that the economies with the lowest inflation have tended to be the ones with the least unemployment. Beyond the short term governments cannot choose to have a bit faster growth in exchange for a bit more inflation. The choice does not exist.

The Virtue of Zero

The rewards of reducing inflation from 5 percent to 0 percent may be smaller than those from crunching inflation from 5,000 percent to 5 percent, but they are still highly desirable. The best inflation rate is one that least affects the behaviour of companies, investors, shoppers and workers. That means zero, because anything higher interferes with the most fundamental function of prices—their ability to provide information about relative scarcities. If prices in general are rising by 5 percent a year, the fact that the price of one particular product rises by 8 percent goes largely unnoticed. Yet that product's relative 3 percent increase ought to attract the attention of potential new producers, and to encourage buyers to look elsewhere—in short, to set in train the changes that maximize economic efficiency. It would do that if the 3 percent rise was like a hillock in an otherwise flat landscape; but, in the mountains of generalized inflation, nobody notices a crag. Even with an annual inflation rate of 5 percent, the general price level doubles every 14 years, obscuring changes in relative prices.

Now imagine a world without inflation. Once it was believable, it would transform the way people behave. Companies would be confident about borrowing long-term money, and lenders confident about providing it. Real interest rates would fall. Firms would invest more because the probable pay-out would be clearer; the same would be true of individuals investing time and money on their education. Governments could budget for infrastructural projects, knowing that their plans would not be derailed by unexpected surges in prices. In general, everyone would think more about the long term because the long term would be easier to see.

Source: *The Economist*, January 22, 1992. © 1992 The Economist Newspaper Ltd. All Rights Reserved. Reprinted with permission. Further reproduction prohibited. www.economist.com.

Analysis: Given a policy of "price stability," zero inflation would seem the best level. That is, no inflation at all. In practical policy terms, however, the gains from the certainty of future prices have to be considered against the costs of potentially higher unemployment.

SUMMARY

- Inflation is an increase in the average price level. Typically it's measured by changes in a price index such as the consumer price index (CPI).
- At the micro level, inflation redistributes income by altering relative prices, income, and wealth. Because not all

prices rise at the same rate and because not all people buy (and sell) the same goods or hold the same assets, inflation doesn't affect everyone equally. Some individuals actually gain from inflation, whereas others suffer a loss of real income or wealth.

- At the macro level, inflation threatens to reduce total output because it increases uncertainties about the future and thereby inhibits consumption and production decisions. Fear of rising prices can also stimulate spending, forcing the government to take restraining action that threatens full employment. Rising prices also encourage speculation and hoarding, which detract from productive activity.
- Fully anticipated inflation reduces the anxieties and real losses associated with rising prices. However, few people can foresee actual price patterns or make all the necessary adjustments in their market activity.
- Inflation in Canada is measured for consumers through the consumer price index (CPI), a monthly measure in the change in the average price of consumer goods and services.
- The CPI is subject to "biases" that may cause the official rate of inflation to be overstated. These biases arise because none of us is "average," we are always free to substitute one good or service with another, and product quality improves while at the same time new products come to market.

- There are several other price indexes in addition to the CPI, such as producer, agricultural, and industrial indexes.
- The GDP deflator is the broadest economic measure of inflation, as it refers to all goods and services included in GDP.
- Since 1991, Canada has had an explicit policy for price stability; current Bank of Canada policy is to maintain the rate of inflation within a 1 to 3 percent range, with a midpoint of 2 percent per year.
- The non-accelerating inflation rate of unemployment (NAIRU) is the level of unemployment in an economy that is consistent with price stability.
- Inflation is caused by either excessive demand (demand-pull inflation) or structural changes in supply (cost-push inflation).
- Worldwide inflation rates have diminished in recent years. Experience with inflation and changing patterns of asset ownership are creating political pressure for greater price stability.

Key Terms

deflation 106
relative price 106
nominal income 108
real income 108
money illusion 110

hyperinflation 111
bracket creep 112
consumer price index (CPI) 112
inflation rate 112
item weight 114

GDP deflator 116
price stability 117
non-accelerating inflation rate of
   unemployment (NAIRU) 118

Questions for Discussion

1. Why would farmers rather store their output than sell it during periods of hyperinflation? How does this behaviour affect prices?
2. How might rapid inflation affect college and university enrollments?
3. Who gains and who loses from rising house prices?
4. If productivity—technological advance—is a good thing, why is deflation a concern? (And what is the connection between productivity and deflation?)
5. If *all* prices increased at the same rate (i.e., no *relative* price changes), would inflation have any redistributive effects?
6. Would it be advantageous to borrow money if you expected prices to rise? Would you want a fixed-rate loan or one with an adjustable interest rate?

7. Are people worse off when the price level rises as fast as their income? Why do people often feel worse off in such circumstances?
8. Identify two groups that benefit from deflation and two that lose.
9. Could demand-pull inflation occur before an economy was producing at capacity? How?
10. Go to http://www.statcan.ca/start.html and click on the Consumer Price Index link. Find the inflation rate for your province. Is the rate of inflation you actually experience likely to be greater or less than your provincial average? Why might your experience of inflation be different?

E X E R C I S E S

PROBLEMS The Student Problem Set to accompany this chapter can be found at the end of the book.

WEB ACTIVITIES Web Activities to accompany this chapter can be found on the Online Learning Centre at **http://www.mcgrawhill.ca/olc/schiller**.

CHAPTER 7

Growth and Productivity: Long-Run Possibilities

LEARNING OBJECTIVES

By the end of this chapter, you should be able to:

7.1 Differentiate between short-run changes in capacity utilization and long-run changes in capacity

7.2 Differentiate between labour productivity and multifactor productivity

7.3 Describe the sources of economic growth

7.4 Describe the evolution of theories of growth

7.5 Explain the role of policy and institutions in sustaining economic growth

> Mr. Speaker, of all the priorities I have mentioned today, the common denominator is prosperity. A better life for all Canadians is the highest priority for this government. To ensure our long-term prosperity, we need to increase our productivity.
>
> —The Honourable James M. Flaherty, P.C., M.P.,
> Minister of Finance—Federal Budget Speech, 2006

Imagine a world with no fax machines, no cellular phones, no satellite TV, and no digital sound. Such a world actually existed—and only 30 years ago! At the time, personal computers were still on the drawing board, and laptops weren't even envisioned. Web sites were a place where spiders gathered, not locations in the Internet. Home video hadn't been seen, and no one had yet popped any microwave popcorn. Biotechnology hadn't yet produced any blockbuster drugs, and people wore the same pair of athletic shoes for a wide variety of sports.

New products are evidence of economic progress. Over time, we produce not only *more* goods and services but also *new* and *better* goods and services. In the process, we get richer: Our material living standards rise.

Rising living standards aren't inevitable, however. According to World Bank estimates, in 2001, 1.1 billion people lived on $1 a day or less and 2.7 billion on $2 a day or less. Worse still, living standards in many of the poorest countries continue to fall, most particularly in areas such as sub-Saharan Africa, where economies have shrunk by 14 percent, but also in central Asia and eastern Europe, where economies are still in transition from communist rule to free markets. The news is better, however, in China, India, south Asia and the Pacific regions, where economic growth has lifted millions of people out of poverty.

This chapter takes a longer-term view of economic performance. Chapters 4, 5, and 6 were concerned with measuring the current economy and understanding where we are now in relation to where we might be given the economy's current production possibilities. In other words, these measures help us to see where we are in the business cycle (discussed back in Chapter 3) by comparing current conditions with the economy's potential—that is, short-run variations in output and prices. This chapter looks at the prospects for *long-run* growth and considers three questions:

- **How important is economic growth?**
- **How does an economy grow?**
- **Is continued economic growth possible? Is it desirable?**

We develop answers to these questions by first examining the nature of economic growth and then examining its sources and potential limits.

7.1 THE NATURE OF GROWTH

Economic growth refers to increases in the output of goods and services. But there are two distinct ways in which output increases, and they have very different implications for our economic welfare.

Short-Run Changes in Capacity Utilization

The easiest kind of growth comes from increased use of our productive capabilities. In any given year there's a limit to an economy's potential output. This limit is determined by the quantity of resources available and our technological know-how. We've illustrated these short-run limits with a *production possibilities* curve, as in Figure 7.1*a*. By using all our available resources and our best expertise, we can produce any combination of goods and services on the production possibilities curve.

We don't always take full advantage of our productive capacity. The economy often produces a mix of output that lies *inside* our production possibilities, like point *A* in Figure 7.1*a*. When this happens, a major *short-run* goal of macro policy is to achieve full employment—to move us from point *A* to some point on the production possibilities curve (such as point *B*). In the process, we produce more output.

Long-Run Changes in Capacity

Once we're fully utilizing our productive capacity, further increases in output are attainable only if we *expand* that capacity. To do so we have to *shift* the production possibilities curve outward as in Figure 7.1*b*. Such shifts imply an increase in *potential* GDP—that is, our productive capacity.

Over time, increases in capacity are critical. Short-run increases in the utilization of existing capacity can generate only modest increases in output. Even high unemployment rates, such as 9 percent, leave little room for increased output. ***To achieve large and lasting increases in output we must push our production possibilities outward.*** For this reason, economists often define *economic growth* in terms of changes in *potential* GDP.

The increase in productive capacity implies having more resources available to the economy or a greater "know-how" that increases the productivity of the available

FIGURE 7.1
Two Types of Growth

Increases in output may result from increased use of existing capacity or from increases in that capacity itself. In part *a* the mix of output at point *A* doesn't make full use of production possibilities. Hence, we can get more output by employing more of our available resources or using them more efficiently. This is illustrated by point *B* (or any other point on the curve).

Once we're on the production possibilities curve, we can get more output only by *increasing* our productive capacity. This is illustrated by the outward *shift* of the production possibilities curve in part *b*.

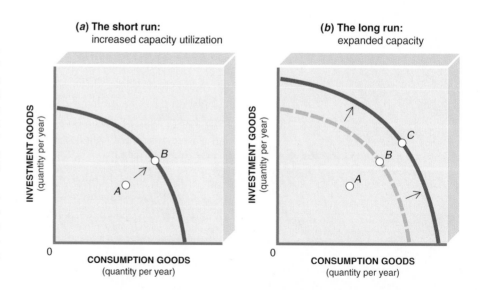

(a) The short run: increased capacity utilization

INVESTMENT GOODS (quantity per year)

CONSUMPTION GOODS (quantity per year)

(b) The long run: expanded capacity

INVESTMENT GOODS (quantity per year)

CONSUMPTION GOODS (quantity per year)

resources. The greater real economic potential means we can produce at point *C* in Figure 7.1*b* rather than point *B,* and as a society, we can consume a larger bundle of real goods and services without demand-side inflationary pressure.

Notice we refer to *real* GDP, not *nominal* GDP, in our concept of economic growth. Nominal GDP can rise even when the quantity of goods and services falls, as was the case in 1991. The total quantity of goods and services produced in 1991 was less than the quantity produced in 1990. Nevertheless, prices rose enough in 1991 to keep nominal GDP growing: Nominal GDP in 1990 was $679.9 billion, rising to $685.4 billion in 1991.

Real GDP refers to the actual quantity of goods and services produced. Real GDP avoids the distortion of inflation by adjusting for changing prices. By using 2002 prices as a *base period,* we observe that real GDP fell from $823.9 billion in 1990 to only $808.2 billion in 1991. Since then real GDP has increased more than 56 percent—an impressive growth achievement.

7.2 MEASURES OF GROWTH

Typically, changes in real GDP are expressed in percentage terms, as a growth *rate.* The **growth rate** is simply the change in real output between two periods divided by total output in the base period. The percentage decline in real output during 1991 was thus $15.7 billion ÷ $823.9, or about 1.9 percent. By contrast, real output grew in 1992 by approximately 1 percent. Notice that although more goods and services were produced in 1992 than had been in 1991, there were still fewer than in 1990!

Figure 7.2 illustrates the recent growth experience of the Canadian economy. In the 1960s, real GDP grew by an average of 5.5 percent per year. Economic growth

The Growth Rate

growth rate: Percentage change in real output from one period to another.

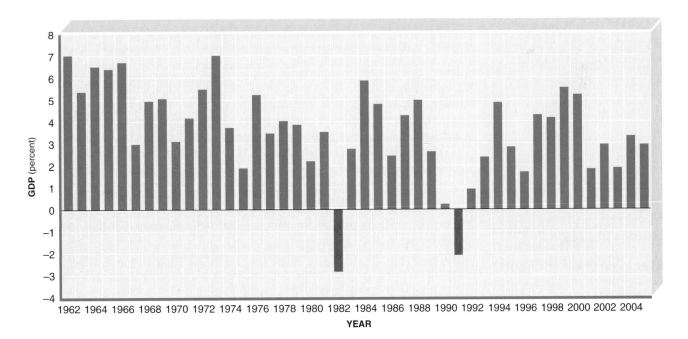

FIGURE 7.2
Real GDP Growth Rates for Canada, 1982–2005

Total output (GDP) typically increases from one year to another. The focus of policy is on the growth rate, that is, how fast real GDP increases from one year to the next. Annual growth rates since 1982 have ranged from a high of 5.68 percent (1984) to a low of minus 2.92 percent (1982). Notice also the recession of 1991 and the slowdown in 2001.

Source: Adapted from Statistics Canada CANSIM database table 380-0017, http://cansim2.statcan.ca. Statistics Canada information is used with the permission of Statistics Canada.

slowed to 4.3 percent in the 1970s, and with the 1982 recession, real GDP growth in the 1980s fell to an average 3.1 percent. The 1990s started out even worse, with negligible growth in 1990 and 1992, and a recession in 1991. The economy performed significantly better after that, however. From 1997 to 2000, real GDP grew by an average of almost 5 percent per year. That acceleration of the growth rate was so impressive that observers began to talk about a "new economy," in which faster growth would be the norm.

The notion of a fast-growth new economy was badly shaken in 2001. In the first quarter of 2001, GDP fell slightly, and although growth was positive for the remaining three quarters, overall growth for the year was only 1.78 percent. Since 2000, average real growth has remained at 2.6 percent, far less than the heady days of 5 percent per year real growth.

The Exponential Process. At first blush, all the anxiety about growth rates seems a bit overblown. Indeed, the whole subject of economic growth looks rather dull when you discover that "big" gains in economic growth are measured in fractions of a percent. However, this initial impression isn't fair. First, even one year's "low" growth implies lost output. If we had just *maintained* output in 1991 at its 1990 level—that is, "achieved" a *zero* growth rate rather than a 2 percent decline—we would have had $16 billion more worth of goods and services, which works out to over $560 worth of goods and services per person. Lots of people would have liked that extra output. In today's $1.4 trillion economy, each 1 percent of economic growth is even more significant.

Second, economic growth is a *continuing* process. Gains made in one year accumulate in future years. It's like interest you earn at the bank: If you leave your money in the bank for several years, you begin to earn interest on your interest. Eventually you accumulate a nice little bankroll.

The process of economic growth works the same way. Each little shift of the production possibilities curve broadens the base for future GDP. As shifts accumulate over many years, the economy's productive capacity is greatly expanded. Ultimately we discover that those "little" differences in annual growth rates generate tremendous gains in GDP.

This cumulative process, whereby interest or growth is compounded from one year to the next, is called an "exponential process." At growth rates of 2.5 percent, GDP doubles in 28 years. With 3.5 percent growth, GDP doubles in only 20 years. In a single generation the *difference* between 2.5 percent growth and 3.5 percent growth amounts to more than $400 billion of output a year. That difference is about 30 percent of 2005's total real GDP. From this longer-term perspective, the difference between 2.5 percent and 3.5 percent growth begins to look very meaningful.

GDP per Capita: A Measure of Living Standards

The exponential process looks even more meaningful when we translate it into *per capita* terms. We can do so by looking at GDP *per capita* rather than total GDP. *GDP per capita* is simply total output divided by total population. In 2005, the total real output (GDP) of Canada was $1,157.7 billion. Since there were approximately 32.3 million of us to share that output, GDP per capita was:

$$\text{GDP per capita} = \frac{\$1,157.7 \text{ billion}}{32.3 \text{ million people}} = \$35,842$$

This does not mean that every man, woman, and child in Canada actually received $35,842 worth of goods and services in 2005; it simply indicates how much output was potentially available to the "average" person. GDP per capita is often used as a basic measure of our standard of living.

Growth in GDP per capita is attained only when the growth of output exceeds population growth. In Canada, this condition is usually achieved. Even when *total* GDP growth slowed in the 1970s and 1980s, *per capita* GDP kept rising because the

WEB NOTE

Statistics Canada maintains both annual and quarterly data on real GDP at: http://www40.statcan.ca/l01/ind01/l3_3764_3012.htm?hili_none.

WEB NOTE

Find growth rates of various countries from the World Bank at www.worldbank.org/data. Click on "Data by Topic," then choose "Macroeconomics and Growth." Under "Economic Growth and Structure," click on "Growth of Output."

Net Growth Rate (%)	Doubling Time (years)
0.0%	Never
0.5	144
1.0	72
1.5	48
2.0	36
2.5	29
3.0	24
3.5	20
4.0	18

TABLE 7.1
The Rule of 72

Small differences in annual growth rates accumulate into large differences in GDP. Shown here are the number of years it would take to double GDP per capita at various net growth rates. *"Net" growth* refers to the GDP growth rate minus the population growth rate.

Doubling times can be approximated by the "rule of 72." Seventy-two divided by the growth rate equals the number of years it takes to double.

population was growing by only 1 percent a year. Hence, even relatively slow economic growth can be enough to keep raising living standards.

The developing nations of the Third World aren't so fortunate. Many of these countries bear both slower *economic* growth and faster *population* growth. They have a difficult time *maintaining* living standards, much less increasing them. Ethiopia, for example, is one of the poorest countries in the world, with GDP per capita of roughly $720. Yet its population continues to grow rapidly (2.6 percent per year), putting constant pressure on living standards. The population of Nigeria grew by an average of 2.8 percent per year in the 1990s, while GDP grew at a slower rate of only 2.4 percent. As a consequence, GDP per capita *declined* nearly 0.4 percent per year.

By comparison with these countries, Canada has been most fortunate. Our GDP per capita has more than doubled since 1980s, despite several recessions. This means that the average person today has twice as many goods and services as the average person had a generation ago.

What about the future? Will we continue to enjoy substantial gains in living standards? A 2003 poll revealed that 40 percent of adults believe their children's living standards will be no higher than today's. That would happen only if population growth outstrips or equals GDP growth. That seems most unlikely. Table 7.1 displays more optimistic scenarios in which GDP continues to grow faster than the population. If GDP *per capita* continues to grow at 1.6 percent per year—as it has between 2000 and 2005—it will take 45 years to double our standard of living. If GDP per capita grows just slightly faster at 2 percent per year, our standard of living will double in only 35 years.

The potential increase in living standards depicted in Table 7.1 won't occur automatically. Someone is going to have to produce more output if we want GDP per capita to rise. One reason our living standard rose in the 1980s is that the labour force grew faster than the population. Those in the World War II baby boom had reached maturity and were entering the labour force in droves. At the same time, more women took jobs outside the home, a trend that continued into the 1990s. As a consequence, the **employment rate** increased significantly, as Figure 7.3 shows. With the number of workers growing faster than the population, GDP per capita was sure to rise.

The employment rate can't increase forever. At the limit, everyone would be in the labour market, and no further workers could be found. Further increases in GDP per capita could only come from increases in output *per worker*.

The most common measure of **productivity** is output per labour-hour, which is simply the ratio of total output to the number of hours worked. As noted earlier, total

GDP per Worker: A Measure of Productivity

employment rate: The percentage of the eligible population 15 years and older that is employed.

productivity: Output per unit of input, for example, output per labour-hour.

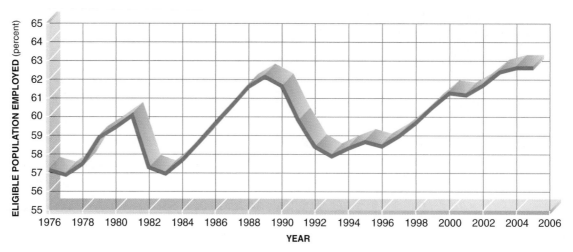

FIGURE 7.3
A Rising Employment Rate

The entry of the baby boom generation into the labour force beginning in the 1960s, and the increased labour-force attachment of women has caused the ratio of employed workers to the population eligible for the labour force (15-years of age and older) to rise. This has boosted per capita GDP.

Source: Adapted from Statistics Canada CANSIM database table 282-0002 http://cansim2.statcan.ca. Statistics Canada information is used with the permission of Statistics Canada.

WEB NOTE

Statistics Canada provides data on labour productivity regularly—search *The Daily* at http://www.statcan.ca/english/dai-quo/ for either "labour productivity" or "multifactor productivity."

GDP in 2005 was $1,157.7 billion. In that same year the labour force was employed for a total of 28.544 billion hours. Hence, the average worker's productivity was

$$\text{Labour productivity} = \frac{\text{total output}}{\text{total labour-hours}}$$

$$= \frac{\$1,157.7 \text{ billion}}{28.544 \text{ billion hours}}$$

$$= \$41 \text{ per hour}$$

The increase in our GDP per capita in recent decades is directly related to the higher productivity of the average Canadian worker. The average worker today produces 50 percent more goods and services as the average worker did in 1980. However, as the following Applications box makes clear, Canada can and should do better. In a comparison with the United States, Canada's productivity fell from 94.1 percent of that of the United States in 2000 to 89 percent in 2005.

A Brief History of Changes in Labour Productivity. For economic growth to continue, the productivity of the average Canadian worker must rise still further. Will it? The 1980s saw **labour productivity** rise at an annual average rate of 1.14 percent. The rate slowed through the early 1990s to an average of just 1 percent (1990–1996). This productivity slowdown constrained GDP growth.

After 1996, labour productivity accelerated sharply to slightly more than 2 percent per year on average. This productivity jump was so impressive that it raised hopes for a "new economy," fueled by information and communication technology advances, better management, and improved public policy that would keep both productivity and GDP growing at faster rates. This euphoria turned to concern, however, as productivity growth from 2002 to 2004 slumped to an average of 0.06 percent per year (Figure 7.4).

labour productivity: Amount of real output (real gross domestic product, GDP) per hour worked.

Multifactor Productivity. While a focus on labour productivity makes sense because its focus is us, economists recognize that an economy's productive potential depends not just on labour but on all resources available to that economy. Thus, we also have

APPLICATIONS

Standard-of-Living Gap with U.S. Closing: but StatsCan Report Shows Improvement Was Based Mainly on Hiring Binge

The main reason is that Canadian employers have been on a hiring binge, and more Canadians than ever are working. Unemployment levels are at 30-year lows, while the proportion of the population that is employed are at all-time highs. And that has increased the country's economic output substantially.

"We're doing well on employment. We've had these favourable shocks," agrees Andrew Sharpe, who heads the Centre for the Study of Living Standards, based in Ottawa. He pointed to rising commodity prices and rising terms-of-trade that have boosted corporate profits immensely over the past few years, leading to prolonged job creation. "But it's not going to last indefinitely," he added. "There's a sustainability issue."

That's where productivity comes in. Especially as Canada's population ages, the economy will become increasingly depen-

dent on productivity improvements to increase its standard-of-living and keep up with the United States, economists say.

The study shows that the productivity problem is bigger than ever. By StatsCan's measure, productivity in Canada was 94.1 percent of that of the United States in 2000, but had dropped to 89 percent in 2005. While the study does not include more recent data, other StatsCan reports show Canada's productivity has been slowly eroding since that time.

"Labour productivity growth is much higher in the United States than Canada since 2000 . . . We're losing ground in terms of productivity."

Source: Heather Scoffield, "Standard-of-living gap with U.S. closing," *The Globe and Mail* (March 27, 2007), p. B3. Reprinted with permission from *The Globe and Mail*.

Analysis: Canada's standard-of-living has been rising because of high commodity prices and high rates of employment. But in the long run, the only sustainable continuing increases in standard-of-living come from productivity gains. If commodity prices begin to fall and employment gains slow, Canada's standard-of-living will head in the opposite direction for all the same reasons.

a broader measure of overall productivity for the economy, called **multifactor productivity.** The measure of multifactor productivity takes total output (GDP) and divides it by all factors of production. The benefit of a multifactor productivity measure is to provide us with better insight into overall resource efficiency and technological change or "know-how."

> **multifactor productivity:** An estimate of real gross domestic product (GDP) per bundle of inputs—labour, capital, and intermediate inputs.

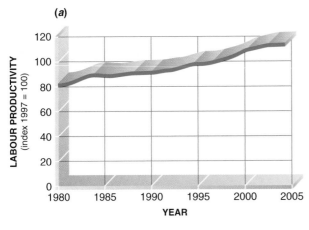

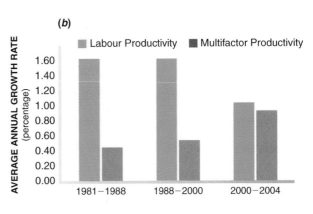

FIGURE 7.4
Productivity Gains in the Canadian Economy

(*a*) Increasing productivity (output per worker) is the critical factor in raising per capita real GDP over time. Figure 7.4*a* illustrates the increasing labour productivity over the 1981–2004 period. Although labour productivity has increased approximately 40 percent over this period, 1997–2002 provided much of this increase with the period after 2002 being relatively flat. (*b*) Figure 7.4*b* gives a comparison of labour productivity and multifactor

productivity—multifactor productivity measures the efficiency of all resources, or factors of production, within an economy.

Source: Adapted from Statistics Canada CANSIM database table 383-0016 and Statistics Canada publication *The Daily*, Catalogue 11-001, July 15, 2005, http://www.statcan.ca/Daily/English/050715/d050715a.htm. Statistics Canada information is used with the permission of Statistics Canada.

7.3 SOURCES OF GROWTH

The arithmetic of economic growth is simple, and has already been illustrated with the *production possibility curve, PPC*. Future real output growth depends on two factors:

$$\frac{\text{Growth rate of}}{\text{total real output}} = \frac{\text{Growth rate}}{\text{of resources}} + \frac{\text{Growth rate}}{\text{of technology}}$$

The growth rate of resources can be broken down into growth in the labour force and growth in capital investment. Accordingly, how fast real GDP increases in the future depends on how fast the labour force grows and the rate of growth in new capital.

We saw in Chapter 5 that the size of the labour force was related both to the size of the population and the participation rate. We also noted that increases in real GDP were aided by the population growth fuelled by the baby boom as well as increasing participation in the labour force by women. However, as the projections in Figure 7.5 show, future population growth is less certain. Depending upon the assumptions made, the Canadian population could begin to decline after 2039, or, even if it continues to grow, that growth could average less than 1 percent per year.

Capital investment expenditure has increased over the past four decades by an average of 3.8 percent per year—although not all of it was new capital, as some purchases replace capital worn out and no longer capable of producing goods or services.

If we cannot rely on sustained increases in economic resources, then future growth must be dependent on increases in technology or "know-how." We capture these gains as increases in productivity. To assess the potential for productivity gains, we need to examine the sources of productivity improvement. ***The sources of productivity gains include:***

- ***Higher skills***—an increase in the quality of labour skills.
- ***More capital***—an increase in the ratio of capital to labour that results in current labour being more productive.
- ***Technological advances***—the development and use of better capital equipment and products.

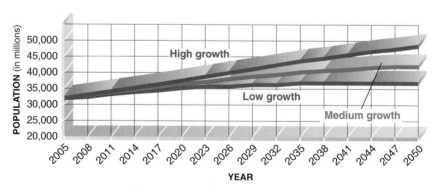

FIGURE 7.5

Population Projections 2005–2050

Each of these projections has been made based on different assumptions about such things as expected life span, birth and death rates, and the rate of immigration. The low growth assumptions have the population peaking in 2039 and declining thereafter. Each of the medium and high growth assumptions have population increasing over the entire term but at relatively low rates: 0.6 percent per year for the medium-growth assumptions and 0.9 percent per year for the high-growth assumptions.

Source: Adapted from Statistics Canada publication *Population Projections for Canada, Provinces and Territories, 2005–2031*, Catalogue 91-520, scenarios 1, 3, and 6. http://www.statcan.ca/english/freepub/91-520-XIE/00105/tablesectionlist.htm. Statistics Canada information is used with the permission of Statistics Canada.

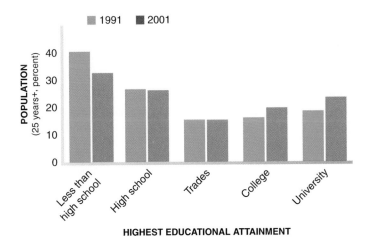

HIGHEST EDUCATIONAL ATTAINMENT

FIGURE 7.6
Highest Educational Attainment

The 1991 and 2001 censuses illustrate the changing educational landscape in Canada and the trend toward increases in educational attainment. Colleges and universities each showed significant increases over the decade.

Source: Adapted from Statistics Canada publication *Education in Canada: Raising the Standard, 2001 Census*, Catalogue 96F0030CXIE20011012. Statistics Canada information is used with the permission of Statistics Canada.

- *Improved management*—better use of available resources in the production process.
- *Improved institutions and institutional quality*—the development of more effective governance structures and policies.

Human-Capital Investment

Continuing advances in education and skills training have greatly increased the quality—the **human capital**—of Canadian labour (Figure 7.6). Between the 1991 and 2001 censuses, the proportion of the Canadian population with less than a high-school education fell from 37 percent of the population over 25-years of age to 29 percent. At the same time the proportion of the population completing trade, college, or university increased from slightly less than 40 percent to greater than 48 percent. There has also been a substantial increase in training by private firms, some even creating their own "universities."

> human capital: The knowledge and skills possessed by the workforce.

Physical-Capital Investment

The knowledge and skills a worker brings to the job don't completely determine his or her productivity. A worker with no tools, no computers, and no machinery won't produce much even if she has a PhD. Similarly, a worker with outmoded equipment won't produce as much as an equally capable worker equipped with the newest machines and the best technology. From this perspective, *a primary determinant of labour productivity is the rate of capital investment.* In other words, improvements in output per *worker* depend in large part on increases in the quantity and quality of *capital* equipment (see the World View box).

The efforts of the average Canadian worker are presently augmented with machinery and equipment worth over $47,000. This huge capital endowment is a prime source of high productivity. To increase productivity, however, the quality and quantity of capital available to the average worker must continue to increase. That requires capital spending to increase faster than the labour force. If the labour force grows at less than 1 percent a year, that's not a hard standard to beat. How much faster capital investment grows is nevertheless a decisive factor in productivity gains.

The 1970s and 1980s exhibited a slowdown in investment in non-residential capital—perhaps not surprising given the recessions occurring over this period. The 1990s, however, saw investment increase by approximately 3.2 percent per year compared with 2.4 percent through the 1980s. Since 2000, growth has actually been higher, at about 4.2 percent per year.

Saving and Investment Rates. The dependence of productivity gains on capital investment puts a new perspective on our choice of consumption or saving. In the short run, the primary concern is current consumption and providing current public services. From a longer-run perspective of economic growth, saving and investment

WORLD VIEW

Comparative Investment and Growth

Investment in new plant and equipment is essential for economic growth. In general, countries that allocate a larger share of output to investment will grow more rapidly. In the 1990s, China had the highest growth rate and one of the highest investment rates.

Country	Growth Rate of Gross Capital Formation (percent) (average, 1990–2000)	Growth Rate of GDP (average, 1990–2000)
Canada	4.5	3.1
China	11.2	10.6
Thailand	–4.0	4.2
Singapore	7.7	7.7
India	7.0	6.0
United States	7.4	3.5
Great Britain	4.6	2.7
South Africa	5.0	2.1

Source: World Bank.

Analysis: Investment increases production possibilities. Countries that devote a larger share of output to investment tend to grow faster.

take on added importance. Saving is a source of investment financing. If we use all our resources and know-how to produce consumer, export, and public sector goods, there wouldn't be anything left for investment. In that case, while we might satisfy short run goals and our productive capacity might be fully utilized, we would confront a long run growth problem. Indeed, if our entire output was consumption goods, our productive capacity would actually shrink since we wouldn't even be replacing worn-out plant and equipment. We must at least add some investment each year just to stay even, in which case our **net investment** would be zero.

net investment: Gross investment less depreciation.

Of course, this saving doesn't have to come from Canadian households. It could just as easily come from households in other countries who want to lend to Canadians to invest or to add or increase their own investment in the Canadian economy.

FIGURE 7.7
Saving and Investment

This figure illustrates the relationship between saving and investment in the economy. Gross saving as a proportion of GDP is practically the same as investment as a proportion of GDP.

Source: Adapted from Statistics Canada, CANSIM Table 380-0032, Saving, investment and net lending. Statistics Canada information is used with the permission of Statistics Canada.

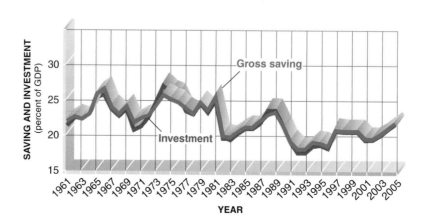

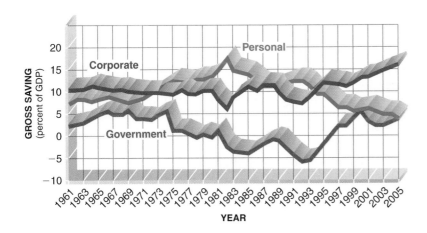

FIGURE 7.8
Gross Saving by Sector

Gross household saving has fallen from a peak in 1982 of 17 percent of GDP to less than 5 percent in 2005. Gross corporate saving has increased since the mid-1990s from an average of approximately 10 percent to almost 17 percent. Government saving has returned to about 5 percent after years of deficits.

Source: Statistics Canada CANSIM Table 380-0032, Saving, investment and net lending. Statistics Canada information is used with the permission of Statistics Canada.

Household and Business Saving. Household personal saving rates in Canada, according to Statistics Canada, have been declining since 1982 when Canadian households saved more than 20 percent of the income available to them. By 1990, the proportion had fallen to less than 13 percent, and by 2000 the rate of saving was less than 5 percent. The possibility exists for Canadian households to actually **dissave,** by spending more on consumption than their available disposable income. Despite the meagre flow of household saving, private investment growth actually accelerated beginning in the 1990s, doubling from $108 billion in 1994 to $223 billion in 2006. Virtually all of that investment was financed with *business saving* and *foreign investment*. The retained earnings and depreciation allowances that create business savings generated a huge cash flow for investment in the 1990s.

Figure 7.8 illustrates the changes in saving as a percentage of GDP for each of the household, corporate, and government sectors.

dissaving: Consumption expenditure in excess of disposable income; a negative saving flow.

Foreign Investment. In addition to this business-saving flow, foreign investors poured money into Canadian plant, equipment, software, and financial assets—Statistics Canada estimates that by the end of 2005, the market value of **foreign direct investment** into Canada was $771.3 billion. Canadians also provided investment for other countries as well; by the end of 2005, the market value of Canadian investment abroad was $808.3 billion.[1] These two income flows more than compensated for the low level of household saving. Many people worry, though, that foreign investments may get diverted elsewhere and that business saving will drop when profits diminish. Then continued investment growth will be more dependent on a flow of funds from household saving.

foreign direct investment: An investment in productive facilities from outside the country that results in ownership or control.

The accumulation of more and better capital equipment does not itself guarantee higher productivity or faster GDP growth. The human factor is still critical: How well resources are organized and managed will affect the rate of growth. Hence, entrepreneurship and the quality of continuing management are also major determinants of economic growth.

It's difficult to characterize differences in management techniques or to measure their effectiveness. However, much attention has been focused in recent years on the alleged shortsightedness of managers. The rumour is that firms focus too narrowly on short-term profits, neglecting long-term gains in productivity. They also emphasize quantity over quality of output. And they fail to include workers in key decisions, thus depriving themselves of important insights and goodwill. By contrast, firms in

Management Training

[1]Statistics Canada, "Latest developments in the Canadian economic accounts," May 24, 2006, Catalogue 13-605-XIE, http://www.statcan.ca/english/freepub/13-605-XIE/13-605-XIE2006002.htm, accessed August 30, 2006.

Japan and elsewhere concentrate on longer-term gains, quality control, and strong bonds between labour and management. As a consequence, Japanese firms enjoy remarkably good labour and customer relations, intense worker loyalty, and faster productivity gains.

If all these accusations about corporate management were true, the economy would surely be in a sorry state. At best, these contrasts between management practices serve as precautionary tales. The time horizons used for developing investment and production plans can affect long-run growth prospects. Management-labour relations can also materially affect productivity. Furthermore, management familiarity with *global* markets will affect a firm's ability to grow and prosper in both foreign and domestic markets. Corporations in the Canada spend millions of dollars on management training to help keep company executives up to speed on these and other determinants of long-run productivity. Such investments in managerial talent are an important source of economic growth.

Research and Development

A fourth and vital source of productivity advance is research and development (R&D), a broad concept that includes scientific research, product development, innovations in production techniques, and the development of management improvements. R&D activity may be a specific, identifiable activity such as in a research lab, or it may be part of the process of learning by doing. In either case, the insights developed from R&D generally lead to new products and cheaper ways of producing them. Over time, R&D is credited with the greatest contributions to economic growth. Figure 7.9 shows both the amount of R&D as a percent of GDP and its source.

Globalization

Another impetus for economic growth has occurred through globalization—a greater integration of the world's markets, the freer flow of ideas and innovation, reductions in trade barriers, and increases in foreign investment. The greater opportunity to

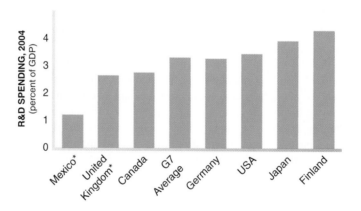

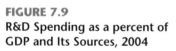

FIGURE 7.9

R&D Spending as a percent of GDP and Its Sources, 2004

Figure 7.9*a* provides a comparison of R&D spending among several countries as well as a G7 average. (Data for Mexico and for the United Kingdom is from 2003.) Figure 7.9*b* illustrates a breakdown between government and industry as a source of R&D spending. (Data for Mexico and for the United Kingdom is from 2003.)

Source: *OECD in Figures, 2005,* pages 70–71, http://213.253.134/oecd/pdfs/browseit/ 0105061E.PDF. ©OECD, 2007.

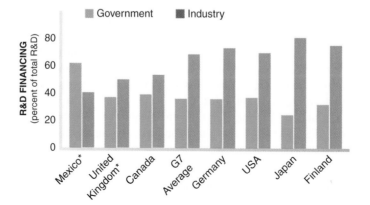

export goods and services has led to significant economic growth for countries such as India and China and resulted in reductions in domestic poverty. As Nicolas Stern, a former Senior Vice President and Chief Economist at the World Bank writes:

> Some anxieties about globalization are well-founded, but reversing globalization would come at an intolerably high price, destroying the prospects of prosperity for many millions of poor people. We do not agree with those who would retreat into a world of nationalism and protectionism. That way leads to deeper poverty and it is fundamentally hostile to the well-being of people in the developing countries. Instead, we must make globalization work for the poor people of the world.[2]

WEB NOTE

The Organization of Economic Cooperation and Development, OECD, provides a comparison of R&D spending across (mostly) developed economies. Visit http://www.oecdwash.org/DATA/online.htm and click on "OECD in Figures" for the most current year.

7.4 THEORIES OF GROWTH

The previous section provided a list of sorts of sources of economic growth. But knowing something about where growth comes from doesn't necessarily tell us how to ensure we get it or what to do first. The simple answer would be, well, do it all! But what would we have to give up? (Remember opportunity cost?) And would that make us better off?

While we have demonstrated how important growth is, as we hope to live in bigger houses, drive better cars, and listen to music on the latest device, it might be even more important to the millions of people living in poverty in developing or under-developed countries, such as those in sub-Saharan Africa or in Central America.

Developing a theory of growth has been central for many economists over the years, and we have an evolution of theory as a result (though perhaps no conclusive answers). That evolution of theory begins with what we can call the *classical growth model*. Simply put, that model stated that growth depended upon a greater accumulation of physical capital—sometimes referred to as **capital deepening**—that would lead to increased productivity of labour in the economy and therefore an increase in potential output, that is, pushing the production possibility curve outward. Some of the initial attempts at spurring development around the world were to encourage such capital accumulation, and foreign aid was often targeted as one way to achieve this. Alas, development and economic growth didn't always follow.

capital deepening: Increasing the amount of capital available to each worker.

In the mid-1950s, economists such as Robert Solow and Trevor Swan published papers that lead to a deeper understanding of growth and to a theory called the *neo-classical growth model*. The starting point here is that continued accumulation of physical capital, or capital deepening, cannot yield sustained growth. The reason for this is the *law of diminishing returns* (a broader discussion of this can be found in your microeconomic text). The importance of the idea here is that providing more and more capital to any worker will lead to the point where the worker is simply unable to operate all the machinery. Therefore, the capital is underused (or not used at all) and productivity isn't increased.

If there is too much physical capital for any one worker, the obvious answer would seem to be to get more workers. In other words, we increase our total potential output by balancing the additional physical capital with more labour. But more workers imply more population (assuming that the economy is fully utilizing its available labour) and the growth we're interested in is per capita growth—a larger share for each of us. More population means the economy's potential is shared among a larger base, so if the population grows by 10 percent and the population grows as well by 10 percent, the per capita change is zero!

---

[2]Nicholas Stern, Former Senior Vice President and Chief Economist, The World Bank, "Globalization, Growth, and Poverty: Building and Inclusive World Economy," World Bank (2001), http://econ.worldbank.org/WBSITE/EXTERNAL/EXTDEC/EXTRESEARCH/EXTPRRS/EXTGGP/0,,menuPK:477838~pagePK:64168092~piPK:64168088~theSitePK:477826,00.html, accessed May 28, 2007.

technical progress: Increases in technology or productivity rather than increases in the quantity of capital or labour.

So if the accumulation of physical capital isn't enough to sustain growth, and a more balanced approach of more physical capital and more labour leaves us exactly the same at the per capita level, what does lead to sustained per capita growth?

Solow's answer to this question was **technical progress,** or in our terminology, increases in "know-how." The problem was, the neo-classical model didn't explain how we could accomplish this! In fact, in the model, technical progress was exogenous or outside of the model itself. Technical progress, advances in knowledge, was what the economy needed, but we didn't know where it came from or how to get it. Thus, the logical next step was to find a *new growth theory* that promoted and explained these advances in knowledge.

New Growth Theory. The evident contribution of "advances in knowledge" to economic growth has spawned a new perspective called "new growth theory." "Old growth theory," it is said, emphasized the importance of bricks and mortar, that is, saving and investing in new plant and equipment. By contrast, "new" growth theory emphasizes the importance of investing in ideas. Paul Romer, a Stanford economist, asserts that new ideas and the spread of knowledge are the primary engines of growth. Romer's treatment of ideas as if they were goods makes the process of advancing knowledge endogenous to the growth model (in this case, economists use the word *endogenous* to indicate that they are including ideas as part of the model rather than outside the model as in the neo-classical theory). However, the use of an idea is not the same as the use of a normal good. The important thing about an idea is that its use isn't restricted by any physical presence or specific industry. The same idea could be used by one worker in one industry or a thousand workers in many different industries without impairing any worker's usage. This then leads to ideas exhibiting increasing (instead of diminishing) returns. Unfortunately, neither Romer nor anyone else is exactly sure how one spawns new ideas or best disseminates knowledge. The only evident policy lever appears to be to support research and development, (a staple of "old" growth theory), focus on education, facilitate the importation of ideas from other countries, and carefully balance restrictions on using ideas that arise from copyright and patent legislation.

There's an important link between R&D and capital investment. As noted earlier, part of each year's gross investment compensates for the depreciation of existing plant and equipment. However, new machines are rarely identical to the ones they replace. When you get a new computer, you're not just *replacing* an old one; you're *upgrading* your computing capabilities with more memory, faster speed, and a lot of new features. Indeed, the availability of *better* technology is often the motive for such capital investment. The same kind of motivation spurs businesses to upgrade machines and structures. Hence, advances in technology and capital investment typically go hand in hand.

Limitless Growth?

Suppose we pulled all the right policy levers and were able to keep the economy on a fast-paced growth track. Could the economy keep growing forever? Wouldn't we use up all available resources and ruin the environment in the process? How much long-term growth is really possible—or even desirable?

The Malthusian Formula for Destruction. The prospect of an eventual limit to economic growth originated in the eighteenth-century warnings of the Reverend Thomas Malthus. Malthus argued that continued economic growth was impossible because food production couldn't keep pace with population growth.

When Malthus first issued his warnings, in 1798, the population of England (including Wales) was about 9 million. Annual production of barley, oats, and related grains was approximately 162 million bushels, and wheat production was around 50 million bushels, just about enough to feed the English population (a little had to be imported from other countries). Although the relationship between food

APPLICATIONS

A Theory of Canada's Economic Growth

A Canada-focused theory of growth was articulated by University of Toronto professor Harold Innis (1894–1952). Beginning with a history of the fur trade published in 1930, Innis suggested that Canada's development and economic growth came from the export of "staple" goods—in his time, fur, fish, lumber, and wheat. Although this is clearly related to "export-driven growth," Innis's specific idea was called "Staple Growth Theory" or the "Staple Thesis."

While the Canadian economy has changed considerably since Innis's writing, Canada's recent growth is still somewhat connected to basic commodities, although now energy products such as oil (as illustrated in the figure) play a larger role. Today, the manufacture of cars and car parts also represent a significant component of Canadian exports.

Source: Statistics Canada CANSIM table 228-0003. Statistics Canada information is used with the permission of Statistics Canada.

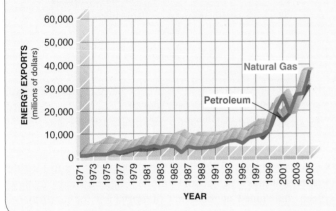

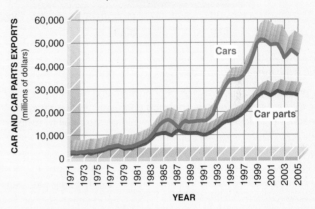

Analysis: Although the Canadian economy has changed considerably since the 1930s, recent economic growth has still been driven by the combination of higher commodity prices and exports of "staples" such as petroleum and natural gas as well as car and car parts manufacturing.

and population was satisfactory in 1798, Malthus reasoned that starvation was not far off. First of all, he observed that "population, when unchecked, goes on doubling itself every 25 years, or increases in a geometrical ratio."[3] Thus, he foresaw the English population increasing to 36 million people by 1850, 144 million by 1900, and more than 1 billion by 1975, unless some social or natural restraints were imposed on population growth.

Limits to Food Production. One natural population check that Malthus foresaw was a scarcity of food. England had only a limited amount of land available for cultivation and was already farming the most fertile tracts. Before long, all available land would be in use and only improvements in agricultural productivity (output per acre) could increase food supplies. Some productivity increases were possible, Malthus concluded, but "the means of subsistence, under circumstances the most favorable to human industry, could not possibly be made to increase faster than in an arithmetical ratio."[4]

With population increasing at a *geometric* rate and food supplies at an *arithmetic* rate, the eventual outcome is evident. Figure 7.10 illustrates how the difference between a **geometric growth** path and an **arithmetic growth** path ultimately leads to starvation. As Malthus calculated it, per capita wheat output would decline from 5.5 bushels in

geometric growth: An increase in quantity by a constant proportion each year.

arithmetic growth: An increase in quantity by a constant amount each year.

[3]Thomas Malthus, *An Essay on the Principle of Population* (1798; reprint ed., Homewood, IL: Richard D. Irwin, 1963), p. 4.
[4]Ibid., p. 5.

(a) Malthus's projections of population and food supply

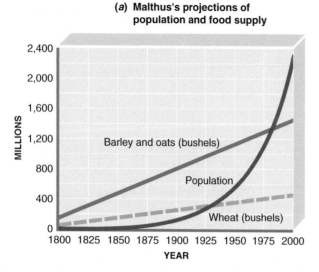

(b) Malthus's projections of declining per capita food output

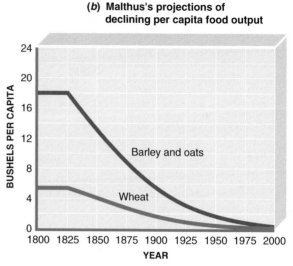

FIGURE 7.10
The Malthusian Doomsday

By projecting the growth rates of population and food output into the future, Malthus foresaw England's doomsday. At that time, the amount of available food per capita would be too small to sustain human life. Fortunately, Malthus overestimated population growth and underestimated productivity growth.

Source: Mathus' arithmetic applied to actual data for 1800 (see text).

1800 to only 1.7 bushels in 1900 (Figure 7.10b). This wasn't enough food to feed the English people. According to Malthus's projections, either England died off about 100 years ago or it has been maintained at the brink of starvation for more than a century only by recurrent plagues, wars, or the kind of "moral restraint" that's commonly associated with Victorian preachments.

Malthus's logic was impeccable. As long as population increased at a geometric rate while output increased at an arithmetic rate, England's doomsday was as certain as two plus two equals four. Malthus's error was not in his logic but in his empirical assumptions. He didn't know how fast output would increase over time, any more than we know whether people will be wearing electronic wings in the year 2203. He had to make an educated guess about future productivity trends. He based his estimates on his own experiences at the very beginning of the Industrial Revolution. As it turned out (fortunately), he had no knowledge of the innovations that would change the world, and he grossly underestimated the rate at which productivity would increase. *Output, including agricultural products, has increased at a geometric rate, not at the much slower arithmetic rate foreseen by Malthus.* As we observed earlier, output has grown at a long-term rate of roughly 3 percent a year. This *geometric* growth has doubled output every 25 years or so. That rate of economic growth is more than enough to raise living standards for a population growing by only 1 percent a year.

Resource Constraints. As Yale historian Paul Kennedy has suggested, maybe Malthus's doomsday predictions were just premature, not wrong. Maybe growth will come to a screeching halt when we run out of arable land, water, oil, or some other vital resource.

Malthus focused on arable land as the ultimate resource constraint. Other doomsday prophets have focused on the supply of whale oil, coal, oil, potatoes, and other "essential" resources. All such predictions ignore the role of markets in both promoting more efficient uses of scarce resources and finding substitutes for them. If, for example, the world were really running out of oil, what would happen to oil prices? Oil prices would rise substantially, prompting consumers to use oil more efficiently and prompting producers to develop alternative fuel sources. If productivity and the availability of substitutes increase fast enough, the price of "scarce" resources might actually fall rather than rise. This possibility prompted a famous "Doomsday bet" between University of Maryland business professor Julian Simon and Stanford ecologist Paul Ehrlich. In 1980, Paul Ehrlich identified five metals that he predicted would become so scarce as to slow economic growth. Simon wagered that the price of those metals would actually *decline* over the ensuing decade as productivity and available substitutes increased. In 1990, their prices had fallen, and Ehrlich paid Simon for the bet.

Environmental Destruction. The market's ability to circumvent resource constraints would seem to augur well for our future. Doomsayers warn, though, that other limits to growth will emerge, even in a world of "unlimited" resources and unending productivity advance. The villain this time is pollution. Over 20 years ago, Paul Ehrlich warned about this second problem:

> Attempts to increase food production further will tend to accelerate the deterioration of our environment, which in turn will eventually *reduce* the capacity of the Earth to produce food. It is not clear whether environmental decay has now gone so far as to be essentially irreversible; it is possible that the capacity of the planet to support human life has been permanently impaired. Such technological "successes" as automobiles, pesticides, and inorganic nitrogen fertilizers are major contributors to environmental deterioration.[5]

The "inevitability" of environmental destruction led G. Evelyn Hutchinson to conclude in 1970 that the limits of habitable existence on Earth would be measured "in decades."[6]

It's not difficult for anyone with the basic five senses to comprehend the pollution problem. Pollution is as close these days as the air we breathe. Moreover, we can't fail to observe a distinct tendency for pollution levels to rise along with GDP and population expansion. If one projects such pollution trends into the future, things are bound to look pretty ugly.

Although pollution is universally acknowledged to be an important and annoying problem, we can't assume that the *rate* of pollution will continue unabated. On the contrary, the growing awareness of the pollution problem has already led to significant abatement-policy efforts. Environment Canada and the provincial ministries, for example, are unquestionably a force working for cleaner air and water. Indeed, active policies to curb pollution are as familiar as auto-exhaust controls and DDT bans. A computer programmed 10 or 20 years ago to project present pollution levels wouldn't have foreseen these abatement efforts and would thus have overestimated current pollution levels.

This isn't to say that we have in any final way "solved" the pollution problem or that we're even doing the best job we possibly can. It simply says that geometric increases in pollution aren't inevitable. There's simply no compelling reason why we have to continue polluting the environment; if we stop, another doomsday can be averted. Julian Simon was so confident of our ability to do so that he offered another doomsday wager in 1996. He offered a $100,000 bet that by any measure human well-being will improve in the next decade.

The Possibility of Growth. Julian Simon may have been right that there are no limits to growth, at least none emanating from resource constraints or pollution thresholds. As Robert Solow summed up the issue:

> My real complaint about the Doomsday school [is that] it diverts attention from the really important things that can actually be done, step by step, to make things better. The end of the world *is* at hand—the earth, if you take the long view, will fall into the sun in a few

WEB NOTE

Check out the Environment Canada website for information on "what they do": http://www.ec.gc.ca/envhome.html.

---

[5]Paul R. Ehrlich and Anne H. Ehrlich, *Population, Resources, Environment: Issues in Human Ecology,* 2nd ed. (San Francisco: W. H. Freeman, 1972), p. 442.
[6]Evelyn Hutchinson, "The Biosphere," *Scientific American,* September 1970, p. 53: Dennis L. Meadows et al., *The Limits to Growth* (New York: Universe Books, 1972), Chapter 4.

"And so, extrapolating from the best figures available, we see that current trends, unless dramatically reversed, will inevitably lead to a situation in which the sky will fall."

Analysis: Most doomsday predictions fail to recognize the possibilities for behavioural change—or the role of market incentives in encouraging it.

billion years anyway, unless some other disaster happens first. In the meantime, I think we'd be better off passing a strong sulfur-emissions tax, or getting some Highway Trust Fund money allocated to mass transit, or building a humane and decent floor under family incomes, or overriding President Nixon's veto of a strong Water Quality Act, or reforming the tax system, or fending off starvation in Bengal—instead of worrying about the generalized "predicament of mankind."[7]

Karl Marx expressed these same thoughts nearly a century earlier. Marx chastised "the contemptible Malthus" for turning the attention of the working class away from what he regarded as the immediate problem of capitalist exploitation to some distant and ill-founded anxiety about "natural" disaster.[8]

The Desirability of Growth. Let's concede, then, that continued, perhaps even "limitless" growth is *possible*. Can we also agree that it's *desirable?* Those of us who commute on congested highways, worry about global warming, breathe foul air, and can't find a secluded camping site may raise a loud chorus of nos. But before reaching a conclusion let's at least determine what it is people don't like about the prospect of continued growth. Is it really economic growth per se that people object to, or instead the specific ways GDP has grown in the past? To state the question this way may provoke a few second thoughts.

First of all, let's distinguish very clearly between economic growth and population growth. Congested neighbourhoods, dining halls, and highways are the consequence of too many people, not of too many goods and services. Indeed, if we had *more* goods and services—if we had more houses and transit systems—much of the population congestion we now experience might be relieved. Maybe if we had enough resources to meet our existing demands *and* to build a solar-generated "new town" in the middle of Saskatchewan, people might move out of the crowded neighbourhoods of Toronto and Montreal. Well, probably not, but at least one thing is certain; with fewer goods and services, more people will have to share any given quantity of output.

Which brings us back to the really essential measure of growth, GDP per capita. Are there any serious grounds for desiring *less* GDP per capita, a reduced standard

---

[7]Robert M. Solow. "Is the End of the World at Hand?" *Challenge,* March 1973, p. 50.
[8]Cited by John Maddox in *The Doomsday Syndrome* (New York: McGraw-Hill, 1972), pp. 40 and 45.

of living? And don't say yes just because you think we already have too many cars on our roads or calories in our bellies. That argument refers to the *mix* of output again and doesn't answer the question of whether we want *any* more goods or services per person. Increasing GDP per capita can take a million forms, including the educational services you're now consuming. The rejection of economic growth per se implies that none of those forms is desirable.

7.5 POLICY LEVERS

Once the sources of growth are known, policies for accelerating long-run economic growth can be developed. Although the pace of economic growth is primarily set by market forces, government policy may be able to affect that pace. Most of the policy options are distinctly *micro* in nature, although *macro* policy decisions are also important.

Governments at all levels already play a tremendous role in human-capital development by building, operating, and subsidizing schools. The quantity and quality of continuing investments in schools will have a major effect on future productivity. Government policy also plays an *indirect* role in schooling decisions by offering subsidized student loans.

Immigration policy is also a determinant of the nation's stock of human capital. In 2005, more than 244,000 people immigrated to Canada (see Figure 7.11). This increased labour inflow not only relieved *short-run* wage and cost pressures but also enhanced the foundation for *long-run* growth. By regulating the number and skills of immigrants, the federal government can affect the size and quality of the labour force. Canada's immigration policy is designed explicitly to raise the skill level of its labour force, by awarding points for education, job skills, work experience and other productivity attributes.

This "skilled worker" class of immigrant is just one of five possible classifications that enable an individual to immigrate to Canada. Others are for investors, entrepreneurs, and self-employed persons; family sponsors; Provincial nominees; or Quebec-selected skilled workers.

Increasing Human-Capital Investment

> **WEB NOTE**
>
> Learn about immigrating to Canada at the Citizen and Immigration website: http://www.cic.gc.ca/english/ immigrate/index.asp.

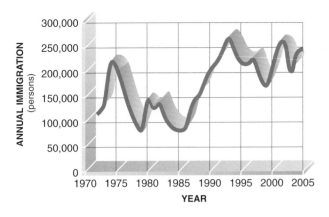

Immigration Selection Factors—Skilled Worker	
Factors	**Points**
Education	25
Official Languages	24
Experience	21
Age	10
Arranged Employment	10
Adaptability	10
Total Possible Points	100

FIGURE 7.11
Canadian Immigration

The chart on the left tracks Canadian immigration from 1972–2005. Although immigration rises and falls from year to year, on average it has been approximately 221,000 per year since the mid-1990s.

On the right, the table shows the selection factors and weighting for potential immigrants to be considered a "skilled worker." The number of points required to "pass" is 67.

Source: Canadian immigration statistics come from Statistics Canada (CANSIM) table 051-0011. The six selection factors has been adapted from the Citizenship and Immigration website at http://www.cic.gc.ca/english/skilled/qual-5.html.

APPLICATIONS

Head Offices Can Locate Anywhere, So Make Canada Competitive

Sports fans know that you can't win a game unless you play sound offence. For government, playing offence means creating an environment that fosters the building and retaining of strong enterprises.

In the new global economy, companies can locate their head office anywhere. The Irish have shown the way. Only a few years ago, Ireland was an economic backwater. What changed? They decided to play offence—taxes were slashed, regulations were streamlined, entrepreneurship was unleashed. Ireland has been transformed into a place where business wants to be. Growth, employment, and living standards have moved way up world rankings.

What is it that prevents Canada from being one of the best places to headquarter and build a business? The biggest negative is our tax rates. In most provinces, the Fraser Institute's measure of "tax freedom day," the date after which the average person's income is actually theirs to keep, comes more than halfway through the year. And Canadian corporate tax policy is simply uncompetitive with other desirable head office locations.

Source: Based on Gwyn Morgan, "Head offices can locate anywhere, so make Canada competitive," *The Globe and Mail* (May 14, 2007) p. B2.

Analysis: The development of better information and communication technologies and easier transportation solutions means business can choose the "best" location for any aspect of their businesses. The "cost" of the operation is impacted by taxes and they are therefore a concern. But businesses also have other concerns such as where skilled workers want to live, so quality of life is another factor.

Increasing Physical-Capital Investment

As in the case of human capital, the possibilities for increasing physical-capital investment are also many and diverse.

Investment Incentives. The tax code is a mechanism for stimulating investment. Faster depreciation schedules (capital cost allowance rates), tax credits for new investments, and lower business tax rates all encourage increased investment in physical capital. As the Applications box illustrates, incentives to move corporate headquarters and build new businesses can depend on competitive tax regimes. These become increasingly more important in a more globalized world, where transportation and communications become less of an issue.

WEB NOTE

See if you would qualify for Canadian immigration by completing one of the self-assessment worksheets provided by Canada's Department of Citizenship and Immigration at www.cic.gc.ca/english/immigrate/index.asp under the "Who Can Apply" link with each category.

Savings Incentives. In principle, the government can also deepen the savings pool that finances investment. Here again, the tax code offers some policy levers. Tax preferences for registered retirement savings plans (RRSPs) and other retirement plans or registered education savings plans (RESPs) may increase the marginal propensity to save or at least redirect savings flows to longer-term investments.

Infrastructure Development. The government also directly affects the level of physical capital through its public works spending. Each level of government, federal, provincial, city, or municipal, spends funds on highways, bridges, sewer systems, and buildings among other things. In 2005, governments collectively in Canada spent some $34 billion on gross capital formation.

crowding out: A reduction in private-sector borrowing (and spending) caused by increased government borrowing.

crowding in: An increase in private-sector borrowing (and spending) caused by decreased government borrowing.

Fiscal Responsibility. In addition to these many supply-side interventions, the government's *macro* policies also affect the rate of investment and growth. Of particular interest in this regard is the federal government's budget balance. If Canadian governments borrow more funds from the national savings pool, other borrowers may end up with less. The outcome of government borrowing—competing for funds in the financial market—may be the **crowding out** of private investment. On the other hand, if governments themselves "save," that is, if they have budget surpluses, they instead add to the national savings pool and facilitate **crowding in** of private investment. Beginning in 1998, the federal Government moved into a surplus position, while the combination of provincial, local, and territorial governments have experienced both deficits (1998–1999, and 2003–2005) and surpluses (2000–2002 and 2006). These surpluses help to increase the available investment funds and reduce pressure on interest rates to rise.

Expectations are a critical factor in both consumption and investment behaviour. People who expect to lose their job next year are unlikely to buy a new car or house this year. Likewise, if investors expect interest rates to jump next year, they may be less willing to initiate long-run capital projects.

Maintaining Stable Expectations

A sense of political and economic stability is critical to any long-run current trend. Within that context, however, specific perceptions of government policy may also alter investment plans. Investors may be looking for a greater commitment to low inflation. They may also be looking for governments to roughly balance their budgets so taxes needn't rise. Such possibilities imply that macro policy must be sensitive to long-run expectations. It also implies that short-run goals may at times conflict with longer-run growth and investment objectives.

Last, but not least, the prospects for economic growth depend on the institutional context of a nation's economy. We first encountered this proposition in Chapter 1. In the World View on page 15, nations were ranked on the basis of an Index of Freedom. Studies have shown how greater economic freedom—secure property rights, open trade, lower taxes, less regulation—typically fosters faster growth. In a paper produced by the International Monetary Fund, IMF, the suggestion is made that growth and institutional quality go hand-in-hand. They go on to explain that by "economic institutions," they mean the broad set of laws, rules, and practices of government.[9] Further, they note that "good economic institutions create effective property rights, including both protection against expropriation by the state (or powerful elites), and enforceable contracts between private parties." In less regulated economies there's more scope for entrepreneurship and more opportunity to invest. Recognizing this, nations around the world, from India to China, to Russia, to Latin America, have deregulated industries, privatized state enterprises, and promoted more open trade and investment.

Institutional Context

[9]International Monetary Fund, "Can PRGF Policy Levers Improve Institutions and Lead to Sustained Growth?" (August 8, 2005) http://www.imf.org/external/np/pp/eng/2005/080805L.pdf, p. 4.

SUMMARY

- Economic growth refers to increases in real GDP. Short-run growth may result from increases in capacity utilization (like less unemployment). In the long run, however, growth requires increases in capacity itself—rightward shifts of the production possibility curve.
- GDP per capita is a basic measure of living standards. GDP per worker is a basic measure of productivity.
- The rate of economic growth is set by the growth rate of resources (labour and capital) plus the growth rate of technology or know-how (productivity). Over time, increases in productivity have been the primary cause of rising living standards.
- Productivity gains come from many sources, including better labour quality, increased capital investment, research and development, improved management, and institutions and institutional quality (government policy).
- Productivity growth accelerated after 1990 due to fast investment growth, especially in information technology.

- Sustaining rapid productivity gains is the critical challenge for long-run GDP growth.
- Canadian household saving has diminished from approximately 20 percent of disposable income prior to 1982 to less than 5 percent by 2000.
- Theories of growth have evolved, beginning with a classical accumulation theory where growth depended on the accumulation of more resources, particularly more physical capital.
- The *neo-classical growth model* suggested that accumulation of resources cannot lead to sustained growth due to the law of diminishing returns, and that even "balanced growth in resources" left per capita income constant. Long-run sustained growth therefore depended on *technical progress*.
- New growth theories focus on better understanding how technical progress—advances in knowledge—could be initiated and self-sustaining. The further benefit of

"ideas" as a growth generator is the potential for increasing, rather than diminishing, returns.

- The argument that there are identifiable and imminent limits to growth—perhaps even a cataclysmic doomsday—are founded on one of two concerns: (1) the depletion of resources and (2) pollution of the ecosystem.
- The general weakness of doomsday arguments is that they regard existing patterns of resource use or pollution as unalterable. As a consequence, they consistently underestimate the possibilities for technological advance or adaptation. Even optimistic projections of technological possibilities turn out to be pessimistic.
- Continued economic growth is desirable as long as it brings a higher standard of living for people and an increased ability to produce and consume socially desirable goods and services.

Key Terms

growth rate 125
employment rate 127
productivity 127
labour productivity 128
multifactor productivity 129

human capital 131
net investment 132
dissaving 133
foreign direct investment 133
capital deepening 135

technical progress 136
geometric growth 137
arithmetic growth 137
crowding out 142
crowding in 142

Questions for Discussion

1. In what specific ways (if any) does a college education increase a worker's productivity?
2. Why do productivity gains slow down in recessions?
3. Why don't we consume all our current output instead of sacrificing some present consumption for investment?
4. The Canadian "points system" (see Figure 7.11) places the greatest weight on factors that offer the potential for the individual to contribute to Canadian economic growth—should it?
5. How would a growing federal budget surplus affect the prospects for long-run economic growth? Why might a growing surplus *not* be desirable?
6. Should fiscal policy encourage more consumption or more saving? Does it matter?
7. In 1866, Stanley Jevons predicted that economic growth would come to a halt when England ran out of coal, a doomsday that he reckoned would occur in the mid-1970s. How did we avert that projection?
8. Figure 7.5 illustrates projections of Canada's population growth being at less than 1 percent per year even in the high growth estimate. How might this affect Canada's economic growth? Our standard of living?
9. Is limitless growth really possible? What forces do you think will be most important in slowing or halting economic growth?
10. Would you accept Julian Simon's second (1996) doomsday wager (page 139)? What dimensions of human well-being might worsen in 10 years?

EXERCISES

PROBLEMS   The Student Problem Set to accompany this chapter can be found at the end of the book.

WEB ACTIVITIES   Web Activities to accompany this chapter can be found on the Online Learning Centre at **http://www.mcgrawhill.ca/olc/schiller**.

PART 3

A Model of the Real Economy

One of the (often) conflicting goals of macroeconomics is to promote long run economic growth while at the same time managing the short run deviations from that long run growth path. These short run cycles affect jobs, prices, international trade, and financial balances. Long run economic growth affects future prosperity. Chapters 8 and 9 build a model of the real economy that is future oriented, enabling economists to understand and explain such short run and long run tradeoffs.

Chapters 10 and 11 discuss the role and function of government as part of the real economy.

Aggregate Demand and Aggregate Supply

The bumpy growth record of the Canadian economy lends some validity to the notion of a recurring business cycle. Every decade seems to contain at least one boom or bust cycle. But the historical record doesn't really answer our key questions. Are business cycles *inevitable?* Can we do anything to control them? **Keynes and the classical economists weren't debating whether business cycles occur but whether they're an appropriate target for government intervention.** That debate continues.

To determine whether and how the government should try to control the business cycle, we first need to understand its origins. What causes the economy to expand or contract? What marketplace forces dampen (self-adjust) or magnify economic swings?

Figure 8.1 sets the stage for answering these questions. This diagram provides a bird's-eye view of how the macro economy works. This basic macro model emphasizes that the performance of the economy depends on a surprisingly small set of determinants.

On the right side of Figure 8.1 the primary measures of macroeconomic performance are arrayed. These basic **macro outcomes include**

- *Output:* total value of goods and services produced (real GDP).
- *Jobs:* levels of employment and unemployment.
- *Prices:* average price of goods and services.
- *Growth:* year-to-year expansion in production capacity.
- *Foreign balances:* international value of the dollar; trade and payment balances with other countries.

These macro outcomes define our economic welfare; we measure our economic well-being in terms of the value of output produced, the number of jobs created, price stability, and rate of economic expansion. We also seek to maintain a certain balance in our international trade and financial relations. The economy's performance is rated by the "scores" on these five macro outcomes.

On the left side of Figure 8.1 three very broad forces that shape macro outcomes are depicted. These **determinants of macro performance are**

- *Internal market forces:* population growth, spending behaviour, invention and innovation, and the like.
- *External shocks:* natural disasters, political uncertainty, trade disruptions, and so on.
- *Fiscal and monetary policies:* tax policy, government spending, changes in the availability of money, and regulation, for example.

LEARNING OBJECTIVES

By the end of this chapter and its appendix, you should be able to:

8.1 Describe the components of the aggregate demand (AD) curve and explain the three reasons for its downward slope

8.2 Differentiate between the short run aggregate supply (SRAS) and the long run aggregate supply (LRAS) curves

8.3 Explain the slope of the short run aggregate supply curve from the cost and profit effects and the slope of the long run aggregate supply curve from the PPC

8.4 Describe the real economy equilibrium in the short and long runs

8.5 Explain the causes and impact in the real economy of shifts in the aggregate demand curve

8A.1 Describe aggregate expenditure, AE

8A.2 Explain the connection between aggregate expenditure and aggregate demand

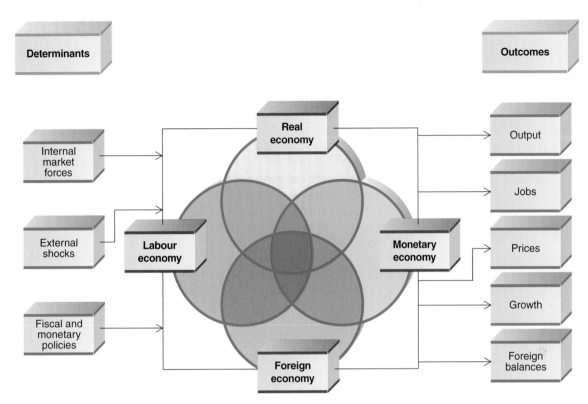

FIGURE 8.1
The Macroeconomic System

The primary outcomes of the macroeconomic system are the output of goods and services (the real economy), jobs (the labour market), prices (real and monetary economies), and foreign balances (the foreign economy). These outcomes result from the interplay of internal market forces—and the inter-relationships among the parts of the system—such as changes in population, innovations, and spending or saving decisions; external shocks such as international disputes, weather, trade disruptions and exchange rates; and fiscal policy such as tax, expenditure, regulatory decisions, and monetary policy decisions affecting interest rates.

In the absence of external shocks or government policy, an economy would still function: It would still produce output, create jobs, develop prices, and maybe even grow. The economy operated with minimal government intervention for much of its history. Even today, many less-developed countries operate in relative isolation from government or international events. In these situations, macro outcomes depend exclusively on internal market forces.

The crucial macro controversy is whether such pure, market-driven economies are inherently stable or unstable. Classical economists viewed internal market forces as self-stabilizing and saw no need for the box in Figure 8.1 labelled "Fiscal and monetary policies." Keynes argued that fiscal and monetary policies were both effective and necessary. Without such intervention, Keynes believed, the economy was doomed to bouts of repeated macro failure.

Modern economists hesitate to give policy intervention that great a role. Nearly all economists recognize that policy intervention affects macro outcomes. But there are great arguments about just how effective any policy lever is. Some economists even echo the classical notion that policy intervention may be either ineffective or, worse still, inherently destabilizing.

In this and the next chapter, we focus on better understanding the workings of the real economy. We start with the following questions.

- **What differentiates short run and long run aggregate supply?**
- **What are the components of aggregate demand?**
- **What determines the level of expenditure for each component?**

8.1 AGGREGATE DEMAND AND SUPPLY

To determine which views of economic performance are valid, we need to examine the inner workings of the macro economy. All Figure 8.1 tells us is that macro outcomes depend on certain identifiable forces. But the figure doesn't reveal *how* the actions and interactions of the four parts of the macroeconomic system—the overlapping circles—translate the determinants into outcomes.

When economists peer into the mechanics of the macro economy they see the forces of supply and demand at work. All the macro outcomes depicted in Figure 8.1 are the result of market transactions—an interaction between supply and demand. Hence, ***any influence on macro outcomes must be transmitted through supply or demand.***

By conceptualizing the inner workings of the macro economy in supply and demand terms, economists have developed a remarkably simple model of how the economy works. To operationalize that model, however, we need to know more about the macroeconomic dimensions of supply and demand.

Aggregate Demand

aggregate demand: The total quantity of output (real GDP) demanded at alternative price levels in a given time period, *ceteris paribus*.

Economists use the term *aggregate demand* to refer to the collective behaviour of all buyers in the marketplace. Specifically, **aggregate demand** refers to the various quantities of output (real GDP) that all people, taken together, are willing and able to buy at alternative price levels in a given period. Our view here encompasses the collective demand for *all* goods and services rather than the demand for any single good.

To understand the concept of aggregate demand better, imagine that everyone is paid on the same day. With their incomes in hand, people then enter the product market. The question becomes: How much output will people buy?

To answer this question, we have to know something about prices. If goods and services are cheap, people will be able to buy more with their available income. On the other hand, high prices will limit both the ability and willingness to purchase goods and services. Note that we're talking here about the *average* price level, not the price of any single good.

Figure 8.2 illustrates this simple relationship between average prices and real spending. The horizontal axis depicts the various quantities of (real) output that might be purchased. The vertical axis shows various price levels that might exist.

The aggregate demand curve illustrates how the real value of purchases varies with the average level of prices. The downward slope of the aggregate demand curve suggests that with a given (constant) level of income, people will buy more goods

FIGURE 8.2
Aggregate Demand

Aggregate demand refers to the total output (real GDP) demanded at alternative price levels, *ceteris paribus*. The vertical axis measures the average level of all prices rather than the price of a single good. Likewise, the horizontal axis refers to the real value of all goods and services, not the quantity of only one product.

The downward slope of the aggregate demand curve is due to the real-balances, foreign-trade, and interest-rate effects.

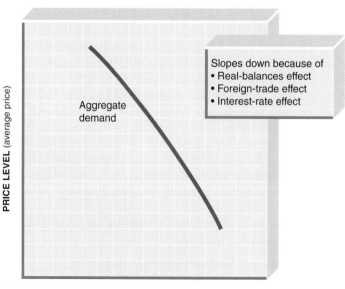

Slopes down because of
• Real-balances effect
• Foreign-trade effect
• Interest-rate effect

Aggregate demand

PRICE LEVEL (average price)

REAL OUTPUT (quantity per year)

and services at lower price levels. Why would this be the case? ***Three separate reasons explain the downward slope of the aggregate demand curve:***

* ***The real-balances effect.***
* ***The foreign-trade effect.***
* ***The interest-rate effect.***

Real-Balances Effect. The most obvious explanation for the downward slope of the aggregate demand curve is that cheaper prices make dollars more valuable. Suppose you had $1,000 in your savings account. How much output could you buy with that savings balance? That depends on the price level. At current prices, you could buy $1,000 worth of output. But what if the price level rose? Then your $1,000 wouldn't stretch as far. ***The real value of money is measured by how many goods and services each dollar will buy.*** When the *real* value of your savings declines, your ability to purchase goods and services declines as well.

Suppose inflation pushes the price level up by 25 percent in a year. What will happen to the real value of your savings balance? At the end of the year, you'll have

$$\frac{\text{Real value of savings}}{\text{at year-end}} = \frac{\text{savings balance}}{\dfrac{\text{price level at year-end}}{\text{price level at year-start}}}$$

$$= \frac{\$1,000}{\dfrac{125}{100}} = \frac{\$1,000}{1.25}$$

$$= \$800$$

In effect, inflation has wiped out a chunk of your purchasing power. At year's end, you can't buy as many goods and services as you could have at the beginning of the year. The quantity of output you demand will decrease. In Figure 8.2 this would be illustrated by a movement up the aggregate demand curve.

A declining price level (deflation) has the opposite effect. Specifically, lower price levels make you "richer": ***The cash balances you hold in your pocket, in your bank account, or under your pillow are worth more when the price level falls.*** As a result, you can buy *more* goods, even though your *nominal income* hasn't changed. In other words, changes in the price level of goods and services lead to a change in real income. Lower prices enable the same nominal income—an increase in real income—to purchase more real goods and services whereas higher prices result in the ability to purchase fewer goods and services—a reduction in real income.

Lower price levels increase the purchasing power of other dollar-denominated assets as well. Bonds, for example, tend to rise in value when the price level falls. This may tempt consumers to use some of their bonds to buy goods and services. With greater real wealth, consumers might also decide to save less and spend more of their current income. In either case, the quantity of goods and services demanded at any given income level will increase. These real-balances effects create an inverse relationship between the price level and the real value of output demanded—that is, a downward-sloping aggregate demand curve.

Foreign-Trade Effect. The downward slope of the aggregate demand curve is reinforced by changes in imports and exports. Consumers have the option of buying either domestic or foreign goods. A decisive factor in choosing between them is their relative price. If the average price of Canadian-produced goods is rising moe quickly than foreign-produced goods, Canadians may buy more imported goods and fewer domestically produced products. Conversely, falling price levels in Canada may convince consumers to buy more "Made in Canada" output and fewer imports.

International consumers are also swayed by relative price levels. When our price levels decline, overseas tourists flock to Niagara Falls and Whistler. Global consumers may also buy more Canadian-manufactured goods such as airplanes and lumber when our price levels decline. Conversely, the quantity of Canadian output demanded by international consumers declines when our price level rises. These changes in imports and exports contribute to the downward slope of the aggregate demand curve.

Interest-Rate Effect. Changes in the price level also affect the amount of money people need to borrow and so tend to affect interest rates. At lower price levels, consumer borrowing needs are smaller. As the demand for loans diminishes, interest rates tend to decline as well. This "cheaper" money stimulates more borrowing and loan-financed purchases. These interest-rate effects reinforce the downward slope of the aggregate demand curve, as illustrated in Figure 8.2.

Of course, the rate of interest also impacts consumers' (and firms') willingness and ability to purchase, particularly with what are often referred to as "big-ticket" items—houses, cars, and furniture. An increase in the rate of interest means that more dollars are required to pay interest and therefore fewer dollars remain to fund additional consumption.

Aggregate Supply

Although lower price levels tend to increase the volume of output demanded in aggregate (AD), they have the opposite effect on the aggregate quantity *supplied* in the short run. As we have observed, in the long run our aggregate supply (LRAS) is determined by the economy's production possibilities, which is defined in turn by the economy's available resources and technology. Within those long run limits, however, producers must decide how much output they're *willing and able* to supply. Their short run aggregate supply (SRAS) decisions are influenced by changes in the price level.

Profit Effect. The primary motivation for supplying goods and services is the chance to earn a profit. Producers can earn a profit so long as the prices they receive for their output exceed the costs they pay in production. Hence, ***changing price levels will affect the profitability of supplying goods.***

If the price level declines, profits tend to drop. In the short run, producers are saddled with some relatively constant costs like rent, interest payments, negotiated wages, and inputs already contracted for. If output prices fall, producers will be hard-pressed to pay these costs, much less earn a profit. Their response will be to reduce the rate of output.

Higher output prices have the opposite effect. Because many costs are relatively constant in the short run, higher prices for goods and services tend to widen profit margins. As profit margins widen, producers will want to produce and sell more goods. Thus, ***we expect the rate of output to increase when the price level rises.*** This expectation is reflected in the upward slope of the short run aggregate supply curve in Figure 8.3. The **short run aggregate supply (SRAS)** reflects the various quantities of real output that firms are willing and able to produce at alternative price levels, in a given time period.

Cost Effect. The upward slope of the short run aggregate supply curve is also explained by rising costs. The profit effect depends on some costs remaining constant when the average price level rises. Not all costs will remain constant, however. Producers may have to pay overtime wages, for example, to increase output, even if *base* wages are constant. Tight supplies of other inputs may also unleash cost increases. Such cost pressures tend to multiply as the rate of output increases. As time passes, even costs that initially stayed constant may start creeping upward.

All these cost pressures will make producing output more expensive. Producers will be willing to supply additional output only if prices rise at least as fast as costs.

short run aggregate supply (SRAS): The total quantity of output (real GDP) producers are willing and able to supply at alternative price levels in a given time period, *ceteris paribus*.

WEB NOTE

The slope of the aggregate supply curve depends in part on what producers pay for their inputs. Find out about producer prices at http://www.statcan.ca/start.html and search for "Producer Price Index" for the latest data.

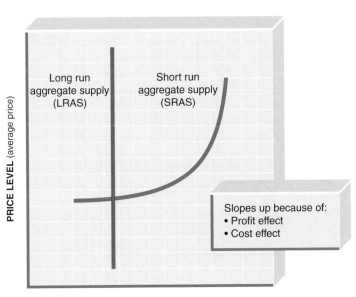

FIGURE 8.3
Aggregate Supply

Aggregate supply is the real value of output (real GDP) producers are willing and able to bring to the market at alternative price levels, *ceteris paribus.* The upward slope of the short run aggregate supply curve reflects both profit effects (the lure of widening profit margins) and cost effects (increasing cost pressures). The long run aggregate supply curve reflects the resource and technology constraint in the economy.

The upward slope of the short run aggregate supply curve in Figure 8.3 illustrates this cost effect. Notice how the aggregate supply curve is practically horizontal at low rates of aggregate output and then gets increasingly steeper. At high output levels the aggregate supply curve almost turns straight up. This changing slope reflects the fact that *cost pressures are minimal at low rates of output but intense as the economy approaches capacity.*

Approaching *capacity* implies that we are approaching (or have reached) a point where we are using all our resources and technology beyond what is *normal* and, in fact, beyond what is sustainable. Therefore, in the long run the economy's ability to produce is constrained not only by the quantity of resources available and the current level of technology, but also by how intensively those resources are used to achieve some *normal capacity utilization;* for example, where a work week consists of 35–40 hours rather than 60–70 or more.

Of course, illustrating the **long run aggregate supply (LRAS)** curve as a fixed vertical curve is a simplification. As the economy's potential grows (as described in the previous chapter) and the production possibility curve shifts outward, that vertical curve itself shifts to the right.

When all is said and done, what we end up with here, as shown in Figure 8.4, is one rather conventional looking (aggregate) demand curve and two curves reflecting the economy's willingness and ability to alter production in the short run (short run aggregate supply curve) and the economy's long run potential given its resources and technology (long run aggregate supply curve). But these particular curves have special significance. Instead of describing the behaviour of buyers and sellers in a single product market, *aggregate supply and demand curves summarize the market activity of the whole (real) economy.* These curves tell us what *total* amount of goods and services will be supplied or demanded at various price levels.

These graphic summaries of buyer and seller behaviour provide some important clues about the economy's performance. The most important clue is point *E* in Figure 8.4, where the aggregate demand and supply curves intersect. This is the only point at which the behaviour of buyers and sellers is compatible both in the short run and the long run. We know from the aggregate demand curve that people are willing and able to buy the quantity Q_E when the price level is at P_E. From the short run aggregate supply curve we know that firms are prepared to sell quantity Q_E at the price level P_E and the economy has the potential to produce Q_E in the long run. Hence,

long run aggregate supply (LRAS): The total quantity of output (real GDP) that an economy is able to produce given its resources and technology being used at a normal capacity utilization.

Real Economy Equilibrium

FIGURE 8.4
Macro Equilibrium

The aggregate demand and supply curves intersect at only one point (E). At that point, the price level (P_E) and output (Q_E) combination is compatible with both buyers' and sellers' intentions. The economy will gravitate to those equilibrium price (P_E) and output (Q_E) levels. At any other price level (e.g., P_1), the behaviour of buyers and sellers is incompatible.

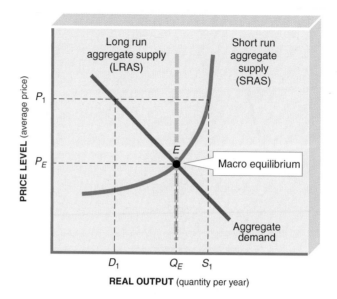

real economy equilibrium: The combination of price level and real output that is compatible with both aggregate demand and aggregate supply.

buyers and sellers are willing to trade exactly the same quantity (Q_E) at that price level. We call this situation the **real economy equilibrium**—the unique combination of prices and output compatible with both buyers and sellers' intentions.

To appreciate the significance of the equilibrium, suppose that another price or output level existed. Imagine, for example, that prices were higher, at the level P_1 in Figure 8.4. How much output would people want to buy at that price level? How much would business want to produce and sell? How much can the economy produce in the long run?

The aggregate demand curve tells us that people would want to buy only the quantity D_1 at the higher price level P_1. In contrast, business firms would want to sell a larger quantity, S_1. This is a *dis*equilibrium situation in which the intentions of buyers and sellers are incompatible. The aggregate *quantity supplied* (S_1) exceeds the aggregate *quantity demanded* (D_1). Accordingly, a lot of goods will remain unsold at price level P_1, and producers' inventories will begin to rise.

To sell these goods, producers will have to reduce their prices. As prices drop, producers will decrease the volume of goods sent to market. At the same time, the quantities that consumers seek to purchase will increase. This adjustment process will continue until point E is reached and the quantities demanded and supplied are equal. At that point, the lower price level P_E will prevail.

The same kind of adjustment process would occur if a lower price level first existed. At lower prices, the aggregate quantity demanded would exceed the aggregate quantity supplied. The resulting shortages would permit sellers to raise their prices. As they did so, the aggregate quantity demanded would decrease, and the aggregate quantity supplied would increase. Eventually, we would return to point E, where the aggregate quantities demanded and supplied are equal.

Equilibrium is unique; it's the only price-output combination that is mutually compatible with aggregate supply and demand. In terms of graphs, it's the only place the aggregate supply and demand curves intersect. At point E there's no reason for the level of output or prices to change. The behaviour of buyers and sellers is compatible. By contrast, any other level of output or prices creates a *dis*equilibrium that requires market adjustments. All other price and output combinations, therefore, are unstable. They won't last. Eventually, the economy will return to point E.

The Desired Adjustment

Figure 8.5 illustrates again this general view of macro equilibrium. In the figure, short run aggregate supply (SRAS) and demand (AD$_1$) establish an equilibrium at E_1. At this particular equilibrium, the value of real output, Q_E, is significantly short of the economy's full-employment potential at Q_F. Accordingly, the economy depicted in

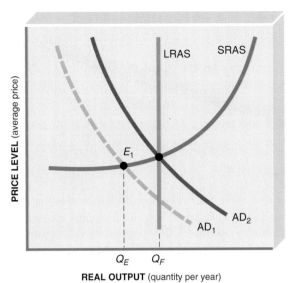

FIGURE 8.5
Escaping a Recession

Aggregate demand (AD) might be insufficient to ensure full employment (Q_F), as illustrated by the intersection of AD_1 and the short run aggregate supply curve. The question is whether and how AD will increase—that is, *shift rightward*—say to AD_2. To answer these questions, the components or demand must be examined.

Figure 8.5 is saddled with excessive unemployment. This is the kind of situation the Canadian economy confronted in 1991.

All economists recognize that such a *short-run* macro outcome is possible. We also realize that the unemployment problem depicted in Figure 8.5 would disappear if either the AD or SRAS curve shifted rightward. A central macro debate is over whether the curves *will* shift on their own (self-adjust). If not, the government might have to step in and do some heavy shifting.

To assess the possibilities for self-adjustment, we need to examine the nature of aggregate demand more closely. Who's buying the output of the economy? What factors influence their purchase decisions?

We can best understand the nature of aggregate demand by breaking it down into its various components. ***The four components of aggregate demand are***

- *Consumption (C)*
- *Investment (I)*
- *Government spending (G)*
- *Net exports (X−M)*

Each of these components represents a stream of spending that contributes to aggregate demand. What we want to determine is how these various spending decisions are made. We also want to know what factors might *change* the level of spending, thereby *shifting* aggregate demand.

Components of Aggregate Demand

8.2 CONSUMPTION

Consider first the largest component of aggregate demand, namely, **consumption.** Consumption refers to expenditures by households (consumers) on final goods and services. ***Consumer expenditures account for greater than half of total spending.*** Hence, whatever factors alter consumer behaviour are sure to have an impact on aggregate demand.

The aggregate demand curve asserts that the *real* value of output demanded depends on the price level. Keynes, however, argued that consumers don't really think in such terms. The typical consumer simply decides how much he or she is going to *spend,* in dollars. The most decisive influence on that spending decision is available income: ***Most consumers simply spend most of whatever income they have.***

consumption: Expenditure by consumers on final goods and services.

Income and Consumption

FIGURE 8.6
Canadian Consumption Expenditure and Disposable Income

The two trend lines over the 1961–2005 period illustrate the relatively close relationship between Canadian's consumption expenditure on goods and services and their annual disposable income. Clearly, consumption rises with income.

Source: Adapted from Statistics Canada CANSIM database table 380-0019, http://cansim2.statcan.ca. Statistics Canada information is used with the permission of Statistics Canada.

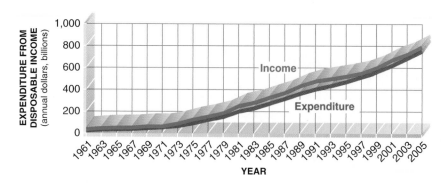

Figure 8.6 seems to confirm Keynes's view. Year after year, consumer spending has risen in tandem with income. Accordingly, if we know how much income consumers have, we should be able to predict roughly how much they'll spend on consumption.

Disposable income is the key concept here. As noted in Chapter 4, *disposable income* is the amount of income consumers actually take home after all taxes have been paid, transfers (e.g., Employment Insurance, GST rebates) have been received, and depreciation charges and retained earnings have been subtracted. Since taxes are collected from all households, but government transfers some of these funds back to households identified by legislation, we can simply illustrate this exchange as "net Taxes."

$$\text{Disposable Income} = \text{National Income} - \text{net Taxes} - CCA - \text{Retained Earnings}$$
$$Y_D = Y - tY - CCA - RE$$
$$Y_D = (1 - t)Y - CCA - RE$$

What will consumers do with their disposable income? There are only two choices: They can either spend their disposable income on consumption, or they can save (not spend) it. At this point we don't care what form household *saving* might take (e.g., cash under the mattress, bank deposits, stock purchases); all we want to do is distinguish that share of disposable income spent on consumer goods and services from the remainder that is *not* spent. By definition, then, **all disposable income is either consumed (spent) or saved (not spent)**; that is,

$$\text{Disposable income} = \text{consumption} + \text{saving}$$
$$(Y_D) = (C) + (S)$$

Consumption vs. Saving

What intrigued Keynes about this formula was the recognition that consumers might *not* spend all their income. This could pose a problem for macro equilibrium. Specifically, too much saving might leave aggregate demand short of its full-employment potential. This possibility led Keynes to take a closer look at the relationship of consumer spending to disposable income.

Keynes discovered two different ways of describing the consumption-income relationship. The first way focuses on the ratio of *total* consumption to *total* disposable income. The second method focuses on the relationship of *changes* in consumption to *changes* in disposable income.

The proportion of *total* disposable income spent on consumer goods and services is referred to as the **average propensity to consume (APC).** To determine the APC, we simply observe how much consumers spend in a given time period out of that period's disposable income. The second measure of consumption behaviour is referred to as the *marginal propensity to consume, MPC.*

average propensity to consume (APC): Total consumption in a given period divided by total disposable income.

The Marginal Propensity to Consume

The **marginal propensity to consume (MPC)** tells us how much consumer expenditure will *change* in response to *changes* in disposable income. With the delta symbol, Δ, representing "change in," MPC can be written as

$$\text{MPC} = \frac{\text{change in consumption}}{\text{change in disposable income}} = \frac{\Delta C}{\Delta Y_D}$$

APPLICATIONS

Canadians Love Spending Money

Spend-happy Canadians are having a tough time making $100 cash last the work week, with most frittering away the funds in four days, and some burning through it in 48 hours or less.

While 67 percent of those surveyed said spending "makes them happy or gives them a rush," John Dale, Mackenzie executive vice-president, notes burning through $100 every four days works out to $760 a month—cash that could be . . . saved . . .

Dale said he finds it unsettling that 42 percent of survey respondents said they have never stopped themselves from buying something they wanted so they could [save] the money instead.

[Dale] cites 2003 Statistics Canada data that shows Canadians only use eight percent of earned RRSP contribution room and notes the Canadian savings rate hit a negative number last year.

Source: Gina Teel, "Canadians love spending money," *The Windsor Star* (January 30, 2006) p. B5. Material reprinted with the express permission of CANWEST NEWS SERVICE, a CanWest Partnership.

Analysis: When consumer spending exceeds disposable income, consumer saving is negative; households are *dissaving*. Dissaving is financed either through past saving or credit (future saving).

To calculate the marginal propensity to consume, we could ask how consumer spending in 2005 was affected by the *last* dollar of disposable income. That is, how did consumer spending change when disposable income increased from $760,379,999 to $760,380,000? If consumer spending increased by 80 cents when this last $1.00 was received, we'd calculate the *marginal* propensity to consume as

$$\text{MPC} = \frac{\Delta C}{\Delta Y_D} = \frac{\$0.80}{\$1.00} = 0.8$$

> **marginal propensity to consume (MPC):** The fraction of each additional (marginal) dollar of disposable income spent on consumption; the change in consumption divided by the change in disposable income.

Once we know how much of their income consumers will spend, we also know how much they'll save. Remember that all **disposable income is, by definition, either consumed (spent on consumption) or saved.** Saving is just whatever income is left over after consumption expenditures. Accordingly, if the MPC is 0.80, then 20 cents of each additional dollar is being saved and 80 cents is being spent (see Figure 8.7). The **marginal propensity to save (MPS)**—the fraction of each additional dollar saved (that is, *not* spent)—is simply

$$\text{MPS} = 1 - \text{MPC}$$

As Table 8.1 illustrates, if we know how much of their income consumers spend, we also know how much of it they save.

The Marginal Propensity to Save

> **marginal propensity to save (MPS):** The fraction of each additional (marginal) dollar of disposable income not spent on consumption; 1 − MPC.

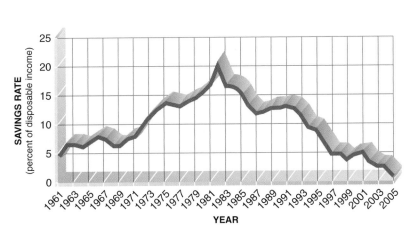

YEAR

FIGURE 8.7

Canadian Saving Rate

The Canadian saving rate rose from 1961 to a peak in the early 1980s and has declined since. By 2005, the rate of disposable income saved fell to just above 1 percent.

Source: Adapted from Statistics Canada CANSIM database table 380-0019, http://cansim2.statcan.ca. Statistics Canada information is used with the permission of Statistics Canada.

TABLE 8.1
Marginal Propensities

Marginal measures are important as they describe the behaviour of consumers given a change in income: in this case, the fraction of the change that impacts consumption (spending) and the fraction of the change that impacts saving (not spending).

MPC. The marginal propensity to consume (MPC) is the *change* in consumption that accompanies a *change* in disposable income; that is,

$$MPC = \frac{\Delta C}{\Delta Y_D}$$

MPS. The marginal propensity to *save* (MPS) is the fraction of each additional (marginal) dollar of disposable income *not* spent—that is, saved. This is summarized as

$$MPS = \frac{\Delta S}{\Delta Y_D}$$

MPS equals 1 – MPC, since every additional dollar is either spent (consumed) or not spent (saved).

8.3 THE CONSUMPTION FUNCTION

The MPC and MPS are simply statistical measures of observed consumer behaviour. What we really want to know is what drives these measures. If we know, then we'll be in a position to *predict* rather than just *observe* consumer behaviour. This ability would be of immense value in anticipating and controlling short-run business cycles.

Autonomous Consumption

Keynes had several ideas about the determinants of consumption. Although he observed that consumer spending and income were highly correlated (Figure 8.6), he knew consumption wasn't *completely* determined by current income. In extreme cases, this is evident. People who have no income in a given period continue to consume goods and services. They finance their purchases by dipping into their savings accounts (past income) or using credit (future income) instead of spending current income. We also observe that people's spending sometimes *changes* even when income doesn't, suggesting that income isn't the *only* determinant of consumption. Other, *non*income determinants of consumption include

- *Expectations:* People who anticipate a pay raise, a tax refund, or a birthday cheque often start spending more money even before the extra income is received. Conversely, workers who anticipate being laid off tend to save more and spend less. Hence, *expectations* may alter consumer spending before income itself changes.
- *Wealth:* The amount of wealth an individual owns also affects a person's ability and willingness to consume. A homeowner may take out a home equity loan to buy a plasma TV, a vacation, or a new car. In this case, consumer spending is being financed by wealth, not current income. *Changes* in wealth will also *change* consumer behaviour. When the stock market rises, stockholders respond by saving less and spending more of their current income. This **wealth effect** was particularly evident in the late 1990s, when a persistent rise in the stock market helped fuel a consumption spree. More recently, rising real estate values—prices of houses and condominiums—have added to this wealth effect. Consumers have used their real estate "wealth" to borrow more and increase current consumption (note the continuing fall in national saving rates in Figure 8.7).
- *Credit:* The availability of credit allows people to spend more than their current income. On the other hand, the need to repay past debts may limit current consumption. Here again, *changes* in credit availability or cost (interest rates) may alter consumer behaviour.
- *Taxes:* Taxes are the link between total and disposable income. The tax cuts that began with the 2000–2001 federal budget and continued with the 2006 federal budget, as well as in several provincial budgets over the same period, put more income

wealth effect: A change in consumer spending caused by a change in the value of assets.

into consumer hands with more income from future paycheques (via tax-rate cuts). These tax reductions stimulated more aggregate demand. Were income taxes to go up, disposable incomes and consumer spending would decline.

- *Price levels:* Rising price levels reduce the real value of money balances and may cause people to curtail spending. (This is the real-balances effect, which also helps explain the downward slope of aggregate demand.)

Income-Dependent Consumption

In recognition of these many determinants of consumption, Keynes distinguished between two kinds of consumer spending: (1) spending *not* influenced by current income and (2) spending that *is* determined by current income. This simple categorization is summarized as

$$\text{Total consumption} = \frac{\text{autonomous}}{\text{consumption}} + \text{income-dependent consumption}$$

where *autonomous* consumption refers to that consumption spending independent of current income. The level of autonomous spending depends instead on expectations, wealth, credit, taxes, price levels, and other nonincome influences.

These various determinants of consumption are summarized in an equation called the **consumption function,** which is written as

$$C = a + bY_D$$

> **consumption function:** A mathematical relationship indicating the rate of desired consumer spending at various income levels.

where C = current consumption
    a = autonomous consumption
    b = marginal propensity to consume
    Y_D = disposable income

At first blush, the consumption function is just a mathematical summary of consumer behaviour. It has important *predictive* power, however: ***The consumption function provides a precise basis for predicting how changes in disposable income (Y_D) will affect consumer spending (C).*** It also shows how changes in *non*income forces will affect consumer spending.

One Consumer's Behaviour

To see how the consumption function works, consider the plight of Justin, a college student who has no income. How much will Justin spend? Obviously he must spend *something,* otherwise he'll starve to death. At a very low rate of income—in this case, zero—consumer spending depends less on current income than on basic survival needs, past savings, and credit. The *a* in the consumption function expresses this autonomous consumption: let's assume it's $50 per week. Thus, the weekly rate of consumption expenditure in this case is

$$C = \$50 + bY_D$$

Now suppose that Justin finds a job and begins earning $100 per week. Will his spending be affected? The $50 per week he'd been spending didn't buy much. Now that he's earning a little income, Justin will want to improve his lifestyle. That is, ***we expect consumption to rise with income.*** The marginal propensity to consume tells us how fast spending will rise.

Suppose Justin responds to the new-found income by increasing his consumption from $50 per week to $125. The *change* in his consumption is therefore $75. Dividing this *change* in his consumption ($75) by the *change* in income ($100) reveals that his marginal propensity to consume is 0.75.

Once we know the level of autonomous consumption ($50 per week) and the marginal propensity to consume (0.75), we can predict consumer behaviour with uncanny accuracy. In this case, Justin's consumption function is

$$C = \$50 + 0.75Y_D$$

FIGURE 8.8

Justin's Consumption Function

The rate of consumer spending (C) depends on disposable income (Y_D). The marginal propensity to consume indicates how much consumption will increase with each added dollar of income. In this case, when disposable income rises from $100 to $200, consumption increases by $75 (from point B to point C). The MPC = 0.75.

The consumption function can be expressed in an equation, a table, or a graph. Point B on the graph, for example, corresponds to row B in the table. Both indicate that this consumer desires to spend $125 per week when his income is $100 per week. The difference between income and consumption equals (dis)saving. When disposable income rises beyond $200, Justin begins to save.

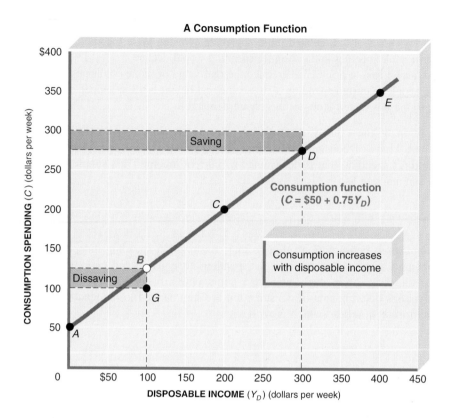

A Consumption Function

Consumption function
($C = \$50 + 0.75Y_D$)

Consumption increases with disposable income

		Consumption ($C = \$50 + 0.75\,Y_D$)			
	Disposable Income (Y_D)	Autonomous Consumption	+ Income Dependent Consumption	=	Total Consumption
A	$ 0	$50	$ 0		$ 50
B	100	50	75		125
C	200	50	150		200
D	300	50	225		275
E	400	50	300		350
F	500	50	375		425

With these numerical values we can advance from simple *observation* (what he's spending now) to *prediction* (what he'll spend at different income levels). Figure 8.8 summarizes this predictive power.

We've already noted that Justin will spend $125 per week when his income is only $100. This observation is summarized in row B of the table in Figure 8.8 and by point B on the graph. Notice that his spending exceeds his income by $25 at this point. The other $25 is still being begged, borrowed, or withdrawn from savings. Without peering further into Justin's personal finances, we simply say that he's *dissaving* $25 per week. **Dissaving occurs whenever current consumption exceeds current income.** As the Applications box on p. 155 revealed, dissaving is occurring because "Canadians love spending money."

If Justin's income continues to rise, he'll stop dissaving at some point. Perhaps he'll even start saving enough to pay back all the people who have sustained him through these difficult months. Figure 8.8 shows just how and when this will occur.

Observe, what happens when his disposable income rises to $200 per week (row C in the table in Figure 8.8). The upward slope of the consumption function (see graph) tells us that consumption spending continues to rise with income. In fact, ***the slope of the consumption function equals the marginal propensity to consume.*** In this case, we see that when income increases from $100 to $200, consumption rises from $125 (point *B*) to $200 (point *C*). Thus the *change* in consumption ($75) equals three-fourths of the *change* in income. The MPC is still 0.75.

Point *C* has further significance. At an income of $200 per week Justin is no longer dissaving but is now breaking even—that is, disposable income equals consumption, so saving equals zero.

What would happen to spending if income increased still further? According to Figure 8.8, Justin will start *saving* once income exceeds $200 per week.

Repeated studies of consumers suggest that there's nothing remarkable about Justin. The consumption function we've constructed for him can be used to depict all consumers simply by changing the numbers involved. Instead of dealing in hundreds of dollars per week, we now play with billions of dollars per year. But the basic relationship is the same. This aggregate relationship between consumption spending and disposable income was already observed in Figure 8.6.

The Aggregate Consumption Function

Although the consumption function is a handy device for predicting consumer behaviour, it's not infallible. People change their behaviour. Neither autonomous consumption (the *a* in the consumption function) nor the marginal propensity to consume (the *b* in $C = a + bY_D$) is set in stone. Whenever one of these parameters changes, the entire consumption function *shifts* to a new position.

Shifts of the Consumption Function

Consider first the value for *a*. We noted earlier that autonomous consumption depends on wealth, credit, expectations, taxes, and price levels. If any of these nonincome determinants changes, the value of the *a* in the consumption function will change as well.

Shifts of Aggregate Demand. Shifts of the consumption function are reflected in shifts of the aggregate demand curve. The Conference Board of Canada reported in August 2006 that the Consumer Confidence Index had fallen for the second consecutive month. Suppose that the result of this *decreased confidence* shifted the consumption function in Figure 8.9 downward from a_1 to a_2. A decrease in consumer spending at any given income level implies a decrease in aggregate demand as well. Recall that the aggregate demand curve depicts how much real output will be demanded at various price levels, *with income held constant*. When the consumption function

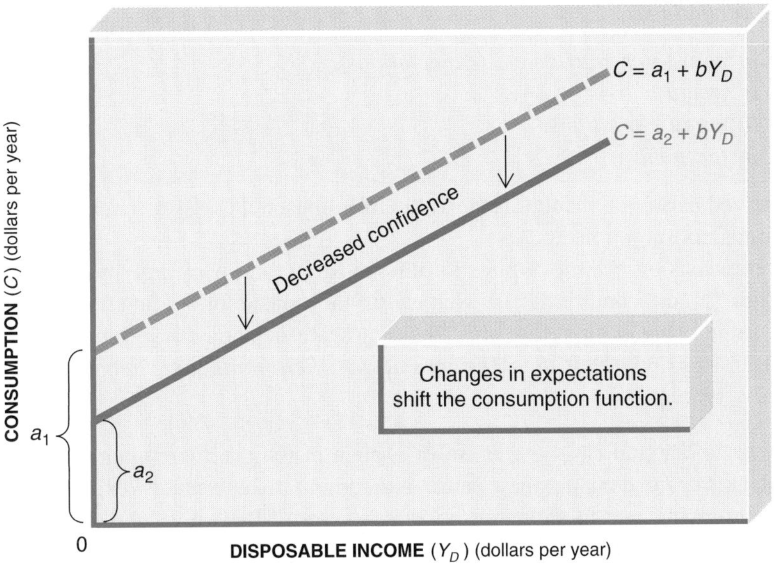

FIGURE 8.9
A Shift in the Consumption Function

Consumers' willingness to spend current income is affected by their confidence in the future. If consumers become more worried or pessimistic, autonomous consumption may decrease from a_1 to a_2. This change will shift the entire consumption function downward.

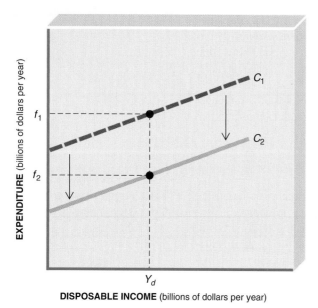

FIGURE 8.10
AD Effects of Consumption Shifts

A downward shift of the consumption function implies that households want to spend less of their income. Here consumption at the disposable income level Y_d decreases from f_1 to f_2. This decreased expenditure is reflected in a leftward shift of the aggregate demand curve. At the initial price level P_1 consumers demanded Y_1 real output. At that same price level, consumers now demand less real output, $Y_2 [= Y_1 - (f_1 - f_2)]$. (*Note:* Both disposable income and the price level are being held constant here.)

shifts downward, households spend less of their income. Hence, less real output is demanded at any given price level. To summarize,

- *A downward shift of the consumption function implies a decrease (a leftward shift) in the aggregate demand curve.*
- *An upward shift of the consumption function implies an increase (a rightward shift) in aggregate demand.*

These relationships are illustrated in Figure 8.10.

Shift Factors   A change in consumer confidence is only one factor that might shift the aggregate demand curve. *Shift factors include all nonincome (autonomous) determinants of consumption, including*

- *Changes in consumer confidence (expectations).*
- *Changes in wealth.*
- *Changes in credit conditions.*
- *Changes in tax policy.*

As we observed earlier, a change in the value of a household's assets (wealth) will alter autonomous consumption.

The same emphasis on *change* applies to other shift factors. A *change* in tax rates or interest rates (credit conditions) is what *shifts* the consumption function up or down. These same changes therefore shift the aggregate demand curve left or right (Figure 8.10). In short, *shifts of the AD curve occur when nonincome determinants of consumption change.*

Shifts and Cycles   Shifts of aggregate demand can be a cause of change in the macro economy. Recurrent shifts of aggregate demand may cause real output to alternately expand and contract, thereby giving rise to short-run business cycles. What we've observed here is that those aggregate demand shifts may originate in consumer behaviour. Changes in consumer confidence, in wealth, or in credit conditions alter the rate of consumer spending. If consumer spending increases abruptly, demand-pull inflation may follow. If consumer spending slows abruptly, a recession may occur.

8.4 INVESTMENT

Although consumer spending can change, the economy need not suffer every time the consumption function shifts. There are, after all, three other sources of aggregate demand: investment (I), government spending (G), and net exports ($X - M$). These components of aggregate demand could potentially offset any shortfalls or instability in consumer spending. To assess this possibility, we will first examine how the level of investment is determined and how stable it is.

As we observed in Chapter 4, investment spending accounts for roughly 20 percent of total output. That spending includes not only expenditures on new plant, equipment, and business software (all referred to as *fixed investment*) but also spending on inventories (called *inventory investment*). Residential construction is also counted in investment statistics because houses and apartment buildings continue to produce housing services for decades. All these forms of **investment** represent a demand for output.

Expectations. Expectations play a critical role in investment decisions. No firm wants to purchase new plant and equipment unless it is convinced people will later buy the output produced by that plant and that equipment. Nor do producers want to accumulate inventories of goods unless they expected consumers to eventually buy them. Thus, *favourable expectations of future sales are a necessary condition for investment spending.*

Interest Rates. A second determinant of investment spending is the rate of interest. Business firms typically borrow money to purchase plant and equipment. The higher the rate of interest, the costlier it is to invest. Accordingly, we anticipate a lower rate of investment spending when interest rates are high, more investment at lower rates, *ceteris paribus*.

Technology and Innovation. A third determinant of investment is changes in technology and innovation. When scientists learned how to miniaturize electronic circuitry, an entire new industry of electronic calculators, watches, and other goods sprang to life. In this case, the demand for investment goods shifted to the right as a result of improved miniaturized circuits and imaginative innovation (for example, the use of the new technology in pocket calculators). More recently, technological advances and cost reductions have stimulated an investment spree in digital music players, laptop computers, cellular phones, video conferencing, fibre-optic networks, and anything associated with the Internet.

The curve I_1, in Figure 8.11, depicts the general shape of the investment function. To find the rate of investment spending in this figure, we simply have to know the rate of interest. At an interest rate of 8 percent, for example, we expect to see $150 billion of investment (point A in Figure 8.11). At 6 percent interest, we'd expect $300 billion of investment (point B).

These predictions about investment spending depend on a critical assumption; namely, that investor expectations are stable. In truth, that's a very tenuous assumption. While no one is entirely sure what shapes investors' expectations, experience shows that they are often quite volatile.

Altered Expectations. Business expectations are essentially a question of confidence in future sales. An upsurge in current consumer spending could raise investor

Determinants of Investment

> **investment:** Expenditures on (production of) new plant, equipment, and structures (capital) in a given time period, plus changes in business inventories.

Shifts of Investment

FIGURE 8.11
Investment Demand

The rate of desired investment depends on expectations, the rate of interest, and innovation. A *change* in expectations will *shift* the investment-demand curve. With given expectations, a change in the rate of interest will lead to *movements* along the existing investment-demand curve. In this case, an increase in investment beyond $150 billion per year (point *A*) may be caused by lower interest rates (point *B*) or improved expectations (point *C*). Keynes emphasized the role of investor expectations in maintaining full-employment spending.

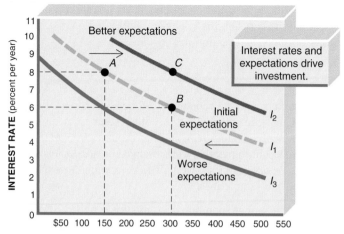

expectations for future sales, shifting the investment function rightward (to I_2). New business software might induce a similar response. New business tax breaks might have the same effect. If any of these things happened, businesses would be more eager to invest. They'd borrow *more* money at any given interest rate (e.g., point *C* in Figure 8.11) and use it to buy more plant, equipment, and inventory.

Business expectations could worsen as well. A transportation strike or spike in oil prices might worsen sales expectations. These kinds of events will shift the investment function leftward, as to I_3 in Figure 8.7. **When investment spending declines, the aggregate demand curve shifts to the left.**

Empirical Volatility. Figure 8.12 shows that changes in investment are more than just a theoretical threat to macro stability. What is depicted here are the quarter-to-quarter changes in both consumer spending and investor spending for the years 1999–2006. Quarterly changes in investment expenditure are generally larger than those for consumption. For example, we can see the impact on investment of the

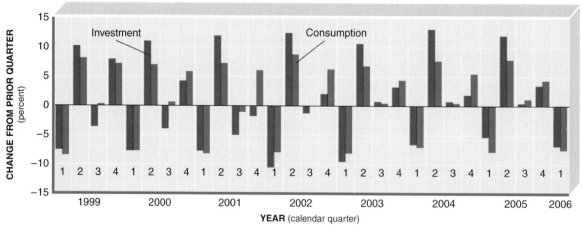

FIGURE 8.12

Investment and Consumption Expenditures: Quarterly Data: From 1999:1 to 2006:1

Notice that although both components swing from quarter-to-quarter, investment is almost always more volatile. That is, the change in investment spending expenditure is generally greater than changes in consumption expenditure. (Note the "Christmas hang-

over" in each first quarter—consumers reduce consumption and pay off bills and firms reduce inventory to prepare for slower sales.)

Source: Adapted from Statistics Canada CANSIM database table 380-0002, http://cansim2.statcan.ca. Statistics Canada information is used with the permission of Statistics Canada.

decline in share values on the NASDAQ exchange in the third quarter of 2000. The impact of the World Trade Center attack in 2001 shows a significant decline in investment spending in the first quarter of 2002, followed by a recovery in the second quarter of 2002. In both of these cases, the quarterly change in investment was greater than the quarterly change in consumption—on both the positive and negative sides.

8.5 GOVERNMENT

The apparent volatility of investment spending heightens rather than soothes anxiety about short-run macro instability. Together, consumption and investment account for roughly 75 percent of total output. As we have seen, the investment component of aggregate demand can be both uncertain and unstable. The consumption component of aggregate demand may shift abruptly as well. As we have seen, such shifts can sow the seeds of an undesirable macro equilibrium. Will the other components of aggregate demand improve the odds of macro success? What determines the level of government spending? How stable is it?

Government Spending

At present, the government sector (federal, provincial, and local) spends over $300 billion on goods and services, all of which is part of aggregate demand (unlike income transfers, which are not).

As Figure 8.13 illustrates, over the 1985–2005 period, the federal government accounted for approximately 20 percent of government spending on goods and services, provincial governments were responsible for approximately 50 percent, and local governments took care of the remaining 30 percent. Total government spending has been moderately pro-cyclical, with expenditure rising as the economy (and government revenue) expands and declining somewhat when the economy (and government revenue) slumps. Again, Figure 8.13 shows these changes with expenditure rising through 1996, then falling slightly from 1997 to 1999, and then climbing again. This doesn't auger well for macro stability, much less "self-adjustment." *If consumption and investment spending decline, the subsequent decline in government spending will aggravate rather than offset the leftward shift of the AD curve.*

Federal and provincial spending on goods and services isn't constrained by tax receipts. Both can *borrow* money, thereby allowing spending to exceed revenue. This

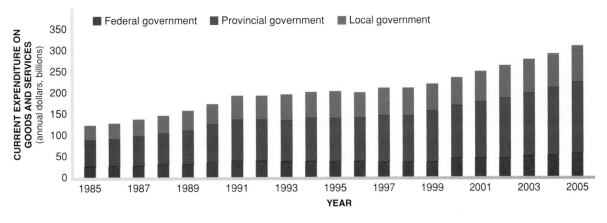

FIGURE 8.13

Government Expenditure on Goods and Services by Level of Government 1985–2005

This graph shows total annual government expenditures on goods and services in Canada over the 1985–2005 period, divided into federal, provincial, and local government components. (Note that

these numbers do not include any transfers from one level of government to another.)

Source: Adapted from Statistics Canada CANSIM database table 380-0022, http://cansim2.statcan.ca. Statistics Canada information is used with the permission of Statistics Canada.

gives federal and provincial governments a unique *counter*-cyclical power. If private-sector spending and incomes decline, tax revenues will fall in response, but governments can *increase* their spending despite declining tax revenues. In other words, governments can help reverse AD shifts by changing their own spending. This is exactly the kind of government action that Keynes advocated. We examine its potential more closely in Chapter 10. For our purposes, since government expenditure tends to change by a relatively small amount year-over-year compared to the size of the entire economy—the result of pre-existing policy and legislation—we can simply take the level of government expenditure to be given, or autonomous.

$$\text{Government Expenditure} = G$$

8.6 THE FOREIGN SECTOR

Net Exports

The fourth and final source of aggregate demand is net exports, X, minus imports, M. Our gross exports depend on the spending behaviour of foreign consumers and businesses. If foreign consumers and investors behave like us, their demand for our products will be subject to changes in *their* income, expectations, wealth, and other factors. In the Asian currency crisis of 1997–1999, this was alarmingly evident: Once incomes in Asia began falling, exports to Asia fell sharply. So did the number of Asian students applying to colleges (a demand for Canadian-produced educational services). This decline in export spending represented a leftward shift of aggregate demand. The same kind of shift can occur in Canada's aggregate demand when the U.S. economy slows, as seen in Figure 8.14 (also see the World View box).

Conversely, when consumer confidence, asset prices (stock market and real estate values), and exchange rates rise (see the Applications box), Canadian consumers, investors, and governments are likely to increase their purchases of foreign produced goods and services. This has been evident over the past few years as the Canadian economy has expanded, stock markets and housing prices have risen, and the Canadian exchange rate (in relation to the U.S. dollar) has reached 30-year highs.

Imports, too, can change, and for the same reasons. Most imports are consumer goods and services. Imports, therefore, just get caught up in the ebb and flow of consumer spending. When consumer confidence slips or the stock market dips, import spending declines along with the rest of consumption (and investment). Conversely, when consumer confidence, asset prices (stock market and real estate values), and exchange rates rise (see the Applications box), Canadian consumers, investors, and governments are likely to increase their purchases of foreign-produced goods and services; imports. This has been evident over the past few years as the Canadian economy has expanded, stock markets and housing prices have risen, and the Canadian exchange rate (in U.S dollar terms) has reached 30-year highs. As a consequence, net exports can be both uncertain and unstable, creating further shifts of aggregate demand.

FIGURE 8.14
Canada's Net Exports 1985–2005

Canada's net exports are influenced by other economic phenomena. Exports are somewhat dependant on foreign income, wealth, confidence, and exchange rates while imports depend on all those things in a Canadian context. Trade relationships and agreements also play a role. After 1989, the adoption of the Free Trade Agreement (FTA) with the United States, and its later extension to Mexico as the North American Free Trade Agreement (NAFTA) had a significant positive impact on our exports and net exports following the 1989–1993 recession in both Canada and the United States.

Source: Adapted from Statistics Canada CANSIM database table 380-0027, http://cansim2.statcan.ca. Statistics Canada information is used with the permission of Statistics Canada.

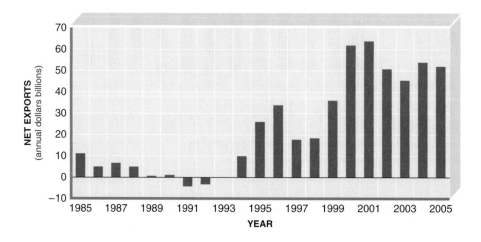

WORLD VIEW

Growth Outlook Cut; Canada to Feel U.S. Slump

The International Monetary Fund has dramatically downgraded its growth projections this year for the U.S. economy because of what it sees as a deepening housing crisis. In an unexpected move, the IMF said yesterday the continuing slump in housing prices in the once red-hot market will clip as much as three-quarters of a percentage point off its forecast for U.S. growth this year, with the fallout to spill over to NAFTA partners Canada and Mexico.

"Risks to the outlook [for Canada] stem largely from the external sector, most notably a weaker-than-expected U.S. economy, a sharp decline in commodity prices or a renewed appreciation of the Canadian dollar," the IMF said.

Although the IMF noted there have been some "tentative signs of stabilization" in the troubled housing sector, the "housing correction still has a way to run," it added. "A turnaround in residential construction is still several quarters away." It also downplayed a spillover from the troubled subprime mortgage market into other sectors, but did not rule it out completely. "Such a development could imply a deeper and more prolonged slowdown or even a recession in the United States, with potential spillovers to other countries," the IMF said.

Source: Peter Morton, "Growth outlook cut: Canada to feel U.S. slump," *The National Post* (April 12, 2007), p. FP6. Material reprinted with the express permission of National Post Company, a CanWest Partnership.

Analysis: In 2005, approximately 81 percent of Canadian exports and 79 percent of Mexican exports went into the United States. So, if and when the U.S. economy slows down, or goes into recession, Canadian and Mexican export demand declines—a leftward shift of the aggregate demand (AD) curve.

APPLICATIONS

Loonie's Flight Could Clip Economy's Wings

With the loonie hurtling through the US92-mark, parity with the U.S. dollar looms like a bug-zapper on a muggy Canadian night. The draw may be irresistible but will the economy be a smouldering, electrified, shell once it finally gets there?

. . . Economists say . . . growth would likely slow overall while the East–West divide that has rent the economy for the past few years would intensify. Cross-border shopping would likely swing into high gear while Canada's tourism sector would take a hit. [And] each cent higher heaps further pain on manufacturing,

said Peter Dungan, economics professor at the Institute for Policy Analysis at the University of Toronto.

Don Drummond, chief economist at the Toronto Dominion Bank, said Canadian manufacturers haven't even taken advantage of the main opportunity offered to them by a stronger dollar. "The one sliver lining to a stronger dollar should have been a boost to machinery and equipment imports," he said.

Source: Jacqueline Thorpe, "Loonie's flight could clip economy's wings," *The National Post* (May 23, 2007) p. FP1.

Analysis: A higher valued Canadian dollar—a higher foreign exchange rate—has an impact on both imports and exports. Since Canadian goods priced in Canadian dollars become more expensive for foreign households, they buy fewer Canadian goods. At the same time, foreign goods become less expensive to Canadian households and more foreign goods are purchased. Net exports would fall.

Since imports are largely a consumption decision, we can isolate a relationship between national income and the consumption of imported goods and services. The question here is what proportion of each additional dollar of national income[1] will be spent on imports. This is just another marginal measure—in this case, the **marginal propensity to import (MPIm),** and is indicated by "*m*."

$$\text{Net Exports, } NX = (X - M) = (X - mY)$$

marginal propensity to import (MPIm): The fraction of each additional (marginal) dollar of national income spent on imported goods and services.

[1]Note that unlike household consumption where expenditure is based on disposable income, import consumption expenditures arise from total national income, representing the consumption of imports from government and businesses as well as households.

8.7 THE FOUR COMPONENTS OF AGGREGATE DEMAND REVISITED

The preceding sections explored each component of aggregate demand deeply: consumption, investment, government, and net exports. In each section, we discussed some of the economic phenomena that shaped the expenditure from each of these participants and explicitly showed these deeper relationships.

We began by noting that aggregate demand (AD) could be summarized as:

$$Y = C + I + G + NX$$

Analyzing each of the components in turn, we found the following:

1. Household consumption, C, was described by the consumption function such that consumption depended on some autonomous amount, a and the marginal propensity to consume, MPC, or b from disposable income. Disposable income is simply the income left in the hands of households to "dispose of" as they wish:

$$C = a + bY_D$$

Disposable income itself was determined as:

$$Y_D = (1 - t)Y$$

Combining these two pieces enables us to "explain" consumption in terms of national income, Y, as:

$$C = a + b(1 - t)Y$$

2. Although we have argued and illustrated that investment, I, is one of the more volatile aspects of aggregate demand, the economic phenomena that create the volatility are largely beyond our scope at this point (we'll revisit investment again a little later in the book). So, for convenience, we'll simply take investment, I, as a given, or autonomous, amount.

$$\text{Investment} = I$$

3. Government expenditure at federal, provincial, territorial, and local levels is mainly predetermined by existing policy and legislation. (This doesn't mean that governments don't make new spending decisions like international expositions or the Olympic games, only that these are the exception rather than the rule). Therefore, like investment, we can take government expenditure, G, as another autonomous amount.

$$\text{Government Expenditure} = G$$

4. Finally, we have net exports, NX. The export side, X, depends on the economies of our trading partners and the decisions of foreign consumers, businesses, and governments. Because at this point we only want to focus on the Canadian economy, we'll yet again take exports as an autonomous amount.

$$\text{Exports} = X$$

Imports, M, on the other hand, depend on the Canadian economy. Therefore, we can draw a relationship between Canadian income and Canadian consumers, businesses, and government purchases of foreign goods and services—the marginal propensity to import, MPIm, or m.

$$\text{Imports} = mY$$

Combining these imports and exports, we can describe net exports as:

$$NX = X - M = X - mY$$

Substituting each of these final descriptions into the original statement provides us with the following model of aggregate demand, AD:

$$Y = C + I + G + NX$$

$$Y = a + b(1 - t)Y + I + G + X - mY$$

When we get over the shock of looking at this string of symbols, we'll notice that we actually know the numbers for just about all of it. The values for each of the autonomous parts are given to us—a, I, G, and X—and the marginal propensities, b and m, and the current level of taxes, t, are simply parameters used to illustrate current relationships. In fact, the only thing we don't know is the final value of national income, Y. A little rearranging gives us:

$$Y = \frac{1}{(1 - b(1 - t) + m)}(a + I + G + X)$$

The first term, Y, is the unknown here, the total value of aggregate demand in the economy. The second term (the ugly looking fraction) is referred to as the **multiplier** for the reason that it multiplies the final term, which is simply the sum of the dollar values of known consumption, investment, government, and exports.

The important thing here is not the algebra, but the fact that the multiplier provides us with a way of considering the impact of government policy and domestic consumption behaviour on aggregate demand and therefore on the position of the aggregate demand curve.

An increase in the marginal propensity to consume (MPC, or b), as we noted before, increases national income, Y, as consumption expenditure from disposable income increases. An increase in the marginal propensity to import (MPIm or m), leads to a decrease in net exports—an increase in imported goods and services—and consequently a decrease in aggregate demand. Finally, government fiscal policy, the rate of taxes in the economy, also impacts aggregate demand; a decrease in taxes increases disposable income and increases consumption and increases aggregate demand. Of course, each of these outcomes assume that there are no changes in expenditure from any other participant.

The actual value of the multiplier in the economy is debated in the profession—estimates range from perhaps 0.9 to 1.15. This is simply another way of expressing the controversy noted earlier—how effective any policy lever is. A multiplier that is less than 1 implies that any autonomous injection (whether originating from government policy, investment, or net exports) results in less economic activity than the value of the injection; a multiplier that is greater than 1 implies greater economic activity.

multiplier: The multiple by which an initial change in aggregate spending will alter total expenditure after an infinite number of spending cycles.

SUMMARY

- The downward slope of the aggregate demand curve is explained by the real-balances effect, the foreign-trade effect, and the interest-rate effect.
- The upward slope of the short run aggregate supply curve (SRAS) is explained by the profit effect and the cost effect. In the long run, the aggregate supply curve (LRAS) is vertical, following the production possibility curve concept that any economy's potential is constrained by the resources and technology available to it at any point of time.

- Too much or too little aggregate demand, relative to full employment, can be *undesirable*. Too little aggregate demand can result in cyclical unemployment, while too much aggregate demand can result in demand-pull inflation.
- Aggregate demand reflects the spending plans of consumers (C), investors (I), government (G), and foreign buyers (net exports = $X - M$).
- Consumer spending is affected by nonincome (autonomous) factors and current income, as summarized in the consumption function: $C = a + bY_D$.

- Autonomous consumption (*a*) depends on wealth, expectations, taxes, credit, and price levels. Income-dependent consumption depends on the marginal propensity to consume (MPC), the *b* in the consumption function.
- Consumer saving is the difference between disposable income and consumption (that is, $S = Y_D - C$). All disposable income is either spent (*C*) or saved (*S*).
- The consumption function shifts up or down when autonomous influences such as wealth and expectations change. Shifts of the consumption function at a constant price level are reflected in shifts of the aggregate demand curve.

- Investment spending depends on interest rates, expectations for future sales, and innovation. Changes in expectations may abruptly alter investment spending.
- Government spending and net exports are influenced by a variety of cyclical and noncyclical factors and may also change abruptly.
- Even a "perfect" macro equilibrium may be upset by abrupt shifts of spending behaviour. Recurrent shifts may cause a business cycle.
- The multiplier value depends upon the marginal propensities to consume (MPC) and import (MPIm) as well as the level of taxes in the economy. The actual value of the multiplier is the focus of ongoing debate.

Key Terms

aggregate demand   148
short run aggregate supply
   (SRAS)   150
long run aggregate supply
   (LRAS)   151
real economy equilibrium   152
consumption   153

average propensity to consume
   (APC)   154
marginal propensity to consume
   (MPC)   155
marginal propensity to save
   (MPS)   155
wealth effect   156

consumption function   157
investment   161
marginal propensity to import
   (MPIm)   165
multiplier   167
aggregate expenditure (A)   169
expenditure equilibrium (A)   172

Questions for Discussion

1. What percentage of last month's income did you spend? How much more would you spend if you won a $1,000 lottery prize? Why might your average and marginal propensities to consume differ?
2. Why do rich people have a higher marginal propensity to save than poor people?
3. How do households dissave? Where do they get the money to finance their extra consumption? Can everyone dissave at the same time?
4. What events might change consumer confidence?
5. The Applications box on page 165 illustrates that a "rising loonie" can be both good news and bad news. Which industries would you expect to increase investment as the loonie rises? Which industries would you expect to decrease investment as the loonie rises? Why would these industries take opposite courses of action?

6. If provincial governments were unable or unwilling to borrow any money, how would their expenditures be affected by a recession? How would their expenditures be affected by an economic "boom"?
7. What factors influence the level of (a) Canadian exports to Mexico, (b) Canadian imports from Mexico?
8. Why wouldn't market participants always want to buy all the output produced?
9. If business expectations increase, how will producers respond and what will be the likely impact on the level of business inventories?
10. How might the real economy equilibrium be affected by (a) a stock market crash, (b) a federal election campaign, (c) a recession in Mexico, (d) a spike (sharp increase) in oil prices? (See Figure 8.4.)

EXERCISES

PROBLEMS   The Student Problem Set to accompany this chapter can be found at the end of the book.

WEB ACTIVITIES   Web Activities to accompany this chapter can be found on the Online Learning Centre at **http://www.mcgrawhill.ca/olc/schiller**.

APPENDIX

THE KEYNESIAN CROSS

The Keynesian view of the macro economy emphasizes the potential changes of the private sector and the undependability of a market-driven adjustment. We have illustrated this theory with shifts of the AD curve. The advantage of the AS/AD model is that it illustrates how both real output and the price level are simultaneously affected by AD shifts. At the time Keynes developed his theory of change, however, inflation was not a threat. In the Great Depression prices were *falling*. With unemployment rates approaching 20 percent, no one worried that increased aggregate demand would push price levels up. The only concern was to get back to full employment.

Because inflation was not seen as an adequate threat, early depictions of Keynesian theory didn't use the AS/AD model. Instead, they used a different basic graph, called the "Keynesian cross." The Keynesian cross focuses on the relationship of total spending to the value of total output, without an explicit distinction between price levels and real output. As we'll see, the Keynesian cross doesn't change any conclusions we've come to, it simply offers an alternative, and historically important, framework for explaining macro outcomes.

Keynes said that in a really depressed economy we could focus exclusively on the rate of *spending* in the economy, without distinguishing between real output and price levels. All he worried about was whether **aggregate expenditure**—the sum of consumer, investor, government, and net export buyers' spending plans—would be compatible with the dollar value of full-employment output.

For Keynes, the critical question was how much each group of market participants would spend at different levels of nominal *income*. As we saw earlier, Keynes showed that consumer spending directly varies with the level of disposable income.

Figure 8A.1 puts the consumption function into the larger context of the real economy. In this figure, the focus is exclusively on *nominal* incomes and spending.

Focus on Aggregate Expenditure

> **aggregate expenditure:** The level of total expenditure related to each level of national income.

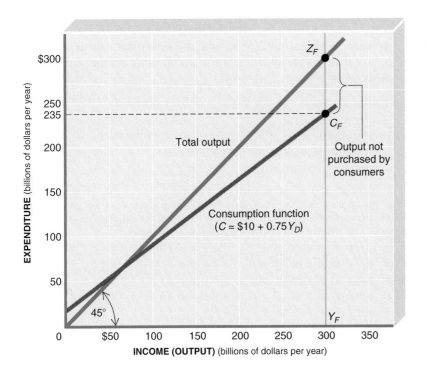

FIGURE 8A.1
The Consumption Shortfall

To determine how much output consumers will demand at full-employment output (Y_F), we refer to the consumption function. First locate full-employment output on the horizontal axis (at Y_F). Then move up until you reach the consumption function. In this case, the amount C_F (equal to $235 billion per year) will be demanded at full-employment output ($300 billion per year). This leaves $65 billion of output not purchased by consumers.

Y_F indicates the dollar value of full-employment output at current prices. In this figure, $300 billion is assumed to be the value of Y_F. The 45-degree line shows all points where total spending equals total income.

Suppose that the consumption function, an illustrated in Figure 8A.1, is given as:

$$C = \$10 + 0.75(Y_D)$$

Notice again that consumers *dissave* at lower income levels but *save* at higher income levels.

The Consumption Shortfall

What particularly worried Keynes was the level of intended consumption at full employment. At full employment, $300 billion of income (output) is generated. But consumers plan to spend only

$$C = \$10 + 0.75(\$300 \text{ billion}) = \$235 \text{ billion}$$

and save the rest ($65 billion).[1] Were product-market sales totally dependent on consumers, this economy would be in trouble: Consumer spending falls short of full-employment output. In Figure 8A.1, this consumption shortfall is the vertical difference between points Z_F and C_F.

Nonconsumer Spending

The evident shortfall in consumer spending need not doom the economy. There are other market participants, and their spending will add to aggregate expenditure. Keynes, however, emphasized that the spending decisions of investors, governments, and net export buyers are made independently. They *might* add up to just the right amount—or they might *not*.

To determine how much other market participants might spend, we'd have to examine their behaviour. Suppose we did so and ended up with the information in Figure 8A.2. The data in that figure reveal how many dollars will be spent at various income levels. By vertically stacking these expenditure components, we can draw on *aggregate* (total) expenditure curve as in Figure 8A.2. The aggregate expenditure curve shows how *total* spending varies with income.

Keynes used the aggregate expenditure curve to assess the potential for the economy to produce too little. He was particularly interested in determining how much market participants would spend if the economy were producing at full-employment capacity.

With the information in Figure 8A.2, it is easy to answer that question. At full employment (Y_F), total income is $300 billion. From the table, we see that total spending at that income level is:

$$\text{Consumer spending at } Y_F = \$10 + 0.75(\$300) = \$235$$
$$\text{Investment spending at } Y_F = 15$$
$$\text{Government spending at } Y_F = 20$$
$$\text{Net export spending at } Y_F = 5$$
$$\text{Aggregate spending at } Y_F = \$275$$

[1]In principle, we first have to determine how much *disposable* income is generated by any given level of *total* income, then use the consumption function to determine how much consumption occurs. If Y_D is a constant percentage of Y, this two-step computation boils down to

$$Y_D = (1 - t)Y$$

where d = the share of total income received as disposable income, and

$$C = a + b(1 - t)Y$$
$$= a + (b \times d)Y$$

The term $b(1 - t)Y$ is the marginal propensity to consume out of *total* income.

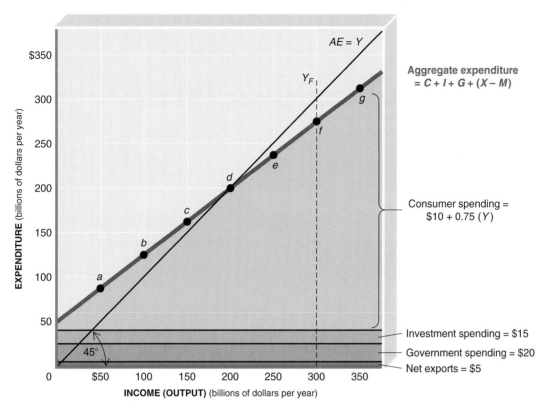

FIGURE 8A.2
Aggregate Expenditure

The aggregate expenditure curve depicts the desired spending of market participants at various income (output) levels. In this case, I, G, and (X − M) don't vary with income, but C does. Adding these four components gives us total desired spending. If total income were $100 billion, desired spending would total $125 billion, as shown in row b in the table and by point b in the graph.

	At Income (output) of	Consumers Desire to Spend	+	Investors Desire to Spend	+	Governments Desire to Spend	+	Net Export Spending	=	Aggregate Expenditure
a	$ 50	$ 47.50		$15		$20		$5		$ 87.50
b	100	85.00		15		20		5		125.00
c	150	122.50		15		20		5		162.50
d	200	160.00		15		20		5		200.00
e	250	197.50		15		20		5		237.50
f	300	235.00		15		20		5		275.00
g	350	272.50		15		20		5		312.50

In this case, we end up with less aggregate expenditure in product markets ($275 billion) than the value of full-employment output ($300 billion). This is illustrated by point f in Figure 8A.3.

The economy illustrated in Figure 8A.3 is in trouble. If full employment were achieved, it wouldn't last. At full employment, $300 billion of output would be produced. But only $275 of output would be sold. There isn't enough aggregate expenditure at current price levels to sustain full employment. As a result, $25 billion of unsold output piles up in warehouses and on store shelves. That unwanted inventory pileup is a harbinger of trouble. Producers may react to the spending shortfall by cutting back on production and laying off workers.

FIGURE 8A.3
Expenditure Equilibrium

There's only one rate of output at which desired expenditure equals the value of output. This expenditure equilibrium occurs at point E, where the aggregate expenditure and 45-degree lines intersect. At this equilibrium, $200 billion of output is produced and willingly purchased.

At full-employment output (Y_F = $300) aggregate expenditure is only $275 billion. This spending shortfall leaves $25 billion of output unsold.

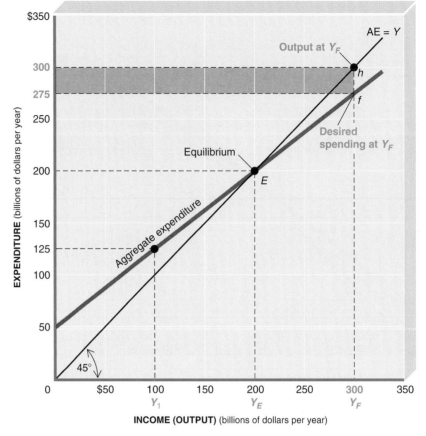

expenditure equilibrium: The rate of output at which desired spending equals the value of output.

A Single Equilibrium. You might wonder whether the planned spending of market participants would ever be exactly equal to the value of output. It will, but not necessarily at the rate of output we seek.

Figure 8A.3 illustrates where this **expenditure equilibrium** exists. Recall the significance of the 45-degree line in that figure. The 45-degree line represents all points where expenditure *equals* income. At any point on this line there would be no difference between total spending and the value of output.

The juxtaposition of the aggregate expenditure function with the 45-degree line is called the Keynesian cross. *The Keynesian cross relates aggregate expenditure to total income (output),* without explicit consideration of (changing) price levels. As is evident in Figure 8A.3, the aggregate expenditure curve crosses the 45-degree line only once, at point E. At that point, therefore, desired spending is *exactly* equal to the value of output. In Figure 8A.3 this equilibrium occurs at an output rate of $200 billion. Notice how much market participants desire to spend at that rate of output. We have

$$\begin{array}{lr}
\text{Consumer spending at } Y_E = \$10 + 0.75(\$200) = & \$160 \\
\text{Investment spending at } Y_E = & 15 \\
\text{Government spending at } Y_E = & 20 \\
\text{Net export spending at } Y_E = & \underline{5} \\
\text{Aggregate spending at } Y_E = & \$200
\end{array}$$

At Y_E we have spending behaviour that's completely compatible with the rate of production. At this equilibrium rate of output, no goods remain unsold. At that one rate of output where desired spending and the value of output are exactly equal, an expenditure equilibrium exists. *At macro equilibrium producers have no incentive to change the rate of output because they're selling everything they produce.*

Unfortunately, the equilibrium depicted in Figure 8A.3 isn't the one we hoped to achieve. At Y_E the economy is well short of its full-employment goal (Y_F).

The expenditure equilibrium won't always fall short of the economy's productive capacity. Indeed, market participants' spending desires could also *exceed* the economy's full-employment potential. This might happen if investors, the government, or foreigners wanted to buy more output or if the consumption function shifted upward. The resulting scramble for goods may start a bidding war that pushes price levels even higher.

The Keynesian analysis of aggregate *expenditure* looks remarkably similar to the Keynesian analysis of aggregate *demand*. In fact, it is. Figure 8A.4 shows the connection between the aggregate expenditure (AE) analysis and the aggregate demand (AD) analysis. Both

Two Paths to the Same Conclusion

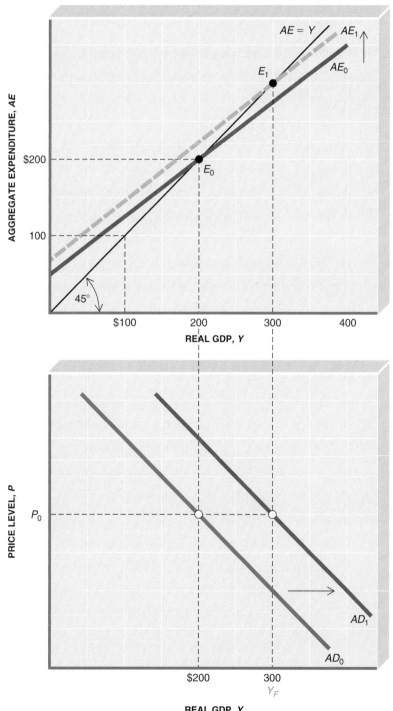

FIGURE 8A.4

Connecting the Aggregate Expenditure and Aggregate Demand Analyses

In the previous figure (Figure 8A.3) the desirable full-employment equilibrium was $300 billion, but the economy was in equilibrium at $200 billion. Figure 8A.4 aligns the aggregate expenditure curve, AE_0, with the aggregate demand curve, AD_0, at the current equilibrium position, E_0, at $200 billion and at a price level, P_0. To reach the desirable full-employment equilibrium at $300 billion, the AE curve is "shifted" upwards—either by increasing autonomous consumption expenditure, investment expenditure, government expenditure, or net exports. This would move us to the position of AE_1, which aligns with the new AD_1 curve that has shifted to the right.

approaches show the economy in the same situation and both approaches respond to changes in autonomous expenditure that "pushes" the economy to the desirable full-employment level of GDP. The key difference between the two forms of analysis is the level of detail about outcomes in the real economy. In the aggregate expenditure analysis, the focus was simply on total spending, the product of output and prices. In the aggregate demand analysis, the larger impact of changes in the real economy on output and prices are distinguished. This is made clearer once you add aggregate supply back into the analysis. The shift of the aggregate demand curve in Figure 8A.4 from AD_0 to AD_1 assumes that the price level remains at P_0. Would this really be the outcome? The answer depends on the "upward slope" of the short run aggregate supply (SRAS) curve. If it was relatively flat, there would be little pressure on the price level to rise. As it becomes steeper, the price level would rise above P_0 and real income (GDP) would fall below the $300 billion full-employment level. In a world where changes in both real output and price levels are important, the AD/AS analysis framework is more useful.

Change and Adjustment in the Real Economy

John Maynard Keynes took a dim view of a market-driven macro economy. He emphasized that (1) a change in the real economy can lead to undesirable outcomes, and worse yet, (2) the adjustment back to a stable and desirable equilibrium might be slow and uncertain. As noted earlier, the first prediction wasn't all that controversial. The classical economists had conceded the possibility of occasional recession or inflation. In their view, however, the economy would quickly self-adjust, restoring full employment and price stability. Keynes's second proposition challenged this view. The most distinctive, and frightening, proposition of Keynes's theory was that there'd be no automatic self-adjustment; the economy could stagnate in *persistent* unemployment or be subjected to *continuing* inflation.

The more modern view of the real economy incorporates some of Keynes' criticisms and concerns by separating *aggregate supply* into a short run and a long run perspective. Since the long run aggregate supply curve (LRAS) is determined by the resources and technology available to the economy—the production possibility curve—it acts as a fixed point that the real economy tends toward. As we've seen, however, each of the short run aggregate supply curve (SRAS) and aggregate demand curve (AD) can shift either outward or inward, creating a new short run equilibrium that may not coincide with the economy's long run potential.

In Chapter 7, we differentiated between changes in the long run potential of an economy—a change in the *capacity* of the economy—and changes in the short run, which are characterized as a change in the *capacity utilization*—that is, a change in the employment level of the economy's available resources and technology. In the short run, therefore, the level of economic activity can be *undesirable* by not fully employing all its available resources or by employing resources and technology beyond the level of economic activity that is sustainable. That is, operating either inside or outside the production possibility curve.

In the case where the short run equilibrium is below the full-employment level, governments have been quicker to try and stimulate the economy. In the run up to the 1993 election in Canada, the Liberal party "red book" pledged up to $4 billion dollars in additional spending to increase AD, to push it back to the full employment level. After the September 11, 2001 attacks in the United States and the resulting economic slowdown, the federal government again saw the need to provide support to AD, but without ignoring the long run perspective. As then Finance Minister Paul Martin explained:

> What I should now like to do is set out a series of [expenditures] which, while providing important stimulus in a time of economic slowdown, focus as well directly on the need to advance the long-term economic plan we have set in train to build for the future.[1]

While Chapter 7 focused on long run economic growth, the focus of this chapter will be on short run *change* and adjustments that move the economy to a desirable equilibrium from an undesirable short run equilibrium. We'll be especially concerned with the following questions:

- **Why might the macroeconomy *change* in the short run?**
- **Could market responses actually *worsen* short run macro outcomes?**
- **How does the macroeconomy self-adjust in the long run (returning to a desired equilibrium)?**

9.1 SHORT RUN CHANGE IN THE REAL ECONOMY

There are two potential problems with any short run equilibrium in the real economy:

- *Undesirability*: The price-output relationship may not satisfy the economic policy goals of full-employment or stable prices; and
- *Instability*: Even if the short run equilibrium is currently optimal, it may be displaced by economic shocks or political uncertainty at home or abroad.

Undesirability. The short run equilibrium depicted in Figure 9.1 is simply the intersection of two curves. All we know for sure is that people want to buy the same quantity of output that businesses want to sell at the price level P_E. This quantity (Q_E) may be more or less than our full-employment capacity. This contingency is illustrated in Figure 9.1. The output level Q_F represents our **full-employment GDP** potential. In this case, the equilibrium rate of output (Q_E) falls far short of capacity production. We've failed to achieve our goal of full employment.

Similar problems may arise from the equilibrium price level. Suppose that P^* represents the most desired price level. In Figure 9.1 we see that the equilibrium price level P_E

full-employment GDP: The total market value of final goods and services that would be produced in a given time period if the economy were operating at full employment; also referred to as potential GDP.

FIGURE 9.1
An Undesired Equilibrium

Equilibrium establishes only the level of prices and output that are compatible with both buyers' and sellers' intentions. These outcomes may not satisfy our policy goals. In this case, the equilibrium price level is too high (above P^*) and the equilibrium output rate falls short of full employment (Q_F).

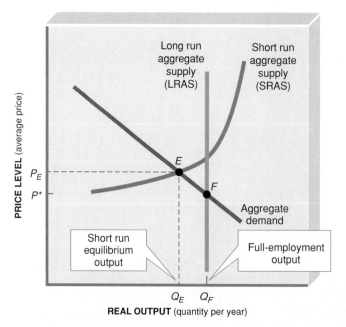

[1]The Honourable Paul Martin P.C., M.P., Minister of Finance, Budget Speech, Monday, December 10, 2001.

exceeds P^*. If market behaviour determines prices, the price level will rise above the desired level. The resulting increase in the average level of prices is what we call *inflation.*

It could be argued, of course, that our apparent undesirable outcome is simply an artifact. We could have drawn the short run aggregate supply and aggregate demand curves to intersect at point F in Figure 9.1. At that intersection we'd be assured of both price stability and full employment. Why didn't we draw them there, instead of intersecting at point E?

On the graph we can draw curves anywhere we want. In the real world, however, ***only one set of aggregate supply and aggregate demand curves will correctly express buyers' and sellers' behaviour.*** We must emphasize here that these "correct" curves may *not* intersect at point F, thus denying us price stability or full employment, or both. That is the kind of economic outcome illustrated in Figure 9.1.

Instability. Figure 9.1 is only the beginning of our macro worries. Suppose, just suppose, that the aggregate supply and aggregate demand curves actually intersected in the perfect spot. That is, imagine that equilibrium yielded the optimal levels of both employment and prices. If this happened, could we settle back and stop fretting about the state of the economy?

Unhappily, even a "perfect" equilibrium doesn't ensure a happy ending. The short run aggregate supply and aggregate demand curves aren't permanently locked into their respective positions. They can *shift*—and they will, whenever the behaviour of buyers and sellers changes.

SRAS Shifts. Suppose the Organization of Petroleum Exporting Countries (OPEC) decreased their daily production of oil, resulting in an increase in the price of oil, as it did in early 2004. These oil price hikes directly increased the cost of production in a wide range of industries, making producers less willing and able to supply goods at prevailing prices. Thus, the short run aggregate supply curve *shifted to the left,* as in Figure 9.2a.

The impact of a leftward supply shift on the economy is evident in Figure 9.2a. Whereas macro equilibrium was originally located at the optimal point F, the new

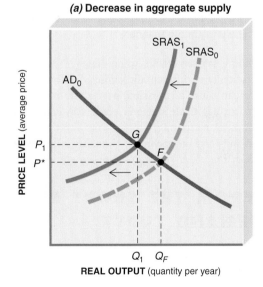

(a) Decrease in aggregate supply

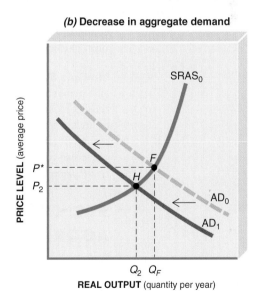

(b) Decrease in aggregate demand

FIGURE 9.2
Real Economy Disturbances

(a) **Aggregate supply shifts**   A decrease (leftward shift) of the aggregate-supply curve tends to reduce real GDP and raise the average price. When supply shifts from $SRAS_0$ to $SRAS_1$, the equilibrium moves from F to G. At G, output is lower and prices are higher than at F. Such a supply shift may result from higher import prices, changes in tax policy, or other events.

(b) **Aggregate demand shifts**   A decrease (leftward shift) in aggregate demand tends to reduce output and the price level. When demand shifts from AD_0 to AD_1, both real output and the price level decline. A fall in aggregate demand may be caused by decreased export demand, changes in expectations, taxes, or other events.

APPLICATIONS

Strong Loonie and U.S. Weakness Cut Growth

Canadian growth slumped to its slowest pace in almost three years in the second quarter, undercut by a weaker U.S. economy, a persistently strong loonie and a cooling housing sector.

"We've had a combination of a strong Canadian dollar and high input costs acting as headwinds on the manufacturing sector . . . and now we're getting a slowdown in our major

trading partner," said Craig Alexander, deputy chief economist at Toronto-Dominion Bank.

Exports were the main drag in the second quarter as U.S. growth slowed by nearly half to 2.9%. Exports of autos, wood products, agriculture and fish all declined.

Source: Jacqueline Thorpe, "Strong Loonie and U.S. weakness cut growth," *The National Post* (September 1, 2006), p. FP1. Material reprinted with the express permission of National Post Company, a CanWest Partnership.

Analysis: Any reductions in exports to the United States from a weaker U.S. economy and the higher exchange rate for the Canadian dollar reduces Canada's net exports (NX) and therefore the aggregate demand for Canadian goods and services, a leftward shift of the AD curve as in Figure 9.2b.

equilibrium is located at point *G*. At point *G*, less output is produced and prices are higher. Full employment and price stability have vanished before our eyes.

AD Shifts. In May, 2005, the Canada–U.S. exchange rate was a little more than $0.785 ($US) for each Canadian dollar. By September, 2006, the Canadian dollar was trading at almost $0.90 ($US). This meant that Canadian exports were about 16 percent more expensive in the United States—and that U.S. imports were 16 percent cheaper for Canadians. Suppose this encouraged Canadians to buy more U.S. goods and services while Americans purchased fewer goods and services from Canada, reducing Canada's net exports. Some firms relying on sales to the U.S. market may also delay or cancel expansion plans, also leading to a reduction in AD. As a result, the AD curve shifted left, as illustrated in Figure 9.2b. So long as the Canadian dollar continues to remain "high"—or continues to appreciate—the AD curve will be kept from shifting back to the right in a timely manner.

Multiple Shifts. The situation gets even crazier when the aggregate supply and aggregate demand curves shift repeatedly in different directions. A leftward shift of the short run aggregate demand curve can cause a recession, as the rate of output falls. A later rightward shift of the short run aggregate demand curve can cause a recovery, with real GDP (and employment) again increasing. Shifts of the short run aggregate supply curve can cause similar upswings and downswings. Thus, *business cycles are likely to result from recurrent shifts of the short run aggregate supply and demand curves.*

9.2 CHANGE FROM THE SHORT RUN AGGREGATE DEMAND CURVE

We have demonstrated how the economy could end up at the wrong equilibrium—with too much or too little aggregate demand. Such an undesirable outcome might result from an initial imbalance between *aggregate demand* at the current price level and full-employment GDP. Or the economy could fall into trouble from a shift in aggregate demand that pushes the economy out of a desirable full-employment–price-stability equilibrium. Whatever the sequence of events might be, the bottom line is the same: Total spending doesn't match total output at the desired full-employment–price-stability level.

The Circular Flow. The circular flow of income illustrates both how such an undesirable outcome comes about and how it might be resolved. Recall that all income originates in product markets, where goods and services are sold. If the economy were

WEB NOTE

To look up Canada–U.S. exchange rates for the past 10 years, go to the Bank of Canada Web site at http://www.bankofcanada.ca/en/rates/exchange.html and click on "Daily rates: 10-year lookup."

APPLICATIONS

Canadian Consumers Confident Even as Family Finances Falter

Canadian consumers' confidence in the economy is pushing them to consider buying big-ticket items, even as they worry about their household budgets, a new report suggests. And while consumers stress over gas prices, their record debt loads are the real problem, a credit counselor says.

Canadians are benefiting from a strong economy, including a healthy real estate market, buoyant stock markets, a 30-year low in unemployment and a rising dollar that gives them more purchasing power, Mr. Antunes said. "Consumers are feeling more optimistic about future job prospects and believe it is a good time to make a major purchase, but they are not as optimistic about the current state of their family finances," said Mr. Antunes.

"People are overly confident, they're eternal optimists, they always think next month will be better," Ms. Campbell [spokeswoman for Credit Counselling Canada] said. Buoyed by a strong economy, many consumers believe they can maintain or even increase their debt load, she added.

Source: Based on Anne Howland, "Canadian consumers confident even as family finances falter," *The Ottawa Citizen* (May 31, 2007), p. C3.

Analysis: As Canadian consumers remain confident about the economy, they may increase their marginal propensity to spend thus reducing their overall saving. The result is a rightward shift of the AD curve and an increase in national income (Y).

producing at *full-employment GDP,* then enough income would be available to buy everything a fully employed economy produces. As we've seen, however, aggregate demand isn't so certain. It could happen that market participants opt *not* to spend all their income, leaving some goods unsold. Alternatively, they might try to buy *more* than full-employment output, pushing prices up.

To see how such imbalances might arise, Keynes distinguished *leakages* from the circular flow and *injections* into that flow, as illustrated in Figure 9.3.

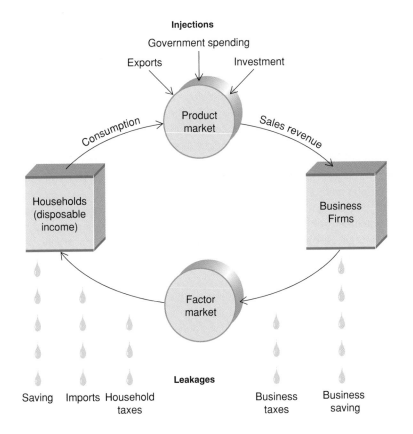

FIGURE 9.3
Leakages and Injections

The income generated in production doesn't return completely to product markets in the form of consumer spending. Consumer saving, imports, taxes, and business saving all leak from the circular flow, reducing aggregate demand. If this leakage isn't offset, some of the output produced will remain unsold.

Business investment, government purchases of goods and services, and exports inject spending into the circular flow, adding to aggregate demand. The focus of macro concern is whether desired injections will offset desired leakage at full employment.

FIGURE 9.4

Leakage and AD

The disposable income consumers receive is only about 60 percent of total income (GDP), due to taxes and income held by businesses. Consumers also tend to save some of their disposable income and buy imported products. As a result of these leakages, consumers will demand less output at the current price level (*P* = 100) than the economy produces at full-employment GDP (*Q_F*). In this case, consumers demand only $235 billion of output at the price level *P* = 100 (point *C_F*) when $300 billion of output (income) is produced (point *F*).

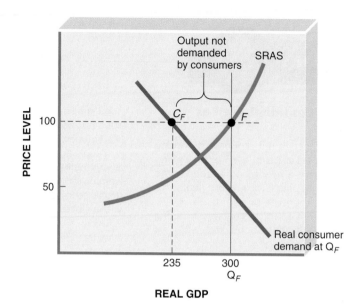

Consumer Saving

leakage: Income not spent directly on domestic output but instead diverted from the circular flow, for example, saving, imports, taxes.

As we observed in Chapter 8, consumers typically don't spend *all* the income they earn in product markets; they *save* some fraction of it. This is the first leak in the circular flow. Some income earned in product markets isn't being instantly converted into spending. This circular flow **leakage** creates the potential for a spending shortfall.

Suppose the economy were producing at full employment, with $300 billion of output at the current price level, indexed at *P* = 100. This initial output rate is marked by point *F* in Figure 9.4. Suppose further that *all* of the income generated in product markets went to consumers. In that case, would consumers *spend* enough to *maintain* full employment? We already observed in Chapter 8 that such an outcome is unlikely. Typically, consumers *save* a small fraction of their incomes.

If the consumption function were $C_F = \$10$ billion $+ 0.75Y_d$, consumers will spend only

$$C_F = \$10 \text{ billion} + 0.75(\$300 \text{ billion})$$

$$= \$235 \text{ billion}$$

at the current price level. This consumption behaviour is illustrated in Figure 9.4 by the point C_F. Consumers would demand more real output with their current income if prices were to fall. Hence, the consumption component of aggregate demand slopes downward from point C_F. Our immediate concern, however, focuses on how much (real) output consumers will purchase at the current price level. At the price level *P* = 100 consumers choose to save $65 billion, leaving consumption ($235 billion) far short of full employment GDP ($300 billion).

The decision to save some fraction of household income isn't necessarily bad, but it does present a potential problem. Unless other market participants, such as business, government, and foreigners, buy this unsold output, goods will pile up on producers' shelves. As undesired inventory accumulates, producers will reduce the rate of output and unemployment will rise.

Business Saving

gross business saving: Depreciation allowances and retained earnings.

The business sector also keeps part of the income generated in product markets. Some revenue is set aside to cover the costs of maintaining, repairing, and replacing plant and equipment. The revenue held aside for these purposes is called a depreciation allowance or capital cost allowance (CCA). In addition, corporations keep some part of total profit (retained earnings) for other business uses rather than turn all profits over to the business owners in the form of stockholder dividends. The total value of depreciation allowances and retained earnings is called **gross business saving**. Whatever businesses save in these forms represents further leakage from the circular flow—income that doesn't automatically flow directly back into product markets.

Governments are also in a position to save. These savings are the result of government taking in more revenue (net taxes) than they use for expenditure—a budget surplus. At times, government's expenditures may exceed their revenue, where they are dissaving—a budget deficit. We will discuss these outcomes more fully in Chapter 10, coming up next.

Saving isn't the only source of leakage. ***Imports also represent leakage from the circular flow.*** When consumers buy imported goods, their spending leaves (that is, leaks out of) the domestic circular flow and goes to foreign producers. As a consequence, income spent on imported goods and services is not part of the aggregate demand for domestic output.

In the real world, ***taxes are a form of leakage as well.*** A lot of revenue generated in market sales gets diverted into federal, provincial, territorial, and local government coffers. Sales taxes are taken out of the circular flow in product markets. Then payroll taxes and income taxes are taken out of wages. Households never get the chance to spend any of that income. They start with disposable income, which is much less than the total income generated in product markets. In 2005, disposable income was only $787 billion while total income (GDP) was $1,371 billion. Hence, consumers couldn't buy everything produced with their current incomes even if they saved nothing.

Although leakage from the circular flow is a potential source of unemployment problems, we shouldn't conclude that the economy will sink as soon as consumers start saving some of their income, buy a few imports, or pay their taxes. Consumers aren't the only ones who buy goods and services in product markets; business firms and government agencies also contribute to total spending. So do international consumers who buy our exports. So before we run out into the streets screaming "The circular flow is leaking!" we need to look at what other market participants are doing.

Imports and Taxes

The top half of Figure 9.3 completes the picture of the circular flow by depicting **injections** of new spending. When businesses buy plant and equipment, they add to the dollar value of product market sales. Government purchases and exports also inject spending into the product market. These ***injections of investment, government, and export spending help offset leakage from saving, imports, and taxes.*** As a result, there may be enough aggregate demand to maintain full employment at the current price level, even if consumers aren't spending every dollar of income.

The critical issue is whether spending injections will actually equal spending leakage at full employment. If so, the economy will stabilize at full employment and we can stop worrying about macro problems. If not, we've still got some work to do.

Injections into the Circular Flow

injection: An addition of spending to the circular flow of income.

As we noted earlier, classical economists had no worries. They assumed that spending injections would always equal spending leakage. That was the foundation of their belief in the economy's self-adjustment. One mechanism assuring the equality of leakages and injections was the interest rate.

Self-Adjustment?

Flexible Interest Rates. Ignore all other injections and leakages for the moment and focus on just consumer saving and business investment (Figure 9.5). If consumer

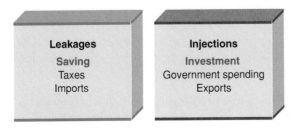

Leakages	Injections
Saving	Investment
Taxes	Government spending
Imports	Exports

FIGURE 9.5
Leakages and Injections

Macro stability depends on the balance between injections and leakages.

saving exceeds business investment, unspent income must be piling up somewhere (in bank accounts, for example). These unspent funds will be a tempting lure for business investors. In the classical view, businesses are always looking for funds to finance expansion or modernization. So they aren't likely to leave a pile of consumer savings sitting idle. Moreover, the banks and other institutions that are holding consumer savings will be eager to lend more funds as consumer savings piles up. To make more loans, they can lower the interest rate. As we observed in Chapter 8 (Figure 8.11), lower interest rates prompt businesses to borrow and invest more. Hence, *classical economists concluded that if interest rates fell far enough, business investment (injections) would equal consumer saving (leakage).* From this perspective, any spending shortfall would soon be closed by this self-adjustment of leakage and injection flows. Aggregate demand would be maintained at full-employment GDP, because investment spending would soak up all consumer saving.

Changing Expectations. Keynes argued that classical economists ignored the role of expectations in business investments. As Figure 8.11 illustrated, the level of investment *is* sensitive to interest rates. But the whole investment function *shifts* when business expectations change. Keynes thought it preposterous that investment spending would *increase* in response to *declining* sales. A decline in investment is more likely, Keynes argued.

Flexible Prices. There is another way the economy could self-adjust. Look at Figure 9.4 again. It says consumers will demand only $235 billion of output *at the current price level.* But what if prices *fell?* Then consumers would buy more output. In fact, if prices fell far enough, consumers might buy *all* the output produced at full employment. In Figure 9.4, the price level $P = 70$ elicits such a response.

Expectations (again). Keynes again chided the classical economists for their naiveté. Sure, a nationwide sale might prompt consumers to buy more goods and services. But how would businesses react? They had planned on selling Q_F amount of output at the price level $P = 100$. If prices must be cut to move their merchandise, businesses are likely to rethink their production and investment plans. Keynes argued that declining (retail) prices were likely to prompt investment cutbacks.

Flexible Exchange Rates. Another mechanism that helps equalize leakages and injections is the exchange rate. If the values of imports and exports aren't equal, classical economists suggest that pressure is exerted on the exchange rate to change. In Canada's case, the increase in net exports after NAFTA (as Figure 8.14 illustrated), was one component in the appreciation of the Canadian dollar from $0.62 ($US) in January 2002 to $0.90 ($US) by September 2006, and over $0.94 ($US) by June 2007. The appreciation of the Canadian dollar simultaneously makes Canadian goods more expensive in U.S. markets—and therefore reduces exports—while making U.S. goods less expensive in Canada—increasing imports. The result would be bringing imports and exports closer and net exports closer to zero. Keynesians might suggest that this process is both lengthy and uncertain. Current inventory must be sold at original prices before consumers will see the new lower domestic prices, and since exchange rates are affected by many things, such realignment might be incomplete. Flexible exchange rates can also impact the willingness of Canadian producers to produce. As the Applications box on page 183 illustrates, for goods sold on international markets and priced in U.S. dollars, changes in the exchange rate can result in changes in Canadian dollar profits.

The Multiplier Process

Keynes not only rejected the classical notion of self-adjustment, he also argued that things were likely to get *worse,* not better, once a spending shortfall emerged.

Rising Dollar Gnaws at Resource Sector

Forestry, mining firms start to take financial hits already seen by manufactures. Having cut a swath through Canada's manufacturing sector, the surging dollar is beginning to do similar damage to resource producers, which are no longer seeing their commodities rise in price at the same pace as recent years.

Most deeply affected is the forest products industry, followed by base metals producers and other miners. "Anybody that has a manufacturing base in Canada and is selling products that are predominantly U.S.-dollar-based is impacted," said Paul Quinn, a forestry analyst with Salman Partners Inc. in Vancouver. "So the whole forest sector is taking a whack on the chin." Every 1-cent increase in the Canadian dollar against the United States greenback means a $19-million hit to Canfor Corp's bottom line, a company spokesman said yesterday.

Cameco Corp., the world's largest uranium miner, has the bulk of its operations in Canada and is sensitive to currency fluctuations because the metal used to fuel nuclear reactors is priced in U.S. dollars. The company says that every 1-cent decrease in the U.S.-to-Canadian dollar exchange rate results in a corresponding decrease in annual net earnings of about $4-million.

Source: A. Hoffman, D. Parkinson, and W. Stueck, "Rising dollar gnaws at resource sector," *The Globe and Mail* (June 5, 2007), p. B1. Reprinted with permission from *The Globe and Mail*.

Analysis: Since sales in U.S. dollars return fewer Canadian dollars after the exchange, companies such as these effectively see reduced prices for their goods. The impact has been reduced business revenues (as noted in the story), profits, and sales expectations. The result might be reduced economic activity in these industries.

To understand Keynes's fears, imagine that the economy is initially at the desired full-employment GDP equilibrium, as represented again by point *F* in Figure 9.6. Included in that full-employment equilibrium GDP is

Consumption	= $235 billion
Investment	= 40 billion
Government	= 15 billion
Net exports	= 10 billion
Aggregate demand at current price level	= $300 billion

Everything looks good in this macro economy. This is pretty much how the Canadian economy has performed, beginning in about 2004. As noted by the Bank of Canada in their July 2006 Policy Update: "The economy is currently judged to be operating just above its production capacity."[2]

The bank goes on to suggest, however, that "with some anticipated moderation in U.S. economic growth combined with . . . exchange rate increases" that net exports could be weaker. Suppose that net exports are indeed weaker, and as a result, aggregate demand, AD shifts inward—to the left.

Undesired Inventory. When net export demand is cut back, unsold goods start piling up. Such a reduction in sales can also lead firms to reduce their investment expenditure, putting off expansion plans or not replacing equipment. Unsold cars and trucks, machinery, software, and beef quickly reach worrisome levels.

Ironically, this additional inventory is counted as part of investment spending. (Recall that our definition of investment spending includes changes in business inventories.) This additional inventory is clearly undesired, however, as producers had planned on selling these goods.

WEB NOTE

For an overview of Canadian economic developments for the most recent quarter, go to http://www.statcan.ca/start.html and search for "Canadian Economic Accounts Quarterly Review."

[2]*Monetary Policy Report Update,* (Bank of Canada, July 13, 2006). p. 1, http://www.bankofcanada.ca/en/mpr/pdf/mpr_update130706.pdf, accessed September 26, 2006.

FIGURE 9.6
AD Shift

When spending drops, aggregate demand shifts to the left. In the short run, this causes output and the price level to fall. The initial equilibrium at *F* is pushed to a new equilibrium at point *b*.

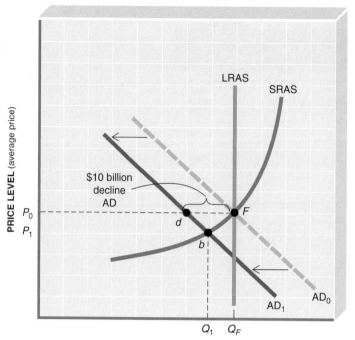

REAL OUTPUT (in billions of dollars per year)

To keep track of these unwanted changes in investment, we **distinguish desired *(or planned) investment from* actual *investment*.** *Desired* investment represents purchases of new plant and equipment plus any *desired* changes in business inventories. By contrast, *actual* investment represents purchases of new plant and equipment plus *actual* changes in business inventories, desired or otherwise. In other words,

$$\frac{\text{Actual}}{\text{investment}} = \frac{\text{desired}}{\text{investment}} + \frac{\text{undesired}}{\text{investment}}$$

Falling Output and Prices. How are business firms likely to react when they see undesired inventory piling up on car lots and store shelves? They could regard the inventory pileup as a brief aberration and continue producing at full-employment levels. But the inventory pileup might also set off sales alarms, causing businesses to alter their pricing, production, and investment plans. If that happens, they're likely to start cutting prices in an attempt to increase the rate of sales. Producers are also likely to reduce the rate of new output. Figure 9.6 illustrates these two responses. Assume that investment spending declines by $10 billion at the existing price level P_0. This shifts the aggregate demand curve leftward from AD_0 to AD_1 and immediately moves the economy from point *F* to point *d*. If no other changes were to occur, the economy would gravitate first toward a new **short-run equilibrium GDP** at point *b*, where the aggregate demand curve, AD_1 intersects with the short-run aggregate supply curve, SRAS. At point *b*, the rate of output (Q_1) is less than the full-employment level (Q_F) and the price level has fallen from P_0 to P_1.

short-run equilibrium GDP: The value of total final output produced at the price level where AD intersects with SRAS.

Household Incomes

The decline in GDP depicted in Figure 9.6 isn't pretty. But Keynes warned that the picture would get uglier when *consumers* start feeling the impact of the production cutbacks.

So far we've treated the production cutbacks that accompany a GDP gap as a rather abstract problem. But the reality is that when production is cut back, people suffer. When producers decrease the rate of output, workers lose their jobs or face pay cuts, or both. As the previous Applications box explained, the rising value of the Canadian dollar has "cut a swath through Canada's manufacturing sector" and is having an impact on forestry and other resource producers. The result could be pressure on these

Brace for Economic Slowdown, Economist Warns

Canadian companies should prepare for the worst, and plan as if a serious global slowdown is in the making, says the chief economist of the federal export-financing agency—rejecting the more optimistic stand of the Bank of Canada that the slowdown will be mild.

"Economic bubbles burst so quickly that the effect is hard to predict," Mr. Poloz told reporters yesterday. "It would be a mistake to underestimate the potential impact of the recent slowing."

Since there's a good chance that EDC's growth estimate of 2.4 per cent could be wrong, Mr. Poloz put together an alternative forecast to help companies deal with a more pessimistic scenario. In this case, troubles in the U.S. housing sector take a turn for the worse. Consumers are spooked and scale back spending, and the United States flirts with recession.

Mexico and Asia would be hit first, with demand for consumer goods dropping off sharply. Commodity prices would slide and currencies in many emerging markets would suffer from a flight to quality.

In Canada, exports would contract sharply, probably by 3.4 percent in 2007—steeper than the 2 percent annualized decline recorded during each of the past two recessions. The slowdown would eventually be felt across all industries, not just manufacturing and exports where the pain is centred for now, Mr. Poloz said. "The shock would affect everybody."

Source: Heather Scofield, "Brace for economic slowdown, economist warns," *The Globe and Mail* (November 7, 2006), p. B4. Reprinted with permission from *The Globe and Mail.*

Analysis: Multiplier effects can spill over national borders. A slowdown in the United States could reduce demand for Mexican and Asian and Canadian exports, setting off a sequence of spending cuts for these and other countries who rely on Mexican, Asian, and Canadian consumers to buy their goods and services in turn.

firms to reduce operations. As workers get laid off or have their wages cut, household incomes decline. Thus, *a reduction in investment spending implies a reduction in household incomes.*

We saw in Chapter 8 the kind of threat a reduction in household income poses. Those consumers who end up with less income won't be able to purchase as many goods and services as they did before. However, not all of these expenditure reductions from households will be at the expense of domestic production. Households also purchase goods and services imported from foreign countries.

As well as households, other macroeconomic sectors also purchase goods and services from foreign producers—government may purchase airplanes made in the United States or Europe to fight forest fires or to transport the Prime Minister around the country, and firms may purchase new machinery (capital equipment) from Japan. In both of these cases, the reduction in national income, *Y*, could lead to a reduction in such import expenditures. These reductions spread the pain, reducing economic activity in foreign countries as suggested in the accompanying World View article.

However, to the extent that expenditure on domestic production is reduced, aggregate demand will fall further, leading to still larger stocks of unsold goods, more job layoffs, and further reductions in income. It's this sequence of events—called the *multiplier process*—that makes a sudden decline in aggregate demand so frightening. What starts off as a relatively small spending shortfall quickly snowballs into a much larger problem.

We can see the multiplier process at work by watching what happens to the $10 billion decline in aggregate demand spending as it makes its way around the circular flow (Figure 9.7). At first (step 1), the only thing that happens is that $10 billion of unsold goods appear (in the form of undesired inventories). Producers adjust to this problem by cutting back on production, laying off workers, and reducing prices (step 2). In either case, the total income generated in the economy falls $10 billion per year

Income-Dependent Consumption

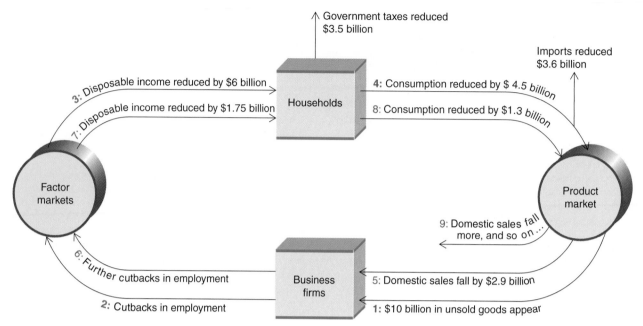

FIGURE 9.7
The Multiplier Process

A decline in investment (step 1) may lead to a cutback in production and income (step 2). A reduction in total income (step 3) will in turn lead to a reduction in consumer spending (step 4). These additional cuts in spending cause a further decrease in income, leading to additional spending reductions, and so on. This sequence of adjustments is referred to as the *multiplier process.*

as the cutbacks occur. As we noted on page 180, consumer disposable income represents about 60 percent of total income because of taxes and earnings retained by businesses, so disposable income will fall by $6 billion (step 3).

How will consumers respond to this drop in disposable income? ***If disposable income falls, we expect consumer spending to drop as well.*** In fact, the consumption function tells us just how much spending will drop. The *marginal propensity to consume (MPC)* is the critical variable in this process. Since we've specified that $C = \$10$ billion $+ 0.75Y_d$, we anticipate that consumers will reduce their spending by $0.75 for every $1.00 of lost disposable income. In the present example, the loss of $6 billion of disposable income will induce consumers to reduce their rate of spending by $4.5 billion per year ($0.75 \times \$6$ billion). This drop in spending is illustrated by step 4 in Figure 9.7. However, not all of this sales reduction comes from domestic producers as consumers also buy fewer imported goods and services.

The multiplier process doesn't stop here. A reduction in consumer spending quickly translates into more unsold output (step 5). As additional goods pile up on producers' shelves, we anticipate further cutbacks in production, employment, and disposable income (step 6).

As disposable incomes are further reduced by job layoffs (step 7), more reductions in consumer spending, for both domestic and foreign production, are sure to follow (step 8). Again the marginal propensity to consume (MPC) tells us how large such reductions will be. With an MPC of 0.75, we may expect spending to fall by another $1.3 billion per year ($0.75 \times \$1.75$ billion) in step 8.

The Multiplier

The multiplier process continues to work until the reductions in income and sales become so small that no one's market behaviour is significantly affected. We don't have to examine each step along the way. As you may have noticed, all the steps begin to look alike once we've gone around the circular flow a few times. Instead of examining each step, we can look ahead to see where they are taking us. Each time the multiplier process works its way around the circular flow, the reduction in spending equals the previous drop in income multiplied by the MPC.

The ultimate impact of an AD shift on total spending can be determined by computing the change in income and consumption at each cycle of the circular flow, for an infinite number of cycles. The entire computation can be simplified considerably by using a single figure, the multiplier. The *multiplier* tells us the extent to which the rate of total spending will change in response to an initial change in the flow of expenditure. As we developed the multiplier in Chapter 8, it also accounts for the fact that not all income removed from the domestic economy results in a reduction of domestic expenditure. First, the reduction in disposable income, Y_d, is less than the reduction in national income, Y, since some would have gone to taxes. Secondly, not all disposable income is used as expenditure (although it seems that way); the reduction in disposable income will also be reflected as reduced savings. Finally, not all expenditure goes to domestic production; therefore, some of the reduction in expenditure will be a reduction in the expenditure on imported goods and services from households, governments, and firms.

Taking all this into consideration, the multiplier can be computed as:

$$\text{multiplier} = \frac{1}{1 - b(1 - t) + m}$$

Where b represents the marginal propensity to consume, MPC; t is the proportion of net taxes paid from national income; and m is the marginal propensity to import (MPIm), the proportion of expenditure flowing to foreign producers.[3]

In our example, the initial change in spending occurs when aggregate demand drops by \$10 billion per year at full-employment output (\$300 billion per year). If Canadian households devote 75 percent, or \$0.75 of each additional dollar to expenditure (the marginal propensity to consume, MPC), and the government's net taxes represent \$0.35 of each dollar of national income, while Canadian households, governments, and firms spend \$0.36 on imported goods and services, the total reduction in domestic national income would be:

$$\begin{aligned} \text{Total change in spending} &= \text{multiplier} \times \text{initial change in aggregate expenditure} \\[6pt] &= \frac{1}{(1 - 0.75(1 - 0.35) + 0.36)} \times \$10 \text{ billion per year} \\[6pt] &= 1.146 \times \$10 \text{ billion per year} \\[6pt] &= \$11.46 \text{ billion per year} \end{aligned}$$

In other words, *the cumulative decrease in total spending (\$135 billion per year) resulting from a shortfall in aggregate demand at full employment is equal to the initial shortfall (\$10 billion per year) multiplied by the multiplier (1.146).* As the World View on page 185 illustrates, the cumulative process of expenditure adjustments can also have worldwide effects. Since Canada has a relatively open economy that is one of the world's largest per-capita traders, slowdowns and economic problems in other countries can have a significant impact on the Canadian economy.

Figures 9.1 and 9.2 hardly inspire optimism about the macro economy. Figure 9.1 suggests that the odds of the market generating an equilibrium at full employment and price stability are about the same as finding a needle in a haystack. Figure 9.2 suggests that if we're lucky enough to find the needle, we'll probably drop it again. From this perspective, it appears that our worries about the business cycle are well founded.

Competing Theories of Short-Run Change

WEB NOTE

Do sports teams create multiplier effects for cities? Read about this at www.brookings.edu/press/review/summer97/noll.htm.

---

[3]The multiplier summarizes the geometric progression considering the proportion of income spent on domestic goods and services.

The classical economists had no such worries. As we saw earlier, they believed that the economy would gravitate toward full employment. Keynes, on the other hand, worried that the macro equilibrium might start out badly and get worse in the absence of government intervention.

Modern macroeconomics recognizes each of these positions: Keynes' concern of short-run disequilibria and relatively slow self-correction, but also the Classical sense of a long-run constraint, the tendency of the economy to move toward this long-run position and the importance of pushing out the economy's production possibilities for future economic "well offness."

The AS/AD model doesn't really settle this controversy. It does, however, provide a convenient framework for comparing these and other theories about how the economy works. Essentially, ***macro controversies focus on the speed of adjustment between the short run and long run and the potential of government intervention to aid the adjustment process.*** These differing views can be classified as demand-side explanations, supply-side explanations, or some combination of the two.

Demand-Side Theories

Keynesian Theory. Keynesian theory is the most prominent of the demand-side theories. Keynes argued that a deficiency of spending would tend to depress an economy. This deficiency might originate in consumer saving, inadequate business investment, or insufficient government spending. Whatever its origins, the lack of spending would leave goods unsold and production capacity unused. This contingency is illustrated by point E_1 in Figure 9.8a. Notice that the equilibrium at E_1 leaves the economy at Q_1, below its full-employment potential (Q_F). Further, Keynes suggested that the "usual" self-correction mechanism (falling prices and wages) wouldn't occur, as they were "*downwardly sticky*." Thus, ***Keynes concluded that inadequate aggregate demand would cause persistently high unemployment.***

Keynes developed his theory during the Great Depression, when the economy seemed to be stuck at a very low level of equilibrium output, far below full-employment GDP. The only way to end the depression, he argued, was for someone to start demanding more goods. He advocated a big hike in government spending to start the economy moving toward full employment. At the time his advice was largely ignored. When Canada mobilized for World War II, however, the sudden surge in government spending shifted the aggregate demand curve sharply to the right, restoring full employment (e.g., a reverse shift from AD_1 to AD_0 in Figure 9.8a). In times of peace,

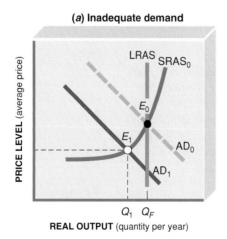

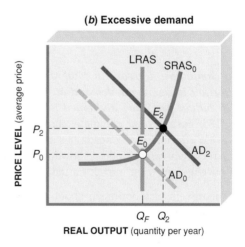

FIGURE 9.8
Demand-Side Theories

Inadequate demand may cause unemployment. In part (*a*), the demand AD_1 creates an equilibrium at E_1. The resulting output Q_1 falls short of full employment Q_F.

In part (*b*), excessive aggregate demand causes inflation. The price level rises from P_0 to P_2 when aggregate demand expands to AD_2. Demand-side theories emphasize how inadequate or excessive AD can cause macro failures.

U.S. Growth Weakest in Four Years; But It's Bouncing Back

WASHINGTON—U.S. economic growth in the opening quarter this year was the weakest in more than four years as business sold off inventories and Americans imported more foreign goods, the government reported yesterday.

The U.S. Commerce Department revised down its estimate for first-quarter expansion in gross domestic product to a 0.6% annual rate from the 1.3% it estimated a month ago. It was the slowest quarterly growth since the fourth quarter of 2002 when the economy edged ahead at a 0.2% rate and was below Wall Street economists' forecasts for a 0.8% quarterly growth rate.

Source: Glenn Somerville, "U.S. growth weakest in four years; But it's bouncing back," *The National Post* (June 1, 2007), p. FP7.

India and China Continue Rapid Economic Expansion

India's Central Statistical Organization (CSO) reported in May 2007 that real (GDP) economic growth for 2006–2007

reached 9.4 percent, the highest rate of growth in a decade and an increase over the 9.2 percent of a year earlier. Much of the increase in economic activity came from increased government expenditure, investment expenditure (gross fixed capital formation), and from consumption expenditure that has been characterized as a "mammoth middle-class" demand.

China's National Bureau of Statistics announced in October 2007 that the economy had experienced "steady and fast growth" for the first three quarters of 2007. The annualized rate of GDP growth for China represented a year-over-year increase of 11.5 percent. The Bureau pointed to accelerating industrial production, consumption expenditures in the domestic market, and the "rapid growth" of foreign trade as reasons for the continuing economic expansion.

Source: Based on "National Economy Kept Steady and Fast Growth in the First Three Quarters of 2007," Li Xiaochao, National Bureau of Statistics of China, October 25, 2007; National Bureau of Statistics China, http://www.stats.gov.cn/english/; Revised Estimates of Annual National Income 2006–07 and Quarterly Estimates of Gross Domestic Product 2006–07, Press Information Bureau Government of India http://mospi.nic.in/pressnote_31may07.htm May 31, 2007.

Analysis: Why do short-term growth rates vary across countries? In these stories, shifts of aggregate demand are emphasized, as illustrated in Figure 9.8.

Keynes also advocated changing government taxes and spending to shift the aggregate demand curve in whatever direction is desired.

The accompanying World View contrasts GDP growth in the United States, India, and China. Notice the role that aggregate demand plays in the stories. In the United States, an increase in imports (decreasing net exports) and a sell-off of inventory has slowed down economic growth. In India, a "mammoth middle-class demand" for goods and services has increased consumer demand, and in China, retail sales (consumer spending), capital spending, and factory output (investment) all increased economic growth by shifting their respective aggregate demand curves to the right.

Monetary Theories. Another demand-side theory emphasizes the role of money in financing aggregate demand. Money and credit affect the ability and willingness of people to buy goods and services. If credit isn't available or is too expensive, consumers won't be able to buy as many cars, homes, or other expensive products. "Tight" money might also curtail business investment. In these circumstances, aggregate demand might prove to be inadequate, as illustrated in Figure 9.8*a*. In this case, an increase in the money supply may be required to shift the aggregate demand curve into the desired position.

Both the Keynesian and monetarist theories also regard aggregate demand as a prime suspect for inflationary problems. In Figure 9.8*b*, the curve AD$_2$ leads to an equilibrium at E_2. At first blush, that equilibrium looks desirable, as it offers more

FIGURE 9.9
Supply-Side Theories

Inadequate supply can keep the economy below its full-employment potential and cause prices to rise as well. $SRAS_1$ leads to output Q_3 and increases the price level from P_0 to P_3. Supply-side theories emphasize how AS shifts can worsen or improve macro outcomes.

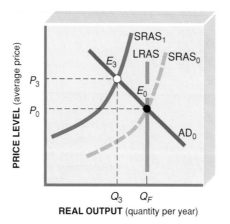

output (Q_2) than the full-employment threshold (Q_F). Notice, however, what's happening to prices: The price level rises from P_0 to P_2. Hence, **_excessive aggregate demand may cause inflation._**

The more extreme monetary theories attribute all our macro successes and failures to management of the money supply. According to these *monetarist* theories, the economy will tend to stabilize at something like full-employment GDP. Thus, only the price level will be affected by changes in the money supply and resulting shifts of aggregate demand. We'll examine the basis for this view in a moment. At this juncture we simply note that **_both Keynesian and monetarist theories emphasize the potential of aggregate-demand shifts to alter some macro outcomes._**

Supply-Side Theories

Figure 9.9 illustrates an entirely different explanation of the business cycle. Notice that the aggregate *supply* curve is on the move in Figure 9.9. The initial equilibrium is again at point E_0. This time, however, aggregate demand remains stationary, while aggregate supply shifts. The resulting decline of aggregate supply causes output and employment to decline (to Q_3 from Q_F).

Figure 9.9 tells us that aggregate supply may be responsible for downturns as well. Our failure to achieve full employment may result from the unwillingness of producers to provide more goods at existing prices. That unwillingness may originate in simple greed, in rising costs, in resource shortages, or in government taxes and regulation. Inadequate investment in infrastructure (e.g., roads, sewer systems) or skill training may also limit supply potential. Whatever the cause, if the short run aggregate supply curve is $SRAS_1$ rather than $SRAS_0$, full employment will not be achieved with the demand AD_0.

The inadequate supply illustrated in Figure 9.9 causes not only unemployment but inflation as well. At the equilibrium E_3, the price level has risen from P_0 to P_3. Hence, a decrease in aggregate supply can cause multiple macro problems. On the other hand, an increase—a rightward shift—in aggregate supply can move us closer to both our price-stability and full-employment goals. Chapter 14 examines the many ways of inducing such a shift.

Another group of economists, who advocate Real Business Cycle theory, suggest that disturbances in the economy are the result of "real" changes in the economy. While these disturbances can arise from either the aggregate demand side (changes in consumer behaviour or business investment, for instance) or from the supply side, they see the supply side disturbances as most significant. Supply side shocks can be positive or negative and include changes in technology or productivity, innovations, changes in the governmental regulatory framework, or rapid change in the price of widely used resources such as energy.

In 2004, economists Finn Kydland and Edward Prescott were awarded the Sveriges Riksbank Prize in Economic Sciences in Memory of Alfred Nobel (often referred to simply as the "Nobel Prize in Economics") for their work on Real Business Cycle theory.

WEB NOTE

Visit the Nobel Prize Web site for information about all the prize-winning economists since the prize's inception in 1969 at http://nobelprize.org/nobel_prizes/economics/.

Not everyone blames either the demand side or the supply side exclusively. The various macro theories tell us that both supply and demand can cause us to achieve or miss our policy goals. These theories also demonstrate how various shifts of the aggregate supply and demand curves can achieve any specific output or price level. One could also shift *both* the SRAS and AD curves to explain unemployment, inflation, or recurring business cycles. Such eclectic explanations draw from both sides of the market.

Eclectic Explanations

9.3 CLOSING RECESSIONARY AND INFLATIONARY GAPS

The key features of the Keynesian adjustment process are

- *Producers cut output and employment when output exceeds aggregate demand at the current price level (leakage exceeds injections).*
- *The resulting loss of income causes a decline in consumer spending.*
- *Declines in consumer spending lead to further production cutbacks, more lost income, and still less consumption.*

Figure 9.10 illustrates the ultimate impact of the multiplier process. Notice that the AD curve shifts *twice*. The first shift—from AD_0 to AD_1—represents the $10 billion drop in aggregate demand. As we saw earlier in Figure 9.7, this initial shift of aggregate demand will start the economy moving toward a new equilibrium at point *b*.

Sequential AD Shifts

Along the way, however, the multiplier kicks in and things get worse. *The decline in household income caused by investment cutbacks sets off the multiplier process, causing a secondary shift of the AD curve.* We measure these multiplier effects at the initial price level of P_0. In Figure 9.10 this is illustrated by the *second* shift of the aggregate demand curve, from AD_1 to AD_2.

Although aggregate demand has fallen (shifted) by $11.46 billion, real output doesn't necessarily drop that much. *The impact of a shift in aggregate demand is reflected in both output and price changes.* This is evident in Figure 9.11, which is a close-up

Price and Output Effects

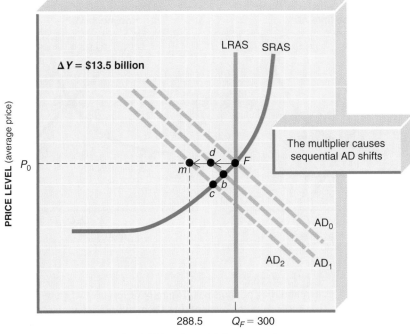

FIGURE 9.10
Multiplier Effects

A decline in investment spending reduces household income, setting off negative multiplier effects. Hence, the *initial* shift of AD_0 to AD_1 is followed by a *second* shift from of AD_1 to AD_2. The second shift represents reduced consumption.

FIGURE 9.11
Recessionary GDP Gap

The real GDP gap is the difference between equilibrium GDP (Q_E) and full-employment GDP (Q_F). It represents the lost output due to a recession.

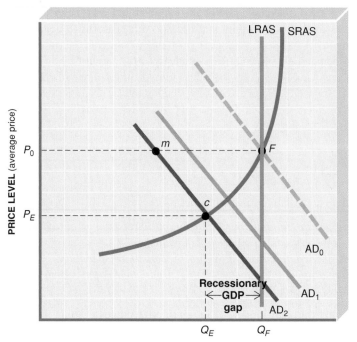

REAL OUTPUT (in billions of dollars per year)

view of Figure 9.10. When AD shifts from AD_0 to AD_2 the macro equilibrium moved down the sloped SRAS curve to point c. At point c the new equilibrium output is Q_E and the new price level is P_E.

Undesired Equilibrium

Figure 9.12*a* depicts the perfect macro equilibrium that everyone hopes for. Aggregate demand and aggregate supply, short run and long run, intersect at E_1. At that macro equilibrium we get both full employment (Q_F) and price stability (P^*)—an ideal situation.

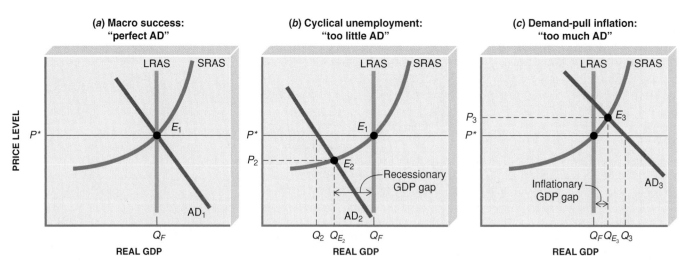

FIGURE 9.12
Macro Failures

Keynesian theory emphasizes that the combined spending decisions of consumers, investors, governments, and net exporters may not be compatible with the desired full employment (Q_F)– price stability (P^*) equilibrium (as they are in Figure *a*). Aggregate demand may be too small (Figure *b*) or too great (Figure *c*) causing cyclical unemployment (*b*) or demand-pull inflation (*c*). Worse yet, even a desirable macro equilibrium (*a*) may be upset by abrupt *shifts* of aggregate demand.

Keynes didn't think such a perfect outcome was likely. Why should aggregate demand intersect with aggregate supply exactly at point E_1? As we've observed, consumers, investors, government, and foreigners make independent spending decisions, based on many influences. Why should all these decisions add up to just the right amount of aggregate demand? Keynes didn't think they would. ***Because market participants make independent spending decisions, there's no reason to expect that the sum of their expenditures will generate exactly the right amount of aggregate demand.*** Instead, there's a high likelihood that we'll confront an imbalance between desired spending and full-employment output levels—that is, too much or too little aggregate demand.

Recessionary GDP Gap. Figure 9.12*b* illustrates one of the undesired equilibriums that Keynes worried about. *Full-employment GDP* is still at (Q_F) and stable prices are at the level P^*. In this case, however, the rate of output demanded at price level P^* is only Q_2, far short of full-employment GDP (Q_F). How could this happen? Quite simple: The spending plans of consumers, investors, government, and export buyers don't generate enough aggregate demand at current (P^*) prices.

The economy depicted in Figure 9.12*b* is in trouble. At full employment, a lot more output would be produced than market participants would be willing to buy. As unsold inventories rose, production would get cut back, workers would get laid off, and prices would decline. Eventually, the economy would settle at E_2, where AD$_2$ and SRAS intersect. *Equilibrium GDP* would be equal to Q_{E_2} and the equilibrium price level would be at P_2.

E_2 is clearly not a happy equilibrium. What particularly concerned Keynes was the **recessionary GDP gap,** the amount by which equilibrium GDP falls short of full-employment GDP. In Figure 9.12*b*, the recessionary GDP gap equals Q_F minus Q_{E_2}. This gap represents unused productive capacity: lost GDP and unemployed workers. It is the breeding ground of *cyclical unemployment.*

As long as the short run aggregate supply curve is upward-sloping, the shock of any AD shift will be spread across output and prices. In Figure 9.11, the net effect on real output is shown as the real GDP gap. ***The recessionary GDP gap equals the difference between equilibrium real GDP (Q_E) and full-employment real GDP (Q_F).*** It represents the amount by which the economy is underproducing during a recession.

Figure 9.11 not only illustrates how much output declines when AD falls but also provides an important clue about the difficulty of restoring full employment. Suppose the recessionary GDP gap were $20 billion, as illustrated in Figure 9.13. How much more AD would we need to get back to full employment?

Upward-Sloping SRAS. Suppose aggregate demand at the equilibrium price level (P_E) were to increase by exactly $20 billion (including multiplier effects), as illustrated by the shift to AD$_3$. Would that get us back to full-employment output? Not according to Figure 9.13. ***When AD increases, both output and prices go up.*** Because the SRAS curve is upward-sloping, the $20 billion shift from AD$_2$ to AD$_3$ moves the new macro equilibrium to point *g* rather than point *f*. We'd like to get to point *f* with full employment and price stability. But as demand picks up, producers are likely to raise prices. This leads us up the SRAS curve to point *g*. At point *g*, we're still short of full employment and have experienced a bit of inflation (an increased price level). ***So long as the short-run AS is upward-sloping, there's a trade-off between unemployment and inflation.*** We can get lower rates of unemployment (more real output) only if we accept some inflation.

"Full" Employment vs. "Natural" Unemployment. The short-term trade-off between unemployment and inflation is the basis for the definition of "full" employment. We don't define full employment as *zero* unemployment; we define it as the rate of unemployment *consistent with price stability and the economy operating at its*

recessionary GDP gap: The amount by which equilibrium GDP falls short of full-employment GDP.

Short-Run Inflation-Unemployment Trade-Offs

FIGURE 9.13
**The Inflation-Unemployment
Trade-Off**

If the short-run AS curve is upward-sloping, an AD increase will raise output *and* prices. If AD increases by the amount of the recessionary GDP gap only (AD$_2$ to AD$_3$), full employment (Q_F) won't be reached. Macro equilibrium moves to point *g*, not point *f*.

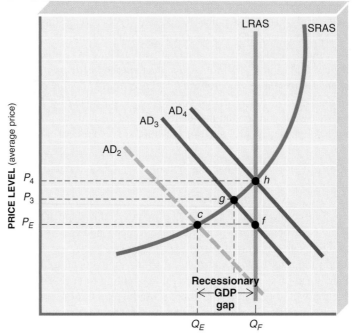

REAL OUTPUT (in billions of dollars per year)

full employment: The lowest rate of unemployment compatible with price stability and the economy operating at potential national income (LRAS).

potential—that is, operating at its LRAS curve. As noted in Chapter 5, **full employment** is typically defined as a 5 to 7 percent rate of unemployment. What the upward-sloping SRAS curve tells us is that *the closer the economy gets to capacity output, the greater the risk of inflation.* To get back to full employment in Figure 9.13, aggregate demand would have to increase to AD$_4$, with the price level rising to P_4.

Not everyone accepts this notion of full employment. As we saw in Chapter 8, neoclassical and monetarist economists prefer to focus on *long*-run outcomes. In their view, the long-run AS curve is vertical. In that long-run context, there's no inflation-unemployment trade-off: An AD shift doesn't change the "natural" (institutional) rate of unemployment but does alter the price level.

Inflationary GDP Gap. Aggregate demand won't always fall short of potential output. But Keynes saw it as a distinct possibility. He also realized that aggregate demand might even *exceed* the economy's full-employment/price stability capacity. This contingency is illustrated in Figure 9.12*c*.

In Figure 9.12*c*, the AD$_3$ curve represents the combined spending plans of all market participants. According to this aggregate demand curve, market participants demand more output (Q_3) at current prices than the economy can produce (Q_F). To meet this excessive demand, producers will use overtime shifts and strain capacity. This will push prices up. The economy will end up at the macro equilibrium E_3. At E_3 the price level is higher (inflation) and short-run output exceeds sustainable levels.

What we end up with in Figure 9.12*c* is another undesirable equilibrium. In this case we have an **inflationary GDP gap,** wherein equilibrium GDP (Q_{E_3}) exceeds full-employment GDP (Q_F). This is a fertile breeding ground for **demand-pull inflation.**

As we've observed, a sudden shift in aggregate demand can have a cumulative effect on macro outcomes that's larger than the initial imbalance. This multiplier process works both ways: Just as a *decrease* in investment (or any other injection) can send the economy into a recessionary tailspin, an *increase* in investment might initiate an inflationary spiral.

Figure 9.14 illustrates the consequences of a sudden jump in investment spending. We start out again in the happy equilibrium (point *F*), where full employment (Q_F) and price stability (P_0) prevail.

inflationary GDP gap: The amount by which equilibrium GDP exceeds full-employment GDP.

demand-pull inflation: An increase in the price level initiated by excessive aggregate demand.

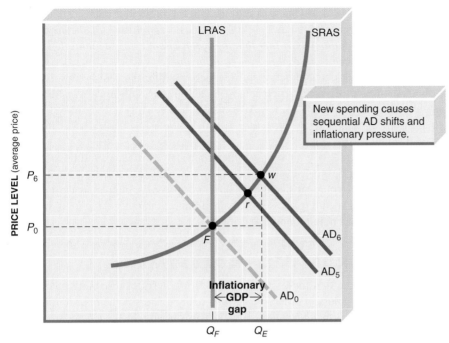

FIGURE 9.14
Demand-Pull Inflation

An increase in investment or other autonomous spending sets off multiplier effects shifting AD to the right. AD shifts to the right *twice,* first (AD_0 to AD_5) because of increased investment, then (AD_5 to AD_6) because of increased consumption. The increased AD moves the economy up the short-run AS curve, causing some inflation. How much inflation results depends on the slope of the SRAS curve.

Increased Investment

Then investors suddenly decide to step up the rate of investment. Perhaps their expectations for future sales have risen. Maybe new technology has become available that compels firms to modernize their facilities. Whatever the reason, investors decide to raise the level of investment at the current price level (P_0). This change in investment spending shifts the aggregate demand curve from AD_0 to AD_5.

Inventory Depletion. One of the first things you'll notice when AD shifts like this is that available inventories shrink. Investors can step up their *spending* more quickly than firms can increase their *production*. A lot of the increased investment demand will have to be satisfied from existing inventory. When this happens, *desired* investment (including desired inventory) will fall below actual investment. The decline in inventory is a signal to producers that it might be a good time to raise prices a bit. Thus, **inventory depletion is a warning sign of impending inflation.** As the economy moves up from point F to point r in Figure 9.14, that inflation starts to become visible.

Household Incomes

Whether or not prices start rising quickly, household incomes will get a boost from the increased investment. Producers will step up the rate of output to rebuild inventories and supply more investment goods (equipment and structures). To do so, they'll hire more workers or extend working hours. The end result for workers will be fatter paycheques.

Induced Consumption

What will households do with these heftier paycheques? By now, you know what the consumer response will be. The marginal propensity to consume prompts an increase in consumer spending. Eventually, consumer spending increases by a *multiple* of the income change.

Figure 9.14 illustrates the secondary shift of AD caused by multiplier-induced consumption. Notice how the AD curve shifts a second time, from AD_5 to AD_6.

A New Equilibrium

The ultimate impact of the investment surge is reflected in the new equilibrium at point w. As before, the shift of AD has affected both real output and prices. Real output does increase beyond the full-employment level, but it does so only at the expense of accelerating inflation. This is a classic case of *demand-pull inflation.* The initial increase in investment was enough to kindle a little inflation. The multiplier effect worsened the problem by forcing the economy further along the ever-steeper SRAS curve. The *inflationary GDP gap* ends up as $Q_E - Q_F$.

Booms and Busts

The Keynesian analysis of leakages, injections, and the multiplier paints a fairly grim picture of the prospects for macro stability. ***The basic conclusion of the Keynesian analysis is that the economy is vulnerable to abrupt changes in spending behaviour and won't self-adjust to a desired macro equilibrium.***

When the aggregate demand curve shifts, macro equilibrium will be upset. Moreover, the responses of market participants to an abrupt AD shift are likely to worsen rather than improve market outcomes. As a result, the economy may gravitate toward an equilibrium of stagnant recession (point *c* in Figure 9.10) or persistent inflation (point *w* in Figure 9.14).

As Keynes saw it, the combination of alternating AD shifts and multiplier effects also causes recurring business cycles. A drop in consumer or business spending can set off a recessionary spiral of declining GDP and prices. A later increase in either consumer or business spending can set the ball rolling in the other direction. This may result in a series of economic booms and busts.

9.4 LONG-RUN SELF-ADJUSTMENT

Some economists argue that these various theories of short-run instability aren't only confusing but also pointless. As they see it, what really matters is the *long*-run trend of the economy, not *short*-run fluctuations around those trends. In their view, month-to-month or quarter-to-quarter fluctuations in real output or prices are just statistical noise. The *long*-term path of output and prices is determined by more fundamental factors.

This emphasis on long-term outcomes is reminiscent of the classical theory: the view that the economy will self-adjust. A decrease in aggregate demand is only a *temporary* problem. Once producers and workers make the required price and wage adjustments, the economy will return to its long-run equilibrium growth path.

The monetarist theory we encountered earlier has a similar view of long-run stability. According to the monetarist theory, the supply of goods and services is determined by institutional factors such as the size of the labour force and technology. These factors determine a natural rate of output that's relatively immune to short-run fluctuations in aggregate demand. If this argument is valid, the long-run aggregate supply curve is vertical, not sloped.

Figure 9.15 illustrates the classical/monetarist view of long-run stability. The vertical long-run AS curve is anchored at the natural rate of output Q_N. The natural rate

FIGURE 9.15
The "Natural" Rate of Output

Monetarists and neoclassical theorists assert that the level of output is fixed at the natural rate Q_N by the size of the labour force, technology, and other institutional factors. As a result, fluctuations in aggregate demand affect the price level but not real output.

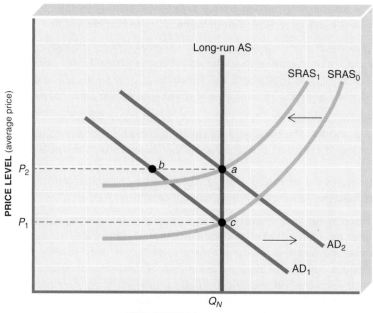

Q_N is itself determined by demographics, technology, market structure, and the institutional infrastructure of the economy.

If the long-run AS curve is really vertical, as the classical and monetarist theories assert, some startling conclusions follow. The most startling implication is that **aggregate demand shifts affect prices but not output in the long run.** Notice in Figure 9.15 how the shift from AD$_1$ to AD$_2$ raises the price level but leaves output anchored at Q_N.

What has happened here? Didn't we suggest earlier that an increase in aggregate demand would spur producers to increase output? And aren't rising prices an extra incentive for doing so?

Monetarists concede that *short-run* price increases tend to widen profit margins. This profit effect is an incentive to increase the rate of output. In the *long run,* however, costs are likely to catch up with rising prices. Workers will demand higher wages, landlords will increase rents, and banks will charge higher interest rates as the price level rises. Hence, a rising price level has only a *temporary* profit effect on supply behaviour. In the *long run,* cost effects will dominate. In the *long run,* a rising price level will be accompanied by rising costs, giving producers no special incentive to supply more output. Accordingly, output will revert to its natural rate Q_N. In other words, these *cost effects* lead to an inward shift of the short run aggregate supply curve as producers face higher production costs. The economy returns to equilibrium at point *a* where real output (Y) is equal to the long run aggregate supply curve, (LRAS), Q_N and prices have risen to P_2.

Classical economists use the vertical AS curve to explain also how the economy self-adjusts to temporary setbacks. If AD declines from AD$_2$ to AD$_1$ in Figure 9.15, the economy may move from point *a* to point *b*, leaving a lot of unsold output. As producers respond with price cuts, however, the volume of output demanded increases as the economy moves from point *b* to point *c*. At point *c*, full employment is restored. Thus flexible prices (and wages) enable the economy to maintain the natural rate of output Q_N.

Short- vs. Long-Run Perspectives

All this may well be true. But as Keynes pointed out, it's also true that "in the long run we are all dead." How long are we willing to wait for the promised "self-adjustment"? In the Great Depression, people waited for 10 years—and still saw no self-adjustment.

Whatever the long run may hold, it's in the short run that we must consume, invest, and find a job. However stable and predictable the long run might be, short-run variations in macro outcomes will determine how well we fare in any year. Moreover, **the short-run aggregate supply curve is likely to be upward-sloping,** as shown in our earlier graphs. This implies that both aggregate supply and aggregate demand influence short-run macro outcomes.

By distinguishing between short-run and long-run aggregate supply curves, competing economic theories achieve a standoff. Theories that highlight the necessity of policy intervention emphasize the importance of short-run macro outcomes. On the other hand, theories that emphasize the "natural" stability of the market point to the predictability of long-run outcomes. Even this fragile truce, however, is easily broken when the questions turn to the duration of the "short" run or the effectiveness of any particular policy option.

9.5 A BRIEF PRIMER ON POLICY OPTIONS

Macro Policy Options

The aggregate supply–demand model is a convenient summary of how the macro economy works. The model raises more questions than it answers, however. We could draw the AS and AD curves—or shift them—to create any outcome we wanted. The real challenge for macro theory is to determine which curves (or shifts) best represent market reality. We'll spend a lot of time sifting through evidence and looking for the "correct" theory. At the outset of that quest, however, we might consider how the AS/AD model also helps define our macro policy options for the economy.

Basic Policy Strategies

The basic choice between market-driven and government-directed behaviour underlies all policy options. The aggregate supply–demand (AS/AD) framework adds a new dimension to this dichotomy. We can now identify *three distinct macro policy strategies:*

- *Shift the aggregate demand curve.* Find and use policy tools that stimulate or restrain total spending.
- *Shift the aggregate supply curves.* Find and implement policy levers that reduce the cost of production or otherwise stimulate more output at every price level.
- *Laissez faire.* Don't interfere with the market; let markets self-adjust.

Specific Policy Options

These very different policy strategies generate a variety of specific policy options, including the following:

Classical Approaches. The classical approach to economic policy embraced the laissez-faire perspective. Prior to the Great Depression, most economists were convinced that the economy would self-adjust to full employment. If the initial equilibrium rate of output were too low, the resulting imbalances would alter prices and wages, inducing changes in market behaviour. The aggregate supply and demand curves would "naturally" shift, until they reached the intersection where full employment (Q_F) prevails.

Recent versions of the classical theory—dubbed the "new classical economics"—stress not only the market's "natural" ability to self-adjust to *long-run* equilibrium but also the inability of the government to improve *short-run* market outcomes. New classical economists point to the increasing ability of market participants to anticipate government policies and to take defensive actions that thwart them.

Fiscal Policy. The Great Depression cast serious doubt on the classical self-adjustment concept. According to Keynes's view, the economy would *not* self-adjust. Rather, it might stagnate until aggregate demand was forcibly shifted. An increase in government spending on goods and services might provide the necessary shift. Or a cut in taxes might be used to stimulate greater consumer and investor spending. These budgetary tools are the hallmark of fiscal policy. Specifically, **fiscal policy** is the use of government tax and spending powers to alter economic outcomes.

fiscal policy: The use of government taxes and spending to alter macroeconomic outcomes.

Fiscal policy is an integral feature of modern economic policy. Every year the federal Parliament and provincial Legislatures introduce, debate, and pass budgets. They argue about whether the economy needs to be stimulated or restrained. They then argue about the level of spending or taxes required to ensure the desired outcome. This is the heart of fiscal policy.

Monetary Policy. The government budget doesn't get all the action. As suggested earlier, the amount of money in circulation may also affect macro equilibrium. If so, then the policy arsenal must include some levers to control the money supply. These are the province of monetary policy. **Monetary policy** refers to the use of money and credit controls to alter economic outcomes.

monetary policy: The use of money and credit controls to influence macroeconomic outcomes.

The Bank of Canada has direct control over monetary policy. The Bank is a federal crown corporation that acts with considerable independence from government itself. According to the Bank of Canada Act, the bank's responsibility is "to regulate credit and currency in the best interests of the economic life of the nation."[4] In practice, the Bank of Canada increases or decreases the money supply to achieve its policy goals.

Supply-Side Policy. Fiscal and monetary policies focus on the demand side of the market. Both are motivated by the conviction that appropriate shifts of the aggregate demand curve can bring about desired changes in output or price levels. **Supply-side policies** offer an alternative; they seek to shift the aggregate supply curves.

supply-side policy: The use of tax incentives, (de)regulation, and other mechanisms to increase the ability and willingness to produce goods and services.

[4]Bank Act of Canada, http://www.bankofcanada.ca/en/about/act_loi_boc_bdc.pdf, accessed October 3, 2006.

There are scores of supply-side levers. The most common are tax reductions (on personal income and business profits as well as on payroll taxes and capital taxes), or reductions in "red tape" intended to increase the ease of adding to economic activity. This was clearly a theme in the 2006 Federal Budget Speech.[5]

To ensure our long-term prosperity, we need to increase our productivity.

- It means reducing red tape, reducing business taxes and eliminating the capital tax to help our Canadian companies compete in the global economy and create jobs for Canadians at home;
- Incentives for Canadians to enter and stay in the workforce such as the new $1,000 Canada Employment Credit;
- Reductions in taxes on small business;
- Creating a climate for job creation and growth by reducing corporate tax rates.

Trade Policy. International trade and money flows offer yet another option for shifting aggregate supply and demand. A reduction in trade barriers makes imports cheaper and more available. This shifts the aggregate supply to the right, reducing price pressures at every output level. Changing the international value (exchange rate) of the dollar alters the relative price of Canadian-made goods, thereby shifting both aggregate demand and supply. Hence, trade policy is another tool in the macroeconomic toolbox.

Eclecticism. Few governments commit themselves entirely to one macroeconomic strategy. Federal Liberal governments have acted both to cut taxes and stimulate economic activity through regional spending. The current Conservative government's budget, as illustrated earlier, has also moved to reduce taxes in many areas and committed to reducing red tape, but continues also to support fishers, forestry, and agriculture industries through various programs.

In part, the eclectic use of policy options reflects a "do-whatever-it-takes-to-win" attitude on the part of politicians. But "politics" isn't the only explanation for the lack of clear-cut policy strategies. No economic theory has proved infallible. As we'll see, different theories provide important insights into how the economy works, but each falls short in explaining one or more of our economic problems. In these circumstances, policymakers are reluctant to put all their economic eggs in one basket. They prefer more "flexible" strategies. So we're likely to witness an eclectic mix of classical, fiscal, monetary, and supply-side policies in the economy tomorrow rather than single-minded adherence to any one theory.

[5]James M. Flaherty, P.C., M.P., Minister of Finance, Federal Budget speech, May 2, 2006, http://www.fin. gc.ca/budget06/speech/speeche.htm.

SUMMARY

- The long-term growth rate of the Canadian economy is approximately 3 percent per year. But output doesn't increase 3 percent every year. In some years, real GDP grows much faster than that; in other years growth is slower. Sometimes total output actually declines.

- These short-run variations in GDP growth are a central focus of macroeconomics. Macro theory tries to explain the alternating periods of growth and contraction that characterize the business cycle; macro policy attempts to control the cycle.

- All the influences on macro outcomes are transmitted through aggregate supply or aggregate demand. Aggregate supply and demand determine the equilibrium rate of output and prices. The economy will gravitate to that unique combination of output and price levels.

- The circular flow of income has offsetting leakages (consumer saving, taxes, business saving, imports) and injections (autonomous consumption, investment, government spending, exports).

- When desired injections equal leakage, the economy is in equilibrium.
- An imbalance of injections and leakages will cause the economy to expand or contract. An imbalance at full-employment GDP will cause cyclical unemployment or demand-pull inflation. How serious these problems become depends on how the market responds to the initial imbalance.
- Classical economists believed (changing) interest rates and price levels would equalize injections and leakages (especially consumer saving and investment), restoring full-employment equilibrium.
- Keynes showed that spending imbalances might actually *worsen* if consumer and investor expectations changed.
- An abrupt change in autonomous spending (injections) shifts the AD curve, setting off a sequential multiplier process that magnifies changes in equilibrium GDP.
- The multiplier itself indicates the cumulative change in demand that follows an initial (autonomous) disruption of spending flows.
- Macro equilibrium may not be consistent with the employment and price level goals set by government. This results in an undesirable macro equilibrium.
- Macro equilibrium may be disturbed by changes in aggregate supply (SRAS) or aggregate demand (AD). Such changes are illustrated by shifts of the SRAS and AD curves, and they lead to a new equilibrium.
- Competing economic theories try to explain the shape and shifts of the aggregate supply and demand curves, thereby explaining the business cycle. Specific theories tend to emphasize demand or supply influences.
- As long as the short-run aggregate supply curve slopes upward, AD shifts will affect both real output and prices.
- The recessionary GDP gap measures the amount by which equilibrium GDP falls short of full-employment GDP.
- The inflationary gap measures the amount by which equilibrium GDP exceeds the long-run full-employment GDP.
- In the long run the LRAS curve tends to be vertical, implying that changes in aggregate demand affect prices but not output. In the short run, however, the SRAS curve is sloped, making macro outcomes sensitive to both supply and demand.
- Macro policy options range from laissez faire (the classical approach) to various strategies for shifting the aggregate demand curve or the aggregate supply curves or both.

Key Terms

full-employment GDP 176	short-run equilibrium GDP 184	demand-pull inflation 194
leakage 180	recessionary GDP gap 193	fiscal policy 198
gross business saving 180	full employment 194	monetary policy 198
injection 181	inflationary GDP gap 194	supply-side policy 198

Questions for Discussion

1. If business cycles were really inevitable, what purpose would macro policy serve?
2. What events might prompt consumers to demand fewer goods at current prices?
3. If equilibrium is compatible with both buyers' and sellers' intentions, how can it be undesirable?
4. The World View on page 189 provides data on economic activity for the United States, India, and China. Use an AD/AS model and explain the impact on the Canadian economy of (*a*) a slowdown in growth of the U.S. economy; (*b*) the purchase of more inexpensive textiles produced in Chinese factories; and, (*c*) the sale of wheat and electronics to satisfy the "mammoth middle-class demand" in India.
5. How would a sudden jump in Canadian prices affect (*a*) imports from Mexico, (*b*) exports to Mexico, and (*c*) Canadian aggregate demand?
6. Why might rising prices stimulate short-run production but have no effect on long-run production?
7. How might a tax cut affect both AD *and* AS?
8. How might declining prices affect a firm's decision to borrow and invest?
9. Why wouldn't investment and saving flows at full employment always be equal?
10. When unwanted inventories pile up in retail stores, how is production affected? What are the steps in this process?
11. How can equilibrium output exceed full-employment output (as in Figure 9.14)?

12. What forces might turn an economic bust into an economic boom? What forces might put an end to the boom?

13. What might trigger an abrupt decline in consumer spending?

14. Will the price level always rise when AD increases? Why or why not?

EXERCISES

PROBLEMS   The Student Problem Set to accompany this chapter can be found at the end of the book.

WEB ACTIVITIES   Web Activities to accompany this chapter can be found on the Online Learning Centre at **http://www.mcgrawhill.ca/olc/schiller**.

PART 4

Fiscal Policy Levers

It is important to remember that when it comes to setting monetary policy, the Bank always tries to develop a complete picture of the economy. We do not react unduly to any individual piece of information. Rather, we put all the pieces together to get to the underlying trends in the economy.

David Dodge,
Governor, Bank of Canada
21 June 2006[1]

The Monetary Economy has as its focus the supply and demand for money. The first chapter in this section—Chapter 12—introduces the nature and function of money in an economy. Chapter 13 looks at monetary policy tools and instruments and how monetary policy seeks to alter aggregate demand and thereby real economy equilibrium.

[1]Bank of Canada. (2006, October). *Monetary policy report*. Publications Distribution, Communications Department, Bank of Canada, Ottawa, Ontario. Available online at http://www.bankofcanada.ca/en/mpr/mpr_previous.html

Fiscal Policy

I n the previous two chapters we've drawn a distinction between an economy's long-run trend and its short-run deviation from that trend. The economy's long-run potential national income, Y^*, is constrained by its available resources and productivity, while any short-run deviation arises from "shocks" to either the short run aggregate supply curve or the aggregate demand curve.

From a Keynesian perspective, such short run deviation is the result of aggregate demand being unstable; too little aggregate demand causes unemployment; too much aggregate demand causes inflation. If the market itself won't correct these imbalances—wages and prices being inflexible or at least slow to adjust—government can intervene to manage the level of aggregate demand. This implies increasing aggregate demand when it's deficient (fiscal stimulus) and decreasing aggregate demand when it's excessive (fiscal restraint).

This chapter examines some tools governments can use to alter macroeconomic outcomes. The questions we confront are:

- **How does government spending and tax policy impact aggregate demand?**
- **How does the choice of a government's policy balance short-run and long-run macroeconomic objectives?**
- **What are the risks of government intervention?**

As we'll see, the government's tax and spending activities affect not only the *level* of output and prices but the *mix* of output as well. In fact, the language of government regarding current fiscal policy would seem to refer to this mix in budgets and speeches that focus on "government investment" in health, education, and Canadians generally.

LEARNING OBJECTIVES

By the end of this chapter, you should be able to:

10.1 Describe the major expenditures of the Federal Government

10.2 Explain how changes in the price level impact the change in real GDP from any shift in AD

10.3 Describe the multiplier effect from any initial change in government spending

10.4 Describe the "risks" associated with government intervention

10.5 Explain the "second crisis" of how the government spends or whom it taxes

10.1 TAXES AND SPENDING

In 1907, the total revenue of the federal government was $96 million. Of this total, customs duties, (taxes on imports and exports) and excise taxes, (mainly taxes on alcohol and tobacco) totalled $73 million, or more than ¾ of federal government revenue in the absence of any taxes on income. Personal and corporate income taxes began to be collected in 1918 but didn't become a larger part of federal government revenue until 1940.

As seen in Table 10.1, by 2006 (March year ending), federal government revenue reached $229.6 billion, and income tax accounted for more than 60 percent of that total. Consumption taxes (GST) added another 20 percent of total revenue. Those custom duties and excise taxes that were so important in 1907 now represent less than 5 percent of federal government revenue.

Federal government expenditures in 1907 were as modest as their revenue, amounting to $110 million dollars, $72 million spent on transportation and communications and economic development, $6 million on general government, $9 million as payments to provinces and municipalities, and $11 million for public debt charges. In contrast, in 2006 federal government expenditures were $216.2 billion, with $80.2 billion going to social services, $24.7 billion transferred to the provinces (general purpose transfers), $24.2 billion for protection of persons and property, $21.5 billion to health, and $21.3 billion to debt charges. The largest component of the 1907 budget, transportation, communications, and economic development, accounted for only a little more than 1 percent of the 2006 budget.

The focus of this chapter is not so much on the dollars spent by government but rather on how government expenditure *directly* affects aggregate demand.

Purchases vs. Transfers. To understand how government spending affects aggregate demand, we must again distinguish between government *purchases* and *income transfers*.

Government Revenue

Government Expenditures

TABLE 10.1
Federal Government Revenue and Expenditures

Federal Government 2006 (millions of dollars)			
Revenue		**Expenditure**	
Income taxes	144,562	General government services	9,059
Consumption taxes	48,490	Protection of persons and property	24,275
Other taxes	670	Transportation and communication	2,266
Contributions to social security plans	22,063	Health	21,531
Sales of goods and services	6,016	Social services	80,281
Investment income	6,613	Education	4,937
Other revenue from own sources	553	Resource conservation and industrial development	8,206
General purpose transfers	603	Environment	2,100
Specific purpose transfers	88	Recreation and culture	4,044
		Labour, employment, and immigration	1,857
		Housing	2,033
		Foreign affairs and international assistance	6,065
		Regional planning and development	339
		Research establishments	3,013
		General purpose transfers	24,785
		Debt charges	21,353
		Other expenditures	14
Total revenue	229,660	Total expenditures	216,156
Surplus	13,504		

Source: "Federal government revenue and expenditures," adapted from Statistics Canada CANSIM database table 385-0001, http://cansim2.statcan.ca, last modified 2006-08-02. Fiscal year ending March 31. Statistics Canada information is used with the permission of Statistics Canada.

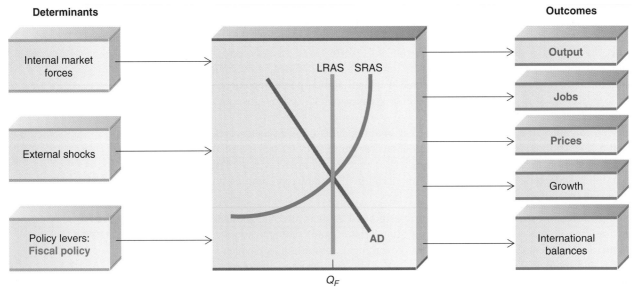

FIGURE 10.1
Fiscal Policy

Fiscal policy refers to the use of the government tax and spending powers to alter macro outcomes. Fiscal policy works principally through shifts of the aggregate demand curve.

Government spending on transportation and communications, education, and housing entail the purchase of goods and services in product markets; they're part of aggregate demand. By contrast, the government doesn't buy anything when it mails out Canada Pension cheques. Those cheques simply transfer income from taxpayers to retired workers. **Income transfers** don't become part of aggregate demand until the transfer recipients decide to spend that income.

As we'll observe in Chapter 11, not all federal government spending entails the purchase of goods and services. In fact, much of federal spending is a general purpose transfer to the provinces, an income transfer to households, or an interest payment on the public debt.

income transfers: Payments to individuals for which no current goods or services are exchanged, such as pension, welfare, and employment insurance payments.

Fiscal Policy

The federal government's tax and spending powers give it a great deal of influence over aggregate demand. *The government can alter aggregate demand by*

- *Purchasing more or fewer goods and services.*
- *Increasing or decreasing taxes.*
- *Changing the level of income transfers.*

Fiscal policy entails the use of these various budget levers to influence macroeconomic outcomes. *From a macro perspective, the federal budget is a tool that can change aggregate demand and macroeconomic outcomes.* Figure 10.1 puts this tool into the framework of the basic AS/AD model.

Although fiscal policy can be used to pursue any of our economic goals, we begin our study by exploring its potential to ensure full employment. We then look at its impact on inflation. Along the way we also observe the potential of fiscal policy to alter the mix of output and the distribution of income.

10.2 FISCAL STIMULUS AND RESTRAINT

The basic premise of fiscal policy is that the real economy's short-run equilibrium may not be a desirable one. This is clearly the case in Figure 10.2. The real economy equilibrium occurs at Q_E, where $1,460 billion of output is being produced. Full-employment GDP, however, occurs at Q_F, where the real value of output is

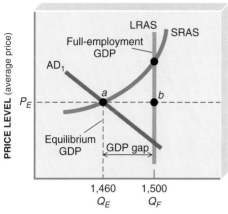

$1,500 billion. Accordingly, the economy depicted in Figure 10.2 is experiencing a *recessionary GDP gap* of $40 billion.

The Keynesian model of the adjustment process helps us not only understand how an economy can get into such trouble but also see how it might get out. Keynes emphasized how the aggregate demand curve *shifts* with changes in spending behaviour. He also emphasized how new injections of spending into the circular flow multiply into much larger changes in total spending. From a Keynesian perspective, then, the way out of recession is obvious: Get someone to spend more on goods and services. Should desired spending increase, the aggregate demand curve would *shift* to the right, leading the economy out of recession. That additional spending impetus could come from increased government purchases or from tax cuts that induce increased consumption or investment. Such a **fiscal stimulus** might propel the economy out of recession.

Although the general strategy for Keynesian fiscal policy is clear, the scope of desired intervention isn't so evident. Two strategic policy questions must be addressed:

* By how much do we want to shift the AD curve to the right?
* How can we induce the desired shift?

At first glance, the size of the desired AD shift might seem obvious. If the GDP gap is $40 billion, why not just increase aggregate demand by that amount?

The Naive Keynesian Model. Keynes thought that policy might just work. The intent of the expansionary fiscal policy is to achieve full employment. In Figure 10.3, this goal would be attained at point *b*. When the AD curve shifts rightward by $40 billion, the new AD₂ curve in fact passes through point *b*, creating the possibility of achieving our full-employment goal.

Will the economy move so easily from point *a* to point *b*? Only under very special conditions. The economy would move from point *a* to point *b* in Figure 10.3 only if the *aggregate supply* curve were horizontal. In other words, we'd achieve full employment at the current price level (P_E) with the shift to AD₂ only if prices didn't rise when the economy expanded. This is the expectation of the naive Keynesian model. In fairness to Keynes, we must recall that he developed this approach during the Great Depression, when prices were *falling*. No one was worried that prices would rise if demand increased.

Price-Level Changes. Even in today's economy, prices may not rise every time aggregate demand increases. Over some ranges of real output, the AS curve may actually be horizontal. Eventually, however, we expect the AS curve to slope upward. When it does, any increase in aggregate demand affects both real output *and* prices. In those

Keynesian Strategy

The Fiscal Target

FIGURE 10.3

The AD Shortfall

If aggregate demand increased by the amount of the recessionary GDP gap, which is the shift from AD_1 to AD_2, equilibrium would occur at point c, leaving the economy short of full employment (Q_F). (Some of the increased demand pushes up prices instead of output.) To reach full-employment equilibrium (point d), the AD curve must shift to AD_3, thereby eliminating the entire AD shortfall. The AD shortfall—the horizontal distance between point a and point e—is the fiscal policy target for achieving full employment.

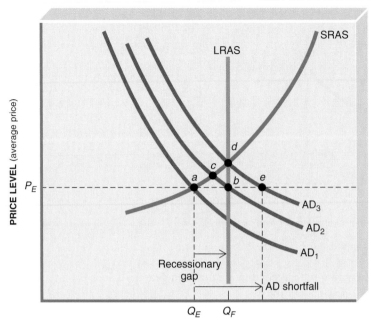

AD shortfall: The amount by which aggregate demand must be increased to achieve full employment after allowing for price-level changes.

circumstances, an increase in aggregate demand doesn't translate dollar-for-dollar into increased real GDP. Instead, *when the AD curve shifts to the right, the economy moves up the short run aggregate supply (SRAS) curve, not horizontally to the right. As a result both real output and the price level change.*

Figure 10.3 illustrates the consequences of the upward-sloping aggregate supply curve. Suppose we actually increased aggregate demand by $40 billion, an amount equal to the initial GDP gap. When the aggregate demand curve shifts from AD_1 to AD_2, the economy moves to the macro equilibrium at point c, not to point b. As demand picks up, we expect cost pressures to increase, pushing the price level up the upward-sloping SRAS curve. At point c, the SRAS and AD_2 curves intersect, establishing a new equilibrium. At that equilibrium, the price level is higher than it was initially (P_E). Real output is higher as well but still short of the full-employment target (Q_F). Hence, the naive Keynesian policy fails to achieve full employment. To do better, we must recognize that *shifting (increasing) aggregate demand by the amount of the GDP gap will achieve full employment only if the price level doesn't rise.*

The AD Shortfall. Although the naive Keynesian approach doesn't work, we needn't forsake fiscal policy. Figure 10.3 simply tells us that the naive Keynesian policy prescription (increasing AD by the amount of the GDP gap) probably won't cure all our unemployment ills. It also suggests, however, that a *larger* dose of fiscal stimulus might just work. *So long as the SRAS curve slopes upward, we must increase aggregate demand by more than the size of the recessionary GDP gap to achieve full employment.*

Figure 10.3 illustrates this new policy target. The **AD shortfall** is the amount of additional aggregate demand needed to achieve full employment *after allowing for price-level changes*. Notice in Figure 10.3 that full employment (Q_F) is achieved only when the AD curve intersects the SRAS curve at point d. To get there, the aggregate demand curve must shift from AD_1 all the way to AD_3. That third aggregate demand curve passes through point e as well. Hence, aggregate demand must increase until it passes through point e. This *horizontal distance between point **a** and point **e** in Figure 10.3 measures the AD shortfall.* Aggregate demand must increase (shift) by the amount of the AD shortfall in order to achieve full employment. Thus, *the AD shortfall is the fiscal target.* That's how much *additional* aggregate demand is required to reach full employment (Q_F).

Were we to increase AD by enough to attain full employment, it's apparent in Figure 10.3 that prices would increase as well. We'll examine this dilemma later; for the time being we focus on the policy options for increasing aggregate demand by the desired amount.

The simplest way to shift aggregate demand is to increase government spending. If the government were to step up its purchases of highways, schools, health care, and other goods, the increased spending would add directly to aggregate demand. This would shift the aggregate demand curve rightward, moving us closer to full employment. Hence, *increased government spending is a form of fiscal stimulus.*

Multiplier Effects. It isn't necessary for the government to make up the entire shortfall in aggregate demand. Suppose that the fiscal target was to increase aggregate demand by $80 billion, the AD shortfall illustrated in Figure 10.3. Were government spending to increase by that amount, the AD curve would actually shift *beyond* point e in Figure 10.3. In that case we'd quickly move from a situation of a recessionary gap (point a) to an inflationary gap.

The origins of this apparent riddle lie in the circular flow of income. When the government buys more goods and services, it creates additional income for market participants. The recipients of this income will in turn spend it. Hence, each dollar gets spent and respent many times. This is the multiplier adjustment process we encountered in Chapters 8 and 9. As a result of this process, *every dollar of new government spending has a multiplied impact on aggregate demand.*

How much "bang" the economy gets for each government "buck" depends on the value of the *multiplier*. Specifically,

$$\frac{\text{Total change}}{\text{in spending}} = \text{multiplier} \times \text{new spending injection}$$

The multiplier acts to increase the impact of any initial fiscal stimulus. On page 187 in Chapter 9, we calculated the multiplier taking into account the marginal propensity to consume, MPC, the proportional rate of tax, t, and the marginal propensity to import, MPIm. The value of the multiplier was 1.146. This implies that for each $1 of new government spending, the total expenditure in the economy would increase by $1.15.

Figure 10.4 illustrates that leveraged impact of government spending. Aggregate demand shifts from AD_1 to AD_2 when the government buys additional goods and

More Government Spending

FIGURE 10.4
The Multiplier Effect

Fiscal stimulus will begin the multiplier process. As a result of this, aggregate demand will increase (shift) in two distinct steps. First, the initial direct increase in government expenditure (AD_1 to AD_2) and second, induced or indirect changes to consumption (AD_2 to AD_3). There are two important things to take note of here: (1) the full multiplier effect assumes a constant price level (point e on the graph), and (2) the upward sloping short-run aggregate supply curve implies that the price level will increase as AD shifts rightward. The final effect of the multiplier is therefore reduced as the price level rises such that the final equilibrium level of national income (Y) at point f (Q_F) is less than at point e.

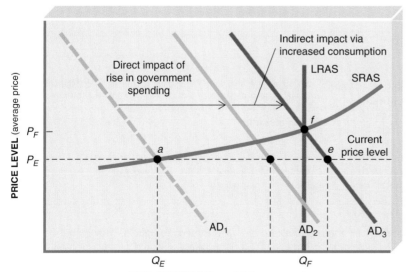

REAL OUTPUT (billions of dollars per year)

services. Multiplier effects then increase consumption spending by $40 further. This additional consumption shifts aggregate demand from AD_2 to AD_3. Thus, ***the impact of fiscal stimulus on aggregate demand includes both the new government spending and all subsequent increases in consumer spending triggered by the additional government outlays.***

The Desired Stimulus. Multiplier effects make changes in government spending a powerful policy lever. The multiplier also increases the risk of error, however. Whereas too little fiscal stimulus may leave the economy in a recession, too much can rapidly lead to excessive spending and inflation.

Determining the correct fiscal stimulus would be pretty straightforward if we knew the exact dimensions of aggregate demand (AD) and the exact level of full-employment national income. This would enable us to calculate the right level of fiscal stimulus using the following formula:

$$\text{Desired fiscal stimulus} = \frac{\text{AD shortfall}}{\text{multiplier}}$$

WEB NOTE

To see what happened to real GDP in South Korea after the 2001 fiscal stimulus, check out GDP data at www.koreaeconomy.org.

In practice, we rarely know the exact size of the shortfall in aggregate demand. Nevertheless, the foregoing formula does provide a useful rule of thumb for determining how much fiscal stimulus is needed to achieve any desired increase in aggregate demand. Such calculations helped the South Korean government decide how much fiscal stimulus was needed in 2001 to keep its economy out of recession (see the World View box).

Tax Cuts

Although injections of government spending can close a GDP gap, increased government purchases aren't the only way to get there. The increased demand required to raise output and employment levels from Q_E to Q_F could emerge from increases in autonomous consumption or investment as well as from increased government spending. It could also come from abroad, in the form of increased demand for our exports. In other words, any "Big Spender" would help, whether from the public sector or the private sector. Of course, the reason we're initially at Q_E instead of Q_F in Figure 10.3 is that consumers, investors, and export buyers have chosen *not* to spend as much as required for full employment.

Consumer and investor decisions are subject to change. Moreover, fiscal policy can encourage such changes. By reducing taxes—changing the revenue rather than the

WORLD VIEW

Seoul Plans Spending to Boost Economy

South Korea's finance minister, Jin Nyum, said the government, state-run companies and funds would increase third-quarter spending on infrastructure and other projects by 4.3 trillion won ($3.35 billion) to a total 30.3 trillion won, in a move to bolster an economy that has been hurt by declining exports. He spoke after President Kim Dae Jung met with economic ministers. Among planned steps to boost the economy are a cut in interest rates on loans to companies that participate in state projects and increased financial support to exporters. The government is also considering a tax cut, Mr. Jin said.

Source: *The Wall Street Journal*, August 8, 2001. Reprinted by permission of The Wall Street Journal. © 2001 Dow Jones Company, Inc. All rights reserved worldwide. www.wsj.com

Analysis: Fear of a pending decline in aggregate demand prompted South Korea's government to increase government spending on roads, bridges, and telecom networks. The government hoped such a fiscal stimulus would offset a decline in export sales and avert recession.

Campbell Delivers on Dramatic Tax Cuts

VICTORIA—Premier Gordon Campbell carried through with his promise of a dramatic tax cut Wednesday by slashing the provincial portion of personal income taxes by about 25 per cent over the next two years.

The cuts will leave $1.35 billion in the pockets of British Columbians in 2001/2002 and another $1.5 billion in 2002/2003.

"We believe that you should keep even more of every dollar that you earn because we know when you do that, you will spend it effectively in your community. That will create more jobs, more opportunities and a healthier economic environment."

Provincial treasury officials said Tuesday their financial models show the tax cuts would punch about a $1-billion hole in the budget delivered last March.

But that model does not take into account the stimulative effect on the economy that Campbell believes will occur as a result of the tax cuts.

"Since 1995, nearly all provinces have cut personal income taxes. Without exception, audited financial statements have shown these tax cuts have produced significantly higher tax revenues over time as the economy grows.

"In turn, that prosperity has meant greater revenue to support critical public services like health care and public education."

Sources: Craig McInnes, "Campbell delivers on dramatic tax cuts," *Vancouver Sun* (June 7, 2001), p. A1. Material reprinted with the express permission of Pacific Newspaper Group Inc., a CanWest Partnership.

Analysis: The decision to cut taxes is a reduction in the revenue raised by government. In this case, the tax cuts reduce revenue by approximately $1 billion, meaning that government would face a greater deficit or would need to reduce other spending or raise other taxes. The argument that tax cuts lead to higher future revenue is uncertain (see the Applications box on page 211), but would depend on the future economic growth attributable to the cuts.

expenditure side—government increases the *disposable income* of the private sector. The question here, however, is how a tax cut affects *spending*. By how much will consumption increase for every dollar of tax cuts?

The answer lies in the marginal propensity to consume. Consumers won't spend every dollar of tax cuts; they'll *save* some of the cut and spend the rest. But even the proportion that they spend won't be spent on Canadian production; some of the additional consumption will be of imported goods and services. Therefore, each dollar of the tax cut will face two leakages, one to saving and the other to imports. Hence, *a tax cut contains less fiscal stimulus than an increase in government spending of the same size.*

The lesser stimulative power of tax cuts is explained by consumer saving and by household consumption of imports. First, only part of a tax cut gets spent. Consumers save the rest. This is evident in Figure 10.5, which illustrates the successive rounds of the multiplier process. Notice that the tax cut is used to increase both consumption and saving. Secondly, since imports are a leakage, only that part of the tax cut that's used to consume Canadian production enters the circular flow as a spending injection. Hence, *the initial spending injection is less than the size of the tax cuts.* By contrast, every dollar of government purchases goes directly into the circular flow. Accordingly, tax cuts are less powerful than government purchases because the initial *spending* injection is smaller.

The different effects of tax cuts and increased government spending have an important implication for government budgets. Because some of the power of a tax cut "leaks" into savings and imports, tax cuts don't "offset" government spending of equal value. This unexpected result is described in Table 10.2.

Taxes and Investment. A tax cut may also be an effective mechanism for increasing *investment* spending. As we implied in Chapters 8 and 9, investment decisions are guided by expectations of the future. If a cut in corporate taxes raises potential

FIGURE 10.5
The Tax Cut Multiplier

Only part of the tax cut ends up increasing consumption of Canadian-produced goods and services; some of the tax cut is saved (the households' marginal propensity to save, MPS), and some of the tax cut is spent on imports, (M). Accordingly, the initial spending injection is less than the tax cut. This makes tax cuts less stimulative than government purchases of the same size. The multiplier still goes to work on that new consumer spending, however.

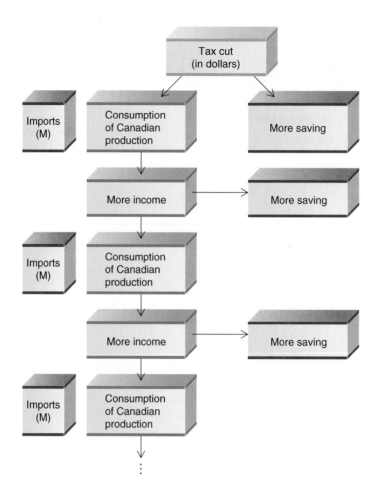

WEB NOTE

See other perspectives on tax cuts from the Canadian Centre for Policy Alternatives (CCPA) at http://www.policyalternatives.ca (use the "quick search" for tax cuts) or from the Fraser Institute at http://www.fraserinstitute.ca/ (search "tax cuts").

after-tax profits, it should encourage additional investment. Once an increase in the rate of investment spending enters the circular flow, it has a multiplier effect on total spending like that which follows an initial change in consumer spending.

The 2006 federal budget included a number of tax changes intended to strengthen and promote investment spending by focusing on corporate and small business taxes. The "Budget in Brief" lists these changes as:

- To create an environment for jobs and growth, Budget 2006 proposes to make Canada's tax system more internationally competitive by:
  - Reducing the general corporate income tax rate to 19 per cent from 21 per cent by 2010.
  - Eliminating the corporate surtax for all corporations as of January 1, 2008.
  - Eliminating the federal capital tax as of January 1, 2006, two years ahead of schedule.
- To support the growth of small business, Budget 2006 proposes to:
  - Increase the amount of small business income eligible for the 12 per cent tax rate to $400,000 from $300,000 as of January 1, 2007.
  - Reduce the 12 per cent tax rate applying to qualifying small business income to 11.5 percent in 2008 and 11 per cent in 2009.[1]

Increased Transfers

A third fiscal policy option for stimulating the economy is to increase transfer payments. If Old Age Security pension recipients, welfare recipients, employment insurance beneficiaries, and veterans get larger benefit cheques, they'll have more

---

[1]Department of Finance, Canada, *The Budget in Brief 2006: Budget 2006—Focusing on Priorities* (May 2, 2006), http://www.fin.gc.ca/budget06/brief/briefe.htm.

Many taxpayers and politicians demand that any new government spending be balanced with new taxes. Such balancing at the margin, it's asserted, will keep the budget deficit from rising, while avoiding further economic stimulus.

However, changes in government spending (*G*) are more powerful than changes in taxes (*T*) or transfers. This implies that an increase in *G* apparently offset with an equal rise in *T* will actually increase aggregate demand.

To see how this curious result comes about, suppose that the government decided to spend $5 billion per year on a new fleet of submarines and to pay for them by raising income taxes by the same amount. Thus

$$\text{Change in } G = +\$5 \text{ billion per year}$$
$$\text{Change in } T = +\$5 \text{ billion per year}$$
$$\text{Change in budget balance} = 0$$

How will this pay-as-you-go (balanced) budget initiative affect total spending?

The increase in the rate of government spending represents a new injection of $5 billion. But the higher taxes don't increase leakage by the same amount. Households will pay taxes by reducing *both* domestic and foreign consumption and by saving. The initial reduction in annual consumer spending on domestic goods and services equals only MPC(1 − MPIm) × $5 billion.

The reduction in consumption is therefore less than the increase in government spending, implying a net increase in *aggregate* spending. The *initial* change in aggregate demand brought about by this balanced budget expenditure is

$$\text{Initial increase in government spending} = \$5 \text{ billion}$$
$$\text{less Initial reduction in consumer spending} = \text{MPC(1} - \text{MPIm)} \times \$5 \text{ billion}$$
$$\text{Net initial change in total spending} = [1 - \text{MPC(1} - \text{MPIm)}] \times \$5 \text{ billion}$$

Like any other changes in the rate of spending, this initial increase in aggregate spending will start a multiplier process in motion. The *cumulative* change in expenditure will be larger, as indicated by the multiplier. The *new* multiplier will reflect the *new* tax rate—since any income generated in successive rounds will be subject to taxes—as well as additional imports purchased.

$$\frac{\text{The}}{\text{multiplier}} \times \frac{\text{initial change}}{\text{in spending per year}} = \frac{\text{cumulative change}}{\text{in total spending}}$$

TABLE 10.2
A Balanced Budget Multiplier

An increase in government expenditure, *G*, paid for by a tax increase of equal size shifts aggregate demand. This table explains why.

APPLICATIONS

Ontario's Tax Cuts Since 1995: The Real Tally

For the fourth provincial election in a row, tax cuts have moved into a central role in the election campaign of the Ontario Conservative Party. As usual, the political rhetoric is liberally sprinkled with evocative claims: [such as] Ontario's economic growth in the late 1990s [was] attributable to tax cuts.

An analysis of Ontario's tax cut program from 1995 to 2003 and the changes promised and expected in the future, however, reveals a very different reality from the picture painted in the rhetoric. Contrary to the government's claims: there is no evidence to support the Government's claim that Ontario's economic performance is attributable to tax cuts. Indeed, the evidence points to factors external to Ontario that have nothing to do with Ontario's tax system whatsoever.

Source: Hugh Mackenzie, "Ontario's tax cuts since 1995: The real tally," *Behind the Issues: Ontario 2003* (Canadian Centre for Policy Alternatives, CCPA, September 1, 2003). Used with permission.

Analysis: Contrary to the claims often made by governments (like the B.C. Government argued in the Applications box on page 209) that tax cuts pay for themselves through faster economic growth, the message in this article suggests that is not the case.

disposable income to spend. The resulting increase in consumption will boost aggregate demand.

Increased transfer payments don't, however, increase injections dollar-for-dollar. Here again, because these transfer payments become part of a household's disposable income, only part of the additional income will be injected into the circular flow; some of the additional income will go to saving (MPS) and some of the consumption will go to foreign producers (MPIm). Hence, *the initial fiscal stimulus (AD shift) of increased transfer payments is*

$$\begin{array}{c}\text{Initial fiscal}\\\text{stimulus (injection)}\end{array} = \text{MPC} \times (1 - \text{MPIm}) \times \begin{array}{c}\text{increase in}\\\text{household transfers}\end{array}$$

This initial stimulus sets the multiplier in motion, shifting the aggregate demand curve further to the right.

Fiscal Restraint

fiscal restraint: Tax hikes or spending cuts intended to reduce (shift) aggregate demand.

The objective of fiscal policy isn't always to increase aggregate demand. At times the economy is already expanding too fast and **fiscal restraint** is more appropriate. In these circumstances, policymakers are likely to be focused on inflation, not unemployment. Their objective will be to *reduce* aggregate demand, not to stimulate it.

The means available to the federal government for restraining aggregate demand emerge again from both sides of the budget. The difference here is that we use the budget tools in reverse. We now want to reduce government spending, increase taxes, or decrease transfer payments.

The Fiscal Target

As before, our first task is to determine how much we want aggregate demand to fall. To determine this, we must consult Figure 10.6. The initial equilibrium in this case occurs at point E_1, where the SRAS and AD_1 curves intersect. At that equilibrium the unemployment rate falls below the rate consistent with full employment (Q_F) and we produce the output Q_1. The resulting strains on production push the price level to P_E, higher than we're willing to accept. Our goal is to maintain the price level at P_F, which is consistent with our notion of full employment *and* price stability.

In this case, we have an *inflationary GDP gap*—that is, equilibrium GDP exceeds full-employment GDP by the amount $Q_1 - Q_F$. If we want to restore price stability (P_F),

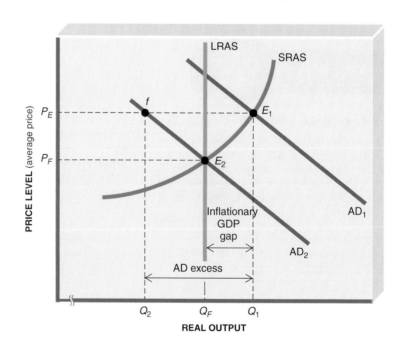

FIGURE 10.6
Excess Aggregate Demand

Too much aggregate demand (AD_1) causes the price level to rise (P_E) above its desired level (P_F). To restore price stability, the AD curve must shift leftward by the entire amount of the excess AD (here shown as $Q_1 - Q_2$). If AD shifts by that much (from AD_1 to AD_2), the excess AD is eliminated and equilibrium moves from E_1 to E_2.

however, we need to reduce aggregate demand by *more* than this GDP gap. The **AD excess** takes into account potential changes in the price level. Observe that *the AD excess exceeds the inflationary GDP gap.* In Figure 10.6, the AD excess equals the horizontal distance from E_1 to point f. This excess aggregate demand is our fiscal policy target. To restore price stability, we must shift the AD curve leftward until it passes through point f. The AD_2 curve does this. The shift to AD_2 moves the economy to a new equilibrium at E_2. At E_2 we have less output but also a lower price level (less inflation).

> **AD excess:** The amount by which aggregate demand must be reduced to achieve full-employment equilibrium after allowing for price-level changes.

Knowing the dimensions of excess aggregate demand, we can compute the desired fiscal restraint as

$$\text{Desired fiscal restraint} = \frac{[\text{excess AD}]}{\text{multiplier}}$$

In other words, first we determine how far we want to shift the AD curve. Generally, the desired AD reduction will equal the excess AD. Then we compute how much government spending or taxes must be changed to achieve the desired shift, taking into account multiplier effects.

Budget Cuts

The first option to consider is budget cuts. By how much should we reduce government expenditure on goods and services? The answer is simple in this case: We first calculate the desired fiscal restraint, as computed above. Then we cut government expenditure by that amount.

The GDP gap in Figure 10.6 amounts to ($Q_1 - Q_F$). If aggregate demand is reduced by that amount, however, some of the restraint will be dissipated in price-level reductions. To bring *equilibrium* GDP down to the full-employment (Q_F) level, even more of a spending reduction is needed.

This cumulative reduction in spending would eliminate excess aggregate demand. We conclude, then, that *the budget cuts, increased by the multiplier value, should equal the size of the desired fiscal restraint,* the distance from E_1 to f in Figure 10.6.

Tax Hikes

Tax increases can also be used to shift the aggregate demand curve to the left. The direct effect of a tax increase is a reduction in disposable income. People will pay the higher taxes by reducing their consumption of Canadian- and foreign-produced goods (imports) *and* by saving less. Only the reduced Canadian consumption results in less aggregate demand in Canada, (although the reduced incomes of foreigners may lead to fewer exports sold as well). As consumers tighten their belts, they set off the multiplier process, leading again to a much larger, cumulative shift of aggregate demand.

Because people pay higher tax bills by reducing both consumption and saving, *taxes must be increased more than a dollar to get a dollar of fiscal restraint.*

Reduced Transfers

The third option for fiscal restraint is to reduce transfer payments. *A cut in transfer payments works like a tax hike, reducing the disposable income of transfer recipients.* With less income, consumers spend less, as reflected in the MPC. The appropriate size of the transfer cut can be computed exactly as the desired tax increase.

Although the process of fiscal restraint would operate in the same fashion—although in the reverse direction—as fiscal stimulus, it tends not to be used in actual practice. There are a number of reasons for this which will be discussed in the following "Fiscal Guidelines" section.

In practice, fiscal restraint most often takes the form of reducing the rate of increase in the growth of government spending or making relatively small changes within government revenue (i.e., taxes) and transfer programs. This approach results in changes to future income that you might receive rather than changes to current income that you are receiving, and is therefore far less visible.

10.3 FISCAL GUIDELINES

The essence of fiscal policy entails deliberate shifting of the aggregate demand curve. The steps required to formulate fiscal policy are straightforward:

- *Specify the amount of the desired AD shift* (excess AD or AD shortfall).
- *Select the fiscal policy tools needed to induce the desired shift.*

As we've seen, the fiscal policy toolbox contains a variety of tools for managing aggregate demand. When the economy is in a slump, the government can stimulate the economy with more government purchases, tax cuts, or an increase in transfer payments. When the economy is overheated, the government can reduce inflationary pressures by reducing government purchases, raising taxes, and cutting transfer payments. Table 10.3 summarizes the policy options and the desired use of each. As confusing as this list of options might at first appear, the guidelines are pretty simple. To use them all one needs to know is the size of the AD shortfall or excess and the marginal propensity to consume and import.

A Warning: Crowding Out

The fiscal policy guidelines in Table 10.3 are a useful guide. However, they neglect a critical dimension of fiscal policy. Notice that we haven't said anything about how the government is going to *finance* its expenditures. Suppose the government wanted to stimulate the economy with a $5 billion increase in federal purchases. How would it pay for those purchases? If the government raised taxes for this purpose, the fiscal stimulus would be largely offset by resultant declines in consumption and investment. If, instead, the government *borrows* the money from the private sector, less credit may be available to finance consumption and investment, again creating an offsetting reduction in private demand. In either case, government spending may "crowd out" some private expenditure. If this happens, some of the intended fiscal stimulus may be offset by the *crowding out* of private expenditure. We examine this possibility further in Chapter 11 when we look at the budget deficits that help finance fiscal policy.

Time Lags

Another limitation on fiscal policy is *time*. In the real world it takes time to recognize that the economy is in trouble. A blip in the unemployment or inflation rate

---

TABLE 10.3
Fiscal Policy Primer

The goal of fiscal policy is to eliminate GDP gaps by shifting the AD curve rightward (to reduce unemployment) or leftward (to curb inflation). The desired shifts may be measured by the AD shortfall or the AD excess. In either case the desired fiscal initiative is equal to the desired shift divided by the multiplier. Once the size of the desired stimulus or restraint is known, the size of the appropriate policy options is easily calculated.

Macro Problem: Weak Economy (unemployment)
Policy Strategy: Fiscal Stimulus

$$\text{Desired fiscal stimulus} = \frac{\text{AD shortfall}}{\text{multiplier}}$$

Policy Options

- Increase government purchases
- Cut taxes
- Increase transfers

Macro Problem: Overheated Economy (inflation)
Policy Strategy: Fiscal Restraint

$$\text{Desired fiscal restraint} = \frac{\text{excess AD}}{\text{multiplier}}$$

Policy Options

- Reduce government purchases
- Increase taxes
- Reduce transfer payments

may not signal a trend. Before intervening, we may want to be more certain that a recessionary or inflationary GDP gap is emerging. Then it will take time to develop a policy strategy and to get Parliament to pass it. Once implemented, we'll have to wait for the many steps in the multiplier process to unfold. In the best of circumstances, the fiscal policy rescue may not arrive for quite a while. In the meantime, the very nature of our macro problems could change if the economy is hit with other internal or external shocks.

Before putting too much faith in fiscal policy, we should also remember who designs and implements tax and spending initiatives: federal and provincial governments. Once a tax or spending plan arrives on the floor of the house, politics take over. However urgent fiscal restraint might be, members of Parliament or legislatures are reluctant to sacrifice any spending projects in their own regions. And if taxes are to be cut, they want *their* constituents to get the biggest tax savings. And no one in government wants a tax hike or spending cut *before* the election. This kind of political influence can alter the content and timing of fiscal policy.

Political Influence

The guidelines for fiscal policy don't say anything about how the government spends its revenue or whom it taxes. The important thing is that the right amount of spending take place at the right time. In other words, insofar as our stabilization objectives are concerned, the content of total spending is of secondary interest; the level of spending is the only thing that counts.

The Concern for Content

The "Second Crisis." But it does matter, of course, whether federal expenditures are devoted to military hardware, urban transit systems, or tennis courts. Our economic goals include not only full employment and price stability but also a desirable mix of output, an equitable distribution of income, and adequate economic growth. These other goals are directly affected by the content of total spending. The relative emphasis on, and sometimes exclusive concern for, stabilization objectives—to the neglect of related GDP content—has been designated by Joan Robinson as the "second crisis of economic theory." She explained that once there was agreement that maintaining employment levels was a responsibility of government:

> The question should have changed. Now that we all agree that government expenditure can maintain employment, we should argue about what the expenditure should be for.[2]

With $220 billion to spend each year, the federal government has great influence not only on short-run prices and employment but also on the mix of output, the distribution of income, and the prospects for long-run growth. In other words, fiscal policy helps shape the dimensions of the economy in the future.

Public vs. Private Spending. One of the most debated issues in fiscal policy is the balance between the public and private sectors. Critics fear that depending on government spending to stabilize the economy will lead to an ever-larger public sector. The 1970s and 1980s saw government's influence in the economy rising through additional program spending and stabilization policies. The share of government expenditures on goods and services peaked at about 24 percent of GDP in 1992. Since then, governments have restrained spending, and government expenditure as a share of GDP has fallen to 19 percent in 2005—about the same level it was in 1969 although still higher than the 15 percent level of the early 1960s.

In 1993, the liberal government of Jean Chrétien favoured additional government spending on infrastructure to stimulate the economy, whereas the conservative government of Stephen Harper prefers tax cuts that bolster private spending.

---

[2]From "The Second Crisis of Economic Theory," by Joan Robinson, *American Economic Review*, May 1972, p. 6. Used by permission of American Economic Association.

In the May 2, 2006 budget speech, Finance Minister, the Honourable James M. Flaherty, P.C., M.P. made the following claim:

> Canadians pay too much in tax. It's holding families back. It makes it harder for small businesses to create jobs and opportunities. It discourages innovation and investment. It is limiting our productivity.
>
> This government could have chosen to spend all of the extra money collected from taxpayers. But that would not have been responsible. That money will be put to best use if we return it to the pockets of Canadians.
>
> Providing immediate and substantial tax relief for all Canadians is a priority for this government.[3]

Output Mixes Within Each Sector. In addition to choosing whether to increase public or private spending, fiscal policy must also consider the specific content of spending within each sector. Suppose we determine that stimulation of the private sector is preferable to additional government spending as a means of promoting full employment. We still have many choices. We could, for example, cut corporate taxes, cut individual taxes, reduce excise taxes, or increase Old Age Security pensions. Each alternative implies a different mix of consumption and investment and a different distribution of income.

Governments often try and mix a little of each approach—the 2006 budget includes personal and corporate tax reductions as well as increased government spending in specific areas and additional transfers to households (see the 2006 budget by using the Web note link).

WEB NOTE

To see federal government budgets and fiscal updates beginning from 1994, go to http://www.fin.gc.ca/access/budinfoe.html.

[3]James M. Flaherty, P.C. M.P., Minister of Finance, The Budget Speech (May 2, 2006), http://www.fin.gc.ca/budget06/speech/speeche.htm, accessed October 13, 2006.

SUMMARY

- The economy's short-run macro equilibrium may not coincide with full employment and price stability. Keynes advocated government intervention to shift the AD curve to a more desirable equilibrium.
- Fiscal policy refers to the use of the government's tax and spending powers to achieve desired macro outcomes. Options for fiscal stimulus include increasing government purchases, reducing taxes, and raising income transfers.
- Fiscal restraint may originate in reductions in government purchases, increases in taxes, or cuts in income transfers.
- Government purchases add directly to aggregate demand; taxes and transfers have an indirect effect by inducing changes in consumption and investment. This makes changes in government spending more powerful per dollar than changes in taxes or transfers.
- Fiscal policy initiatives have a multiplied impact on total spending and output. An increase in government spending, for example, will result in more disposable income, which will be used to finance further consumer spending.
- The objective of fiscal policy is to close GDP gaps. To do this, the aggregate demand curve must shift by more than the size of the GDP gap to compensate for changing price levels. The desired shift is equal to the aggregate demand shortfall (or excess).
- Because of the multiplier effect, the desired fiscal stimulus or restraint may be different than the size of the AD shortfall or excess; less where the multiplier is greater than one and greater where the multiplier is less than one.
- Changes in government spending and taxes alter the content of GDP and thus influence what to produce. Fiscal policy affects the relative size of the public and private sectors as well as the mix of output in each sector.

Key Terms

income transfers   206
fiscal stimulus   207

AD shortfall   208
fiscal restraint   214

AD excess   215

Questions for Discussion

1. How can you tell if the economy is in equilibrium? How could you estimate the GDP gap?
2. Will an extra $20 billion per year spent on housing have the same impact on the economy as an extra $20 billion spent on highways? Explain.
3. What happens to aggregate demand when transfer payments and the taxes to pay them both rise?
4. Why are the AD shortfall and AD excess larger than their respective GDP gaps? Are they ever the same size?
5. Will consumers always spend the same percentage of any tax cut? Why might they spend more or less than usual?
6. How does the slope of the SRAS curve affect the size of the AD shortfall? If the SRAS curve were horizontal, how large would the AD shortfall be in Figure 10.3?
7. According to the World View on page 210, what prompted South Korea's fiscal stimulus in 2001? Had the government not intervened, what might have happened?
8. How quickly should government act to remedy an AD excess or shortfall? What are the risks of quick fiscal policy responses?
9. Why do critics charge that fiscal policy has a "big-government bias"?
10. The Applications box on page 211 announces a personal income tax cut of 25 percent for BC residents and explains that "these tax cuts have produced significantly higher tax revenues over time." Explain both why tax revenue might fall in the first year but eventually be higher than before the cuts.

EXERCISES

PROBLEMS   The Student Problem Set to accompany this chapter can be found at the end of the book.

WEB ACTIVITIES   Web Activities to accompany this chapter can be found on the Online Learning Centre at **http://www.mcgrawhill.ca/olc/schiller**.

Deficits, Surpluses, and Debt

The Honourable Jim Flaherty, Minister of Finance, today [March 19, 2007] tabled a balanced budget that moves to restore fiscal balance in Canada, cuts taxes for working families, reduces the national debt and invests in key priorities like improving health care and environmental protection.[1]

In November 2005, the Honourable Ralph Goodale, then Liberal Minster of Finance, noted in the government's "plan for growth and prosperity" that Canada's macroeconomic advantage would be found in:

> . . . the Government's commitment to balanced budgets or better and its balanced approach to the allocation of surpluses—including unanticipated surpluses in excess of the Contingency Reserve—between debt reduction, tax relief and investments in key economic and social priorities.[2]

The point being made in each of these statements is that the government budget balance plays a significant role in promoting future economic growth as well as current economic stability. Each quotation commits the government to balanced budgets "or better," tax relief, and overall debt reduction. The purpose of such a strategy is to encourage innovation and investment and to achieve "key economic and social priorities."

So, if conservative and liberal governments, broadly speaking, share similar goals, why does there seem so much controversy and disagreement? As in most of economics, the goals generally aren't the issue, rather it is the tactics chosen to achieve them. In the case of government, the issues arise from choosing more or less spending, more or less taxation, and more or less repayment of the public debt.

This chapter begins by determining the government's budget balance (BB) and then considers the impact of balanced and unbalanced (surplus or deficit) budget outcomes. In the case of deficits, we go on to ask questions about how that deficit is financed and explore the impact of government-held debt on current and future budgets. More specifically, we begin with these questions:

- **How is the government's budget balance determined?**
- **What issues, if any, arise from a budget in either surplus or deficit?**
- **Who pays for the accumulated national (public) debt?**

As we'll see, the answers to these questions add another dimension to fiscal policy debates.

[1]News release, Department of Finance, "Budget, 2007: A stronger, better, safer Canada" (March 19, 2007), http://www.fin.gc.ca/news07/07-022e.html.
[2]http://www.fin.gc.ca/ec2005/agenda/agTOCe.html, accessed October 22, 2006.

LEARNING OBJECTIVES

By the end of this chapter, you should be able to:

11.1 Determine the government's budget balance

11.2 Explain deficit, surplus, and balanced with respect to a government's budget balance

11.3 Explain the differences between a cyclical and structural deficit

11.4 Explain the economic impact of a budget deficit and a budget surplus

11.5 Differentiate between measuring debt levels and measuring debt as a percentage of GDP

11.1 THE GOVERNMENT BUDGET BALANCE (BB)

Keynesian theory highlights the potential of *fiscal policy* to solve our macro problems. The guidelines are simple. Use fiscal stimulus—stepped-up government spending, tax cuts, increased transfers—to eliminate unemployment. Use fiscal restraint—less spending, tax hikes, reduced transfers—to keep inflation under control. From this perspective, the federal budget is a key policy lever for controlling the economy.

The federal government's budget balance, (BB) is simply a measure of the relative sizes of government's revenue (the taxes and any other revenue that it receives) and its expenditure.

Table 11.1 illustrates the revenue and Table 11.2 the expenditure of the federal government for the year ending March 31, 2006. With respect to the government revenue, the vast majority comes from taxes on income, both personal and corporate, and taxes on the consumption of goods and services (GST). In fact, these account for a little more than 86 percent of total revenue. Contributions to social security plans (employment insurance and the Canada and Quebec pension plans) account for an additional 8 percent of the total. This reality is consistent with our earlier model for government revenue, as a proportion of national income itself:

$$\text{Government revenue} = \text{Tax rate } (t) \times \text{National income } (Y)$$

$$= tY$$

The expenditure side is a little more complex, but we can simplify the categories down to three: general expenditures (G), transfers to provinces and households, (tr) and interest payments on the public debt (D).

$$\text{Government expenditure} = \text{General } (G) + \text{Transfers } (tr) + \text{Interest Payments } (D)$$

$$= \quad G \quad + \quad tr \quad + \quad D$$

To determine the federal government's budget balance we subtract the expenditures from the revenues:

$$\text{Budget balance } (BB) = \text{Revenue} - \text{Expenditure}$$

$$BB = [tY] - [G + tr + D]$$

$$BB = tY - G - tr - D$$

Federal Government Revenues (billions of dollars)		
	2006 Revenue	**Percent of Total**
Income taxes	$144.562	64.36
Consumption taxes	48.490	21.59
Other taxes	0.670	0.30
Contributions to social security plans	17.527	7.80
Sales of goods and services	6.016	2.68
Investment income	6.096	2.71
Other revenue from own sources	0.553	0.25
General purpose transfers	0.603	0.27
Specific purpose transfers	0.088	0.04
Total	$224.607	100.00*

(*Percent may not add to 100 due to rounding)

Source: "Federal and Provincial Budget Balance 1989–2006," adapted from Statistics Canada CANSIM database table 385-0017, http://cansim2.statcan.ca. "Federal government revenues and expenditure: Year ending March 31, 2006," adapted from Statistics Canada CANSIM database table 385-0002, http://cansim2.statcan.ca. Statistics Canada information is used with the permission of Statistics Canada.

WEB NOTE

For a more detailed explanation for each "line" of federal government revenue and expenditure, go to http://www.statcan.ca/english/sdds/document/1735_D9_T9_V1_E.pdf.

TABLE 11.1
Federal Government Revenues: Year Ending March 31, 2006

Table 11.1 illustrates where the federal government revenue arises. The largest source of revenue for the federal government is income taxes; they represent about 64 percent of total revenue. Another 22 percent comes from consumption taxes, such as the Goods and Services Tax, GST.

TABLE 11.2
**Federal Government Expenditure:
Year Ending March 31, 2006**

On the expenditure side illustrated in Table 11.2, some 79 percent of expenditures come from five areas: defense, social services (which includes social assistance, Canada pensions, GST rebates, family allowance, and child tax benefit payments among others), health, transfers to the provinces, and the payment on the federal portion of the national debt.

	Federal Government Expenditures: (billions of dollars)	
	2006 Expenditure	**Percent of Total**
General government services	$ 9.059	4.29
Protection of persons and property	24.275	11.50
Transportation and communications	2.266	1.07
Health	21.531	10.20
Social services	64.577	30.59
Education	4.937	2.34
Resource conservation and industrial development	8.206	3.89
Environment	2.100	1.00
Recreation and culture	4.044	1.92
Labour, employment, and immigration	1.857	0.88
Housing	2.033	0.96
Foreign affairs and international assistance	6.065	2.87
Regional planning and development	0.339	0.16
Research establishments	3.013	1.43
General purpose transfers	24.785	11.74
Debt charges	32.004	15.16
Other expenditures	0.014	0.00
Total	$211.103	100.00*

(*Percent may not add to 100 due to rounding)

Source: "Federal and Provincial Budget Balance 1989–2006," adapted from Statistics Canada CANSIM database table 385-0017, http://cansim2.statcan.ca. "Federal government revenues and expenditure: Year ending March 31, 2006," adapted from Statistics Canada CANSIM database table 385-0002,http://cansim2.statcan.ca. Statistics Canada information is used with the permission of Statistics Canada.

The overall budget balance can result in two possibilities: it can be balanced, that is, the value of revenue and expenditure is exactly equal, or it can be unbalanced, being in deficit where expenditure is larger than revenue and being in surplus where revenue is greater than expenditure.

$$BB = 0 \quad \text{Balanced budget}$$
$$BB < 0 \quad \text{Budget deficit}$$
$$BB > 0 \quad \text{Budget surplus}$$

Budget Surpluses and Deficits

deficit spending: The use of borrowed funds to finance government expenditures that exceed tax revenues.

budget deficit: Amount by which government spending exceeds government revenue in a given time period.

Use of the budget to stabilize the economy implies that federal expenditures and receipts won't always be equal. In a recession, for example, the government has sound reasons both to cut taxes and to increase its own spending. By reducing tax revenue and increasing expenditure simultaneously, however, the federal government will throw its budget out of balance. This practice is called **deficit spending,** a situation in which the government borrows funds to pay for spending that exceeds tax revenue. The size of the resulting **budget deficit** is equal to the difference between expenditures and receipts.

During an economic boom the government may want to reduce pressure from aggregate demand by increasing taxes or reducing its own spending. By increasing its revenue and reducing its expenditure will again throw its budget out of balance. In this case, the government would accumulate a **budget surplus**.

As Figure 11.1 shows, the federal government has been in a surplus position since 1998. Table 11.3 provides a more detailed look at the balances for 2002 to 2006. However, as Figure 11.1 illustrates, prior to 1998 the federal government ran a budget deficit. In fact, the federal government ran a deficit each year beginning in 1975.

	2002	2003	2004	2005	2006
Total revenue	192.288	190.914	199.107	211.800	224.607
Total expenditure	184.941	189.249	196.992	206.680	211.103
Surplus (deficit)	7.348	1.665	2.115	5.120	13.504

Source: Adapted from Statistics Canada CANSIM database table 385-0002, http://cansim2.statcan.ca. Statistics Canada information is used with the permission of Statistics Canada.

TABLE 11.3
Federal Government: Budget Balance (billions of dollars)

Budget deficits arise when government outlays (spending) exceed revenue (receipts). When revenue exceeds outlays, a budget surplus exists.

Provincial governments have had a more mixed history, at various times moving between deficit and surplus budgets. As of March 31, 2007 only one territory, the Northwest Territories, and four provinces, Newfoundland, Nova Scotia, Quebec, and Ontario, reported deficits. All other territories and provinces reported surpluses ranging from $12 million in the Yukon Territories to $7.5 billion in Alberta.

budget surplus: An excess of government revenue over government expenditure in a given time period.

Keynesian View. As far as Keynes was concerned, budget deficits and surpluses are just a routine byproduct of countercyclical fiscal policy. Deficits can easily arise when the government uses fiscal stimulus to increase aggregate demand, just as fiscal restraint (tax hikes; spending cuts) may cause a budget surplus. As Keynes saw it, *the goal of macro policy is not to balance the budget but to balance the economy (at full employment).* If a budget deficit or surplus was needed to shift aggregate demand to the desired equilibrium, then so be it. In Keynes's view, a balanced budget would be appropriate only if all other injections and leakages were in balance and the economy was in full-employment equilibrium. As the World View confirms, other nations evidently subscribe to that conclusion as well.

Theory aside, the federal government would have considerable difficulty balancing their budgets each year. Parliament doesn't have as much control over spending and revenue as people assume. Hence, neither deficits nor surpluses are necessarily the result of fiscal policy decisions. To understand the limits of budget management, we have to take a closer look at how budget outlays and receipts are actually determined.

Discretionary vs. Automatic Spending

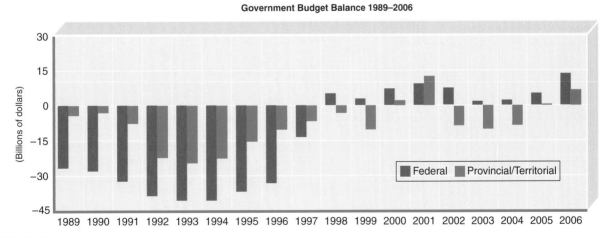

Government Budget Balance 1989–2006

FIGURE 11.1
Federal and Provincial Budget Balance 1989–2006

As illustrated in Figure 11.1, the federal government began a string of surplus budgets beginning in 1998. While individual provinces and territories have experienced surplus and deficit budgets, collectively they have been in deficit for five of the nine years between 1998 and 2006.

Source: Adapted from Statistics Canada CANSIM database table 385-0017, http://cansim2.statcan.ca. Statistics Canada information is used with the permission of Statistics Canada.

Budget Imbalances: Advanced Economies

The figure to the right illustrates the budget imbalances in 2005 for Canada and 10 other "advanced economies." While much of the attention is directed at the Canadian surplus and the U.S. deficit, more countries experienced deficits in this year than experienced surpluses.

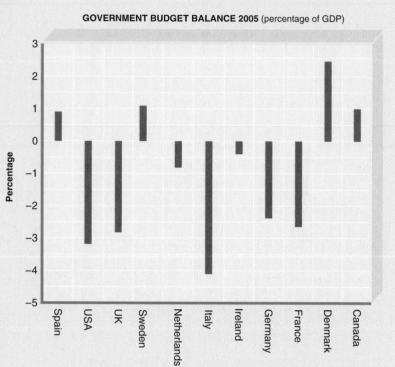

GOVERNMENT BUDGET BALANCE 2005 (percentage of GDP)

Source: James B. Davies, Susanna Sandstrom, Anthony Shorrocks, and Edward N. Wolf, "Wealth shares for countries with wealth distribution data, official exchange rate basis," The World Distribution of Household Wealth (December 2006). Used with the permission of the International Monetary Fund.

Analysis: To compare budget balances to those of other industrialized countries, we must adjust for differences in size by forming the ratio of deficits or surpluses to GDP.

fiscal year (FY): The 12-month period used for accounting purposes.

The federal government prepares a budget document for each **fiscal year (FY)** which runs from April 1 to March 31st of the following year. Generally, the budget document is presented to parliament prior to the beginning of the fiscal year, usually either in February or March (The January 2006 federal election delayed the introduction of the budget for the 2006–2007 budget until May). The budget begins by reviewing past fiscal performance, presents current and future estimates of the economic environment, and then provides a blueprint for the federal government's budgetary revenue and expenditure. For example, Table 11.4 from the *Budget in Brief* document shows budgetary revenue

	Actual Estimate		Projection	
	2004–2005	2005–2006	2006–2007	2007–2008
Budgetary revenues	$211.9	$220.9	$227.1	$235.8
Program expenses	176.3	179.2	188.8	196.5
Public debt charges	34.1	33.7	34.8	34.8
Total expenses	210.5	212.9	223.6	231.4
Planned debt reduction	1.5	8.0	3.0	3.0
Remaining surplus		0.6		1.4

TABLE 11.4
Summary Statement of Transactions (including May 2006 budget measures, billions of dollars)

Note: Totals may not add up due to rounding.

Source: Government of Canada, *The Budget in Brief, 2006*, http://www.fin.gc.ca/budget06/brief/briefe.htm, accessed October 25, 2006.

in 2006–2007 to be estimated at $227.1 billion and program expenses (expenditure) at $188.8 billion with another $34.8 billion representing interest charges on the public debt.

While this budget includes any changes to program spending or revenue from taxes, it of course also includes commitments from earlier budgets and program spending for programs continuing.

To the extent that past years' commitments determine the current year's level of spending, any government will have less scope to use **discretionary fiscal policy,** that is, spending decisions not locked in by prior legislative commitments (such as employment insurance and transfers to the provinces for health, education, and social services, for example). *To a large extent, current revenues and expenditures are the result of decisions made in prior years.* In this sense, much of each year's budget is considered *"uncontrollable."*

This doesn't mean that discretionary fiscal policy is no longer important; it simply means that the potential for *changing* budget outlays in any year is much smaller than it might first appear. Yet, the ability to *change* tax or spending levels is the force behind Keynesian fiscal policy. Recall that deliberate changes in government spending or taxes are the essence of *fiscal restraint* and *fiscal stimulus.* If most of the budget is uncontrollable, those policy levers are less effective.

Automatic Stabilizers. Most of the uncontrollable line items in the federal budget have another characteristic that directly affects budget deficits: their value *changes* with economic conditions. Consider employment insurance benefits. The employment insurance program, established in 1940 as the Unemployment Insurance Commission (UIC), provides that persons who lose their jobs will receive some income (the basic benefit rate is 55 percent of your average insured earnings, to a maximum of $413 per week) from the government. The law establishes the *entitlement* to employment insurance benefits but not the amount to be spent in any year. Each year's expenditure depends on how many workers lose their jobs and qualify for benefits. During the recession of the early 1990s, for example, employment insurance (EI) benefits reached $15.4 billion in the 1992–1993 fiscal year. In the most recent fiscal year, 2005–2006, with higher benefits per person, total EI payments were $8.4 billion. Such year-to-year changes in federal government spending are *automatic,* not *discretionary* and fluctuate as a result of the state of the economy.

Welfare benefits also fluctuate in response to economic conditions. In a recession, as people exhaust their EI eligibility or lose jobs where they haven't established eligibility, they turn to welfare for help. They were *entitled* to welfare benefits according to eligibility rules already written; no new legislation is required to approve this increase in provincial government spending (since welfare is a provincial responsibility).

Notice that *outlays for unemployment compensation and welfare benefits increase when the economy goes into recession.* This is exactly the kind of fiscal policy that Keynes advocated. The increase in *income transfers* helps offset the income losses due to recession. These increased transfers therefore act as **automatic stabilizers**— injecting new spending into the circular flow during economic contractions. Conversely, transfer payments decline when the economy is expanding and fewer people qualify for employment insurance or welfare benefits. Hence, no one has to pull the fiscal policy lever to inject more or less entitlement spending into the circular flow; much of it happens automatically.

Automatic stabilizers also exist on the revenue side of the federal budget. Income taxes are an important stabilizer because they move up and down with the value of spending and output. As we've observed, if household incomes increase, a jump in consumer spending is likely to follow. The resultant multiplier effects might create some demand-pull inflation. The tax code lessens this inflationary pressure. When you get more income, you have to pay more taxes. Hence, income taxes siphon off some of the increased purchasing power that might have found its way to product markets. Progressive income taxes are particularly effective stabilizers, as they siphon off increasing proportions of purchasing power when incomes are rising and decreasing proportions when aggregate demand and output are falling.

> **discretionary fiscal spending:** Those elements of the federal budget not determined by past legislative commitments.

> **automatic stabilizer:** Federal or provincial expenditure or revenue item that automatically responds countercyclically to changes in national income, like employment insurance benefits, income taxes.

Cyclical Balance

Automatic stabilizers imply that policymakers don't have total control of each year's budget. In reality, *the size of the federal deficit or surplus is sensitive to expansion and contraction of the macro economy.*

This implies that a government's budget balance is in part the result of an economy's cyclical behaviour. As the economy moves toward recession, these automatic transfers increase, increasing total government expenditure. As the economy recovers from recession, these automatic transfers decrease, decreasing total government expenditure.

That part of the deficit attributable to cyclical disturbances (unemployment and inflation) is referred to as the **cyclical balance.** As we've observed,

> **cyclical balance:** That portion of the budget balance attributable to short-run deviations from the economy's potential GDP.

- *The cyclical balance widens when GDP growth slows or inflation decreases.*
- *The cyclical balance shrinks when GDP growth accelerates or inflation increases.*

If observed budget balances don't necessarily reflect fiscal policy decisions, how are we to know whether fiscal policy is stimulative or restrictive? Clearly, some other indicator is needed.

Structural Balance

To isolate the effects of fiscal policy, economists break down the actual budget balance into *cyclical* and *structural* components:

$$\text{Actual budget balance} = \text{cyclical balance} + \text{structural balance}$$

> **structural balance:** Revenue at full employment minus expenditure at full employment under prevailing fiscal policy.

The cyclical portion of the budget balance reflects the impact of the business cycle on federal tax revenues and spending. The **structural balance** reflects fiscal policy decisions. Rather than comparing actual outlays to actual receipts, the structural balance compares the outlays and receipts that would occur if the economy were at full employment.[3] This technique eliminates budget distortions caused by cyclical conditions. Any remaining changes in spending or outlays must be due to policy decisions. Hence, *part of the balance arises from cyclical changes in the economy; the rest is the result of discretionary fiscal policy.*

Figure 11.2 illustrates the *actual* and *cyclically-adjusted* budget balances for the federal government from 1990 through 2005. The *structural* component of the deficit is represented by the cyclically-adjusted budget balance. In 1990, for example, the

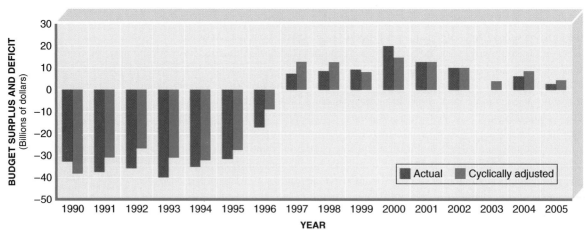

FIGURE 11.2

Actual vs. Cyclically-Adjusted Budget Balance

The federal government's actual budget balance includes both a cyclical and a structural component. Changes in the structural component result from policy changes, while changes in the cyclical component result from changes in the economy.

Source: Fiscal Reference Tables; September 2009 Department of Finance, Government of Canada.

[3]The structural deficit is also referred to as the "full-employment," "high-employment," or "standardized" deficit.

actual budget balance was a deficit of $33.3 billion whereas, if the economy had been operating at its potential, the budget balance would have been a deficit of $38.4 billion. The fact that the actual deficit was less indicates that the economy was operating above potential, generating additional tax revenue to offset some of that structural deficit. In contrast, in 2005, the cyclically-adjusted budget balance was greater than the actual by approximately $2.4 billion. In 2005, had the economy been operating at potential, the federal budget surplus would have been $2.4 billion greater than it actually was.

Figure 11.2 also illustrates an important change in government policy between the early 1990s and the period after 1997. In the early 1990s, the federal budget would have been in deficit even when the economy was operating at its potential—a structural deficit. The policy response was a change in approach; the federal government altered program expenditures and revenue sources to focus on balanced or surplus budgets. The result is apparent after 1997.

By distinguishing between the structural budget and the actual budget, we can evaluate fiscal policy more accurately. Only changes in the structural deficit are relevant. In fact, *only changes in the structural budget balance measure the thrust of fiscal policy.* By this measure we categorize fiscal policy in the following ways:

- *Fiscal stimulus is measured by the increase in the structural deficit* (or shrinkage in the structural surplus).
- *Fiscal restraint is gauged by the decrease in the structural deficit* (or increase in the structural surplus).

11.2 ECONOMIC EFFECTS OF DEFICITS

No matter what the origins of budget deficits, most people are alarmed by them. Should they be? What are the *consequences* of budget deficits?

Crowding Out

We've already encountered one potential consequence of deficit financing: *If the government borrows funds to finance deficits, the availability of funds for private-sector spending may be reduced.* This is the *crowding-out* problem noted in Chapter 10. If crowding out occurs, the increase in government expenditure will be at least partially offset by reductions in consumption and investment.

If the economy were operating at full employment, and if all borrowing came from domestic savers (and all investment came from domestic savers as well), crowding out would be inevitable. At full employment, we'd be on the production possibilities curve, using all available resources. As Figure 11.3 reminds us, additional government purchases can occur only if private-sector purchases are reduced. In real terms, *crowding out implies less private-sector output.*

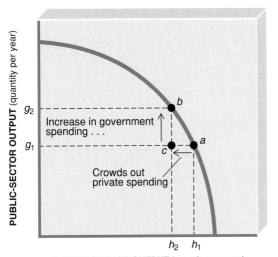

FIGURE 11.3
Crowding Out

If the economy is fully employed, an increase in public-sector expenditure (output) will reduce private-sector expenditure (output). In this case a deficit-financed increase in government expenditure moves the economy from point *a* to point *b*. In the process the quantity $h_1 - h_2$ of private-sector output is crowded out to make room for the increase in public-sector output (from g_1 to g_2). If the economy started at point *c*, however, with unemployed resources, crowding out need not occur.

However, all the "ifs" in the previous paragraph are important. In an open economy like Canada's, flows of funds for borrowing and lending aren't restricted to the domestic economy. Private firms and governments alike can, and do, lend and borrow outside the domestic economy. So, for crowding out to have a significant impact, the world economy would also have to be "at potential."

That doesn't imply, however, that financing deficits is cost free. If governments borrow from foreign economies, the inflow of funds includes an exchange of currencies, from the country of origin to the destination: in our case, the Canadian dollar. Such an inflow can exert upward pressure on the Canadian exchange rate, making imports less expensive and exports more expensive. Net exports (NX) would be impacted, and through net exports, the GDP.

Crowding out is complete only if the economy is at full employment. If the economy is in recession, it's possible to get more public-sector output (like highways, schools, and health care) without cutbacks in private-sector output. This possibility is illustrated by the move from point *c* to point *b* in Figure 11.3.

Tax cuts have crowding-out effects as well. The purpose of tax cuts was to stimulate consumer spending. As the economy approaches full employment, however, how can more consumer output be produced? At the production possibilities limit, the added consumption will force cutbacks in either investment or government services.

What Figure 11.3 emphasizes is that *the risk of crowding out is greater the closer the economy is to full employment.* This implies that deficits are less appropriate at high levels of employment but more appropriate at low levels of employment.

Opportunity Cost

Even if crowding out does occur, that doesn't mean that deficits are necessarily too big. Crowding out simply reminds us that there's an *opportunity cost* to government spending. We still have to decide whether the private-sector output crowded out by government expenditure is more or less desirable than the increased public-sector output.

Interest-Rate Movements

Although the production possibilities curve illustrates the inevitability of crowding out at full employment, it doesn't explain *how* the crowding out occurs. Typically, the mechanism that enforces crowding out is the rate of interest. When the government borrows more funds to finance larger deficits, it puts pressure on financial markets. That added pressure may cause interest rates to rise. If they do, households will be less eager to borrow more money to buy cars, houses, and other debt-financed products. Businesses, too, will be more hesitant to borrow and invest. Hence, *rising interest rates are both a symptom and a cause of crowding out.*

Rising interest rates may also crowd out *government* spending in the wake of tax cuts. We know consumers will use their tax cuts to buy more goods and services. In the process, they'll undoubtedly borrow more money as well, to make larger purchases (plasma TVs, cars, etc.). This added borrowing will push interest rates up. As interest rates rise, government borrowing costs rise as well, since the interest cost of the public debt is dependent on both the size of the debt and the interest rate in the economy. For example, as interest rates declined in Canada through the early 2000s, federal government debt charges fell from $40.1 billion in fiscal year 2002 to $32.0 billion in fiscal year 2006[4] although the net federal debt fell by only $340 million.[5] Thus higher interest costs leave less room in government budgets for financing new projects or expanding current ones.

How much interest rates rise again depends on how close the economy is to its productive capacity. If there is lots of excess capacity, interest-rate induced crowding out isn't very likely. As capacity is approached, however, interest rates and crowding out are both likely to increase.

[4]Statistics Canada, CANSIM Table 385-0002, http://www40.statcan.ca/l01/cst01/govt02b.htm, accessed November 1, 2006.
[5]Statistics Canada, CANSIM Table 385-0010, http://www40.statcan.ca/l01/cst01/govt03a.htm, accessed November 1, 2006.

11.3 ECONOMIC EFFECTS OF SURPLUSES

Although budget deficits have seemed the "problem" and continue to be the focus of much political talk, more recently, the federal government has consistently delivered budget surpluses. These surpluses also impose economic effects, and we need to ponder those as well. Essentially, these effects are the mirror image of those discussed for budget deficits.

When the government takes in more revenue than it spends, it adds to leakage in the circular flow. But the federal government doesn't hide the surplus under the finance minister's mattress or put it into a bank account. Rather, government directs the surplus towards one or more of the following uses:

Crowding In

- *Spend it on goods and services.*
- *Cut taxes.*
- *Increase income transfers.*
- *Pay off old debt ("save it").*

The first three options effectively wipe out the surplus by changing budget outlays or receipts. There are important differences here, though. The first option—increased government spending—not only reduces the surplus but enlarges the public sector. Cutting taxes or increasing income transfers, by contrast, puts the money into the hands of consumers and enlarges the private sector.

In the May 2006 budget speech, Finance Minister James Flaherty stated that "this government is focused. And nowhere are we more focused than in the area of tax relief." The Minister goes on to note that "this budget delivers more than twice as much tax relief as new spending. For every new tax dollar we spend, this government is returning two tax dollars to hard-working Canadians."[6]

APPLICATIONS

Surplus Hits $13B, Cuts Debt: Reduced Spending Put More in Coffers: Flaherty

OTTAWA—The amount of money Ottawa annually spends dropped for the first time in almost a decade in the past fiscal year, allowing the Conservative government to post a larger-than-expected surplus of $13.2 billion that will help slash the federal debt.

The $13.2 billion surplus is the second largest in the past nine years, and the entire amount will be used to pay down the federal debt, as required by law. As a result, the debt stands at $481.5 billion, or 14 percent below its peak of $562.9 billion in 1996–97.

Dale Orr, managing director of economic forecaster Global Insight Canada, said paying down the debt by $13.2 billion will have long-term positive impacts, such as reducing both the tax burden for future generations and the cost of financing debt.

But not all federal finance observers were thrilled with the news. John Williamson, federal director of the Canadian Taxpayers Federation, said the larger-than-expected surplus was due to over taxation . . . Annual surpluses represent over-taxation by government and the money should go back to taxpayers in the form of lower income taxes."

Source: Paul Viera, "Surplus hits $13B, cuts debt," *National Post* (September 26, 2006). Material reprinted with the express permission of National Post Company, a CanWest Partnership.

Analysis: The policy debate around the public debt has a number of perspectives. One aspect alluded to in the story above is the reduction in the "cost of financing debt," the annual interest payment of the federal government. Any reduction in the financing cost leaves additional funds for other uses—a fiscal dividend. Another aspect noted in the story is the reduction of the tax burden in the future as less revenue is required if interest payments are less. A third aspect is discussed below, that if gains from absolute debt reduction are small then the issue is really one of reducing the debt:GDP ratio, which can also arise from GDP growth rather than absolute reduction of the debt.

[6]Budget Speech (May 2, 2006), http://www.fin.gc.ca/budget06/speech/speeche.htm, accessed November 1, 2006.

The fourth budget option is to use the surplus to pay off some of the debt accumulated from earlier deficits. This has a similar but less direct *crowding-in* effect. If government pays off some of its accumulated debt, households that were holding that debt (government bonds) will end up with more money. If they use that money to buy goods and services, then private-sector output will expand.

Even people who haven't lent any money to government will benefit from the debt reduction. When the government reduces its level of borrowing, it takes pressure off market interest rates. As interest rates drop, consumers will be more willing and able to purchase big-ticket items such as cars, appliances, and houses, thus changing the mix of output in favor of private-sector production.

Cyclical Sensitivity

Like crowding out, the extent of crowding in depends on the state of the economy. In a recession, a surplus-induced decline in interest rates isn't likely to stimulate much spending. If consumer and investor confidence are low, even a surplus-financed tax cut might not lift private-sector spending much.

11.4 THE ACCUMULATION OF DEBT

public debt: The accumulated debt of Canadian governments—federal, provincial, and territorial.

The current accumulated **public debt** is simply the sum of all previous budget balances. Budget deficit years add to the debt while budget surplus years don't—and may actually lead to reductions in the debt level depending on which of the four potential uses for the surplus is chosen.

There are two ways to think about the accumulated public debt: first is the absolute dollar amount, while the other is as a percentage of current nominal GDP. While newspaper headlines tend to focus on the dollar value—the scariest approach—a more logical approach is to look at debt as a proportion of total national income. Figure 11.4 takes this second approach, providing an historical overview of the debt:GDP ratio

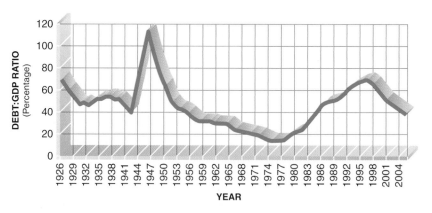

FIGURE 11.4
Historical View of the Debt:GDP* Ratio

Throughout the 1920s and 1930s, the federal debt exceeded 40 percent of national income. The debt ratio rose sharply through World War II, reaching a peak of 113 percent in 1946. The ratio then fell consistently until the mid-1970s when the combination of new and better entitlement programs (health, social services, and unemployment benefits) and a series of economic "shocks" (recessions in the 1970s, 1980s, and early 1990s) reversed that trend. Since 1996, the debt ratio has again been falling, declining to 38 percent in 2005.

*In the period 1926–1960, GNP is used to calculate the ratio, the remaining period uses GDP.
Source: Adapted from Statistics Canada publication *Historical Statistics of Canada*, Catalogue 11-516-XIE, and CANSIM database tables 385-0010 and 380-0017, http://cansim2.statcan.ca. Statistics Canada information is used with the permission of Statistics Canada.

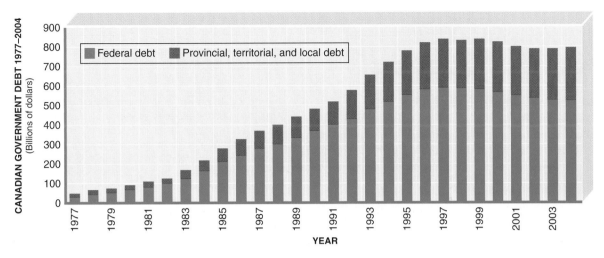

FIGURE 11.5
The National Debt

The federal government debt reached a peak in 1997 of $588.4 billion and since that time has been reduced to $523.4 billion in 2005. The payment made in September 2006 (see the Applications box on page 227) would reduce the federal debt further. The opposite experience has occurred at the provincial/territorial level. Whereas in 1977, total provincial/territorial debt amounted to only $13.6 billion dollars, or about 40 percent of the federal debt, by 2004 that total had grown to $263.3 billion, or about 50 percent of the federal debt.

Source: Adapted from Statistics Canada CANSIM database tables 385-0010 and 385-0017, http://cansim2.statcan.ca. Statistics Canada information is used with the permission of Statistics Canada.

from 1926 to 2005. Figure 11.5 gives the debt position of the federal and provincial/territorial governments from 1977–2004.

As illustrated in Figure 11.4, the federal government debt as a proportion of national income increased to around 50 percent of national income during the depression of the 1930s and then "spiked" upward during World War II, reaching a peak of 113 percent of total national income in 1946. The post-war recovery reduced the proportion—through surpluses and growth of national income—so that by 1974, the ratio of debt to national income was only 14 percent. Between 1977 and 1996, the ratio again increased as the economy suffered through a period of unusual economic dislocation (oil shocks in the 1970s leading to recessions in 1981–1984 and again from 1989–1991 and high interest rates through the 1980s that increased the cost of the existing debt), reaching 69 percent of national income in 1996. Since 1997, the proportion of debt to national income has been declining, falling to 38 percent in 2005.

As the Applications box on page 229 notes, the $13.2 billion paydown of the debt reduces the dollar figure of the debt to $481.5 billion. This, coupled with economic growth (greater GDP) will also reduce the debt-to-GDP ratio further. As noted in the May 2006 budget speech:

> As a result of our debt reduction plan, the ratio of debt to GDP is projected to fall to about 31.7 per cent by 2007–08. This will allow us to reduce the debt-to-GDP ratio to 25 per cent by 2013–14.[7]

Figure 11.5 illustrates the change in the dollar amount of debt over the 1977–2004 period for both the federal government, and consolidated amounts for the provincial/territorial governments. The federal government debt reached its highest point in 1997 at $588.4 billion and, as noted above, has fallen ever since. The consolidated provincial/territorial government debt has increased over this entire time period, with the exception of 1982, 2000, and 2001, climbing to $263.3 billion in 2004.

---

[7]Budget Speech (May 2006). http://www.fin.gc.ca/budget06/speech/speeche.htm, accessed November 1, 2006.

Debt Museum an Argentine First

A group of financial journalists and academics have found a novel way to make the best of Argentina's chronic economic woes. They are starting a museum. The Museum of Foreign Debt, which opens next month in Buenos Aires, is the world's first national museum devoted to overspending. Its aim is to explain how this South American country of 30 million people has so regularly plumbed the depths of fiscal management, including the most recent meltdown nearly two years ago.

Mr. Pristupin hopes that when they tire of tango and the city's Parisian-style cafes, foreign tourists will make the trek to the museum's temporary quarters in the economics department at the University of Buenos Aires, where they can watch video installations chronicling significant moments in the country's debt history, and view exhibits that chart the cycle of Argentina's economic breakdown.

One of the videos at the Museum of Foreign Debt shows then Argentine president Adolfo Rodriguez Saa announcing Argentina's latest default in December, 2001, a tumultuous time in the country's history during which violent protests erupted on the streets of Buenos Aires and the country went through five presidents in a two-week period.

Immediately after the speech, Argentina stopped payments on its US$142-billion debt. The default, coupled with more than four years of deep recession, left more than 57% of the population under the poverty line and nearly 20% unemployed.

Source: Isobel Vincent, "Debt museum an Argentine first," *The National Post* (September 27, 2003) p. A12.

Analysis: Fiscal policy decisions, deficits, and debt, can have impacts beyond government's financial position, creating political upheaval and social dislocation.

The different debt experiences of the federal and provincial/territorial governments can be summarized by looking at their respective budget balances, particularly over the 1998–2006 period where the federal government has run annual budget surpluses. Figure 11.6 illustrates that the provincial/territorial governments ran budget deficits in five of the nine years. In two other years the provincial/territorial budget balance was essentially balanced, resulting in little budget surplus.

Finally, we can think about Canada's federal debt in an international context. Figure 11.7 illustrates IMF staff estimates for the general government net debt in a few advanced economies. While Canada's net debt is expected to continue to

FIGURE 11.6
Federal and Provincial/Territorial Budget Balances 1998–2006

This figure illustrates the different experiences of the federal and consolidated provincial/territorial governments for the period 1998–2006. The federal government ran a budget surplus over this entire period, while provincial/territorial governments ran deficits in five of the nine years and essentially balanced budgets in two other years.

Source: Adapted from Statistics Canada CANSIM database table 385-0001, http://cansim2.statcan.ca. Statistics Canada information is used with the permission of Statistics Canada.

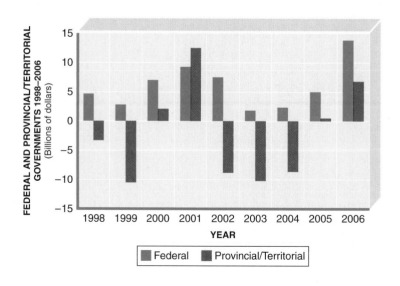

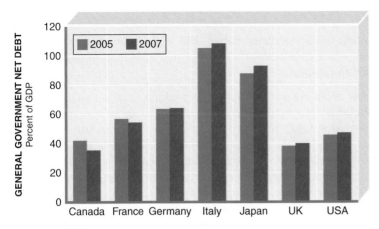

FIGURE 11.7
General Government Net Debt for 2005 and 2007

This figure indicates the level and change in government debt between 2005 and 2007. Canada is estimated to have the lowest debt as a percent of GDP, and of the countries shown only Canada and France have declines in debt as a percentage of GDP between 2005 and 2007.

Source: Editorial, "U.S. republicans and their fiscal sins," *The Globe and Mail* (November 7, 2006), p. A20. Reprinted with permission from *The Globe and Mail*.

decline—to 35.8 percent in 2007 from 41.9 percent in 2005—the other countries (with the exception of France) continue to have increasing debt totals, ranging in 2007 from 38.8 percent of GDP in the United Kingdom to 107.5 percent of GDP in Italy and 92.4 percent of GDP in Japan.

U.S. Republicans and Their Fiscal Sins

As they head into midterm elections today that could cost them control of one or both houses of Congress, the Republicans face the wrath of U.S. voters on several fronts. . . . But if there is one reason to throw the Republicans out, it is their disastrous fiscal management.

That's why the most important person out on the hustings in this election is a non-partisan accountant named David Walker, who is not seeking elected office. Mr. Walker is the U.S. Comptroller General, and he has chosen the midterm elections as a platform for his dire warnings about the nation's coming fiscal calamity and the grave threat it poses to the economic health of future generations. "This is about the future of our country, our kids and grandkids," he said in a speech during what he calls "the fiscal wake up tour."

Mr. Walker knows whereof he speaks. As the head of the Government Accountability Office, he is the U.S. equivalent of

Canada's Auditor General. And he does not like what he sees. The budget deficit for the fiscal year that ended Sept. 30 declined to a four-year low of $248 billion ($US) from a record $413 billion in 2004. But it is the rapidly accumulating debt that poses the greatest long-term risk. If unchecked, that debt and the accompanying costs will vacuum up most of Washington's income and shred the value of the U.S. dollar. Mr. Walker estimates that unless action is taken to restore fiscal responsibility, the current debt of about $8.5 trillion ($US) will climb to about $46-trillion in coming decades, when adjusted for inflation. "We the people have to rise up to make sure things get changed," he said. If not, Americans, who already live beyond their means, will face increasing economic hardship, high interest rates, rising taxes, lower benefits and a declining standard of living.

Source: Editorial, "U.S. Republicans and their fiscal sins," *The Globe and Mail* (November 7, 2006), p. A20. Reprinted with permission from *The Globe and Mail*.

Analysis: Unlike Canada, where the debt is falling in both dollars and as a percentage of GDP, the United States is experiencing an increasing level of debt. As illustrated in Figure 11.7, the U.S. general government net debt has increased between 2005 and 2007. One impact mentioned in the article has been very evident as the value of the U.S. dollar in terms of the Canadian dollar has fallen from $1.14 ($Cdn) in November 2006 to $1.07 ($Cdn) by May 2007.

11.5 WHO OWNS THE DEBT?

To the average citizen, the accumulated public debt is both incomprehensible and frightening. Who can understand debts that are measured in *billions* of dollars? Who can ever be expected to pay them?

Liabilities = Assets

> **liability:** An obligation to make future payment; debt.

> **asset:** Anything having exchange value in the marketplace; wealth.

Ownership of the Debt

> **internal debt:** Government debt held by Canadian households and institutions.

> **external debt:** Government debt held by foreign households and institutions.

The first thing to note about the national debt is that it represents not only a liability but an asset as well. When government borrows money, it issues bonds. Those bonds are a **liability** for the government since it must later repay the borrowed funds. But those same bonds are an **asset** to the people who hold them. Bondholders have a claim to future repayment. They can even convert that claim into cash by selling their bonds in the bond market. Therefore, *national debt creates as much wealth (for bondholders) as liabilities (for the government).* Neither money nor any other form of wealth disappears when the government borrows money.

The fact that total bond assets equal total bond liabilities is of little consolation to taxpayers confronted with $481.5 billion of national debt and who worry when, if ever, they'll be able to repay it. The fear that either the government or its taxpayers will be "bankrupted" by the national debt always lurks in the shadows. How legitimate is that fear?

Figure 11.8 shows who owns the bonds the federal government has issued. The largest portion of federal government debt is held within the Canadian economy itself, referred to as **internal debt.** Approximately 75 percent of the debt is held by households and firms—often financial firms—inside the Canadian economy. Another 11 percent is held as assets at the Bank of Canada, an arm of the federal government itself, and the remaining 13 percent is held by foreigners, referred to as **external debt.** Thus, approximately 86 percent of the federal debt outstanding in 2005–2006 is held by Canadians themselves. This means that the interest paid on this debt is paid to other Canadians, and becomes a component of income for Canadians to use for either consumption or savings. The level of foreign ownership of Canada's debt has changed over the years. In 1970–1971, foreigners held only 2.8 percent of Canada's debt but by 1993–1994, this proportion had increased to 27 percent.[8] Since then, the proportion held by foreigners has decreased to the current 2005–2006 level of 13 percent.

Separately from the issue of who holds the government debt—and who gets the interest payment—there is an issue of the currency that the debt is owed in. For instance, the federal government could issue bonds payable in Euros or U.S. dollars rather than Canadian dollars. If bonds are sold in foreign currency, then the interest payments and the principle repayment must also be in that currency. Foreign currency can only be obtained through trade (our goods and services for their currency) or by buying that

FIGURE 11.8
Who Holds Canada's Federal Debt

The federal debt is mostly held by other Canadians: 75 percent outside of government and another 11 percent held as assets by the Bank of Canada, an arm of the federal government. The remaining 13 percent is held by foreigners.

Source: Government of Canada, fiscal reference tables—Sept 2006 from Ministry of Finance: Table 14 and the Bank of Canada Weekly Financial Statistics: Assets and Liabilities.

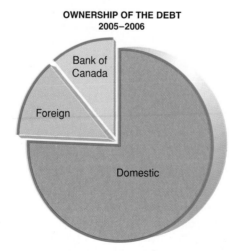

OWNERSHIP OF THE DEBT
2005–2006

Bank of Canada

Foreign

Domestic

[8]Department of Finance, *Fiscal Reference Tables,* Table 14 (October 1996).

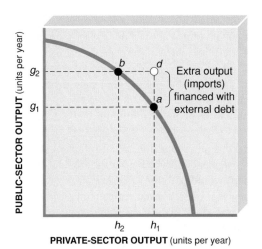

FIGURE 11.9
External Financing

A closed economy must forsake some private-sector output to increase public-sector output (see Figure 11.3). External financing temporarily eliminates that opportunity cost. Instead of having to move from *a* to *b*, external borrowing allows us to move from *a* to *d*. At point *d* we have more public output and no less private output.

foreign currency on international markets (in the same way you might buy Euros for a trip to Europe or U.S. dollars for a trip to the United States). Each of these alternatives can create other economic problems, some of which we will look at a little later in Chapter 16, International Finance, in the context of the value of the Canadian dollar.

No Crowding Out. When we borrow funds from abroad, we increase our ability to consume, invest, and finance government activity. In effect, other nations are lending us the income necessary to *import* more goods. If we can buy imports with borrowed funds (without offsetting exports), our real consumption will exceed our production possibilities. As Figure 11.9 illustrates, external borrowing allows us to enjoy a mix of output that lies *outside* our production possibilities curve. Specifically, ***external financing allows us to get more public-sector goods without cutting back on private-sector production (or vice versa).*** When we use external debt to finance government spending, we move from point *a* to point *d* in Figure 11.9. Imported goods and services eliminate the need to cut back on private-sector activity, a cutback that would otherwise force us to point *b*. External financing eliminates this opportunity cost. The move from point *a* to point *d* reflects the additional imports financed by external debt.

The imports needn't be public-sector goods. A tax cut at point *b* might increase consumption and imports by $h_1 - h_2$, moving the economy to point *d*. At *d* we have *more* consumption and *no less* government activity.

External financing appears to offer the proverbial free lunch. It would be a free lunch if foreign lenders were willing to accumulate Canadian bonds forever. They would then own stacks of paper (bonds), and we'd consume some of their output (our imports) each year. ***As long as outsiders are willing to hold Canadian bonds, external financing imposes no real cost.*** No goods or services are given up to pay for the additional output received.

Repayment. Foreign investors may not be willing to hold bonds indefinitely. At some point they'll want to collect their bills. To do this, they'll cash in (sell) their bonds, then use the proceeds to buy Canadian goods and services. When this happens, Canada will be *exporting* goods and services to pay off its debts. Recall that the external debt was used to acquire imported goods and services. Hence, ***external debt must be repaid with exports of real goods and services.***

11.6 BURDEN OF THE DEBT

It may be comforting to know that most of our national debt is owned internally, and some of it by the government itself. Figure 11.8 won't still the fears of most taxpayers, however, especially those who don't hold any bonds. From their perspective, the total debt still looks frightening.

External Debt

Refinancing

"What's this I hear about you adults mortgaging my future?"

From The Wall Street Journal—permission, Cartoon Features Syndicate.

Analysis: The fear that present generations are passing the debt burden to future generations is exaggerated.

Debt Service

refinancing: The issuance of new debt in payment of debt issued earlier.

debt charges: The interest required to be paid each year on outstanding debt.

Opportunity Costs

The Real Trade-Offs

How much of a "burden" the debt really represents isn't so evident. For nearly 30 years (1970–1997), the federal government kept piling up more debt without apparent economic damage. As we saw earlier (Figure 11.4), deficits and debt stretched out over even longer periods in earlier decades.

How was the government able to pile debt upon debt? Quite simple: As debts have become due, the federal government has simply borrowed new funds to pay them off. New bonds have been issued to replace old bonds. This **refinancing** of the debt is a routine feature of debt management.

The ability to refinance its debt raises an intriguing question. What if the debt could be eternally refinanced? What if no one *ever* demanded to be paid off more than others were willing to lend? Then the national debt would truly grow forever.

Two things are worrisome about this scenario. First, eternal refinancing seems like a chain letter that promises to make everyone rich. In this case, the chain requires that people hold ever-larger portions of their wealth in the form of bonds. People worry that the chain will be broken and that they'll be forced to repay all the outstanding debt. Parents worry that the scheme might break down in the next generation, unfairly burdening their own children or grandchildren (see cartoon).

Aside from its seeming implausibility, the notion of eternal refinancing seems to defy a basic maxim of economics, namely, that "there ain't no free lunch." Eternal refinancing makes it look as though government borrowing has no cost, as though federal spending financed by the national debt is really a free lunch.

There are two flaws in this way of thinking. The first relates to the interest charges that accompany debt. The second, and more important oversight relates to the real economic costs of government activity.

With over $480 billion in accumulated debt, the federal government must make enormous interest payments every year. **Debt charges** refer to these annual interest payments. In the fiscal year ending March 31, 2006, the federal government paid over $32 billion and the provincial/territorial governments another $24 billion in interest charges. These interest payments force governments to reduce outlays for other purposes or to finance a larger budget each year. In this respect, *interest payments restrict the government's ability to balance the budget or fund other public-sector activities.*

Although the debt-servicing requirements may pinch government's spending purse, the real economic consequences of interest payments are less evident. Who gets the interest payments? What economic resources are absorbed by those payments?

As noted, most of the nation's outstanding debt is internal—that is, owned by domestic households and institutions. Therefore, most interest payments are made to people and institutions within Canada. *Most debt servicing is simply a redistribution of income from taxpayers to bondholders.* In many cases, the taxpayer and bondholder are the same person. In all cases, however, the income that leaks from the circular flow in the form of taxes to pay for debt servicing returns to the circular flow as interest payments. Total income is unchanged. Thus, debt servicing may not have any direct effect on the level of aggregate demand.

Opportunity costs are incurred when real resources (factors of production) are used. The amount of that cost is measured by the other goods and services that could have been produced with those resources, but weren't. Although the *process* of debt servicing absorbs few resources and so has negligible opportunity cost, to understand the true burden of the national debt, we have to look at what that debt financed. *The true burden of the debt is the opportunity cost of the activities financed by the debt.* To assess that burden, we need to ask what the government did with the borrowed funds.

Although the national debt poses no special burden to the economy, the transactions it finances have a substantial impact on the basic questions of WHAT, HOW, and FOR WHOM to produce. The mix of output is influenced by how much deficit spending the government undertakes. The funds obtained by borrowing allow the federal government to bid for scarce resources. Private investors and consumers will have less access to loanable funds and be less able to acquire incomes or goods. The larger the deficit, the more the private sector gets squeezed. Hence, deficit financing allows the government to obtain more resources and change the mix of output. In general, *deficit financing tends to change the mix of output in the direction of more public-sector goods.*

The deficits of the 1980s helped finance increased transfer payments (e.g, employment insurance), and spending in health and education. The same result could have been financed with higher taxes. Taxes are more visible and always unpopular, however. By borrowing rather than taxing, the federal government's claim on scarce resources is less apparent. Either financing method allows the public sector to expand at the expense of the private sector. This resource reallocation reveals the true burden of the debt: *The burden of the debt is really the opportunity cost (crowding out) of deficit-financed government activity.*

Opportunity costs are incurred at the time a government activity takes place, not when the resultant debt is paid. In other words, *the primary burden of the debt is incurred when the debt-financed activity takes place.*

The real costs of government projects can't be postponed until a later year. In other words, the real burden of the debt can't be passed on to future generations. On the contrary, future generations will benefit from the sacrifices made today to build colleges, parks, highways, dams, and other public-sector projects. Future taxpayers will be able to *use* these projects without incurring the opportunity costs of their construction.

Economic Growth. Although future generations may benefit from current government spending, they may also be adversely affected by today's opportunity costs. Of particular concern is the possibility that government deficits might crowd out private investment. Investment is essential to enlarging our production possibilities and attaining higher living standards in the future. If federal deficits and debt-servicing requirements crowd out private investment, the rate of economic growth will slow, leaving future generations with less productive capacity than they would otherwise have. Thus, *if debt-financed government spending crowds out private investment, future generations will bear some of the debt burden.* Their burden will take the form of smaller-than-anticipated productive capacity.

There's no certainty that such crowding out will occur. Also, any reduction in private investment may be offset by public works (such as highways and schools) that benefit future generations. So future generations may not suffer a net loss in welfare even if the national debt slows private investment and economic growth. From this perspective, *the whole debate about the burden of the debt is really an argument over the mix of output.* If we permit more deficit spending, we're promoting more public-sector activity. On the other hand, limits on deficit financing curtail growth of the public sector. Battles over deficits and debts are a proxy for the more fundamental issue of private versus public spending.

Repayment. All this sounds a little too neat. Won't future generations have to pay interest on the debts we incur today? And might they even have to pay off some of the debt?

We've already observed that the collection of taxes and processing of interest payments absorb relatively few resources. Hence, the mechanisms of repayment entail little burden.

Notice also who *receives* future interest payments. When we die, we leave behind not only the national debt but also the bonds that represent ownership of that debt. Hence, future grandchildren will be both taxpayers *and* bondholders. If interest payments are made 30 years from today, only people who are alive and holding bonds at

WEB NOTE

For a discussion on the "Vanishing Efficiency Gains of Debt Repayment" visit the Centre for Policy Alternatives Web site at http://www.policyalternatives.ca/News/2005/11/PressRelease1228/.

that time will receive interest payments. ***Future interest payments entail a redistribution of income among taxpayers and bondholders living in the future.***

The same kind of redistribution occurs if and when our grandchildren decide to pay off the debt. Tax revenues will be used to pay off the debt. The debt payments will go to people then holding bonds. The entire redistribution will occur among people living in the future.

Eliminating the Debt

Although external and internal debts pose very different problems, most policy discussions overlook these distinctions. In policy debates, the aggregate size of the national debt is usually the only concern. The key policy questions are whether and how to limit or reduce the national debt.

Deficit Ceilings. *The only way to stop the growth of the national debt is to eliminate the budget deficits that create debt.* The first step in debt reduction, therefore, is a balanced annual budget. A balanced budget will at least stop the debt from growing further. *The only way to reduce the size of the federal debt is to run surplus budgets and use that surplus to pay down the debt.* As the Applications box on page 229 showed, reducing the actual size of the debt requires budget surpluses that are then dedicated to paying down existing debt.

Over the past decade, successive governments have adopted several approaches to the "debt issue." As was noted in the introduction to this chapter, the November 2005 policy of the Liberal government was to set out a specific split of any surplus between additional government spending and paying down the debt. Although the Conservative budget from March 2007 doesn't explicitly set out a debt policy, the commitment was to balanced budgets. The $13.2 billion paydown of the debt described by the Applications box was accompanied by a statement from the Minister of Finance that "paying down the debt makes good sense."[9]

[9]Paul Viera, "Surplus hits $13B, cuts debt," *National Post* (September 26, 2006).

SUMMARY

- Budget imbalances result from both discretionary fiscal policy (structural deficits and surpluses) and cyclical changes in the economy (cyclical deficits and surpluses).
- Fiscal restraint is measured by the reduction in the structural deficit; fiscal stimulus occurs when the structural deficit increases.
- Automatic stabilizers increase federal spending and reduce tax revenues during recessions. When the economy expands, they have the reverse effect, thereby shrinking the cyclical deficit.
- Deficit financing of government expenditure may crowd out private investment and consumption. The risk of crowding out increases as the economy approaches full employment. If investment becomes the opportunity cost of increased government spending or consumer tax cuts, economic growth may slow.
- Crowding in refers to the increase in private-sector output made possible by a decline in government borrowing.

- Each year's deficit adds to the national debt. The national debt grew sporadically until World War II and then skyrocketed. Recessions and increased government spending since 1980 increased the national debt to $588 billion.
- Budget surpluses may be used to finance tax cuts or more government spending, or used to reduce accumulated national debt.
- Every dollar of federal government debt represents a dollar of assets to the people who hold Government of Canada bonds. Government of Canada bonds are held by government agencies (the Bank of Canada), financial institutions (chartered banks), and Canadian and foreign households.
- The real burden of the debt is the opportunity cost of the activities financed by the debt. That cost is borne at the time the deficit-financed activity takes place. The benefits of debt-financed activity may extend into the future.
- External debt permits the public sector to expand without reducing private-sector output. External debt also makes it possible to shift some of the real debt burden on to future generations.

Key Terms

deficit spending 222
budget deficit 222
budget surplus 223
fiscal year (FY) 224
discretionary fiscal spending 225

automatic stabilizer 225
cyclical balance 226
structural balance 226
public debt 230
liability 234

asset 234
internal debt 234
external debt 234
refinancing 236
debt charges 236

Questions for Discussion

1. In what ways do future generations benefit from this generation's deficit spending? Cite three examples.
2. What's considered "too much" debt or "too large" a deficit? Are you able to provide any guidelines for deficit or debt?
3. If deficit spending "crowds out" some private investment, could future generations be worse off? If external financing eliminates crowding out, are future generations thereby protected?
4. What should the government do with a budget surplus?
5. How long would it take to pay off the national debt? How would the economy be affected?
6. The Applications box on page 229 highlighted the federal government's $13.2 billion paydown of the federal debt. Had they decided to use that revenue for additional spending or transfers, what would have been the impact on future government budget balances?
7. The November 2005 fiscal update promised to "*maintain the Government's commitment to balanced budgets or*

better and its balanced approach to the allocation of surpluses—including unanticipated surpluses in excess of the Contingency Reserve—between debt reduction, tax relief and investments in key economic and social priorities." What should that appropriate balance be and what are the economic implications of that balance?
8. Should the federal government create legislation that requires the federal budget to always balance in any fiscal year? Why or why not?
9. Should the federal government create legislation that requires the federal debt to be paid off by some particular date? Why or why not?
10. The federal government has stated that the purpose of their "debt reduction plan" is to reduce the size of the federal debt relative to the size of the economy to 25 percent by the fiscal year 2013–2014. How could they achieve this goal without actually paying off any of the debt?

EXERCISES

PROBLEMS   The Student Problem Set to accompany this chapter can be found at the end of the book.

WEB ACTIVITIES   Web Activities to accompany this chapter can be found on the Online Learning Centre at **http://www.mcgrawhill.ca/olc/schiller**.

Money and Banks

Sophocles, the ancient Greek playwright, had very strong opinions about the role of money. As he saw it, "Of evils upon earth, the worst is money. It is money that sacks cities, and drives men forth from hearth and home; warps and seduces native intelligence, and breeds a habit of dishonesty."

In modern times, people may still be seduced by the lure of money and fashion their lives around its pursuit. Nevertheless, it's hard to imagine an economy functioning without money. Money affects not only morals and ideals but also the way an economy works.

This and the following chapter examine the role of money in the economy today. We begin with a very simple question:

- **What is money?**

As we'll discover, money isn't exactly what you might think it is. There's a lot more money in the economy than there is cash. And there's a lot more income around than money. So money is something quite different from either cash or income. Once we've established the characteristics of money, we go on to ask:

- **How is money created?**
- **What role do banks play in the circular flow of income and spending?**
- **How does money supply and money demand determine an interest rate in the monetary economy?**

In Chapter 13, we will look at how the Bank of Canada administers monetary policy through control of the money supply and the implications of monetary policy on aggregate demand in the real economy and therefore on national income, GDP.

LEARNING OBJECTIVES

By the end of this chapter, you should be able to:

12.1 Describe the three essential characteristics of money

12.2 Describe how purchasing power is created through commercial bank loans

12.3 Demonstrate how the target reserve ratio, the excess reserve ratio, and the cash drain impact the creation of purchasing power

12.4 Describe the various measures of the supply of money in the economy

12.5 Describe the three demands for holding money in the economy

12.6 Demonstrate the equilibrium condition in the loanable funds market

12.1 WHAT IS "MONEY"?

To appreciate the significance of money for a modern economy, imagine for a moment that there were no such thing as money. How would you get something for breakfast? If you wanted eggs for breakfast, you'd have to tend your own chickens or go see Farmer Brown. But how would you pay Farmer Brown for his eggs? Without money, you'd have to offer him some goods or services that he could use. In other words, you'd have to engage in primitive **barter**—the direct exchange of one good for another—to get eggs for breakfast. You'd get those eggs only if Farmer Brown happened to want the particular goods or services you had to offer.

barter: The direct exchange of one good for another, without the use of money.

The use of money greatly simplifies market transactions. It's a lot easier to exchange money for eggs at the supermarket than to go into the country and barter with farmers every time you crave some eggs. Our ability to use money in market transactions, however, depends on the grocer's willingness to accept money as a *medium of exchange.* The grocer sells eggs for money only because he can use the same money to pay his help and buy the goods he himself desires. He too can exchange money for goods and services.

Without money, the process of acquiring goods and services would be much more difficult and time-consuming. This was evident when the value of the Russian ruble plummeted. Trading goods for Farmer Brown's eggs seems simple compared to the complicated barter deals Russian factories had to negotiate when paper money was no longer accepted (see World View). And Russian workers certainly would've preferred to be paid in cash rather than in bras and coffins.

WORLD VIEW

The Cashless Society

Bartering Chokes Russian Economy

NARO-FOMINSK, RUSSIA—Natalya Karpova, a supervisor at a fabric factory here on the outskirts of Moscow, heard good news a couple of weeks ago. Three carloads of concrete utility poles had arrived at the train station.

This was a matter of utmost importance to Karpova, because her factory was a year behind on its electric bill and had no cash on hand. The electric company agreed to accept utility poles instead, but how to pay for utility poles with no rubles?

Simple. First, her factory shipped fabric 200 miles to a sewing factory in Nizhny Novgorod. In exchange for the fabric, that factory sewed shirts for the security guards who work at a nearby automobile manufacturer. In exchange for the shirts, the auto factory shipped a car and truck to a concrete plant. In exchange for the vehicles, the concrete plant delivered the poles to the electric company.

Thus did the Narfomsholk fabric factory pay for the power to run its dye machines.

But only for a while. "Now they want a steam shovel," said Karpova, with a little sigh.

This is how Karpova's factory and much of Russia's industry survives these days: barter. By some estimates, it accounts for almost three-fourths of all transactions.

Barter is poisoning the development of capitalism in Russia because it consumes huge amounts of time that would be better spent producing goods.

Many workers have no expectation of a real paycheck. Unpaid wages now amount to an estimated $11 billion. Instead of money, the workers are stuck with whatever the factory or farm is handing out, usually what it produces. The practice is so common now that only the more bizarre substitutes for wages draw notice, such as bras or coffins.

—Sharon LaFraniere

Source: *Washington Post*, September 3, 1998. © 1998, The Washington Post. Reprinted with permission. www.washingtonpost.com

Analysis: When the Russian ruble lost its value, people would no longer accept it in payment. Market transactions had to be bartered, a clumsy and inefficient process.

Many Types of Money

WEB NOTE

To see the complete text of *A History of the Canadian Dollar* by James Powell, go to http://www.bankofcanada.ca/ en/dollar_book/index.html.

WEB NOTE

Take a virtual tour of the Canadian Currency Museum at the Bank of Canada. Enter the Museum and learn about the history of money in Canada at http://www.currencymuseum. ca/eng/exhibits/index.php.

WEB NOTE

Visit the Salt Spring Island Currency Web site at http:// www.saltspringdollars.com/ background.htm to see the currency and explore the history of this island currency.

Modern Concepts

money: Anything that is accepted as a medium of exchange and serves as both a store of value and as a unit of measurement.

Although markets can't function well without money, they can get along without *dollars.* James Powell, in *History of the Canadian Dollar,* writes that:

> The first regular system of exchange in Canada involving Europeans occurred in Tadoussac in the early seventeenth century. Here, French traders bartered each year with the Montagnais people (also known as the Innu), trading weapons, cloth, food, silver items, and tobacco for animal pelts, especially those of the beaver.[1]

Powell also notes that in 1608, the beaver pelt was a "universally accepted medium of exchange" in Samuel De Champlain's colony. Throughout the seventeenth century, Moose skins and Spanish *piastres* were also used when "official money" was in short supply. In 1685, when New France found itself again short of money, playing cards were used instead!

So have all these "other" forms of money been left in the distant past? Actually, no. On September 15, 2001, the Salt Spring Island community (Salt Spring is one of the Gulf Islands between the British Columbia mainland and Vancouver Island) introduced "Salt Spring Island" dollars at their Farmer's Institute Fall Fair. The mission statement as provided on the Web site states that:

> The purposes of the Society are to design, issue and maintain a local currency for Salt Spring Island with the goal of raising funds for worthwhile community projects while promoting local commerce and goodwill.

On Salt Spring Island, at least, the Salt Spring dollars are accepted interchangeably with Canada's official currency.

This historical perspective on **money** highlights its essential characteristics. ***Anything that serves all the following purposes can be thought of as money:***

- *Medium of exchange:* is accepted as payment for goods and services (and debts).
- *Store of value:* can be held for future purchases.
- *Unit of measurement:* serves as a way of measuring the prices of goods and services.

The bills and coins we carry around today aren't the only form of "money" we use. Most people realize this when they offer to pay for goods with a cheque rather than cash. People do distinguish between "cash" and "money," and for good reason. The "money" you have in a chequing account can be used to buy goods and services or to pay debts, or it can be retained for future use. In these respects, your chequing account balance is as much a part of your "money" as are the coins and dollars in your pocket or purse. You can access your balance by writing a cheque or using an ATM or debit card. Cheques are more convenient than cash because they eliminate trips to the bank. Cheques are also safer: Lost or stolen cash is gone forever; chequebooks and credit cards are easily replaced at little or no cost. We might use cheques even more frequently if everyone accepted them.

There's nothing unique about cash, then, insofar as the market is concerned. ***Chequing accounts can and do perform the same market functions as cash.*** Accordingly, we must include chequing account balances in our concept of money. The essence of money isn't its taste, colour, or feel but, rather, its ability to purchase goods and services.

Credit cards are another popular *medium of exchange.* People use credit cards for about one-third of all purchases over $100. This use is not sufficient, however, to qualify credit cards as a form of "money." Credit card balances must be paid by cheque or cash. The same holds true for balances in online electronic credit accounts ("e-cash"). Electronic purchases on the Internet or online services are ultimately paid

---

[1]James Powell, *A History of the Canadian Dollar,* (Ottawa: Publications Division, Bank of Canada, 2005), http://www.bankofcanada.ca/en/dollar_book/index.html, accessed November 20, 2006.

by withdrawals from a bank account (by cheque or computer). Online payment mechanisms and credit cards are a payment *service,* not a final form of payment (credit card companies charge fees and interest for this service). The cards themselves are not a store of value, in contrast to cash or bank account balances. A credit card, as the name suggests, is pre-approved credit, that is, consumer debt that must be paid off through either past or future saving. While credit cards enable current consumption, they do so by shifting it from the past or from the future.

The Diversity of Bank Accounts. To determine how much money is available to purchase goods and services, we need to count up all our coins and currency—as well as our bank account balances. This effort is complicated by the variety of bank accounts people have. In addition to simple no-interest chequing accounts at full-service banks, people have bank accounts that pay interest, offer automatic transfers, require minimum holding periods, offer overdraft protection, or limit the number of cheques that can be written. People also have "bank" accounts in credit unions, brokerage houses, and other nontraditional financial institutions (see Table 12.1 on page 246).

Although all bank account balances can be spent, they're not all used the same way. People use regular chequing accounts all the time to pay bills or make purchases. But consumers can't write cheques on most savings accounts. And few people want to cash in a certificate of deposit just to go to the movies. Hence, *some bank accounts are better substitutes for cash than others.*

The second purpose of money is to act as a *store of value.* That is, money can be held, or stored, to be used to purchase goods and services in the future. Those coins in your pocket, bills in your wallet, or deposits in a financial institution could be spent today, but they don't need to be. They could easily be left where they are and used at some other time. The point here is that "money" retains its nominal ability to purchase goods or services. A $2 coin today is still a $2 coin tomorrow and can be used tomorrow to purchase $2 worth of goods or services. This is the purpose of money, however, that is most impacted by inflation. As prices rise, a $2 coin is able to purchase fewer goods or services. In extreme cases of "hyperinflation," the purchasing power of money diminishes so quickly that storing money becomes unattractive.

The third purpose of money is to be a *unit of measurement.* Goods or services can be compared by their prices that are measured in money terms. A $10 CD has the same relative price as a $10 movie ticket but is five times the relative price of a $2 cup of coffee. One way to think about how useful and convenient this measurement system turns out to be is to think of travelling for the first time to a foreign country such as Guatemala. If you wander into the local market to buy a cup of coffee and find that its price is 4.50 quetzals, how do you know if that's a "good deal"? Well, if the next shop is selling CDs at 25 quetzals, the relative price is pretty much the same as you're used to. But if you know that the Canadian dollar equivalent of 4.5 quetzals was $0.62 Canadian, you would recognize it as a good buy. Being able to compare what else we could purchase with the equivalent amount helps us to better understand our opportunity cost.

12.2 CREATING PURCHASING POWER

Once we've decided what money is, we still have to explain where it comes from. Part of the explanation is simple. Currency must be printed. In Canada, banknotes (paper money) are printed by the Canadian Banknote Company and BA International, while coins are struck by the Royal Canadian Mint. This "physical currency," however, represents only a small fraction of our economy's total purchasing power—or total money supply. Much of the economy's total purchasing power comes from transactions accounts. So, where do all the transactions accounts come from? How do people

Analysis: People see very little of their money—most deposits and loans are computer entries in the banking system.

acquire transactions deposits? How does the total amount of such deposits—and therefore the total money supply of the economy—change?

Deposit Creation

Most people assume that all transactions account balances come from cash deposits. But this isn't the case. Direct deposits of paycheques, for example, are carried out by computer, not by the movement of cash (see cartoon). Moreover, the employer who issues the paycheque probably didn't make any cash deposits. It's more likely that she covered those paycheques with customers' cheques that she deposited or with loans granted by the bank itself.

The ability of banks to lend money opens up a whole new set of possibilities for creating purchasing power. *When a bank lends someone money, it simply credits that individual's bank account.* The money appears in an account just as it would with a cash deposit. And the owner of the account is free to spend that money as with any positive balance. Hence, *in making a loan, a bank effectively creates money because transactions account balances are counted as part of the money supply.*

To understand the origins of our money supply then, we must recognize two basic principles:

- Transactions account balances are a large portion of the money supply.
- Banks can create transactions account balances by making loans.

> **deposit creation:** The creation of transactions deposits by bank lending.

The following two sections examine this process of **deposit creation** more closely. We determine how banks actually create deposits and what forces might limit the process of deposit creation.

Bank Regulation. Financial institutions in Canada—banks and similar institutions—are regulated by the Office of the Superintendent of Financial Institutions (OSFI). The mandate of the OSFI is to:

- Supervise institutions to ensure that they maintain minimum funding and are complying with regulation
- Ensure that management takes action as a response to any material deficiencies
- Advance and administer the regulatory framework
- Watch for broader system or sector issues that might impact financial institutions

The OSFI, however, goes on to note in their mandate of "the need to allow institutions to compete effectively and take reasonable risks. [OSFI] legislation also recognizes that management, boards of directors and plan administrators are ultimately responsible and that financial institutions and pension plans can fail."[2]

[2]Office of the Superintendent of Financial Institutions, *Our Mandate,* http://www.osfi-bsif.gc.ca/osfi/index_e.aspx?DetailID=2, accessed December 1, 2006.

Canada's Banking System Has Created a Fortress of Solvency

Alberta's been booming for so long now that everyone's forgotten how tough things were there during the recession in the early 1980s, which was felt most strongly in the oil and gas sector, particularly for investors and the banks that specialized in financing activity in the oil patch.

Such a bank was the Canadian Commercial Bank. . . . The recession hit the bank hard: lots of non-performing loans in the oil patch and in California real estate. By 1983, it was in trouble, though regulators thought the situation was still manageable and encouraged five of the big banks to provide it with a special liquidity facility. But by 1985, the Canadian dollar was dropping and interest rates were rising putting even more pressure on the bank's portfolio of real estate loans and making it more expensive for it to roll over its maturing wholesale deposit liabilities. So in March, 1985, the Alberta and federal governments, together with the six big domestic banks, provided a further support package.

Over that summer, the bank continued to lose deposits and most days needed liquidity support from the Bank of Canada to clear its transactions. By the Labour Day weekend, CCB was into the Bank of Canada for $1.3 billion. The Inspector-General of Banks announced on Sunday, Sept. 1, that he had informed the Minister of Finance the CCB was unable to meet its liabilities as they came due, that the bank was no longer viable, and that there was thus no basis for the Bank of Canada to provide further liquidity support. The Bank of Canada pulled the plug on CCB.

In the years after CCB's failure, major changes were made in the Canadian financial system's machinery, most of them invisible to the general public. The glitches in the settlement system arising from CCB's failure were corrected. The Inspectorate of Banks was eliminated [and reconstituted as the] Office of the Superintendent of Financial Institutions, OSFI—with more staff, a bigger budget, and closer oversight from the Bank of Canada and the Department of Finance. A CCB will never happen again.

Source: Harry Koza, "Canada's banking system has created a fortress of solvency," *The Globe and Mail* (March 16, 2007), p. B9. Used with permission of Harry Koza.

Analysis: While bank failures don't happen in Canada very often—the one previous to this was in 1923—they do and can occur and make regulatory agencies like the OSFI important in maintaining confidence in the Canadian financial system.

The Banking System

To understand how money is "created" through banks, we'll simplify reality greatly by taking the banking system as a whole and not worrying about individual banks. This doesn't alter the impact on the money supply since it is simply the sum of all bank's activities in any case. Imagine that you've been saving some of your income by putting loose change into a piggy bank. Now, after months of saving, you break the bank and discover that your thrift has yielded $100. You immediately deposit this money in a new chequing account. How will this deposit affect the money supply?

Your initial deposit will have no immediate effect on the money supply. The coins in your piggy bank were already counted as part of the money supply because they represented cash held by the public. ***When you deposit cash or coins in a bank, you're only changing the composition of the money supply, not its size.*** The public (you) now holds $100 less of coins but $100 more of transactions deposits. Accordingly, no money is created by the demise of your piggy bank (the initial deposit). This accounting outcome is reflected in the following "T account" of the banking system and the composition of the money supply:

Banking System		Money Supply	
Assets	Liabilities	Cash held by the public	− $100
		Transactions deposits at bank	+ $100
+ $100 in coins	+ $100 in deposits	Change in money supply	0

TABLE 12.1
Financial Institutions in Canada

These institutions to a greater or lesser level perform "banking" functions and provide "purchasing power" to the Canadian economy. Therefore, they are all counted in the Canadian total money supply.

Financial Institutions in Canada	
Commercial Banks	Financial institutions that engage in deposits, loans, and other financial services, they include domestic chartered banks as well as subsidiaries of foreign banks and foreign bank branches in Canada. (See the World View on page 248 for a comparison of bank's world rankings.)
Credit Unions and Caisses Populaires	A co-operative financial institution that is owned by its members and operates for their benefit. Credit unions and caisses populaires are subject to provincial regulation and are usually small and locally oriented.
Trust and Mortgage Loan Companies	A financial institution that operates under either provincial or federal legislation and conducts the same activities as a bank. Like a bank, it operates through a network of branches. However, because of its fiduciary role, a trust company can administer estates, trusts, pension plans, and agency contracts, which banks cannot do.
Government Savings Institutions	These are government-operated deposit taking institutions that are provincially legislated. Examples include the Province of Ontario Savings Office and Alberta Treasury Branches.
Money Market Mutual Funds	These are funds administered by financial institutions where depositors purchase shares of a fund that in turn buys government bonds and treasury bills.
Insurance Companies	Insurance companies are non-bank financial institutions specializing in insuring risk. They are generally divided into two categories—life and health or property and casualty—and may be either federally or provincially regulated.

The T account shows that your coins are now held by a bank. In exchange, the bank has credited your chequing account $100. This balance is a liability for the bank since it must allow you to withdraw the deposit on demand.

The total money supply is unaffected by your cash deposit because two components of the money supply change in opposite directions (i.e., less cash, more bank deposits). This initial deposit is just the beginning of the money creation process, however. Banks aren't in business for your convenience; they're in business to earn a profit. To earn a profit on your deposit, the bank will have to put your money to work. This means using your deposit as the basis for making a loan to someone who's willing to pay the bank interest for use of money. If the function of banks was merely to store money, they wouldn't pay interest on their accounts or offer free chequing services. Instead, you'd have to pay them for these services. Banks pay you interest and offer free (or inexpensive) chequing because they can use your money to make loans that earn interest.

The Initial Loan. Typically, a bank doesn't have much difficulty finding someone who wants to borrow money. Someone is always eager to borrow money. The question is: How much money can a bank lend? Can it lend your entire deposit? Or must it keep some of your coins in reserve, in case you want to withdraw them?

To answer this question, suppose that the bank decided to lend the entire $100 to Campus Radio. Campus Radio wants to buy a new antenna but doesn't have any money in its own chequing account. To acquire the antenna, Campus Radio must take out a loan.

When the bank agrees to lend Campus Radio $100, it does so by crediting the account of Campus Radio. Instead of giving Campus Radio $100 cash, the bank simply adds $100 to Campus Radio's chequing account balance. That is, the loan is made with a simple bookkeeping entry as follows:

Bank		Money Supply	
Assets	Liabilities	Cash held by the public	no change
		Transactions deposits at bank	+ $100
$100 in coins	$100 your account balance	Change in money supply	+ $100
$100 in loans	$100 Campus Radio account		

This simple bookkeeping procedure is the key to creating money. When the bank lends $100 to the Campus Radio account, it "creates" money. Keep in mind that transactions deposits are counted as part of the money supply. Once the $100 loan is credited to its account, Campus Radio can use this new money to purchase its desired antenna, without worrying that its cheque will bounce.

Or can it? Once the bank grants a loan to Campus Radio, both you and Campus Radio have $100 in your chequing accounts to spend. But the bank is holding only $100 of **reserves** (your coins). In other words, the increased account balance obtained by Campus Radio doesn't limit your ability to write cheques. There's been a net *increase* in the value of transactions deposits but no increase in bank reserves.

bank reserves: Assets held by a bank to fulfill its deposit obligations.

Secondary Deposits. What happens if Campus Radio actually spends the $100 on a new antenna? Won't this "use up all" the reserves held by the bank, endangering your cheque-writing privileges? The answer is no.

Consider what happens when Atlas Antenna receives the cheque from Campus Radio. What will Atlas do with the cheque? Atlas could go to their bank and exchange the cheque for $100 of cash (your coins). But Atlas may prefer to deposit the cheque in its own chequing account. This way, the money is kept in a safe place and should Atlas later want to spend the money, it can simply write its own cheque. In the meantime, the bank continues to hold its entire reserves (your coins), and both you and Atlas have $100 to spend.

Fractional Reserves. Notice what's happened here. The money supply has increased by $100 as a result of deposit creation (the loan to Campus Radio). Moreover, the bank has been able to support $200 of transaction deposits (your account and either the Campus Radio or Atlas account) with only $100 of reserves (your coins). In other words, *bank reserves are only a fraction of total deposits.* In this case, the bank's reserves (your $100 in coins) are only 50 percent of total deposits. Thus the bank's **reserve ratio** is 50 percent—that is,

reserve ratio: The ratio of a bank's reserves to its total transactions deposits.

$$\frac{\text{Reserve}}{\text{ratio}} = \frac{\text{bank reserves}}{\text{total deposits}}$$

The ability of a bank to hold reserves that are only a fraction of total deposits results from two facts: (1) people use cheques for most transactions, and (2) each individual bank has many other clients coins that can be substituted for yours. In reality, many banks are available, and people withdraw cash from their accounts and write cheques to people who have accounts in other banks. In addition, the prudent management of a financial institution requires banks to hold some **target reserve** level against normal day-to-day activity. As a result of revisions to the Bank Act in the 1990s, financial institutions were left to decide on the appropriate level of these target reserves rather than maintaining a legislated level of required reserves as had been the case up to this time.

target reserves: The minimum amount of reserves a bank desires to hold; equal to target reserve ratio times transactions deposits.

Suppose, for instance, that the bank desired to have targeted reserves equal to 75 percent of total deposits, including those created through loans.

The bank's dilemma is evident in the following equation:

$$\frac{\text{target}}{\text{reserves}} = \frac{\text{target reserve}}{\text{ratio}} \times \frac{\text{total}}{\text{deposits}}$$

To support $200 of total deposits, the bank would need to satisfy this equation:

$$\frac{\text{target}}{\text{reserves}} = 0.75 \times \$200 = \$150$$

But the bank has only $100 of reserves (your coins) and so would violate the reserve target if it increased total deposits to $200 by lending $100 to Campus Radio.

The bank can still issue a loan to Campus Radio. But the loan must be less than $100 to keep the bank within the limits of the reserve formula. Thus, *a minimum reserve directly limits deposit-creation possibilities.* It's still true, however, as we'll now illustrate, that the banking system, taken as a whole, can create multiple loans (money) from a single deposit.

A Multibank World   Let's relax the original simplifying assumption of a banking system, and illustrate the process of deposit creation in a multibank environment. In this case, we will assume

WORLD VIEW

Banks Worldwide Ranked by Asset Size

The following table shows the world's 10 largest banks by asset size as well as the "big six" Canadian chartered banks and their ranking. Note that the largest Canadian bank—the Royal Bank of Canada—ranks number 40 in the world.

Asset Rank 2006	Bank	Country	Assets ($ Billions Cdn)
1	UBS	Switzerland	$2.289
2	Barclays Bank	U.K.	$2.280
3	BNP Paribas	France	$2.211
4	Citigroup	U.S.A.	$2.194
5	HSBC Holdings	U.K.	$2.168
6	Crédit Agricole Group	France	$2.119
7	Royal Bank of Scotland	U.K.	$1.994
8	Mitsubishi UFJ Financial Group	Japan	$1.841
9	Deutsche Bank	Germany	$1.728
10	Bank of America Corp.	U.S.A.	$1.701
40	Royal Bank of Canada	Canada	$0.557
47	Toronto-Dominion Bank	Canada	$0.408
49	Scotiabank	Canada	$0.393
56	Bank of Montreal	Canada	$0.325
58	CIBC	Canada	$0.316
119	National Bank of Canada	Canada	$0.117

Source: Top 150 banks worldwide ranked by asset size. Canadian Bankers Association. Retrieved November 21, 2007 from http://www.cba.ca/en/content/stats/070821-Bank%20Rankings%20July%202007%20Input.pdf

Analysis: As the table above shows, the Royal Bank of Canada is Canada's largest bank but only the 40th largest bank in world terms when ranked by asset size. In fact the Royal Bank is only ¼ the size of Barclays Bank from the United Kingdom. As it becomes easier to move money (capital) around the world, the Canadian economy gets access to larger pools of loanable funds while Canadian banks may find themselves facing greater competition.

		Deposit in Bank	Excess Reserves	Change in Bank Loans	Change in Purchasing Power
Step 1	You break your piggy bank	+$100.00	+$95.00		$0
Step 2	Loan to Campus Radio	+$95.00	+$90.25	+$95.00	+$95.00
Step 3	Campus Radio buys an antenna from Atlas	−$95.00	−$90.25		
Step 4	Atlas deposits cheque from Campus Radio	+$95.00	+$90.25		
Step 5	Loan to Herman's Hardware	+$90.25	+$85.74	+$90.25	+$90.25
	Totals	$285.25		$185.25	$185.25

TABLE 12.2
Creating Money Through Deposits

Since we are assuming a desired or target reserve ratio 5 percent, the implication is that 95 percent of any deposit represents an excess reserve.

that each bank has the same target reserve ratio of 5 percent. Now when you deposit $100 in your chequing account, the bank must hold at least $5 as cash reserves.[3]

Excess Reserves. The remaining $95 the bank obtains from your deposit is regarded as **excess reserves.** These reserves are "excess" in that your bank desires to hold in reserve only $5 (equal to $5 percent of your initial $100 deposit):

$$\frac{\text{excess}}{\text{reserves}} = \frac{\text{total}}{\text{reserves}} - \frac{\text{target}}{\text{reserves}}$$

The $95 of excess reserves isn't needed and may be used to support additional loans. Hence, the bank can now lend $95. In view of the fact that banks earn profits (interest) by making loans, we assume that the bank will try to use these excess reserves as soon as possible.

To keep track of the changes in reserves, deposit balances, and loans that occur in a multibank world we'll have to do some bookkeeping. Table 12.2 shows the process from the initial deposit of $100.00 from your piggy bank, the resulting excess reserves, and finally the creation of money from the banking system.

When you deposit your $100 of coins into the bank, the bank uses those funds as a source of earnings by making loans and charging interest on those loans. As we've noted, however, the bank will keep aside some desired or targeted reserves so it has sufficient funds to cover its own day-to-day expenses (and give depositors back their money if they ask for it). Since the bank has decided to hold 5 percent in targeted reserves, that means they will hold on to $5.00 from your $100.00 deposit. The result is that there is an additional $95.00 of excess reserves not needed. Suppose that it decides to lend the $95.00 to Campus Radio and adds this amount into Campus Radio's account. The bank's loan portfolio has increased by the $95.00 it has loaned to Campus Radio and its deposits have increased from $100 to $195. Since the bank now has higher deposits, it must also increase its targeted reserves by 5 percent of the additional $95 deposit, or $4.75. Since it still has the original $100 in coins (remember it "loaned" money to Campus Radio by creating an account deposit), there will still be $90.25 in excess reserves.

Changes in Purchasing Power. Before thinking about what might happen next, let's consider what has happened to purchasing power in the economy during these first two steps. First you deposited $100 of cash into your bank account. This initial transaction

excess reserves: Bank reserves in excess of targeted reserves.

---

[3]The reserves themselves may be held in the form of cash in the bank's vault but are usually held as credits with the Bank of Canada or by holding government securities.

did not change the value of the purchasing power. Only where the purchasing power was located was affected—$100 less cash held by you and $100 more cash held in your account at the bank. Not until Step 2, when the bank makes a loan, does all the excitement begin. In making the loan to Campus Radio, the bank automatically increases the total purchasing power by $95. Why? Because Campus Radio now has more money in its account than it did before and no one else has any less. And Campus Radio can use these funds to purchase goods and services, just like anyone else.

The second step is the heart of creating purchasing power. Purchasing power effectively appears out of thin air when a bank makes a loan. To understand how this works, you have to keep reminding yourself that purchasing power is more than the coins and currency that we carry around. Deposits also represent purchasing power because they are denominated in money terms. Hence, the creation of deposits via new loans creates additional purchasing power meaning more "money" is available in the economy.

Individual Banks and the Banking System. We can see why individual banks don't matter in this process by considering what happens if Campus Radio spends their $95 by buying an antenna from Atlas Antenna who deals with a different bank. In Step 3, when Campus Radio pays for the new antenna with a cheque, its bank, Bank One, would have its deposits reduced by $95 dollars and its excess reserves reduced to $0. Bank One would have $100 of deposits remaining and $5 of targeted reserves (or 5 percent of deposits). In Step 4, when Atlas deposits Campus Radio's cheque into its bank, Bank Two, deposits there rise by $95 once they get the money from Bank One[4] and Bank Two now has excess reserves of $90.25. So, while the individual banks are affected, the banking system is left unchanged with $195 of deposits, $9.75 of desired targeted reserves, and $90.25 of remaining excess reserves.

More Deposit Creation. In Step 5, Bank Two takes advantage of its newly acquired excess reserves by making a loan to Herman's Hardware, crediting Herman's account for the $90.25 loan. This third deposit (yours, Atlas's, and now Herman's) increases deposits in the banking system to $285.25, and the total level of desired targeted reserves to 5 percent of $285.25 or $14.26. Since we started with $100 in coins, this means there is still excess reserves in the banking system of $85.74 remaining.

So far, we've seen how shifting $100 from your piggy bank into a deposit at Bank One has increased total bank deposits by $285.25 and increased total purchasing power by $185.25 (since the original $100 was already purchasing power). But there are still excess reserves in Bank Two that can be loaned out. How much additional purchasing power can be created before the process comes to an end? That's the question that the next section answers.

12.3 THE MONEY MULTIPLIER

By now it's perhaps obvious that the process of deposit creation won't come to an end quickly. On the contrary, it can continue indefinitely, just like the income multiplier process in Chapter 8. Indeed, people often refer to deposit creation as the money multiplier process, with the **simple money multiplier** expressed as the reciprocal of the target reserve ratio.[5] That is,

> **simple money multiplier:** The number of deposit (loan) dollars that the banking system can create from $1 of excess reserves; equal to 1 ÷ target reserve ratio.

$$\frac{\text{simple money}}{\text{multiplier}} = \frac{1}{\text{target reserve ratio}}$$

---

[4] In actuality, banks rarely "go" anywhere; such interbank reserve movements are handled through the Canadian Payments Association (CPA) in one of two systems: the Large Value Transfer System (LVTS) or the Automated Clearing Settlement System (ACSS). The effect is the same, however. The nature and use of bank reserves are discussed more fully in Chapter 13.

[5] The simple money multiplier $(1/r)$ is the sum of the infinite geometric progression $1 + (1 - r) + (1 - r)^2 + (1 - r)^3 + \cdots + (1 - r)^\infty$.

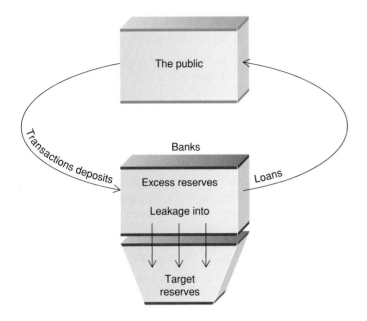

FIGURE 12.1
The Money Multiplier Process

Part of every new bank deposit leaks into target reserves. The rest—excess reserves—can be used to make loans. These loans, in turn, become deposits elsewhere. The process of money creation continues until all available reserves become target reserves.

Figure 12.1 illustrates the money multiplier process. When a new deposit enters the banking system, it creates both excess and target reserves. The target reserves represent leakage from the flow of money since they can't be used to create new loans. Excess reserves, on the other hand, can be used for new loans. Once those loans are made, they typically become transactions deposits elsewhere in the banking system. Then some additional leakage into reserves occurs, and further loans are made. The process continues until all excess reserves have leaked into target reserves. Once excess reserves have completely disappeared, the total value of new loans will equal initial excess reserves multiplied by the money multiplier.

The potential of the money multiplier to create loans is summarized by the equation

$$\begin{matrix} \text{excess} \\ \text{reserves} \\ \text{of banking} \\ \text{system} \end{matrix} \times \begin{matrix} \text{simple} \\ \text{money} \\ \text{multiplier} \end{matrix} = \begin{matrix} \text{potential} \\ \text{deposit creation} \end{matrix}$$

Notice how the money multiplier worked in our previous example. The value of the money multiplier was equal to 20, since we assumed that the target reserve ratio was 0.05. Moreover, the initial level of excess reserves was $95, as a consequence of your original deposit (step 1). According to the money multiplier, then, the deposit-creation potential of the banking system was

$$\begin{matrix} \text{excess} \\ \text{reserves} \\ (\$95) \end{matrix} \times \begin{matrix} \text{simple} \\ \text{money multiplier} \\ (20) \end{matrix} = \begin{matrix} \text{potential} \\ \text{deposit} \\ \text{creation } (\$1,900) \end{matrix}$$

When all the banks fully utilized their excess reserves at each step of the money multiplier process, the ultimate increase in the money supply was in fact $1,900.

While you're struggling through Table 12.2, notice the critical role that excess reserves play in the process of deposit creation. A bank can make additional loans only if it has excess reserves. Without excess reserves, all of a bank's reserves are required, and no further liabilities (transactions deposits) can be created with new loans. On the other hand, a bank with excess reserves can make additional loans. In fact,

Excess Reserves as Lending Power

- *Each bank may lend an amount equal to its excess reserves and no more.*

As such loans enter the circular flow and become deposits elsewhere, they create new excess reserves and further lending capacity. As a consequence,

- *The entire banking system can increase the volume of loans by the amount of excess reserves multiplied by the simple money multiplier.*

By keeping track of excess reserves, then, we can gauge the lending capacity of any bank or, with the aid of the money multiplier, the entire banking system.

The fact that we've called the money multiplier so far the simple money multiplier should tip you off that more is coming. The simple money multiplier includes two assumptions—that banks choose to hold no excess reserves and that all funds are deposited back into the banking system. If we relax each of these assumptions, the money multiplier itself gets smaller. Why? Because removing each of these assumptions results in the banking system having fewer excess reserves to loan out.

In the case of excess reserves, financial market uncertainty or economic conditions might encourage financial institutions to hold a higher target level of reserves, adding some former "excess reserves" to their holdings.

cash drain: Cash received by individuals or firms that they do not re-deposit back into financial institutions.

In the second case, individuals or firms who receive the money may decide to hold on to some cash rather than re-depositing it all back into the financial system. Such a decision is described as a **cash drain.** Literally, cash is being drained from the banking system so that less is available to be loaned out.

Adding these other two pieces results in a more realistic money multiplier, or a real money multiplier, RMM:

$$\frac{\text{real money}}{\text{multiplier}} = \frac{1}{\text{target reserve} + \text{excess reserve} + \text{cash drain}}$$

So, if financial institutions held a target reserve of 5 percent, added additional excess reserves of 5 percent, and the cash drain represented 15 percent, the final money multiplier would be 4 and the total change in the money supply would be $400.00.

$$\frac{\text{real money}}{\text{multiplier}} = \frac{1}{0.05 + 0.05 + 0.15}$$

$$\frac{\text{total change in}}{\text{money supply}} = \frac{\text{excess loanable}}{\text{reserves}} \times \frac{\text{real money}}{\text{multiplier}}$$

$$\frac{\text{total change in}}{\text{money supply}} = 4 \times \$100 = \$400$$

12.4 MEASURING MACROECONOMIC PURCHASING POWER

M1: Cash and Transactions Accounts

money supply: The level of purchasing power (currency and deposits) available to an economy. Measured and defined as M1 through M3.

Several different measures of money have been developed to accommodate the diversity of bank accounts and other payment mechanisms. The narrowest definition of the **money supply** is designated **M1,** *which includes*

- *Currency outside banks*
- *Personal chequing accounts*
- *Current accounts*

As Figure 12.2 indicates, the largest components of this "narrow" definition of the money supply (M1) are the transaction account balances, which are the balances in bank accounts that are readily accessed on demand, i.e., demand deposits.

The distinguishing feature of all transactions accounts is that they permit direct payment to a third party (by cheque or debit card), without requiring a trip to the

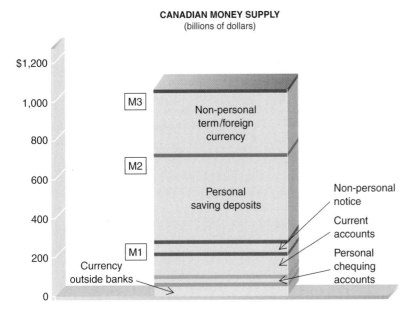

CANADIAN MONEY SUPPLY
(billions of dollars)

FIGURE 12.2
Composition of the Money Supply

Cash—currency in circulation—is only a small part of the total money supply. People also have access to "demand" deposits, that are included in the narrowest definition of the money supply, M1; as well as "notice" deposits, M2; and term deposits or foreign currency deposits, which make up the broadest definition of the money supply, M3. The total purchasing power in the economy (M3) is approximately 22 times larger than the physical money in circulation.

Source: Bank of Canada, Weekly financial statistics, November 10, 2006, http://www.bankofcanada.ca/en/wfsgen.html, accessed November 15, 2006.

bank to make a special withdrawal. Because of this feature, **transactions accounts** are the readiest substitutes for cash in market transactions. M1 therefore represents the most "liquid" purchasing power in the economy—the quickest and easiest to exchange for real goods and services.

Transactions accounts aren't the only substitute for cash. People can and do dip into savings accounts on occasion. In fact, people often have their savings accounts attached to their debit cards! However, we make a technical distinction between the transaction accounts and these "less liquid" accounts because of the "notice" requirement that may or may not be enforced. Any notice required implies a delay in being able to make the final transaction. The fact that notice is seldom required in practice means that there may be little practical difference in the relative **liquidity** of M1 and M2. As a result, savings account balances are almost as good a substitute for cash as transactions account balances. M2 includes

- All of M1
- Non-personal (business) notice accounts
- Personal saving deposits

Finally, we have a broad measure of the money supply, designated as M3, which includes

- All of M2
- Non-personal (business) term deposits
- Foreign currency accounts

M3 represents the least liquid form of purchasing power as term deposits can be locked in for a specified period of time (for instance, one year) and may include a penalty of lost interest income for early redemption. Foreign currency requires an exchange into the domestic currency prior to being spent.

To add an additional complication to these measures, households often move deposits from one account type to another depending upon the interest return offered by the various accounts. When interest rates are high—and the opportunity cost of holding money in its most liquid forms is therefore high—households may shift deposits from transactions accounts to savings accounts or even to term deposits or other types

> **transactions account:** A bank account that permits direct payment to a third party, for example, with a cheque.

M2: M1 Plus Personal Savings and Business Notice Accounts

> **liquidity:** The ease with which money or money-denominated assets can be exchanged for goods or services.

M3: M2 Plus Term Deposits and Foreign Currency

TABLE 12.3

Additional Measures of the Money Supply

The standard measures of the money supply include data only from Canada's chartered banks, although, as we have seen, there are many other financial intermediaries. These additional measures include purchasing power held at other near- or non-bank institutions. These additions would increase the total money supply by approximately $1,000 billion.

Additional Measures of the Canadian Money Supply
M1+ includes currency held by the public outside of banks and all chequable deposits at chartered banks, credit unions and caisses populaires, and trust and mortgage loan companies.
M1++ includes M1+ and all non-chequable notice deposits at chartered banks, credit unions and caisses populaires, and trust and mortgage loan companies.
M2+ includes all deposits at non-bank deposit-taking institutions, money-market mutual funds, and individual annuities at life insurance companies.
M2++ includes M2+ plus Canada Savings Bonds and the cumulative net contributions to mutual funds (other than Canadian dollar money market mutual funds, which are already included in M2+)

Sources: D. Maclean, "Analyzing monetary aggregates," *Bank of Canada Review* (Summer, 2001). Bank of Canada Monetary Aggregates, http://www.bankofcanada.ca/en/graphs/notes-1-aggreg. html, accessed November 11, 2006.

of accounts at non-chartered banks ("near banks") or financial institutions as described in Table 12.3.

The purchasing power available through these near banks and financial institutions are added on to the measurements as "plusses", that is, M1+, M1++, M2+, and M2++. The difference this makes in the total measure of the money supply can be quite significant. For instance, while the measure for M2 was $704.3 billion, the equivalent measure of M2++ was $1,422.5 billion.

Our concern about the specific nature of money stems from our broader interest in *aggregate demand.* What we want to know is how much purchasing power consumers have, since this will affect their ability to purchase goods and services. What we've observed, however, is that money isn't so easily defined. How much spending power people have depends not only on the number of coins in their pockets but also on their willingness to write cheque, make trips to the bank, or convert other assets into cash.

In an increasingly complex financial system, the core concept of "money" isn't easy to pin down. Nevertheless, the official measures of the money supply (particularly M1 and M2) are fairly reliable benchmarks for gauging how much purchasing power market participants have.

12.5 COMMERCIAL BANKS AND THE CIRCULAR FLOW

The bookkeeping details of bank deposits and loans are rarely exciting and often confusing. But they do demonstrate convincingly that banks can create money. In that capacity, **banks perform two essential functions for the macro economy:**

- **Banks transfer money from savers to spenders by lending funds (reserves) held on deposit.**
- **The banking system creates additional money by making loans in excess of total reserves.**

In performing these two functions, banks change the size of the money supply—that is, the amount of purchasing power available for buying goods and services. Market participants may respond to these changes in the money supply by altering their spending behaviour and shifting the aggregate demand curve.

Figure 12.3 on the next page is a simplified perspective on the role of banks in the circular flow. As before, income flows from product markets through business firms

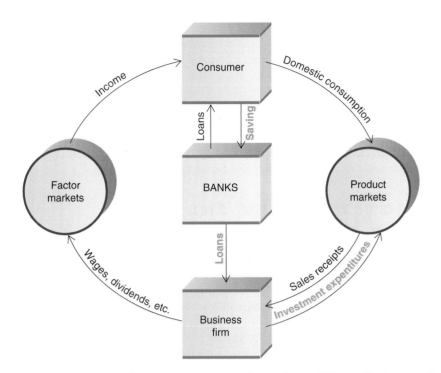

FIGURE 12.3
Banks in the Circular Flow

Banks help transfer income from savers to spenders by using their deposits to make loans to business firms and consumers who want to spend more money than they have. By lending money, banks help maintain any desired rate of aggregate demand.

to factor markets and returns to consumers in the form of disposable income. Consumers spend most of their income but also save (don't spend) some of it.

The leakage represented by consumer saving is a potential source of stabilization problems, particularly unemployment. If additional spending by business firms, foreigners, or governments doesn't compensate for consumer saving at full employment, a recessionary GDP gap will emerge, creating unemployment (see Chapters 8 and 9). Our interest here is in the role the banking system can play in encouraging such additional spending.

Suppose for the moment that *all* consumer saving was deposited in piggy banks rather than depository institutions (banks) and that no one used cheques. Under these circumstances, banks couldn't transfer money from savers to spenders by holding deposits and making loans.

In reality, a substantial portion of consumer saving *is* deposited in banks. These and other bank deposits can be used as the basis of loans, thereby returning purchasing power to the circular flow. In fact, the primary economic function of banks isn't to store money but to transfer purchasing power from savers to spenders. They do so by lending money to businesses for new plant and equipment, to consumers for new homes or cars, and to government entities that desire greater purchasing power. Moreover, because the banking system can make *multiple* loans from available reserves, banks don't have to receive all consumer saving to carry out their function. On the contrary, *the banking system can create any desired level of money supply if allowed to expand or reduce loan activity at will.*

There are three major constraints on the deposit creation of the banking system.

Deposits. The first constraint is the willingness of consumers and businesses to continue using and accepting cheques rather than cash in the marketplace. If people preferred to hold cash rather than chequebooks, banks wouldn't be able to acquire or maintain the reserves that are the foundation of bank lending activity.

Borrowers. The second constraint on deposit creation is the willingness of consumers, businesses, and governments to borrow the money that banks make available. The chain of events we've observed in deposit creation depends on the willingness of

Financing Injections

Constraints on Deposit Creation

Campus Radio to borrow $95, of Herman's Hardware to borrow $90.25, and so on. If no one wanted to borrow any money, deposit creation would never begin. By the same reasoning, if all excess reserves aren't borrowed (lent), deposit creation won't live up to its theoretical potential.

Regulation. A third constraint on deposit creation is the Bank Act, which applies to all federally regulated financial institutions. Although revisions over the years—particularly 1967 and 1991—have removed any specific *required* reserve, banks are required to have sufficient reserves to cover all their day-to-day payments on average. These and other tools of monetary policy are discussed in Chapter 13.

12.6 MONEY DEMAND AND THE LOANABLE-FUNDS MARKET

The best place to learn how monetary policy works is the money *market*. You must abandon any mystical notions you may harbour about money and view it like any other commodity that's traded in the marketplace. Like other goods, there's a supply of money and a demand for money. Together they determine the "price" of money, or the **interest rate.**

> interest rate: The price paid for the use of money.

At first glance, it may appear strange to call interest rates the price of money. But when you borrow money, the "price" you pay is measured by the interest rate you're charged. When interest rates are high, money is "expensive." When interest rates are low, money is "cheap."

Money Balances

Even people who don't borrow must contend with the price of money. Money, as we've seen, comes in many different forms. A common characteristic of all money is that it can be held as a store of value. People hold cash and maintain positive bank balances for this purpose. Most of the money in our common measures of *money supply* (M1–M3) is in the form of bank balances. There's an opportunity cost associated with such money balances, however. Money held in transactions accounts earns little or no interest. Money held in savings accounts and money market mutual funds does earn interest but usually at relatively low rates. By contrast, money used to buy bonds or stocks or to make loans is likely to earn a higher interest rate of return.

The Price of Money. The nature of the "price" of money should be apparent: People who hold *cash* are forgoing an opportunity to earn interest. So are people who hold money in chequing accounts that pay no interest. In either case, *forgone interest is the opportunity cost (price) of money people choose to hold.* How high is that price? It's equal to the market rate of interest.

Money held in interest-paying bank accounts does earn some interest. In this case, the opportunity cost of holding money is the *difference* between the prevailing rate of interest and the rate paid on deposit balances. As is the case with cash and regular chequing accounts, opportunity cost is measured by the forgone interest.

The Demand for Money

> demand for money: The quantities of money people are willing and able to hold at alternative interest rates, *ceteris paribus.*

Once we recognize that money does have a price, we can easily formulate a demand for money. As is the case with all goods, the **demand for money** is a schedule (or curve) showing the quantity of money demanded at alternative prices (interest rates).

While at first glance it might seem irrational to hold money balances that pay little or no interest, there are many good reasons for doing so.

> transactions demand for money: Money held for the purpose of making everyday market purchases.

Transactions Demand. Even people who've mastered the principles of economics hold money. They do so because they want to buy goods and services. In order to transact business in product or factor markets, we need money in the form of either cash or a positive bank account balance. Debit cards and ATM cards don't work unless there's money in the bank. Payment by e-cash also requires a supporting bank balance. Even when we use credit cards, we're only postponing the date of payment by a few weeks or so. Accordingly, we recognize the existence of a basic **transactions demand**

for money. Since transactions vary positively with the level of income, we can model this relationship as some proportion, e, of national income, Y: $e(Y)$.

Precautionary Demand. Another reason people hold money is their fear of the proverbial rainy day. A sudden emergency may require money purchases over and above normal transactions needs. Moreover, such needs may arise when the banks are closed or in a community where one's cheques aren't accepted. Also, future income is uncertain and may diminish unexpectedly. Therefore, people hold a bit more money (cash or bank account balances) than they anticipate spending. This **precautionary demand for money** is the extra money being held as a safeguard against the unexpected. As with the transaction demand above, the precautionary demand varies positively with national income as well. The relationship can be presented as some proportion, f, of national income, Y: $f(Y)$.

Speculative Demand. People also hold money for speculative purposes. Suppose you were interested in buying stocks or bonds but hadn't yet picked the right ones or regarded their present prices as too high. In such circumstances, you might want to hold some money so that you could later buy a "hot" stock or bond at a price you think attractive. Thus, you'd be holding money in the hope that a better financial opportunity would later appear. In this sense, you'd be *speculating* with your money, forgoing present opportunities to earn interest in the hope of hitting a real jackpot later. These money balances represent a **speculative demand for money.** Unlike the transactions and precautionary demands above, the speculative demand varies negatively with interest rates rather than national income. Therefore the relationship here would be how the demand for money changes, g, when there is a change in the interest rate, i: $g(i)$.

The Market Demand Curve. These three motivations for holding money combine to create a *market demand* for money. The question is, what shape does this demand curve take? Does the quantity of money demanded decrease sharply as the rate of interest rises? Or do people tend to hold the same amount of money, regardless of its price?

People do cut down on their money balances when interest rates rise. At such times, the opportunity cost of holding money is simply too high. This explains why so many people move their money out of transactions deposits (M1) and into money market mutual funds (M2+) when interest rates are extraordinarily high (for example, in 1980–1982). Corporations are even more careful about managing their money when interest rates rise. Better money management requires watching chequing account balances more closely and even making more frequent trips to the bank, but the opportunity costs are worth it.

Figure 12.4 illustrates the total market demand for money. Like nearly all demand curves, the market demand curve for money slopes downward. The downward slope

precautionary demand for money: Money held for unexpected market transactions or for emergencies.

speculative demand for money: Money held for speculative purposes, for later financial opportunities.

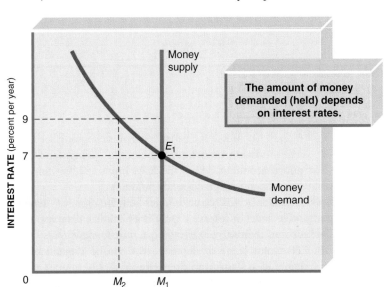

FIGURE 12.4
Loanable Funds Market Equilibrium

All points on the market demand curve represent the quantity of money people are willing to hold at a specific interest rate. The equilibrium interest rate occurs at the intersection (E_1) of the money supply and money demand curves. At that rate of interest, people are willing to hold as much money as is available. At any other interest rate (for example, 9 percent), the quantity of money people are *willing* to hold won't equal the quantity available, and people will adjust their portfolios.

indicates that ***the quantity of money people are willing and able to hold (demand) increases as interest rates fall* (ceteris paribus).** Finally, we can bring each of the transactions, precautionary, and speculative relationships together to express the demand for money as:

$$M^D = e(Y) + f(Y) - g(i)^6$$

And, since in equilibrium the demand for money will equal the supply of money:

$$M^D = M^S$$

we can also state that

$$M^S = e(Y) + f(Y) - g(i)$$

Equilibrium

Once a money demand curve and a money supply curve are available, the action in money markets is easy to follow. Figure 12.4 summarizes this action. The money demand curve in Figure 12.4 reflects existing demands for holding money. The money supply curve is drawn at an arbitrary level of M_1. In practice, its position depends on bank of Canada policy (Chapter 13), the lending behaviour of private banks, and the willingness of consumers and investors to borrow money.

The intersection of the money demand and money supply curves (E_1) establishes an **loanable funds market equilibrium.** Only at this interest rate is the quantity of money supplied equal to the quantity demanded. In this case, we observe that an interest rate of 7 percent equates the desires of suppliers and demanders.

At any rate of interest other than 7 percent, the quantity of money demanded wouldn't equal the quantity supplied. Look at the imbalance that exists, for example, when the interest rate is 9 percent. At that rate, the quantity of money supplied (M_1 in Figure 12.4) exceeds the quantity demanded (M_2). All the money (M_1) must be held by someone, of course. But the demand curve indicates that people aren't *willing* to hold so much money at that interest rate (9 percent). People will adjust their **portfolio decisions** by moving money out of cash and bank accounts into bonds or other assets that offer higher returns. This will tend to lower interest rates (recall that buying bonds tends to lower their yields). As interest rates drop, people are willing to hold more money. Ultimately we get to E_1, where the quantity of money demanded equals the quantity supplied. At that equilibrium, people are content with their portfolio choices. Any change in the demand for money (households, firms, or government wishing to make additional transactions, for instance) or in the supply of money (such as monetary policy, which we will discuss in Chapter 13) will lead to pressure on the interest rate for loanable funds to change.

loanable funds market equilibrium: The interest rate at which the quantity of money demanded in a given time period equals the quantity of money supplied.

portfolio decisions: The choice of where (how) to hold idle funds.

[6]The transactions demand, e, is a function of national income, Y; precautionary demand, f, is also a function of Y; and speculative demand, g, is a function of the rate of interest, i. Therefore, money demand can be modelled as:

$$M^D = e(Y) + f(Y) - g(i)$$

SUMMARY

- In a market economy, money serves a critical function in facilitating exchanges and specialization. *Money* refers to anything that serves these three purposes: generally accepted as a medium of exchange, used as a store of value, and acts as a unit of measurement.

- Banks have the power to create money (purchasing power) by making loans. In making loans, banks create new transactions deposits, which become part of the money supply.

- Because people use deposit account balances to buy goods and services, such balances are also regarded as

money. M1 includes cash on hand plus chequing accounts; M2 is slightly less liquid, including savings and other notice accounts; M3 is the least liquid, adding term accounts and foreign currency holdings.

- A bank's ability to make loans—create money—depends on its level of reserves. Only if a bank has reserves in excess of their *target reserves* can it make new loans.

- The total value of deposits that can be created by the banking system from excess reserves (the money multiplier) depends on the target reserve ratio, any excess reserve ratio banks desire to hold, and the cash drain ratio from the economy itself.

• Banks operate in the circular flow by facilitating the transfer of purchasing power from savers to spenders.

• The market interest rate represents the *price of money* in the economy—it is the price a borrower pays to a saver to use the saver's money.

• The demand for money arises from transactions demand, precautionary demand, and speculative demand.

• The equilibrium in the loanable-funds market is the intersection of the demand for money and the supply of money—this is the market interest rate. Any change to either the demand for money or the supply of money causes pressure on the interest rate to change.

Key Terms

barter   241
money   243
deposit creation   244
bank reserves   247
reserve ratio   247
target reserves   247
excess reserves   249
simple money multiplier   250

cash drain   252
money supply (M1, M2, M3)   252
transactions account   253
liquidity   253
interest rate   256
demand for money   256
transactions demand for
   money   257

precautionary demand
   for money   257
speculative demand for
   money   257
loanable funds market
   equilibrium   258
portfolio decisions   258

Questions for Discussion

1. Why are chequing account balances, but not credit cards, regarded as "money"?

2. How are an economy's production possibilities affected when workers are paid in bras and coffins rather than cash? (See the World View, page 241 about bartering in Russia.)

3. What percentage of your monthly bills do you pay with (*a*) cash, (*b*) cheque, (*c*) credit card, and (*d*) automatic transfers? How do you pay off the credit card balance? How does your use of cash compare with the composition of the money supply (Figure 12.2)?

4. If you can purchase airline tickets with online computer services, should your electronic account be counted in the money supply? Explain.

5. Does the fact that your bank keeps only a fraction of your account balance in reserve make you uncomfortable? Why don't people rush to the bank and retrieve their money? What would happen if they did?

6. If people never withdrew cash from banks, how much money could the banking system potentially create?

Could this really happen? What might limit deposit creation in this case?

7. If Internet e-cash systems could make loans, how would the money supply be affected?

8. Suppose that large numbers of people withdrew all their "foreign currency" deposits in the banking system, exchanged them into Canadian dollars and re-deposited the money into their chequing accounts. What money measures (M1, M2, or M3) would be affected in this transaction? How would it affect the specific money measure? How would it affect the Canadian money supply? What if the funds were used to buy Canada Savings Bonds instead?

9. Suppose a bank has a target reserve ratio of 10 percent and desires to hold excess reserves of 5 percent. If the economy's cash drain was 10 percent, what would be the total "deposit creation" from each additional dollar of excess reserves?

10. What proportions of your money balance are held for transactions, precautionary, and speculative purposes? Can you think of any other purpose for holding money?

EXERCISES

PROBLEMS   The Student Problem Set to accompany this chapter can be found at the end of the book.

WEB ACTIVITIES   Web Activities to accompany this chapter can be found on the Online Learning Centre at **http://www.mcgrawhill.ca/olc/schiller**.

The Bank of Canada and Monetary Policy

Whereas it is desirable to establish a central bank in Canada to regulate credit and currency in the best interests of the economic life of the nation, to control and protect the external value of the national monetary unit and to mitigate by its influence fluctuations in the general level of production, trade, prices and employment, so far as is possible within the scope of monetary action, and generally to promote the economic and financial welfare of Canada.

—Preamble to the Bank of Canada Act, 1934

In the previous chapter we described what money is and how it is created—the supply of money. We've also gotten a few clues about the limits of money creation and the motives for holding money in an economy—the demand for money. Finally, we brought the supply of money and the demand for money together to describe the market for loanable funds, and the equilibrium "price" of money in the economy—the interest rate.

This chapter examines the mechanics of controlling the money supply in the economy—*monetary policy*—and the impact that such policy has on commercial banks and bond markets, and thereby on the real economy's aggregate demand. The basic issues addressed are:

- *What is the Bank of Canada and what are its responsibilities?*
- *How is monetary policy implemented?*
- *What is the relationship between the money supply, interest rates, and aggregate demand?*
- *How effective is monetary policy compared to fiscal policy?*

This chapter begins with a description of the creation of the Bank of Canada and its role and responsibilities. We then take a look at the monetary policy tools available to the Bank of Canada that are used to discharge their responsibilities and the monetary policy instrument at the centre of monetary policy discussions.

It is also important for us to develop an understanding of the relationship between this monetary economy and the real economy. In fact, the directness of this relationship is a matter of debate among economists. Some argue that changes in the money supply directly affect macro outcomes; others argue that the effects of such changes are indirect and less certain.

LEARNING OBJECTIVES

By the end of this chapter, you should be able to:

13.1 Explain the development and the inflation-control policy goal of the Bank of Canada

13.2 Describe the two monetary policy tools available to the Bank of Canada and how each policy tool is used to implement monetary policy

13.3 Describe the target for the overnight rate of interest in relation to the operating band and the commercial bank's prime rate of interest

13.4 Explain how monetary policy is transmitted through to the real economy under closed and open economy assumptions

13.5 Explain how monetary policy and fiscal policy interact

13.6 Describe the constraints on the effectiveness of monetary policy

Paralleling these arguments about *how* monetary policy works are debates over the relative effectiveness of monetary and fiscal policy. Some economists argue that monetary policy is more effective than fiscal policy; others contend the reverse is true. This chapter will conclude with these different views of money, the impact of more or less money in the economy—and assesses their implication for macro policy.

13.1 THE BANK OF CANADA

There have been Royal Commissions on such specific matters as individual bank failures, and many parliamentary committees on Canadian banking and currency in general, but this is the first Royal Commission ever appointed to consider certain broad aspects of the Canadian banking and currency system. . . . the Commission considered that its main problem was in connection with the desirability of establishing a central bank.[1]

Although the question regarding the advisability of a central bank had been asked before, the experience of the depression and criticism of Canada's financial structure encouraged Prime Minister R. B. Bennett in 1933 to set up a Royal Commission lead by Lord Macmillan to study the question. The terms of the commission were to study "the organisation and working of our entire banking and monetary system [and] to consider the arguments for or against a central banking institution . . ."[2]

The *Report of the Royal Commission on Banking and Currency in Canada* was delivered later that same year. The government acted quickly to accept the recommendation to create a central bank and the subsequent Bank of Canada Act was given royal assent on July 3, 1934. Less than a year later, the Bank of Canada opened in Ottawa as a private company, with its shares owned by the public. The Bank remained a private company only until 1938, when its shares were bought back from the public by the federal government and the Bank became a Crown Corporation, responsible to the federal government, which it remains.

The Bank of Canada Act has been amended a number of times over the years, the most recent changes occurred in 2001. Throughout these changes, the preamble to the Act remains for the Bank of Canada to "promote the financial and economic welfare of Canada."

The responsibilities of the Bank of Canada can be summarized in four points:

1. Act as Canada's "monetary authority"—"The goal of monetary policy is to contribute to solid economic performance and rising living standards for Canadians by keeping inflation low, stable, and predictable.";[3]
2. Design and issue Canada's only "official" currency and protect the currency from counterfeiting;
3. Promote a stable and safe financial system, both within Canada and internationally; and
4. Provide banking services to the federal government and members of the Canadian Payments Association, (CPA).

As the monetary authority in Canada, the Bank of Canada can administer monetary policy to affect three economic variables: the rate of inflation, the domestic rate of interest (the loanable funds equilibrium), or the exchange rate. The unfortunate complexity of monetary policy is that it can work towards only one of these three goals at any one time.

---

[1]C. A. Curtis, "The Canadian Macmillan Commission," *The Economic Journal* 44, no. 173 (March 1934) 48–59, http://www.jstor.org, accessed December 20, 2006.

[2]Bank of Canada, "Who We Are," (2006), http://www.bankofcanada.ca/en/about/history.html, accessed December 20, 2006.

[3]Bank of Canada Web site. (2006), http://www.bankofcanada.ca/en/faq/faq_bank_roles.html#6, accessed December 20, 2006.

The current focus of the Bank of Canada as a policy goal is inflation control:

In February 1991, the federal government and the Bank of Canada jointly announced a series of targets for reducing total CPI inflation to the mid-point of a range of 1 to 3 percent by the end of 1995. That inflation control target range was extended a number of times.[4]

In November 2006, the federal government and the Bank of Canada again extended the **inflation control target:**

The Government and the Bank of Canada have renewed Canada's inflation-control target for a further five-year period, ending 31 December 2011. Under this agreement, the Bank will continue to conduct monetary policy aimed at keeping inflation, as measured by the consumer price index (CPI), at 2 percent, with a control range of 1 to 3 percent around this target.[5]

Although the Bank of Canada is a Crown Corporation it has considerable independence from the federal government. Such independence is important (and common among central banks around the world) so that monetary policy decisions are seen to be separate from the political dimension and fiscal policy choices.

In part, this independence is reflected in the fact that the Governor and Senior Deputy-Governor are appointed by the Bank's Board of Governors rather than by the government itself. The appointments are for a term of seven years and individuals can be re-appointed at the end of any term. The current Governor of the Bank of Canada is Mark Carney, who was appointed February 1, 2008.

At the top of the Bank of Canada's organizational chart (Figure 13.1) is a Board of Directors. The Board includes 12 directors (appointed for three-year terms by the federal

> **inflation control target:** The level of inflation, as measured by the consumer price index (CPI), that is the goal of monetary policy by the Bank of Canada. Currently, the target is 2 percent, with a control range of 1 to 3 percent.

WEB NOTE

See more information about the Bank's management structure and who holds these key positions at http://www.bankofcanada.ca/en/about/corp.html.

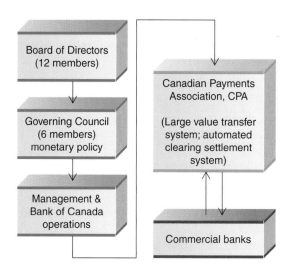

FIGURE 13.1
The Structure of the Bank of Canada

The general direction of the Bank of Canada is set by its Board of Directors, 12 outside members appointed by the federal government, plus the Deputy Minister of Finance, the Governor, and the Senior Deputy-Governor of the Bank of Canada.

The Governing Council of the Bank is made up of 6 members, including the Governor of the Bank of Canada, the Senior Deputy-Governor, and four additional Deputy-Governors. It is this Governing Council that sets monetary policy for the Bank.

The Governing Council is also part of the Bank's Management team that administers the day-to-day operations of the Bank. These operations include working with the Canadian Payments Association to ensure that financial clearing and settlement occurs smoothly.

[4]Bank of Canada, *Monetary Policy Report* (October 19, 2006), http://www.bankofcanada.ca/en/mpr/pdf/mproct06.pdf, accessed January 4, 2007.
[5]Bank of Canada, *Renewal of the Inflation-Control Target* (November 2006), http://www.bankofcanada.ca/en/press/background_nov06.pdf, accessed January 3, 2007.

Minister of Finance) from outside the bank, as well as the Governor and the Senior Deputy-Governor of the Bank of Canada. The Deputy Minister of Finance also sits on the Board as a non-voting member. The Board of Directors is responsible for the governance of the Bank. The monetary policy direction is determined by the Bank's Governing Council, which is made up of the Governor and Senior-Deputy Governor plus four additional Deputy-Governors. As well as monetary policy direction, the Governing Council is responsible for Canada's payments systems and the day-to-day management of the Bank.

There are two payments systems in Canada through which all non-cash payments are settled:[6]

- *Large Value Transfer System (LVTS):* The LVTS is an electronic wire-transfer system that processes large-value or time-critical payments quickly and continuously throughout the day. In 2004, the LVTS handled an average of 17,193 payments— worth an average total of $130 billion—each day.
- *Automated Clearing Settlement System (ACSS):* The ACSS handles most ordinary payments, such as regular cheques, automatic bill payments, and debit card transactions. In 2004, the ACSS handled an average of 19.8 million payment items per day, with an average total value of over $16.65 billion.

While the Bank of Canada works with commercial banks through the payments systems, and also acts as a "lender of last resort" (that is, the Bank will lend funds to other banks if required), the actual regulation of financial institutions is administered by the Office of the Superintendent of Financial Institutions, OSFI, as we discussed earlier.

13.2 MONETARY POLICY TOOLS

It is important to remember that when it comes to setting monetary policy, the Bank always tries to develop a complete picture of the economy. We do not react unduly to any individual piece of information. Rather, we put all the pieces together to get to the underlying trends in the economy.[7]

Our immediate interest isn't in the structure of the Bank of Canada, but in the way the Bank is able to operate monetary policy to alter the money supply. The Bank of Canada exercises control over the money supply through two monetary policy tools:

1. Re-depositing
2. Open-market operations

The Bank's first monetary policy tool arises from its role as the "government banker and treasury manager" for the federal government. Funds flowing to and from the federal government are managed by the Bank of Canada. The Bank of Canada also manages Canada's foreign currency reserves.

Re-depositing

Flow of Funds. As the fiscal agent for the federal government, the Bank receives funds coming to the federal government. Since this represents a flow of money from inside the real economy to the Bank, which is outside the real economy (Figure 13.2), the result would be a reduction of the money supply. The Bank can **"sterilize"** such an action by re-depositing these funds back into commercial banks inside the real economy. The re-depositing of these funds leaves the reserves of the commercial banks unchanged and therefore the money supply unchanged.

The Bank could, however, also use this opportunity to alter the money supply in the economy either by re-depositing less than the amount received—thus reducing the

sterilization: To combine two actions so that there is no effect; in the case of money flowing from commercial banks to the Bank of Canada, the sterilization occurs through the Bank of Canada re-depositing their funds back into an account at the commercial banks.

[6]Bank of Canada Web site, (2006), http://www.bankofcanada.ca/en/financial/financial_gen.html, accessed December 22, 2006.

[7]David Dodge, Governor, Bank of Canada *Monetary Policy Report* (Ottawa: Bank of Canada, October 2006), http://www.bankofcanada.ca/en/mpr/mpr_previous.html.

WEB NOTE

Watch a video that explains the management structure of the Bank, and its roles and responsibilities at http://www.bankofcanada.ca/en/video_corp/ videos.html.

FIGURE 13.2

The Bank of Canada and the Real Economy

Since the Bank of Canada is "outside" the real economy, any money flowing from the real economy (or financial institutions "inside" the real economy) to the Bank represents a reduction in the money supply. Conversely, any money flowing from the Bank of Canada to the real economy represents an increase in the money supply.

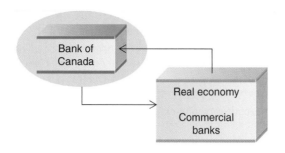

supply of money in the economy—or re-deposit additional funds held at the Bank of Canada as well as that received—thus increasing the money supply.

Foreign Currency Reserves. As the manager of Canada's foreign exchange reserves, the Bank can also impact the money supply in Canada. Again, the Bank's decision regarding re-depositing, or sterilization of the funds could result in the money supply increasing, decreasing, or staying the same. Although the role of the Bank in the foreign exchange market will be treated in greater depth in Chapter 16, it is important to consider the results of any transaction here.

Since the Bank holds both Canadian dollars and foreign currency—U.S. dollars, $; Euros, €; and Japanese Yen, ¥; for instance—it is able to be both a buyer and seller of Canadian dollars. That is, it could sell some of its U.S. dollars and buy Canadian dollars in exchange, or sell some of its Canadian dollars and buy euros. Suppose the Bank chose to buy Canadian dollars by selling off some of its U.S. dollar holdings. The result would be fewer Canadian dollars available to the real economy (and coincidentally, more U.S. dollars, but more about that in Chapter 16). The Bank could choose to maintain this decrease in the money supply, or sterilize the action by re-depositing these Canadian dollars back into commercial banks.

In spite of the Bank's ability to use re-depositing to impact the money supply, it generally doesn't. In the Bank's own words: "the transfer of government deposits, which has been the traditional instrument for neutralizing public sector flows and for setting the level of settlement balances in Canada, would continue to be used for this purpose."[8]

Open Market Operations

If re-depositing is a possible monetary policy tool, but isn't actively used as such, then *open market operations are the principal mechanism for directly altering the reserves of the banking system.* Since reserves are the lifeblood of the banking system, open market operations are of immediate and critical interest to private banks and the larger economy.

Portfolio Decisions. To appreciate the impact of open market operations, you have to think about the alternative uses for idle funds. Just about all of us have some idle funds, even if they amount to just a few dollars in our pocket or a minimal balance in our chequing account. Other consumers and corporations have great amounts of idle funds, even millions of dollars at any time. Here we're concerned with what people decide to do with such funds.

People (and corporations) don't hold all their idle funds in transactions accounts or cash. Idle funds are also used to purchase stocks, build up savings account balances, and purchase bonds. These alternative uses of idle funds are attractive because they

---

[8]Bank of Canada, *A Proposed Framework for the Implementation of Monetary Policy in the Large Value Transfer System Environment,* (March 1996), http://www.bankofcanada.ca/en/lvts/dp2.html, accessed January 2, 2007.

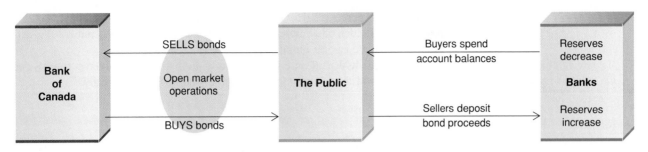

FIGURE 13.3
Open Market Operations

People may hold assets in the form of bank deposits (money) or bonds. When the Bank of Canada buys bonds from the public, it increases the flow of deposits (and reserves) to the banks. When the Bank of Canada sells bonds, it diminishes the flow of deposits and therewith the banks' capacity to lend (create money).

promise some additional income in the form of interest, dividends, or capital appreciation, such as higher stock prices. Deciding where to place idle funds is referred to as the *portfolio decision.*

Like you (or corporations), the Bank of Canada can also buy or sell bonds on the open-market. Unlike each of you (or corporations) that are all inside the real economy, the Bank of Canada is outside. Any transaction between the real economy and the Bank serves to move money either into or out of the real economy. The purpose of these operations is to alter the level of reserves held by commercial banks and thereby, the supply of money in the real economy. Figure 13.3 depicts the general nature of the Bank's open-market operations. ***When the Bank of Canada buys bonds from the public, it increases reserves in the commercial banking system. When the Bank sells bonds to the public, it decreases reserves in the commercial banking system.***

The Bond Market. To understand how open market operations work, let's look closer at the bond market. Not all of us buy and sell bonds, but a lot of consumers and corporations do: Daily volume in bond markets exceeds $17 billion. What's being exchanged in this market, and what factors influence decisions to buy or sell?

In our discussion thus far, we've portrayed banks as intermediaries between savers and spenders. Banks aren't the only mechanism available for transferring purchasing power from nonspenders to spenders. Funds are lent and borrowed in bond markets as well. In this case, a corporation may borrow money directly from consumers or other institutions. When it does so, it issues a bond as proof of its promise to repay the loan. A **bond** is simply a piece of paper certifying that someone has borrowed money and promises to pay it back at some future date. In other words, a bond is nothing more than an IOU. In the case of bond markets, however, the IOU is typically signed by a giant corporation or a government agency rather than a friend. It's therefore more widely accepted by lenders.

Because most corporations and government agencies that borrow money in the bond market are well known and able to repay their debts, their bonds are actively traded. If I lend $1,000 to General Motors on a 10-year bond, for example, I don't have to wait 10 years to get my money back; I can resell the bond to someone else at any time. If I do, that person will collect the face value of the bond (plus interest) from GM when it's due. The actual purchase and sale of bonds take place in the bond market. Although a good deal of the action occurs on Bay Street in Toronto, the bond market has no unique location. Like other markets we've discussed, the bond market exists whenever and however bond buyers and sellers get together.

Bond Yields. People buy bonds because bonds pay interest. If you buy a General Motors bond, GM is obliged to pay you interest during the period of the loan. For

bond: A certificate acknowledging a debt and the amount of interest to be paid each year until repayment; an IOU.

yield: The rate of return on a bond; the annual interest payment divided by the bond's price.

example, an 8 percent 2015 GM bond in the amount of $1,000 states that GM will pay the bondholder $80 interest annually (8 percent of $1,000) until 2015. At that point GM will repay the initial $1,000 loan (the "principal").

The current **yield** paid on a bond depends on the promised interest rate (8 percent in this case) and the actual purchase price of the bond. Specifically,

$$\text{Yield} = \frac{\text{annual interest payment}}{\text{price paid for bond}}$$

If you pay $1,000 for the bond, then the current yield is

$$\text{Yield} = \frac{\$80}{\$1,000} = 0.08, \text{ or } 8\%$$

which is the same as the interest rate printed on the face of the bond. But what if you pay only $900 for the bond? In this case, the interest rate paid by GM remains at 8 percent, but the *yield* jumps to

$$\text{Yield} = \frac{\$80}{\$900} = 0.089, \text{ or } 8.9\%$$

Buying a $1,000 bond for only $900 might seem like too good a bargain to be true. But bonds are often bought and sold at prices other than their face value (a bond priced higher than its face value is said to sell at a *premium* while a bond priced below its face value is said to sell at a *discount*). In fact, *a principal objective of open market activity is to alter the price of bonds, and therewith their yields.* By doing so, the Bank of Canada makes bonds a more or less attractive alternative to holding money.

open market operations: Purchases and sales of government bonds by the Bank of Canada for the purpose of altering bank reserves.

Open Market Activity. The basic premise of open market activity is that participants in the bond market will respond to changes in bond prices and yields. As we've observed, *the less you pay for a bond, the higher its yield.* Accordingly, the Bank of Canada can induce people to *buy* bonds by offering to sell them at a lower price (e.g., a $1,000, 8 percent bond for only $900). Similarly, the Bank of Canada can induce people to *sell* bonds by offering to buy them at higher prices. In either case, the Bank hopes to move reserves into or out of the banking system. In other words, **open market operations** entail the purchase and sale of government securities (bonds) for the purpose of altering the flow of reserves into and out of the banking system.

13.3 IMPLEMENTING MONETARY POLICY

The previous section explained the tools the Bank of Canada can use to alter the supply of money in the Canadian economy—the way the Bank can administer monetary policy. This section takes the next step by exploring how monetary policy is implemented through interest rates, and the next section completes the picture by tracing the monetary policy impacts back to the real economy through aggregate demand.

The Bank of Canada Web site notes that it "carries out monetary policy by influencing short-term interest rates. It does this by raising and lowering the target for the overnight rate."[9] Figure 13.4 illustrates the relationship among the overnight rate, the bank rate, and the commercial bank prime rate of interest.

The target for the overnight rate is used to indicate the direction of monetary policy deemed appropriate by the Bank of Canada (see the Applications Box on the next page).

[9]Bank of Canada, *Monetary Policy,* (2006), http://www.bankofcanada.ca/en/monetary/target.html, accessed January 2, 2007.

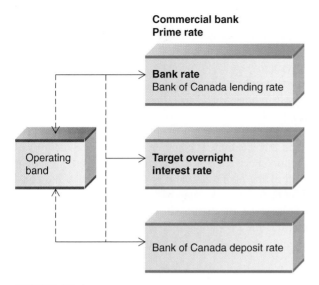

Commercial bank Prime rate

Bank rate
Bank of Canada lending rate

Operating band

Target overnight interest rate

Bank of Canada deposit rate

FIGURE 13.4
Short Term Interest Rates in the Economy

The target overnight interest rate is given as the mid-point of a ½ percentage point operating band (this ½ percentage point is more often referred to as a 50-basis point spread). The top of the operating band is the bank rate (¼ percent above the target rate), the rate of interest charged by the Bank of Canada for short term loans. The bottom of the operating band is the rate of interest paid on deposits at the Bank of Canada. The prime rate is that set by the commercial banks as the rate of lending to their most credit-worthy clients (and might also be thought of as a near risk-free commercial rate). While there is no structural relationship between the commercial "prime rate" and the Bank of Canada's target overnight rate, the overnight rate does imply the trend that commercial banks take into account when setting their own rates.

APPLICATIONS

Bank of Canada Raises Rates

The Bank of Canada raised its key interest rate to 4.5 per cent, the first increase in more than a year, and said more rate hikes may be needed to dampen inflation.

The central bank boosted its overnight lending rate Tuesday from 4.25 per cent, as expected. The move swiftly prompted some of the major [commercial] banks to boost their mortgage and prime lending rates.

In a lengthy statement, the central bank said more "modest" increases are likely after inflation topped its expectations. Core inflation, which strips out the most volatile items in the consumer price index, has been running ahead of the bank's 2 per cent target for the past 10 months.

"We are expecting another 25-basis point rate hike on Sept. 5 [2007] to 4.75 per cent, followed by a brief pause to gauge the effect of both the higher interest rates and the

recent appreciation of the Canadian dollar," said Ted Carmichael, chief economist of J.P. Morgan Securities Canada Inc., in a note.

The bank acknowledged Tuesday that both economic growth and inflation have been hotter than it had anticipated in April. Domestic demand has remained "the key driver" of Canadian economic growth, buoyed by strong commodity prices. "The bank judges that the economy is now operating further above its production potential than was projected" in April, the bank said.

Source: Tanya Grant, "Bank of Canada raises rates," *The Globe and Mail Update*, http://www.reportonbusiness.com/servlet/story/RTGAM.20070710.wboc0710/BNStory/Business/home, accessed July 10, 2007. Reprinted with permission from *The Globe and Mail*.

Analysis: The Bank of Canada uses its monetary policy instrument to focus on its monetary policy goal of low and stable price inflation—keeping inflation at an annual average of 2 percent.

target for the overnight rate: Sometimes referred to as the key interest rate or the key policy rate, the target for the overnight rate sets the target for major financial institutions to borrow or lend among themselves for one day (overnight). This target rate also influences other consumer lending rates (loans and mortgage rates).

prime rate: The rate of interest commercial banks charge their most credit-worthy (lowest risk) clients.

Since November of 2000, this target has been announced by the Bank of Canada on eight pre-set dates throughout the year. The **target for the overnight rate** is the midpoint of an *operating band* that extends ¼ percent above the target rate and ¼ percent beneath it. For example, if the overnight rate is 4¼ percent, the operating band would be from 4 to 4½ percent. More commonly in the financial press, this ½ of 1 percent band is referred to as being 50-basis points wide. Each "basis-point" therefore represents 1/100th of one percentage point.

Remember that one of the functions of the central bank is to act as a "lender of last resort" to commercial banks in the economy. If commercial banks need additional funds, they are able to borrow for short terms—or overnight—to have sufficient liquidity. The bank rate at the top of the operating band is the loan rate to the commercial banks. At other times, commercial banks may have surplus funds on reserve at the central bank. When this is the case, the Bank will pay interest on those funds at the rate indicated by the bottom of the operating band. The top and bottom of the band then represents the borrowing and lending rates in the economy to the commercial banks.

The prime rate, while influenced by the target for the overnight rate and the operating band, is not directly connected to either. It represents not only the influence of target for the overnight rate, but also the level of risk in the economy and the competitive situation among the financial system. Generally though, the **prime rate** represents the lowest rate offered to the most credit-worthy clients of the commercial banks—those clients that present the lowest risk of non-payment to the financial institutions. All other rates then are a combination of the prime rate and additional risk associated with each individual borrower.

This brings us back to the loanable funds market and the equilibrium rate of interest that we dealt with in Chapter 12. The equilibrium rate of interest in the economy came about as a consequence of the supply of money and the demand for money in the economy. The equilibrium interest rate is influenced, as we saw, by the Bank's target for the overnight rate of interest, but it in turn is adjusted through changes in the supply of money, principally through open-market operations—the buying and selling of government securities—undertaken by the Bank of Canada. So, the implementation of monetary policy happens through adjusting the total supply of money in the economy.

Decreasing the Money Supply

Figure 13.5 illustrates the Bank's impact on the rate of interest as a result of selling bonds to the public. When the Bank of Canada sells a bond into the real economy, money, held as reserves by commercial banks, flows out of the economy into the central bank. If the central bank chooses to hold the money in its own

FIGURE 13.5

Open-Market Operations in the Loanable Funds Market

When the Bank of Canada sells bonds into the market, it reduces reserves at the commercial banks (replacing money with the bond) reducing the money supply in the economy and competing the interest rate upward.

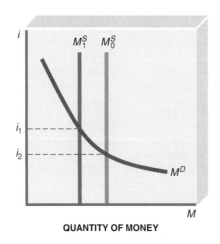

QUANTITY OF MONEY

vault, the money supply is reduced by the amount of the bond, and by the factor of the money multiplier. In Figure 13.5, this reduction of the money supply is shown as a leftward shift of the money supply curve, from M_0^S to M_1^S. Since the demand for money is unchanged, the equilibrium rate of interest in the economy must rise. Money becomes relatively more scarce, and therefore, relatively more expensive.

We can also see this transaction in numbers. The question here then becomes, What change in the money supply is required if the Bank intends to reduce the money supply by, say, $2 billion? We begin by remembering the basic relationship between the money supply and the monetary base:

$$\Delta \text{ Money supply} = [\text{money multiplier}][\Delta \text{ money}]$$

The money multiplier takes into account the banks desired reserve ratio, any desired excess reserves, and the cash drain in the economy. Suppose that the multiplier turns out to be 4.00. Since we know the Bank of Canada's intention is to reduce the money supply by $2 billion, we can substitute those values into the relationship.

$$-\$2 \text{ billion} = [4.00][\Delta \text{ money}]$$

Notice that the change in money is negative, indicating the reduction in money supply. If it was an increase, the value would be positive. Now we just need to rearrange the relationship so that what we don't know—the change in money—is expressed in terms of what we do know.

$$\Delta \text{ Money} = \frac{-\$2 \text{ billion}}{4.00} = -\$0.5 \text{ billion or } -\$500 \text{ million}$$

So the Bank of Canada can reduce the total money supply in the economy by selling $500 million of bonds into the economy and holding the $500 million in payment at the Bank outside of the real economy.

Open-market operations can also be used to increase the money supply in the real economy. To accomplish this, the Bank of Canada would purchase bonds from the bond market. When the Bank of Canada buys a bond from the real economy, the bond moves out of the economy and into the central bank, and the money payment for the bond is deposited in commercial banks, increasing reserves. The money supply is increased by the amount of the payment, and by the factor of the money multiplier. This increase in the money supply would be shown as a rightward shift of the money supply curve. Since the demand for money is unchanged, the equilibrium rate of interest in the economy must fall. Money becomes relatively less scarce, and therefore, relatively less expensive.

Increasing the Money Supply

Although our discussion here has been framed entirely in terms of the money supply either increasing or decreasing, this is really just a simplification of what really occurs. A growing economy, which as we have seen, Canada's economy generally is, needs a steadily increasing supply of money to finance market exchanges. As the economy produces more goods and services, more money is required to purchase those goods and services. Hence, the Bank of Canada rarely seeks an outright reduction or increase in the money supply. What it does is regulate the *rate of growth* in the money supply. If the Bank of Canada wished to slow the rate of consumer and investor spending, it restrains the growth of money and credit. To slow economic growth (and potential price inflation), China pursued this sort of monetary restraint in 2004 (see the World View box on the next page).

If the Bank wished to stimulate the rate of consumer and investor spending, it would increase the *growth* of money and credit. Figure 13.6 provides a snapshot of the changing year-over-year growth rate of the money supply—using the M1++ monetary aggregate—from 1996 through 2006.

No Letup Seen in Red-Hot Chinese Market

China has raised interest rates twice this year, and further hikes are almost a given. But the big question is: What impact, if any, will that have on the red-hot Chinese stock market, which seems poised to continue to soar.

Chinese Premier Wen Jiabao warned Wednesday that the government would take "appropriate" steps to keep the high-flying Chinese economy from overhearing. He told a meeting of the State Council that monetary policy should be tightened "appropriately," a statement interpreted by government economists as a clear signal that more interest rate increases are in the cards, with the next one coming possibly by the end of [June].

"Given the recently established hypersensitivity to inflation and interest rate risks, will global investors be able to continue to look through further monetary tightening by the Chinese government?" Mr Liu asked in his report. In an interview, he said that if the Chinese central bank were to raise rates today, investors would likely say "so what" and thus it likely wouldn't have much impact on the market. But if there were two or three more rate hikes afterward, then "I think people will gradually realize that the Chinese government is getting more and more serious on these things."

Source: Angela Barnes, "No letup seen in red-hot Chinese market, *The Globe and Mail* (June 15, 2007) p. B10. Reprinted with permission from *The Globe and Mail*.

Analysis: Central banks raise interest rates (slow growth in the money supply) when they sense inflationary pressure in the economy. Decision makers, however, have to believe that the bank is "serious" about controlling inflation for any change to have a full effect.

FIGURE 13.6

**Monetary Aggregates: M1++
(1-year growth rate)**

The graph illustrates the changing nature of the monetary growth rate, from less than 2 percent in 1996 and 1998 to more than 15 percent in 2002.

Source: Bank of Canada, "Summary of key monetary variables," http://www.bankofcanada.ca/en/graphs/m_1_plus_plus.html, accessed January 3, 2007.

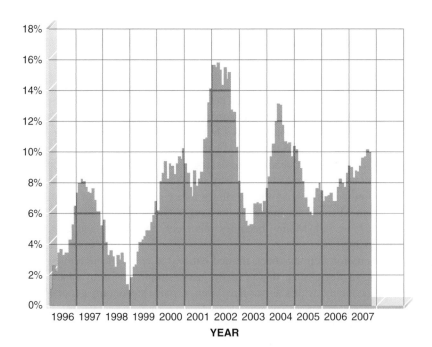

13.4 THE MONETARY TRANSMISSION MECHANISM

Now that we know about the monetary policy tools, the monetary policy instrument, and how the Bank of Canada goes about implementing monetary policy, we need to understand how the impact of monetary policy is transmitted into the real economy. A change in the interest rate isn't the end of this story, by any means! The ultimate objective of monetary policy is to alter macroeconomic outcomes: prices, output, and employment. This results from a change in aggregate demand. Therefore, the next

APPLICATIONS

Focusing Monetary Policy on Price Stability

Since 1991 the federal government and the Bank of Canada have agreed to focus monetary policy on price stability—maintaining inflation at 2 percent per year and within a 1 to 3 percent range. In November 2006, the government and the Bank agreed to a further 5-year extension of this mandate through to December 31, 2011. The Bank concludes its backgrounder document *Renewal of the Inflation-Control Target* with two questions it believes requires further research, and with some rationale for these questions:

- What are the costs and benefits of an inflation target lower than 2 percent? Would an inflation target lower than 2 percent generate significant net benefits for the economy and for Canadian households?
- What are the costs and benefits of replacing the current inflation target with a longer-term, price level target? Would a price-level target produce significant net benefits for the economy and for Canadian households?

Targeting a low, stable, and predictable inflation rate of 2 percent per annum removes much of the uncertainty and economic costs associated with high and volatile inflation, such as Canadians experienced in the 1970s and 1980s. It does not, however, eliminate all of the costs associated with inflation. A 2 percent rate of inflation causes the price level to double approximately every 35 years. Although the erosion in purchasing power is difficult to notice year by year, it can still pose a serious problem on a cumulative basis. This erosion is particularly acute for those pensioners on a fixed income. It can also distort price signals, because of potential confusion between movements in relative prices and a change in the aggregate price level, and it can impose "menu costs" by creating the need to regularly adjust prices. The key questions are whether the benefits of reducing the target rate of inflation below 2 percent are significant, and whether the prospective benefits would outweigh the possible transition costs associated with achieving a lower ongoing inflation rate. . . .

The reasons traditionally given for not targeting an inflation rate closer to zero have centred primarily on three issues: (i) the measurement error embedded in existing price indexes; (ii) the labour market consequences of the presence of downward nominal wage rigidities; and (iii) the problems posed by the constraint that nominal interest rates cannot go below zero.

The main difference between price-level targeting and inflation targeting is the way in which past deviations from the target are treated. Inflation targeting, as it is currently practiced, effectively ignores past deviations from the target–that is bygones are bygones. It allows "one-off" price-level movements and aims only at bringing future (i.e., projected) inflation back to the target. In contrast, with a price-level target (which could rise over time), the short-run inflation objective would be adjusted from time to time in order to unwind any cumulative deviations of the actual price level from the target price level that had occurred. If the actual price level were below (or above) the price-level target, the central bank would have to aim for a slightly higher (or lower) inflation rate over a period of time in order to bring the actual price level back to the target.

Source: Bank of Canada, *Renewal of the Inflation-Control Target: Background Information,* http://www.bankofcanada.ca/en/press/2006/pr06-19. html, accessed January 3, 2007.

Analysis: Even a low rate of inflation like 2 percent diminishes the purchasing power of money, reducing it by half over 35 years and creating serious difficulties for anyone on a fixed income. Moving to a lower target rate of inflation (such as 1 percent) or to a "price level target" instead of an inflation target will have their own opportunity costs and economic consequences.

question is how changes in interest rates (the loanable funds market) affect consumer, investor, government, and net export spending.

Figure 13.7 traces the impact path of monetary policy into the real economy and the variables that are affected, that is, the **monetary transmission mechanism.** As illustrated, monetary policy affects the real economy's aggregate demand through two channels. First, changes to Canadian interest rates alter the willingness and ability of consumers, investors, and governments to spend. Second, changes in Canadian interest rates can affect the international value of the Canadian dollar—Canadian dollar exchange rates. In turn, a change in the rate of exchange changes the prices of and the demand for Canadian goods and services in foreign markets (from foreign consumers, investors, and governments) as well as changing the prices of and the demand for foreign goods and services in Canadian markets (from Canadian consumers, investors, and governments).

monetary transmission mechanism: The impact path of how monetary policy is "transmitted" into the real economy through aggregate demand.

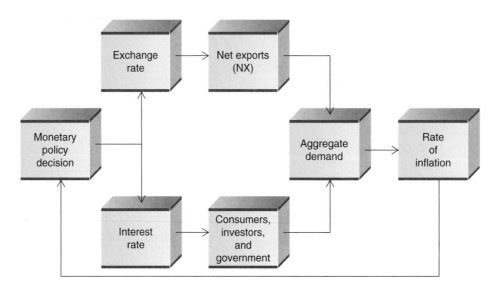

FIGURE 13.7
The Monetary Transmission Mechanism

Monetary policy impacts are transmitted into the real economy through two channels: first, monetary policy impacts domestic interest rates, altering the spending decisions of Canadian consumers, investors, and governments. Second, monetary policy impacts the international value of the Canadian dollar—the exchange rate—altering the price of and demand for Canadian goods in foreign markets (exports) and the price of and demand for foreign goods in Canada (imports). In a "closed economy" setting, only the first impact is considered while in an "open economy" both channels come into play.

Let's first consider only the "closed economy" impact of monetary policy. That is, for the time being we will ignore any impact on Canadian exchange rates (which will be considered in detail in Chapter 16 along with the foreign economy and a full "open economy" view). In fact, for simplicity, we will consider a policy of monetary stimulus (an increase in the money supply) with a focus on investor behaviour.

Monetary Stimulus

Investment. Will lower interest rates encourage spending? In Chapter 8 we observed that investment decisions are sensitive to the rate of interest. Specifically, we demonstrated that lower rates of interest reduce the cost of buying plant and equipment, making capital investment more profitable. Lower interest rates also reduce the opportunity cost of holding inventories. Accordingly, a lower rate of interest should result in a higher rate of desired investment spending, as shown by the movement down the investment-demand curve in Step 2 of Figure 13.8.

Aggregate Demand. The increased investment brought about by lower interest rates represents an injection of new spending into the circular flow. That jump in spending will kick off multiplier effects and result in an even larger increase in aggregate demand. Step 3 in Figure 13.8 illustrates this increase by the rightward *shift* of the aggregate demand curve. Market participants, encouraged by lower interest rates, are now willing to buy more output at the prevailing price level.

Consumers too may change their behaviour when interest rates fall. As interest rates fall, mortgage payments decline. Monthly payments on home equity and credit card balances may also decline. These lower interest changes can free up billions of consumer dollars. This increased net cash flow and lower interest rates may encourage consumers to buy new cars, appliances, or other "big-ticket" items (see the Applications box). Governments may also conclude that lower interest rates increase the desirability of public works. All such responses would add to aggregate demand.

Step 1: An increase in the money supply lowers the rate of interest.

Step 2: Lower interest rates stimulate investment.

Step 3: More investment increases aggregate demand (including multiplier effects).

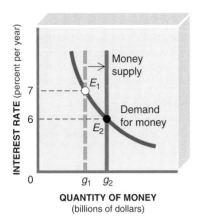

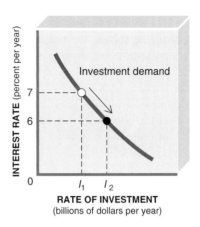

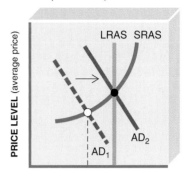

FIGURE 13.8
Monetary stimulus

An increase in the money supply may reduce interest rates and encourage more investment. The increase in investment will trigger multiplier effects that increase aggregate demand by an even larger amount.

From this perspective, ***the Bank of Canada's objective of stimulating the economy is achieved in three distinct steps:***

- *An increase in the money supply.*
- *A reduction in interest rates.*
- *An increase in aggregate demand.*

Like fiscal policy, monetary policy is a two-edged sword, at times seeking to increase aggregate demand and at other times trying to restrain it. When inflation threatens, the objective of monetary policy is to reduce the rate of total spending, which puts

Monetary Restraint

APPLICATIONS

Teetering on the Brink of Bankruptcy: Rise in Interest Rates Could Push Many over the Edge

Today's debt-addicted society has become so used to cheap credit that any significant rise in interest rates could increase personal bankruptcies at a pace not seen in 5 to 10 years, one economist suggests.

CIBC World Markets economist Benjamin Tal, who regularly takes the financial pulse of Canadian households, warns it would take only a one-percentage hike in rates to start exposing cracks in the seemingly solid financial situation many households currently enjoy.

"The implications of the credit boom of the last five, six, or seven years is that we have a generation of borrowers that has never experienced high interest rates and, therefore, people have been borrowing much more. As a society, we have become more vulnerable to the risk of higher interest rates," Tal said.

A recent CIBC World Markets [study] noted that household credit is rising by about 10 per cent on a year-over-year basis. During the first three months of 2007, household debt rose 2.7 per cent while personal disposable income increased 2 per cent, it said.

Source: E. Beauchesne and A. Howland, "Teetering on the brink of bankruptcy: Rise in interest rates could push many over the edge," *Winnipeg Free Press* (July 6, 2007), p. A14. Material reprinted with the express permisson of CanWest News Service, a CanWest Partnership.

Analysis: Low interest rates over the past five years have encouraged market participants to borrow and spend more money. This has shifted the aggregate demand curve rightward. Higher interest rates, however, would increase borrowing costs thus increasing consumer saving from disposable income and reducing current consumption, shifting the AD curve leftward.

the Bank of Canada in the position of "leaning against the wind." If successful, the resulting reduction in spending will keep aggregate demand from increasing inflationary pressures.

Higher Interest Rates. The mechanics of monetary policy designed to combat inflation are similar to those used to increase spending only the direction is reversed. In this case, we seek to discourage spending by increasing the rate of interest. The Bank can push interest rates up by selling bonds to reduce the money supply and help establish a new and higher equilibrium rate of interest.

The ultimate objective of a restrictive monetary policy is to reduce aggregate demand. For monetary restraint to succeed, spending behaviour must be responsive to interest rates.

Reduced Aggregate Demand. Figure 13.8 showed the impact of interest rates on investment and aggregate demand. If the interest rate rises from 6 to 7 percent, investment declines from I_2 to I_1 and aggregate demand shifts *leftward*. At higher rates of interest, many marginal investments will no longer be profitable. Likewise, many consumers will decide that they can't afford the higher monthly payments associated with increased interest rates; purchases of homes, cars, and household appliances will be postponed. Governments may also decide to cancel or postpone projects. Thus, *monetary restraint is achieved with*

- *A decrease in the money supply.*
- *An increase in interest rates.*
- *A decrease in aggregate demand.*

The resulting leftward shift of the aggregate demand curve lessens inflationary pressures.

Figure 13.9 gives a historical picture of Canadian monetary policy over the past decade. From 1997 through to the beginning of 2001, the Bank of Canada was restraining Canadian spending, reducing pressure on inflation in the Canadian economy. The approach changed in early 2001 from restraining demand to a more stimulative stance, and the target for the overnight rate of interest fell from 5.50 percent to 2.00 percent by January of 2002. Between January 2002 and August 2004, the target rate remained relatively consistent. The Bank returned to a more restrictive monetary policy in September 2004, and the target for the overnight rate had risen back to 4.25 percent by May 2006, where it has remained through the end of the year.

So far in this chapter we've only looked at the impact of monetary policy decisions on interest rates in the economy and then on how monetary policy decisions can impact aggregate demand through the monetary transmission mechanism, which in turn changes economic outcomes in the real economy. This is an explicit example of how different parts of the macroeconomic system interact with each other. This leads

Fiscal Policy and the Monetary Transmission Mechanism

FIGURE 13.9
Bank of Canada: Target for the Overnight Rate of Interest

The path of the target for the overnight rate over the past decade illustrates the Bank of Canada's shifting between a policy of restraint (Jan 1997–Feb 2001 and Jan 2005–Dec 2006) and a more stimulative approach (Feb 2001–Feb 2002 and March 2003–Dec 2004).

Source: Bank of Canada, "Target for the overnight rate," http://www.bankofcanada. ca/en/rates/interest-look.html, accessed January 3, 2007.

TARGET OVERNIGHT RATE

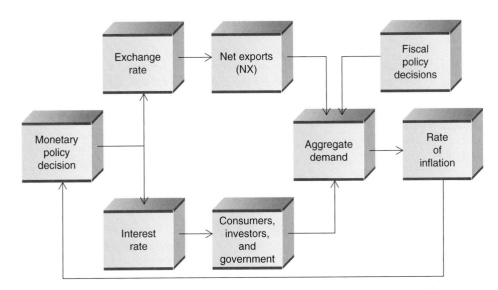

FIGURE 13.10
Fiscal Policy and the Monetary Transmission Mechanism

Since fiscal policy is a component of aggregate demand, AD, any change in government spending or tax policy can directly impact the level of aggregate demand in the economy. If the change in AD exerts pressure on the price level, that is, is inflationary, monetary policy decisions may be taken to offset or reduce this pressure.

to the question of how changes outside of the monetary economy could initiate monetary policy decisions. To answer this question with an example, let's look at how fiscal policy decisions in the real economy may do this.

Figure 13.10 illustrates a policy change originating in the real economy itself, specifically, a change in fiscal policy—a change in government spending plans or taxation. Since government expenditure is a component of aggregate demand, AD, any change in the level of government spending will shift the AD curve. Suppose, for example, the government intends to stimulate the economy by increasing its own spending. The result is a rightward shift of the AD curve and a new higher equilibrium level of GDP. Assuming that the economy was at Y^* (potential GDP) to begin with, the extra aggregate demand will result in an inflationary gap and inflationary pressure in the economy.

So far, none of this changes anything in the monetary economy. However, remember that the demand for money curve includes both transactional money and precautionary money. The level of money for transactions and precaution is dependent on the level of national income, Y. If national income, GDP, rises, then the demand for transactional and precautionary money will also rise, an increase or rightward shift of the money demand curve. The Bank of Canada (the monetary authority) can react in one of two ways: it can either increase the supply of money in the economy to accommodate the additional demand, or it can hold the money supply constant, in other words, do nothing.

If the Bank of Canada holds the supply of money constant, the excess demand for money will cause the domestic interest rate to rise. Ignoring the foreign market for the time being, the increase in the interest rate will reduce the investment spending in the economy, which in turn reduces overall aggregate demand. The result is that the "net" stimulus arising from additional government expenditure is less than the total additional government expenditure by the reduction in investment expenditure (and perhaps fewer new cars purchased by consumers). This reduction is referred to as *crowding-out*.[10]

If the Bank of Canada acts "in sympathy" to the increased demand for money by simultaneously increasing the supply of money, there would be no interest rate impact and therefore no change in investment or consumer expenditure and therefore no crowding out. This is not without its own problems though, as we will see ahead in Section 13.6, as the increase in the money supply can reinforce the inflationary pressure in the economy.

---

[10]Chapter 12 (page 258) provided the relationship of money supply to money demand as $M^S = e(Y) + f(Y) - g(i)$. If M^S remains constant while, for instance, Y increases, then the interest rate, i, must rise to balance the equation.

13.5 MONETARY POLICY CONSTRAINTS

The mechanics of monetary policy are simple enough. They won't always work as well as we might hope, however. Several constraints can limit the Bank of Canada's ability to alter the money supply, interest rates, or aggregate demand.

Constraints on Monetary Stimulus

Short- vs. Long-Term Rates. One of the most visible constraints on monetary policy is the distinction between short-term interest rates and long-term interest rates. Monetary policy (through the target for the overnight rate of interest) has its greatest impact on short-term interest rates. Yet, most spending decisions are more affected by long-term interest rates such as mortgages, installment loans, and bond financing. As a consequence, the success of the Bank of Canada's intervention depends in part on how well changes in long-term interest rates mirror changes in short-term interest rates.

Figure 13.11 compares average bond yields for 1–3 years, 5 years, and 10 years with the target for the overnight rate of interest for January of each year. Between January of 2001 and January of 2002, the target for the overnight rate fell from 5.5 percent to 2.0 percent. Over the same time frame, the longer 10-year bond yield actually rose by 0.03 percent, from 5.39 to 5.42 percent. The shorter the term, the more closely the bond yield mirrors changes in the overnight rate.

Reluctant Lenders. There are several reasons why long-term rates might not closely mirror changes in short-term rates. The first potential constraint is the willingness of private banks to increase lending activity. The Bank of Canada can reduce the cost of funds to the banking system; but the money supply won't increase as much as expected unless banks lend more money.

If commercial banks instead choose to accumulate excess reserves, the money supply won't increase as much as intended. This is simply another example of the money multiplier function. As the proportion of money held as excess reserves by commercial banks increases, the money multiplier decreases and, therefore, the change in the total money supply is smaller than intended. During the Great Depression banks also held onto their excess reserves instead of using them for new loans. In such cases, long-term rates stay relatively high even when short-term rates are falling.

Liquidity Trap. There are circumstances in which even *short-term* rates may not fall when the Bank of Canada wants them to. The possibility that interest rates may not respond to changes in the money supply is illustrated by the liquidity trap. When

FIGURE 13.11
Selected Canadian Interest Rates over Different Terms

Figure 13.11 compares the 1–3 year, 5 year, and 10 year bond yields with the target for the overnight rate of interest from 2001 to 2006. Rates are for January of each year. The target for the overnight rate (the shortest term) varies the most. The next shortest term, 1–3 years, most closely mirrors the target for the overnight rate but as the terms lengthen, the variance becomes less and the similarity diminishes.

Source: Bank of Canada, "Selected Canadian Bond Yields." http://www.bankofcanada.ca/en/rates/bonds.html, and "Canadian Interest Rates," http://www.bankofcanada.ca/en/rates/interest-look.html, accessed January 4, 2007.

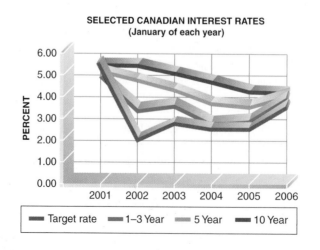

SELECTED CANADIAN INTEREST RATES
(January of each year)

(a) A liquidity trap can stop interest rates from falling.

(b) Inelastic investment demand can also impede monetary policy.

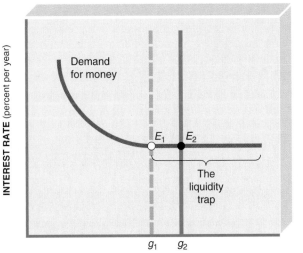

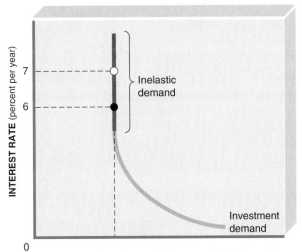

FIGURE 13.12
Constraints on Monetary Stimulus

(a) Liquidity Trap If people are willing to hold unlimited amounts of money at the prevailing interest rate, increases in the money supply won't push interest rates lower. A liquidity trap— the horizontal segment of the money demand curve—prevents interest rates from falling.

(b) Inelastic Demand A lower interest rate won't always stimulate investment. If investors have unfavorable expectations for future sales, small reductions in interest rates may not alter their investment decisions. Here the rate of investment remains constant when the interest rate drops from 7 to 6 percent. This kind of situation blocks the second step in the Keynesian approach to monetary policy (see Figure 13.8b).

interest rates are low, the opportunity cost of holding money is cheap. At such times people may decide to hold all the money they can get, waiting for income-earning opportunities to improve. Bond prices, for example, may be high and their yields low. Buying bonds at such times entails the risk of capital losses (when bond prices fall) and little reward (since yields are low). Accordingly, market participants may decide just to hold any additional money the Bank of Canada supplies. At this juncture—a phenomenon Keynes called the **liquidity trap**—further expansion of the money supply has no effect on the rate of interest. The horizontal section of the money demand curve in Figure 13.12a portrays this situation.

What happens to interest rates when the initial equilibrium falls into this trap? Nothing at all. Notice that the equilibrium rate of interest doesn't fall when the money supply is increased from g_1 to g_2 (Figure 13.12a). People are willing to hold all that additional money without a reduction in the rate of interest. This is the behaviour that neutralized Japan's monetary stimulus in 1999–2001 (see the World View on the next page).

Low Expectations. Even if both short- and long-term interest rates do fall, we've no assurance that desired *spending* will increase as expected. Keynes put great emphasis on *expectations*. Recall that investment decisions are motivated not only by interest rates but by expectations as well. During a recession—when unemployment is high and the rate of spending low—corporations have little incentive to expand production capacity. With little expectation of future profit, investors are likely to be unimpressed by "cheap money" (low interest rates) and may decline to use the lending capacity that banks make available.

liquidity trap: The portion of the money demand curve that is horizontal; people are willing to hold unlimited amounts of money at some (low) interest rate.

Why Japan Is Stuck

Free Money Can't Budge the Economy

Decades from now, people may still be arguing over one of the most intriguing economic mysteries of the 1990s: How did a country as rich and sophisticated as Japan fall into a liquidity trap, a bizarre state of affairs in which even near-zero interest rates fail to get banks lending, businesses investing, consumers spending, and the real economy moving?

By any measure, Japan's economic crisis this decade has been a nightmare. A vortex of falling asset prices, banking crises, declining corporate profits, and rising government debt has sucked the economy down. . . .

Until recently it was barely credible that an advanced economy could face Japan's dilemma. True, academics once thought a lot about liquidity traps, which Depression-era economist John Maynard Keynes raised as a possibility in the 1930s. But interest in the issue waned in the inflationary postwar decades. And periodic recessions responded to the usual measures.

Blunt Tools. Then came the great Japanese recession. Today, the BOJ is virtually giving money away, and nobody wants it. Japan has vast savings but no credit creation. Japan may have waited far too long to apply classic remedies. Fiscal and monetary tools become blunted once a depression psychology, such as Japan now suffers, sets in.

Japan has cut its official discount rate to 0.5 percent and short-term rates to nearly zero. Yet the economy isn't growing. Here's why:

Banks

Burdened by bad debts and short of capital, they aren't lending; instead, they are putting excess reserves in the bond market.

Companies

They have little incentive to borrow to finance new investment because industrial Japan is already saddled with excess capacity.

Consumers

They are so anxious that they are saving, not spending, even though bank deposits yield less than 1 percent.

Source: *Business Week*, April 12, 1999. Reprinted by permission. Copyright 1999 by The McGraw-Hill Companies.

Analysis: When consumers and businesses are very pessimistic, they are likely to hold more money rather than spend it. Such a liquidity trap blunts monetary stimulus.

Investment demand that's slow to respond to the stimulus of cheap money is said to be *inelastic* because it won't expand. Consumers too are reluctant to borrow when current and future income prospects are uncertain or distinctly unfavourable. Accordingly, even if the Bank of Canada is successful in lowering interest rates, there's no assurance that lower interest rates will stimulate borrowing and spending.

When the Japanese central bank cut the discount rate from an extraordinary low ½ percent to an unheard of ¼ percent, no one responded. In the lengthening recession Japanese consumers were trying to save more of their money and producer expectations were glum. So even *really* cheap loans didn't budge the aggregate demand curve.

The vertical portion of the investment demand curve in Figure 13.12b illustrates the possibility that investment spending may not respond to changes in the rate of interest. Notice that a reduction in the rate of interest from 7 percent to 6 percent doesn't increase investment spending. In this case, businesses are simply unwilling to invest any more funds. As a consequence, aggregate spending doesn't rise. The Bank of Canada's policy objective remains unfulfilled, even though the Bank has successfully lowered the rate of interest. Recall that the investment demand curve may also *shift* if expectations change. If expectations worsened, the investment demand curve would shift to the left and might result in even *less* investment at 6 percent interest (see Figure 13.12b).

Time Lags. Even when expectations are good, businesses won't respond *instantly* to changes in interest rates. Lower interest rates make investments more profitable. But it still takes time to develop and implement new investments. Hence, *there is always a time lag between interest-rate changes and investment responses.*

The same is true for consumers. Consumers don't rush out the door to refinance their homes or buy new ones the day the Bank of Canada reduces interest rates. They might start *thinking* about new financing, but aren't likely to *do* anything for a while. The Bank of Canada writes in the October 2006 *Monetary Policy Report* that "the transmission mechanism is complex and involves long and variable lags." They go on to suggest that these lags may be as long as 18–24 months or six to eight quarters.

Expectations. Time lags and expectations could also limit the effectiveness of monetary restraint. In pursuit of "tight" money, the Bank of Canada could drain bank reserves and force interest rates higher. Yet market participants might continue to borrow and spend if high expectations for rising sales and profits overwhelm high interest rates in investment decisions. Consumers too might believe that future incomes will be sufficient to cover larger debts and higher interest charges. Both groups might foresee accelerating inflation that would make even high interest rates look cheap in the future. This was apparantly the case in Britain in 2004, as the World View below documents.

Limits on Monetary Restraint

Global Money. Market participants might also tap global sources of money. If money gets too tight in domestic markets, business may borrow funds from foreign banks or institutions. General Motors, Alcan Aluminum, Encana Resources, and other firms can borrow funds from foreign subsidiaries, banks, and bond markets. The result might be a smaller change in aggregate demand than desired by the Bank of Canada in response to a change in Canadian interest rates.

How Effective? In view of all these constraints on monetary policies, some observers have concluded that monetary policy is an undependable policy lever. Keynes, for example, emphasized that monetary policy wouldn't be very effective in ending a deep recession. He believed that the combination of reluctant bankers, the liquidity trap, and low expectations would render monetary stimulus ineffective. Using monetary policy to stimulate the economy in such circumstances would be akin to "pushing on a string."

WORLD VIEW

Rising Rates Haven't Thwarted Consumers

THE BANK OF ENGLAND continued its tightening of monetary policy on June 10. And with the British economy still expanding at a decent clip, more hikes are on the way.

As expected by most economists, the BOE raised its lending rate by a quarter-point, to 4.5%. It was the fourth bump up since November, 2003. In explaining the move, the BOE's statement pointed to above-trend output growth, strong household, business, and public spending, as well as a labor market that "has tightened further.". . .

The BOE is the first of the world's major central banks to raise rates, but the moves have done little to curb borrowing, especially by consumers. Home buying remains robust. . . .

The easy access to credit and the strong labor markets are boosting consumer spending.

Source: *BusinessWeek*, June 28, 2004. Reprinted by permission. Copyright 2004 by The McGraw-Hill Companies.

Analysis: Strong expectations and rising incomes may fuel continued spending even when interest rates are rising.

The limitations on monetary restraint aren't considered as serious. The Bank of Canada has the power to reduce the money supply. If the money supply shrinks far enough, the rate of spending will have to slow down.

13.6 MONEY NEUTRALITY

The Keynesian view of money emphasizes the role of interest rates in fulfilling the goals of monetary policy. *In the Keynesian model, changes in the money supply affect macro outcomes primarily through changes in interest rates.* The three-step sequence of (1) money supply change, (2) interest rate movement, and (3) aggregate demand shift makes monetary policy subject to several potential uncertainties. As we've seen, the economy doesn't always respond as expected to monetary policy.

An alternative view of the effectiveness of monetary policy altering real economy macroeconomic outcomes comes from classical economists and again differentiates between the short run and the long run. Generally speaking, monetary policy in this view is seen as an important force in controlling inflation but ineffective in altering the level of national output or GDP.

The Equation of Exchange

The long run potential impact of monetary policy on output can be expressed through a simple equation called the **equation of exchange,** written as:

$$MV = PQ$$

where M refers to the quantity of money in circulation and V to its **velocity** of circulation. Total spending in the economy is equal to the average price (P) of goods times the quantity (Q) of goods sold in a period. This spending is financed by the supply of money (M) times the velocity of its circulation (V).

Suppose, for example, that only two participants are in the market and that the money supply consists of one crisp $20 bill. What's the limit to total spending in this case? If you answer "$20," you haven't yet grasped the nature of the circular flow. Suppose I begin the circular flow by spending $20 on eggs, bacon, and a litre of milk. The money I spend ends up in Farmer Brown's pocket because he is the only other market participant. Once in possession of the money, Farmer Brown may decide to satisfy his long-smoldering desire to learn something about economics and buy one of my books. If he acts on that decision, the $20 will return to me. At that point, both Farmer Brown and I have sold $20 worth of goods. Hence, $40 of total spending has been financed with one $20 bill.

As long as we keep using this $20 bill to buy goods and services from each other, we can continue to do business. Moreover, the faster we pass the money from hand to hand during any period of time, the greater the value of sales each of us can register. If the money is passed from hand to hand eight times, then I'll be able to sell $80 worth of textbooks and Farmer Brown will be able to sell $80 worth of produce during that period, for a total nominal output of $160. *The quantity of money in circulation and the velocity with which it travels (changes hands) in product markets will always be equal to the value of total spending and income (nominal GDP).* Figure 13.13 illustrates the velocity of M+. The relationship is summarized as

$$M \times V = P \times Q$$

In this case, the *equation of exchange* confirms that

$$\$20 \times 8 = \$160$$

The value of total sales for the year is $160.

The equation of exchange simplifies the explanation of how monetary policy works. There's no need to follow the effects of changes in M through the money

equation of exchange: Money supply (M) times velocity of circulation (V) equals level of aggregate spending ($P \times Q$).

velocity of money (V): The number of times per year, on average, a dollar is used to purchase final goods and services; $PQ \div M$.

WEB NOTE

For a fun way of thinking about velocity visit "Where's Willey" at http://www.whereswilly.com/.

markets to interest rates and further to changes in total spending. The basic consequences of monetary policy are evident in the equation of exchange. The two sides of the equation of exchange must always be in balance. Hence, we can be absolutely certain that *if* **M** *increases, prices* **(P)** *or output* **(Q)** *must rise, or* **V** *must fall.*

The equation of exchange is an incontestable statement of how the money supply is related to macro outcomes. The equation itself, however, says nothing about *which* variables will respond to a change in the money supply. The *goal* of monetary policy is to change the macro outcomes on the right side of the equation. It's *possible,* however, that a change in *M* might be offset with a reverse change in *V*, leaving *P* and *Q* unaffected. Or it could happen that the *wrong* macro outcome is affected. Prices (*P*) might rise, for example, when we're trying to increase real output (*Q*).

There are some important assumptions that transform the equation of exchange from a simple identity to a behavioural *model* of macro performance. The first assumption is that the velocity of money (*V*) is stable. How fast people use their money balances depends on the institutional structure of money markets and people's habits. Neither the structure of money markets nor people's habits are likely to change when *M* is altered. Accordingly, an increase in *M* won't be offset by a reduction in *V*. Instead, the impact of an increased money supply will be transmitted to the right-hand side of the equation of exchange, which means that **total spending must rise if the money supply (M)** *grows and* **V** *is stable.*

A second assumption asserts that *Q* is also stable. The result is that only price (*P*) can be affected by any change in the money supply (*M*).

What does it mean for *Q* to be stable? The argument here is that the quantity of goods produced is primarily dependent on production capacity, labour market efficiency, and other "structural" forces. These structural forces establish a *"natural" rate of unemployment* that's fairly immune to short-run policy intervention. This is the *long-run* aggregate supply curve we first encountered in Chapter 8 (which simply reflects the production possibility curve—that output (*Q*) is constrained by the level of resources and technology available to the economy at any point in time.) From this perspective, there's no reason for producers to depart from this "natural" rate of output when the money supply increases. Producers are smart enough to know that both prices and costs will rise when spending increases. Hence, rising prices won't create any new profit incentives for increasing output. Firms will just continue producing at the "natural" rate with higher (nominal) prices and costs. As a result, increases in aggregate spending—whether financed by more *M* or faster *V*—aren't likely to alter real output levels. *Q* will stay constant.

As the "simple economics" in the accompanying cartoon suggests, a decrease in *M* should directly reduce the price level. When *M increases,* total spending rises, but the higher nominal value of spending is completely absorbed by higher prices. In this view, monetary policy affects only the rate of inflation.

Stable Velocity

"Natural" Unemployment

The Dropouts—Used by permission of Howard Post.

Analysis: If the money supply shrinks (or its growth rate slows), price levels will rise less quickly.

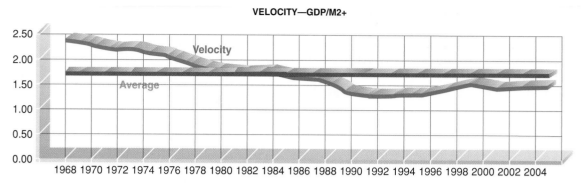

VELOCITY—GDP/M2+

FIGURE 13.13
The Velocity of M2+

The velocity of money (the ratio of GDP to M2+) has averaged about 1.73 in the period from 1968–2005. However, velocity seems to have declined somewhat over this period, with more noticeable declines during recessionary periods—see 1978–1981 and 1988–1992.

Source: Adapted from Statistics Canada CAMSIM database 176-0020 and CANSIM tables 380-0002, http://cansim2.statcan.ca, and calculations by the author. Statistics Canada information is used with the permission of Statisitics Canada.

Figure 13.14 illustrates the argument in the context of aggregate supply and demand. The assertion that real output is fixed at the production possibility curve—with the normal utilization of resources such as labour (implying a natural rate of unemployment)—is reflected in the vertical aggregate supply curve. With real output stuck at Q^*, any increase in aggregate demand directly raises the price level.

There are fundamental differences here, not only about how the economy works but also about how successful macro policy might be. To appreciate those differences, consider the responses to inflationary and recessionary gaps from an equation of exchange perspective.

Fighting Inflation. Consider again the options for fighting inflation. The objective of policy is to reduce aggregate spending. From a Keynesian perspective, the way to achieve this reduction is to shrink the money supply and drive up interest rates. But the counter argument is that nominal interest rates are already likely to be high. Furthermore, if an effective anti-inflation policy is adopted, interest rates will come *down*, not go up.

Real vs. Nominal Interest. To understand this conclusion, we have to distinguish between *nominal* interest rates and *real* ones. Nominal interest rates are the ones we

FIGURE 13.14
A Vertical Long-run Aggregate Supply Curve

The rate of real output is set by structural factors. Furthermore, firms aren't likely to be fooled into producing more just because prices are rising if costs are rising just as much. Hence, long-run aggregate supply remains at the "natural" level Q^*. Any increases in aggregate demand, therefore, raise the price level (inflation) but not output.

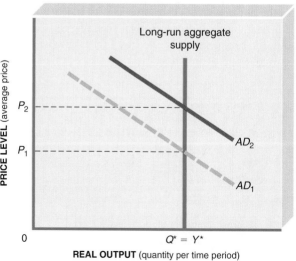

actually see and pay. When a bank pays 5½ percent interest on your bank account, it's quoting (and paying) a nominal rate.

Real interest rates are never actually seen and rarely quoted. These are "inflation-adjusted" rates. Specifically, the **real interest rate** equals the nominal rate *minus* the anticipated rate of inflation; that is,

$$\begin{matrix} \text{Real} & & \text{nominal} & & \text{anticipated} \\ \text{interest} & = & \text{interest} & - & \text{inflation} \\ \text{rate} & & \text{rate} & & \text{rate} \end{matrix}$$

Recall what inflation does to the purchasing power of the dollar: As inflation continues, each dollar purchases fewer goods and services. As a consequence, dollars borrowed today are of less real value when they're paid back later. The real rate of interest reflects this inflation adjustment.

Suppose you lend someone $100 at the beginning of the year, at 8 percent interest. You expect to get more back at the end of the year than you start with. That "more" you expect refers to *real* goods and services, not just dollar bills. Specifically, you anticipate that when the loan is repaid with interest at the end of the year, you'll be able to buy more goods and services than you could at the beginning. This expectation of a *real* gain is at least part of the reason for making a loan.

Your expected gain won't materialize, however, if all prices rise by 8 percent during the year. If the inflation rate is 8 percent, you'll discover that $108 buys you no more at the end of the year than $100 would have bought you at the beginning. Hence, you'd have given up the use of your money for an entire year without any real compensation. In such circumstances, the *real* rate of interest turns out to be zero; that is,

$$\begin{matrix} \text{Real} & & 8\% \text{ nominal} & & \\ \text{interest} & = & \text{interest} & - & 8\% \text{ inflation} \\ \text{rate} & & \text{rate} & & \text{rate} \end{matrix}$$

$$= 0\%$$

The nominal rate of interest, then, really has two components: (1) the real rate of interest, and (2) an inflation adjustment. If the real rate of interest was 4 percent and an inflation rate of 9 percent was expected, the nominal rate of interest would be 13 percent. If inflationary expectations *improved,* the *nominal* interest rate would *fall.* This is evident in the rearranged formula:[11]

$$\begin{matrix} \text{Nominal} & & \text{real} & & \text{anticipated rate} \\ \text{interest rate} & = & \text{interest rate} & + & \text{of inflation} \end{matrix}$$

If the real interest rate is 4 percent and anticipated inflation falls from 9 to 6 percent, the nominal interest rate would decline from 13 to 10 percent.

A central assumption of this perspective is that the real rate of interest is fairly stable. This is a critical point. ***If the real rate of interest is stable, then changes in the nominal interest rate reflect only changes in anticipated inflation.*** From this perspective, high nominal rates of interest are a symptom of inflation, not a cure.

Consider the implications of all this for monetary policy. Suppose we want to close an inflationary GDP gap. A reduced money supply (*M*) will deflate total spending. But Keynesians rely on a "quick fix" of *higher* interest rates to slow consumption and investment spending. Others, by contrast, assert that nominal interest rates will *fall* if the Bank of Canada tightens the money supply. Once market participants are convinced that the Bank is going to reduce money supply growth, inflationary expectations diminish. When inflationary expectations diminish, nominal interest rates will begin to fall.

real interest rate: The nominal rate of interest minus anticipated inflation rate.

---

[11]The formula given is known as the Fisher equation, named after Irving Fisher (1867–1947), and is an approximation of the actual value that is little different at low levels of inflation.

Short- vs. Long-Term Rates (again). The argument is supported by the different movements of short-term and long-term interest rates. As we observed earlier, short-run rates (like the target for the overnight rate) are very responsive to Bank of Canada intervention. But long-term rates are much slower to respond. This suggests that banks and borrowers look beyond current economic conditions in making long-term financial commitments.

If the Bank is reducing money-supply growth, short-term rates may rise quickly. But long-term rates won't increase unless market participants expect inflation to worsen. Given the pivotal role of long-term rates in investment decisions, the Bank may have to stall GDP growth—even spark a recession—to restrain aggregate demand enough to stop prices from rising. Rather than take such risks, *some economists advocate steady and predictable changes in the money supply.* Such a policy, they believe, would reduce uncertainties and thus stabilize both long-term interest rates and GDP growth.

Fighting Unemployment. The link between anticipated inflation and nominal interest rates also constrains expansionary monetary policy. The Keynesian cure for a recession is to expand M and lower interest rates. But if an increase in M will lead—via the equation of exchange—to higher P, and if everyone believed this would happen, then an unexpectedly large increase in M would immediately raise people's inflationary expectations. Even if short-term interest rates fell, long-term interest rates might actually rise. This would defeat the purpose of monetary stimulus.

From this perspective, expansionary monetary policies aren't likely to lead us out of a recession. On the contrary, such policies might double our burden by heaping inflation on top of our unemployment woes. The rate of real output and employment is more dependent on structural characteristics of the economy than on changes in the money supply. All monetary policy should do is ensure a stable and predictable rate of growth in the money supply. Then people could concentrate on real production decisions without worrying so much about fluctuating prices.

13.7 THE CONCERN FOR CONTENT

Monetary policy, like fiscal policy, can affect more than just the *level* of total spending. We must give some consideration to the impact of the Bank of Canada's actions on the *content* of the GDP if we're going to be responsive to the "second crisis" of economic theory.[12]

The Mix of Output

When interest rates change, not all spending decisions will be affected equally. Investment decisions that are highly sensitive to interest rates are more susceptible to monetary policy than others. The construction industry, especially the residential housing market, stands out in this respect. The sensitivity of housing costs to interest rate changes forces the construction industry to bear a disproportionate burden of restrictive monetary policy. Accordingly, when the Bank of Canada pursues a policy of tight money—high interest rates and limited lending capacity—it not only restrains total spending but reduces the share of housing in that spending. Utility industries, public works projects, and provincial and local finances are also disproportionately affected by monetary policy.

In addition to altering the content of demand and output, monetary policy affects the competitive structure of the market. When money is tight, banks must ration available credit among loan applicants. Large and powerful corporations aren't likely to run out of credit because banks will be hesitant to incur their displeasure and lose their business. Thus, General Motors and IBM stand a much better chance of obtaining

---

[12]See the quotation from Joan Robinson in Chapter 10, calling attention to the exclusive focus of economists on the *level* of economic activity (the "first crisis"), to the neglect of content (the "second crisis").

tight money than does the corner grocery store. Moreover, if bank lending capacity becomes too small, GM and IBM can always resort to the bond market and borrow money directly from the public. Small businesses seldom have such an alternative.

Monetary policy also affects the distribution of income. When interest rates fall, borrowers pay smaller interest charges. On the other hand, lenders get smaller interest payments. Hence, a lower interest rate redistributes income from lenders to borrowers. When interest rates declined sharply in 2001, homeowners refinanced their mortgages and saved billions of dollars in interest payments. The decline in interest rates, however, *reduced* the income of retired persons, who depend heavily on interest payments from certificates of deposit, bonds, and other assets.

Income Redistribution

SUMMARY

- The essence of monetary policy lies in the Bank of Canada's control over the money supply. By altering the physical money available in the economy, the Bank can influence the purchasing power available to the economy.

- There are sharp disagreements about the relative effectiveness of monetary versus fiscal policy. Some economists argue that monetary policy is a more effective policy tool than fiscal policy; others contend the reverse is true.

- The responsibility of the Bank of Canada can be summarized as (1) act as Canada's monetary policy authority; (2) design and issue Canada's official currency; (3) promote a safe and stable financial system; and (4) act as the federal government's banker.

- Beginning in February 1991, and recently extended to December 2011, the policy goal of the Bank of Canada is to maintain an inflation-control target of 2 percent within an operating range of 1 to 3 percent.

- The Bank of Canada exercises control over the money supply through two monetary policy tools: (1) re-depositing government funds either into or out of the commercial banking system; or (2) open-market operations: the buying and selling of bonds between the Bank of Canada and the commericial banking system.

- Open-market operations are the main monetary policy tool: when the Bank of Canada buys bonds from the public, it increases money reserves in the commercial banking system. When the Bank sells bonds to the public, it decreases reserves in the commercial banking system.

- The Bank of Canada implements monetary policy by changing its target for the overnight rate and influencing other short-term interest rates.

- The monetary transmission mechanism illustrates the impact of monetary policy on the "real" economy. The impact can arise from both changes in expenditure from households, government, and investors resulting from a change in the domestic interest rate and from a change in net exports resulting from a change in the domestic exchange rate.

- Monetary policy can be operated in sympathy with fiscal policy or separately. If monetary policy follows fiscal policy, any inflationary pressure is accentuated. If operated separately, the intended fiscal policy outcome can sustain some level of crowding out.

- Monetary policy is constrained by: (1) the relationship between short and long term rates; (2) the reluctance of lenders to lend; (3) the existence of a liquidity trap; (4) public expectations; (5) "lags" in the effectiveness of monetary policy; and (6) global sources of money.

- The impact of monetary policy is subject to "long and variable lags" that may be as long as 18–24 months or 6–8 quarters before it is fully integrated into the economy.

- The neutrality of money emphasizes long term linkages. Using the equation of exchange ($M \times V = P \times Q$), and assuming that the velocity of money (V) and the production possibilities of an economy (Q) are stable, at least in the short run, changes in the money supply, (M) will directly affect the price level in the economy (P).

Key Terms

inflation-control target   262
sterilization   263
bond   265
yield   266
open-market operations   266

target for the overnight rate   268
prime rate   268
monetary transmission
   mechanism   271

liquidity trap   277
equation of exchange   280
velocity of money (V)   280
real interest rate   283

Questions for Discussion

1. Why do "high" interest rates so adversely affect the demand for housing and yet have so little influence on the demand for pizzas?

2. If the Bank of Canada mailed everyone a brand new $100 bill, what would happen to the price level (P) and output in the real economy (GDP)?

3. Can there be any inflation without an increase in the money supply? How?

4. How might the existence of money multiplier effects increase the risk of inflation when the target for the overnight rate is reduced?

5. On September 18, 2007, the United States Federal Reserve (the Fed) reduced their key interest rate by ½ percent (50 basis points) to offset problems arising from a "credit crunch." How might this monetary policy decision result in more credit in the market?

6. Could long term interest rates rise when short term rates are falling? What would cause such a pattern?

7. How did the Bank of Japan hope to increase the money supply in 2001? (See the World View, page 278). If *M* did increase, would the economy necessarily recover?

8. Why did China raise reserve requirements in 2004? How did they expect consumers and businesses to respond? (See the World View, page 270).

9. In the October 2006 *Monetary Policy Report Summary,* the Bank of Canada suggested that the Canadian economy was operating slightly above its potential. How could the Bank use open-market operations to bring the economy back to potential?

10. The Bank of Canada has had price stability as its policy goal (an inflation target of 2 percent per year within an oeprating range of 1 to 3 percent) since 1991 and recently renewed through 2011. The climb of the Canadian dollar towards parity with the U.S. dollar has prompted many in export industries (such as lumber and automobiles) to call on the Bank of Canada to reduce the exchange rate. Why are these two goals incompatible?

EXERCISES

PROBLEMS The Student Problem Set to accompany this chapter can be found at the end of the book.

WEB ACTIVITIES Web Activities to accompany this chapter can be found on the Online Learning Centre at **http://www.mcgrawhill.ca/olc/schiller**.

PART 5

Short-Run Aggregate Supply and Short Run Policy Options

he purpose of fiscal and monetary policy is to alter macroeconomic outcomes—national income, unemployment, inflation, economic growth, or international balances (the exchange rate or foreign reserves). So far, this discussion has mainly focused on managing aggregate demand (AD). We need to now fill in a little more of the puzzle by moving the focus to the short run aggregate supply (SRAS) curve—supply-side policies—and how shifts of the SRAS curve impact these outcomes. In the short run, any increase (shift right) in the short run aggregate supply promotes more output and less inflation. Supply-side policy also emphasizes the connection between the short and long runs and notes that aggregate supply is critical to long run economic growth.

Chapter 14 takes a look at the theory underlying supply-side policy recommendations.

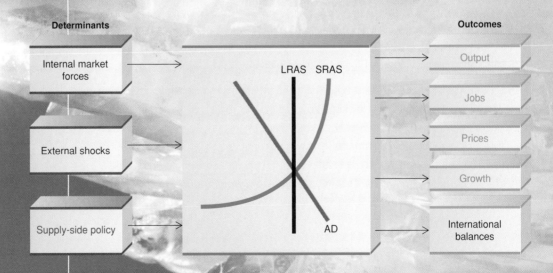

Aggregate Supply and Supply-Side Economics

I n Chapter 7, "Growth and Productivity," we connected the production possibility curve, PPC, with the long run aggregate supply (LRAS) curve. This suggested that, for long-run, economic growth (increasing the potential of the economy), the economy needed to add additional resources and/or technology (productivity). The long-run constraint on the economy's potential was again illustrated in Chapter 8, "Aggregate Supply and Aggregate Demand," through the strictly vertical long run aggregate supply curve.

However, as we approached our discussion of policy and policy implications, our attention focused entirely on aggregate demand, AD. This "demand-side" focus was the consequence of the Keynesian revolution that began in the 1930s and fully took hold after 1945. Keynesian policy was operated through the management of aggregate demand in the real economy and was a response to the economic conditions that were faced by policy-makers.

The impetus for examining the short-run aggregate supply (SRAS) curve of the macro economy sprang up in the "stagflation" of the 1970s. The prevailing policy prescriptions and Keynesian approach to the macro economy no longer seemed able to provide appropriate policy direction. Robert E. Lucas (University of Chicago) and Thomas J. Sargent (New York University) wrote in 1978 that:

> Existing Keynesian macroeconometric models are incapable of providing reliable guidance in formulating monetary, fiscal, and other types of policy. This conclusion is based in part on the spectacular recent failure of these models . . .[1]

Stagflation exists when both unemployment and inflation are increasing at the same time. Between 1972 and 1983, for example, inflation—as measured by the consumer price index, CPI, varied from approximately 6 percent to over 12 percent from an annual rate of less than 3 percent in 1971. Over this same period, the unemployment rate rose from a little more than 6 percent to over 12 percent. How could this happen? *No shift of the aggregate demand curve can increase inflation and unemployment at the same time.*

LEARNING OBJECTIVES

By the end of this chapter, you should be able to:

14.1 Describe the formation of expectations

14.2 Explain the impact of expectations on macroeconomic outcomes

14.3 Illustrate an inflation–unemployment trade-off in an AD/AS framework

14.4 Describe the "expectations augmented" Phillips Curve

14.5 Explain the impact of a shift of the short run aggregate supply curve

14.6 Describe the policy levers emphasized for the SRAS curve

[1] As reproduced in B. Snowdon and H.R. Vane, *Modern Macroeconomics: Its Origins, Development and Current State,* (Massachusetts: Edward Elgar Publishing, 2005), p. 219.

If aggregate demand increases (shifts right), the price level may rise but unemployment should decline with increased economic activity. If aggregate demand decreases (shifts left) inflation should subside but unemployment increase. In other words, most demand-side theories predict that inflation and unemployment move in opposite directions in the short run.

When this didn't happen, an alternative explanation was sought. The explanation was found on the supply-side of the macro economy—referred to as a "new classical counter revolution"—and summarized through three central tenets:

1. That participants in the economy—households and firms, for instance—are able to form accurate expectations about the future and will then act on those expectations.
2. That participants in the labour market—workers and firms—respond only to changes in relative prices and not simply to changes in nominal prices.
3. A return to the "market clearing" perspective of classical theory. That is, that the macro economy (like a micro economy) will return to its equilibrium position relatively quickly following any disturbance.[2]

Any policies that alter the willingness or ability to supply goods at various price levels will shift the short run aggregate supply curve. This chapter identifies some of those policy options and examines how they affect macro outcomes. As we'll see, the short run aggregate supply curve plays a critical role in determining how difficult it is to achieve the goals of full employment and price stability in the short run while the long run aggregate supply curve acts as the economy's level of sustainable long-run total output. The focus, then, will be on the following two questions:

- *How does the short run aggregate supply curve affect macroeconomic outcomes?*
- *How can the aggregate supply curves be shifted?*

We begin this chapter by taking a closer look at the formation of expectations and the implications of these expectations when economy participants act upon them. The following section will look at the response of workers and firms and the connection of inflation and unemployment in the macro economy. This analysis is referred to as an expectations augmented Phillips curve.

The third section of the chapter will revisit the modern view of the AD/AS model and review the long-run aggregate supply and aggregate demand curves to establish context and then turn our attention to the shape of the short run aggregate supply curve as well as how the response of households and firms to changes in AD might be reflected in changes to the position of the SRAS curve. This discussion provides perspective on the last of the three "new classical" tenets given above.

Finally, we will identify policies that are emphasized in new classical theory to shift the SRAS curve (and the LRAS curve) in the desired, rightward, direction.

> **stagflation:** The simultaneous occurrence of substantial unemployment and inflation.

14.1 EXPECTATIONS AND MACROECONOMIC OUTCOMES

Expectations play a crucial role not only in consumer behaviour but also in the behaviour of firms in the economy with respect to their decisions about production and investment and their willingness and ability to supply output at various prices. If producers expect more "business-friendly" government policies, they may be willing to invest in more plant and equipment. In contrast, the prospect of increasing government regulation or higher taxes deters investors from expanding production capacity.

---

[2]B. Snowdon and H.R Vane, *Modern Macroeconomics: Its Origins, Development and Current State,* (Massachusetts: Edward Elgar Publishing, 2005), p. 223.

Hence, expectations can affect not only the shape of the short run aggregate supply curve, but also its position. And it is this second impact—the position of the curve—that we are most interested in here.

Keynes' approach to expectations was to see them as dependent on the past rather than focused on an uncertain future. Therefore, current policies didn't change current expectations and the expectations themselves were formed unsystematically. In fact, Keynes described expectations as arising from "animal spirits":

> There is the instability due to the characteristic of human nature that a large proportion of our positive activities depend on spontaneous optimism rather than on a mathematical expectation, whether moral or hedonistic or economic. Most, probably, of our decisions to do something positive, the full consequences of which will be drawn out over many days to come, can only be taken as a result of animal spirits—of a spontaneous urge to action rather than inaction.[3]

If expectations are formed unsystematically, then there can be no systematic change in consumer or firm behaviour as a result of current policy. Rather, participants will only alter their own behaviour after an economic phenomena—such as inflation—has already occurred. Such a *backward-looking approach* to forming expectations is also referred to as **adaptive expectations.**

The emergence of new classical economics as a force in macroeconomics in the 1970s also added a new perspective on both the formation of expectations by households and firms and on the impact that expectations have in the economy generally and on the effectiveness of demand-oriented policy.

New classical economists saw decision makers as being rational, and able to accurately predict the future state of the economy. The term given to this assumption was **rational expectations.** Having formed these expectations, households and firms would then act on these expectations, altering macroeconomic outcomes by altering their behaviour.

Figure 14.1 illustrates how the rational expectations of economic participants can impact the effectiveness of aggregate demand management policy. For example, suppose that an increase in government spending, fiscal policy, shifts the aggregate demand curve from AD_0 to AD_1. As we have seen before, the result would be an increase in national income, Y to Y_1. What we also see is that prices would also rise. If suppliers perceive this rise in price to be a rise in the relative price of their good, then they would be willing to increase production to satisfy the new aggregate demand (AD_1). However, if suppliers fully understand the impact of this policy, they would recognize that it is only a change in nominal prices, and that they would expect nominal wages and other input prices to also rise. This prompts a "correction" of the SRAS curve, from $SRAS_0$ to $SRAS_1$. The final result is that the economy remains at potential national income, Y^*, but the economy has sustained a bout of inflation, raising the price level in the economy from P_0 to P_1.

The implication of the general upward-sloping shape of the short run aggregate supply curve is that any shift of the aggregate demand curve will result in both an increase in output as well as an increase in the price level, or inflation. If we then add rational expectations to the mix, where suppliers respond to the fiscal stimulus as an inward shift of the SRAS curve, the final result is only inflationary pressure in the economy, with no gain in national income.

As we've seen, the basic short-run objective of fiscal and monetary policy is to attain full employment and price stability. The strategy is to shift the aggregate demand

adaptive (backward-looking) expectations: Expectations of the future that are formed from past experience, adapted by the difference between the expected value and actual value (the error of the estimate).

rational expectations: Hypothesis that people's spending decisions are based on all available information, including the anticipated effects of government intervention.

[3]J.M. Keynes, "Chapter 12, The State of Long Term Expectation, Part VII," *The General Theory of Employment, Interest and Money,* http://etext.library.adelaide.edu.au/k/keynes/john_maynard/k44g/chapter12.html.

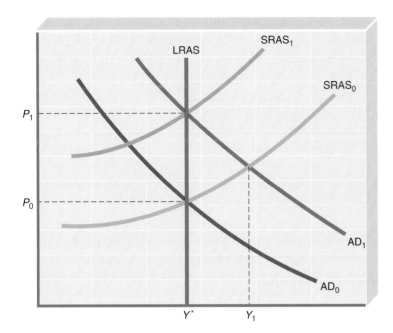

FIGURE 14.1
The SRAS Curve with Fully Rational Expectations

Since firms "rationally expect" input prices to rise along with output prices (only a change in nominal prices rather than relative prices) the SRAS curve shifts inward to $SRAS_1$ and the economy remains at Y^* with a higher price level, P_1

curve to a more favourable position. Now the question turns to the *response* of producers to an aggregate demand shift. Will they increase real output? Raise prices? Or some combination of both?

14.2 THE INFLATION-UNEMPLOYMENT TRADE-OFF

Until now we've used the upward-sloping SRAS curve depicted in Figure 14.1 to characterize producer behaviour. Because it allows for varying output/price responses at different levels of economic activity, this SRAS curve is generally regarded as the most realistic for short-run outcomes. However, even if expectations are not fully rational and there is a delay in the supplier correction, the upward-sloping section of the SRAS curve has some disturbing implications. Because both prices and output respond to aggregate demand-side shifts, the economy can't both increase employment and maintain price stability at the same time—at least not with fiscal and monetary policy. Consider the simple geometry of policy stimulus and policy restraint.

Demand Stimulus. Monetary and fiscal stimulus shift the aggregate demand curve rightward. This is the aggregate demand-side effect evident in Figure 14.1. However, *all rightward shifts of the aggregate demand curve increase both prices and output if the aggregate supply curve is upward-sloping.* This implies that fiscal and monetary efforts to reduce unemployment will also cause some inflation.

Demand Restraint. Monetary and fiscal restraint shift the aggregate demand curve leftward. *If the aggregate supply curve is upward-sloping, leftward shifts of the aggregate demand curve cause both prices and output to fall.* Therefore, fiscal and monetary efforts to reduce inflation will also increase unemployment. Consider the aggregate demand curve in Figure 14.1 shifting from AD_1 to AD_0.

FIGURE 14.2
The Phillips Curve

The Phillips curve illustrates a trade-off between full employment and price stability. In the 1960s it appeared that efforts to reduce unemployment rates below 5.5 percent (point *C*) led to increasing rates of inflation (points *A* and *B*). Inflation threatened to reach unacceptable heights long before everyone was employed.

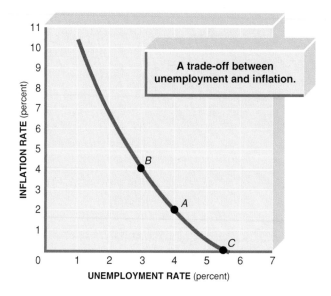

Phillips curve: A historical (inverse) relationship between the rate of unemployment and the rate of inflation; commonly expresses a trade-off between the two.

The Phillips Curve. The message of the upward-sloping aggregate supply curve is clear: *Demand-side policies alone can never succeed completely; they'll always cause some unwanted inflation or unemployment.*

Our macro track record provides ample evidence of this dilemma. Consider, for example, our experience with unemployment and inflation during the 1960s, as shown in Figure 14.2. This figure shows a **Phillips curve,** indicating that prices generally started rising before the objective of expanded output had been completely attained. Inflation struck before full employment was reached.

The Phillips curve was developed by the New Zealand economist, Alban W. Phillips, to summarize the relationship between unemployment and inflation in England for the years 1826–1957.[4] Few ideas in economics became as central to policy-making as the "notion of a trade-off between inflation and the underemployment of (labour) resources."[5] The Phillips curve was raised from the status of an obscure graph to that of a policy issue by the discovery that a similar relationship apparently existed in other countries and at other times. Suppose, for instance, that an unemployment rate of 4 percent was likely to be accompanied by an inflation rate of 2 percent. This relationship is expressed by point *A* in Figure 14.2. By contrast, lower rates of unemployment were associated with higher rates of inflation, as at point *B*. Alternatively, complete price stability appeared attainable only at the cost of an unemployment rate of 5.5 percent (point *C*). A seesaw kind of relationship existed between inflation and unemployment: When one went up, the other fell.

The trade-off between unemployment and inflation originates in the upward-sloping SRAS curve. Figure 14.3*a* illustrates this point. Suppose the economy is initially at equilibrium *A*, with fairly stable prices but low output. When aggregate demand expands to AD₂, prices rise along with output, so we end up with higher inflation but less unemployment. This is also shown in Figure 14.3*b* by the move from point *a* to point *b* on the Phillips curve. The move from point *a* to point *b* indicates a decline in unemployment (more output) but an increase in inflation (higher price level). If

---

[4]A. W. Phillips. "The Relationship Between Unemployment and the Rate of Change of Money Wage Rates in the United Kingdom, 1826–1957," *Economica* (November 1958). Phillips's paper studied the relationship between unemployment and *wage* changes rather than *price* changes; most later formulations (and public policy) focus on prices.

[5]J. C. R. Rowley. and D. A. Wilton, "Empirical Foundations for the Canadian Phillips Curve," *Canadian Journal of Economics* 7 no. 2 (May 1974), pp. 240–259.

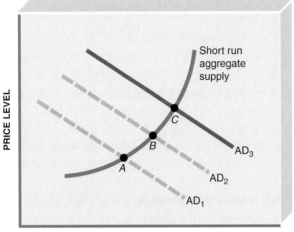

(*a*) Increases in aggregate demand cause . . .

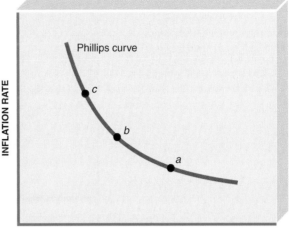

(*b*) A trade-off between unemployment and inflation.

FIGURE 14.3
The Phillips Curve Trade-Off

If the aggregate supply curve slopes upward, increases in aggregate demand always cause both prices and output to rise. Thus, higher inflation becomes a cost of achieving lower unemployment. In (*a*), increased demand moves the economy from point *A* to point *B*. At *B*, unemployment is lower, but prices are higher. This trade-off is illustrated on the Phillips curve in (*b*). Each point on the Phillips curve represents a different AS/AD equilibrium from the graph on the left.

demand is increased further, to AD_3, a still lower unemployment rate is achieved but at the cost of higher inflation (point *c*).

Rowley and Wilton's review of studies on a Canadian Phillips curve (see footnote 5 on page 292) suggests the following consensus: first, a relationship between inflation and unemployment appears to exist; but, second, the relationship isn't necessarily stable over time. The breakdown of the Phillips curve relationship in the 1970s was characterized by the stagflation experience we described in the opening to this chapter. The Canadian economy experienced both high unemployment and high inflation. One approach to explaining this result was the inclusion of expectations changing behaviour in the economy and the existence of a "natural rate" of unemployment.

As illustrated by point *C* in Figure 14.2, price stability was associated with a rate of unemployment of 5.5 percent. This "natural rate" (or the non-accelerating inflation rate of unemployment, NAIRU) is the rate the economy will tend towards. Figure 14.4 illustrates the Phillips curve relationship with the natural rate. At point *c* the economy has a rate of unemployment consistent with the natural rate and price stability—no inflationary pressure. A fiscal stimulus that shifts the aggregate demand curve to the right initially increases national income, Y, and therefore unemployment, to point *b*, but also initiates inflation. Since the resulting inflation is expected by participants in the economy, the Phillips curve shifts upward to point *d*. Unemployment remains unchanged at the "natural rate," but the economy now has a "new normal" expectation of inflation.

In a later study, Pierre Fortin suggested that the institutional arrangements within a country could have important effects on the inflation–unemployment relationship, noting that his "own work has identified effects of demography, minimum wages, and employment insurance in the Canadian context."[6]

---

[6]Pierre Fortin, "The Phillips curve, macroeconomic policy, and the welfare of Canadians," *Canadian Journal of Economics* 24, no 4 (November 1991) pp. 774–803.

FIGURE 14.4
Expectations Augmented Phillips Curve

Expectations result in the Phillips curve shifting upward, where inflation exists in the economy but the rate of unemployment remains unchanged at the natural rate.

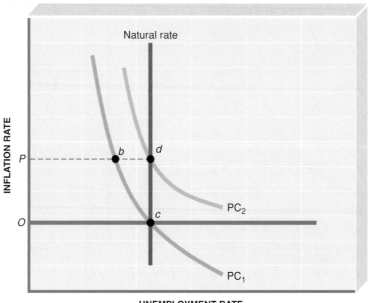

14.3 SHIFTS OF THE SHORT RUN AGGREGATE SUPPLY CURVE

The breakdown of an inflation-unemployment trade-off implied by incorporating a natural rate with rational expectations seemed to spell the end for reducing unemployment as a policy goal. Many economists argued, however, that the economy can attain lower levels of unemployment without initiating higher inflation. This certainly appeared to be the case in the 1990s. Beginning in about 1994, unemployment fell from a high of 11.4 percent to below 7.0 percent by 2000 and to 6.1 percent by the end of 2006, with inflation remaining more or less constant. How could this happen? There is no aggregate demand shift that can reduce both unemployment and inflation.

Rightward AS Shifts: All Good News

Only a rightward shift of the SRAS curve can reduce unemployment and inflation at the same time. When the short run aggregate supply increases from $SRAS_1$ to $SRAS_2$ in Figure 14.5, macro equilibrium moves from E_1 to E_2. At E_2 real output is higher, so the unemployment rate must be lower. At E_2 the price level is also lower, indicating reduced inflation. Hence, a rightward shift of the SRAS curve offers the best of two worlds—something aggregate *demand* shifts (Figure 14.1) can't do.

FIGURE 14.5
Shifts of the Short Run Aggregate Supply Curve

A rightward shift of the SRAS curve ($SRAS_1$ to $SRAS_2$) reduces both unemployment and inflation. A leftward shift has the opposite effect, resulting in stagflation.

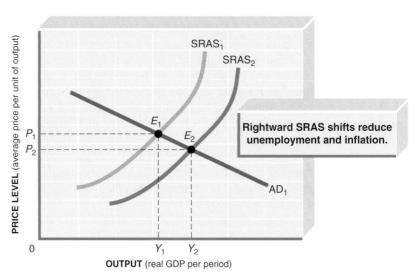

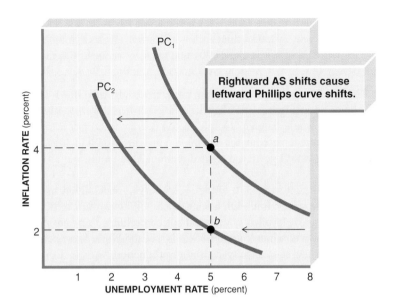

FIGURE 14.6
A Phillips Curve Shift

If the Phillips curve shifts leftward, the short-run unemployment inflation trade-off eases. With PC₁, 5 percent unemployment ignites 4 percent inflation (point *a*). With PC₂, 5 percent unemployment causes only 2 percent inflation (point *b*).

Phillips Curve Shift. As we saw in Figure 14.3, the Phillips curve is a direct by-product of the SRAS curve. Accordingly, ***When the SRAS curve shifts, the Phillips curve shifts as well.*** As Figure 14.6 illustrates, the Phillips curve shifts to the left, the opposite of the SRAS shift in Figure 14.5. No new information is conveyed here. The Phillips curve simply focuses more directly on the implied change in the unemployment–inflation trade-off. ***When the Phillips curve shifts to the left, the unemployment–inflation trade-off eases.***

The Misery Index. To keep track of simultaneous changes in unemployment and inflation, Arthur Okun (1928–1980), a U.S. economist, developed what he referred to as a "discomfort index." Others renamed it a "misery index." The misery index is simply the sum of the annual rate of inflation and unemployment rate. Figure 14.7 illustrates a Canadian misery index. Beginning with the stagflation in the 1970s, the index reached a peak of almost 22 percent by 1982. Since that time, the index has fallen to, and remained near 10 percent, with the exception of the recessionary period of 1989 to 1991 when it spiked above 15 percent.

The Great Divide

Analysis: Leftward shifts of the short run aggregate supply curve push price levels up and output down. The remedy for such stagflation is a rightward shift of aggregate supply.

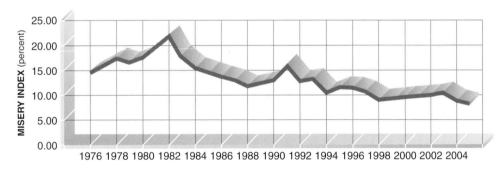

FIGURE 14.7
Canada's Misery Index

Stagflation in the 1970s was characterized by high inflation and high unemployment. The misery index illustrates this, reaching a peak in 1982 of almost 22 percent. With the exception of a spike to over 15 percent during the 1989–1991 recessionary period, the index has remained fairly stable at about 10 percent.

Source: Part of data is adapted from Statistics Canada, CANSIM database table 362–0002 and table 282–0002. http://cansim2.statcan.ca. Statistics Canada information is used with the permission of Statistics Canada.

The reduction in the Canadian misery index can be attributed both to the success of the Bank of Canada's focus on inflation (and inflation-control targets) from 1991, and strong economic growth beginning in the 1990s that steadily reduced the rate of unemployment to a 30-year low of 6.1 percent by December, 2006.

Leftward SRAS Shifts: All Bad News

WEB NOTE

To see information on the misery index in the United States and its potential link to the crime rate, check out Wikipedia at http://en.wikipedia.org/wiki/Misery_index_(economics).

Whereas rightward SRAS shifts appear to be a dream come true, leftward SRAS shifts are a real nightmare. Imagine in Figure 14.5 that the SRAS shift is reversed, that is, from SRAS$_2$ to SRAS$_1$. What would happen? Output would decrease and prices would rise, exactly the kind of dilemma depicted in the accompanying cartoon on the previous page. In other words, nothing would go in the right direction. This would be rampant stagflation.

A natural disaster can trigger a leftward shift of the SRAS curve, especially in smaller nations. In 2003, an earthquake struck Iran with a vengeance, killing upward of 40,000 people. In addition, the earthquake levelled homes and office buildings, tore up roads and water systems, and shut down communications networks (see the World View below). This supply-side shock diminished the capacity for future production.

In a larger, more diversified economy like that of Canada, leftward shifts of the short run aggregate supply curve are less dramatic. When the Organization of Petroleum Exporting Countries (OPEC) abruptly raised oil prices in the 1970s, or today as world economic growth and emerging economies such as India and China have raised oil prices, many industries experience higher production costs that reduce the ability and willingness to supply output at given price levels. The end result is an increase in both inflation and unemployment. Oil shocks also divert consumer spending from domestic goods and services to imported oil (a form of circular flow leakage). This kind of external shock contributed to the big increase in macro misery during the years 1975–1982.

The September 11, 2001, terrorist attacks on the World Trade Center and Pentagon in the United States were another form of external shock. The attacks directly destroyed some production capacity (office space, telecommunications links, transportation links). But they took an even greater toll on the *willingness* to supply goods and services. In the aftermath of the attacks, businesses, perceiving new risks to investment and production, held back from making new commitments. Increased security measures also made transporting goods more expensive. All of these responses shifted the SRAS curve leftward and the Phillips curve rightward, adding to macro misery.

WORLD VIEW

Quake Victims Snatch Up Aid As Death Toll Reaches 28,000

BAM, Iran—Survivors of Iran's earthquake scavenged the rubble for their battered belongings and desperately jostled for aid handouts Tuesday as some officials speculated the death toll could reach 50,000.

While the chief U.N. official in Bam, Ted Peran, put the death toll at 28,000, Iranian President Mohammad Khatami said it was expected to climb above 30,000 — roughly a third of the city's population. Other government officials said they feared more than 50,000 had been killed. At least 12,000 people were injured in the earthquake, which had a magnitude of 6.6. . . .

Along the ruined streets of Bam, crowds of people surrounded aid trucks. Women in black chadors, some carrying infants, scrambled for old clothes tossed from the back of a truck. Some young men tried to clamber onto the truck to help themselves, but they were pushed back.

Others scavenged in the rubble in search of their belongings. One man extracted a pair of trousers and a bottle of water from a pile of rocks where his house used to be.

—Matthew Pennington,
The Associated Press

Source: *Associated Press*, December 29, 2003. Reprinted with permission of the Associated Press.

Analysis: A natural disaster that destroys both human and physical capital shifts the aggregate supply curve to the left, reducing output and raising price levels.

14.4 POLICY LEVERS FOR THE SRAS CURVE

From the supply side of macro markets, the appropriate response to negative external shocks is clear: shift the SRAS curve rightward. As the forgoing graphs have demonstrated, *rightward shifts of the aggregate supply curve always generate desirable macro outcomes.* The next question, of course, is how to shift the aggregate supply curve in the desired (rightward) direction. Supply-side economists look for clues among the forces that influence the supply-side response to changes in demand. Among those forces, the following policy options have been emphasized:

- Tax incentives for saving, investment, and work.
- Human capital investment.
- Deregulation.
- Trade liberalization.
- Infrastructure development.

All these policies have the potential to change supply decisions *independently* of any changes in aggregate demand. If they're effective, they'll result in a rightward shift of the aggregate supply curve and an *improved* trade-off between unemployment and inflation.

Although we've talked explicitly of technological advancement as a long run determinant of economic growth, each of these policies can also be connected to better technology. Investment in new machinery can increase the productivity of machines; a more educated workforce (human capital investment) can result in more productive labour. Deregulation and trade liberalization—between provinces as well as between countries—can increase competitive pressure to become more productive, and new infrastructure can move goods, services, and factors of production to where they are required. The important role of innovation and entrepreneurship is the focus of the Applications box on page 300.

Tax Incentives

The most talked-about supply-side policy option for improving the unemployment–inflation trade-off is tax cuts. Both the February 2000 federal budget and the October 2000 budget update announced a series of tax reductions:

> Canadians have one more reason to celebrate New Year's Day.
>
> On January 1, 2001, new federal tax cuts come into effect as part of the Government's $100-billion Five-Year Tax Reduction Plan—the largest tax cut in Canada's history.[7]

These tax cuts included reductions in personal income tax that will leave Canadians with "more money in their pockets," and reductions to business taxes to spur greater entrepreneurship and competitiveness "to secure a more prosperous future for Canadians." Tax cuts are, of course, a staple of Keynesian economics. *In Keynesian economics, tax cuts are used to increase aggregate demand.* By putting more disposable income in the hands of consumers, Keynesian economists seek to increase expenditure on goods and services. Output is expected to increase in response. From a Keynesian perspective, the form of the tax cut is not very important, as long as disposable income increases.

But the importance of tax cuts take on a whole new role on the supply side of the economy as **tax incentives.** Taxes not only alter disposable income but also affect the incentives to work and produce. High tax rates destroy the incentives to work and produce, so they end up reducing total output. Low tax rates, by contrast, allow people to keep more of what they earn and so stimulate greater output. *The direct effects of taxes on the supply of goods are the concern of supply-side economists.* Figure 14.8 shows the difference between demand-side and supply-side perspectives on tax policy.

tax incentives: Changes in tax policy that can lead to changes in the behavior of labour and producers by altering the "incentives" for particular behaviours.

---

[7]Department of Finance, Canada, http://www.fin.gc.ca/toce/2000/update01-1e.html, accessed February 8, 2007.

FIGURE 14.8

Two Theories for Getting the Economy Moving

Keynesians and supply-siders both advocate cutting taxes to reduce unemployment. But they have very different views on the kind of tax cuts required and the impact of any cuts enacted.

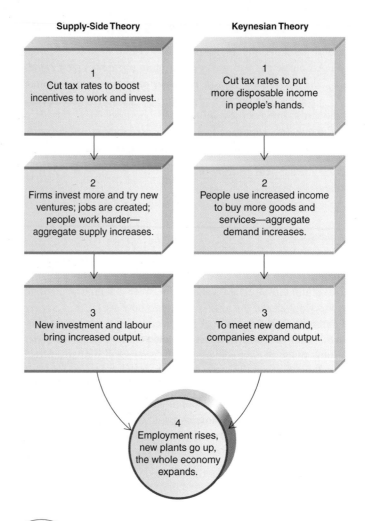

Supply-Side Theory

1 Cut tax rates to boost incentives to work and invest.

2 Firms invest more and try new ventures; jobs are created; people work harder—aggregate supply increases.

3 New investment and labour bring increased output.

Keynesian Theory

1 Cut tax rates to put more disposable income in people's hands.

2 People use increased income to buy more goods and services—aggregate demand increases.

3 To meet new demand, companies expand output.

4 Employment rises, new plants go up, the whole economy expands.

APPLICATIONS

A Decimated Sector Becomes a Footnote

It's almost a miracle that Genfast Manufacturing Co. was able to hang on so long. The maker of car engine bolts in Brantford, Ont. had been facing intense pressure from the auto sector to lower its prices. The soaring Canadian dollar took a huge chunk out of its sales. Asian competitors were breathing down its neck.

Genfast's experience of hanging on by its finger nails is the story of manufactures in Central Canada. As the Canadian dollar has appreciated, the number of plant closings and layoffs has climbed too. The sector is being decimated.

Jay Myers, chief economist for the Canadian Manufactures & Exporters [Association], looks to Germany for inspiration. Like Ontario and Quebec, manufacturing is central to its economy, and Germany, too, has been dealing with a strong currency.

And yet, manufacturing is surging ahead there, driving strong economic growth through exports of goods to Asia, of all places, Mr. Myers points out.

"The reason is, they're extremely innovative, and their goods sell on their quality and engineering," he said. He believes global forces will push Canadian firms in that direction too, rather than kill them off. "People wrote off manufacturing in 1990, and said we'd be a services economy. And what they found is that manufacturing is versatile."

Source: Heather Scoffield, "A decimated sector becomes a footnote," *The Globe and Mail* (June 30, 2007) p. B4. Reprinted with permission from *The Globe and Mail*.

Analysis: Canada is a large exporting country, and Canadian manufacturers are sensitive to changes in the exchange rate of the Canadian dollar. When the dollar rises, it makes Canadian goods more expensive, as with Genfast. However, the competitive pressures and less expensive imports of new capital and technology can enhance productivity.

Federal Government 2006	(%)
Up to $35,595	15.50
$35,595 up to $71,190	22.00
$71,190 up to $115,739	26.00
over $115,739	29.00

Provincial Governments 2007	Lowest %	Highest %
British Columbia	5.70	14.70
Alberta	10.00	10.00
Saskatchewan	11.00	15.00
Manitoba	10.90	17.40
Ontario	6.05	11.16
Quebec	16.00	24.00
New Brunswick	10.12	17.95
Nova Scotia	8.79	17.50
Prince Edward Island	9.80	16.70
Newfoundland	10.57	18.02

Sources: Federal tax rates: the actual rate for the lowest tax bracket for 2006 is the average of a 15 percent rate for January to June (from the November 2005 *Economic and Fiscal Update*), and a 15.5 rate established in the May 2006 *Federal Budget*, or 15.25 percent. Provincial tax rates: Alberta Government, "Major provincial tax rates, 2007," *Budget 2007*, http://www.finance.gov. ab.ca/publications/budget/budget2007/tax.html#major_provincial, accessed July 11, 2007.

TABLE 14.1

Federal and Provincial Government Marginal Personal Income Tax Rates

To calculate the combined rate, simply add together the federal and appropriate provincial marginal tax rates. For instance, the lowest rate in Saskatchewan would be 15.50 + 11.00 = 26.50 percent while the highest would be 44.00 percent (29.00 + 15.00). (Note that these rates don't include any surtaxes that are added in Ontario, Nova Scotia, Prince Edward Island, and Newfoundland).

Marginal Tax Rates. Supply-side theory places special emphasis on *marginal* tax rates. The **marginal tax rate** is the tax rate imposed on the last (marginal) dollar of income received. In our progressive income tax system, marginal tax rates increase as more income is received.

Canadian governments take a larger share out of each additional dollar earned as income rises from one level to the next. Table 14.1 shows the federal government's personal income marginal tax rates for 2006[8] and a comparison of the lowest and highest provincial marginal tax rates for 2007. In the 2000 federal budget, the middle marginal tax rate of 26 percent was reduced to 23 percent over five years. The November 2005 economic and fiscal update further reduced the lowest rate to 15 percent and the May 2006 budget revised the lowest rate to 15.5 percent.

While many provinces have acted to reduce their marginal tax rates for both personal income and corporate profits, it is important to note that some of these reductions have been offset by increases in provincial user fees. So although the personal/corporate income tax burden may be smaller, some of the reduction is simply shifted to higher costs for other government services and therefore does not enhance the incentive to increase production.

Labour Supply. The marginal tax rate directly changes the financial incentive to *increase* one's work. ***If the marginal tax rate is high, there's less incentive to work more***—the federal government will get most of the added income. Confronted with high marginal tax rates, workers may choose to stay home rather than work an extra shift. Families may decide that it doesn't pay to send both parents into the labour

marginal tax rate: The tax rate imposed on the last (marginal) dollar of income.

[8]Note that the actual marginal rate of personal income tax paid by Canadians is a combination of the federal and provincial rates. Since each province sets their own rate, the rates will be different for each province.

market. When marginal tax rates are low, by contrast, those extra work activities generate bigger increases in disposable income.

Entrepreneurship. Marginal tax rates affect not only labour-supply decisions but also decisions on whether to start or expand a business. Most small businesses are organized as sole proprietorships or partnerships and subject to *personal,* not *corporate,* tax rates. Hence, a decline in personal tax rates will affect the risk/reward balance for potential entrepreneurs. Columbia Business School professors William Gentry and Glenn Huber have demonstrated that progressive marginal tax rates discourage entry into self-employment. Syracuse professor Douglas Holtz-Eakin and Princeton economist Harvey Rosen have shown that the growth rate, investment, and employment of small businesses are also affected by marginal tax rates. As Holtz-Eakin concluded, "taxes matter."

Investment. Taxes matter for corporations too. Corporate entities account for nearly 90 percent of business output and 84 percent of business assets. Like small proprietorships, corporations, too, are motivated by *after*-tax profits. Hence, corporate *investment* decisions will be affected by corporate tax rates. If government imposes a high tax rate on corporate profits, the payoff to investors will be diminished. Potential investors may decide to consume their income rather than to invest in plant and equipment. If that happens, total investment will decline and output will suffer. Accordingly, *if high tax rates discourage investment, aggregate supply will be constrained.*

Tax-Induced Supply Shifts. If tax rates affect supply decisions, then *changes* in tax rates will shift aggregate supply. Specifically, supply-siders conclude that *a reduction in marginal tax rates will shift the aggregate supply curve to the right.* The increased

APPLICATIONS

Remaking Our Economy

According to the non-partisan Conference Board of Canada, our national prosperity is a mansion built on sand. We're not innovative enough. Our entrepreneurs—indeed, Canadians as a whole—are too "complacent" and unwilling to take risks. We are 14th out of 17 advanced nations in "innovation"—the ability to bring new products from the laboratory to the marketplace. And we finished dead last in private-sector research and development.

These indicators may seem abstract, but they matter in a very real sense. Nations profit when their scientists, financiers and entrepreneurs develop the next computer operating system, the next industry-standard microchip, the next home entertainment system or the next generation of jet or automobile engine. Too often, Canada is importing these breakthroughs from other countries instead of developing them ourselves.

For government, the key is infrastructure. Rather than trying to micromanage economic outcomes, Ottawa and the provinces need to focus on building roads, harbours and rail lines to service industry. The federal government has done some of this. Infrastructure Canada has helped cities upgrade their mass transit and spent hundreds of millions expanding crucial border crossings with the United States to help businesspeople and goods flow faster to our largest foreign markets.

Corporations too are to blame, as are universities and unions. There are plenty of research tax breaks, according to the Conference Board, just too few entrepreneurs willing to risk taking advantage of them. Canada also suffers from too few postgraduate researchers in commercially viable disciplines, while unions have recently reverted to economy-crippling strikes rather than realizing that when businesses do well, so do their members.

Source: Editorial, "Remaking Our Economy," *The National Post,* (June 14, 2007), p. A20. Material reprinted with the express permission of National Post Company, a CanWest Partnership.

Analysis: Entrepreneurship and commercial innovation from research and development are important to increase the economy's potential—shifting the SRAS and LRAS outward—and increasing Canadian's standard of living.

APPLICATIONS

Alberta to Cut "Prosperity Bonus" Cheques

Ralph Klein's government will send Albertans a "prosperity bonus," one of a number of measures in its long-awaited announcement on how it will spend the billions of dollars it's reaping from energy royalties.

Based on private-sector forecasts that the province's [2005] year-end surplus is headed toward $7-billion, the pool of money for bonuses could be as high as $1.4-billion.

In recent months, the Conservative government has been criticized for its lack of vision about how to use a growing surplus without creating jealousy among the country's cash-strapped provinces. Calling it an "unprecedented windfall," Mr. Klein

told reporters yesterday after emerging from a closed-door caucus meeting in Cold Lake that the government plans to "spread the money around three ways" and they will be just about even.

The debt-free province, which has the lowest taxes in the country, wants to use its unallocated surplus on infrastructure projects and rebates.

Source: Katherine Harding, "Alberta to cut prosperity cheques," *The Globe and Mail* (September 13, 2005), p. A5. Reprinted with permission from *The Globe and Mail*.

Analysis: Tax cuts, rebates, and infrastructure spending can impact demand-side or supply-side incentives. Given that the province already has the "lowest taxes in the country," the additional fiscal spending on one-time "prosperity cheques" and infrastructure may temporarily shift the AD curve to the right. Critics insisted that this was a lost opportunity to provide additional incentives on the supply-side that might result in permanently higher growth.

supply will come from three sources: more work effort, more entrepreneurship, and more investment. This increased willingness to produce will reduce the rate of unemployment. The additional output will also help reduce inflationary pressures. Thus we end up with less unemployment *and* less inflation.

From a supply-side perspective, the form of the tax cut is critical. For example, **tax rebates** (see the Applications box above) are a one-time windfall to consumers and have no effect on marginal tax rates. As a consequence, disposable income rises, but not the incentives for work or production. Rebates directly affect only the demand side of the economy.

To stimulate aggregate *supply,* tax *rates* must be reduced, particularly at the margin. These cuts can take the form of reductions in personal income tax rates or reductions in the marginal tax rates imposed on businesses. In either case, the lower tax rates will give people a greater incentive to work, invest, and produce.

As we noted earlier, marginal personal tax rates were reduced in each category beginning in 2001, and changes continued to be made in succeeding years. In the recent May 2006 federal budget, tax changes were again central to the budget. The *Budget in Brief* stated that this budget "delivers more tax relief than the last four federal budgets."[9] It goes on to state that the government's intention is to "create an environment for jobs and growth" by making "Canada's tax system more internationally competitive" and by supporting "the growth of small business." The government then announced a series of tax cut proposals aimed at reducing both corporate and small business tax rates.

Table 14.2 illustrates the distinction between Keynesian and supply-side tax cuts. Under both tax systems (A and B), a person earning $200 pays $80 in taxes before the tax cut and $60 after the tax cut. But under system A, the marginal tax rate is always 50 percent, which means that government is getting half of every dollar earned

tax rebate: A lump-sum refund of taxes paid.

[9]Department of Finance, Canada, *The Budget in Brief 2006,* http://www.fin.gc.ca/budget06/brief/briefe.htm, accessed February 8, 2007.

TABLE 14.2

Average vs. Marginal Tax Rates

The same amount of taxes can be raised via two very different systems. Here a person earning $200 pays $80 in taxes under either system (A or B). Thus, the *average* tax rate (total tax ÷ total income) is the same in both cases ($80 ÷ $200 = 40%) but the *marginal* tax rates are very different. System A has a high marginal rate (50%), whereas system B has a low marginal tax rate (30%). System B provides a greater incentive for people to earn over $100.

Tax System	Initial Tax Schedule	Tax on Income of $200	Tax Rate — Average	Tax Rate — Marginal	Disposable Income
		Initial Alternatives			
A	$30 + 50% of income over $100	$80	40%	50%	$120
B	$50 + 30% of income over $100	$80	40%	30%	$120

The average tax rate could be cut to 30 percent under either system. Under both systems, the revised tax would be $60 and disposable income would be increased to $140. Keynesians would be happy with either form of tax cut. But supply-siders would favour system B because the lower marginal tax rate gives people more incentive to earn higher incomes.

Tax System	Initial Tax Schedule	Tax on Income of $200	Tax Rate — Average	Tax Rate — Marginal	Disposable Income
		Alternative Forms of Tax Cut			
A	$10 + 50% of income over $100	$60	30%	50%	$140
B	$30 + 30% of income over $100	$60	30%	30%	$140

above $100. By contrast, system B imposes a marginal tax rate of only 30 percent—$0.30 of every dollar above $100 goes to the government. Under system B, people have a greater incentive to earn more than $100. Although both systems raise the same amount of taxes, system B offers greater incentives to work extra hours and produce more output.

Tax Elasticity of Supply. Virtually all economists agree that tax rates influence people's decisions to work, invest, and produce. But the policy-relevant question is, *how much* influence do taxes have? Do reductions in the marginal tax rate shift the aggregate supply curve far to the right? Or are the resultant shifts quite small?

The response of labour and capital to a change in tax rates is summarized by the **tax elasticity of supply.** Like other elasticities, this one measures the proportional response of supplies to a change in price (in this case, a tax *rate*). Specifically, the tax elasticity of supply is the percentage change in quantity supplied divided by the percentage in tax rates, that is,

> **tax elasticity of supply:** The percentage change in quantity supplied divided by the percentage change in tax rates.

$$\text{Tax elasticity of supply} = \frac{\% \text{ change in quantity supplied}}{\% \text{ change in tax rate}}$$

Normally we expect quantity supplied to go up when tax rates go down. This implies an inverse (or negative) relationship between the two variables—*quantity supplied* and the *tax rate*. The inverse relationship means that the "sign" of the elasticity calculation, *E*, will be negative, although it's usually expressed in absolute terms (without the minus sign). The (absolute) value of *E* must be greater than zero, since we expect *some* response to a tax cut. The policy issue boils down to the question of how large *E* actually is.

If the tax elasticity of supply were large enough, a tax cut might actually *increase* tax revenues. Suppose the tax elasticity were equal to 1.5. In that case a tax cut of 10 percent would cause output supplied to increase by 15 percent (= $1.5 \times 10\%$). Such a large increase in the tax base (income) would result in *more* taxes being paid even though the tax *rate* was reduced. One of U.S. President Ronald Reagan's economic advisors, Arthur Laffer, actually thought such an outcome was possible. More recently, some Canadian politicians have also adopted this thinking, often predicting an increase in tax revenues as a result of tax cuts. In reality, the tax elasticity of supply turned out to be much smaller (around 0.15) and tax revenues fell. The aggregate supply curve *did* shift to the right, but not very far, when marginal tax rates were cut.

Although the relatively low tax elasticity of supply reduced government tax revenues, the federal and some provincial governments have continued to pursue lower tax rates as a policy to increase total economic activity. Even though initially tax revenues might fall, the prospect of faster economic growth in the future means a faster revenue recovery and greater future government revenue without the disincentives inherent in higher marginal tax rates.

Savings Incentives. Supply side economists emphasize the importance of *long-run* responses to changed tax incentives. On the demand side, an increase in income translates very quickly into increased spending. On the supply side, things don't happen so fast. It takes time to construct new plants and equipment. People are also slow to respond to new work and investment incentives. Hence, the full benefits of supply-side tax cuts—or the damage done by tax hikes—won't be immediately visible.

Of particular concern to supply-side economists is the rate of saving in the economy. Demand-side economists emphasize spending and tend to treat *saving* as a leakage problem. Supply-siders, by contrast, emphasize the importance of saving for financing investment and economic growth. At full employment, a greater volume of investment is possible only if the rate of consumption is cut back. In other words, additional investment requires additional saving. Hence, **supply-side economists favour tax incentives that encourage saving as well as greater tax incentives for investment.** This kind of perspective contrasts sharply with the Keynesian emphasis on stimulating consumption, as the accompanying cartoon emphasizes.

Analysis: In the short run, consumer saving may reduce aggregate demand. However, saving also finances increased investment, which is essential to long-run growth.

Investment Incentives. An alternative lever for shifting aggregate supply is to offer tax incentives for investment. The 2001 tax cuts focused on *personal* income tax rates. In contrast, the May 2006 federal budget elimination of the federal capital tax provided an incentive to increase investment in the economy. The amount of investment depends on comparing the "cost" of the investment itself—including any tax implications—with the expected returns to be earned from the investment. The elimination of the capital tax would reduce the "cost" of investment by the amount of the tax and increase the willingness to invest.

Tax incentives also apply to individuals. Other taxes, such as capital gain taxes (taxes levied on the increase in value of property and corporate stock) and taxes on dividends (returns to shareholders), alter people's investment decisions.

Governments also target programs in certain areas to encourage additional investment. The November 2006 economic and fiscal update, for instance, suggested "accelerating capital cost allowance to encourage bioenergy in the pulp and paper sector." This would encourage firms to invest more now to take advantage of reducing the after-tax cost of these new investments.

Human Capital Investment

A nation's ability to supply goods and services depends on its *human* capital as well as its *physical* capital. If the size of the labour force increased, more output could be produced in any given price level. Similarly, if the *quality* of the workforce were to increase, more output could be supplied at any given price level. In other words, increases in *human capital*—the skills and knowledge of the workforce—add to the nation's potential output. This represents an increase in the *productivity* of the labour force—labour productivity—an increase in the *technology* available to the economy.

A mismatch between the skills of the workforce and the requirements of new jobs is a major cause of the unemployment–inflation trade-off. When aggregate demand increases, employers want to hire more workers. But the available (unemployed) workers may not have the skills employers require. This is the essence of *structural unemployment.* The consequence is that employers can't increase output as fast as they'd like to. Prices, rather than output, increase.

The larger the skills gap between unemployed workers and the requirements of emerging jobs, the worse will be the Phillips curve trade-off. To improve the trade-off, the skills gap must be reduced. This is another supply-side imperative. ***Investments in human capital reduce structural unemployment and shift the aggregate supply curve rightward.***

Worker Training. The tax code is a policy tool for increasing human capital investment as well as physical capital investment. In this case tax credits are made available to employers who offer more worker training. Such credits reduce the employer's after-tax cost of training.

An example in the May 2006 federal budget illustrates how fiscal policy can increase worker improvement. The government offered a "new tax credit of up to $2,000 for employers who hire apprentices." This encouraged firms to hire additional apprentices, increasing employment and output, while also providing "learning-by-doing" for the apprentices themselves.

Government policy can encourage new hiring in other forms as well. For instance, the B.C. Government introduced a "training wage" that enabled employers to hire individuals with little experience at a rate $2 beneath the existing "minimum wage" rate. In effect, employees "subsidized" their own employment as a way of increasing their experience and their general productivity.

Education Spending. Another way to increase human capital is to expand and improve the efficacy of the education system. The public school system in Canada—from primary to university—is a provincial responsibility. Figure 14.9 presents the change in post-secondary funding in British Columbia over the 2005–2006 to 2008–2009 budget years.

But that doesn't mean the federal government has no role to play. For instance, in the May 2006 budget, the federal government added a tax credit for the cost of textbooks,

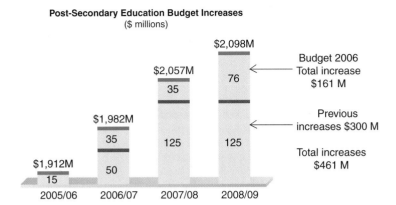

Post-Secondary Education Budget Increases
($ millions)

FIGURE 14.9
British Columbia Post-Secondary Funding

Provincial governments see education as an important way to increase human capital. As an example, the B.C. government is intending to increase current and future funding for post-secondary education from the 2005/2006 to the 2008/2009 budget years. The graph shows both increases in funding announced in prior years as well as the additional funding included in the May 2006 provincial budget.

Source: Copyright © Province of British Columbia. All rights reserved. Reprinted with permission of the Province of British Columbia. www.ipp.gov.bc.ca

eliminated the limit on scholarships and bursary funds students can receive without paying federal taxes, and expanded the eligibility for Canada Student Loans. Each of these policies is intended to reduce the "cost" of post-secondary education and thereby encourage more participation and more future labour productivity.

Transfer Payments. Welfare programs also discourage workers from taking available jobs. Unemployment and welfare benefits provide a source of income when a person isn't working. Although these *income transfers* are motivated by humanitarian goals, they also inhibit labour supply. Transfer recipients must give up some or all of their welfare payments when they take a job, which makes working less attractive and therefore reduces the number of available workers. The net result is a leftward shift of the aggregate supply curve.

Recognizing that income transfers reduce aggregate supply doesn't force us to eliminate all welfare programs. Welfare programs are also intended to serve important social needs. The AS/AD framework reminds us, however, that the structure of such programs will affect aggregate supply.

Deregulation

Government intervention affects the shape and position of the aggregate supply curve in other ways. The government intervenes directly in supply decisions by *regulating* employment and output behaviour. In general, such regulations limit the flexibility of producers to respond to changes in demand. Government regulation also tends to raise production costs. The higher costs result not only from required changes in the production process but also from the expense of monitoring government regulations and filling out endless government forms.

Factor Markets

Government intervention in factor markets increases the cost of supplying goods and services in many ways.

Minimum Wages Minimum wage laws are one of the most familiar forms of factor-market regulation.

The goal of the minimum wage law is to ensure workers a decent standard of living. But the law has other effects as well. By prohibiting employers from using lower-paid workers, it limits the ability of employers to hire additional workers. Teenagers, for example, may not have enough skills or experience to merit the minimum wage. Employers may have to rely on more expensive workers rather than hire unemployed teenagers. In the absence of a minimum wage, employers would hire and train more teenagers and other low-skill workers. With minimum wage requirements, the costs of production increase. In fact, it was precisely these issues that prompted the B.C. government to introduce its "training wage" as a policy intended to encourage the employment of more younger people who have fewer skills and less experiences.

Here again the issue is not whether minimum wage laws serve any social purposes but how they affect macro outcomes. By shifting the aggregate supply curve

APPLICATIONS

Take Down Competition Barriers, Study Says; Deregulation Urged

OTTAWA–Governments across Canada should reduce barriers to competition and to the movement of labour within the country, as well as encourage more investment in both labour and technology, a new study concludes. The report by the Centre for the Study of Living Standards [CSLS], released yesterday, is based on a review of the relatively stronger productivity performances of a half-dozen other industrial countries, including the United States, Australia, Ireland, Britain, Finland and Sweden.

While Canada's economy has performed well in most respects, its productivity performance—which is key to boosting living standards—has been relatively "dismal" the report says. All of the six countries were more productive than Canada, where output per hour worked last year was only 78.1 percent of that of U.S. workers, said Andrew Sharpe, economist and head of the centre. The relative productivity of the others, as percentage of U.S. output per hour worked, was Ireland at 98.1, Finland 81.7, Sweden 86.4, Britain, 84,4, and Australia, 78.2. Since 1973, Canada has had the third-lowest productivity growth of nearly two dozen industrial countries, the report says.

Source: Eric Beauchesne, "Take down competition barriers, study says; Deregulation urged," *The National Post* (April 11, 2007) p. FP6. Material reprinted with the express permission of CanWest News Service, a CanWest Partnership.

Analysis: Where deregulation can boost competition within an economy, the result can be increases innovation and greater productivity. The report notes that "competition and productivity are closely linked."

leftward, minimum wage laws make it more difficult to achieve full employment with stable prices.

Mandatory Benefits. Government directed benefits can have the same kind of effect on the short run aggregate supply curve. The federal government, for example, requires firms (and workers) to pay Employment Insurance premiums. Provincial governments also require firms to contribute to certain programs, such as Worker's Compensation. These payments increase payroll costs and therefore add to the cost of production, leaving producers less willing to supply output at any given price level.

Employment Standards. The federal government and provincial governments each impose a regulatory framework on factor markets. The federal government regulates any area of federal responsibility—generally those involving inter-provincial or international industries. For example, the federal government regulates air, rail, and inter-provincial truck transport, federally chartered banks, and radio, telephone, and television communications, among other industries:

> The Canada Labour Code (Labour Standards) and accompanying Regulations apply to employees and employers in works, undertakings, or businesses under the legislative authority of the Parliament of Canada.[10]

Provincial and territorial governments regulate labour standards and occupational health and safety regulations within their own jurisdiction. For example, Ontario's Employment Standards Act sets out the regulations for employers and employees effective in Ontario. They do note the federal/provincial jurisdictions, stating that:

> Most employers and employees in Ontario are covered by this provincial law. The [Employment Standards Act] ESA does not apply to you if you operate or work in a business that is regulated by the Government of Canada, such as: airlines, banks, shipping companies, radio and television stations, inter-provincial transport of goods and people.[11]

[10]Summary," *Canada Labour Code,* http://www.hrsdc.gc.ca/asp/gateway.asp?hr=/en/lp/lo/lswe/ls/publications/1.shtml&hs=lxn, accessed February 13, 2007.

[11]Ministry of Labour, Ontario. *Employment Standards* (2006), http://www.labour.gov.on.ca/english/es/, accessed February 13, 2007.

APPLICATIONS

EU, Canada Bid for Open Skies

The European Commission wants to establish an open aviation market between Canada and 27 European Union countries—paving the way for more transatlantic flights and cheaper air fares—even though similar efforts with the United States have so far failed to take off.

The EU's executive agency, based in Brussels, said yesterday it has proposed to open negotiations with Ottawa on a "comprehensive aviation agreement" between Canada and the EU that seeks to end market restrictions for airlines and promote regulatory homogeneity.

"Right now there are 17 different air service agreements in place," said Roy Christensen, a spokesman for the European Commission in Canada. "The idea is to replace them with one

agreement that covers not only the 17 [European] countries, but all 27 EU member states.

A single accord that allows market forces to determine where airlines can fly and how often could help boost annual traffic between Canada and the EU to 14 million by 2011 from eight million today, according to a study launched by the European Commission. The study also predicted the creation of 3,700 new jobs and consumer benefits totaling $109-million in the form of lower air fares.

Source: Chris Sorensen, "EU, Canada bid for open skies: 17 agreements in place: Ottawa receptive to EU proposal for aviation deal," *The National Post* (January 10, 2007) p. FP 4. Material reprinted with the express permission of National Post Company, a CanWest Partnership.

Analysis: Regulations in the aviation industry add costs to airlines—and complying with different regulations for different destinations can increase production costs further. Reducing and "homogenizing" regulations could reduce costs, increase competition, and shift the SRAS curve to the right.

The government's regulation of factor markets tends to raise production costs and inhibit supply. The same is true of regulations imposed directly on product markets.

Product Markets

Food and Drug Standards. The federal government sets regulations for agricultural goods (food, drugs, and vitamins) through the Canadian Food Inspection Agency (CFIA) and Health Canada.

The CFIA is "dedicated to safeguarding food, animals and plants, which enhances the health and well-being of Canada's people, environment and economy."[12] For example, the Canada Agricultural Products Act (1985) regulates honey. Section 4.1 of the act notes that "Subject to subsections (2) and (3), no person shall market honey in import, export or inter-provincial trade as food unless the honey: (a) is not adulterated; (b) is not contaminated; (c) is edible; (d) is prepared in a sanitary manner; and (e) meets all other requirements of the Food and Drugs Act and the Food and Drug Regulations."[13]

Health Canada's *Access to Therapeutic Products: The Regulatory Process in Canada* document describes its purpose and writes that:

> Therapeutic products such as pharmaceutical drugs, vitamins, vaccines and medical devices play an important role in helping Canadians lead healthy lives. More than 22,000 pharmaceutical products and 40,000 medical devices are available in Canada. Canadians trust that the products they use have passed Health Canada's rigorous safety standards and will help to deliver desired health outcomes.[14]

Health Canada also sets standards for testing new drugs and evaluates the test results when approving drugs for sale in Canada. As with the CFIA, the goal of regulation is to minimize health risk to consumers.

[12]Canadian food inspection agency, Web site, http://www.inspection.gc.ca/english/toce.shtml, accessed February 13, 2007.

[13]"Honey Regulations," the Canada Agricultural Products Act, http://laws.justice.gc.ca/en/showdoc/cr/C.R.C.-c.287/bo-ga:s_4//en#anchorbo-ga:s_4, accessed February 13, 2007.

[14]Health Canada, *Access to Therapeutic Products: The Regulatory Process in Canada,* http://www.hc-sc.gc.ca/ahc-asc/pubs/hpfb-dgpsa/access-therapeutic_acces-therapeutique_e.html#1, accessed February 13, 2007.

Like all regulation, however, the CFIA and Health Canada standards entail real costs. The tests required for new drugs are expensive and time-consuming. Getting a new drug approved for sale can take years of effort and require a huge investment. The net results are that (1) fewer new drugs are brought to market and (2) those that do reach the market are more expensive than they would have been in the absence of regulation. In other words, the aggregate supply of goods is shifted to the left.

Other examples of government regulation are commonplace. Environment Canada works with the Canada Environmental Protection Act (CEPA) to regulate vehicle engine and equipment emissions, protect the marine environment from pollution from land, and manage the control and movement of hazardous waste and recyclable materials. The Investment Canada Act (ICA) prescribes the rules for non-Canadians investing in the Canadian economy, and the Canadian parliament restricts foreign imports, which raises their prices. As a final example, the Canadian Competition Bureau administers the Canada Competition Act, which "is a federal law governing most business conduct in Canada. It contains both criminal and civil provisions aimed at preventing anti-competitive practices in the marketplace."[15]

Reducing Costs. Many—perhaps most—of these regulatory activities are beneficial. In fact, all were originally designed to serve specific public purposes. As a result of such regulation, we get safer drugs, cleaner air, and less deceptive advertising. We must also consider the costs involved, however. All regulatory activities impose direct and indirect costs. These costs must be compared to the benefits received. ***The basic contention of supply-side economists is that regulatory costs are now too high.*** To improve our economic performance, they assert, we must **deregulate** the production process, thereby shifting the aggregate supply curve to the right again. According to a recent World Bank study, this supply-side insight has global validity (see the World View box).

> **deregulation:** The reduction or removal of regulations or regulatory oversight that adds costs to the production of goods and services.

Government regulation of international trade also influences the shape and position of aggregate supply. Trade flows affect both factor and product markets.

Easing Trade Barriers

Factor Markets. In factor markets, Canadian producers buy raw materials, equipment parts, and components from foreign suppliers. Tariffs (taxes on imported goods) make such inputs more expensive, thereby increasing the cost of Canadian production. Regulations or quotas that make foreign inputs less accessible or more expensive similarly constrain the Canadian aggregate supply curve. For example, the quota on sugar imported into the United States increases the cost of U.S.-produced soft drinks, cookies, and candy. Just that one trade barrier has cost U.S. consumers over $2 billion ($US) in higher prices—and of course Canadian consumers face increased costs on imported products.

Product Markets. The same kind of trade barriers affect product markets directly. With completely unrestricted ("free") trade, foreign producers would be readily available to supply products to Canadian consumers. If Canadian producers were approaching capacity or incurring escalating cost pressures, foreign suppliers would act as a safety valve. By increasing the quantity of output available at any given price level, foreign suppliers help flatten out the aggregate supply curve.

Despite the success of the North American Free Trade Agreement (NAFTA) and the World Trade Organization (WTO) in reducing trade barriers, many imports are still subject to tariffs. Nontariff barriers (regulation, quotas, and so forth) also still constrain aggregate supply. This was evident in the multiyear battle over Mexican trucking. Although NAFTA authorized Mexican trucking companies to compete freely in the United States by 2000, U.S. labour unions (Teamsters) and trucking companies vigourously protested their entry, delaying the implied reduction in transportation costs for four years.

[15]Canadian Competition Bureau, Web site, http://www.competitionbureau.gc.ca/internet/index.cfm?itemID=148&lg=e.

WORLD   VIEW

World Bank Faults Tight Regulation

Study to Argue Fewest Rules Foster Strongest Economies; Goal Is to Promote Changes

WASHINGTON—The World Bank, hoping to spur officials in developing countries to consider changes, plans to release a new survey finding that the least amount of business regulation fosters the strongest economies.

The bank, in cooperation with academics, management-consulting firms and law firms, measured the costs of five basic business-development functions in 130 nations. Titled "Doing Business," the report analyzes how regulation and legal systems affect companies' ability to register with the government, obtain credit, hire and fire workers, enforce contracts and work through bankruptcy courts.

The least regulated and most efficient economies are concentrated among countries with well-established common-law traditions, including Australia, Canada, New Zealand, the United Kingdom and the U.S. On par with the best performers are Singapore and Hong Kong. . . .

The countries with the most inefficient across-the-board regulations and laws are Bolivia, Burkina Faso, Chad, Costa Rica, Guatemala, Mali, Mozambique, Paraguay, the Philippines and Venezuela . . .

"In much of Africa, Latin America and the former Soviet Union, excess regulation stifles productive activity," the authors said.

The report uses its comparisons to advance the thesis that heavier regulation is usually associated with more inefficiency in public institutions, causing longer delays and higher cost. The consequence often is more unemployment and corruption, and less productivity and investment.

—Michael Schroeder and Terence Roth

Let's Make a Deal

Number of days to enforce a commercial business contract:

Fastest Countries	Days	Slowest Countries	Days
Tunisia	7	Guatemala	1,460
Netherlands	39	Serbia and Montenegro	1,028
New Zealand	50	Slovenia	1,003
Singapore	50	Poland	1,000
Botswana	56	Ethiopia	895

Top 10 countries whose regulation systems make it easiest for companies to register, obtain credit, hire and fire workers, enforce contracts and work through the bankruptcy courts.

* Australia
* Canada
* Denmark
* Netherlands
* New Zealand
* Norway
* Singapore
* Sweden
* U.K.
* U.S.

Source: *The Wall Street Journal*, October 7, 2003. Reprinted by permission of The Wall Street Journal, © 2003 Dow Jones & Company. All rights reserved worldwide.

Analysis: More government regulation raises business costs and constrains productivity. Countries with less obtrusive regulation grow faster.

Immigration. Another global supply-side policy lever is immigration policy. Skill shortages in Canadian labour markets can be overcome with education and training. But even faster relief is available in the vast pool of foreign workers. Citizenship and Immigration Canada attempts to reduce current shortages through a "skilled worker" classification and add to economic growth through a "business" classification. Temporary visas for farm workers also help avert cost-push inflation in the farm sector. By regulating the flow of immigrant workers, Parliament has the potential to alter the shape and position of the SRAS curve.

Another way to reduce the costs of supplying goods and services is to improve the nation's infrastructure, that is, the transportation, communications, judicial, and other systems that bind the pieces of the economy into a coherent whole. The inter-provincial

Infrastructure Development

Canada's New Government to Help Employers Address Labour Shortages in Western Canada

VANCOUVER—The Honourable Monte Solberg, Minister of Citizenship and Immigration, and the Honourable Diane Finley, Minister of Human Resources and Social Development Canada, today announced improvements to the Temporary Foreign Worker Program to make it easier for employers in Alberta and British Columbia to hire foreign workers when there are no Canadian citizens or permanent residents available to fill the position.

Source: Citizenship and Immigration Canada, Vancouver, News Release November 15, 2006, http://www.cic.gc.ca/english/index.asp.

Analysis: When the domestic labour market is unable to supply enough workers or workers with specific skills, foreign workers can be added to the domestic labour market.

highway system, for example, enlarged the market for producers looking for new sales opportunities. Improved air traffic controls and larger airports have also made international markets and factors of production readily accessible. Without highways and international airports, the process of supplying goods and services would be more localized and much more expensive.

It's easy to take infrastructure for granted until you have to make do without it. In recent years, Canadian producers have rushed into China, Russia, and Eastern Europe looking for new profit opportunities. What they discovered is that even simple communication is difficult where telephones are relatively scarce and unreliable.

In China, there are about 50 telephones per 100 people (mainline and cellular); Russia has about 72. By contrast, Canada has about 100 telephones for every 100 people.[16]

Cars and taxicabs are almost as hard to locate in Russia or China, and conference facilities are primitive. There are few established clearinghouses for marketing information, and labour markets are fragmented and localized. Getting started sometimes requires doing everything from scratch.

Although Canada has a highly developed infrastructure, it, too, could be improved. There are roads and bridges to repair, more airports to be built, faster rail systems to construct, and space-age telecommunications networks to install. Spending on this kind of infrastructure will not only increase aggregate demand (fiscal stimulus) but also shift aggregate supply.

"I blame government, labor, business, and my ex-wife."

Analysis: Because many constraints on aggregate supply contribute to stagflation, it's hard to single out any one cause (or cure).

[16]The data relates to the years 2003 and 2004 and comes from the World Bank's *Human Development Report* statistical tools available at http://hdr.undp.org/en/statistics/.

SUMMARY

- Fiscal and monetary policies seek to attain full employment and price stability by altering the level of aggregate demand. Their success depends on microeconomic responses, as reflected in the price and output decisions of market participants.
- The expectations of market participants play a crucial role in the macroeconomy. The more quickly that expectations form and are acted on, the quicker the macroeconomy is altered in line with those expectations. Adaptive expectations, or backward-looking expectations, are relatively slow to respond. Rational expectations are relatively quick.
- The market's response to shifts in aggregate demand is reflected in the shape and position of the short run aggregate supply curve. If the SRAS curve slopes upward, a trade-off between unemployment and inflation exists.
- The Phillips curve illustrates the unemployment–inflation trade-off. The expectations-augmented Phillips curve added to a natural rate of unemployment suggests a rightward shift of the Phillips curve. The natural rate of unemployment becomes associated with a new, higher rate of inflation.
- If the short run aggregate supply curve shifts to the left, or inward, the trade-off between unemployment and inflation worsens. Stagflation—a combination of substantial inflation and unemployment—results.
- Supply-side policies attempt to alter price and output decisions directly. If successful, they'll shift the short run aggregate supply curve to the right. A rightward shift of the SRAS implies less inflation *and* less unemployment.
- Marginal tax rates are a major concern of supply-side economists. High tax rates discourage extra work, investment, and saving. A reduction in marginal tax rates should shift the SRAS to the right.
- The tax elasticity of supply measures the response of quantity supplied to changes in tax rates. Empirical evidence suggests that the tax elasticity is low—relatively inelastic—and that shifts in the short run aggregate supply curve are therefore small.
- Investment in human capital increase productivity and therefore shift aggregate supply also. Worker's training and formal education enhancements are policy levers.
- Government regulation often raises the cost of production and limits output. Deregulation is intended to reduce costly restrictions on price and output behaviour, thereby shifting the short run aggregate supply curve to the right.
- Trade barriers shift the short run aggregate supply curve leftward by raising the cost of importing and raising the price of imported products. Reducing trade barriers increases short run aggregate supply.
- Public infrastructure is part of the economy's capital resources. Investments in infrastructure (such as transportation systems) facilitate market exchanges and expand the production possibilities.

Key Terms

stagflation 288
adaptive (backward-looking)
  expectations 290
rational expectations 290

Phillips curve 292
tax incentives 297
marginal tax rate 299
tax rebate 301

tax elasticity of supply 302
deregulation 308

Questions for Discussion

1. Why might prices rise when aggregate demand increases? What factors might influence the extent of price inflation?
2. What were the unemployment and inflation rates last year? Where would they lie on Figure 14.6? Can you explain the implied shift from curve PC_2?
3. Why would a business prefer to locate in Tunisia rather than Guatemala, according to the World View on p. 309?
4. Which of the following groups are likely to have the highest tax elasticity of labour supply? (*a*) college students, (*b*) single parents, (*c*) primary earners in two-parent families, (*d*) secondary earners in two-parent families. Why are there differences?
5. How is the short run aggregate supply curve affected by (*a*) minimum wage laws, (*b*) Canada Pension Plan payroll taxes and retirement benefits?
6. If all workplace-safety regulations both (*a*) improve workers well-being and (*b*) raise production costs, how should the line between "good" regulations and "bad" regulations be drawn?
7. How do each of the following infrastructure items affect aggregate supply? (*a*) highways, (*b*) schools, (*c*) sewage systems, (*d*) courts and prisons.
8. How would the volume and timing of capital investments be affected by (*a*) a permanent cut in the capital-gains tax, (*b*) a temporary 10-percent tax credit?

9. British Columbia's "training wage" was introduced for inexperienced workers to encourage firms to hire more of them—particularly youth between 18–24 years of age. Why should this increase employment?

10. The Applications box on page 307 indicates the desire of the European Commission to negotiate a "comprehensive aviation agreement" with Canada. How might such an agreement lead to reduced prices for consumers *and* more profitable airlines?

EXERCISES

PROBLEMS   The Student Problem Set to accompany this chapter can be found at the end of the book.

WEB ACTIVITIES   Web Activities to accompany this chapter can be found on the Online Learning Centre at **http://www.mcgrawhill.ca/olc/schiller**.

PART 6

The Foreign Economy: Trade and Finance

Our interactions with the rest of the world have a profound impact of the mix of output (WHAT), the methods of production (HOW), and the distribution of income (FOR WHOM). Trade and global money flows can also affect the stability of the macro economy. Chapter 15 explores the pattern and motives of international trade in goods and services while Chapter 16 focuses on international finance and exchange rates.

International Trade

Free trade, one of the greatest blessings a government can confer on a people, is in almost every country unpopular.

Thomas Babington Macaulay,
English historian and statesman, (1824)

I n 2006, Canadians imported some $487.7 billion dollars worth of goods and services. We enjoy pineapples from Hawaii, cars from Japan, movies from the United Kingdom and t-shirts from China. And yet, free trade, as Macaulay suggests, is unpopular. We also sold about $524.7 billion dollars worth of Canadian produced goods and services to households in other countries in 2006, and no one is concerned because that production represents our jobs and our income. So perhaps it isn't "free trade" that is the issue so much as "free imports"? And perhaps that's understandable. After all, imports compete with goods and services that we have, or do, or could produce ourselves. In other words, imports compete with domestic jobs! So, we're left with exports, good; and imports, bad. But wait a minute. Our exports must then also be competition for, and replacements of, jobs in other countries. Would these other countries be better off not buying Canadian goods and services? Well, you see the problem. So, after all this, we are back to examining Macaulay's original proposition that if free trade is a blessing, why isn't it more popular?

Let's begin here by introducing—without discussion—a few of the arguments economists often put forward in favour of a free trade regime. At the conclusion of this chapter, you can look back and see if these arguments are persuasive.

As we noted above, increased trade leads to increased competition in many markets. Increased competition leads to the most efficient allocation of resources and therefore aids economic growth. Jagdish Bhagwati, in his book *In Defense of Globalization*, writes that the "freeing of trade is pursued because it is argued on both theoretical and empirical grounds, that it produces prosperity and has a favorable impact on poverty as well."[1] Amartya Sen expresses the importance of trade as one "freedom" that is fundamental to development in less developed countries.[2] He suggests that "the ability of the market mechanism to contribute to high economic growth and to overall economic progress has been widely—and rightly—acknowledged in the contemporary development literature."

[1] Jagdish Bhagwati, *In Defense of Globalization* (Oxford University Press: New York, 2004), p. 82.
[2] Amartya Sen, *Development as Freedom* (Anchor Books: New York, 1999), p. 6.

LEARNING OBJECTIVES

By the end of this chapter, you should be able to:

15.1 Describe the importance of trade to Canada's economy

15.2 Demonstrate the motivation to trade using a production possibility curve model and the mutual gain that arises from trade

15.3 Explain the concepts of absolute and comparative advantage and why absolute costs don't matter but comparative costs do

15.4 Explain why protectionist pressure arises in the economy and describe several arguments used to promote trade protection

15.5 Describe several barriers to trade and demonstrate the impact of barriers to trade through supply and demand

15.6 Describe the evolution of Canada's trade agreements, the WTO, and NAFTA

Therefore, the argument concludes, trade can make Canadians better off, can increase economic growth, can lead to a reduction in poverty, and can assist and accelerate development in emerging economies. The purpose of this chapter, then, is to explain how these advantages of international trade arise.

This chapter begins with a survey of international trade patterns—what goods and services we trade, and with whom. Then we address basic issues related to such trade:

* **What benefit, if any, do we get from international trade?**
* **How much harm do imports cause, and to whom?**
* **Should we protect ourselves from "unfair" trade by limiting imports?**

After examining the arguments for and against international trade, we draw some general conclusions about trade policy. As we'll see, international trade tends to increase *average* incomes, although it may diminish the job and income opportunities for specific industries and workers.

15.1 TRADE PATTERNS

In 2005 the United States imported $1,732.4 billion ($US) worth of merchandise (goods) from around the world.[3] This represented approximately 21 percent of the world's total merchandise imported. Compare this to Canada's total *imports* of $388.2 billion ($Cdn) (about $319.7 billion ($US)), or about 3.9 percent of the world's total. This large difference in dollar value, however hides the relative importance of imports in the two economies. In Canada, imports represent about 28 percent of total GDP, whereas in the United States, imports make up about one-half of that amount.

In 2006, although imports represented 34 percent of total gross domestic product, they accounted for even larger shares of specific product markets. Coffee is a familiar example. Since all coffee is imported, Canadians would have a harder time staying awake without imports. Likewise, there'd be no aluminum if we didn't import bauxite, no chrome bumpers if we didn't import chromium, no tin cans without imported tin, and a lot fewer computers without imported components.

We import *services* as well as *goods*. If you fly to Europe on Virgin Airways you're importing transportation services. If you stay in a London hotel, you're importing lodging services. When you go to Barclay's Bank to cash traveller's cheques, you're importing foreign financial services. These and other services now account for approximately 17 percent of total Canadian imports, or about $79.5 billion ($Cdn) in 2005.

Exports

While we're buying goods (merchandise) and services from the rest of the world, global consumers are buying our *exports*. In 2005, Canada exported $453.1 billion ($Cdn) worth of goods, including wheat, softwood lumber, cars and car parts, crude petroleum, aluminum, and natural gas.[4] We also exported approximately $66.6 billion in services, for example software licenses, tourism, engineering, and financial services.

In the case of *exports,* in 2005 Germany was the world's largest exporter of goods in dollar terms with sales of $969.9 billion ($US). The United States ranked second at $904.4 billion ($US). Although Canada ranked 9th in dollar terms, this hides the importance of exports as a proportion of our total GDP. In 2005, exports of goods represented a little more than 33 percent of total GDP compared to the U.S. ratio of

[3]World Trade Organization, "Leading Exporters and Importers in World Merchandise Trade: Table 1.6," *World Trade in 2005—Overview,* http://www.wto.org/english/res_e/statis_e/its2006_overview_e.htm, accessed February 24, 2007.

[4]World Trade Organization, "Leading exporters and importers in world merchandise trade: Table 1.6," *World Trade in 2005—Overview,* (2006) http://www.wto.org/english/res_e/statis_e/its2006_e/its06_overview_e.htm, accessed February 24, 2007.

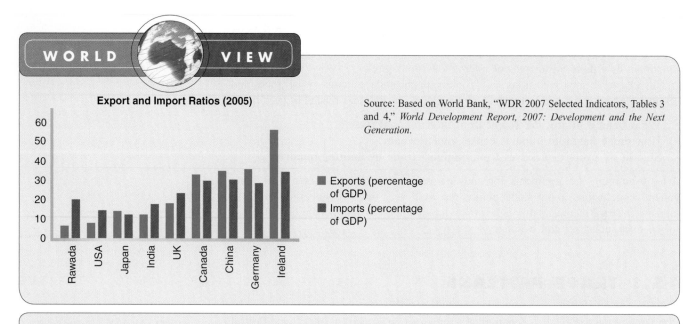

Source: Based on World Bank, "WDR 2007 Selected Indicators, Tables 3 and 4," *World Development Report, 2007: Development and the Next Generation.*

Analysis: The relatively low export and import ratio of the United States and Japan reflects the relatively large size of their domestic economies and their ability to produce a broader range of goods. The higher ratios of Canada, China, Germany, and particularly Ireland illustrate a greater importance of trade as a component of GDP.

a little greater than 7 percent of GDP. If we include exported services as well, Canada's proportion to GDP increases to almost 38 percent.

The World View box illustrates the proportion of GDP represented by exports and imports for a number of countries. Ireland is one of the most export-oriented countries, with a ratio of goods exports to GDP of almost 56 percent. Since Ireland is also a large tourist destination, adding in tourism services can push its export ratio over 90 percent! By contrast, Rwanda exports very little as a proportion of GDP; less than 6 percent. This reality may indicate that Rwanda has few goods to sell to other countries, or that other countries may not allow Rwanda to sell goods in their markets. Where the latter is the case—due to government policy—Sen's freedom to trade is violated and Rwandan development may be hindered and delayed.

Trade Balances

Although we export a lot of goods, we also import other goods and these two values may not be equal, resulting in an imbalance in our trade. The trade balance is simply the difference between the value of exports and the value of imports, that is,

$$\text{Trade balance} = \text{Exports (X)} - \text{Imports (Im)}$$

In 2006, our total exports exceeded our total imports by $37 billion, meaning that Canada had a positive trade balance or **trade surplus** for this year.

Although the overall trade balance includes both goods and services, these international flows are usually reported separately, with the *merchandise* trade balance distinguished from the *services* trade balance. As Table 15.1 shows, Canada had a merchandise trade surplus of $51.3 billion in 2005 but a **trade deficit** in services of $14.3 billion, adding up to the overall $37 billion surplus.

When Canada has a trade surplus with the rest of the world, other countries must have an offsetting trade deficit. On a global scale, imports must equal exports, since every good exported by one county must be imported by another. Hence, ***any imbalance in Canada's trade must be offset by reverse imbalances elsewhere.***

Even when Canada's overall balance in the trade account is in surplus, the bilateral balance—that is, accounts with other individual countries—varies greatly. Table 15.2,

trade surplus (deficit): The amount by which the value of exports exceeds (is less than) the value of imports in a given time period.

Product Category	Exports, X ($ billions)	Imports, Im ($ billions)	Surplus (Deficit)
Merchandise (goods)	$455.696	$404.391	$51.305
Services	69.010	83.269	(14.259)
Total Trade	$524.706	$487.660	$37.046

Source: Adapted from Statistics Canada Web site http://www40.statcan.ca/01/cst01/econ04.htm and also available from Statistics Canada CANSIM table 380-0017. Statistics Canada information is used with the permission of Statistics Canada.

TABLE 15.1
Canada's Trade Balance, 2006

Both merchandise (goods) and services are traded between countries. Canada typically has a merchandise surplus and a services deficit. When combined, they resulted in an overall trade surplus in 2006.

Canada's Trade by Country or Country Group	Exports to ($ billions)	Imports from ($ billions)	Merchandise Trade Balance ($ billions)
United States	$360.963	$264.889	$96.024
Japan	$10.455	$11.882	−$1.427
United Kingdom	$11.560	$9.543	$2.016
Other EU Countries	$21.270	$32.495	−$11.224
Other OECD Countries	$17.561	$23.683	−$6.123
Other Countries	$33.887	$61.902	−$28.015

Notes: 1. United States includes Puerto Rico and Virgin Islands.
2. Other OECD countries excludes the United States, Japan, United Kingdom, and other EU (European Union) countries.
3. Other countries are countries not included in OECD or EU.

Source: Adapted from Statistics Canada Web site http://www40.statcan.ca/101/cst01/gblec02a.htm. Statistics Canada information is used with the permission of Statistics Canada.

TABLE 15.2
Canada's Bilateral Merchandise Trade Balances, 2006

The Canadian trade surplus is the net result of trade surpluses and trade deficits with individual countries. Canada had a huge merchandise trade surplus with the United States, which was reduced by merchandise trade deficits in much of the rest of the world.

for example, shows that our 2006 aggregate merchandise trade surplus ($51.3 billion) included a huge bilateral surplus with the United States ($96.0 billion) and bilateral deficits with Japan and the European Union countries taken together.

15.2 MOTIVATION TO TRADE

Many people wonder why we trade so much, particularly since (1) we import many of the things we also export (like computers, airplanes, clothes), (2) we *could* produce many of the other things we import, and (3) we worry so much about trade imbalances. Why not just import those few things that we can't produce ourselves, and export just enough to balance that trade?

Although it might seem strange to be importing goods we could produce ourselves, such trade is entirely rational. Our decision to trade with other countries arises from the same considerations that motivate individuals to specialize in production: satisfying their remaining needs in the marketplace. Why don't you become self-sufficient, growing all your own food, building your own shelter, recording your own songs? Presumably because you've found that you can enjoy a much higher standard of living (and better music) by working at just one job then buying other goods in the marketplace. When you do so, you're no longer self-sufficient. Instead, you are *specializing* in production, relying on others to produce the array of goods and services you want. When countries trade goods and services, they are doing the same thing—*specializing* in production, then *trading* for other desired goods. Why do they do this? Because *specialization increases total output.*

To see how nations benefit from trade, we'll examine the production possibilities of two countries. We want to demonstrate that two countries that trade can together produce more output than they could in the absence of trade. If they can, ***the gain***

Specialization

from trade is increased world output and a higher standard of living in all trading countries. This is the essential message of the *theory of comparative advantage.*

Production and Consumption without Trade

Consider the production and consumption possibilities of just two countries—say, Canada and France. For the sake of illustration, assume that both countries produce only two goods: bread and wine. Let's also set aside worries about the law of diminishing returns and the substitutability of resources, thus transforming the familiar *production possibilities* curve into a straight line, as in Figure 15.1.

The "curves" in Figure 15.1 suggest that Canada is capable of producing much more bread than France. With our labour, land, and other resources, we assume that Canada is capable of producing up to 100 zillion loaves of bread per year. To do so, we would have to devote all our resources to that purpose. This capability is indicated by point *A* in Figure 15.1*a* and in row *A* of the accompanying production possibilities schedule. France (Figure 15.1*b*), on the other hand, confronts a *maximum* bread production of only 15 zillion loaves per year (point *G*).

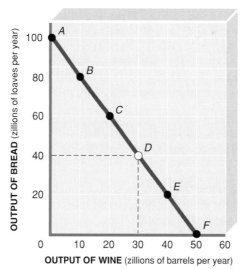

(a) Canadian production possibilities

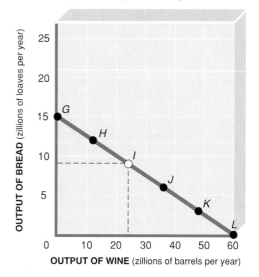

(b) French production possibilities

Canadian Production Possibilities		
	Bread (zillions of loaves)	+	Wine (zillions of barrels)
A	100	+	0
B	80	+	10
C	60	+	20
D	40	+	30
E	20	+	40
F	0	+	50

French Production Possibilities		
	Bread (zillions of loaves)	+	Wine (zillions of barrels)
G	15	+	0
H	12	+	12
I	9	+	24
J	6	+	36
K	3	+	48
L	0	+	60

FIGURE 15.1

Consumption Possibilities Without Trade

In the absence of trade, a country's consumption possibilities are identical to its production possibilities. The assumed production possibilities of Canada and France are illustrated in the graphs and the corresponding schedules. Before entering into trade, Canada chose to produce and consume at point *D*, with 40 zillion loaves of bread and 30 zillion barrels of wine. France chose point *I* on its own production possibilities curve. By trading, each country hopes to increase its consumption beyond these levels.

The capacities of the two countries for wine production are 50 zillion barrels for Canada (point *F*) and 60 zillion for France (point *L*), largely reflecting France's greater experience in tending vines. Both countries are also capable of producing alternative *combinations* of bread and wine, as evidenced by their respective production possibilities curves (points *A–F* for Canada and *G–L* for France).

In the absence of contact with the outside world, the production possibilities curve for each country would also define its **consumption possibilities.** Without imports, a country cannot consume more than it produces. Thus, the only immediate issue in a closed economy is which mix of output to choose—*what* to produce and consume—out of the domestic choices available.

Assume that Canadians choose point *D* on their production possibilities curve, producing and consuming 40 zillion loaves of bread and 30 zillion barrels of wine. The French, on the other hand, prefer the mix of output represented by point *I* on their production possibilities curve. At that point they produce and consume 9 zillion loaves of bread and 24 zillion barrels of wine.

To assess the potential gain from trade, we must focus the *combined* output of Canada and France. In this case, total world output (points *D* and *I*) comes to 49 zillion loaves of bread and 54 zillion barrels of wine. What we want to know is whether world output would increase if France and Canada abandoned their isolation and started trading. Could either country, or both, consume more output by engaging in a little trade?

Because both countries are saddled with limited production possibilities, trying to eke out a little extra wine and bread from this situation might not appear very promising. Such a conclusion is unwarranted, however. Take another look at the production possibilities confronting Canada, as reproduced in Figure 15.2*a*. Suppose Canada were to produce at point *C* rather than point *D*. At point *C* we could produce 60 zillion loaves of bread and 20 zillion barrels of wine. That combination is clearly possible, since it lies on the production possibilities curve. We didn't choose that point earlier because we assumed the mix of output at point *D* was preferable. The mix of output at point *C* could be produced, however.

We could also change the mix of output in France. Assume that France moved from point *I* to point *K*, producing 48 zillion barrels of wine and only 3 zillion loaves of bread.

> **consumption possibilities:** The alternative combinations of goods and services that a country could consume in a given time period.

Production and Consumption with Trade

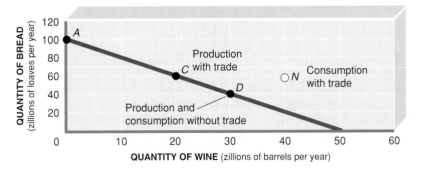

(a) Canadian production and consumption

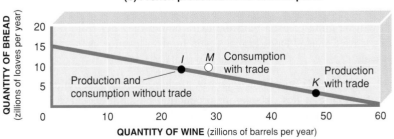

(b) French production and consumption

FIGURE 15.2
Consumption Possibilities with Trade

A country can increase its consumption possibilities through international trade. Each country alters its mix of domestic output to produce more of the good it produces best. As it does so, total world output increases, and each country enjoys more consumption. In this case, trade allows Canada's consumption to move from point *D* to point *N*. France moves from point *I* to point *M*.

Two observations are now called for. The first is simply that output mixes have changed in each country. The second, and more interesting, is that total world output has increased. When Canada and France were at points *D* and *I*, their *combined* output consisted of

	Bread (zillions of loaves)	Wine (zillions of barrels)
Canada (at point *D*)	40	30
France (at point *I*)	9	24
Total pretrade output	49	54

After moving along their respective production possibilities curves to points *C* and *K*, the combined world output becomes

	Bread (zillions of loaves)	Wine (zillions of barrels)
Canada (at point *C*)	60	20
France (at point *K*)	3	48
Total output with trade	63	68

Total world output has increased by 14 zillion loaves of bread and 14 zillion barrels of wine. *Just by changing the mix of output in each country, we've increased total world output.* This additional output creates the potential for making both countries better off than they were in the absence of trade.

Canada and France weren't producing at points *C* and *K* before because they simply didn't want to *consume* those particular output combinations. Nevertheless, our discovery that points *C* and *K* allow us to produce *more* output suggests that everybody can consume more goods and services if we change the mix of output in each country. This is our first clue as to how specialization and trade can benefit an economy.

Suppose we're the first to discover the potential benefits from trade. Using Figure 15.2 as our guide, we suggest to the French that they move their mix of output from point *I* to point *K*. As an incentive for making such a move, we promise to give them 6 zillion loaves of bread in exchange for 20 zillion barrels of wine. This would leave them at point *M*, with as much bread to consume as they used to have, plus an extra 4 zillion barrels of wine. At point *I* they had 9 zillion loaves of bread and 24 zillion barrels of wine. At point *M* they can have 9 zillion loaves of bread and 28 zillion barrels of wine. Thus, by altering their mix of output (from point *I* to point *K*) and then trading (point *K* to point *M*), the French end up with more goods and services than they had in the beginning. Notice in particular that this new consumption possibility (point *M*) lies *outside* France's domestic production possibilities curve.

The French will be quite pleased with the extra output they get from trading. But where does this leave Canada? Does France's gain imply a loss for us? Or do we gain from trade as well?

Mutual Gains   As it turns out, *both* Canada and France gain by trading. Canada, too, ends up consuming a mix of output that lies outside our production possibilities curve.

Note that at point *C* we produce 60 zillion loaves of bread per year and 20 zillion barrels of wine. We then export 6 zillion loaves to France. This leaves us with 54 zillion

TABLE 15.3
Gains from Trade

When nations specialize in production, they can export one good and import another and end up with more goods to consume than they had without trade. In this case, Canada specializes in bread production.

	Production	+	Imports	−	Exports	=	Consumption	Production and Consumption with No Trade
			Production and Consumption with Trade					
Canada at . . .	Point C						Point N	Point D
Bread	60	+	0	−	6	=	54	40
Wine	20	+	20	−	0	=	40	30
France at . . .	Point K						Point M	Point I
Bread	3	+	6	−	0	=	9	9
Wine	48	+	0	−	20	=	28	24

loaves of bread to consume. In return for our exported bread, the French give us 20 zillion barrels of wine. These imports, plus our domestic production, permit us to *consume* 40 zillion barrels of wine. Hence, we end up consuming at point N, enjoying 54 zillion loaves of bread and 40 zillion barrels of wine. Thus, by first changing the mix of output (from point D to point C), then trading (point C to point N), we end up with 14 zillion more loaves of bread and 10 zillion more barrels of wine than we started with. International trade has made us better off, too.

Table 15.3 recaps the gains from trade for both countries. Notice that Canadian imports match French exports and vice versa. Also notice how the trade-facilitated consumption in each country exceeds no-trade levels.

There's no sleight of hand going on here; the gains from trade are due to specialization in production. When each country goes it alone, it's a prisoner of its own production possibilities curve; it must make production decisions on the basis of its own consumption desires. When international trade is permitted, however, each country can concentrate on the exploitation of its production capabilities. *Each country produces those goods it makes best and then trades with other countries to acquire the goods it desires to consume.*

The resultant specialization increases total world output. In the process, each country is able to escape the confines of its own production possibilities curve, to reach beyond it for a larger basket of consumption goods. *When a country engages in international trade, its consumption possibilities always exceed its production possibilities.* These enhanced consumption possibilities are emphasized by the positions of points N and M outside the production possibilities curves (Figure 15.2). If it weren't possible for countries to increase their consumption by trading, there'd be no incentive for trading, and thus no trade.

15.3 PURSUIT OF COMPARATIVE ADVANTAGE

Although international trade can make both countries better off, it's not so obvious which goods should be traded, or on what terms. In our previous illustration, Canada ended up trading bread for wine in terms that were decidedly favourable to us. Why did we export bread rather than wine, and how did we end up getting such a good deal?

Opportunity Costs

The decision to export bread is based on *comparative advantage,* that is, the *relative* cost of producing different goods. Recall that we can produce a maximum of 100 zillion loaves of bread per year or 50 zillion barrels of wine. Thus, the domestic *opportunity cost* of producing 100 zillion loaves of bread is the 50 zillion barrels of wine we forsake to devote our resources to bread production. In fact, at every point on Canada's production possibilities curve (Figure 15.2*a*), the opportunity cost of a loaf of bread is $\frac{1}{2}$ barrel of wine. We're effectively paying half a barrel of wine to get a loaf of bread.

Although the cost of bread production in Canada might appear outrageous, even higher opportunity costs prevail in France. According to Figure 15.2*b*, the opportunity cost of producing a loaf of bread in France is a staggering four barrels of wine. To produce a loaf of bread, the French must use factors of production that could otherwise be used to produce four barrels of wine.

Comparative Advantage. A comparison of the opportunity costs prevailing in each country exposes the nature of comparative advantage. Canada has a comparative advantage in bread production because less wine has to be given up to produce bread in Canada than in France. In other words, the opportunity costs of bread production are lower in Canada than in France. ***Comparative advantage refers to the relative (opportunity) costs of producing particular goods.***

A country should specialize in what it's *relatively* efficient at producing, that is, goods for which it has the lowest opportunity costs. In this case, Canada should produce bread because its opportunity cost ($\frac{1}{2}$ barrel of wine) is less than France's (four barrels of wine). Were you the production manager for the whole world, you'd certainly want each country to exploit its relative abilities, thus maximizing world output. Each country can arrive at that same decision itself by comparing its own opportunity costs to those prevailing elsewhere. ***World output, and thus the potential gains from trade, will be maximized when each country pursues its comparative advantage.*** Each country does so by exporting goods that entail relatively low domestic opportunity costs and importing goods that involve relatively high domestic opportunity costs. That's the kind of situation depicted in Table 15.3.

Absolute Costs Don't Matter

In assessing the nature of comparative advantage, notice that we needn't know anything about the actual costs involved in production. Have you seen any data suggesting how much labour, land, or capital is required to produce a loaf of bread in either France or Canada? For all you and I know, the French may be able to produce both a loaf of bread and a barrel of wine with fewer resources than we're using. Such an *absolute advantage* in production might exist because of their much longer experience in cultivating both grapes and wheat or simply because they have more talent.

We can envy such productivity, and even try to emulate it, but it shouldn't alter our production or trade decisions. All we really care about are *opportunity costs*—what *we* have to give up in order to get more of a desired good. If we can get a barrel of wine for less bread in trade than in production, we have a comparative advantage in producing bread. As long as we have a *comparative* advantage in bread production we should exploit it. It doesn't matter whether France could produce either good with fewer resources. For that matter, even if France had an absolute advantage in *both* goods, we'd still have a *comparative* advantage in bread production, as we've already confirmed. The absolute costs of production were omitted from the previous illustration because they were irrelevant.

15.4 TERMS OF TRADE

terms of trade: The rate at which goods are exchanged; the amount of good A given up for good B in trade.

It definitely pays to pursue one's comparative advantage by specializing in production. It may not yet be clear, however, how we got such a good deal with France. We're clever traders, but beyond that, is there any way to determine the **terms of trade,** the quantity of good A that must be given up in exchange for good B? In our previous illustration, the terms of trade were very favourable to us; we exchanged only 6 zillion loaves of bread for 20 zillion barrels of wine (Table 15.3). The terms of trade were thus 6 loaves = 20 barrels.

The terms of trade with France were determined by our offer and France's ready acceptance. But why did France accept those terms? France was willing to accept the offer because the terms of trade permitted France to increase its wine consumption without giving up any bread consumption. The offer of 6 loaves for 20 barrels was an improvement over France's domestic opportunity costs. France's domestic possibilities required it to give up 24 barrels of wine to produce 6 loaves of bread (see Figure 15.2*b*). Getting bread via trade was simply cheaper for France than producing bread at home. France ended up with an extra 4 zillion barrels of wine (Table 15.3).

Our first clue to the terms of trade, then, lies in each country's domestic opportunity costs. *A country won't trade unless the terms of trade are superior to domestic opportunities.* In our example, the opportunity cost of 1 barrel of wine in Canada is 2 loaves of bread. Accordingly, we won't export bread unless we get at least 1 barrel of wine in exchange for every 2 loaves of bread shipped overseas.

All countries want to gain from trade. Hence, we can predict that *the terms of trade between any two countries will lie somewhere between their respective opportunity costs in production.* That is, a loaf of bread in international trade will be worth at least $\frac{1}{2}$ barrel of wine (Canada's opportunity cost) but no more than 4 barrels (the French opportunity cost). In our example, the terms of trade ended up at 1 loaf = 3.33 barrels (that is, at 6 loaves = 20 barrels). This represented a very large gain for Canada and a small gain for France. Figure 15.3 illustrates this outcome and several other possibilities.

Limits to the Terms of Trade

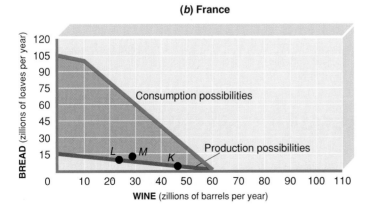

(a) Canada

(b) France

FIGURE 15.3
Searching for the Terms of Trade

Assume Canada can produce 100 zillion loaves of bread per year (point *A*). If we reduce output to only 85 zillion loaves, we could move to point *X*. At point *X* we have 7.5 zillion barrels of wine and 85 zillion loaves of bread.

Trade increases consumption possibilities. If we continued to produce 100 zillion loaves of bread, we could trade 15 zillion loaves to France in exchange for as much as 60 zillion barrels of wine. This would leave us *producing* at point *A* but *consuming* at point *Y*. At point *Y* we have more wine and no less bread than we had at point *X*.

A country will end up on its consumption possibilities curve only if it gets *all* the gains from trade. It will remain on its production possibilities curve only if it gets *none* of the gains from trade. The terms of trade determine how the gains from trade are distributed, and thus at what point in the shaded area each country ends up.

Note: The kink in the consumption possibilities curve at point *Y* occurs because France is unable to produce more than 60 zillion barrels of wine.

The Role of Markets and Prices

Relatively little trade is subject to such direct negotiations between countries. More often than not, the decision to import or export a particular good is left up to the market decisions of individual consumers and producers.

Individual consumers and producers aren't much impressed by such abstractions as comparative advantage. Market participants tend to focus on prices, always trying to allocate their resources to maximize profits or personal satisfaction. Consumers tend to buy the products that deliver the most utility per dollar of expenditure, while producers try to get the most output per dollar of cost. Everybody's looking for a bargain.

So what does this have to do with international trade? Well, suppose that Henri, an enterprising Frenchman, visited Canada before the advent of international trade. He observed that bread was relatively cheap while wine was relatively expensive—the opposite of the price relationship prevailing in France. These price comparisons brought to his mind the opportunity for making a fast euro. All he had to do was bring over some French wine and trade it in Canada for a large quantity of bread. Then he could return to France and exchange the bread for a greater quantity of wine. *Alors!* Were he to do this a few times, he'd amass substantial profits.

Henri's entrepreneurial exploits will not only enrich him but will also move each country toward its comparative advantage. Canada ends up exporting bread to France, and France ends up exporting wine to Canada, exactly as the theory of comparative advantage suggests. The activating agent isn't the Ministry of Trade and its 620 trained economists but simply one enterprising French trader. He's aided and encouraged, of course, by consumers and producers in each country. Canadian consumers are happy to trade their bread for his wines. They thereby end up paying less for wine (in terms of bread) than they'd otherwise have to. In other words, the terms of trade Henri offers are more attractive than the prevailing (domestic) relative prices. On the other side of the Atlantic, Henri's welcome is equally warm. French consumers are able to get a better deal by trading their wine for his imported bread than by trading with the local bakers.

Even some producers are happy. The wheat farmers and bakers in Canada are eager to deal with Henri. He's willing to buy a lot of bread and even to pay a premium price for it. Indeed, bread production has become so profitable in Canada that a lot of people who used to grow and mash grapes are now growing wheat and kneading dough. This alters the mix of output in the direction of more bread, exactly as suggested in Figure 15.2*a*.

In France, the opposite kind of production shift is taking place. French wheat farmers are planting more grape vines so they can take advantage of Henri's generous purchases. Thus, Henri is able to lead each country in the direction of its comparative advantage while raking in a substantial profit for himself along the way.

Where the terms of trade and the volume of exports and imports end up depends partly on how good a trader Henri is. It will also depend on the behaviour of the thousands of individual consumers and producers who participate in the market exchanges. In other words, trade flows depend on both the supply and the demand for bread and wine in each country. ***The terms of trade, like the price of any good, depend on the willingness of market participants to buy or sell at various prices.*** All we know for sure is that the terms of trade will end up somewhere between the limits set by each country's opportunity costs.

WEB NOTE

Find out more about Canada's trade negotiations and agreements at Foreign Affairs and International Trade Canada: http://www.international.gc.ca/tna-nac/menu-en.asp.

15.5 PROTECTIONIST PRESSURES

Although the potential gains from world trade are impressive, not everyone will participate in the celebration. On the contrary, some people will see the threat in establishing new trade routes. These people and groups will not only boycott the celebration but actively seek to discourage Canadians from continuing to trade at all!

APPLICATIONS

Chrysler Deals to Get Small Cars from China

The Chrysler Group has agreed in principle to import Chinese-built subcompact cars to North America and Europe, a milestone that could lead to the first Chinese cars on North American roads if Chinese automakers don't act on their own faster.

The deal between Chrysler and Chery Automobile Co., if approved by the DaimlerChrysler supervisory board this month, would give Chrysler a subcompact model it lacks.

While a domestic automaker importing Chinese vehicles may raise some political concerns, Chrysler CEO Tom LaSorda has said such a partnership is the only way Chrysler could sell a vehicle profitably.

Source: Based on Justin Hyde, Joe Guy Collier, and Jason Roberson, "Chrysler deals to get small cars from China," *National Post* (January 5, 2007), p. DT2.

Analysis: Goods imported from other countries compete with the same or similar goods produced in Canada and can alter the mix of production in both countries.

Microeconomic Pressures

Consider, for example, the auto workers at Chrysler in Windsor. As the Applications box above explains, Chrysler has agreed to a deal to sell cars imported from China in North America. Suppose Canadians are able to buy cars more cheaply from China than they can from Windsor. Before long we begin to hear talk about unfair foreign competition, or about the higher quality of the Canadian-built cars, or about the desire for "fair" trade. The car industry may also emphasize the importance of maintaining an adequate production of cars and a strong automobile industry here at home, just in case other countries use our lack of car production to force us to agree to other deals.

Import-Competing Industries. Joining with the auto workers will be the other automotive parts producers and merchants whose livelihood depends upon the domestic Canadian car industry. If they are clever enough, the auto workers will also get the Premier of Ontario to join their demonstration. After all, the Premier must recognize the needs of the local constituents, and there are almost certainly no Ontarians producing cars in China. Canadian consumers are, of course, benefiting from these reduced car prices, but they're unlikely to demonstrate over a couple of hundred dollars on the price of a car. On the other hand, those few hundred dollars per car translate into millions of dollars for the domestic car companies and their workers.

Of course, while Canadian consumers are buying cars made in China, Chinese consumers are buying goods and services from Canada. And the affected Chinese industries and workers are no happier about international trade than are the Canadian auto workers. They would dearly love to sink all those boats bringing Canadian goods and services from Canada, thereby protecting their own market position.

If we're to make sense of trade policies, then, we must recognize one central fact of life: Some producers have a vested interest in restricting international trade. In particular, *workers and producers who compete with imported products—who work in import-competing industries—have an economic interest in restricting trade.* This helps explain why Canadian auto workers are unhappy with DaimlerChrysler's deal with China and why the domestic car industry is unhappy with car imports. It also explains why farmers in the United States are unhappy with imports of Canadian wheat for pasta production, or why U.S. lumber producers are unhappy with imports of Canadian softwood lumber for home construction.

Export Industries. Although imports typically mean fewer jobs and less income for some domestic industries, exports represent increased jobs and income for other industries. Producers and workers in export industries gain from trade. Thus, on a microeconomic level there are identifiable gainers and losers from international trade. *Trade not only alters the mix of output but also redistributes income from import-competing industries to export industries.* This potential redistribution is the source of political and economic friction. It is this friction that makes the case for Macauley's contention that we began this chapter with, that free trade is "in almost every country, unpopular."

Net Gain. We must be careful to note, however, that the microeconomic gains from trade are greater than the microeconomic losses. It's not simply a question of robbing Peter to enrich Paul. We must remind ourselves that consumers in general enjoy a higher standard of living as a result of international trade. As we saw earlier, trade increases world efficiency and total output. Accordingly, we end up slicing up a larger pie rather than just reslicing the same old smaller pie.

This point is made by U.S. economist Paul Krugman when he describes the perspectives of business people and economists. Business people tend to focus on the impact of individual exports or imports, often a win–lose situation for any particular industry. The focus of economists is on the "gains from trade," the fundamental increase in total world spending described above.

> Why don't economists subscribe to what sounds like common sense to businesspeople? The idea that free trade means more global jobs seems obvious: More trade means more exports and therefore more export-related jobs. But there is a problem with that argument. Because one country's exports are another country's imports, every dollar of export sales is, as a matter of sheer mathematical necessity, matched by a dollar of spending shifted from some country's domestic goods to imports. Unless there is some reason to think that free trade will increase total world spending, overall world demand will not change.[5]

That total world spending will increase is, in fact, the point made with comparative advantage. As countries shift their resources towards goods and services in which they have comparative advantage, total world production can rise, thus increasing income and spending. In other words, trade is beneficial because it increases total production (and thereby additional employment and consumption).

The gains from trade will mean nothing to workers who end up with a smaller slice of the (larger) pie. It's important to remember, however, that the gains from trade are large enough to make everybody better off. Whether we actually choose to distribute the gains from trade in this way is a separate question, to which we shall return shortly. Note here, however, that *trade restrictions designed to protect specific microeconomic interests reduce the total gains from trade.* Trade restrictions leave us with a smaller pie to split up.

Additional Pressures

Import-competing industries are the principal obstacle to expanded international trade. Selfish micro interests aren't the only source of trade restrictions, however. Other arguments are also used to restrict trade.

National Security. The national security argument for trade restrictions is twofold. We can't depend on foreign suppliers to provide us with essential defense-related goods, it is said, because that would leave us vulnerable in time of war. The domestic agricultural industry often promotes a similar argument. If Canada was to become dependant on foreign sources of food, we could be "made" to make decisions we otherwise wouldn't make at the threat of the food being withheld.

[5]Paul Krugman, "A country is not a company," *Harvard Business Review,* (96)2, pp. 40–47.

U.S. Appliance Firms Guilty of Dumping in Canada

OTTAWA—Prices for some major appliances could more than double as a result of a ruling that the U.S. companies behind Whirlpool, Frigidaire, Kelvinator and Amana have unfairly dumped exports on the $1-billion-a-year Canadian appliance market.

The Canadian International Trade Tribunal has confirmed a ruling from the Canadian Customs and Revenue Agency that refrigerators, dishwashers and dryers were sold at below-market prices.

Camco Inc. of Hamilton, which makes appliances under the GE, Hotpoint, Kenmore, Beaumark and other brand names, complained last November that it was losing sales to unfair competition from White Consolidated Industries Inc. and Whirlpool Corp., two major U.S. manufacturers.

A four-month investigation, following a probe by customs officials, confirmed the goods had been sold for less than the price in the home [U.S.] market or at a loss.

"It [the ruling] will have a substantial positive impact for Camco. We're confident we will regain a substantial share of the profit we've lost over the past two years," James Fleck, Camco president, said yesterday. "It's a level playing field and an opportunity to regain the market share we've lost."

Depending on the model, prices will have to increase anywhere from a few dollars to almost 150%.

Source: Ian Jack, "U.S. appliance firms guilty of dumping in Canada," *National Post*, August 9, 2000, p. C3. Material reprinted with the express permission of National Post Company, a CanWest Partnership.

Analysis: Dumping results in unfair competitive pressure as selling prices don't necessarily reflect market conditions or costs. These and other pressures in the appliance industry caused the Hamilton Camco plant to close in 2004, while the company itself was sold to Controladora Mabe SA. a Mexico-based company.

Dumping. Another argument against free trade arises from the practice of **dumping.** Foreign producers "dump" their goods when they sell them in Canada at prices lower than those prevailing in their own country, perhaps even below the costs of production.

> **dumping:** The sale of goods in export markets at prices below domestic prices.

Dumping may be unfair to import-competing producers, but it isn't necessarily unwelcome to the rest of us. As long as foreign producers continue dumping, we're getting foreign products at low prices. How bad can that be? There's a legitimate worry, however. Foreign producers might hold prices down only until domestic producers are driven out of business. Then we might be compelled to pay the foreign producers higher prices for their products. In that case, dumping could consolidate market power and lead to monopoly-type pricing. The fear of dumping, then, is analogous to the fear of predatory pricing. The Applications box illustrates both the concern of manufacturers and the benefit to consumers. The loss of market share and profitability to Camco Inc. may result in a reduction in production, or a complete cessation. Consumers, on the other hand, will pay "from a few dollars to almost 150%" more for their refrigerators, dishwashers, or dryers as additional duties are imposed.

The potential costs of dumping are serious. It's not always easy to determine when dumping occurs, however. Those who compete with imports have an uncanny ability to associate any and all low prices with predatory dumping.

Infant Industries. Actual dumping threatens to damage already established domestic industries. Even normal import prices, however, may make it difficult or impossible for a new domestic industry to develop. Infant industries are often burdened with abnormally high startup costs. These high costs may arise from the need to train a whole workforce and the expenses of establishing new marketing channels. With time to grow, however, an infant industry might experience substantial cost reductions and establish a comparative advantage. When this is the case, trade restrictions might help nurture an industry in its infancy. Trade restrictions are justified, however, only if there's tangible evidence that the industry can develop a comparative advantage reasonably quickly.

Improving the Terms of Trade. A final argument for restricting trade rests on how the gains from trade are distributed. As we observed, the distribution of the gains from trade depends on the terms of trade. If we were to buy fewer imports, foreign producers might lower their prices. If that happened, the terms of trade would move in our favour, and we'd end up with a larger share of the gains from trade.

One way to bring about this sequence of events is to put restrictions on imports, making it more difficult or expensive for Canadians to buy foreign products. Such restrictions will reduce the volume of imports, thereby inducing foreign producers to lower their prices. Unfortunately, this strategy can easily backfire: Retaliatory restrictions on imports, each designed to improve the terms of trade, will ultimately eliminate all trade and therewith all the gains people were competing for in the first place.

15.6 BARRIERS TO TRADE

The microeconomic losses associated with imports give rise to a constant clamour for trade restrictions. People whose jobs and incomes are threatened by international trade tend to organize quickly and air their grievances. The World View box below depicts the efforts of farmers in Montana and North Dakota to limit imports of Canadian wheat and livestock. They hope to convince Congress to impose restrictions on imports. More often than not, Congress grants the wishes of these well-organized and well-financed special interests.

Embargoes

> **embargo:** A prohibition on exports or imports.

The surefire way to restrict trade is simply to eliminate it. To do so, a country need only impose an embargo on exports or imports, or both. An **embargo** is nothing more than a prohibition against trading particular goods.

As the World View box on the next page illustrates, some embargo decisions arise not from a concern for domestic jobs, but more from domestic sensibilities. While the reason underlying the decision may be valid, the article makes the point that economic consequences are still imposed on both potential consumers—replacement with more expensive or less desirable products—and on the export producers—loss of jobs, incomes, and way of life.

Tariffs

> **tariff:** A tax (duty) imposed on imported goods.

A more frequent trade restriction is a **tariff,** a special tax imposed on imported goods. Tariffs, also called *customs duties,* were once the principal source of revenue for governments. In modern times, tariffs have been used primarily as a means to protect specific industries from import competition. In Canada, while most tariffs are imposed

Farmers Stage Protests over Import of Products

Farmers claiming that imports of Canadian grain and other agricultural products are depressing U.S. prices threatened on Tuesday more blockades at border crossings unless the U.S. government acts to slow the flow of goods.

Farmers also want Canadian wheat and livestock tested for diseases and additives that are banned here.

Blockades and other protests have appeared at various border crossings in North Dakota and Montana for several days. In Montana, 20 long-haul truckers were ticketed Monday, the first day of a state crackdown on border inspections. And farmers in North Dakota dumped grain on U.S. Highway 281, stopping truck traffic for eight hours.

"We've got an oversupply of wheat, hogs and cattle already," said Curt Trulson, a farmer in Ross, N.D. "We don't need any more foreign commodities."

Source: *USA Today,* September 23, 1998. USA TODAY. © 1998, USA Today. Reprinted with permission. www.usatoday.com

Analysis: Import-competing industries cite lots of reasons for restricting trade. Their primary concern, however, is to protect their own jobs and profits.

Inuit Call for Rethink of Seal-Ban Proposal

A council representing Inuit from Canada, Russia, Alaska and Greenland has warned European legislators that a renewed push to ban seal products could devastate native communities.

Some members of the European Parliament say the annual seal hunt in Canada is cruel and unsustainable and they've passed a non-binding declaration calling for a ban on imports of seal products. It will be up to the European Commission to determine whether it becomes law.

Meanwhile, the German Parliament unanimously endorsed an import ban the day after the Inuit Circumpolar Council,

which represents 150,000 Inuit living in the Arctic, sent a letter asking legislators to rethink their position.

"The proposed legislation would hurt our Inuit economy, our Inuit culture, and our Inuit spirituality in unimaginable ways," council chairwoman Patricia Cochran said in a letter dated Oct. 18.

"Inuit base their hunt, all hunts, on the principle of sustainable use, not on the principle of subjective 'public decency' as some European governments seem to be doing," she wrote.

Source: *The Globe and Mail* (October 31, 2006). p. A15. Used with the permission of the Canadian Press.

Analysis: Although bans, or embargoes, may have more to do with political, social, or cultural sensibilities, the economic impacts are no less consequential.

---

on goods coming from other countries, in some cases there are also tariffs for goods moving from one province to another.

The tariff imposed on imported goods is also dependent on the particular country of origin. In the most recent customs tariff provided by the Canada Border Services Agency, countries are separated into four categories (although an individual country can be simultaneously in more than one category). Some countries have been designated for a General Preferential Tariff treatment, some countries are beneficiaries of the Least Developed Country tariff treatment, some countries are designated beneficiary countries for purposes of the Commonwealth Caribbean Countries tariff treatment, and others receive no beneficial treatment and are subject to the full tariff.[6]

The attraction of tariffs to import-competing industries should be obvious. *A tariff on imported goods makes them more expensive to domestic consumers and thus less competitive with domestically produced goods.* Among tariffs in place for Canada in 2007 were $0.374 per litre on sparkling wine and $0.2816 per litre on cider. These tariffs enable Canadian-produced sparkling wine and cider to sell at a higher price, and therefore contribute higher sales revenue and profits for domestic producers. In the same manner, ski jackets (made from synthetic material) face a tariff of 18 percent while a new guitar has 6 percent added.[7] In each case, domestic producers in import-competing industries gain. The losers are domestic consumers, who end up paying higher prices.

"Beggar Thy Neighbour." Microeconomic interests aren't the only source of pressure for tariff protection. Imports represent leakage from the domestic circular flow and a potential loss of jobs at home. From this perspective, the curtailment of imports looks like an easy solution to the problem of domestic unemployment. Just get people to "buy Canadian" instead of buying imported products, so the argument goes, and domestic output and employment will surely expand.

Tariffs designed to expand domestic employment are more likely to fail than to succeed. If a tariff wall does stem the flow of imports, it effectively transfers the

WEB NOTE

For more information about Canada's most recent customs tariffs, go to the Canada Border Services Agency site at http://www.cbsa-asfc.gc.ca/trade-commerce/tariff-tarif/menu-e.html#current.

---

[6]See the Canada Border Services Agency Web site at http://www.cbsa-asfc.gc.ca/menu-eng.html for more information.

[7]All tariff amounts have been taken from documents on the Canada Border Services Agency Web site. These are from the Departmental Consolidation of the Customs Tariff, 2007. http://www.cbsa-asfc.gc.ca/general/publications/tariff2007/01-99/tblmod-1-e.html, accessed March 2, 2007.

"Beggar-Thy-Neighbour" Policies in the 1930s

President Herbert Hoover, ignoring the pleas of 1,028 economists to veto it, signed the Smoot-Hawley Tariff Act on June 17, 1930. It was a hollow celebration. The day before, anticipating the signing, the stock market suffered its worst collapse since November 1929, and the law quickly helped push the Great Depression deeper.

The new tariffs, which by 1932 rose to an all-time high of 59 percent of the average value of imports (today it's 5 percent), were designed to save American jobs by restricting foreign competition. Economists warned that angry nations would retaliate, and they did.

- Spain passed the Wais tariff in July in reaction to U.S. tariffs on grapes, oranges, cork, and onions.
- Switzerland, objecting to new U.S. tariffs on watches, embroideries, and shoes, boycotted American exports.
- Italy retaliated against tariffs on hats and olive oil with high tariffs on U.S. and French automobiles in June 1930.
- Canada reacted to high duties on many food products, logs, and timber by raising tariffs threefold in August 1932.

- Australia, Cuba, France, Mexico, and New Zealand also joined in the tariff wars.

From 1930 to 1931 U.S. imports dropped 29 percent, but U.S. exports fell even more, 33 percent, and continued their collapse to a modern-day low of $2.4 billion in 1933. World trade contracted by similar proportions, spreading unemployment around the globe.

In 1934 the U.S. Congress passed the Reciprocal Trade Agreements Act to empower the president to reduce tariffs by half the 1930 rates in return for like cuts in foreign duties on U.S. goods. The "beggar-thy-neighbour" policy was dead. Since then, the nations of the world have been reducing tariffs and other trade barriers.

Source: World Bank, *World Development Report 1987;* and *The Wall Street Journal,* April 28, 1989, Reprinted by permission of The Wall Street Journal, © 1989 Dow Jones & Company. All rights reserved. www.worldbank.org; www.wsj.com

Analysis: Tariffs inflict harm on foreign producers. If foreign countries retaliate with tariffs of their own, world trade will shrink and unemployment will increase in all countries.

---

unemployment problem to other countries, a phenomenon often referred to as "beggar thy neighbour." The resultant loss of business in other countries leaves them less able to purchase our exports (see the World View box).

Quotas

quota: A limit on the quantity of a good that may be imported in a given time period.

Tariffs reduce the flow of imports by raising import prices. The same outcome can be attained more directly by imposing import **quotas,** numerical restrictions on the quantity of a particular good that may be imported. As explained in the Applications box on the next page, the intention to limit the importation of milk-protein concentrates will increase the revenue of dairy fanners in Canada by $2-million a month, but might result in a reduction of cheese production in Canada or higher prices faced by consumers. Although quotas restrict the quantity of imports while tariffs increase the price of importing, both result in the same effect—protection of the domestic producer and higher domestic prices for consumers.

Comparative Effects

Quotas, like all barriers to trade, reduce world efficiency and invite retaliatory action. Moreover, their impact can be even more damaging than tariffs. To see this, we may compare market outcomes in four different contexts: no trade, free trade, tariff-restricted trade, and quota-restricted trade.

No-Trade Equilibrium. Figure 15.4a depicts the supply-and-demand relationships that would prevail in an economy that imposed a trade *embargo* on foreign textiles. In this situation, the *equilibrium price* of textiles is completely determined by domestic demand and supply curves. The no-trade equilibrium price is p_1, and the quantity of textiles consumed is q_1.

APPLICATIONS

Ottawa Moves on Dairy Protection: Import Restriction

OTTAWA—The federal Conservative government has moved to restrict the import of a key ingredient used to make cheese.

The decision, announced yesterday by Agriculture Minister Chuck Strahl, came about due to the failure by the country's dairy processors to resolve a dispute regarding the import of milk-protein concentrates. Dairy farmers claimed they lost, collectively, about $2-million a month in sales in the last fiscal year because of increased imports of milk-protein substitutes, and have called on Ottawa to restrict imports of the product for the past three years.

"We are very pleased with the outcome," said Jacques Laforge, president of the 16,000-member Dairy Farmers of Canada. "It stops the erosion of our revenue. What we've lost, we've lost. But this freezes the damage."

Don Jarvis, president of the Dairy Processors Association of Canada, said his members—such as Saputo Inc., Kraft Canada Inc. and Agripur—bought milk-protein from abroad because it is not readily available in Canada and was in most cases cheaper. He said yesterday's decision could have an impact on the availability and pricing of cheese.

Source: P. Vieira, "Ottawa moves on dairy protection: Import restriction," *National Post* (February 8, 2007), p. FP7. Material reprinted with the express permission of National Post Company, a CanWest Partnership.

Analysis: The quote from the president of the Dairy Farmers of Canada crystallizes the point here: "it stops the erosion of our revenue." Dairy farmers are able to receive higher prices for milk-protein concentrates because the restriction on imports imposed by the federal government reduces supply and thereby raises the price of imported substitutes.

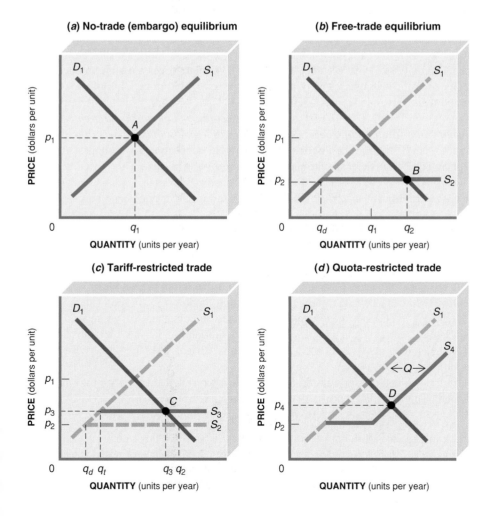

FIGURE 15.4
The Impact of Trade Restrictions

In the *absence of trade,* the domestic price and sales of a good will be determined by domestic supply and demand curves (point *A* in part *a*). Once trade is permitted, the market supply curve will be altered by the availability of imports. With *free trade* and unlimited availability of imports at price p_2, a new market equilibrium will be established at world prices (point *B*).

Tariffs raise domestic prices and reduce the quantity sold (point *C*). *Quotas* put an absolute limit on imported sales and thus give domestic producers a great opportunity to raise the market price (point *D*).

Free-Trade Equilibrium. Suppose now that the embargo is lifted. The immediate effect of this decision will be a rightward shift of the market supply curve, as foreign supplies are added to domestic supplies (Figure 15.4b). If an unlimited quantity of textiles can be bought in world markets at a price of p_2, the new supply curve will look like S_2 (infinitely elastic at p_2). The new supply curve (S_2) intersects the old demand curve (D_1) at a new equilibrium price of p_2 and an expanded consumption of q_2. At this new equilibrium, domestic producers are supplying the quantity q_d while foreign producers are supplying the rest ($q_2 - q_d$). Comparing the new equilibrium to the old one, we see that *free trade results in reduced prices and increased consumption.*

Domestic textile producers are unhappy, of course, with their foreign competition. In the absence of trade, the domestic producers would sell more output (q_1) and get higher prices (p_1). Once trade is opened up, the willingness of foreign producers to sell unlimited quantities of textiles at the price p_2 puts a lid on domestic prices.

Tariff-Restricted Trade. Figure 15.4c illustrates what would happen to prices and sales if the United Textile Producers were successful in persuading the government to impose a tariff. Assume that the tariff raises imported textile prices from p_2 to p_3, making it more difficult for foreign producers to undersell domestic producers. Domestic production expands from q_d to q_t, imports are reduced from $q_2 - q_d$ to $q_3 - q_t$, and the market price of textiles rises. Domestic textile producers are clearly better off, whereas consumers and foreign producers are worse off. In addition, the government will collect increased tariff revenues.

Quota-Restricted Trade. Now consider the impact of a textile *quota.* Suppose we eliminate tariffs but decree that imports can't exceed the quantity Q. Because the quantity of imports can never exceed Q, the supply curve is effectively shifted to the right by that amount. The new curve S_4 (Figure 15.4d) indicates that no imports will occur below the world price p_2 and above that price the quantity Q will be imported. Thus, the *domestic* demand curve determines subsequent prices. Foreign producers are precluded from selling greater quantities as prices rise further. This outcome is in marked contrast to that of tariff-restricted trade (Figure 15.4c), which at least permits foreign producers to respond to rising prices. Accordingly, *quotas are a greater threat to competition than tariffs, because quotas preclude additional imports at any price.* Suppose that restricting the imports of milk-protein concentrates—as suggested in the Applications box—increases the price of cheese by 20 percent. This would result in $10 worth of cheese now being priced at $12. Canadian consumers end up paying more for cheese, and having fewer dollars remaining to buy other goods and services.

A slight variant of quotas has been used in recent years. Rather than impose quotas on imports, the government asks foreign producers to "voluntarily" limit their exports. A form of this "**voluntary restraint agreement**" was part of the Canada–United States softwood lumber agreement negotiated in Fall 2006. One of the options in the agreement was for producers to "restrain" exports to a maximum market share of between 30 and 34 percent, depending upon the prevailing market price in the United States.

In the 1980s, Canada negotiated with Japanese automakers to "voluntarily" limit their sales of cars in Canada. The result was a shortage of Japanese cars in the market, and higher prices (and profit margins) for each car than they otherwise would have been.

All these voluntary export restraints, as they're often called, represent an informal type of quota. The only difference is that they're negotiated rather than imposed. But these differences are lost on consumers, who end up paying higher prices for these goods.

"TELL ME AGAIN HOW THE QUOTAS ON JAPANESE CARS HAVE PROTECTED US"

—from *Herblock at Large* (Pantheon Books, 1987).

Analysis: Trade restrictions that protect import-competing industries also raise consumer prices.

Voluntary Restraint Agreements

voluntary restraint agreement (VRA): An agreement to reduce the volume of trade in a specific good; a voluntary quota.

Nontariff Barriers

Tariffs and quotas are the most visible barriers to trade, but they're only the tip of the iceberg. Indeed, the variety of protectionist measures that have been devised is testimony to the ingenuity of the human mind. At the turn of the twentieth century, the Germans were committed to a most-favoured-nation policy, a policy of extending equal treatment

WORLD VIEW

High Court Opens U.S. Roads to Mexican Trucks

The Supreme Court ruled yesterday that the Bush administration can open U.S. roads to Mexican trucks as soon as it wants, overruling a lower court judgment that the government must first study the environmental effects.

Under NAFTA, which went into effect in 1994, the United States was supposed to phase out restrictions on Mexican trucks crossing the border by 2000, provided those trucks meet U.S. safety standards. But under pressure from members of Congress and the Teamsters union, which feared losing jobs to low-wage Mexican drivers, the Clinton administration maintained the existing barriers, citing safety concerns. As a result, Mexican trucks have been confined to a 20-mile zone along the border, where they transfer their loads to U.S. carriers in cities such as San Diego and Laredo, Tex.

The Bush administration vowed to open the border in 2001 after a NAFTA panel held that Washington was violating the agreement.

—Paul Blustein

Source: *The Washington Post*, June 8, 2004. © 2004 The Washington Post. Reprinted with permission. www.washingtonpost.com

Analysis: Nontariff barriers like extraordinary safety requirements on Mexican trucks limit import competition.

to all trading partners. The Germans, however, wanted to lower the tariff on cattle imports from Denmark without extending the same break to Switzerland. Such a preferential tariff would have violated the most-favoured-nation policy. Accordingly, the Germans created a new and higher tariff on "brown and dappled cows reared at a level of at least 300 meters above sea level and passing at least one month in every summer at an altitude of at least 800 meters." The new tariff was, of course, applied equally to all countries. But Danish cows never climb that high, so they weren't burdened with the new tariff.

With the decline in tariffs over the last 20 years, nontariff barriers have increased. Canada uses product standards, licensing restrictions, restrictive procurement practices, and other nontariff barriers to restrict imports.

APPLICATIONS

B.C. Premier Shines Spotlight on Free Trade

It wasn't even on the agenda, but the seemingly dry subject of provincial free trade stole some of the spotlight at a meeting between western premiers yesterday. "When are we going to decide we are a country? When are we going to decide that the free movement of goods and people and services is something that is part of what a national identity should be?" British Columbia Premier Gordon Campbell told reporters after the annual conference wrapped up in Iqaluit.

B.C. and Alberta signed a first-of-its-kind interprovincial trade agreement that began coming into effect this spring. The deal, which is opposed by unions in both provinces, aims to slash trade barriers and red tape and increase labour mobility in a bid to create the country's second-largest economic trade zone, behind Ontario. Both governments were confident that the Trade, Investment and Labour Mobility Agreement (TILMA) would become an example for the rest of the country. However, no other provinces have acted on it or joined it.

Source: Katherine Harding, "B.C. Premier shines spotlight on free trade," *The Globe and Mail* (July 7, 2007), p. A7.

Analysis: Barriers to trade are not only an international concern, many barriers exist between provinces across the country, and the motivation, benefits, and costs of reducing or eliminating them are the same as in the international sphere.

15.7 INTERNATIONAL INSTITUTIONS

An Increasingly Global Market

Proponents of free trade and representatives of special interests that profit from trade protection are in constant conflict. But most of the time the trade-policy deck seems stacked in favour of the special interests. Because the interests of import-competing firms and workers are highly concentrated, they're quick to mobilize politically. By contrast, the benefits of freer trade are less direct and spread over millions of consumers. As a consequence, the beneficiaries of free trade are less likely to monitor trade policy—much less lobby actively to change it. Hence, the political odds favour the spread of trade barriers.

Multilateral Trade Pacts

Despite these odds, the long-term trend is toward *reducing* trade barriers, thereby increasing global competition. Two forces encourage this trend. The principal barrier to protectionist policies is worldwide recognition of the gains from freer trade. Since world nations now understand that trade barriers are ultimately self-defeating, they're more willing to rise above the din of protectionist cries and dismantle trade barriers. They diffuse political opposition by creating across-the-board **trade pacts** that seem to spread the pain (and gain) from freer trade across a broad swath of industries. Such pacts also incorporate multiyear timetables that give affected industries time to adjust.

> **trade pact:** A negotiation or agreement between countries governing trade; *bilateral* trade pacts involve two countries, and *multilateral* trade pacts involve more than two countries.

The opposition of import-competing industries to these multilateral, multiyear trade pacts is countered by a second force: the interests of *export*-oriented industries and other multilateral firms. Restrictions on imports of milk-protein concentrates in Canada may result in retaliation by the countries that sold us the concentrates and a reduction in Canadian exports to those countries. Tariffs or export charges, such as in the 2006 Softwood Lumber agreement, increases the price of lumber in the U.S. market, making buildings and housing more expensive for U.S. consumers. An increasing popular awareness of such damage has created a political climate for freer trade.

Global Pacts: GATT and WTO

The granddaddy of the multilateral, multiyear free-trade pacts was the 1947 **General Agreement on Tariffs and Trade (GATT).** Twenty-three nations pledged to reduce trade barriers and give all GATT nations equal access to their domestic markets.

> **General Agreement on Tariffs and Trade (GATT):** A trade pact that covered the rules and regulations governing the international trade in goods; now part of the World Trade Organization, WTO.

Since the first GATT pact, seven more "rounds" of negotiations have expanded the scope of GATT: 117 nations signed the 1994 pact. As a result of these GATT pacts, average tariff rates in developed countries have fallen from 40 percent in 1948 to less than 4 percent today.

> **World Trade Organization (WTO):** An international institution that administers the rules of trade among 151 member nations, including Canada.

WTO. The 1994 GATT pact also created the **World Trade Organization (WTO)** to enforce free-trade rules. If a nation feels its exports are being unfairly excluded from another country's market, it can file a complaint with the WTO. In April 2006 Canada joined the European Union and the United States in complaining about the way China imposes tariffs on imported car parts. In September 2006 the WTO created a panel drawn from other WTO members to make a decision about the complaint. If the panel finds in Canada's favour, they may enable Canada to impose retaliatory tariffs on some Chinese goods or services.

On the other side, in November 2006 the European Union filed a complaint with the WTO regarding Canada's unequal tax treatment of domestically produced versus imported wine and beer. At this stage, the European Communities are asking for "consultations" with Canada. If these consultations prove fruitless, the complaint could move to a "third-party" panel for an adjudication, and if the European Communities were successful, the ability to impose retaliatory tariffs on other Canadian goods or services.

In effect, the WTO is now the world's trade police force. It is empowered to cite nations that violate trade agreements and even to impose remedial action when violations persist. Why do sovereign nations give the WTO such power? Because they are all convinced that free trade is the surest route to GDP growth.

APPLICATIONS

DOHA Talks in Danger of Collapse; Subsidies at Issue: Rich, Poor Countries Remain at Odds

WASHINGTON—Global trade talks [the Doha Round] launched six years ago appear to be sliding quickly into a coma with the world's wealthiest countries fearing there may not be any quick recovery. Trade ministers from Canada, the United States and leading Asian countries wrapped up another stalled set of trade negotiations in Australia yesterday by complaining there appears to be little chance for trade breakthroughs globally, . . . or among Asia–Pacific countries any time soon.

The Doha Round launched in 2001 and aimed at reducing farm subsidies among the richer countries and making it easier

for poorer countries to trade, has virtually gone nowhere in the past six years. The rich and poor countries are still at odds, leading to a near collapse last month in Germany at a meeting of the so-called G4 countries, which are the U.S., the European Union, Brazil and India.

Source: Peter Morton, "DOHA talks in danger of collapse; Subsidies at issue: rich, poor countries remain at odds," *National Post* (July 7, 2007), p. FP7. Material used with express permission of Montreal National Post Company, a CanWest Partnership.

Analysis: Multilateral trade negotiations are complex. Although "rich" countries have pledged to reduce subsidies that distort trade, political consequences and internal lobbies have made it difficult to actually do so.

WTO Protests. Although freer trade clearly boosts economic growth, some people say that it does more harm than good. Environmentalists question the very desirability of continued economic growth. They worry about the depletion of resources, congestion and pollution, and the social friction that growth often promotes. Labour organizations worry that global competition will depress wages and working conditions. And many Third World nations are concerned about playing by trade rules that always seem to benefit rich nations (e.g., copyright protection, import protection, farm subsidies).

Despite some tumultuous street protests (e.g., Seattle in 1999), WTO members continue the difficult process of dismantling trade barriers. The latest round of negotiations began in Doha, Qatar, in 2001. The key issue in the "Doha Round" has been farm subsidies in rich nations. Poor nations protest that farm subsidies in the United States and Europe not only limit their exports but also lower global farm prices (hurting farmers in developing nations). By the end of 2004, the WTO had secured pledges to reduce those farm subsidies (see the Applications box).

Because worldwide trade pacts are so complex, many nations have also pursued *regional* free-trade agreements. In December 1992, the United States, Canada, and Mexico signed the **North American Free Trade Agreement (NAFTA),** a 1,000-page document covering more than 9,000 products. The ultimate goal of NAFTA is to eliminate all trade barriers in goods and services between these three countries. At the time of signing, intraregional tariffs averaged 11 percent in Mexico, 5 percent in Canada, and 4 percent in the United States. NAFTA requires that all tariffs between the three countries be eliminated by 2007. The pact also requires the elimination of specific nontariff barriers. But NAFTA does not enable labour mobility which was included in the British Columbia–Alberta agreement (see the Applications box on page 333).

The NAFTA-initiated reduction in trade barriers substantially increased trade flows between Mexico, Canada, and the United States. It also prompted a wave of foreign investment in Mexico, where both cheap labour and NAFTA access were available. Overall, NAFTA accelerated economic growth and reduced inflationary pressures in all three nations. In the first 10 years of the agreement (1994–2004), Canada's exports by value to its NAFTA partners increased by 87 percent.[8] Over this same period, exports from the

Regional Pacts: NAFTA and EU

North American Free Trade Agreement (NAFTA): A regional agreement among Canada, the United States, and Mexico that implements a free trade area.

[8]Government of Canada, *NAFTA: A decade of strengthening a dynamic relationship,* http://www.dfait-maeci.gc.ca, accessed March 3, 2007.

APPLICATIONS

Regional and Bilateral Free Trade Initiatives

Canada is exploring, negotiating, or has recently completed free trade agreements with a number of countries or country-groups around the world. The purpose of these agreements is to "enhance [Canada's] economic prosperity and provide the foundation for sustainable economic, social and cultural development." The latest agreement announced on June 7, 2007, was with the European Free Trade Association (EFTA), which includes Switzerland, Norway, Iceland, and Liechtenstein. As a trading group, the EFTA would represent Canada's 8th largest export market.

The Minister of International Trade, David Emerson, has also announced the start of negotiations toward free trade agreements with Columbia, Peru, and the Dominican Republic. As well, negotiations are continuing with South Korea, Jordan, and Singapore as well as with larger trade groups such as the Central America Four (CA4) including El Salvador, Guatemala, Honduras, and Nicaragua; the Caribbean Community (CARICOM); and the Andean countries.

Source: Based on Foreign Affairs and International Trade Canada, http://www.international.gc.ca/trade/tna-nac/efta-en.asp, accessed November 14, 2007.

Analysis: One trade strategy has been to negotiate smaller bilateral deals and knit them into a larger framework later on. Part of the motivation for this has been the difficulties in large scale negotiations such as the WTO's Doha Round (see the Applications box on page 335).

United States to Canada and Mexico increased by almost 70 percent and Mexican exports to Canada and the United States increased by more than 200 percent.

As we discussed earlier, exports are only half of the exchange since Mexican and U.S. exports become Canadian imports. Since imports represent, at least in some cases, a replacement of goods that were previously produced in Canada by Canadian workers, one criticism of NAFTA was fear of increased unemployment in the Canadian economy. Canadian economist Richard Harris looked at the evidence across a number of studies and found that the FTA and NAFTA had no significant impact on job losses in Canada and offered one study suggesting that increased trade had accounted for 23 percent of the jobs created between 1971 and 1991.[9] He also quotes economic historian Douglas Irwin, that:

> In fact, the overall effect of trade on the number of jobs is best approximated as zero. Total employment is not a function of international trade, but the number of people in the labour force.

In 1989, Canada also began discussions with 12 other countries that border on the Pacific Ocean. This became the Asia-Pacific Economic Cooperation (APEC) group and has since grown to 21 countries. The purpose of the group is to reduce tariffs and other barriers to trade, to increase investment, and aid economic reform. Through these measures economists expect more efficiency and stronger economic growth.

Since 1994, Canada has concluded agreements with Chile, Costa Rica, and Israel, and continues to negotiate with members of the Caribbean Community (CARICOM) and members of the ANDEAN community in South America, as well as other individual countries.

The *European Union* is another regional pact, but one that virtually eliminates national boundaries among 25 countries. The EU not only eliminates trade barriers but also enhances full intercountry mobility of workers and capital. In 1999, the EU nations also created a new currency (the euro) that has replaced the German mark, the French franc, and other national currencies. In effect, Europe has become one large, unified market. As trade barriers continue to fall around the world, the global marketplace is

WEB NOTE

For more information regarding Canada and the North American Free Trade Agreement (NAFTA), go to http://www.dfait-maeci.gc.ca/nafta-alena/menu-en.asp. For information on APEC, go to http://apec.org/.

WEB NOTE

To see what's new, check out the Foreign Affairs and International Trade Canada site on current trade negotiations and agreements, http://www.international.gc.ca/tna-nac/what-en.asp.

[9]Richard Harris, *The economic impact of the FTA and NAFTA agreements for Canada: A review of the evidence. included in NAFTA@1O*. J. M. Curtis and A. Sydor, (eds.) Public Works and Government Services Canada, http://www.dfait-maeci.gc.ca, accessed March 3, 2007.

APPLICATIONS

Free Trade, Human Rights Top Harper's Colombian Agenda

Free trade talks, human rights and Colombia's efforts to end its decades-old civil war will top the agenda today as Prime Minister Stephen Harper gets down to business on the first stop on his four-nation tour of Latin America and the Caribbean.

Canada is intent on signing a free-trade deal with Colombia. a growing economy that despite its internal strife and notoriety as the world's no. 1 cocaine producer is a increasingly attractive investment destination for Canadian companies, particularly in the mining and oil and gas sectors.

A coalition of Canadian groups ranging from the Canadian Labour Congress to the Canadian chapter of Amnesty International last week called on Mr. Harper to stop all trade talks with Colombia until the issue is fully debated in Canada. "Canada must send a strong message in the Americas that it puts human rights first—for trade deals, investment, development assistance and diplomatic policy—and expects other governments to do the same," the coalition said in a statement.

Source: Alan Freeman, "Free Trade, Human Rights Top Harper's Colombian Agenda," *The Globe and Mail* (July 16, 2007), p. A4. Reprinted with permission of the Globe and Mail.

Analysis: Trade deals can be seen to legitimize foreign governments but can also increase the international scrutiny, comment, and criticism of their actions as well.

likely to become more like an open bazaar as well. The resulting increase in competition should spur efficiency and growth in the economy tomorrow.

Although the focus of this chapter has largely been of the market benefits from trade, we should recognize that a considerable amount of the debate around trade and trade agreements arises from "non-market" concerns. Examples of these would be the human rights records of potential partners, the perception of an unequal distribution of benefits particularly between rich and poor countries, and potential environmental consequences of transporting goods around the world.

As the Applications box above discusses, a potential free trade deal between Columbia and Canada has been criticized for putting trade opportunities before human rights concerns, suggesting that "Canada must send a strong message in the Americas that it puts human rights first—for trade deals. . . ." In other words, that trade deals should be a reward after repairing human rights records rather than come before.

A Broader View of Trade

APPLICATIONS

The "100-Mile" Diet

This "diet" isn't about reducing your weight or improving your health, but, rather, is a response to the greenhouse gasses emitted as food is transported around the world. The salad we have with dinner may include lettuce from California, mangoes from Australia, and sweet peppers from Mexico. Our morning ritual may include coffee grown in India or Guatemala and fruit delivered in the midst of the northern winter from countries in the southern hemisphere. Alisa Smith and James

McKinnon wrote *The 100-mile diet: A year of local eating* about their experiment to shop for food and drink that comes from within 100-miles of their Vancouver apartment.

Source: Based on Alisa Smith and James MacKinnon, *The 100-mile diet: A year of local eating,* (Toronto: Random House Canada, 2007), http://100milediet.org/category/about/.

Analysis: Transportation costs are often assumed away in economic analysis, and the fact that the price of transportation has become so inexpensive makes this assumption reasonable. But the externalities of transportation are also ignored, and these may be becoming more important.

As the Applications box at the bottom of the previous page illustrates, trade requires the transportation of goods and services from where they are produced to where they will be consumed. The externality of transportation, using trains, airplanes, trucks, and ships, may be increased pollution or greenhouse gas emissions. The "100-mile diet" is a response to the distance some goods travel and an attempt to use producers closer to home.

SUMMARY

- International trade permits each country to specialize in areas of relative efficiency, increasing world output. For each country, the gains from trade are reflected in consumption possibilities that exceed production possibilities.
- One way to determine where comparative advantage lies is to compare the quantity of good A that must be given up in order to get a given quantity of good B from domestic production. If the same quantity of B can be obtained for less A by engaging in world trade, we have a comparative advantage in the production of good A. Comparative advantage rests on a comparison of relative opportunity costs.
- A country with absolute advantage is able to produce some good or service with fewer resources (per unit of output). Patterns of trade are not determined by absolute advantage but rather by comparative advantage. Absolute costs don't count!
- The terms of trade—the rate at which goods are exchanged—are subject to the forces of international supply and demand. The terms of trade will lie somewhere between the opportunity costs of the trading partners. The terms of trade determine how the gains from trade are shared.
- Resistance to trade emanates from workers and firms that must compete with imports. Even though the country as a whole stands to benefit from trade, these individuals and companies may lose jobs and incomes in the process.
- Trade barriers take many forms. Embargoes are outright prohibitions against import or export of particular goods. Quotas limit the quantity of a good imported or exported. Tariffs discourage imports by making them more expensive. Other nontariff barriers make trade too costly or time-consuming.
- The World Trade Organization (WTO) seeks to reduce worldwide trade barriers and enforce trade rules. Regional accords such as the European Union (EU) and North American Free Trade Agreement (NAFTA) pursue similar objectives among fewer countries.

Key Terms

trade surplus (deficit) 316
consumption possibilities 319
terms of trade 322
dumping 327
embargo 328

tariff 328
quota 330
voluntary restraint agreement
   (VRA) 332
trade pact 334

General Agreement on Tariffs and
   Trade, GATT 334
World Trade Organization, WTO 334
North American Free Trade
   Agreement, NAFTA 335

Questions for Discussion

1. Suppose a lawyer can type faster than any secretary. Should the lawyer do her own typing? Can you demonstrate the validity of your answer?
2. What would be the effects of a law requiring bilateral trade balances?
3. If a nation exported much of its output but imported little, would it be better or worse off? How about the reverse, that is, exporting little but importing a lot?
4. How does international trade restrain the price behaviour of domestic firms?
5. Suppose we refused to sell goods to any country that reduced or halted its exports to us. Who would benefit and who would lose from such retaliation? Can you suggest alternative ways to ensure import supplies?
6. Domestic producers often base their claim for import protection on the fact that workers in country X are

paid substandard wages. Is this a valid argument for protection?

7. Based on the Applications box on page 325, what might be the impact of the Chrysler deal on Chrysler workers in Canada? What might be the impact on potential purchasers of these Chrysler products?

8. If Canada was to ask Chrysler to "voluntarily" restrict the export of these Chinese-produced cars, what would be the impact in the Canadian market? What would be the effect on Canadian workers? On Canadian buyers?

9. The B.C. Fruit Growers Association (BCFGA) has alleged that Washington state farmers dumped apples into the B.C. market during 2004. What would be the effect of a countervailing duty or tariff on Washington's apples?

10. Canada is currently negotiating trade agreements with several countries. These negotiations generally rely on each country "giving up" some protection. What if Canada simply unilaterally removed all tariffs and non-tariff barriers? Who would lose? Who would win? What would be the net effect on the economy as a whole?

EXERCISES

PROBLEMS The Student Problem Set to accompany this chapter can be found at the end of the book.

WEB ACTIVITIES Web Activities to accompany this chapter can be found on the Online Learning Centre at **http://www.mcgrawhill.ca/olc/schiller**.

International Finance

I n Chapter 15, we found that Canadians purchased some $493.3 billion dollars worth of goods and services while at the same time selling some $526.2 billion worth of Canadian goods and services to foreign households. Of course, foreign households don't have Canadian dollars with which to buy those Canadian goods or services, and Canadians can't use euros, yuan, or yen for their own day-to-day purchases. Equally, Canadian households don't keep reserves of U.S. dollars, Mexican pesos, or Brazilian reals in case they want to purchase goods or services produced in those countries. Canadians also buy financial assets such as stocks and bonds, and production facilities such as factories or mining operations in foreign countries just as foreigners buy stocks, bonds, and production facilities in Canada. Whether purchasing goods or services, or stocks, bonds, or factories, each of these exchanges either begin or end with Canadian dollars.

Suppose you want to buy a Magnavox DVD player. You don't have to know that Magnavox players are produced by the Dutch company Philips Electronics. And you certainly don't have to fly to the Netherlands to pick it up. All you have to do is drive to the nearest electronics store; or you can just "click and buy" at the Internet's virtual mall.

But you may wonder how the purchase of an imported product was so simple. Dutch companies sell their products in euros, the currency of Europe. But you purchase the DVD player in dollars. How is such an exchange possible?

There's a chain of distribution between your dollar purchase in Canada and the euro-denominated sale in the Netherlands. Somewhere along that chain someone has to convert your dollars into euros. The critical question for everybody concerned is how many euros we can get for our dollars—that is, what the **exchange rate** is. If we can get 0.65 euros for every dollar, the exchange rate is 0.65 euros = 1 dollar. Alternatively, we could note that the price of a euro is $1.54 when the exchange rate is 0.65 to 1. Thus, *an exchange rate is the price of one currency in terms of another.*

This chapter examines the exchange of international currency, the value of the exchange of money and money-denominated assets, the effect of exchange rates on trade patterns, and the connections among fiscal policy, monetary policy, exchange rates, and international trade. We will focus on the following questions:

- *What determines the value of one country's money as compared to the value of another's?*
- *What causes the international value of currencies to change?*

LEARNING OBJECTIVES

By the end of this chapter, you should be able to:

16.1 Describe the accounts that make up Canada's balance of international payments, the transactions reported in each account, and the role of official reserves

16.2 Explain the operation of a foreign exchange market and where supply and demand for currency originates and describe the equilibrium as the official exchange rate

16.3 Explain how purchasing power parity (PPP) offers an imperfect long-run value of the exchange rate

16.4 Describe the differences between a fixed and a flexible exchange rate regime

16.5 Explain why and how the Bank of Canada might intervene to "manage" a flexible exchange rate

16.6 Use a Mundell-Fleming model approach to explain the impact on national income of fiscal or monetary policy under fixed or flexible exchange rate regimes

- *What exchange rate policies are available to the government?*
- *How does fiscal and monetary policy interact with exchange rate policy?*

16.1 CANADA'S BALANCE OF INTERNATIONAL PAYMENTS

Canada's **balance of international payments** is described as a record of international transactions between Canadian residents and non-residents within a given time period and from a Canadian perspective. These international transactions include the Canadian dollar value of goods, services, investment income, or financial claims exchanged and are organized into the "current account" and the "capital and financial account."

Table 16.1 depicts the Canadian balance of international payments for 2006. Notice that the vast number of separate transactions are classified into a relatively few summary measures and that while the final "balance" of the two accounts will be zero, neither of the individual accounts (or any of the sub-accounts) necessarily balance.

The current account is made up of the exchange of goods and services between Canada and other countries, transfers, and the exchange of income on investments earned in the current period. Table 16.2 provides a more detailed view of Canada's current account for 2006.

As we discussed in Chapter 15, Canada traditionally has a surplus in the trade of goods and a deficit in the trade of services, and these values are illustrated in the current account. In 2006, Canada enjoyed a trade surplus in goods of $54.3 billion but a services deficit of $17.1 billion. A significant part of the services deficit arises from the fact that Canadians seem to spend more on travel to foreign countries ($23.6 billion), than foreigners spend visiting Canada ($16.4 billion). The current account also shows the income earned on past investments in foreign countries by Canadians and by foreigners in Canada that is paid in the current period. As we explained in Chapter 4 when we looked at the difference between gross domestic product and gross

exchange rate: The price of one country's currency expressed in terms of another's; the domestic price of a foreign currency.

balance of international payments: A record of international transactions between Canadian residents and non-residents within a given time period and from a Canadian perspective.

Current Account Balance

Item	Canada's Balance of International Payments 2006 (billions of dollars)		
	Receipts (Inflow)	Payments (Outflow)	Balance
Current account			
Goods and services	$523.7	$486.5	$37.2
Investment income	58.0	71.0	(13.0)
Transfers	9.8	9.6	0.2
Current account balance	$591.5	$567.1	$24.3
Capital and financial account			
Capital account	$4.9	$0.7	$4.2
Financial account	142.6	164.3	(21.7)
Official reserves		1.0	(1.0)
Capital and financial account balance	$147.5	$166.0	($18.5)
Statistical discrepancy			($5.8)
Balance of international payments			$0.0

Source: Adapted from Statistics Canada CANSIM database tables 376-0001 and 376-0002, http://cansim2.statcan.ca, and available on the Statistics Canada website at: http://www40.statcan.ca/101/cst01/econ01a.htm and http://www40.statcan.ca/101/cst01/econ01b.htm. Statistics Canada information is used with the permission of Statistics Canada.

TABLE 16.1
Canada's Balance of International Payments

The balance of international payments is a summary statement of a country's international transactions. The major components of the summary are the current account (made up of the merchandise trade balance, services, and transfers), the capital and financial account (which includes the sale or purchase of real and financial assets and the change in official foreign reserves at the Bank of Canada), and a statistical discrepancy that brings the two accounts into final balance.

TABLE 16.2
Current Account

The current account records the exchange of goods, services, and transfers as well as the income received from assets owned in the respective countries.

Item	Canada's Current Account Balance 2006 (billions of dollars)		
	Receipts (Inflow)	Payments (Outflow)	Balance
Goods	$458.6	$404.3	$54.3
Services			
Travel	16.4	23.6	(7.2)
Transportation	12.2	19.2	(7.0)
Other services	36.5	39.4	(2.9)
Investment income			
Direct investment	30.6	30.9	(0.3)
Portfolio investment	15.2	25.1	(9.9)
Other investments	12.2	15.0	(2.8)
Transfers	9.8	9.6	0.2
Current account balance	$591.5	$567.1	$24.3

Source: Adapted from Statistics Canada CANSIM database tables 376-0001 and 376-0002, http://cansim2.statcan.ca, and available on the Statistics Canada website at: http://www40.statcan.ca/101/cst01/econ01a.htm. Statistics Canada information is used with the permission of Statistics Canada.

WEB NOTE

The latest statistics on the balance of international payments are available from Statistics Canada at http://www40.statcan.ca/l01/cst01/econ01a.htm and http://www40.statcan.ca/l01/cst01/econ01b.htm.

Capital and Financial Account

national product, the fact that there is greater investment in Canada by foreigners than the other way around implies that more investment income will paid out of Canada ($71.0 billion) than will be received by Canadians ($58.0 billion), resulting in a deficit of $13.0 billion.

The capital and financial account measures the value of international transactions (in Canadian dollars) of real and financial assets (this includes patents or international inheritances as well as stocks and bonds), as well as any change in the Bank of Canada's official foreign reserves. Table 16.3 gives a more detailed description of Canada's capital and financial account for 2006.

Item	Canada's Capital and Financial Account 2006 (billions of dollars)		
	Receipts (Inflow)	Payments (Outflow)	Balance
Capital account	$4.9	$0.7	$4.2
Financial account			
Direct foreign investment	78.3	51.3	27.0
Portfolio investment—bonds	18.0	43.6	(25.6)
Portfolio investment—stocks	10.8	28.3	(17.5)
Portfolio investment—other	3.7	6.8	(3.1)
Other investments	31.7	34.3	(2.6)
Change to official reserves		1.0	(1.0)
Financial account balance	$142.6	$165.3	($22.7)
Statistical discrepancy			($5.8)
Capital and financial account balance			($18.5)

TABLE 16.3
Canada's Capital and Financial Account

The capital and financial account records the exchange in real and financial assets between Canada and foreign countries.

Source: Adapted from Statistics Canada CANSIM database tables 376-0001 and 376-0002, http://cansim2.statcan.ca, and available on the Statistics Canada website at: http://www40.statcan.ca/101/cst01/econ01b.htm. Statistics Canada information is used with the permission of Statistics Canada.

As Table 16.3 illustrates, the bulk of the international transactions occur either as *direct investment* or as *portfolio investment.* Direct investment (or direct foreign investment) is described as where the investor in one country has a significant influence or control of productive resources in another country. For instance, the $6.9 billion purchase of B.C. natural gas distribution company Terasen Gas by Kinder-Morgan Inc. of Houston, Texas, in 2005 represented a foreign direct investment by the U.S. company in Canada. The recent purchase of part of Terasen from Kinder-Morgan Inc by Fortis Inc, located in St. John's, for $3.7 billion would be a reduction in the foreign direct investment in Canada.

Portfolio investment is defined by the fact that the investor has no significant influence in the operations associated with the assets purchased. For instance, a Canadian buying a few shares of Kinder-Morgan Inc., would have no significant influence on the operations or management of the firm. Similarly, the purchase of U.S. government bonds would provide no significant influence in the government's decisions. *Other investments* are similar to portfolio investments except that they tend not to be traded in an established market—such as the Dow-Jones or NASDAQ.

The final entry in the capital and financial account presented in Table 16.3 is the change in the **official reserves** held by the Bank of Canada. The Bank holds *foreign currency reserves* that it can use, along with Canadian dollars, in international markets. For instance, if the Bank chooses to buy up Canadian dollars held by a French citizen, they would spend some of the euros in reserve to buy them. Since this represents an outflow of financial assets, the transaction is recorded in the financial account. In 2006, as Table 16.1 indicates, the level of foreign reserves in Canada fell by $1.0 billion. That is, the Bank of Canada sold foreign currency and bought Canadian dollars. In 2004, the reverse was true, foreign currency reserves at the Bank of Canada increased by $3.4 billion. Figure 16.1 gives the position of foreign currency holdings at the bank of Canada from 1961 to 2005.

> **official (international) reserves:** Foreign currency holdings of the Canadian government including U.S. dollars and other foreign currencies.

The *statistical discrepancy* is the final balancing entry. Although Statistics Canada does a remarkable job, the impossibility of accurately measuring all the transactions that occur among countries is truly daunting. The statistical discrepancy recognizes this difficulty and simply adjusts the accounts so the balance of payments does indeed balance. In 2006, the statistical discrepancy was an outflow of $5.8 billion whereas in 2004, the statistical discrepancy represented an inflow of $3.8 billion.

The net capital and financial outflows were essential to balance Canada's current account surplus. As in any market, the number of dollars demanded must equal the

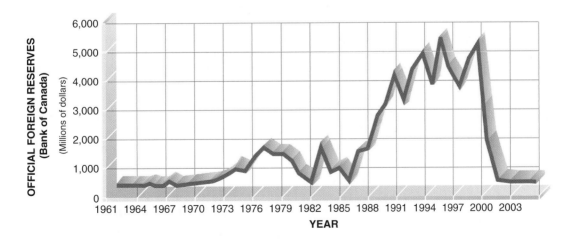

FIGURE 16.1

Official Foreign Reserves at the Bank of Canada, 1961–2005

The Bank of Canada holds foreign reserves accumulated through exports and the sale of financial assets sold to foreigners.

Source: Statistics Canada, CANSIM Table 378-0004. Used with permission of the Bank of Canada.

number of dollars supplied at the equilibrium. Thus, *the current account surplus must equal the capital and financial account deficit.* In other words, there can't be any dollars left lying around unaccounted for. The statistical discrepancy reminds us that our accounting system isn't perfect—that we can't identify every transaction. Nevertheless, all the accounts must eventually "balance out." That, after all, is the character of a market equilibrium.

16.2 CANADIAN EXCHANGE RATES AND THE FOREIGN-EXCHANGE MARKET

Most exchange rates are determined in foreign-exchange markets. Stop thinking of money as some sort of magical substance, and instead view it as a useful commodity that facilitates market exchanges. From that perspective, an exchange rate—the price of a country's currency—is subject to the same influences that determine all market prices: demand and supply.

The Demand for Dollars

Kinder-Morgan Inc.'s purchase of Terasen Gas in 2005 resulted in U.S. investors acquiring a Canadian company. The Fortis purchase from Kinder-Morgan meant that a Canadian company acquired assets owned in the United States. Since the U.S. company operates with U.S. dollars, to buy Terasen required them to buy Canadian dollars, since these are what the Canadian owners wanted. When Fortis made their deal, they needed to buy U.S. dollars because that was what the U.S. owners required. In other words, before the purchases could be made, the buyers had to acquire the appropriate currency. Kinder-Morgan exchanged U.S. dollars for Canadian dollars, and Fortis exchanged Canadian dollars for U.S. dollars.

Canadian tourists also need American dollars. Few American restaurants or hotels accept Canadian currency as payment for goods and services; they want to be paid in U.S. dollars. Accordingly, Canadian tourists must buy American dollars if they want to see the United States.

Europeans love iPods. The Apple Corporation, however, wants to be paid in U.S. dollars. Hence, European consumers must exchange their currencies for U.S. dollars if they want an iPod. Individual consumers can spend euros at their local electronics store. When they do so, however, they're initiating a series of market transactions that will end when Apple Corporation gets paid in U.S. dollars. In this case, some intermediary exchanges the European currency for American dollars.

Some foreign investors also buy Canadian dollars for speculative purposes. If a U.S. firm is intending to buy Canadian goods or services when they need them for production, they may arrange to buy Canadian dollars now to have them "on-hand" for when they're needed. Europeans planning on travelling in Canada in the future may choose to buy dollars now if they believe that they may become more expensive later on.

Finally, the Bank of Canada holds reserves of foreign currencies: U.S. dollars, euros, etc. That gives them the option of intervening in the foreign-exchange market as buyers of Canadian dollars. As we'll see a little later on in this chapter, the Bank of Canada may do this as part of specific policy to "support" the exchange rate of the Canadian dollar.

Each of these motivations gives rise to a demand for Canadian dollars. Specifically, *the foreign-exchange market demand for Canadian dollars originates in*

- Foreign demand for Canadian goods and services (exports and tourism)
- Foreign demand for saving and investment in Canada (portfolio investment and direct investment)
- Currency speculation
- Currency transactions from the Bank of Canada

The supply of Canadian dollars is simply the "other side" of the demand transactions For example, when Kinder-Morgan Inc. bought Canadian dollars to buy Terasen Gas, they sold U.S. dollars—supplying U.S. dollars in order to exchange them for Canadian dollars. When Fortis bought U.S. dollars to pay Kinder-Morgan, they sold Canadian dollars—supplying Canadian dollars to exchange them for U.S. dollars. In other words, the demand for one currency represents a supply of another currency.

When Canadians plan a mid-winter trip to Mexico to escape the ice and snow, they need to buy Mexican pesos to pay for their hotel, meals, and souvenirs. When they do, they'll be demanding pesos by supplying Canadian dollars. Canadian consumers also buy goods and services in Canada that were produced in other countries, such as mangoes from Australia and BMWs from Germany. Even though Canadian consumers pay in Canadian dollars, somewhere along the way, Canadian dollars had to be supplied in exchange for the Australian dollars paid to mango growers and for the euros paid to German auto workers.

Canadian households save some of their income by making *portfolio investments* in foreign countries. Canadian firms make *foreign direct investments* in foreign countries buying gold mines or textile factories. Canadian firms also buy intermediate products and capital equipment for their own production in Canada. The automotive industry buys car parts from U.S. and foreign producers while farmers buy new tractors from European, U.S., or Japanese producers.

Again, finally, the Bank of Canada can use its supply of Canadian dollars to sell them in exchange for foreign currencies. They can do this both to increase their own holdings of foreign currency reserves, and to ensure that there are sufficient Canadian dollars on the foreign exchange market to satisfy the demand at the existing exchange rate. Therefore, the Bank of Canada is in a unique position with respect to the foreign exchange market. It is able to act as both a buyer and seller of Canadian dollars and thereby to manage or balance out the market.

We can summarize each of these foreign-exchange market transactions by noting that *the supply of Canadian dollars originates in*

- Canadian demand for goods and services (imports and tourism)
- Canadian demand for saving and investment in foreign countries (portfolio investment and direct investment)
- Speculation in foreign currency
- Currency transactions from the Bank of Canada

The Value of the Dollar

Whether Canadian consumers will choose to buy a BMW depends partly on what the car costs. The price tag isn't always apparent in international transactions. Remember that the BMW producer and workers want to be paid in their own currency. Hence, the *dollar* price of a BMW depends on two factors: (1) the German price of a BMW and (2) the *exchange rate* between Canadian dollars and euros. Specifically, the Canadian price of a BMW is

$$\frac{\text{Dollar price}}{\text{of BMW}} = \frac{\text{euro price}}{\text{of BMW}} \times \frac{\text{dollar price}}{\text{of euro}}$$

Suppose the BMW company is prepared to sell a BMW for 50,000 euros and that the current exchange rate is 0.65 euros = $1. At these rates, a BMW will cost you

$$\frac{\text{Dollar price}}{\text{of BMW}} = 50,000 \text{ eruros} \times \frac{\$1}{0.65 \text{ euros}}$$
$$= \$77,000$$

If you're willing to pay this much for a shiny new BMW, you may do so at current exchange rates.

Now suppose the exchange rate changes from 0.65 euros = $1 to 0.50 euros = $1. *A higher dollar price for euros will raise the dollar costs of European goods.* In this case, the dollar price of a euro increases from $1.54 to $2.00. At this new exchange rate, the

FIGURE 16.2
The Foreign-Exchange Market

The foreign-exchange market operates like other markets. In this case, the "good" bought and sold is "dollars" (foreign exchange). The price and quantity of dollars actually exchanged are determined by the intersection of market supply and demand.

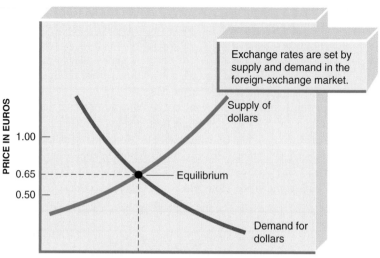

QUANTITY OF DOLLARS EXCHANGED

WEBNOTE

Learn more about the history of the euro at http://www.ecb.int/bc/history/background/html/index.en.html.

BMW plant in Germany is still willing to sell BMWs at €50,000 apiece. And German consumers continue to buy BMWs at that price. But this constant euro price now translates into a higher *dollar* price. Thus a BMW now costs you $100,000.

As the dollar price of a BMW rises, the number of BMWs sold in Canada will decline. As BMW sales decline, the quantity of euros demanded may decline as well. Thus, the quantity of foreign currency demanded declines when the exchange rate rises because foreign goods become more expensive and imports decline.[1] When the U.S. dollar price of European currencies actually increased in 1992, BMW decided to start producing cars in South Carolina. A year later Mercedes-Benz decided to produce cars in the United States as well. Sales of American-made BMWs and Mercedes to Canadians would depend on the exchange rate of U.S. dollars rather than euros.

The Supply Curve. These market responses suggest that the supply of dollars is upward-sloping. If the value of the dollar rises, Canadians will be able to buy more euros. As a result, the dollar price of imported BMWs will decline. Canadian consumers will respond by demanding more imports, thereby supplying a larger quantity of dollars. The supply curve in Figure 16.2 shows how the quantity of dollars supplied rises as the value of the dollar increases.

The Demand Curve. The demand for dollars can be explained in similar terms. Remember that the demand for dollars arises from the foreign demand for exports and investments. If the exchange rate moves from 0.65 euros = $1 to 0.50 euros = $1, the euro price of dollars falls. As dollars become cheaper for Germans, all Canadian exports effectively fall in price. Germans will buy more Canadian products (including trips to Whistler Blackcomb) and therefore demand a greater quantity of dollars. In addition, foreign investors will perceive in a cheaper dollar the opportunity to buy Canadian stocks, businesses, and property at fire-sale prices. Accordingly, they join foreign consumers in demanding more dollars. Not all these behavioural responses will occur overnight, but they're reasonably predictable over a brief period of time.

Equilibrium

Given market demand and supply curves, we can predict the *equilibrium price* of any commodity, that is, the price at which the quantity demanded will equal the quantity supplied. This occurs in Figure 16.2 where the two curves cross. At that equilibrium, the value of the dollar (the exchange rate) is established. In this case, the euro price of the dollar turns out to be 0.65 euros.

---

[1]The extent to which imports decline as the cost of foreign currency rises depends on the *price elasticity of demand*.

Foreign-Exchange Rates

Exchange rates are determined as a "bilateral" equilibrium. That is, there is a Canadian dollar exchange rate determined against each of currency individually. The table presents the Canadian dollar priced in several foreign currencies as well as those same foreign currencies priced in Canadian dollars.

Country	Foreign Currency price of a Canadian Dollar	Canadian dollar price of a Foreign Currency Unit
United States, Dollar ($)	$0.8557	$1.1687
United Kingdom, Pound (£)	£0.4429	$2.2578
Europe, Euro (€)	0.6483€	$1.5426
Japan, Yen (¥)	100.05¥	$0.009995

Source: Bank of Canada currency converter for noon, March 13, 2007.

Analysis: The exchange rates between the Canadian dollar and other currencies are determined by supply and demand in foreign-exchange markets. The rates reported here represent the exchange rates at noon on March 13, 2007.

The value of the dollar can also be expressed in terms of other currencies. The World View above displays a sampling of dollar exchange rates at March 2007.

Notice that while $1 ($Cdn) can buy 100¥ (yen), it can at the same time buy only 0.65€ (euros). This is what we mean by exchange rates being "bilateral." There is an exchange rate between the Canadian dollar and each other world currency. And, as the World View illustrates, that exchange rate can be calculated in either a Canadian dollar value or the value of a Canadian dollar in foreign currency.

For example, the price of a Canadian dollar in yen (¥) is 100.05¥. The price of one yen in Canadian dollar terms is $0.009995. So, what is the relationship between these two values? In fact, these two calculations are simply the inverse of each other:

$$\frac{\$1}{100.05¥} = \$0.009995 \text{ ($Cdn) for each yen}$$

or

$$\frac{1¥}{\$0.009995} = \$100.05¥ \text{ for each dollar ($Cdn)}$$

This may often seem confusing as we talk about both of these calculations in the same breath. But, recognizing the connection between these two perspectives—and remembering that they are just two perspectives of the same transaction—will help to lessen that confusion.

The interesting thing about markets isn't their character in equilibrium but the fact that prices and quantities are always changing in response to shifts in demand and supply. The Canadian demand for BMWs shifted overnight when Japan introduced a new line of sleek, competitively priced cars (i.e., Lexus). The reduced demand for BMWs shifted the supply of dollars leftward. That supply shift raised the value of the dollar vis-á-vis the euro, as illustrated in Figure 16.3 (It also increased the demand for Japanese yen, causing the yen value of the dollar to *fall*.)

WEB NOTE

The Bank of Canada has a currency converter for the most current "noon rates." Check out the Canadian exchange rate with 50+ other currencies at http://www.bankofcanada.ca/en/rates/converter.html.

Market Dynamics

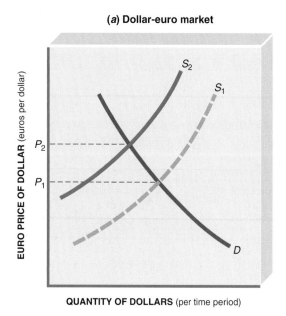

(a) Dollar-euro market

(b) Dollar-yen market

FIGURE 16.3
Shifts in Foreign-Exchange Markets

When the Japanese introduced luxury autos into Canada, the demand for German cars fell. As a consequence, the supply of dollars in the dollar-euro market (part *a*) shifted to the left and the euro value of the dollar rose. At the same time, the increased demand for Japanese cars shifted the dollar supply curve in the yen market (part *b*) to the right, reducing the yen price of the dollar.

Depreciation and Appreciation

depreciation: A fall in the price of one currency relative to another.

appreciation: A rise in the price of one currency relative to another.

Exchange-rate changes have their own terminology. **Depreciation** of a currency occurs when one currency becomes cheaper in terms of another currency. In our earlier discussion of exchange rates, for example, we assumed that the exchange rate between euros and dollars changed from 0.65 euros = $1 to 0.50 euro = $1, making the euro price of a dollar cheaper. In this case, the dollar *depreciated* with respect to the euro.

The other side of depreciation is **appreciation,** an increase in the value of one currency as expressed in another country's currency. ***Whenever one currency depreciates, another currency must appreciate.*** When the exchange rate changed from 0.65 euros = $1 to 0.50 euros = $1, not only did the euro price of a dollar fall, but also the dollar price of a euro rose. Perhaps we can see this better by looking at it from the other perspective—looking at the dollar price of the euro, which is after all, simply the inverse of the euro price of the dollar:

$$0.65€ = \$1 = \frac{\$1}{0.65€} = \$1.53846 \text{ for each euro}$$

$$0.50€ = \$1 = \frac{\$1}{0.50€} = \$2.00000 \text{ for each euro}$$

So, the dollar price of the euro rose from $1.54 to $2.00 for each euro. Hence, the euro appreciated as the dollar depreciated.

Although all exchange rates are determined bilaterally—that is, one currency traded for another, the Bank of Canada does present a *Canadian dollar effective exchange rate index* (CERI), that represents the Canadian dollar exchange rate experience measured against our six major trading partners: The U.S., the European Euro area, Japan, China, Mexico, and the United Kingdom. Each of these six foreign currencies is given a weighting based on the trade of goods, services, and non-energy commodities with Canada. Since the United States represents our largest trading partner, the bilateral Canada–U.S. exchange rate accounts for more than 76 percent of the weight in the

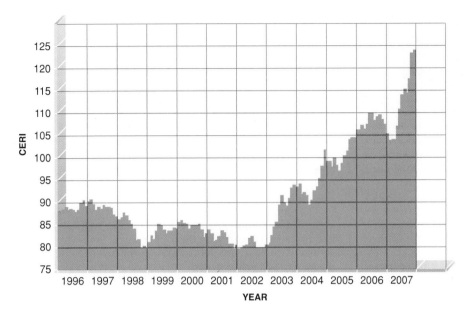

FIGURE 16.4

Canadian Dollar Effective Exchange Rate Index (CERI)

CERI is a weighted effective exchange rate measuring the bilateral exchange rate of the Canadian dollar against the currencies of Canada's six major trading partners. The foreign currencies and their index weights are: the U.S. dollar (76.18 percent), the European euro (9.31 percent), the Japanese yen (5.27 percent), the Chinese yuan (3.29 percent), the Mexican peso (3.24 percent), and the U.K. pound (2.71 percent).

Source: Bank of Canada—Canadian dollar effective exchange rate index: Monetary policy indicators. Retrieved March 16, 2007, from http://www.bankofcanada.ca/en/graphs/V41498903-gr.html. CERI weightings and description have been taken from http://www.bankofcanada.ca/en/rates/ceri.html.

index. Figure 16.4 illustrates this effective exchange rate index beginning in 1996 through February 2007.

Figure 16.4 shows the CERI relatively stable between 1996 and the first quarter of 1998 before *depreciating* in late 1998. The Canadian dollar then *appreciated* through 1999 and until late 2000, when it once again *depreciated* such that by the end of 2002, the CERI was approximately the same as in late 1998. Since the beginning of 2003, however, the Canadian dollar has generally *appreciated*. Between 2003 and the end of 2006, the index rose from 80 to about 108, a increase of more than $1/3$, or 35 percent.

The impact of these changes in the Canadian dollar effective exchange rate is noticed by consumers purchasing imports, producers selling exports, and tourists looking forward to a warm Mexican beach in February, or a trip to New York in the summer. The relatively low and slight *depreciation* of the CERI between 1996 and 2003 raised the price of foreign goods and services while at the same time, reducing the Canadian dollar price of Canadian goods and services sold in foreign markets. The result was good news for Canadian exporters as they sold more exports. Even Canadian producers selling in Canada were happy as foreign competitive goods and services became more expensive in Canadian dollar terms.

Since 2003, however, the situation has been the reverse. The CERI has appreciated, increasing the purchasing power of the Canadian dollar in foreign markets and making goods and services priced in Canadian dollars more expensive in foreign currency terms. The increase in the value of the Canadian dollar would slow down export demand while increasing import demand. Domestic producers would again see more competition from foreign goods and Canadian tourists travelling abroad would enjoy "cheaper" holidays.

APPLICATIONS

Exporters' Hopes Sink on News of Rising Loonie

The higher loonie has been playing havoc with Canadian manufacturers. About half of Canada's manufacturing output is shipped to the United States. A higher loonie raises the price U.S. customers have to pay for Canadian-made goods.

In the latest quarterly survey of business conditions, Statistics Canada reported 27 percent of manufacturers expect to decrease production during the current quarter, while only 14 percent expect an increase. "This represents the most negative balance of opinion since January, 2001," Statistics Canada said.

About 4,000 manufacturing companies participated in the voluntary survey. StatsCan said the grim outlook results from a combination of higher energy costs, declining order levels, limited Canadian production capacity and the higher loonie.

The loonie has risen 28 percent over the past three years. The Canadian dollar is now within a quarter cent of the U.S. 89.29 cents it reached 15 years ago on November 1, 1991, and within half a cent of the U.S.89.35 cents it hit 28 years ago on June 16, 1978.

Source: Drew Hasselback, "Exporters' hopes sink on news of rising loonie, *The National Post* (April 28, 2006), p. FP5. Material reprinted with the express permission of National Post Company, a Can West Partnership.

More Canadians Crossing Border for Shopping Sprees

With a loonie heading toward par with the U.S. greenback and an increasing suspicion that none of the expected benefits are filtering down to consumers in the form of lower prices, Canadians are converting their currency and flooding into border shopping malls.

"The number of Canadian shoppers has certainly increased in the first six months of the year," said Chelsea Premium Outlets marketing director Jean Guinot this week. "And we're delighted. With the chance of parity (with the American dollar), the interest will only grow."

Source: Chris Cobb, "More Canadians crossing border for shopping sprees," *Leader Post* (June 23, 2007) p. B5. Material reprinted with the express permission of Can West News Service, a Can West Partnership.

Analysis: The appreciation of a nation's currency is good for importers, cross-border shoppers, and tourists heading for foreign beaches, but bad for that nation's exporters of goods and services. The higher foreign prices for Canadian manufactured goods can lead to a reduction in the quantity of those goods purchased by foreign households. Since these stories were written, the Canadian dollar has continued to rise, closing at $1.065 ($US) on November 9, 2007.

Market Forces

Exchange rates change for the same reasons that any market price changes: The underlying supply or demand (or both) has shifted. Among the more important sources of such shifts are

- *Relative income changes.* If incomes are increasing faster in country A than in country B, consumers in A will tend to spend more, thus increasing the demand for B's exports and currency. B's currency will appreciate.
- *Relative price changes.* If domestic prices are rising rapidly in country A, consumers will seek out lower-priced imports. The demand for B's exports and currency will increase. B's currency will appreciate.
- *Changes in product availability.* If country A experiences a disastrous wheat crop failure, it will have to increase its food imports. B's currency will appreciate.
- *Relative interest rate changes.* If interest rates rise in country A, people in country B will want to move their deposits to A. Demand for A's currency will rise and it will appreciate.
- *Speculation.* If speculators anticipate an increase in the price of A's currency, for the preceding reasons or any other, they'll begin buying it, thus pushing its price up. A's currency will appreciate.

foreign-exchange markets: Places where foreign currencies are bought and sold

All these various changes are taking place every minute of every day, thus keeping **foreign-exchange markets** active. On an average day, over *$1 trillion* of foreign exchange is bought and sold in the market. Significant changes occur in currency

Money Crisis Pulling Asian Students Home

The financial tsunami that swamped Asian economies in the last few months is sloshing back across the Pacific toward American colleges and universities, where thousands of Asian students are suddenly short of dollars.

Since last July, the Indonesian currency, the rupiah, has lost 80 percent of its value as measured against the U.S. dollar. A half-dozen Asian currencies have lost about half their value against the dollar.

That means, for example, that what would have been $20,000 in Korean money (the won) a year ago is now worth only $10,000. Consequently, Korean and Indonesian students—plus Malaysians, Thais, Singaporeans and Japanese—are struggling to pay their tuition bills. Some can't—so they're going home.

There are about 458,000 foreign students in the USA—about 3 percent of total higher education enrollment, according to the Institute of International Education, a nonprofit cultural exchange organization that conducts an annual census of foreign students. About 57 percent of the students are Asians.

Source: *USA Today,* February 18, 1998. USA TODAY. Copyright 1998. Reprinted with permission. www.usatoday.com

Analysis: When the foreign price of the U.S. dollar rises (dollar appreciation), American exports (including educational services) become more expensive, which causes a decline in enrollments (quantity demanded).

values, however, only when several of these forces move in the same direction at the same time. This is what caused the Asian crisis of 1997–1998.

The Asian Crisis of 1997–1998. In July 1997, the Thai government decided the baht was overvalued and let market forces find a new equilibrium. Within days, the value of the baht plunged against other currencies. This sharp decline in the value of the Thai baht simultaneously increased the Thai price of other currencies. As a consequence, Thais could no longer afford to buy as many imports from other countries.

The devaluation of the baht had a domino effect on other Asian currencies. The plunge in the baht shook confidence in the Malaysian ringget, the Indonesian rupiah, and even the Korean won. People wanted to hold "hard" currencies like the U.S. dollar. Even Canada wasn't immune to this loss of confidence as the value of the Canadian dollar, which was $0.726 ($US) in July, had fallen to $0.694 ($US) by the end of 1997 and to $0.648 ($US) by the end of 1998.

Given the scope and depth of the Asian crisis of 1997–1998, it's easy to understand why people crave *stable* exchange rates. The resistance to exchange-rate fluctuations originates in various micro- and macroeconomic interests.

Resistance to Exchange-Rate Changes

The microeconomic resistance to changes in the value of the dollar arises from two concerns. First, people who trade or invest in world markets want a solid basis for forecasting future costs, prices, and profits. Forecasts are always uncertain, but they're even less dependable when the value of money is subject to change. A Canadian firm that invests $2 million in a ski factory in Sweden expects not only to make a profit on the production there but also to return that profit to Canada. If the Swedish krona depreciates sharply in the interim, however, the profits amassed in Sweden may dwindle to a mere trickle, or even a loss, when the kronor are exchanged back into dollars. From this view, the uncertainty associated with fluctuating exchange rates is an unwanted burden.

Micro Interests

Even when the direction of an exchange rate move is certain, those who stand to lose from the change are prone to resist. *A change in the price of a country's money automatically alters the price of all its exports and imports.*

In a country whose currency appreciates, there'll be opposition to the exchange-rate movements. When the dollar appreciates, Canadians buy more foreign products as their prices in Canadian dollars falls. Canadian firms in competition with the imports will be forced to reduce their prices as well, resulting in reduced profitability. The insistence that the government "do something" about the "high dollar" may turn into a political force for "correcting" foreign-exchange rates.

Macro Interests

Any microeconomic problem that becomes widespread enough can turn into a macroeconomic problem. The higher value of the Canadian dollar makes foreign goods and services less expensive in the Canadian market. As consumers purchase more foreign goods, they support employment of foreign resources rather than Canadian ones. As well, as the price of foreign goods and services declines, Canadian firms are confronted with greater competition. If firms are unable to adjust to this new competition, there may be layoffs in Canada, resulting in higher rates of unemployment and additional calls for the government to "do something."

Canadian investors may also be encouraged to change their behaviour as a result of the dollar's appreciation. Foreign goods and services become less expensive as we saw above, but the production resources that produced those goods and services also becomes less expensive to buy. Canadian firms may see this as an opportune time to invest "overseas," buying or building foreign production facilities, which increases the resources in the foreign economy rather than in Canada.

On the opposite side, the depreciation of the Canadian dollar in the period 1995–2002 saw the Canadian dollar trade in the range of $0.62 and $0.75 ($US). At rates such as these, which were perceived to be very low, there was concern that Canada was "for sale"; that the relatively inexpensive Canadian dollar would make it easier for foreigners to "buy up" Canadian resources and property to the detriment of Canadians. This was another situation where there were calls for the government to "do something"—although not the same "something" as when the dollar appreciated.

The low exchange rate also gave Canadian firms an advantage selling into the U.S. market—and predictably resulted in calls for the U.S. government to "do something" to protect their local business from such "unfair" Canadian competition. Industries such as Canadian softwood lumber producers and prairie wheat farmers faced demands for quotas or tariffs to be placed on their exports to reduce the competitive pressure on U.S. firms.

16.3 A LONG-RUN THEORY OF EXCHANGE RATE VALUES

The previous section described the foreign exchange market and how various transactions between two countries result in the determination of a bilateral *official exchange rate*. But the exchange rate today will likely be different from the exchange rate tomorrow and likely is different from the exchange rate on the day before. That leads us to another question: Is there a way to know which direction and to what level the exchange rate will go in the future? As with a great deal of macroeconomics, the answer is "sort of."

To think about this, we need to go back to the fundamental use of any currency— the purchase of a good or service. Since any particular good is the same in Canada as in another country, the ability to purchase that good should also be the same. Notice here that the emphasis is on ability rather than saying that they should be the same nominal price.

purchasing power parity (PPP): A rate of exchange such that a good in two different countries could be purchased with the same amount of domestic currency.

Purchasing power parity (PPP), suggests that, in the long run, the bilateral exchange rate (e) should simply adjust the two currencies such that the price of the good in one country, converted by the exchange rate into another currency, should be exactly enough to buy that same good in the other country. In other words:

$$P^{USA} = (e)(P^{CDA})$$

Where:

P^{USA} = Price of the good in the United States

e = the Canadian dollar priced in U.S. dollars (Note that $1/e$ = the U.S. dollar priced in Canadian dollars.)

P^{CDA} = Price of the good in Canada

For example, suppose that the purchase price of the just released DVD of your favourite band's concert is selling for $29.95. Since the current price of a Canadian dollar priced in U.S. dollars is $0.86, this same DVD should sell in the United States for:

$$P^{USA} = (0.86)(\$29.95)$$

$$P^{USA} = \$25.76 \ (\$US)$$

More often though, our interest is not in determining the PPP price in another country based on the local price, but rather, determining the bilateral exchange rate that should exist to bring the two prices into "parity."

For example, suppose that we knew the local price of the DVD was $29.95 ($Cdn), and by looking on the web, we found that the DVD was available in the United States for $25.76 ($US). We can use these two prices to find the implied exchange rate that leaves the purchasing power of the two country's currencies at parity—the purchasing power parity exchange rate.

$$\frac{P^{USA}}{P^{CDA}} = e^{PPP}$$

Substituting the actual prices into the formula gives:

$$\frac{\$25.76}{\$29.95} = 0.86$$

In this case, the *official* exchange rate determined in the foreign exchange market turns out to be equivalent to the *purchasing power parity* exchange rate. When this is the case, we would say that the current exchange rate is correctly valued at its long run position. What happens when the rates are not the same? For example, what if the DVD sold in Canada at $26.95 rather than $29.95, but the official exchange rate was still $e = 0.86$?

In this case, American consumers could buy the $26.95 ($Cdn) necessary to buy the DVD in Canada for only $23.18 ($US), (0.86 × $26.95). They could then use the Canadian dollars purchased to buy the DVD in Canada. You should be saying to yourself right about now—"wait a minute, there is a foreign exchange market transaction occurring and that can alter the exchange rate." And, of course, you would be right! When the U.S. consumer purchases Canadian dollars, they add to the demand for Canadian dollars, putting upward pressure on the value of the Canadian dollar—appreciating it. At the same time, the U.S. consumer is increasing the supply of U.S. dollars, putting downward pressure on the value of the U.S. dollar—depreciating it. Where will it end? At the point where the purchasing power parity exchange rate is re-established:

$$\frac{P^{USA}}{P^{CDA}} = e^{PPP}$$

$$\frac{\$25.76}{\$26.95} = 0.96$$

This implies that at the current bilateral exchange rate of $0.86 ($US.) for each Canadian dollar, the Canadian dollar is *undervalued*. That is, the purchasing power of the Canadian dollar is higher than the official exchange rate recognizes. The expectation, then, is that the Canadian dollar would appreciate until it reaches the e^{PPP}.

So, how "good" a predictor of future value is this? And the answer is, "not perfect." The reason for the imperfection arises from three areas:

1. Not all goods and services are tradable between countries.
2. Transportation costs matter.
3. Not all countries produce the same goods and services.

Since the currency exchange rate is adjusted through trade—as households in one country exchange their currency for that of the other country to buy the goods or services—unless a trade can take place, the currency transactions doesn't happen and the "official" exchange rate doesn't adjust. Secondly, transportation costs are seldom zero. That means that a good or service could itself be "cheaper" in another country, but the cost of getting it to the consumer is greater than the difference, so the exchange doesn't happen. And, finally, if different countries produce different goods, there may not be the same good or service available from another country. The result of these three distortions is that the official exchange rate and the purchasing power parity rate may not coincide.

So where is purchasing power parity useful if not in predicting the future value of a currency? One answer is when looking at international comparisons. Statistics generated by the World Bank or the United Nations are often calculated using purchasing power parity values. The purpose of this is to get a more accurate measurement of what goods and services households in different countries are actually able to buy with their currency rather than using an official market exchange rate that may undervalue the particular currency.

16.4 EXCHANGE RATE POLICY REGIMES

Given the potential opposition to exchange-rate movements, governments often feel compelled to intervene in foreign-exchange markets. The intervention is usually intended to achieve greater exchange-rate stability. But such stability may itself give rise to undesirable micro- and macroeconomic effects.

Fixed Exchange Rates

gold standard: An agreement by countries to fix the price of their currencies in terms of gold; a mechanism for fixing exchange rates.

One way to eliminate fluctuations in exchange rates is to fix the rate's value. To fix exchange rates, each country may simply proclaim that its currency is worth so much in relation to that of other countries. The easiest way to do this is for each country to define the worth of its currency in terms of some common standard. Under a **gold standard,** each country determines that its currency is worth so much gold. In so doing, it implicitly defines the worth of its currency in terms of all other currencies, which also have a fixed gold value. In 1944, the major trading nations met at Bretton Woods, New Hampshire, and agreed that each currency was worth so much gold. The value of the U.S. dollar was defined as being equal to 0.0294 ounce of gold, while the British pound was defined as being worth 0.0823 ounce of gold. Thus, the exchange rate between British pounds and U.S. dollars was effectively fixed at $1 = 0.357 pound, or 1 pound = $2.80 (or $2.80/0.0823 = $1/0.0294). The Canadian dollar had been fixed in 1939, at the beginning of World War II, at $0.91 ($US) and was re-valued upward in July of 1946 to full parity with the U.S. dollar. That is, $1 U.S. = $1 Canadian.[2]

Balance-of-Payments Problems. It's one thing to proclaim the worth of a country's currency; it's quite another to *maintain* the fixed rate of exchange. As we've observed, foreign-exchange rates are subject to continual and often unpredictable changes in supply and demand. Hence, two countries that seek to stabilize their exchange rate at some fixed value are going to find it necessary to compensate for such foreign-exchange market pressures.

[2]James Powell, *A History of the Canadian Dollar* (Bank of Canada, 1995), http://www.bank-banque-canada.ca/en/dollar_book/index.html, accessed March 19, 2007.

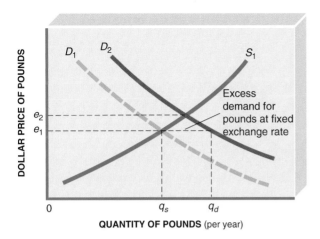

FIGURE 16.5
Fixed Rates and Market Imbalance

If exchange rates are fixed, they can't adjust to changes in market supply and demand. Suppose the exchange rate is initially fixed at e_1. When the demand for British pounds increases (shifts to the right), an excess demand for pounds emerges. More pounds are demanded (q_d) at the rate e_1 than are supplied (q_s). This causes a balance-of-payments deficit for Canada.

Suppose the exchange rate officially established by Canada and Great Britain is equal to e_1, as illustrated in Figure 16.5. As is apparent, that particular exchange rate is consistent with the then-prevailing demand and supply conditions in the foreign-exchange market (as indicated by curves D_1 and S_1).

Now suppose that Canadians suddenly acquire a greater taste for British cars and start spending more income on Jaguars and the like. Although Ford owns Jaguar, the cars are still produced in Great Britain. Hence, as Canadian purchases of British goods increase, the demand for British currency will *shift* from D_1 to D_2 in Figure 16.5. Were exchange rates allowed to respond to market influences, the dollar price of a British pound would rise, in this case to the rate e_2. But we've assumed that government intervention has fixed the exchange rate at e_1. Unfortunately, at e_1, Canadian consumers want to buy more pounds (q_d) than the British are willing to supply (q_s). The difference between the quantity demanded and the quantity supplied in the market at the rate e_1 represents a *market shortage* of British pounds.

The excess demand for pounds implies a **balance-of-payments deficit** for Canada: More dollars are flowing out of the country than into it. The same disequilibrium represents a **balance-of-payments surplus** for Britain, because its outward flow of pounds is less than its incoming flow.

Basically, there are only two solutions to balance-of-payments problems brought about by the attempt to fix exchange rates:

- Allow exchange rates to rise to e_2 (Figure 16.5), thereby eliminating the excess demand for pounds.
- Alter market supply or demand so that they intersect at the fixed rate e_1.

Since fixed exchange rates were the initial objective of policy, only the second alternative is of immediate interest.

The Need for Reserves. One way to alter market conditions would be for someone simply to supply British pounds to Canadian consumers. The Bank of Canada could have accumulated a reserve of foreign exchange in earlier periods. By selling some of those foreign-exchange reserves now, the Bank could help to stabilize market conditions at the officially established exchange rate. The rightward shift of the pound supply curve in Figure 16.6 illustrates the sale of accumulated British pounds—and related purchase of Canadian dollars—by the Bank of Canada. (In 2006, the Bank of Canada decreased their foreign exchange reserves, selling $1.0 billion; see the Official reserves in Table 16.1.)

In a **fixed exchange rate regime,** the central bank—in Canada's case, the Bank of Canada—must act as the residual buyer or seller of Canadian dollars. We saw this policy potential of the Bank of Canada when we looked at the changes in supply and

balance-of-payments deficit: An excess demand for foreign currency at current exchange rates.

balance-of-payments surplus: An excess demand for domestic currency at current exchange rates.

fixed exchange rate regime: A rate "fixed" by government and not allowed to change through market forces.

FIGURE 16.6
The Impact of Monetary Intervention

If the Bank of Canada holds reserves of British pounds, it can use them to buy Canadian dollars in foreign exchange markets. As it does so, the supply of pounds will shift to the right, S_2, thereby maintaining the desired exchange rate, e_1. The Bank of England could bring about the same result by offering to buy Canadian dollars with British pounds.

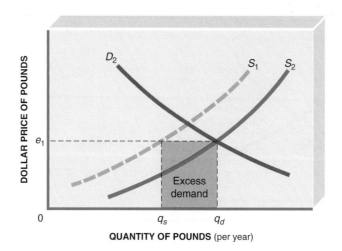

QUANTITY OF POUNDS (per year)

demand in the foreign exchange market in Figure 16.2. The problem is that the Bank of Canada can only get foreign exchange either through trade, capital asset transactions, or by purchasing foreign exchange on the foreign exchange market. This limits the Bank's ability to intervene in the foreign exchange market through the buying or selling of official reserves and may require other domestic policies to support a fixed exchange rate.

Domestic Adjustments. The supply and demand for foreign exchange can also be shifted by changes in basic fiscal, monetary, or trade policies. With respect to trade policy, *trade protection can be used to prop up fixed exchange rates.* We could eliminate the excess demand for pounds (Figure 16.5), for example, by imposing quotas and tariffs on British goods. Such trade restrictions would reduce British imports to Canada and thus the demand for British pounds. Such restrictions on international trade, however, violate the principle of comparative advantage and thus reduce total world output. Trade protection also invites retaliatory trade restrictions.

Fiscal policy is another way out of the imbalance. An increase in income tax rates will reduce disposable income and have a negative effect on the demand for all goods, including imports. A reduction in government spending will have similar effects. In general, *deflationary (or restrictive) policies help correct a balance-of-payments deficit by reducing domestic incomes and thus the demand for imports.*

Monetary policies in a deficit country could follow the same restrictive course. A reduction in the money supply will tend to raise interest rates. The balance of payments will benefit in two ways. The resultant slowdown in spending will reduce import demand. In addition, higher interest rates may induce international investors to move some of their funds into the deficit country. Such moves will provide immediate relief to the payments imbalance.[3] Russia tried this strategy in 1998, tripling key interest rates (to as much as 150 percent). But even that wasn't enough to restore confidence in the ruble, which kept depreciating. Within three months of the monetary policy tightening, the ruble lost half its value.

A surplus country could help solve the balance-of-payments problem. By pursuing expansionary—even inflationary—fiscal and monetary policies, a surplus country could stimulate the demand for imports. Moreover, any inflation at home will reduce the competitiveness of exports, thereby helping to restrain the inflow of foreign demand. Taken together, such efforts would help reverse an international payments imbalance.

[3]Before 1930, not only were foreign-exchange rates fixed, but domestic monetary supplies were tied to gold stocks as well. Countries experiencing a balance-of-payments deficit were thus forced to contract their money supply, and countries experiencing a payments surplus were forced to expand their money supply by a set amount. Monetary authorities were powerless to control domestic money supplies except by erecting barriers to trade. The system was abandoned when the world economy collapsed into the Great Depression.

Even under the best of circumstances, domestic economic adjustments entail significant costs. In effect, ***domestic adjustments to payments imbalances require a deficit country to forsake full employment and a surplus country to forsake price stability.*** China has had to grapple with these domestic consequences of fixing the value of its currency. The artificially low value of the yuan has promoted Chinese exports and accelerated China's GDP growth. It has also caused prices in China to rise faster than the government desires, however. To maintain the yuan's fixed exchange rate, the Chinese government began introducing restrictive monetary and fiscal policies in 2003–2004. There's no easy way out of this impasse. Market imbalances caused by fixed exchange rates can be corrected only with abundant supplies of foreign-exchange reserves or deliberate changes in fiscal, monetary, or trade policies.

The Euro Fix. Members of the European Monetary Union (EMU) eliminated their national currencies, making the euro the common currency of Euroland (Slovenia joined in 2007 and Cyprus and Malta are joining on January 1, 2008, increasing the number of "euro" countries to 15). They went far beyond the kind of exchange-rate fix we're discussing here. Members of the EMU *eliminated* their national currencies, making the euro the common currency of Euroland. They don't have to worry about reserve balances or domestic adjustments. However, they do have to reconcile their varied national interests to a single monetary authority, which may prove to be difficult politically in times of economic stress.

Balance-of-payments problems wouldn't arise in the first place if exchange rates were allowed to respond to market forces. Under a system of **flexible exchange rates** (often called floating exchange rates), the exchange rate moves up or down to choke off any excess supply of or demand for foreign exchange. Notice again in Figure 16.5 that the exchange-rate move from e_1 to e_2 prevents any excess demand from emerging. ***With flexible exchange rates, the quantity of foreign exchange demanded always equals the quantity supplied,*** and there's no imbalance. For the same reason, there's no need for foreign-exchange reserves.

Although flexible exchange rates eliminate balance-of-payments and foreign-exchange reserves problems, they don't solve all of a country's international trade problems. ***Exchange-rate movements associated with flexible rates alter relative prices and may disrupt import and export flows.*** As noted before, depreciation of the dollar raises the price of all imported goods. The price increases may contribute to domestic cost-push inflation. Also, domestic businesses that sell imported goods or use them as production inputs may suffer sales losses. On the other hand, appreciation of the dollar raises the foreign price of Canadian goods and reduces the sales of Canadian exporters. Hence, ***someone is always hurt, and others are helped, by exchange-rate movements.*** The resistance to flexible exchange rates originates in these potential losses. Such resistance creates pressure for official intervention in foreign-exchange markets or increased trade barriers.

After revaluations of the "fixed" Canadian exchange rate in 1946 and 1949, Canada was one of the first countries in the world to abandon fixed rates and move to a flexible exchange rate regime. James Powell, in *A History of the Canadian Dollar* quotes Douglas Abbot, the Minister of Finance, who announced:

> Today the Government, by Order in Council under the authority of the Foreign Exchange Control Act, cancelled the official rates of exchange which had been in effect since September 19th of last year. . . . It has been decided not to establish any new fixed parity for the Canadian dollar at this time, nor to prescribe any new official fixed rates of exchange. Instead, rates of exchange will be determined by conditions of supply and demand for foreign currencies in Canada.[4]

Flexible Exchange Rates

flexible exchange rates: A system in which exchange rates are permitted to vary with market supply-and-demand conditions; floating exchange rates.

---

[4]James Powell, *A History of the Canadian Dollar* (Bank of Canada, 1995), p. 61, http://www.bank-banque-canada.ca/en/dollar_book/1950-62.pdf, accessed March 19, 2007.

"Damn it! How can I relax, knowing that out there, somewhere, somehow, someone's attacking the dollar?"

Analysis: A "weak" dollar reduces the buying power of tourists.

Although Canada again returned to a fixed exchange rate in 1962, a flexible exchange rate regime was re-established in 1970 and continues today.

Speculation. One force that often helps maintain stability in a flexible exchange-rate system is speculation. Speculators often counteract short-term changes in foreign-exchange supply and demand. If an exchange rate temporarily rises above its long-term equilibrium, speculators will move in to sell foreign exchange. By selling at high prices and later buying at lower prices, speculators hope to make a profit. In the process, they also help stabilize foreign-exchange rates.

Speculation isn't always stabilizing, however. Speculators may not correctly gauge the long-term equilibrium. Instead, they may move "with the market" and help push exchange rates far out of kilter.

Managed Exchange Rates. Governments can intervene in foreign-exchange markets without completely fixing exchange rates. That is, they may buy and sell foreign exchange for the purpose of *narrowing* rather than *eliminating* exchange-rate movements. Such limited intervention in foreign-exchange markets is often referred to as **managed exchange rates,** or, popularly, "dirty floats."

> **managed exchange rates:** A system in which governments intervene in foreign-exchange markets to limit but not eliminate exchange-rate fluctuations; "dirty floats."

The basic objective of exchange-rate management is to provide a stabilizing force. The Bank of Canada, for example, may use its foreign-exchange reserves to buy dollars when they're depreciating too much. Or it will buy foreign exchange if the dollar is rising too fast. From this perspective, exchange-rate management appears as a fail-safe system for the private market. Unfortunately, the motivation for official intervention is sometimes suspect. Private speculators buy and sell foreign exchange for the sole purpose of making a profit. But government sales and purchases may be motivated by other considerations. A falling exchange rate increases the competitive advantage of a country's exports. A rising exchange rate makes international investment less expensive. Hence, a country's efforts to manage exchange-rate movements may arouse suspicion and outright hostility in its trading partners.

Although managed exchange rates would seem to be an ideal compromise between fixed rates and flexible rates, they can work only when some acceptable "rules of the game" and mutual trust have been established. As Sherman Maisel, a former governor of the Federal Reserve Board, put it, "Monetary systems are based on credit and faith: If these are lacking, a . . . crisis occurs."[5]

[5]Sherman Maisel, *Managing the Dollar* (New York: W. W. Norton, 1973), p. 196.

16.5 EXCHANGE RATES AND TRADE IN A SMALL OPEN ECONOMY

In 1976, Canada was invited to join the Group of Six, more commonly referred to as the "G6," which had met for the first time in 1975. Canada became a member of the new "G7," along with the United States, the United Kingdom, Japan, Italy, Germany, and France. This Group of Seven represents the seven major industrial democracies in the world or, generally, the seven countries with the largest level of GDP. In 1998, Russia was added to the G7 to form the "G8." (As you can see, economists are not necessarily creative with names.)

Although Canada is a member of these groups, (G7 and G8), Canadian GDP represents only about 4.3 percent of the G8's total GDP based on 2006 estimates. The G8 itself represents approximately 63 percent of total World GDP.[6] When taken in the context of the entire world's GDP, Canada represents less than 3.0 percent of that total. While Canada is considered one of the world's major industrial democracies, it makes up a relatively small proportion of the world's total GDP. So we can consider Canada a "small" economy.

In Chapter 15 and earlier we noted the history of Canada as an "open" economy. That is, Canada's trade with the rest of the world—our imports and exports—accounts for a significant proportion of total GDP. In 2006 the ratio of the combination of imports and exports to total GDP was slightly greater than 70 percent, or more than $1 trillion. This ratio has been called an "openness index" by some economists, and by that measure, Canada can clearly be termed an open economy.

So, when we think about Canada in a world context, Canada can be best described as a "small open economy," Ah, I hear you say, but So what? Why does it matter? Why should we care? Well, simply put, we care because decisions in the rest of the world impact the Canadian economy. And therefore, fiscal policy decisions, monetary policy decisions, and trade policy decisions made in Canada can change what the rest of the world does and therefore can impact Canadian economic performance.

In 1999, the Bank of Sweden prize in Economic Sciences in memory of Alfred Nobel was awarded to the Canadian-born economist, Robert A. Mundell. Part of the press release by the Academy for the award noted Mundell's "pioneering article (1963) [that] addresses the short-run effects of monetary and fiscal policy in an open economy."[7]

Mundell's work, along with that of the English economist Marcus Fleming, is presented in the context of the **Mundell-Fleming model.**

To understand the impact on the Canadian economy resulting from changes in domestic fiscal and monetary policy, the model begins with two basic assumptions:

1. Capital is highly mobile; that is, money investments (capital) are able to flow freely between countries; and,
2. Domestic interest rates will be equivalent to foreign interest rates in equilibrium[8] because of the inflow and/or outflow of capital.

Given these two basic assumptions, we can then evaluate the impact on the Canadian economy resulting from fiscal or monetary policy under the condition of either a fixed exchange rate regime or a flexible exchange rate regime.

> **Mundell-Fleming model:** An analysis of the relationship among the exchange rate regime, direction of capital flows, impact on the exchange rate, impact on net exports, and the final impact on national income.

[6] For an estimate of the G8 proportion of world GDP, see the "G8—economic power" page at the official 2007 Summit Web site: http://www.g-8.de/Webs/G8/EN/G8/Economics/economics.html.

[7] The Prize in Economics Press Release, http://nobelprize.org/nobel_prizes/economics/laureates/1999/press.html, accessed March 20, 2007. Mundell's pioneering article is: R. A. Mundell, "Capital mobility and stabilization policy under fixed and flexible exchange rates," *Canadian Journal of Economics* (29) (1963), pp. 475–485.

[8] This equivalency does not mean that the numbers themselves are exactly equal—only that taking risk and other factors into account, potential investors would see the two interest rates as equivalent and be indifferent between them.

TABLE 16.4

Fiscal Policy and Monetary Policy Under Different Exchange Rate Regimes

In Chapter 13 (Figure 13.7), the monetary transmission mechanism illustrated the impact on the Canadian economy from changes in both the interest rate and the exchange rate. The

Mundell-Fleming "small open-economy" analysis extends our understanding by incorporating international capital flows and exchange rate regimes to the impact of fiscal and monetary policy decisions on national income, Y.

	Fiscal Policy		Monetary Policy	
	Fixed Exchange Rate	Flexible Exchange Rate	Fixed Exchange Rate	Flexible Exchange Rate
Policy Change	$G\uparrow$	$G\uparrow$	$MS\uparrow$	$MS\uparrow$
Interest Rate	$i\uparrow$	$i\uparrow$	$i\downarrow$	$i\downarrow$
Capital Flow	$K_R\uparrow$ (Inflow)	$K_R\uparrow$ (Inflow)	$K_P\uparrow$ (Outflow)	$K_P\uparrow$ (Outflow)
Exchange Rate	$e\uparrow$ Appreciation	$e\uparrow$ Appreciation	$e\downarrow$ Depreciation	$e\downarrow$ Depreciation
Policy Accommodation: Bank of Canada	Bank of Canada sells dollars $MS\uparrow$: e remains fixed	No Bank of Canada policy required	Bank of Canada buys dollars $MS\downarrow$: e remains fixed	No Bank of Canada policy required
Net Exports	No change	$NX\downarrow$ ($X\downarrow$ $Im\uparrow$)	No change	$NX\uparrow$ ($X\uparrow$ $Im\downarrow$)
Impact on Y	Stimulative $Y\uparrow$	Uncertain $G\uparrow Y\uparrow$-$NX\downarrow Y\downarrow$	No change	Stimulative $Y\uparrow$

Table 16.4 provides an example of the effectiveness of fiscal policy and monetary policy under both a fixed exchange rate regime and a flexible exchange rate regime. However, we'll take the time to work through only the flexible exchange rate regime here, since Canada has followed a flexible exchange rate regime since 1970, and that condition is of most interest to us.

Suppose that a government intends to stimulate economic activity—the level of current national income, Y—by increasing their own spending (increasing government expenditure, G). This additional expenditure increases national income, Y, and also increases the demand for money in the economy, M^D. Since there has been no change in the supply of money, M^S (no specific monetary policy), the shift of the M^D curve will result in an increase in the Canadian rate of interest, i_C. Since any change in the Canadian rate of interest will have no effect on foreign interest rates, the Canadian interest rate will rise relative to the foreign interest rate:

$$i_C > i_F$$

The second assumption above states that the domestic and foreign interest rates will be made equivalent through the inflow or outflow of capital, K, from the Canadian economy. In this case, the higher Canadian interest rates attract capital receipts, K_R, or an inflow of capital for portfolio investments. Since Canadian portfolio investments are priced in Canadian dollars, foreigners must first acquire Canadian dollars—increasing the demand for Canadian dollars on the foreign exchange market (and at the same time, increasing the supply of their own currency). This leads to an appreciation of the value of the Canadian dollar on foreign exchange markets—an increase in the foreign currency price of the Canadian dollar, or a decrease in the Canadian dollar price of foreign currency. Capital, K_R, would continue to flow into Canada until the Canadian interest rate benefit was competed away, and the Canadian and foreign interest rates were equivalent.

The appreciation of the Canadian dollar means that Canadian-produced goods and services will now be more expensive in foreign markets. This will reduce the quantity of Canadian exports, X, sold to foreign markets. The higher value of the Canadian dollar also makes foreign produced goods and services less expensive in Canada, thus increasing the quantity of imports, Im, purchased by Canadians. Overall, this will reduce Canadian net exports, NX. Since net exports are a component of total Canadian national income, Y, or GDP, the reduction of net exports leads to a reduction in current Canadian GDP.

Since the purpose of the original fiscal policy was to increase national income, we have to ask if we have achieved our goal. The answer here is: I'm not sure. The initial increase in government expenditure does add to GDP, but the resulting decrease in net exports subtracts from it. The net outcome, then, is uncertain. It will depend on how much net exports change in relation to the original increase in expenditure.

In the case of monetary policy, the analysis is quite a bit simpler. An increase in the money supply, M^S, would reduce the Canadian interest rate, i. This would leave the domestic Canadian interest rate below the foreign rate:

$$i_C < i_F$$

This makes foreign portfolio investments more attractive and would lead to an outflow of capital, K_P, which in turn would begin to depreciate the value of the Canadian dollar. The depreciation of the Canadian dollar means that Canadian-produced goods and services will now be less expensive in foreign markets. This will increase the quantity of Canadian exports, X, sold to foreign markets. The lesser value of the Canadian dollar also makes foreign-produced goods and services more expensive in Canada, thus decreasing the quantity of imports, Im, purchased by Canadians. Overall, this will increase Canadian net exports, NX. Since net exports are a component of total Canadian national income, Y or GDP, the increase of net exports leads to an increase in current Canadian GDP.

In the case of monetary policy, the only impact on national income is the increase arising from net exports. Therefore, GDP would unequivocally increase.

16.6 A COMMON CURRENCY AND GLOBALIZATION

In the press release announcing Mundell as the 1999 winner of the Nobel memorial prize in economics,[9] the reason for his choice was noted as being not only for his work in "small open economies" (as we saw in the Mundell-Fleming model above), but also for his "radical" re-positioning of the exchange rate regime question from a debate between a fixed versus a flexible exchange rate regime, to a question that asks "when does it make sense for countries to pursue a common currency?"

As the Applications box on the next page illustrates, some economists favour the idea of common currencies. Being in favour of a common currency for Canada and the United States arises from two areas. It comes from the desire to see Canada's productivity increase and to reduce the cost of production, thereby increasing the competitiveness of Canadian goods and services in the U.S. market. The argument is that this would be accomplished through reductions of currency risk (the risk that the currency values will change in the time it takes between agreeing to an exchange and actually making it), thus stabilizing relative prices, and by reducing the transactions cost—(the cost of having to sell one currency and purchase another).

A general consensus might be that a common currency makes the most sense where two or more countries represent the most significant proportion of each other's trade (exports and imports) and where the countries involved tend to share similar economic structures. In terms of trade significance, Canada's exports of goods and services to the United States and Mexico in 2006 represented more than 80 percent of Canada's total exports. For the United States, Canada and Mexico represent the destination for approximately 26 percent of total U.S. exports of goods and services in 2006. For

---

[9]Royal Swedish Academy of Sciences, "The Sveriges Riksbank Prize in Economic Sciences in Memory of Alfred Nobel, 1999," press release (October 13, 1999), http://nobelprize.org/nobel_prizes/economics/laureates/1999/press.html, accessed March 22, 2007.

APPLICATIONS

Globalization Creating a "Deadly Brew" for National Currencies

Hardly a day goes by that someone, somewhere isn't griping about currencies.

So, maybe it's time to rethink the whole idea of national currencies. That, at least, is the provocative thesis of Benn Steil, director of international economics at the Council of Foreign Relations in New York. In an article in *Foreign Affairs* magazine, Mr. Steil suggests that scores of countries—from the Americas and Asia to Europe and the Middle East—should simply give up on their own currencies and embrace one of the world's global currencies, such as the euro or the U.S. dollar. "National currencies and global markets simply do not mix," Mr. Steil argued. "Together they make a deadly brew of currency crises and geopolitical tension and create ready pretexts for damaging protectionism."

Get rid of monetary nationalism, along with unlived currencies, and you'll rid the system of a major source of instability, he concluded. "Europeans used to say that being a country required having a national airline, a stock exchange, and a currency," he wrote. "Today, no European country is any worse off without them. Even grumpy Italy has benefited enormously from the lower interest rates and permanent end to lira speculation. China, he suggested, would do well to give up the yuan in favour of a "pan-Asian" currency that would rival the euro and the dollar, while allowing the country to liberalize its financial and capital markets.

Source: Barrie McKenna, "Globalization creating a 'deadly brew' for national currencies," *The Globe and Mail* (July 17, 2007) p. B12. Reprinted with permission from *The Globe and Mail*.

Analysis: Small and relatively weak currencies can lead to increased instability across the international economy, disrupting international trade and investment and slowing economic growth and development. Some of this was highlighted earlier in the text with the discussion of the Thai baht and the larger effect on the confidence in other currencies. Steil is quoted later in the story suggesting that "Canada isn't like Brazil or Turkey, where the threat of a currency crisis is ever present. Canada can certainly sustain a national currency, because Canadians, as well as foreigners, treat the currency as a reliable store of wealth. Canada is at no significant risk of a currency crisis, but that doesn't mean Canada couldn't do better."

common currency zone: A group of two or more countries that agree to share a common currency and therefore a common monetary policy.

Mexico, Canada and the United States are the destination for approximately 88 percent of Mexican goods and services (2005 estimate). While trade within the NAFTA area accounts for a significant proportion of Canadian and Mexican exports, this is less true for the United States.

Another general condition is the similarity of each economy's structure. The importance of this condition is that it implies that all countries will react similarly to shocks caused by international events or international price movements. If countries experience "shock symmetry," then the same monetary policy or exchange rate impact will be appropriate for all. If this is not the case, if each country reacts to shocks differently, or they have "shock asymmetry," then a purely domestic currency will enable exchange rate revaluation to act as a "shock absorber"—so, in Canada's case, the Canadian dollar can appreciate or depreciate to remove some of the impact of the shock. Since the Canadian economy relies more heavily on international commodity prices—oil and nickel, for instance—than does the U.S. economy, the Canadian dollar exchange rate has been able to fulfill this "shock absorber" characteristic.

Finally, the advent of a common currency means the creation of a common monetary policy. In the case of a common currency for NAFTA partners, there would have to be one monetary policy for all three countries: Canada, the United States, and Mexico, (as is true in the Eurozone where the European Central Bank, ECB, will administer a single monetary policy for all 15 Eurozone countries). This means that no individual country could pursue a monetary policy that was only in its own interest. This loss of monetary policy control by countries in a **common currency zone** is seen as a loss both in policy flexibility (fiscal policy becomes the only domestic policy option) and at the same time, a loss in political sovereignty, as monetary policy decisions that affect the local economy are made by a "foreign" institution.

In a speech to the Lunenburg Board of Trade in June, 2006, Tiff Macklem, a Deputy Governor of the Bank of Canada, noted that having a Canadian currency following a flexible exchange rate regime enables the Bank to have a monetary policy suited to Canadian economic circumstances. He then went on to say that:

> There's another important reason for having a flexible exchange rate. Just as a properly moored ship has some play in the mooring lines to absorb changes in the wind and the tide, the floating dollar helps the economy to absorb shocks—especially external shocks that affect our economy differently than the economies of our major trading partners. That is, it helps us adjust to shifting currents in the global economy. It's useful to think of the exchange rate as a relative price, a price that provides a good deal of useful information. Movements in the exchange rate send signals to businesses and consumers, signals that help the economy adjust to changing circumstances.[10]

[10]Remarks by Tiff Macklem, Deputy Governor of the Bank of Canada, to the Lunenburg Board of Trade, Lunenburg, Nova Scotia. (June 8, 2006), http://www.bankofcanada.ca/en/speeches/2006/sp06-9.html, accessed March 22, 2007.

SUMMARY

- Money serves the same purposes in international trade as it does in the domestic economy, namely, to facilitate productive specialization and market exchanges. The basic challenge of international finance is to create acceptable standards of value from the various currencies maintained by separate countries.

- The Canadian balance of international payments is a record of all international transactions for a specific time period and from a Canadian perspective, that is, measured in Canadian dollars.

- The balance of payments includes the current account, the capital and financial account, and the change to official reserves—foreign currency held at the Bank of Canada.

- Exchange rates are "bilateral," (the rate of one country's currency is expressed in terms of another country's), determined separately for each other country, and is determined by supply and demand in the foreign exchange market.

- Foreign currencies have value because they can be used to acquire goods, resources, and financial assets from other countries. The demand for the Canadian dollar arises from exports, X, capital inflow, K_R, currency speculation, and the Bank of Canada. The supply of the Canadian dollar arises from imports, Im, capital outflow, K_P, currency speculation, and the Bank of Canada.

- Exchange rates are affected by market forces, such as relative income changes, relative price changes, changes in product availability including the impact of trade policy, relative interest rate changes, and currency speculation. An appreciation of an exchange rate is a change that makes one country's currency more expensive in terms of another currency. Depreciation occurs when a country's currency is less expensive in terms of another currency.

- Changes in exchange rate are often resisted. Exporters don't want the currency to appreciate as it makes their goods more expensive in foreign markets. Importers and tourists don't want the currency to depreciate as it makes foreign goods and foreign travel more expensive.

- In the long run, currencies should tend toward their purchasing power parity, PPP, level. That is, the "price" of goods and services should be the same once adjusted by the exchange rate. Non-traded goods, transportation costs, and the production of different products reduce the predictive power of PPP.

- A fixed exchange rate regime results in monetary policy being directed to maintaining the fixed rate. Any market imbalances have to be removed through the Bank of Canada buying or selling foreign exchange reserves at the fixed rate.

- A flexible exchange rate regime enables market forces to determine the exchange rate and allows the rate to adjust to different circumstances. There is no need under flexible rates for intervention by the Bank of Canada and monetary policy can therefore be used for another purpose—like controlling inflation.

- The Mundell-Fleming model illustrates the connection between exchange rate regimes (fixed or flexible), flows of capital (inflows or outflows), exchange rates (appreciation or depreciation), and trade (exports or imports) for a small open economy, given that capital is highly mobile and domestic and foreign interest rates in equilibrium are equivalent.

- Being part of a NAFTA common currency zone (similar to the Euro countries) can reduce exchange rate risk and exchange transactions costs. A common currency makes the most sense where the intra-regional trade is significant and where each economy is similarly structured—facing "shock symmetry."

Key Terms

exchange rate 341
balance of international payments 341
official (international) reserves 343
depreciation (currency) 348
appreciation 348

foreign-exchange markets 350
purchasing power parity (PPP) 352
gold standard 354
balance-of-payments deficit 355
balance-of-payments surplus 355

fixed exchange rate regime 355
flexible exchange rates 357
managed exchange rates 358
Mundell-Fleming model 359
common currency zone 362

Questions for Discussion

1. How would the appreciation of the Canadian dollar against the U.S. dollar help Fortis in their purchase of Terasen assets from Kinder-Morgan in the United States.?

2. Why would Tourism Toronto be in favour of a depreciation of the Canadian dollar with respect to the U.S. dollar while the Toronto Maple Leafs would not?

3. Why would a depreciation of the Canadian dollar with respect to the Japanese yen prompt Honda to build a production plant in Canada?

4. If Canada was to fix its exchange rate to the U.S. dollar what would happen to the Canadian rate of inflation if the U.S. inflation rate rose to 5 percent per year?

5. How would each of the following events affect the demand or supply for Mexican pesos?
   a. A colder Canadian winter
   b. An increase in the Canadian rate of inflation
   c. A decrease in the Canadian interest rate relative to the Mexican interest rate

6. When the Canadian dollar depreciated against the U.S. dollar in the 1990s, did this make the price of Canadian softwood lumber "unfair" in the U.S. market?

7. China has recently been under considerable international pressure to allow their currency, the yuan, to appreciate.

Who will gain and who will not if the Chinese government was to allow an appreciation?

8. Suppose that this text was offered for sale on "Amazon.com" in the United States for $64.95 ($US) while on the Canadian site, the price was $72.95 ($Cdn). What would the purchasing power parity exchange rate, e^{PPP}, be? If the current official exchange rate is $1 ($Cdn) = $0.85 ($US), does this imply that the Canadian dollar is overvalued or undervalued? Would you predict the Canadian exchange rate would appreciate or depreciate relative to the U.S. dollar?

9. The Mundell-Fleming model provides an approach to analyze the impact of fiscal and/or monetary policy on national income, Y. Suppose Canada chose a fixed exchange rate regime, what would the analysis look like if:
   a. Government expenditure was decreased?
   b. Open-market operations were used by the Bank of Canada to sell bonds?

10. If Canada, the United States, and Mexico agreed to adopt a common currency (the North American dollar), what would the benefits be and why, and what would the costs be and why?

EXERCISES

PROBLEMS The Student Problem Set to accompany this chapter can be found at the end of the book.

WEB ACTIVITIES Web Activities to accompany this chapter can be found on the Online Learning Centre at **http://www.mcgrawhill.ca/olc/schiller**.

Note: Numbers in parentheses indicate the page numbers on which the definitions appear.

absolute advantage: The ability of a country to produce a specific good with fewer resources (per unit of output) than other countries. (56)

AD excess: The amount by which aggregate demand must be reduced to achieve full-employment equilibrium after allowing for price-level changes. (215)

AD shortfall: The amount by which aggregate demand must be increased to achieve full employment after allowing for price-level changes. (208)

adaptive (backward-looking) expectations: Expectations of the future that are formed from past experience, adapted by the difference between the expected value and actual value (the error of the estimate). (290)

aggregate demand (AD): The total quantity of output (real GDP) demanded at alternative price levels in a given time period, *ceteris paribus.* (148)

aggregate expenditure: The level of total expenditure related to each level of national income. (169)

appreciation: A rise in the price of one currency relative to another. (348)

arithmetic growth: An increase in quantity by a constant amount each year. (137)

asset: Anything having exchange value in the marketplace; wealth. (234)

automatic stabilizer: Federal or provincial expenditure or revenue item that automatically responds countercyclically to changes in national income, like employment insurance benefits, income taxes. (225)

average propensity to consume (APC): Total consumption in a given period divided by total disposable income. (154)

balance of international payments: A record of international transactions between Canadian residents and non-residents within a given time period and from a Canadian perspective. (341)

balance-of-payments deficit: An excess demand for foreign currency at current exchange rates. (355)

balance-of-payments surplus: An excess demand for domestic currency at current exchange rates. (355)

bank reserves: Assets held by a bank to fulfill its deposit obligations. (247)

barter: The direct exchange of one good for another, without the use of money. (241)

base period: The time period used for comparative analysis; the basis for indexing, for example, of price changes. (79)

bond: A certificate acknowledging a debt and the amount of interest to be paid each year until repayment; an IOU. (265)

bracket creep: The movement of taxpayers into higher tax brackets (rates) as nominal incomes grow. (112)

budget deficit: Amount by which government spending exceeds government revenue in a given time period. (222)

budget surplus: An excess of government revenue over government expenditure in a given time period. (223)

business cycle: Alternating periods of economic growth and contraction. (58)

capital: Final goods produced for use in the production of other goods, e.g., equipment, structures. (6)

capital deepening: Increasing the amount of capital available to each worker. (135)

cash drain: Cash received by individuals or firms that they do not re-deposit back into financial institutions. (252)

census metropolitan area (CMA): Large urban centres including adjacent urban and rural areas. (90)

ceteris paribus: The assumption of nothing else changing. (19)

common currency zone: A group of two or more countries that agree to share a common currency and therefore a common monetary policy. (362)

comparative advantage: The ability of a country to produce a specific good at a lower opportunity cost than its trading partners. (56)

complementary goods: Goods frequently consumed in combination; when the price of good *x* rises, the demand for good *y* falls, *ceteris paribus.* (34)

consumer price index (CPI): A measure (index) of changes in the average price of consumer goods and services. (112)

consumption: Expenditure by consumers on final goods and services. (153)

consumption function: A mathematical relationship indicating the rate of desired consumer spending at various income levels. (157)

consumption possibilities: The alternative combinations of goods and services that a country could consume in a given time period. (319)

crowding in: An increase in private-sector borrowing (and spending) caused by decreased government borrowing. (142)

crowding out: A reduction in private-sector borrowing (and spending) caused by increased government borrowing. (142)

cyclical balance: That portion of the budget deficit attributable to short-run deviations from the economy's potential GDP. (226)

cyclical unemployment: Unemployment attributable to a lack of job vacancies, that is, to inadequate aggregate demand. (99)

debt charges: The interest required to be paid each year on outstanding debt. (236)

deficit spending: The use of borrowed funds to finance government expenditures that exceed tax revenues. (222)

deflation: A decrease in the average level of prices of goods and services. (106)

demand: The willingness and ability to buy specific quantities of a good at alternative prices in a given time period, *ceteris paribus.* (31)

demand curve: A curve describing the quantities of a good a consumer is willing and able to buy at alternative prices in a given time period, *ceteris paribus.* (33)

demand for money: The quantities of money people are willing and able to hold at alternative interest rates, *ceteris paribus.* (256)

demand schedule: A table showing the quantities of a good a consumer is willing and able to buy at alternative prices in a given time period, *ceteris paribus.* (32)

demand-pull inflation: An increase in the price level initiated by excessive aggregate demand. (194)

deposit creation: The creation of transactions deposits by bank lending. (244)

depreciation: A fall in the price of one currency relative to another. (348)

depression: A severe and extended recession. (63)

deregulation: The reduction or removal of regulations or regulatory oversight that adds costs to the production of goods and services. (308)

discouraged worker: An individual who isn't actively seeking employment but would look for or accept a job if one were available. (95)

discretionary fiscal spending: Those elements of the federal budget not determined by past legislative commitments. (225)

disposable income (DI): After-tax income of households; personal income less personal taxes. (76)

dissaving: Consumption expenditure in excess of disposable income; a negative saving flow. (133)

dumping: The sale of goods in export markets at prices below domestic prices. (327)

economics: The study of how best to allocate scarce resources among competing uses. (4)

economic growth: An increase in output (real GDP); an expansion of production possibilities. (12)

efficiency: Maximum output of a good from the resources used in production. (10)

embargo: A prohibition on exports or imports. (328)

employment rate: The percentage of the eligible population 15 years and older that is employed. (127)

entrepreneurship: The assembling of resources to produce new or improved products and technologies. (6)

equation of exchange: Money supply (M) times velocity of circulation (V) equals level of aggregate spending ($P \times Q$). (280)

equilibrium price: The price at which the quantity of a good demanded in a given time period equals the quantity supplied. (42)

excess reserves: Bank reserves in excess of targeted reserves. (249)

exchange rate: The price of one country's currency expressed in terms of another's; the domestic price of a foreign currency. (341)

expenditure equilibrium: The rate of output at which desired spending equals the value of output. (172)

exports: Goods and services sold to foreign buyers. (72)

external debt: Government debt held by foreign households and institutions. (234)

factor market: Any place where factors of production (e.g., land, labour, capital) are bought and sold. (29)

factors of production: Resource inputs used to produce goods and services, e.g., land, labour, capital, entrepreneurship. (6)

fiscal policy: The use of government taxes and spending to alter macroeconomic outcomes. (198)

fiscal restraint: Tax hikes or spending cuts intended to reduce (shift) aggregate demand. (214)

fiscal stimulus: Tax cuts or spending hikes intended to increase (shift) aggregate demand. (207)

fiscal year (FY): The 12-month period used for accounting purposes. (224)

fixed exchange rate regime: A rate "fixed" by government and not allowed to change through market forces. (355)

flexible exchange rates: A system in which exchange rates are permitted to vary with market supply-and-demand conditions; floating exchange rates. (357)

foreign direct investment: An investment in productive facilities from outside the country that results in ownership or control. (133)

foreign economy: The world economy outside of the borders of the macroeconomy under consideration. Interactions between a domestic economy (like Canada) and all other countries in the world include the exchange of goods and services (international trade) and the exchange of financial assets and currency transactions (foreign direct investment and exchange rates). (53)

foreign-exchange markets: Places where foreign currencies are bought and sold. (350)

frictional unemployment: Brief periods of unemployment experienced by people moving between jobs or into the labour market. (98)

full employment: The lowest rate of unemployment compatible with price stability and the economy operating at potential national income (LRAS). (194)

full-employment GDP: The total market value of final goods and services that would be produced in a given time period if the economy were operating at full employment; also referred to as potential GDP. (176)

GDP deflator: A price index that refers to all goods and services included in GDP. (116)

GDP per capita: Total GDP divided by total population; average GDP per person. (79)

General Agreement on Tariffs and Trade (GATT): A trade pact that covered the rules and regulations governing the international trade in goods; now part of the World Trade Organization, WTO. (334)

geometric growth: An increase in quantity by a constant proportion each year. (137)

gold standard: An agreement by countries to fix the price of their currencies in terms of gold; a mechanism for fixing exchange rates. (354)

government failure: Government intervention that fails to improve economic outcomes. (17)

gross business saving: Depreciation allowances and retained earnings. (180)

gross domestic product (GDP): The total market value of all final goods and services produced within a nation's borders in a given time period. (68)

growth rate: Percentage change in real output from one period to another. (125)

growth recession: A period during which real GDP grows but at a rate below the long-term trend. (63)

human capital: The knowledge and skills possessed by the workforce. (131)

hyperinflation: Formally defined as a inflation rate of 50 percent per month or more—nearly 1300 percent per year—but more commonly used to describe rates of 200 percent per year or greater. (111)

imports: Goods and services purchased from foreign sellers. (72)

income transfers: Payments to individuals for which no current goods or services are exchanged, e.g., pension, welfare, employment insurance payments. (206)

inflation: An increase in the average level of prices of goods and services. (79)

inflation control target: The level of inflation, as measured by the consumer price index (CPI), that is the goal of monetary policy by the Bank of Canada. Currently, the target is 2 percent, with a control range of 1 to 3 percent. (262)

inflation rate: The annual percentage rate of increase in the average price level. (112)

inflationary GDP gap: The amount by which equilibrium GDP exceeds full employment GDP. (194)

injection: An addition of spending to the circular flow of income. (181)

interest rate: The price paid for the use of money. (256)

intermediate goods: Goods or services purchased for use as input in the production of final goods or in services. (70)

internal debt: Government debt held by Canadian households and institutions. (234)

investment: Expenditures on (production of) new plant, equipment, and structures (capital) in a given time period, plus changes in business inventories. (161)

item weight: The percentage of total expenditure spent on a specific product; used to compute inflation indexes. (114)

labour force: The civilian, non-institutional population, 15-years of age and over, who, during the reference week, were either employed or unemployed as defined by Statistics Canada. (88)

Labour Force Survey (LFS): A monthly survey of 53,000 Canadian households across the 10 provinces; used to determine the size of the Canadian labour force and the rate of unemployment in Canada. (92)

labour market: A part of the larger factor or resource market. Labour is hired by firms and paid wages to produce goods and services. The nature of the market impacts the level of unemployment and the level of wages in the national economy. (53)

labour productivity: Amount of real output (real gross domestic product, GDP) per hour worked. (128)

labour-force participation rate: The percentage of the working-age population working or seeking employment. (89)

laissez faire: The doctrine of "leave it alone," of nonintervention by government in the market mechanism. (14)

law of demand: The quantity of a good demanded in a given time period increases as its price falls, *ceteris paribus*. (33)

law of supply: The quantity of a good supplied in a given time period increases as its price increases, *ceteris paribus*. (39)

leakage: Income not spent directly on domestic output but instead diverted from the circular flow, e.g., saving, imports, taxes. (180)

liability: An obligation to make future payment; debt. (234)

liquidity: The ease with which money or money-denominated assets can be exchanged for goods or services. (253)

liquidity trap: The portion of the money demand curve that is horizontal; people are willing to hold unlimited amounts of money at some (low) interest rate. (277)

loanable funds market equilibrium: The interest rate at which the quantity of money demanded in a given time period equals the quantity of money supplied. (258)

long run aggregate supply (LRAS): The total quantity of output (real GDP) that an economy is able to produce given its resources and technology being used at a normal capacity utilization. (151)

macroeconomics: The study of aggregate economic behaviour, of the economy as a whole. (18)

managed exchange rates: A system in which governments intervene in foreign-exchange markets to limit but not eliminate exchange-rate fluctuations; "dirty floats." (358)

marginal propensity to consume (MPC): The fraction of each additional (marginal) dollar of disposable income spent on consumption; the change in consumption divided by the change in disposable income. (155)

marginal propensity to import (MPIm): The fraction of each additional (marginal) dollar of national income spent on imported goods and services. (165)

marginal propensity to save (MPS): The fraction of each additional (marginal) dollar of disposable income not spent on consumption; (155)

marginal tax rate: The tax rate imposed on the last (marginal) dollar of income. (299)

market demand: The total quantity of a good or service people are willing and able to buy at alternative prices in a given time period; the sum of individual demand. (36)

market failure: An imperfection in the market mechanism that prevents optimal outcomes. (16)

market mechanism: The use of market prices and sales to signal desired outputs (or resource allocations). (13)

market shortage: The amount by which the quantity demanded exceeds the quantity supplied at a given price; excess demand. (43)

market supply: The total quantity of a good that sellers are willing and able to sell at alternative prices in a given time period, *ceteris paribus*. (38)

market surplus: The amount by which the quantity supplied exceeds the quantity demanded at a given price; excess supply. (43)

microeconomics: The study of individual behaviour in the economy, of the components of the larger economy. (18)

mixed economy: An economy that uses both market signals and government directives to allocate goods and resources. (16)

monetary economy: The supply and demand for money determines the level of interest rates, and influences inflation and the exchange rate of the currency. The focus of monetary policy determined by the Bank of Canada. (53)

monetary policy: The use of money and credit controls to influence macroeconomic outcomes. (198)

monetary transmission mechanism: The impact path of how monetary policy is "transmitted" into the real economy through aggregate demand. (271)

money: Anything that is accepted as a medium of exchange and serves as both a store of value and as a unit of measurement. (243)

money illusion: The use of nominal dollars rather than real dollars to gauge changes in one's income or wealth. (110)

money supply: The level of purchasing power (currency and deposits) available to an economy. Measured and defined as M1 through M3. (252)

multifactor productivity: An estimate of real gross domestic product (GDP) per bundle of inputs—labour, capital, and intermediate inputs. (129)

multiplier: The multiple by which an initial change in aggregate spending will alter total expenditure after an infinite number of spending cycles. (167)

Mundell-Fleming model: An analysis of the relationship among the exchange rate regime, direction of capital flows, impact on the exchange rate, impact on net exports, and the final impact on national income. (359)

national-income accounting: The measurement of aggregate economic activity, particularly national income and its components. (67)

natural rate of unemployment: Long-term rate of unemployment determined by structural forces in labour and product markets. (100)

net domestic product (NDP): The total income earned by factors of production within Canada: GDP less Capital Consumption Allowance, CCA, and taxes less subsidies on products and any statistical discrepancy. (75)

net exports: The value of exports minus the value of imports. (73)

net investment: Gross investment less depreciation. (132)

nominal GDP: The value of final output produced in a given period, measured in the prices of that period (current prices). (78)

nominal income: The amount of money income received in a given time period, measured in current dollars. (108)

non-accelerating inflation rate of unemployment (NAIRU): A rate of unemployment that is consistent with price stability (an inflation rate of zero). (118)

North American Free Trade Agreement (NAFTA): A regional agreement among Canada, the United States, and Mexico that implements a free trade area. (335)

not in the labour force: Anyone 15 years of age or older who is unwilling or unable to participate in the labour market, and who is neither employed nor unemployed. (88)

official (international) reserves: Foreign currency holdings of the Canadian government including U.S. dollars and other foreign currencies. (343)

Okun's Law: One percent more unemployment is estimated to equal 2 percent less output. (91)

open market operations: Purchases and sales of government bonds by the Bank of Canada for the purpose of altering bank reserves. (266)

opportunity cost: The most desired goods or services that are forgone to obtain something else. (7)

personal income (PI): Income received by households before payment of personal taxes. (75)

Phillips curve: An historical (inverse) relationship between the rate of unemployment and the rate of inflation; commonly expresses a trade-off between the two. (292)

portfolio decision: The choice of where (how) to hold idle funds. (258)

precautionary demand for money: Money held for unexpected market transactions or for emergencies. (257)

price stability: The absence of significant changes in the average price level; officially defined as a rate of inflation of approximately 2 percent. (117)

prime rate: The rate of interest commercial banks charge their most credit-worthy (lowest risk) clients. (268)

product market: Any place where finished goods and services (products) are bought and sold. (30)

production possibilities: The alternative combinations of final goods and services that could be produced in a given time period with all available resources and technology. (8)

productivity: Output per unit of input, e.g., output per labour-hour. (127)

public debt: The accumulated debt of Canadian government—federal, provincial, and territorial. (230)

purchasing power parity (PPP): A rate of exchange such that a good in two different countries could be purchased with the same amount of domestic currency. (352)

quota: A limit on the quantity of a good that may be imported in a given time period. (330)

rational expectations: Hypothesis that people's spending decisions are based on all available information, including the anticipated effects of government intervention. (290)

real economy: Where the employment of "real" resources (labour, capital, and natural resources) create all the goods and services that are purchased by households, government, firms, and foreigners. Represented as the total value of national output—gross domestic product, GDP. (52)

real economy equilibrium: The combination of price level and real output that is compatible with both aggregate demand and aggregate supply. (152)

real GDP: The value of final output produced in a given period, adjusted for changing prices. (61)

real income: Income in constant dollars; nominal income adjusted for inflation. (108)

real interest rate: The nominal interest rate minus the anticipated inflation rate. (283)

recession: A decline in total output (real GDP) for two or more consecutive quarters. (63)

recessionary GDP gap: The amount by which equilibrium GDP falls short of full-employment GDP. (193)

reference week: One calendar week (Sunday to Saturday) covered by the Labour Force Survey each month. (92)

refinancing: The issuance of new debt in payment of debt issued earlier. (236)

reserve ratio: The ratio of a bank's reserves to its total transactions deposits. (247)

saving: That part of disposable income not spent on current consumption; disposable income less consumption. (76)

Say's Law: Supply creates its own demand. (59)

scarcity: Lack of enough resources to satisfy all desired uses of those resources. (5)

seasonal unemployment: Unemployment due to seasonal changes in employment or labour supply. (97)

shift in demand: A change in the quantity demanded at any (every) given price. (35)

short run aggregate supply (SRAS): The total quantity of output (real GDP) producers are willing and able to supply at alternative price levels in a given time period, *ceteris paribus.* (150)

short-run equilibrium GDP: The value of total final output at the price level where AD intersects with SRAS. (184)

simple money multiplier: The number of deposit (loan) dollars that the banking system can create from $1 of excess reserves; equal to $1 \div$ target reserve ratio. (250)

speculative demand for money: Money held for speculative purposes, for later financial opportunities. (257)

stagflation: The simultaneous occurrence of substantial unemployment and inflation. (288)

sterilization: To combine two actions so that there is no effect; in the case of money flowing from commercial banks to the Bank of Canada, the sterilization occurs through the Bank of Canada re-depositing those funds back into an account at the commercial banks. (263)

structural balance: Revenue at full employment minus expenditure at full employment under prevailing fiscal policy. (226)

structural unemployment: Unemployment caused by a mismatch between the skills (or location) of job seekers and the requirements (or location) of available jobs. (98)

substitute goods: Goods that substitute for each other; when the price of good x rises, the demand for good y increases, *ceteris paribus.* (33)

supply: The ability and willingness to sell (produce) specific quantities of a good at alternative prices in a given time period, *ceteris paribus.* (31)

supply-side policy: The use of tax incentives, (de)regulation, and other mechanisms to increase the ability and willingness to produce goods and services. (198)

target for the overnight rate: Sometimes referred to as the key interest rate or the key policy rate, the target for the overnight rate sets the target for major financial institutions to borrow or lend among themselves for one day (overnight). This target rate also influences other consumer lending rates (loans and mortgage rates). (268)

target reserve: The minimum amount of reserves a bank desires to hold; equal to target reserve ratio times transactions deposits. (247)

tariff: A tax (duty) imposed on imported goods. (328)

tax elasticity of supply: The percentage change in quantity supplied divided by the percentage change in tax rates. (302)

tax incentive: Changes in tax policy that can lead to changes in the behaviour of labour and producers by altering the "incentives" for particular behaviours. (297)

tax rebate: A lump-sum refund of taxes paid. (301)

technical progress: Increases in technology or productivity rather than increases in the quantity of capital or labour. (136)

terms of trade: The rate at which goods are exchanged; the amount of good A given up for good B in trade. (322)

trade pact: A negotiation or agreement between countries governing trade; *bilateral* trade pacts involve two countries, and *multilateral* trade pacts involve more than two countries. (334)

trade surplus (deficit): The amount by which the value of exports exceeds (is less than) the value of imports in a given time period. (316)

transactions account: A bank account that permits direct payment to a third party, for example, with a cheque. (253)

transactions demand for money: Money held for the purpose of making everyday market purchases. (257)

underemployment: People seeking full-time paid employment who work only part-time or are employed at jobs below their capability. (95)

unemployment: The inability of labour-force participants to find jobs. (91)

unemployment rate: The proportion of the labour force that is unemployed. (93)

value added: The increase in the market value of a product that takes place at each stage of the production process. (70)

velocity of money (V): The number of times per year, on average, that a dollar is used to purchase final goods and services; $PQ \div M.$ (280)

voluntary restraint agreement (VRA): An agreement to reduce the volume of trade in a specific good; a "voluntary" quota. (332)

wealth effect: A change in consumer spending caused by a change in the value of assets. (156)

World Trade Organization (WTO): An international institution that administers the rules of trade among 151 member nations, including Canada. (334)

yield: The rate of return on a bond; the annual interest payment divided by the bond's price. (266)

Problems for Chapter 1

Name: _____

1. According to Table 1.1 (or Figure 1.1), what is the opportunity cost of the
   - (*a*) Third metric tonne of wheat? _____
   - (*b*) Fourth metric tonne of wheat? _____

2. (*a*) According to Figure 1.2, what is the opportunity cost of Canada's wheat production at point *C*?
   - (*b*) What would be the gain to Canada's softwood lumber production if Canada cut the output of wheat from three metric tonnes per year to two metric tonne per year (that is, move from point *C* to point *B*)?

3. How much money would be available to spend on health care if the current spending on national defence is reduced from 1% of the $1.5 trillion economy to ½ %?

4. What is the opportunity cost (in dollars) to attend an hour-long econ lecture for
   - (*a*) A minimum-wage teenager $_____
   - (*b*) A $100,000 per year corporate executive $_____

5. Suppose either computers or televisions can be assembled with the following labour inputs:

Units produced	1	2	3	4	5	6	7	8	9	10
Total labour used	3	7	12	18	25	33	42	54	70	90

   - (*a*) Draw the production possibilities curve for an economy with 54 units of labour. Label it P54.
   - (*b*) What is the opportunity cost of the eighth computer?
   - (*c*) Suppose immigration brings in 36 more workers. Redraw the production possibilities curve to reflect this added labour. Label the new curve P90.
   - (*d*) Suppose advancing technology (e.g., the miniaturization of electronic circuits) increases the productivity of the 90-labourer workforce by 20 percent. Draw a third production possibilities curve (PT) to illustrate this change.

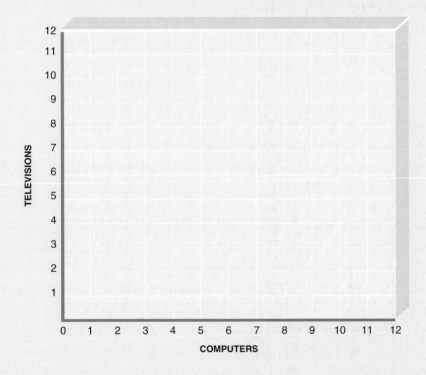

6. Suppose there's a relationship of the following sort between study time and grades:

	(a)	(b)	(c)	(d)	(e)
Study time (hours per week)	0	2	6	12	20
Grade-point average	0	1.0	2.0	3.0	4.0

If you have only 20 hours per week to use for either study time or fun time,

(a) Draw the (linear) production possibilities curve on the graph below that represents the alternative uses of your time.

(b) What is the cost, in lost fun time, of raising your grade-point average from 2.0 to 3.0? Illustrate this effort on the graph (point C to point D).   _____

(c) What is the opportunity cost of increasing your grades from 3.0 to 4.0? Illustrate as point D to point E.   _____

(d) Why does the opportunity cost change? _____

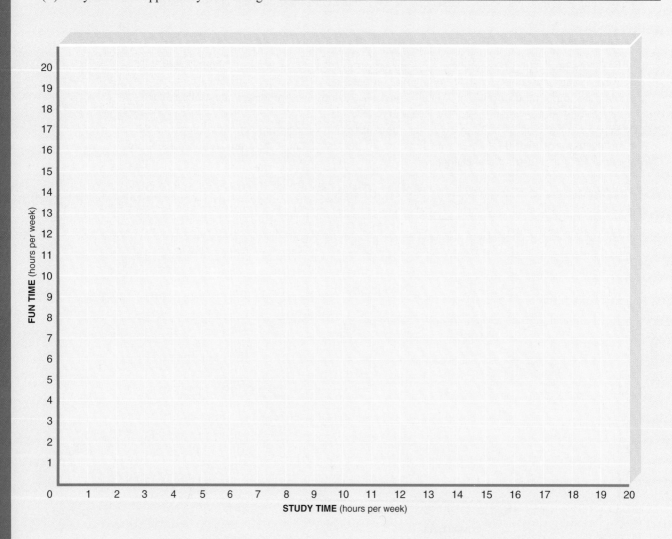

Problems for Chapter 2

Name: _____

1. According to Figure 2.3, at what price would Tom buy 15 hours of web tutoring?

        (a) Without a lottery win. _____

        (b) With a lottery win. _____

2. According to Figures 2.5 and 2.6, what would the new equilibrium price of tutoring services be if Ann decided to stop tutoring? _____

3. Given the following data, identify the amount of shortage or surplus that would exist at a price of

        (a) $5.00 _____

        (b) $3.00 _____

        (c) $1.00 _____

A. Price	$5.00	$4.00	$3.00	$2.00	$1.00		C. Quantity supplied	$5.00	$4.00	$3.00	$2.00	$1.00
B. Quantity demanded												
Al	1	2	3	4	5		Alice	3	3	3	3	3
Betsy	0	1	1	1	2		Butch	7	5	4	4	2
Casey	2	2	3	3	4		Connie	6	4	3	3	1
Daisy	1	3	4	4	6		Dutch	6	5	4	3	0
Eddie	1	2	2	3	5		Ellen	4	2	2	2	1
Market total	__	__	__	__	__		Market total	__	__	__	__	__

4. Graph the official and equilibrium prices for upscale clothes in Vancouver on Boxing Day (see Application, p. 44).

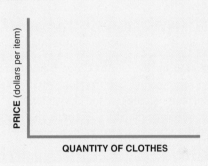

PRICE (dollars per item)

QUANTITY OF CLOTHES

5. In the World View on page 49, menu prices are continuously adjusted. Graph the initial and final (adjusted) prices for the following situations. Be sure to label axes and graph completely.

(a) Customers are ordering too little haddock.   **(b) The kitchen is running out of beef ribs.**

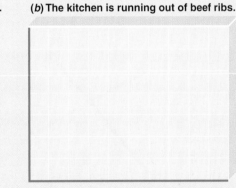

6. As a result of the ice storm in Eastern Canada, the demand for generators increased, driving up the price of generators in this market. What effect, if any, do you think this may have had on the market for generators in other parts of Canada?

7. Biofuels derived from agricultural products such as corn, canola, soybeans, and wheat have received considerable interest as an alternative to fossil fuels since many scientists believe that they reduce greenhouse gases. On the following three graphs, show how an increase in demand for biofuel (say wheat)—*ceteris paribus*—will affect the equilibrium for (*a*) biofuel wheat, (*b*) pasta, and (*c*) coal.

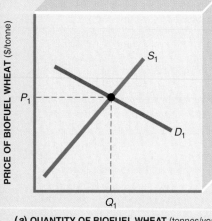
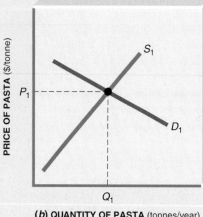
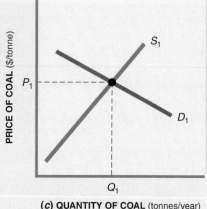

(*a*) **QUANTITY OF BIOFUEL WHEAT** (tonnes/year)   (*b*) **QUANTITY OF PASTA** (tonnes/year)   (*c*) **QUANTITY OF COAL** (tonnes/year)

8. Suppose the population for the city of Calgary has increased dramatically over the past year. In addition, the union representing construction workers has negotiated a 20% increase in the hourly wages paid to carpenters, plumbers, and drywallers.

   Given the above information, if we examine the market for single family housing, which curve will directly affected by

   (*a*) the increase in population? _____
   (*b*) the increase in hourly wage rates? _____

On the following graphs, illustrate the three possible outcomes associated with this simultaneous shift in the market for single family housing.

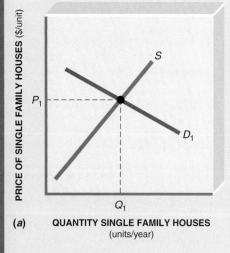
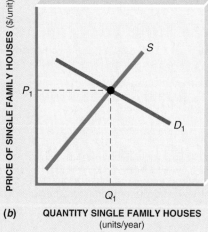
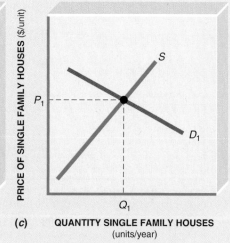

(*a*) **QUANTITY SINGLE FAMILY HOUSES** (units/year)   (*b*) **QUANTITY SINGLE FAMILY HOUSES** (units/year)   (*c*) **QUANTITY SINGLE FAMILY HOUSES** (units/year)

Problems for Chapter 3

Name: _____

1. The macroeconomy is described in the text as being composed of four economies/markets. Which of these economies or markets would I look at if I was interested in:
   (*a*) employment and wages _____
   (*b*) the supply of money _____
   (*c*) price level of goods and services _____
   (*d*) rate of interest _____
   (*e*) exchange rate of the Canadian dollar _____
   (*f*) value of goods and services sold to foreign purchasers _____
   (*g*) value of foreign goods and services purchased by Canadians _____
   (*h*) value of foreign direct investment (FDI) in Canada _____

2. The summary of the October 2007 Monetary Policy Report Update from the Bank of Canada presents the highlights of the update at http://www.bankofcanada.ca/en/mpr/pdf/mprsumoct07.pdf. Read the overview and find one sentence—or part of a sentence—in the summary that relates to each of the component parts of the macroeconomic system: the real economy, the labour market, the monetary economy, and the foreign economy. _____
   _____

3. The World View on page 54 gives a perspective of Canada's economy in relation to other countries in the world. Pick one of the country groups from the "advanced economies" or "other emerging market and developing countries" groups and explain the relative economic size of the countries included.

   Begin at http://www.imf.org/external/pubs/ft/weo/2007/02/weodata/index.aspx, which is the IMF data site—click on the "By Countries" link under the "Download WEO Data" heading and then select a country group from the list provided and follow the steps. Choose the "Gross Domestic Product, current dollars (U.S. dollar)" option (this will give you a comparison across countries in US dollars). Click on "continue" at the bottom and then again on the next page—make sure that all countries are "selected" and then click "prepare report." _____
   _____

4. Look at the current estimate of Canada's total National Income, GDP on the Statistics Canada site: http://www.statcan.ca/start.html. Click on the "Gross domestic product" link in the latest indicators box on the right side of the page. Given the information in *The Daily,* where do you think Canada is in the business cycle and why do you think this? _____
   _____

5. The Bank of Canada's October 2007 Monetary Policy Report Update notes in the opening paragraph of the overview that "the economy is now operating further above its production potential than had been previously expected." Use the production possibility curve (PPC) model and briefly explain what this statement means. _____
   _____

Problems for Chapter 4

Name: _____

1. Suppose that furniture production encompasses the following stages:

Stage 1: Trees sold to lumber company	$1,000
Stage 2: Lumber sold to furniture company	$1,700
Stage 3: Furniture company sells furniture to retail store	$3,200
Stage 4: Furniture store sells furniture to consumer	$5,995

   (a) What is the value added at each stage?

   Stage 1: _____
   Stage 2: _____
   Stage 3: _____
   Stage 4: _____

   (b) How much does this output contribute to GDP? _____

   (c) How would answer (b) change if the lumber were exported to the United States but the furniture was imported back to Canada by the retail furniture store? _____

2. If real GDP increases by 2.6 percent next year and the price level goes up by 2 percent, what will happen to nominal GDP? _____

3. Suppose that your province's production and prices for 2004 and 2005 were as given in the following table:

Products	2004 Quantity	2004 Price	2005 Quantity	2005 Price
Cars	10,000	$16,000.00	12,000	$16,500.00
Cases of Wine	2,000	$120.00	2,500	$125.00
Barrels of Oil	20,000	$55.00	25,000	$70.00
Kg of Carrots	100,000	$2.00	95,000	$2.25

   (a) Given the values in the table, calculate *nominal* GDP for 2004 and 2005 _____

   (b) What was the *nominal* rate of growth in GDP from 2004 to 2005? _____

   (c) Given the values in the table, calculate *real* GDP for 2004 and 2005 (use 2004 as the "base year" for the calculation) _____

   (d) What was the *real* rate of growth in GDP from 2004 to 2005? _____

   (e) What was the rate of inflation between 2004 and 2005? _____

4. Calculate Canada's *nominal* national income for 2006 from both the expenditure and income approaches from the following figures (all figures are in billions):

Capital cost allowance	$184.8
Imports	$487.7
Corporate profits	$198.9
Farm operations	$0.4
Household consumption	$803.5
Government profits	$13.8
Government	$320.1
Wages and salaries	$737.4
Gross investment	$285.7
Interest	$65.3
Inventory adjustment	($1.8)
Exports	$524.7
Unincorp. business profits	$86.0
Taxes less subsidies—factors	$64.4
Taxes less subsidies—products	$97.2

   National income: _____

5. From the calculations in question 4 above, what was the statistical discrepancy for 2006?   _____

6. What is the value of "net investment" for Canada in 2006 from the figures in question 4 above?   _____

7. If Canada's population in 2006 was 32,500,000, what was the GDP per capita for 2006? How does this compare with 2005? (see the GDP per capita discussion on page 79)   _____

8. Compare the values given in Table 4.3 on page 74 for wages and salaries and corporate profits with those fund in Problem 4 above. How do they compare? Which had the larger gain and why?
   (*a*) Wages and Salaries   _____
   (*b*) Corporate Profits   _____

9. Statistics Canada gives *real* national income (GDP) for 2006 as $1,282.2 billion. Using the calculation for *nominal* GDP from question 4 above, and the statistical discrepancy adjustment from question 5 above, find the *GDP deflator* value for 2006.   _____

10. Canada's *real* and *nominal* national income (GDP) for 1996 are given by Statistics Canada (using 2002 constant prices to calculate real national income) as:

Nominal	$ 836.9
Real	$ 913.3

    (*a*) How much has nominal national income increased between 1996 and 2006?   _____
    (*b*) How much has real national income increased between 1996 and 2006?   _____

Problems for Chapter 5

Name: _____

1. According to the Labour Force Survey for September, 2007, there were 26.632 million
   Canadians eligible to be in the labour force, of which 1.054 million were unemployed and
   17.977 million were employed. Given these values, what percent of the labour force was:
   (a) Employed? _____
   (b) Unemployed? _____
   (c) What was the participation rate in September, 2007? _____

2. Between 1976 and 2005, by how much did:
   (a) Canada's population increase (see Figure 5.2) _____
   (b) Canada's labour force increase (see Figure 5.2) _____
   (c) Canada's unemployment rate change (see Figure 5.5) _____

3. If the Canadian labour force is increasing at 1.5 percent per year, how many new jobs have to be
   created each *month* to keep the unemployment rate steady? _____

4. **Web Query:** Look at the latest release of the Labour Force Survey from Statistics Canada
   (look in the "Latest indicators" box on the right side of the Statistics Canada Website at
   http://www.statcan.ca/start.html and click on "unemployment rate").
   (a) What was the unemployment rate in your province? _____
   (b) What was the participation rate in your province? _____
   (c) How does your answers to each of (a) and (b) above compare to the national rate? _____
   (d) What proportion of those employed in your province were employed part-time? _____

5. Between 1980 and 2005, by how much, and in which direction did the labour force participation
   rate (Figure 5.2) change for:
   (a) Men _____
   (b) Women _____

6. Assuming that Okun's Law is correct—that each 1 percent rise in unemployment reduces
   real GDP by 2 percent—how much real output (GDP) was lost in 2002 when Canada's
   unemployment rate rose from 7.2 percent to 7.7 percent? _____

7. Suppose the following data describes the Ontario economy in 2006 and 2007:

	2006	2007
Population	10.27 million	10.40 million
Labour force	6.95 million	7.06 million
Unemployment rate	6.6 percent	6.2 percent

   (a) What is the number of unemployed persons in each year? _____
   (b) How many people are employed in each year? _____
   (c) If the participation rate in Ontario in each year is 67.9 percent, how many people in Ontario
       are eligible to be in the labour force? _____

8. Based on the data given in question 7 above, what would the data look like for 2007 if 50,000
   unemployed become "discouraged workers"?
   (a) What would be the new number of unemployed workers? _____
   (b) What would be the new number of employed workers? _____
   (c) What would be the new rate of unemployment in Ontario? _____

9. Osberg and Lin (2000) estimated that structural unemployment in Canada represented approximately 0.75 percent. If this estimate is still true today, and the labour force in Canada in September 2007 is 17.977 million persons:
   (*a*) What is the estimated number of those categorized as structurally unemployed in Canada?   _____
   (*b*) What government policies might reduce this number?   _____

10. Suppose that the headline in the morning newspaper read: *number of unemployed rises as the unemployment rate falls to 6 percent*. How would you explain this seemingly contradictory headline? How would you explain a situation where the number of unemployed fell yet the unemployment rate rises? _____

   _____

Problems for Chapter 6

Name: _____

1. If tuition keeps increasing at the same rate as given in the April 2006 *Education Matters*—about 6 percent per year—what will the cost of tuition be in five years time at your school? _____

2. Suppose you'll have an annual nominal income of $40,000 for each of the next three years, and the inflation rate is 5 percent per year.
   (a) Find the real value of your $40,000 salary for each of the next three years.

   Year 1: _____
   Year 2: _____
   Year 3: _____

   (b) Suppose that you get a 3 percent raise in each of the next three years, how does this change the "real" value of your salary (your real income) for each year?

   Year 1: _____
   Year 2: _____
   Year 3: _____

3. The consumer price index, CPI, for the city of Whitehorse in the Yukon Territory is given by Statistics Canada as follows for the years 2002–2006:

2002	100.00
2003	101.90
2004	103.00
2005	105.30
2006	106.80

   (a) Which of these years is the "base year"? _____
   (b) What was the rate of inflation experienced in Whitehorse for 2003 through 2006? _____

4. We suggested in the chapter that the CPI tends to overstate the real rate of inflation experienced by each of us:
   (a) Briefly state and explain the four "biases" that effect inflation measurement. _____

   _____

   (b) How do each of these "biases" affect your personal inflation experience? _____

   _____

5. Assuming that the following table describes a typical consumer's complete budget, compute the item weights for each product.

Item	Quantity	Unit Price	Item Weight:
Coffee	20 kilos	$ 3	_____
Tuition	1 year	4,000	_____
Pizza	100 pizzas	8	_____
VCR rental	75 days	15	_____
Vacation	2 weeks	300	_____
		Total:	_____

6. Suppose the prices listed in the table for Problem 5 changed from one year to the next, as shown below. Use the rest of the table to compute the average inflation rate.

   | | Unit Price | | Percent | × | Item | = | Inflation |
Item	Last Year	This Year	Change in Price		Weight		Impact
Coffee	$ 3	$ 4	_____		_____		_____
Tuition	4,000	7,000	_____		_____		_____
Pizza	8	10	_____		_____		_____
VCR rental	15	10	_____		_____		_____
Vacation	300	500	_____		_____		_____
					Average inflation:		_____

7. Use the major component weights for the CPI in Figure 6.2 to determine the percentage change in the CPI that would result from a: (see Table 6.3 for help with this question)
   (*a*) 10 percent increase in "recreation, education, and reading" prices   _____
   (*b*) 6 percent decrease in "shelter"   _____
   (*c*) 20 percent increase in "transportation"   _____
   (*d*) doubling of "health and personal care"   _____

8. The chapter noted that inflationary pressure can arise from both the supply and demand sides of the economy. For each of the following headlines, which "side" of the economy would exert inflationary pressure:
   (*a*) *Vancouver's city workers settle for a 17.5 percent wage increase over 5 years*   _____
   (*b*) *Copper prices hit a new "all-time" high*   _____
   (*c*) *Canadian consumers continue on a "buying binge"*   _____
   (*d*) *Minimum wages should rise to $10 in British Columbia*   _____

9. Since 1991, the goal of the Bank of Canada as given by the federal government has been "price stability." But price stability has been defined as an inflation rate of 2 percent per year on average within a range of 1 to 3 percent:
   (*a*) At an annual rate of 2 percent inflation, what would the price of a $100 MP3 player be in 10 years?   _____
   (*b*) What would the price of the MP3 player be if inflation is 3 percent per year? 1 percent per year?   _____
   (*c*) Are any of the prices in (*a*) or (*b*) above stable?   _____

10. The following table provides the inflation indexes from the CPI, the consumer price index, and the GDP deflator for the period 2000–2006 (2002 = 100.00)

Year	CPI	GDP Deflator
2000	95.40	97.80
2001	97.80	98.10
2002	100.00	100.00
2003	102.80	103.30
2004	104.70	106.60
2005	107.00	110.20
2006	109.10	112.80

   (*a*) Using the values in the table above, draw a graph illustrating each inflation index, the CPI and the GDP deflator. _____

   (*b*) What can you say about the measures of inflation? Are they the same or is one increasing faster than the other is? _____

   (*c*) Why is one different from the other? (Hint: the GDP deflator includes all prices in the economy whereas the CPI only includes consumer prices.) _____

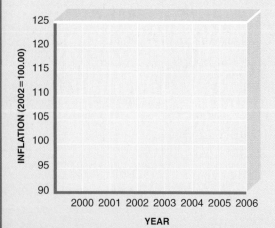

Problems for Chapter 7

Name: _____

1. Using a production possibility curve (PPC) graph to illustrate, show and explain points that would result from the following statements and the effect, if any, on the PPC itself
   (a) *Unemployment is rising*   _____
   (b) *Net investment in the economy is higher*   _____
   (c) *Capacity utilization for capital is down*   _____
   (d) *Productivity has increased*   _____

2. According to the rule of 72 (Table 7.1), how many years will it take for GDP to double if the economy is growing at:
   (a) 3 percent a year?   _____
   (b) 4.5 percent a year?   _____

3. According to the Rule of 72 (Table 7.1), how long will it be before GDP doubles in
   (a) The United States?   _____
   (b) China?   _____
   (c) South Africa?   _____
   (*Note:* See the World View on page 132.)

4. If real GDP is growing at 3 percent a year, how long will it take for
   (a) Real GDP to double?   _____
   (b) Real GDP per capita to double if the population is increasing each year by
                                         (*i*) 0 percent?   _____
                                         (*ii*) 1 percent?   _____
                                         (*iii*) 2 percent?   _____

5. Suppose that each additional 5 percentage points in the rate of investment (investment, *I*, divided by gross domestic product, GDP) will boost economic growth by 1 percentage point. Assume that all investment must be financed with domestic consumer saving. The Canadian economy is now fully employed at (that is, all resources and technology are being used to their normal capacity utilization):

GDP	$1,446.3 billion
Consumption	803.5 billion
Investment	321.1 billion

   If the goal is to raise the economic growth rate by 1.5 percent:
   (a) By how much must investment increase?   _____
   (b) If Canadian consumers are unwilling to save more, where might the extra investment expenditure come from?   _____

6. In 2005, which sector contributed the most to saving? (See Figure 7.8). How might this saving behaviour be related to *optimistic expectations* about the future from both the household and corporate sectors?   _____

7. In the Solow and Swan *neo-classical growth model*, the "law of diminishing returns" matters. Why? And what would be the outcome of all resources growing at the same rate as the population on per-capita economic growth? _____

8. In 2005, the participation rate was 67.2 percent of those eligible to be part of the Canadian labour force (28.5 million people). If the participation rate increased to 70 percent:
   (*a*) How many additional people could be working?   _____
   (*b*) If average real GDP per worker is $75,000, how much greater would real GDP have been?   _____

9. If average real GDP per worker is now $75,000 per year, how much will the average worker produce in five years time if productivity improves by
   (*a*) 1 percent per year?   _____
   (*b*) 2 percent per year?   _____

10. Go to the Statistics Canada page for Real Gross Domestic Product, Expenditure Based at http://www40.statcan.ca/l01/cst01/econ05.htm, or search for "Real gross domestic product, expenditure-based" from the Statistics Canada homepage at http://www.statcan.ca/start.html. For the five years shown, answer the following questions:
   (*a*) What is the range of the annual investment rate ("business gross fixed
         capital formation" divided by "real GDP at market prices")   Highest   _____
                                                                                   Lowest   _____

   (*b*) What is the range of annual real growth rates (*Note that you can only*
         calculate the final four years)   Highest   _____
                                                                                   Lowest   _____

1. Figure 8.4 presents a full aggregate supply and aggregate demand graph in a stable macroeconomic equilibrium at price level, P_E.
   (a) What is the difference in real output at the price level, P_1?   _____
   (b) What would happen to the price level, in the short-run, if the aggregate demand curve shifted to the right?   _____

2. Suppose you have $500 in savings when the price level index is at 100.
   (a) If inflation pushes the price level up by 20 percent, what will be the real value of your savings?   _____
   (b) What happens to the real value of your savings if the price level *declines* by 10 percent?   _____

3. Use the following information to draw aggregate demand and aggregate supply curves on the graph below. Both curves are assumed to be straight lines. (Long-run aggregate supply = $500)

Average Price	Real Output Demanded (per year)	Real Output Supplied in the short-run (per year)
$1,000	0	$1,000
100	$900	100

   (a) At what price level does equilibrium occur?   _____
   (b) What curve would have shifted if a new equilibrium were to occur at an output level of 700 and a price level of 700?   _____
   (c) What curve would have shifted if a new equilibrium were to occur at an output level of 700 and a price level of 500?   _____
   (d) What curve would have shifted if a new equilibrium were to occur at an output level of 700 and a price level of 300?   _____
   (e) Compared to the initial equilibrium (a), how have price levels or output changed in
      (b) Output: _____   Price level: _____
      (c) Output: _____   Price level: _____
      (d) Output: _____   Price level: _____

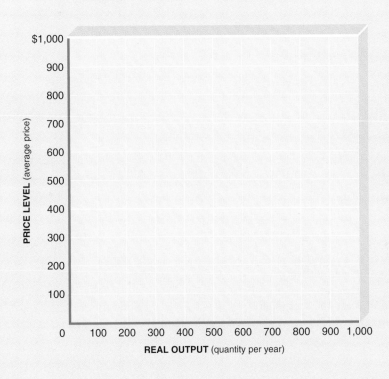

4. Describe the economy's long-run aggregate supply curve (LRAS) in the context of the production possibility curve, PPC, and with the concept of *normal capacity utilization* of resources. _____

5. Using the following data, determine:

National income (GDP)	$1,446.3 billion
Marginal propensity to consume, b	0.90
Proportional rate of taxes	0.40
Autonomous expenditure	$ 50.0 billion

   (a) Disposable income, Y_d _____

   (b) Consumption expenditure, C _____

   (c) Saving, S _____

6. If the disposable income of Canadians rises from $870.0 billion to $900.0 billion and savings rises by $5 billion, what are Canadian's:

   (a) Marginal propensity to consume, MPC   _____

   (b) Marginal propensity to save, s _____

7. Describe why rising real-estate values might increase consumption and reduce saving in the economy. _____

8. Given the data in question 5 above, as well as the following data, determine:

Exports	$524.7
Marginal propensity to import, MPIm	0.34

   (a) Level of Canadian imports MPI   _____

   (b) Level of Canadian net exports, NX   _____

   (c) Whether the trade balance is in surplus or deficit   _____

9. Suppose that the following data describes the economy of Saskatchewan:

Marginal propensity to consume, MPC	0.80
Marginal propensity to import, MPIm	0.30
Proportionate rate of taxes, t	0.35
Autonomous consumption, a	$ 4.5 billion
Government expenditure, G	$ 9.5 billion
Investment expenditure, I	$ 9.0 billion
Exports, X	$12.0 billion

   Using the data, find

   (a) The value of the multiplier, k _____

   (b) The value of total autonomous expenditure   _____

   (c) The equilibrium value of national income, Y _____

10. Suppose that a multiplier is given by the following data

Marginal propensity to consume, MPC	0.85
Marginal propensity to import, MPIm	0.40
Proportional rate of taxes, t	0.45

   Using this information, determine (showing proof of your answer)

   (a) The value of the multiplier, k _____

   (b) What changes to the rate of taxes, t, would increase the multiplier?   _____

   (c) What changes to the marginal propensity to import, MPIm, would decrease the multiplier?   _____

Problems for Chapter 9

Name: _____

1. Illustrate these events with SRAS or AD shifts and explain the impact on the economy in terms of changes in the price level and real output in the short run.

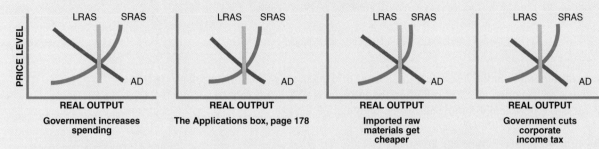

| Government increases spending | The Applications box, page 178 | Imported raw materials get cheaper | Government cuts corporate income tax |

2. Assume that the accompanying graph depicts aggregate supply and demand conditions in an economy. Full employment occurs when $60 billion of real output is produced.

   (*a*) What is the current equilibrium rate of output? _____

   (*b*) How far short of full employment is the equilibrium rate of output? _____

   (*c*) Illustrate a shift of aggregate demand that would change the equilibrium rate of output to $60 billion. Label the new curve AD$_2$.

   (*d*) What is the price level at the new equilibrium? _____

   (*e*) Illustrate a shift of short-run aggregate supply, SRAS, that would, when combined with AD$_1$, move equilibrium output to $60 billion.

   (*f*) What is the price level at this new equilibrium? _____

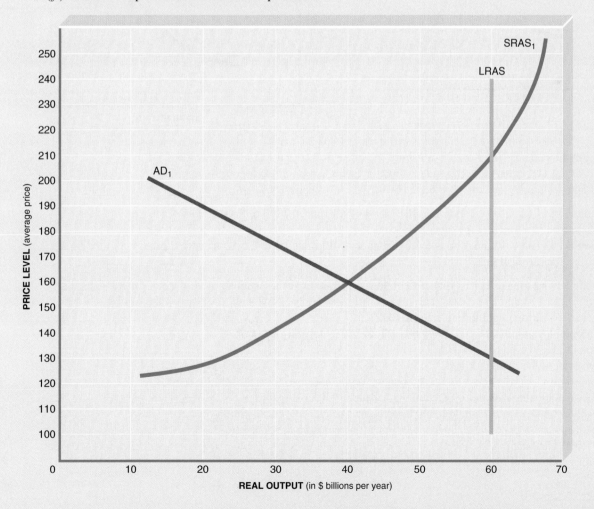

3. If the consumption function is $C = \$20 + 0.9Y_d$,
   (a) What does the saving function look like?   _____
   (b) What is the rate of desired saving when disposable income equals

                                                                (i) $500?   _____
                                                               (ii) $1,000? _____
                                                              (iii) $1,500? _____

4. Illustrate in the graph on the left below the impact of a sudden decline in consumer confidence
   that reduces consumption by $150 billion at the price level P_F.
   (a) What is the new equilibrium level of real output?   _____
   (b) How large is the real GDP gap?   _____
   (c) What has happened to average prices?   _____

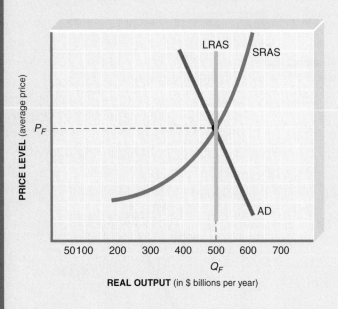

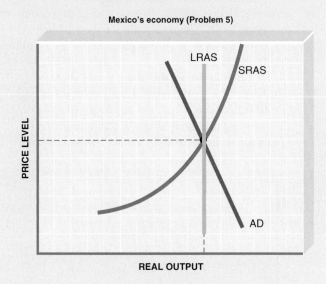

Mexico's economy (Problem 5)

5. Use the graph on the right, above, to illustrate the effect in Mexico of the case where
   "troubles in the U.S. housing sector take a turn for the worse [and, U.S.] consumers are
   spooked and scale back spending." (See the World View on page 185)

6. If the reduction of Mexico's exports into the U.S. market was $10 billion, and the Mexican
   multiplier included a marginal propensity to consume, MPC, equal to 0.70, a proportional rate
   of taxes of 0.25, and a marginal propensity to import, MPIm, equal to 0.30, what would the total
   reduction be for Mexican GDP?   _____

7. The accompanying graph depicts a macro equilibrium. Answer the questions based on the
   information in the graph.
   (a) What is the current equilibrium rate of GDP?   _____
   (b) If full-employment real GDP is $1,000 billion, what problem does this
       economy have?   _____
   (c) How large is the real GDP gap?   _____
   (d) If the multiplier were equal to 1.5, how much additional investment would be needed to
       increase aggregate demand by the amount of the initial GDP gap?   _____
   (e) Illustrate the changes in autonomous investment and induced consumption that occur in d.
   (f) What happens to prices when aggregate demand increases by the amount of
       the initial GDP gap?   _____
   (g) Is full employment restored by the AD shift?   _____

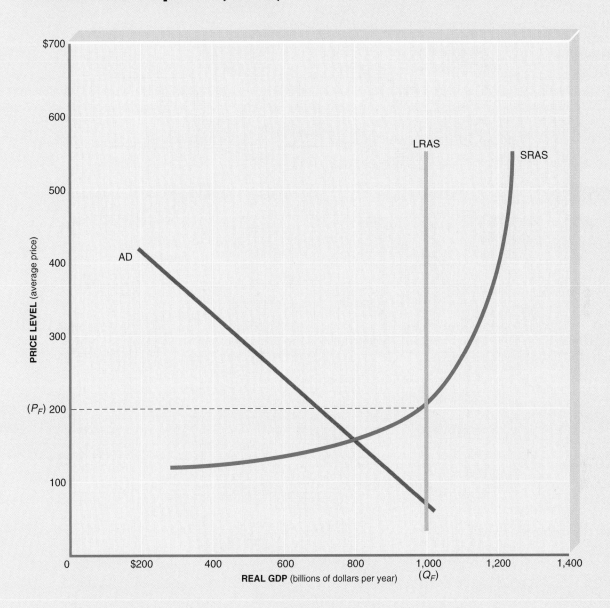

8. Complete the following table:

Price Level	Real Output Demanded (in $ billions) by:								Aggregate Demand	Aggregate Supply
	Consumers	+	Investors	+	Government	+	Net Exports	=		
120	80		15		20		10		___	170
110	92		16		20		12		___	160
100	104		17		20		14		___	150
90	116		18		20		16		___	140
80	128		19		20		18		___	120
70	140		20		20		20		___	95
60	154		21		20		22		___	65

(a) What is the level of equilibrium GDP?   _____

(b) What is the equilibrium price level?   _____

    (c) If full employment occurs at real GDP = $165 billion, what kind of
        GDP gap exists?   _____
    (d) How large is that gap?   _____
    (e) Which macro problem exists here?   _____

9. On the graph below, draw the AD and SRAS and LRAS (given in (d)) curves with these data:

Price level	140	130	120	110	100	90	80	70	60	50
Real output										
Demanded	600	700	800	900	1,000	1,100	1,200	1,300	1,400	1,500
Supplied	1,200	1,150	1,100	1,050	1,000	950	900	800	600	400

    (a) What is the equilibrium
        (i) Real output level?   _____
        (ii) Price level?   _____

Suppose net exports decline by $150 at all price levels, but all other components of aggregate
demand remain constant.
    (b) Draw the new AD curve.
    (c) What is the new equilibrium
        (i) Output level?   _____
        (ii) Price level?   _____
    (d) If full employment GDP (potential GDP, Y^*) is $1,000, what macro problem has
        arisen in this economy? _____

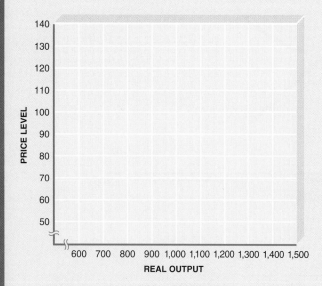

10. Suppose that an economy is currently operating at a short-run equilibrium of $1,200 billion
    whereas the full-employment level of output (potential GDP) is $1,100 billion.
    (a) What gap is this economy experiencing?   _____
    (b) How could this gap be closed through demand-side theory?   _____
    (c) How could this gap be closed through supply-side theory?   _____
    (d) How could real business cycle theory explain this gap?   _____

Problems for Chapter 10

Name: _____

1. Go to the Statistics Canada homepage at http://www.statcan.ca/start.html and enter "Provincial and territorial general government revenue and expenditures" into the search field. Select the table. Find the province or territory that you are living in (listed on the left) and then:
   (a) What are the largest three sources of revenue and total government revenue?   _____
   (b) What are the largest three areas of expenditure and total government expenditure?   _____
   (c) What is the amount of "general" and "specific" transfers from the federal government?   _____
   (d) What was the expenditure for debt charges?   _____
   (e) What is the government's budget balance, BB?   _____

2. Suppose that the marginal propensity to consume, MPC is 0.80 and the marginal propensity to import, MPIm, is 0.40 and the proportional rate of taxes is 0.35.

   If the government wants to stimulate the economy, by how much will aggregate demand at current prices shift initially (before multiplier effects) with
   (a) A $5 billion increase in domestic government purchases?   _____
   (b) A $5 billion tax cut? (increase in disposable income, Y_d)   _____
   (c) A $5 billion increase in income transfers?   _____

   What will the cumulative AD shift be for
   (d) The increased G?   _____
   (e) The tax cut?   _____
   (f) The increased transfers?   _____

3. Suppose the government decides to increase taxes by $20 billion to increase health care spending by the same amount. How will this combined tax-transfer policy affect aggregate demand at current prices?   _____

4. On the accompanying graph, identify and label
   (a) Current macro equilibrium.
   (b) The real GDP gap.
   (c) The AD excess or shortfall.
   (d) The new equilibrium that would occur with appropriate fiscal policy.

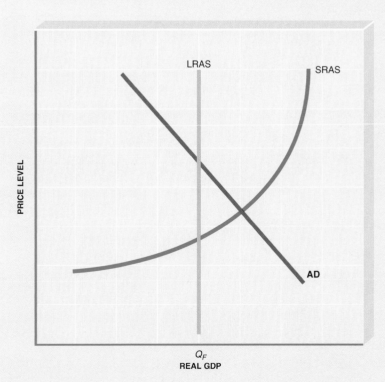

5. According to the World View on page 208,
   (a) By how much did South Korea's government *increase* public-works spending?   _____
   (b) By how much might this fiscal stimulus have increased aggregate demand if the multiplier is 1.15?   _____

6. According to the Applications box on page 209, the cuts to personal incomes taxes by Premier Gordon Campbell in British Columbia will "leave $1.35 billion in the pockets of British Columbians in 2002 and another $1.5 billion in 2003."
   (a) If British Columbia's marginal propensity to consume, MPC, is 0.95, their marginal propensity to import, MPIm, is 0.45, and the new federal/provincial proportional tax rate is 0.33, what will the additional economic activity be as the result of the tax cuts in 2002 and 2003?   _____
   (b) The Applications box on page 211 analyzing the results of tax cuts in Ontario since 1995 suggests that "there is no evidence to support the Government's claim that Ontario's economic performance is attributable to tax cuts." Why might tax cuts not increase economic performance?   _____

7. Suppose that the government chose to increase income transfers rather than government expenditure to stimulate the economy illustrated in Figure 10.4. Would the amount of the income transfers required to shift the AD to the desired location be larger, smaller, or the same as the amount of direct government expenditure? Why?   _____

8. If the federal government's policy was to close any "inflationary" or "recessionary" gaps through fiscal policy, what would the required change in expenditure where:
   (a) The inflationary or recessionary gap is $10 billion and the multiplier is 1.25?   _____
   (b) The inflationary or recessionary gap is $10 billion and the multiplier is 0.95?   _____

9. Governments at all levels are beginning to look at policies that are targeted at reducing greenhouse gas emissions and reducing human impact on climate change. How would the following approaches impact other aspects of the macroeconomy?
   (a) New government spending financed by borrowing?   _____
   (b) New government spending financed by higher taxes?   _____
   (c) New regulations aimed at emitters?   _____

10. Use the following data to complete the graph and to answer the following questions:

Price level	10	20	30	40	50	60	70	80	90	100
Real GDP supplied	$500	600	680	750	820	880	910	940	960	970
Real GDP demanded	$960	920	880	840	800	760	720	680	640	600

(a) If full employment (LRAS) occurs at a real output rate of $880, how large is the real GDP gap? _____

(b) How large is the AD shortfall? _____

(c) What will happen to prices if AD increases enough to restore full employment? _____

(d) Assuming MPC = 0.75, MPIm = 0.35, and t = 0.40, how will macro equilibrium change
if the government purchases increase by $20? Illustrate your answer on the graph. _____

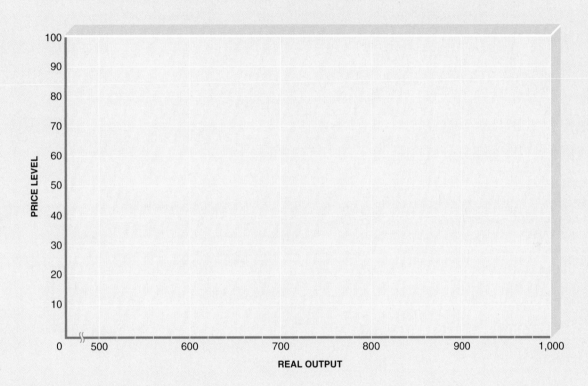

Problems for Chapter 11

Name: _____

1. From 2002 to 2006 how did each of the following change?
   (*a*) Government revenue   _____
   (*b*) Government spending   _____
   (*c*) Budget deficit   _____
   (*Note:* See Table 11.3)

2. Go to the Statistics Canada homepage at http://www.statcan.ca/start.html and enter "Provincial and territorial general government revenue and expenditures" into the search field. Select the table. Find the province or territory that you are living in (listed on the left) and then:
   (*a*) Show the budget balance, BB, calculation as given on page 219 (*Note: for simplicity, we will take "General Transfers" under Expenditures as the only transfers of the Provincial/ Territorial government although these are only transfers to local governments. Other income transfers, such as social assistance are part of Social Services and not shown separately.*)   _____
   (*b*) Is the provincial/territorial government currently in balance, in deficit, or in surplus?   _____

3. The World View on page 222 provides the government budget balance—as a percent of GDP—for 2005. Which country has the largest percentage deficit? Which country has the largest percentage surplus?   _____

4. Go to the International Monetary Fund, IMF, World Economic Outlook reports page at (http://www.imf.org/external/ns/cs.aspx?id=29) and look for the most recent document under the "Data and Statistics" tab at the top of the page, and then the "World Economic Outlook Database" under the "Global Data" heading. Using the countries noted in the World View in question 3 above—how have the government budget balances as a percent of GDP changed? What can you infer about the "fiscal policy" direction of governments in general?   _____

5. Go to the International Monetary Fund, IMF, World Economic Outlook reports page at (http://www.imf.org/external/ns/cs.aspx?id=29) and look for the most recent document under the "Data and Statistics" tab at the top of the page, and then the "World Economic Outlook Database" under the "Global Data" heading. Look under "by countries" and then "advanced economies" then choose "general government net debt (as a percent of GDP). Compare Canada to the other countries for which there are data. How would you describe Canada's debt "problem" in relation to these other countries?   _____

6. Suppose the following data describes an economy:

National income, GDP	$350 billion
Proportional rate of tax, *t*	0.25
Government Expenditure, *G*	$ 54.0 billion
Government Transfers, *tr*	$ 25.0 billion
Current government debt, *d*	$175.0 billion
Current average interest rate, *i*	4.25 percent (0.0425)

   (*a*) What is this government's budget balance, BB?   _____
   (*b*) Is the government in a balanced, deficit, or surplus fiscal position?   _____
   (*c*) What is the government's current debt-to-GDP ratio?   _____
   (*d*) What will the following year's government debt be?   _____
   (*e*) How would the BB change if the interest rate rises to 5.5 percent? _____
   (*f*) If the economy enjoys economic growth of 3 percent next year while nothing else changes, what happens to the debt to GDP ratio?   _____

7. The press release from the Centre for Policy Alternatives included as a Web note on page 235 (http://www.policyalternatives.ca/News/2005/11/PressRelease1228/) states that "Myatt and Ruggeri argue that [the benefits of a lower debt ratio] cannot be used to justify using budget surpluses to pay down the debt because balanced budgets alone are sufficient to shrink the debt-to-GDP ratio—even without debt repayment. Debt repayment simply speeds up the automatic rate of decline in this ratio by a few years."
   (a) Explain how even a balanced budget can result in a reduction of the debt-to-GDP ratio   _____
   (b) Illustrate how debt repayment simply "speeds up" the decline.   _____

8. After the payment toward the public debt made in September 2006 (see the Applications on page 227), the debt amounted to $481.5 billion. If no additional payments are made (or deficits run) what would happen to Canada's debt-to-GDP ratio over the next five years if, beginning with GDP at $1,446.3 billion:
   (a) The economy grows at 1 percent per year?   _____
   (b) The economy grows at 3 percent per year?   _____
   (c) The economy grows at 5 percent per year?   _____

9. Suppose a government has no debt and a balanced budget. Suddenly it decides to spend $10 billion while raising only $8 billion worth of taxes.
   (a) What will be the government's deficit?   _____
   (b) If the government finances the deficit by issuing bonds, what amount of bonds will it issue?   _____
   (c) At a 10 percent rate of interest, how much interest will the government pay each year?   _____
   (d) Add the interest payment to the government's $10 billion expenditures for the next year, and assume that taxes remain at $8 billion. In the second year, compute the
      (i) Deficit.   _____
      (ii) Amount of new debt (bonds) issued.   _____
      (iii) Debt-service requirement.   _____
   (e) Repeat these calculations for the third, fourth, and fifth years, assuming that the government taxes at a rate of $8 billion each year and has noninterest expenditures of $10 billion annually.

	Year 3	Year 4	Year 5
Deficit	_____	_____	_____
New debt	_____	_____	_____
Debt service	_____	_____	_____

   (f) What will happen to the ratio of government debt to government expenditure with each passing year?

Year 2	Year 3	Year 4	Year 5
_____	_____	_____	_____

10. In Figure 11.9, what is the opportunity cost of increasing government spending from g_1 to g_2 if
   (a) No external financing is available?   _____
   (b) Complete external financing is available?   _____

1. In the World View on page 241, the concluding paragraph notes two of "the more bizarre substitutes for wages, such as bras and coffins."
   (a) Explain how bras or coffins could satisfy the three conditions given for something to be thought of as money (see page 242).   _____
   (b) Explain how bras or coffins as *barter goods* can make exchange in the economy difficult.   _____

2. The Applications box on page 245 notes the rarity of bank failures in the Canadian financial system and the importance of maintaining confidence in the system:
   (a) What would be the impact on the economy's total purchasing power if households withdrew their money from the bank and buried it in their backyard instead for safekeeping?   _____
   (b) What would be the impact on the "price of money" (the rate of interest) because of part (a) above?   _____

3. Suppose that your birthday card from your grandparents this year included a $50 bill.
   (a) If your grandparents live in Canada, what is the change in the Canadian money supply because of your birthday? Why?   _____
   (b) If your grandparents live outside of Canada, would your answer to part (a) be different? Why?   _____
   (c) Using Table 12.2 on page 249 as a model, show the impact of each step on deposits in the bank, excess reserves, change in bank loans, and the change in purchasing power if you: _____
       (i) deposit the $50 into your chequing account   _____
       (ii) the bank uses a 10 percent desired reserve ratio and keeps no excess reserves (and there is no cash drain)   _____
       (iii) the bank lends the maximum possible to "Qwickie Mart"   _____
       (iv) Qwickie Mart uses the money to buy donuts from "Duff's Donuts"   _____
       (v) Duff's deposits the payment into their chequing account   _____
       (vi) the bank lends the maximum possible to Lisa   _____
       (vii) Lisa buys saxophone lessons from "Ralph's Musik"   _____
       (viii) Ralph deposits the money into his chequing account   _____
       (ix) the bank lends the maximum possible to Bart   _____

4. Suppose the current exchange value of the Canadian dollar leads Canadian households to purchase $5 million ($US) with cheques totalling $4.76 million drawn on their Canadian bank account and then deposits the U.S. dollars into a U.S. dollar bank account.
   (a) Which measures of the Canadian money supply change? (For example, M1, M2, M2+, etc.)   _____
   (b) How would your answer in part (a) change if $2 million of the payment came from Credit Unions and Caisse Populaires?   _____

5. If the target reserve of banks is 7.5 percent (0.075), what would the money multiplier be:
   (a) When there are no excess reserves or cash drain?   _____
   (b) When banks hold no excess reserves but the cash drain is 15 percent (0.15)?   _____
   (c) When banks hold excess reserves of 5 percent (0.05) and the cash drain is 15 percent (0.15)? _____

6. Figure 12.4 on page 257 gives a loanable funds market where the equilibrium interest rate (the price of money, remember) is 7 percent. Illustrate the situation and explain the change(s) if any where:

   (*a*) The money demand (M^D) decreases (shifts to the left)   _____

   (*b*) The money demand (M^D) increases (shifts to the right)   _____

7. What two possibilities are there that would result in the equilibrium rate of interest in Figure 12.4 on page 257 to be 9 percent? Briefly, explain how each of these possibilities might come about?   _____

8. If the Canadian economy's GDP (national income, Y) is $1,400.0 billion, the transactions demand for money, e, is 0.25, the precautionary demand for money, f, is 0.05, and the speculative demand for money, g, is 100, what level of the money supply, M^S, would be consistent with a loanable funds market equilibrium interest rate of 7 percent? (Look at the footnote at the bottom of page 258 for help.)   _____

9. Given the information in question 8 above, what would happen to the loanable funds market equilibrium interest rate if the money supply, M^S, increased by $3 billion?   _____

10. In 1993–1994, Yugoslavia experienced "the worst episode of hyperinflation in history" (see http://www.sjsu.edu/faculty/watkins/hyper.htm#YUGO). The annual inflation rate was calculated at 5 quadrillion percent—that's a 5 with 15 zeros after it! Explain how inflation (and more spectacularly hyperinflation) diminishes the *store of value* purpose of money.   _____

Problems for Chapter 13

Name: _____

1. Of the two monetary policy tools available to the Bank of Canada, open-market operations are the principal mechanism for directly altering the reserves of the banking system. Explain carefully how open-market operations would be used to:
   (a) Increase the Canadian money supply, M^S _____
   (b) Decrease the Canadian money supply, M^S _____

2. If Canadian households send $10 billion to the federal government as tax payments, and the federal government leaves these funds with the Bank of Canada, what would the Bank of Canada do to *sterilize* the impact on the Canadian Money Supply, M^S? _____

3. Assume that a $1,000 bond issued in 2005 pays $100 in interest each year. What is the current yield on the bond if it can be purchased for
   (a) $1,200?   _____
   (b) $1,000?   _____
   (c) $800?   _____
   (d) $600?   _____

4. Bonds often sell at either a *premium* or a *discount* as a way of adjusting the current *yield* paid on the bond to the current market expectations. Which of the following bonds are selling at a premium, a discount, or at par? (Note: all these bonds are quoted as $100 face value and have been taken from the *National Post* bond listings from November 2, 2007)
   (a) WelFarg 4.38 percent bond selling for $93.98   _____
   (b) Bell 6.55 percent bond selling for $88.42   _____
   (c) Domtar 10.00 percent bond selling for $108.45   _____
   (d) TDBank 5.75 percent bond selling for $100.00   _____
   (e) GrTAA 6.45 percent bond selling for $110.47   _____

5. Each of the bonds listed in question 4 above pay an annual rate of interest based on the coupon rate given (for instance 6.55 percent for the Bell bond) and the face value of the bond (in each case here $100.00). From this information:
   (a) Calculate the adjusted yield for each of the bonds given in Problem 4 above (refer to page 266 if you are not sure what you are doing here)
   (b) What can the comparison between the coupon rate and the current yield tell you about whether the bond sells at a premium, a discount, or at par?   _____

6. If the real money multiplier in the economy happens to be 3.7, what would the value of open-market operations be:
   (a) To decrease the total money supply, M^S, by $10 billion?   _____
   (b) To increase the total money supply, M^S, by $8 billion?   _____
   (c) What would be the effect of parts (a) and (b) on the *target overnight interest rate* and on the commercial bank's *prime rate*?   _____

7. Suppose the following information describes the economy of Quebec:

Price level, P	$100.0
Quantity of goods and services, Q	2.85 billion
Money supply, M	$ 14.25 billion
Velocity of money, V	20.0

   (a) If the money supply increased to $15 billion and velocity and the price level remain constant, what will happen to real output, Q?   _____
   (b) If money is indeed neutral, and real output is fixed at the LRAS level, what would happen to the price level as the money supply increased?   _____
   (c) How much would velocity have to fall for the price level in part (b) to remain constant at $100.0?   _____

Problems for Chapter 13 (cont'd)

Name: _____

8. If the current commercial bank *prime rate* of interest is 6.25 percent and the measure of inflation in Canada is 2.50 percent:

    (*a*) What is the estimated *real interest rate* in Canada? _____

    (*b*) If the *real interest rate* remains at the level determined in part (*a*), and the *prime rate* rises to 7.0 percent, what is the expected rate of inflation? _____

9. The following data describe market conditions:

Money supply (in billions)	$100	$200	$300	$400	$ 500	$ 600	$ 700
Interest rate	8.0	7.5	7.0	6.5	6.0	5.5	5.5
Rate of investment (in billions)	$ 12	$ 12	$ 15	$ 16	$16.5	$16.5	$16.5

    (*a*) At what rate of interest does the liquidity trap emerge? _____

    (*b*) At what rate of interest does investment demand become totally inelastic? _____

10. Use the accompanying graphs to show what happens in the economy when M^S increases from $30 billion to $40 billion.

    (*a*) By how much does *PQ* change if *V* is constant? _____

    (*b*) If aggregate supply were fixed (vertical) at the initial output level, what would happen to the price level? _____

    (*c*) What is the value of *V*? _____

    (*d*) Using the graphs provided, carefully explain the operation of the monetary transmission mechanism (assuming a closed economy setting). _____

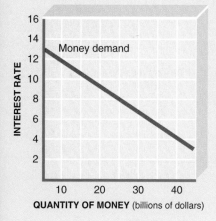

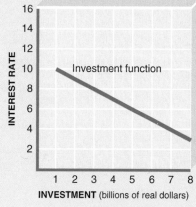

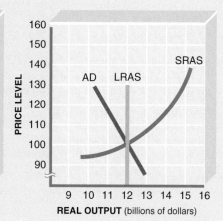

Problems for Chapter 14

Name: _____

1. The World View on page 296 describes the devastation in Iran from a 2003 earthquake. Use an AD/AS graph to illustrate the effect of the earthquake and explain the impact on national income, potential national income, and the price level in the local economy.   _____

2. How does the Canadian Misery Index compare to your provincial or territorial index over the past 10 years? (The data is available free from Statistics Canada at their website: http://www.statcan. ca/start. Look for CANSIM tables 282-0002 and 326-0002.)   _____

3. The Applications box on page 298 talks about the importance of innovation for the German economy, suggesting that "manufacturing is surging ahead there, driving strong economic growth through exports of goods to Asia, of all places." How does such innovation and increases in productivity effect the short-run aggregate supply, SRAS, and the long-run aggregate supply, LRAS, curves? (Draw an AD/AS graph to illustrate your explanation). What could be the effect on the price level of manufactured goods? Why?   _____

PRICE LEVEL

REAL OUTPUT

4. In the Applications box on page 300, the Conference Board of Canada (CBC) offers a number of possible policies that might stimulate Canadian innovation and productivity. What are the policy levers suggested by the Conference Board to improve Canada's future economic potential?   _____

5. The Applications box on page 306 presents findings from a recent report by the Centre for the Study of Living Standards (CSLS) stating that output per worker in Canada in 2006 was only 78.1 percent that of a U.S. worker.

   (a) Since Canada's GDP in 2006 was $1,446.3 billion—assuming that this represented Canada's potential national income, Y^*—what could Canada's potential national income be if worker productivity was equal to that of the United States?   _____

   (b) What would Canada's potential national income be if worker productivity in Canada were equivalent to Sweden's 86.4 percent of the U.S. or Ireland's 98.1 percent of the U.S.?   _____

6. Suppose taxpayers are required to pay a base tax of $50 plus 30 percent on any income over $100, as in the initial tax system B in Table 14.2. Suppose further that the taxing authority wishes to raise by $20 the taxes of people with incomes of $200.

   (a) If marginal tax rates are to remain unchanged, what will the new base tax have to be? $_____

   (b) If the base tax of $50 is to remain unchanged, what will the marginal tax rate have to be?   _____%

7. Suppose households supply 23 billion hours of labour per year and have a tax elasticity of supply of 0.20. If the tax rate is decreased by 5 percent, by how many hours will the supply of labour decline?   _____

8. On the following graph, plot the unemployment and inflation rates for the last 10 years the data is available. Is there any evidence of a Phillips curve trade-off? Explain your answer.   _____

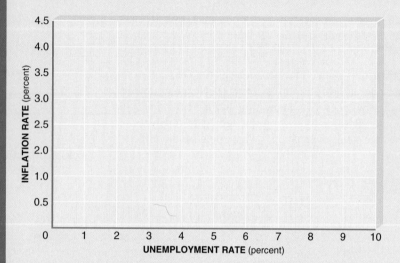

9. In Figure 14.4, expectations shift the Philips curve upward (or to the right) from PC_1 to PC_2 where the rate of unemployment at point d is the same as at point c (at the economy's "natural rate" or its "non-accelerating inflation rate of unemployment," NAIRU). How is the movement from point b to point d affected by *adaptive expectations* as compared to *rational expectations*?   _____

10. Suppose an economy is characterized by the AS/AD curves in the accompanying graph. A decision is then made to increase infrastructure spending by $20 billion a year.

 (a) Illustrate the direct impact of the increased spending on aggregate demand on the graph (ignore multiplier effects).

 (b) If the SRAS and LRAS are unaffected, what is the new short-run equilibrium rate of output? _____

 (c) What is the new short-run equilibrium price level? _____

 (d) Now assume that the infrastructure investments increase both the LRAS and SRAS by $30 billion a year (from the initial equilibrium). Illustrate this effect on the graph.

 (e) After both demand and supply adjustments occur, what is the final equilibrium
   (i) Rate of output? _____
   (ii) Price level? _____

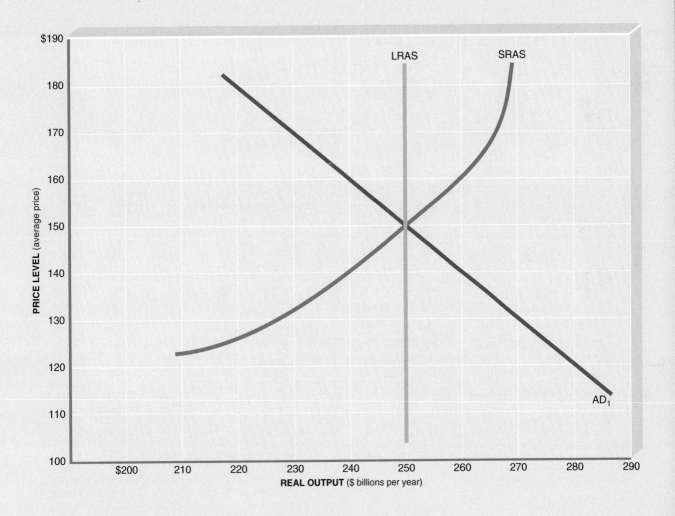

Problems for Chapter 15

Name: _____

1. Suppose Canada can produce a maximum of 200,000 hybrid sport coupes or 160,000 barrels of Okanagan wine. (If we assume a constant opportunity cost):
   (*a*) What is the opportunity cost of one barrel of wine? _____
   (*b*) If another country offers to trade six hybrid sport coupes for four barrels of Okanagan wine, should Canadians accept the offer? _____
   (*c*) What are the implied terms of trade in part (*b*) above? _____

2. What if you are able to cook a meal in 60 minutes or clean the house in 90 minutes while your roommate is able to cook a meal or clean the house in 45 minutes:
   (*a*) Who has the absolute advantage in cooking meals? In cleaning the house? _____
   (*b*) Who has the comparative advantage in cooking meals? In cleaning the house? _____

3. If it takes 64 farm workers to harvest one tonne of strawberries and 16 farm workers to harvest one tonne of wheat, what is the opportunity cost of five tonnes of strawberries?

4. Alpha and Beta, two tiny islands off the east coast of Tricoli, produce pearls and pineapples. The following production possibilities schedules describe their potential output in tonnes per year.

Alpha		Beta	
Pearls	Pineapples	Pearls	Pineapples
0	30	0	20
2	25	10	16
4	20	20	12
6	15	30	8
8	10	40	4
10	5	45	2
12	0	50	0

   (*a*) Graph the production possibilities confronting each island.
   (*b*) What is the opportunity cost of pineapples on each island (before trade)? Alpha: _____
   Beta: _____

   (*c*) Which island has a comparative advantage in pearl production? _____
   (*d*) Graph the consumption possibilities of each island with free trade.

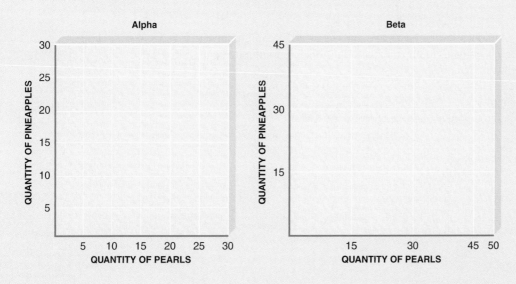

5. In 2004, Canadian cheese producers made about 830 million kilograms of cheese (according to numbers on the Dairy Processors Association home page at http://www.dpac-atlc.ca/english/). The Applications box on page 331 presents the federal government's decision to "restrict the import of a key ingredient used to make cheese." Don Jarvis, president of the Dairy Processors Association suggested that the "decision could have an impact on the availability and pricing of cheese."

   (a) If the restriction on imported milk-protein concentrates increases the price of cheese by $0.75 per kilogram and Canadian consumers bought 700 million kilograms of cheese, what is the cost of the restriction to Canadian consumers each year?   _____

   (b) If Canadian dairy farmers are "losing" $2 million per month because of the trade in milk-protein concentrates, what is the cost of the imports to dairy farmers each year?   _____

   (c) Could consumers pay the farmers their annual loss and still be better off?   _____

6. Suppose the two islands in Problem 4 agree that the terms of trade will be one for one and exchange 10 pearls for 10 pineapples.

   (a) If Alpha produced 6 pearls and 15 pineapples while Beta produced 30 pearls and 8 pineapples before they decided to trade, how much would each be producing after trade? Assume that the two countries specialize just enough to maintain their consumption of the item they export, and make sure each island follows its comparative advantage.   Alpha: _____   Beta: _____

   (b) How much would each island be consuming after specializing and trading?   Alpha: _____   Beta: _____

   (c) How much would the combined production of pineapples increase for the two islands due to trade? _____

   (d) How much would the combined production of pearls increase? _____

   (e) How could both countries produce and consume even more? _____

   (f) Assume the two islands are able to trade as much as they want with the rest of the world, with the terms of trade at one pineapple for one pearl. Draw the ultimate consumption possibilities curve for each island.

7. Suppose the following table reflects the domestic supply and demand for compact disks (CDs):

Price ($)	16	14	12	10	8	6	4	2
Quantity supplied	8	7	6	5	4	3	2	1
Quantity demanded	2	4	6	8	10	12	14	16

   (a) Graph these market conditions on the next page and identify the equilibrium price and sales.   Price/sales: _____

   (b) Now suppose that foreigners enter the market, offering to sell an unlimited supply of CDs for $6 apiece. Illustrate and identify

   (i) The market price   _____

   (ii) Domestic consumption   _____

   (iii) Domestic production   _____

(*c*) If a tariff of $2 per CD is imposed, what will happen to
  (*i*) The market price?   _____
  (*ii*) Domestic consumption?   _____
  (*iii*) Domestic production?   _____

Graph your answers.

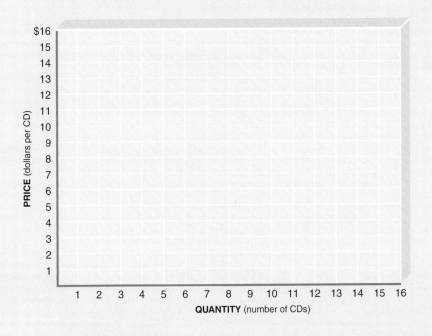

8. Go to the website: http://www.international.gc.ca/tna-nac/reg-en.asp, which provides information on the "regional and bilateral initiatives" of the Government of Canada:
   (*a*) Pick one of the links to Canada's "Free trade negotiations and discussions" and write a paragraph giving the Canadian perspective of the proposed agreement.

9. The Applications box on page 335 suggests that the latest round of WTO negotiations—the DOHA round—are in danger of collapse because of subsidies paid to farmers in "rich" countries. Using a supply and demand format graph to illustrate, explain the impact of rich country subsidies on the willingness and ability to supply agricultural goods and the impact on potential "poor" country exporters.

10. The Applications box on page 333 talks about establishing free trade within Canada as well as between Canada and other countries. Go to the Trade, Investment and Labour Mobility Agreement, TILMA website at http://www.tilma.ca/. Write a paragraph giving the purpose of TILMA and the potential impact in the Alberta and British Columbia economies. Are there opportunities for other provinces and territories to join in? Would this be a good thing? Why or why not?

Problems for Chapter 16

Name: _____

1. If a euro is worth $1.36, what is the euro price of a dollar? _____

2. On November 2, 2007, the Canadian dollar hit a new high of $1.0685 ($US) On November 2, 2006, the Canadian dollar was trading at $0.8801 ($US) On November 2, 2005, the Canadian dollar was trading at $0.8473 ($US).
   - (a) If a full-season ski pass for Mount Tremblant costs $1,269.00, what would the price in U.S. dollars be for each of 2005, 2006, and 2007? (Assume that the pass is the same price each year.) _____
   - (b) In Aspen, Colorado, a premier pass for unlimited skiing sells for $1,879.00 ($US). What would the Canadian dollar price be for each of 2005, 2006, and 2007? (Again, assume that the price has remained the same each year.) _____
   - (c) What has happened to the relative price of the two ski areas over the three years? _____

3. If a PlayStation 3 costs 20,000 yen in Japan, how much will it cost in Canadian dollars if the exchange rate is
   - (a) 122.6 yen = $1? _____
   - (b) 1 yen = $0.008156? _____
   - (c) 100 yen = $1? _____

4. The U.S. dollar price of a Canadian dollar is given by the Bank of Canada as:

November 1, 2002	$0.64
November 2, 2005	$0.85
November 2, 2007	$1.07

   - (a) By how much has the Canadian dollar appreciated between 2002 and 2005? _____
   - (b) By how much has the Canadian dollar appreciated between 2005 and 2007? _____

5. If inflation raises Canadian prices by 2 percent and the Canadian dollar appreciates against the U.S. dollar by 21 percent (as it did between November 2006 and November 2007), by how much does the U.S. price of Canadian exports change? _____

6. The World View on page 347 gives the foreign-exchange rates of the Canadian dollar for a few selected countries. Go to the Bank of Canada's currency converter at http://www.bankofcanada.ca/en/rates/converter.html and find the most recent rates for:
   - (a) United Kingdom, pound _____
   - (b) Europe, Euro area, euro _____
   - (c) Japan, yen _____
   - (d) Has the Canadian dollar appreciated or depreciated against these currencies since March 13, 2007? _____

7. For each of the following possible events, indicate whether the demand or supply curve for Canadian dollars would shift, the direction of the shift, the determinant of the change, the inflow or outflow effect on the balance of payments (and the sub-account affected), and the resulting movement of the equilibrium exchange rate for the value of the Canadian dollar:
   - (a) Canadian-produced cars become more popular in the United States
   - (b) Inflation in Canada increases relative to all other countries
   - (c) The Canadian economy falls into recession
   - (d) Interest rates in Canada are reduced
   - (e) Canadian productivity increases
   - (f) Canadians take advantage of high exchange rates to vacation in the United States
   - (g) The Bank of Canada sells some of its stock of foreign currency and buys Canadian dollars
   - (h) Production in the "Oil Sands" increases and more oil is exported

8. According to the Economist magazine's July, 2007 Big Mac index (http://www.economist.com/finance/displaystory.cfm?story_id=9448015), the Canadian dollar's purchasing power parity rate should be about $0.88 ($US). How much is the Canadian dollar currently over- or under-valued? (Go to the Bank of Canada website at http://www.bankofcanada.ca/en/rates/converter.html for the current rate of exchange.) _____

9. The Mundell-Fleming model enables an analysis of the relationship among the exchange rate regime, the direction of capital flows, the impact on the exchange rate, the impact on net exports, and the final impact on national income, GDP. Given that Canada maintains a flexible exchange rate regime:
   (*a*) What would happen if government spending was reduced?   _____
   (*b*) What would happen if the Bank of Canada purchases bonds through open-market operations?   _____

10. The following schedules summarize the supply and demand for trifflings, the national currency of Tricoli:

Triffling price

(Canadian dollars per triffling)	0	$4	$8	$12	$16	$20	$24
Quantity demanded (per year)	40	38	36	34	32	30	28
Quantity supplied (per year)	1	11	21	31	41	51	61

Use the above schedules for the following:
   (*a*) Graph the supply and demand curves.
   (*b*) Determine the equilibrium exchange rate.   _____
   (*c*) Determine the size of the excess supply or excess demand that would exist if the Tricolian government fixed the exchange rate $22 = 1 triffling.   _____
   (*d*) How might this imbalance be remedied?

_____

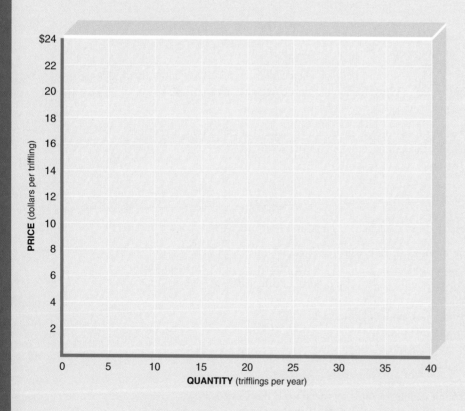